ST. PATRICK
APOSTLE OF IRELAND

A Memoir of his Life and Mission

WITH AN INTRODUCTORY DISSERTATION ON
SOME EARLY USAGES OF THE CHURCH IN IRELAND, AND ITS
HISTORICAL POSITION FROM THE ESTABLISHMENT OF
THE ENGLISH COLONY TO THE PRESENT DAY

BY

JAMES HENTHORN TODD, D.D.

SENIOR FELLOW OF TRINITY COLLEGE,
REGIUS PROFESSOR OF HEBREW IN THE UNIVERSITY, AND
TREASURER OF ST. PATRICK'S CATHEDRAL,
DUBLIN

Ego Dominus primus et novissimus Ego sum. Viderunt insulæ et
timuerunt, extrema terræ obstupuerunt, et appropinquaverunt, et
accesserunt. — *Isai.* xli. 4, 5

Wipf and Stock Publishers
EUGENE, OREGON

Wipf and Stock Publishers
199 West 8th Avenue, Suite 3
Eugene, Oregon 97401

St. Patrick Apostle of Ireland
A Memoir of His Life and Mission
By Todd, James Henthorn
ISBN: 1-59244-200-5
Publication date: March, 2003
Previously published by Hodges, Smith, & Co., January, 1864 .

PREFACE.

THE AUTHOR feels that some apology is required for having occupied in this volume so large a space with merely introductory matter. But Irish history is so little known, that it became necessary to explain at considerable length certain customs or usages of the antient Church of Ireland, which by some writers have been greatly misunderstood, and by others concealed or kept out of view. It was important to make it clear that those usages were not of the nature of heretical or schismatical irregularities, nor all of them, strictly speaking, peculiar to Ireland. Some of them were the result of the insulated position of the country, combined with the social condition of the people under the government of their aboriginal chieftains; some of them were antient customs, which continued to exist in Ireland long after they had been abolished elsewhere; and some had been abolished elsewhere for reasons which did not apply to Ireland.

It was necessary, also, in order to correct certain popular mistakes, to draw attention to the fact that from the eleventh century to the Reformation there were two Churches in Ireland, each ignoring, as far as it could, the existence of the other; and that since the Reformation a third Church has sprung up, deriving its succession from a foreign source; whilst the original Irish Church, properly so called, having merged into the Church of the English pale, has adopted the Reformation, and lost in a great measure its hold upon the descendants of the native tribes. This loss is to be attributed to that old and deep-seated disaffection to England which is the parent of almost all the political and social evils of the country; nor can there be a doubt that this disaffection was mainly caused, not by religious differences, but by the impolitic measures enforced in the twelfth and some following centuries, for compelling the Irish people to adopt manners and laws for which they were wholly unprepared; not to speak of the arbitrary confiscation of landed property, for the benefit of the English colonists, and the sudden overthrow of the authority of the native chieftains.

The remainder of the volume is occupied with the history of the plantation of Christianity in Ireland, as it is recorded in the acts of its first missionaries, Palladius and Patrick. But, notwithstanding the number of pages employed in the narrative, several important questions have been designedly passed over without notice.

It has not been thought necessary, for example, to occupy any space with a refutation of the arguments of those who have affected to cast doubts upon the existence of St. Patrick. Such doubts have proceeded for the most part from writers strongly prejudiced by party feeling, and wholly ignorant of the original sources of the history. Their objections derive whatsoever plausibility they may possess from garbled quotations, misinterpreted authorities, and mistakes about antient customs, especially Irish antient customs. They deal largely in premises from which the conclusions deduced do not follow, and in conclusions which are deduced from no premises at all.

The traditions collected in the Book of Armagh cannot be later than the third half-century after the date usually assigned to the death of St. Patrick. They were collected, for the most part, with a manifest purpose. That purpose was to prop up the incipient claims of Armagh to a jurisdiction over other Churches in Ireland; claims which, it appears, were not then universally allowed. They assume the existence of St. Patrick as admitted by all parties, and never questioned. Had the story of St. Patrick been then of but recent origin, some remarks or legends in the collection would certainly have betrayed the fact. That the collectors of these traditions indulged in the unscrupulous use of legend strengthens the argument. There were men alive at the time whose grandfathers might have conversed with disciples of the Patrick who was said to have converted the Irish in the latter half of the fifth century. Had the existence of this Patrick been a thing to be proved, or ever doubted, some of these men would have been produced as witnesses, and made to tell their experience; but in the whole of this curious record there is not a hint dropped capable of giving support to the hypothesis that the history of Patrick was then a recently invented fable. Had it been so, the resistance to the claims of Armagh could not fail to have brought out some allusion to the fact. It is incredible that a whole nation could have combined thus to deceive themselves; and it is even more incredible that a purely mythological personage should have left upon a whole nation so indelible an impression of imaginary services; an impression which continues to the present day in their fireside lore, their local traditions, their warm-hearted devotion and gratitude; which has left also its lasting memorial in the antient names of hills and headlands, towns and villages, churches and monasteries, throughout the country.

The story of St. Patrick's commission from Pope Celestine is rejected in the following pages, simply because the writer believes that there is no satisfactory evidence for it. He hopes that no reader will suppose him to have been influenced by any controversial prejudice in coming to this conclusion. He is conscious of no such prejudice. He is, indeed, sincerely attached to the Reformed Church of these kingdoms, in which he holds the office of a priest; but he cannot perceive how the question whether Patrick had or had not his mission from Rome affects in any way the controversy which now unhappily divides the western Church. The Rome of the fifth century was not guilty of the abuses which rendered the Reformation necessary in the sixteenth. If we acknowledge, as we must do, the Roman mission of Palladius, as well as the Roman mission of Augustine of Canterbury, it is difficult to see what is to be gained by denying the Roman mission of Patrick.

With the Roman story falls to the ground the fable of St. Patrick's having been a canon regular of the Church of St. John Lateran, at Rome. That is another subject which has been passed over without discussion in the following pages. There is no authority even in the later and most legendary of the Lives for the statement. There were no canons regular, in the fifth century,

Preface. vii

in the Church of St. John Lateran, of whose society Patrick could have been a member. The stories of his having taken the monastic habit under St. Martin of Tours, although countenanced by some of his biographers, and of his having been for a time an Augustinian hermit, are equally without foundation. Such tales belong to the eleventh or twelfth century, when the Augustinian orders were first introduced into Ireland; and to a somewhat later period must be referred the famous institution of St. Patrick's Purgatory. This was a manifest invention of the English ecclesiastics who had come over to settle in Ireland, and were anxious to connect themselves, in the eyes of the people, with traditions of St. Patrick. To the supposed adventure of a knight, named Owain, or Owen, the purgatory first owed its celebrity. Its first historian, Henry of Saltrei, was an English Cistercian monk; and the imposture was supported for some centuries by the Anglo-Irish bishops of the north of Ireland, and even by the English kings. To the primitive Church of Ireland it was entirely unknown.

It may be desirable to say a few words in this place on the uncouth, and seemingly unpronounceable, proper names of persons and places, which must embarrass every reader of Irish history who is unskilled in the Celtic languages. To change the spelling of such names, with a view to represent to English eyes their pronunciation, seemed a course which, besides being unscholarlike, would be very little likely to effect its object. The name, in its new form, would be more barbarous in appearance, and perhaps quite as difficult of pronunciation as it was in its original and correct orthography. Any change in that orthography, made with this view, would destroy the etymology, and render it impossible for the philological student to trace, with any certainty, the real origin and meaning of the name. The reader of the history of Ireland, who is ignorant of the Irish language, must therefore make up his mind to encounter this difficulty, as the reader of the history of France, or Spain, Arabia, Russia, or Poland, has to encounter the corresponding difficulty if he should happen to be ignorant of the languages of those countries.

To assist the reader in his contest with this difficulty, the following rules are here given; and, with a little attention, it is hoped the embarrassment may in this way be most easily overcome:—

VOWELS.

A is always sounded as *a* in *wall*, or *a* in *hat*; never as *a* in *fate*.
E is always as *e* in *grey*, or *e* in *set*; never as *ee* in *meet*.
I is always as *ee* in *meet*, or as *i* in *pin*; never as *i* in *fight*.
O is as *o* in *more*; or, when short, as *o* in *pot*, or *u* in *tub*.
U is like *u* in *rule*, or *oo* in *fool*; and, when short, like *u* in *full*.

DIPHTHONGS.

AI is pronounced as *oi* in *soil*; and, when short, like *ai* in the French *travailler*.
AO like *ay* in *mayor*; by natives of Connaught, like *uee* in *queen*.
AU like *u* long, or *oo*.
EA like *ea* in *bear*, *swear*; or, if short, like *ea* in *heart*.
EE, in old spelling, is the same as EA, and pronounced as *ea* in *bear*, or *ai* in *nail*.
EI, when long, like *ei* in *reign*; when short, like *e* in *serve*.
EO long, like *o* in *pole*, or *oa* in *coal*; if short, like *u* in *cut*.
EU is the same as EA, and often written for it.
IA always long, like *ee* in *beer*.
IO, when long, is the same as IA; when short, like *io* in *action*.
IU, long, both vowels sounded, like *ew* in *few*; short, like *oo* in *good*.
OI. Whether long or short, the two vowels are separately sounded; the *o* predominating when long, and accented thus, *ói*; when short,

and the *i* accented as *oí*, the *i* or *ee* sound predominates, and the combination is sounded like *uee* in *queen*.

OO, in old spelling, is pronounced like *o* in *pole*.

UA is always long, like *wa* in *war*.

UI is pronounced always so as to make each vowel distinctly heard; if accented *úi*, the *u* predominates, as *oò-ee*; if accented *uí*, the sound resembles *wee* in *weep*; if short, or unaccented, the sound is the same, but shortened as much as possible.

CONSONANTS.

B, as in English. BH as *v* or *w*.

C, always hard, as K; never as *c* in *ceiling*. CH as the Greek χ, or German *ch* in *reich*; never as *ch* in *cheer*.

D, as in English. DH nearly as *y*.

F, as in English. FH quiescent, or without sound.

G, as *g* in *gale*; never as *g* in *ginger*. GH final had best be pronounced like *h*, or *gh* in *high*. Its correct pronunciation can only be attained by a native.

L, as in English.

M, as in English. MH like *v*; in the middle of words, like *w*.

N, as in English. The combination NG can only be pronounced by a native.

P, as in English. PH like F, or *ph* in *Philip*.

R, as in English.

S, before or after *a*, *o*, and *u*, like *s* in *sun*, or *hiss*; before or after *e* and *i*, as *sh* in *shine*, *blush*. SH as *h* in *hill*.

T, before the broad vowels *a*, *o u*, is to be pronounced like a slender *th*, as in *thought*; before the small vowels *e*, *i*, like *t* in *tune*. TH is pronounced like the English *h*; at the end of words or syllables, almost quiescent.

These rules are very general, and of course very imperfect; but by an adherence to them, a tolerable approximation to the correct pronunciation may be obtained. Such readers as desire to study the subject more deeply will find full information, with copious examples, explaining especially the provincial and dialectic pronunciations, in Dr. O'Donovan's 'Grammar of the Irish Language:' Dublin, 1845.

In conclusion, the author has to acknowledge much

valuable assistance given to him by the Very Rev. Charles Graves, Dean of the Castle Chapel, Dublin, especially in decyphering the curious passage quoted pp. 454, 455, of this volume, from the Book of Armagh. A page there is nearly obliterated in the original MS., but Dean Graves, with great labour and skill, has succeeded in completely recovering it.

His best thanks are also due to his valued friend the Rev. Dr. Reeves, of Armagh, who has most kindly read and corrected all the sheets from page 265 to the end of the volume; detecting many errors, and supplying from his great stores of information, with the liberality of a true scholar, many particulars and valuable references which the author had overlooked.

The proof sheets of the earlier part of the volume wanted the advantage of this supervision. They were corrected by the author at a distance from books of reference, whilst he was resident on the Continent, for his health, in the early part of the year 1862. They probably contain many errors which might otherwise have been avoided, and for which the author hopes this apology may be accepted.

TRINITY COLLEGE, DUBLIN:
October 31, 1863.

CONTENTS.

INTRODUCTION.

Two periods of Irish Church History — Irregularities attributed to the Church in the first period — Not peculiar to Ireland — Three Orders of Irish Saints — Ecclesiastical tenure of Land, illustrated by the foundation of Trim — Comarbs, or Coarbs — The Muinnter, or Monastic family — Termon Lands — Monastic Officers — Antient Lists of the Successors of St. Patrick — Christianity in Ireland before St. Patrick — Second period — Clanship — Two hostile Churches in Ireland since the Eleventh Century — Bull of Pope Adrian IV. — English rule in Ireland — Hatred of England not caused by Religious differences — The Reformation — The Penal Laws — The Legislative Union . pp. 1—246

APPENDIX TO THE INTRODUCTION . . . . 247—262
   A.—Genealogical Tables :—
      Table I.—Kings of Ireland descended from Eochaidh Muighmeadhoin 249
      Table II.—The Northern Hy Neill . . . 250
      Table III.—The Southern Hy Neill . . . 252
      Table IV.—Relationship between St. Brigid and St. Columba 252
      Table V.—Relationship between St. Brigid and her first bishop, Conlaedh 253
      Table VI.—List of the Kings of Ireland from A.D. 164 to 665 255
   B.—History of the Foundation of Trim from the Book of Armagh . . . . 257—262

CHAPTER I.

The antient Church of Britain, and the Mission of Palladius to the Scots believing in Christ — Certain Portions of the Acts of Palladius transferred to St. Patrick 265

CHAPTER II.

The History and Acts of St. Patrick, Apostle of Ireland, and Founder of the See of Armagh—His Writings—His early History, as gathered from his Writings—Date of his Mission . . p. 346

CHAPTER III.

The Missionary Labours of St. Patrick—His interview with King Laoghaire—His Irish Hymn—His adventures in Connaught—Festival of his Baptism—Story of King Laoghaire's Daughters—Foundation of Armagh—His supposed Revision of the Pagan Laws—His Canons—Date of his Death—Review of his History—His Policy, in first addressing the Chieftains, founded on a Knowledge of the Irish People—Cause of his Rapid Success—His Toleration of the Pagan Superstitions—His Mission not without Danger to Himself—Ecclesiastical Clanship in the Monasteries—Causes of the Popularity of the Monastic Life in Ireland—The *Abgitoria*, or Alphabets written by St. Patrick—Alphabetic Writing and a Pagan Literature in Ireland before St. Patrick—The Christianity established by him a National Institution—His Missionary Character 400

INDEX 517

ERRATA.

Page
45, l. 16, *for* σκολά´οντες *read* σχολάζοντες.
47, l. 22, *for* populus *read* populos.
130, l. 10, *for* Fiac *read* Fiacc.
145, l. 1, *for* Lib. i. *read* Lib. l.
166, heading of page, *for* Fertighus *read* Fertighis.
179, l. 2, col. 2, *for* Arti *read* Artri.
214, note 4, *for* Ui Eochadh *read* Ui Eochach.
215, l. 6, *for* Bridgid *read* Brigid.
249, l. 4, *after* Eochaidh *dele* comma.
249, l. 16 and 22,
250, and 252, } *for* Hy Niall *read* Hy Neill.
313, l. 5, *for* barbaros *read* barbaras.
448, note 2, l. 6, *for* Sanctilegium *read* Sanctilogium.

ST. PATRICK

APOSTLE OF IRELAND.

INTRODUCTORY DISSERTATION

I. THE history of the Irish Episcopal successions divides itself into two distinct and well defined periods. The first period embraces the primitive ages, from the earliest plantation of Christianity in the island to the establishment of archiepiscopal and diocesan jurisdiction in the beginning of the twelfth century. The second period extends from the twelfth century to the present day.

Two periods in Irish Church History.

2. During the former period many seeming, and some real, irregularities existed in the Church of Ireland, which, when they came to be known, excited the wonder of the rest of Christendom. Anselm[1], Archbishop of Canterbury, in one of

Irregularities attributed to the antient Irish Church.

---

[1] *Anselm.* Opp. ed. Bened. Paris, 1721. Epistt. lib. iii. 147. Usser. *Syllog.* Epist. 36 (Works, vol. iv. p. 523). " Item dicitur, episcopos in terra vestra passim eligi, et sine certo episcopatus loco constitui:

* B

By St. Anselm.

his letters to Muirchertagh, or Murtach O'Brien, nominal King of Ireland, in the beginning of the twelfth century, thus describes these abuses: 'It is also said that bishops in your country are elected at random, and appointed without any fixed place of episcopal jurisdiction; and that a bishop, like a priest, is ordained by a single bishop.' He then goes on to reason that 'a bishop cannot be constituted in accordance with the will of God, if he has no certain diocese or people to govern. For even in worldly affairs,' he says, 'we would not give either the name or the office of a shepherd to him who had no flock to feed.'

By St. Bernard.

And so also St. Bernard complains, in language, perhaps, too strong, that throughout the whole of Ireland, up to his own times, there had been 'a dissolution of ecclesiastical discipline, a relaxation of censure, a making void of religion;' that 'instead of Christian piety was everywhere introduced a cruel barbarism, nay, a sort of paganism, substituted under the Christian name. For,' he adds, 'bishops were changed

atque ab uno episcopo episcopum sicut quemlibet presbyterum ordinari.' The Muirchertach to whom this letter was addressed, was great-grandson of the celebrated Brian Borumha, and died in 1119; during his reign, in consequence most probably of his correspondence with Anselm, the synod of Rathbresail made the first attempt to introduce Archiepiscopal jurisdiction, and to fix the boundaries of episcopal sees or dioceses in Ireland.

We may remark here that the uncouth and seemingly barbarous spellings of the Irish names, to those who are ignorant of the Celtic languages, is perhaps the greatest obstacle to the popular knowledge of Irish history, and a reason why educated Englishmen are content to remain in entire ignorance of a people so intimately connected with themselves. The name *Muirchertach* has been *Anglicized* (if we may so say), *Morrogh*, *Murtogh*, *Mortimer*, and *Moriarty*. It is derived from *Muir* (Latin *Mare*) the sea; and signifies, 'expert at sea;' *Marinus*, or *Navalis*.

and multiplied at the pleasure of the metropolitan, a thing unheard of since the beginning of Christianity, without order, without reason, so that one bishopric was not content with a single bishop, but almost every church had its separate bishop.'[1]

3. How far this state of things was in its origin rendered necessary by the civil or political circumstances of the country, may be difficult to prove. But it is certain that in the early period of which we are speaking, bishops, without sees or dioceses, were very numerous in Ireland. Except in Armagh, Trim, and one or two other places, no lands or other endowments were set apart for their support. In some cases the bishops were compelled to demand fees[2] for the

<small>Bishops without sees or dioceses.</small>

---

[1] *Bishop.* S. Bernard. *De Vita Malachiæ*, c. x. 'Inde tota illa per universam Hiberniam, de qua superius diximus, dissolutio ecclesiasticæ disciplinæ, censuræ enervatio, religionis evacuatio: inde illa ubique pro mansuetudine christiana, sæva subintroducta barbaries, imo paganismus quidam inductus sub nomine christiano. Nam (quod inauditum est ab ipso Christianitatis initio) sine ordine, sine ratione, mutabantur et multiplicabantur episcopi pro libitu metropolitani, ita ut unus episcopatus uno non esset contentus, sed singulæ pene ecclesiæ singulos haberent episcopos.' By *the metropolitan* in this passage it is probable that St. Bernard meant the successor of St. Patrick at Armagh: his language implies that there were episcopal districts (episcopatus), although such districts, whether limited by the territorial possessions of the monasteries or of the chieftains, were 'not content' to submit to the ordinary jurisdiction of a single bishop.

[2] *Fees.* Lanfranc, Archbishop of Canterbury, in his letter to 'Terdelvacus,' nominal king of Ireland, mentions, as one of the abuses of the Irish church, that the bishops took money for conferring holy orders: 'Quod sacri ordines per pecuniam ab episcopis dantur.' Ussher, *Sylloge*, Epist. 27. The real name of the king to whom this complaint was addressed was *Tordhealbach* (grandson of Brian Borumha). He was nominal king of Ireland from A.D. 1086 to 1094. His name, so unpronounceable to English tongues, is now commonly written Torlogh or Turlogh, and has been Latinized *Theodoricus*, although without any other reason than the remote resemblance in sound. The name signifies 'Like a chieftain.' Dr. O'Brien (Dictionary, *in voce*) tells us that it signifies, 'Like the God Thor,' but *Thor* was a Saxon, not a Celtic deity, and was unknown to the Irish. The word *tor* signifies a lord, a chieftain. See Irish Nennius, p. 223, *n*.

exercise of their function; but ordinarily they were maintained by the offerings[1] of the clergy or congregations amongst whom they ministered. Those who were connected with the religious houses shared no doubt with the rest of the inmates the common property of the society; and those who ministered in the establishment of one of the petty kings or chieftains, were probably supported by their chief as one of his principal retainers or functionaries, and a part of his regal or patriarchal state.

<small>A real Episcopacy in the Irish Church, although without dioceses.</small>

4. It would be a very great mistake, however, to suppose that there was no real episcopacy or episcopal jurisdiction in Ireland in the times we speak of, or that the distinction between the orders of priest and bishop was not thoroughly understood and carefully preserved in the primitive Irish Church. Seeming irregularities no doubt there were; bishops were sometimes ordained *per saltum*, without having previously passed through the inferior orders; they were consecrated by a single bishop, instead of by three, as the antient canons of the Church are supposed to have re-

---

[1] *Offerings.* These offerings, in later times, were received at episcopal visitations: the collection of canons, entitled ' *Synodus Episcoporum, i.e., Patricii, Auxilii et Isernini*,' published by Spelman, Ware, and Wilkins, although it is evidently of a date much later than that to which it pretends, may be quoted in proof of this remark. Can. 25 is as follows: 'Si quæ a religiosis hominibus donata fuerint diebus illis, quibus Pontifex in singulis habitaverit Ecclesiis, pontificalia dona, sicut mos antiquus, ordinare ad episcopum pertinebunt, sive ad usum necessarium, sive egentibus distribuendum, prout ipse episcopus moderabit.' Villanueva, *Opusc. S. Patricii*, Dublin, 1835, p. 4. In St. Patrick's time there could have been no 'mos antiquus' in Ireland, as to the distribution of offerings made to the bishops under the name of 'pontificalia dona.' But these canons are undoubtedly Irish and antient; probably not later than the tenth or eleventh century.

quired; and they were not set apart to labour in any defined district or diocese, nor bound to yield canonical obedience to any superior episcopal or archiepiscopal authority.

The Degree or Order of the episcopacy was frequently conferred in recognition of the pre-eminence in sanctity or learning of some distinguished ecclesiastic, who nevertheless continued to live, either as a hermit, or as the head of a school in his monastery, without necessarily taking upon him the charge of any district, church, or diocese. But the peculiar functions of his order were never overlooked, nor did the presbyters ever intrude upon the episcopal office; so that the attempt made by some modern writers to represent the primitive government of the Irish Church as a species of Presbyterianism is entirely futile and unfounded. The bishops were always applied to, to consecrate churches, to ordain to the ecclesiastical degrees, or Holy Orders, including the consecration of other bishops; to give Confirmation, and the more solemn benedictions; and to administer the Holy Communion with peculiar rites, of greater pomp and ceremony.

5. It is true that the bishops attached to religious houses were subject to the superior of the monastery, although that superior may have been no more than a priest, or even a layman; but no abbat, in any such monasteries, although exercising a certain jurisdiction over his bishop, ever ventured to usurp any of the spiritual functions of the episcopal office. *Bishops in monasteries subject to the abbat, with full recognition of their superiority in order.*

6   *Episscopacy recognised as*   [INTROD.

Example of deference to episcopal authority.

6. It appears to have been a rule, as indeed it is still more or less in every branch of the Catholic Church, that some peculiar rites were necessary when a bishop took part as celebrant in the office of the holy Eucharist. Adamnan[1], in his life of St. Columba, tells a curious story which will illustrate this, and will also shew in what honour the episcopal office was held in the antient Scotic monasteries. 'Once upon a time,' he says, 'a certain stranger [or pilgrim[2]] from the province of Munster, whose name was Cronan, came to the saint [*i.e.*, to St. Columba, at Hi, or Iona]; he endeavoured from humility, as much as possible, to conceal himself, that none might know him to be a bishop, but he could not escape the penetration of the saint. For on the next Lord's Day, having been invited by St. Columba to consecrate, according to custom, the Body of Christ, he calls the saint that they might break the bread of the Lord together, as if they had been both presbyters. The saint then approaching the altar, suddenly looked into his face, and thus addressed him : "May Christ bless thee, brother; break thou this bread alone, with episcopal rite; we know now that thou art a bishop. Wherefore didst thou attempt to conceal thyself until now, so that due veneration was not

---

[1] *Adamnan.* Vit. S. Columbæ, lib. i. c. 44. (ed. Reeves, p. 85.) cf. Colgan. *Actt. SS.* p. 302.

[2] *Pilgrim.* The word used is *proselytus*; but the same individual is called a pilgrim, *peregrinus*, in the same chapter: and Dr. Reeves shews that Adamnan uses the words as synonymous. Vit. S. Columbæ, *Glossary*, p. 451. The Greek word *proselytus* properly signifies a stranger, *advena*.

rendered unto thee by us?" When he heard this, the humble pilgrim, greatly astounded, worshipped Christ in the saint; and all present who witnessed it, wondering greatly, gave glory to the Lord.'

We are not bound to receive the miraculous part of this story, if indeed there be anything miraculous really implied in it. It proves, however, beyond all doubt, that the author regarded the episcopal office as worthy of the highest honour: and the case is the more remarkable[1], because of the high dignity and reputation of Columba, although himself but a priest; and because Adamnan, who records it, was himself, as the abbat of a Columban monastery, officially excluded from the higher order. It is clear that reverence for the episcopal office was with the monks of Hi a principle, and superseded even the veneration paid to St. Columba himself in his own monastic society.

7. Another very curious anecdote, told by the same author[2], illustrates in a remarkable manner the position of a bishop in an Irish or Scotic monastery, as subject to the jurisdiction of his abbat.

Example of the bishop's subjection to the abbat.

An Irish ecclesiastic, named Findchan, a presbyter, and a soldier of Christ, 'Christi miles,' (*i.e.*, a monk,) became the founder of a monastery at a place called *Artchain*, in the *Ethica Terra*,

---

[1] *Remarkable.* This observation has been made by Dr. Reeves. Adamnan. Note p. 86.

[2] *Author.* Adamnan. *Vit. S. Columbæ* (ed. Reeves), i. 36.

or Tiree.[1] He brought over with him from
'Scotia,' that is, from Ireland, in the habit of a
clerk, one Aedh Dubh, or the Black, hoping
apparently to convert him to a religious life, by
keeping him for a few years under his own instruction in his monastery. Aedh, or Hugh, as
the name is often Englished, seems to have been
a most unfavourable subject for such an experi-
ment. He was of the royal family of the Cruith-
nians, or Picts, of Dalaradia in Ulster, but is
described by our author as a sanguinary murderer:
'valde sanguinarius homo, et multorum trucidator.' In the year 565 he had murdered Diarmait[2], son of Fergus Cerbhaill, (or Carroll,) who
was supreme king of all Ireland by Divine right:
'totius Scotiæ regnatorem Deo auctore ordinatum.' After this unpromising character had
spent some time in 'pilgrimage' at the monastery of his friend, Findchan conceived so good
an opinion of him, that he sent for a bishop, and
caused him to be ordained priest.[3] The bishop
appears to have had some scruples, and insisted

---

[1] *Tiree.* Dr. Reeves (*Adamnan*, p. 48, note; Ulster Journal of Archæology, ii. p. 223, *sq.*); has clearly proved that the *Ethica Terra* of Adamnan was the island *Tir-itha* or Tiree. Father Innes imagined it to be Shetland, an hypothesis wholly irreconcilable with Adamnan's notices of it. *Civ. and Eccl. Hist. of Scotland*, p. 180. c. 36.

[2] *Diarmait.* Diarmait was the son of Fergus Cerbhiall, who was the son of Conall Crimthan, who was the son of Niall of the Nine Hostages. He was king of Ireland 21 years, from 544 to 565. O'Flaherty, *Ogygia*, p. 430.

[3] *Priest.* 'Hic itaque idem Aidus, post aliquantum in peregrinatione transactum tempus, accito episcopo, quamvis non recte, apud supra dictum Findchanum, presbyter ordinatus est. Episcopus tamen, non est ausus super caput ejus manum imponere, nisi primo idem Findchanus, Aidum carnaliter amans, suam capiti ejus pro confirmatione imponeret dexteram.' *Adamnan*, Vit. Columbæ (ed. Reeves, pp. 68, 69.)

that Findchan should share the responsibility, by first putting his own hand on Aedh's head, which accordingly he consented to do, from his singular affection for Aedh: 'Aidum carnaliter amans.' And the blood-stained murderer, the 'sanguinarius trucidator,' was ordained to the sacred office of the priesthood.

When this transaction came to the ears of St. Columba, he was very indignant. He predicted that Findchan's hand, which was guilty of such sacrilege, should miraculously rot, and fall from his body; and that Aedh[1], returning like a dog to his vomit, should again become a murderer, and ultimately be murdered himself.

From this narrative it appears that Findchan, notwithstanding his great anxiety to have his unworthy pupil ordained, did not venture to perform that office himself, being only a presbyter, but *sent for a bishop*, or summoned the bishop who was connected with his monastery, to perform the office. It is to be observed also that the bishop, being subject to the abbat, and bound to obedience, did not dare to refuse, notwithstanding his scruples, and merely stipulated that Findchan should take upon himself the responsibility of the act, by first laying his own hands on the head of the candidate; not as ordaining, or adding anything to the validity of

---

[1] *Aedh*. He was the son of Suibhne Araidhe, and was chief of Dalaradia in 565, when he murdered King Diarmait. In 581 he became, by usurpation, King of Uladh (Ulidia, or Ulster), and in 588 was himself slain, by the son of his predecessor. See Reeves, *Adamn.* pp. 66, 70, notes. The Four Masters place his death in 592, and the murder of King Dairmait in 558, but their chronology is wrong.

the priesthood conferred, but only 'pro confirmatione,' to justify the bishop in the act. In the form of this ordination there was nothing irregular; but the story shews incidentally that it was not at that time the ordinary custom in the Irish Church for the assisting presbyters to join in the imposition of hands, as enjoined by the well-known canon of the fourth council of Carthage. On this occasion there was no attempt to observe that canon; for Findchan was required to lay on hands *first*, not to join in the imposition of the hands of the bishop. And this was done 'pro confirmatione,' as evidence that the bishop was acting not of his own free will, but under the authority of his monastic superior.

And accordingly it is very remarkable that Columba[1], although he condemns in the severest terms this sacrilegious ordination, denouncing against Findchan a fearful punishment, never censures the bishop; evidently assuming that the bishop had done all that was in his power to signify his disapprobation, and to protest against the act.

<small>The abbatial jurisdiction over bishops not peculiar to Columban monasteries.</small>

8. These anecdotes both have reference to Columban monasteries; and the latter illustrates very strikingly the statement of the venerable Bede[2], that the abbat of Hi was always a priest,

---

[1] *Columba.* Innes suggests that Columba pronounced no judgment against the bishop, because 'the holy man would not assume a power over a bishop or pronounce sentence against him, out of respect to his character.' *Civ. and Eccl. Hist. of Scotland*, pp. 182, 183. But the bishop had done nothing worthy of censure; he had acted under the commands of his abbat, to whom he was bound to render obedience.

[2] *Bede.* Hist. Eccles. iii. c. 4. 'Habere autem solet ipsa insula rec-

to whose jurisdiction the whole province and even the bishops themselves were subject, after the example of the founder, Columba, who was not a bishop, but a priest and monk.

This, however, was not peculiar to the monastery of Hi, or its dependent religious houses. Something of the same kind will be found in St. Brigid's celebrated establishment at Kildare. Cogitosus[1], one of the early biographers of St. Brigid, tells us, in his Prologue, that when innumerable people of both sexes flocked to her 'from all the provinces of Ireland,' bringing their voluntary offerings, she erected on the plain of Lifé, or Liffey[2], on the sure foundations of faith, her monastery, 'which is the head of nearly all the

Constitution of St. Brigid's monastery of Kildare.

---

torem semper abbatem presbyterum, cujus juri et omnis provincia, et ipsi etiam episcopi, ordine inusitato, debeant esse subjecti, juxta exemplum primi doctoris illius, qui non episcopus, sed presbyter, extitit, et monachus.'

[1] *Cogitosus.* The *Vita S. Brigidæ* by Cogitosus has been printed by Canisius, *Lectt. Antiq.*, tom. v.; by Messingham, *Florileg. Ins. Sanctor.*; and by Colgan, *Trias Thaumaturga*, p. 518. It is also printed by Surius and the Bollandists at Feb. 1. Messingham supposes Cogitosus to have flourished A.D. 550, assuming him to have said that he was St. Brigid's nephew. But this mistake is corrected by Colgan, who decides that the *Life of St. Brigid* must have been written before the year 594, probably before 580. His argument, however, for this date is inconclusive, and will be noticed presently (see p. 15). The name of Cogitosus occurs as a saint (at Apr. 18) in the Irish unpublished Martyrologies of Tamlacht or Tallaght, and Marianus O'Gorman. But it is not mentioned in the older martyrology of Aengus, the Culdee, written before A.D. 800. It would seem therefore that Cogitosus must have become known to Irish hagiography after this year, and therefore could scarcely have been so old as the sixth century. The Martyrology of Tallaght, as we now have it, was composed about 900 (Colgan, *Actt. SS.* p. 581, c. 12), and Marianus O'Gorman died in the latter half of the 12th century. The name of our author, in its Celtic form, was Cogitois, or Cogitis, and it is not improbable that he alludes to his own name when he begins his *Life of St. Brigid* with the words 'Cogitis me fratres.' If this conjecture be well founded it affords a curious incidental evidence of the authenticity of the work. There cannot be a doubt that Dr. Petrie is correct in making A.D. 800—835 the period within which Cogitosus wrote. (Round Towers, p. 202. Trans. R. Irish Acad. vol. xx.)

[2] *Liffey.* This is now the name of the river which flows through

Irish churches, and the pinnacle towering above all monasteries of the Scots, whose jurisdiction, (*parochia,*) spread throughout the whole Hibernian land, reaches from sea to sea.' She then, he adds, reflected that she ought to provide 'with prudent care, regularly in all things, for the souls of her people,' as well as for 'the churches of the many provinces that adhered to her. She therefore came to the conclusion 'that she could not be without a high priest to consecrate churches, and to settle the ecclesiastical degrees in them.' The result was that she pitched upon a holy man, a solitary, adorned with all virtues, and by whom God had wrought many miracles. She sent for him from his desert, and went herself to meet him. He agreed to her proposals, and she engaged him '*to govern the church with her*' in episcopal dignity, that nothing of sacerdotal order should be wanting in her churches.'

In this way, says our author, he 'was the anointed head and chief of all bishops, and she the most blessed chief of all virgins;' so that by their happy unanimity and government in all virtues, she erected her principal church; and by their united merits 'her chair[1], both epi-

---

this plain. But originally it was the name of the plain, and the river (in contradistinction to the plain) was called *River of the Liffey*, in Irish *Amhain na Lifé*, which has been Anglicized, *Anna Liffey*, and has greatly puzzled some English writers: as if the word *Anna* was a woman's name.

[1] *Chair.* 'Cathedra episcopalis et puellaris.' It must be borne in mind that St. Brigid's establishment at Kildare comprehended both sexes, who were divided from each other in the Cathedral by a partition. See the remarkable description of this arrangement by Cogitosus, c. 35; Colgan, *Triad. Th.* p. 523, and Dr.

scopal and virginal, like a fruitful vine spreading all around with growing branches, established itself in the whole Hibernian island, in which he, as archbishop of the Irish bishops, and she, as abbess whom all abbesses of the Scots venerate, are pre-eminent, in happy succession and in perpetual order.'

9. In this remarkable passage it will be seen that many of the peculiarities of the antient Church of Ireland may be traced. St. Brigid was evidently impressed with the necessity of having in connexion with her newly-founded monastery a high priest or bishop, who should take care 'regularly in all things' for the souls of her followers; consecrate her churches, and 'settle the ecclesiastical degrees' (that is, ordain presbyters and other clergy to minister) 'in them;' that so 'nothing should be wanting of sacerdotal order in her churches,' or dependent religious houses. She regarded the presence of a bishop as essential, not only to ecclesiastical regularity, but also to the very salvation of the souls of her people.

Peculiar usages of the Irish Church exhibited in the monastery of Kildare.

But it is equally clear that she had her bishop under her own jurisdiction. 'She engaged him to govern the church *with her*.' If he was anointed head of all bishops, she was most

---

Petrie's valuable observations on it. *Round Towers*, p. 196, *sq.* (*Trans. of R. Irish Acad.*, vol. xx.) Comp. also Colgan's remarks on the three Prelacies of Kildare. *Ibid.* p. 626, *sq. App. V. ad Vit. S. Brig.*, and the curious story told by the author of the Scholia on the Martyrology of Aengus the Culdee, of St. Brigid having been herself ordained a *bishop* by St. Moel or Mel, bishop of Ardagh. *Obits and Martyrol. of Christ's Church*. Introd. p. xcvi. *sq.*

blessed chief of all virgins; if he had an episcopal chair (*cathedra episcopalis*), she had a virginal chair (*cathedra puellaris*) of equal rank and dignity; if he was always 'archbishop' of the Irish, she was always the abbess whom all other abbesses of the Scots venerated; for as he was pre-eminent among the bishops of all Ireland, so she was pre-eminent among the abbesses of the Scots 'in happy succession and in perpetual order.' In other words, this succession of bishops and abbesses had continued in unbroken pre-eminence, from the days of St. Brigid to the time of her biographer Cogitosus.

Meaning of the title of Archbishop in antient Irish Church History.

10. The mention of the title of archbishop in the foregoing passage, and in some other records of the antient Church of Ireland, has given rise to several mistakes and much confusion. Thus we are told that St. Fiacc, Bishop of Slebhte, or Sletty, was consecrated a bishop by St. Patrick, and afterwards constituted Archbishop of Leinster[1]; that King Brandubh, in a synod of clergy and laity, decreed that the archbishopric of all Leinster should be for ever in the see and chair of St. Moedhog[2], or Mogue, that is, in Ferns, and that St. Moedhog should accordingly be at once consecrated 'archbishop.'

Even Colgan was misled by these statements, and inferred[3] that Sletty, the see of St. Fiacc,

---

[1] *Leinster.* See Colgan, *Triad. Thaum.* p. 4, col. 1.

[2] *Moedhog.* Vit. S. Maidoci, ap. Colgan (*Actt. SS. ad* 31 *Jan.*), c. 24.

[3] *Inferred.* Colgan. *Triad. Thaum.* p. 524, col. 2. Ussher has also fallen into the same error. *Relig. of Ant. Irish*, ch. viii. (Works, vol. iv. p. 321, *sq.*)

was originally, in the lifetime of St. Patrick, the archbishopric of Leinster; that the archiepiscopal jurisdiction was afterwards, by the influence of St. Brigid, transferred to Kildare; that it was again transferred to Ferns about A.D. 598, or at least before 604, in which year Brandubh, King of Leinster, was slain[1]; and that it became permanently fixed in Dublin, after the foundation of that see in the eleventh century.

Upon this Colgan builds an argument to prove that Cogitosus must have lived before the archiepiscopal see was transferred to Ferns, that is to say, before A.D. 598, or at least before 604; because he speaks of its having been in Kildare in his time. Byeus[2], however, the learned Bollandist compiler of the life of St. Fiacc, draws an opposite conclusion from the same premises: namely, that the scholia published by Colgan on St. Fiacc's hymn, and all other authorities in which the title of archbishop is to be found, cannot possibly be earlier than the twelfth century.

Both conclusions, however, are erroneous. The scholiast on St. Fiacc, whose words in the original Irish have recently been published[3] by the Irish Archæological and Celtic Society, does not say that Fiacc was Archbishop of Leinster, but that having been consecrated a bishop by St. Patrick, he became from thenceforth *Ard-epscop*, a chief or eminent Bishop of Leinster.

---

[1] *Slain.* The Four M. date his death 601. Annals of Ulster, 604.
[2] *Byeus.* Acta SS. Bolland. ad 12 Oct., p. 98, num. 7.
[3] *Published.* Prefatory Scholium to Fiacc's Hymn in praise of St. Patrick; *Book of Hymns of the Antient Irish Church*, p. 287, 89.

The life of St. Brigid by Cogitosus, and the life of St. Moedhoc, (attributed to a St. Evin, whose age is uncertain,) if not written originally in the Irish language, were both written by Irishmen to whom the vernacular word was familiar; and it is most natural that the authors, if they wrote in Latin, or the translators, if the original were in Irish, should have rendered the word *Ard-epscop* by the seemingly equivalent *Archbishop*.[1]

The Irish word, however, did not imply any thing of jurisdiction: and is not synonymous in this respect with our present use of the term *Archbishop*. It denotes only an eminent, or celebrated bishop; and there is nothing in it inconsistent with the existence of several *Ard-*, or chief bishops, at the same time, in the same district, as Leinster. But it would be clearly impossible to suppose two or more Archbishops of Leinster, or of all Ireland, in the modern sense of the word, exercising jurisdiction, at the same time, over the bishops of the same province. It does not, therefore, at all follow that there might not have been co-existing *Ard*-bishops, at Sletty, at Kildare, and at Ferns. This entirely destroys

---

[1] *Archbishop*. In every page of the Irish annals we meet with such words as *Ard-righ*, a chief or eminent king. *Ard-file*, a chief poet. *Ard-anchoire*, an eminent or remarkable anchorite. *Ard-eagnaidhe*, an eminent sage or man of learning. In none of these cases is the notion of jurisdiction over other kings, poets, anchorites, or men of learning implied. In the Book of Armagh (182, b. 2) the word *húasal-ter-chomrictid* is glossed 'archi-synagogus,' and we have also *húasal lieig* (glossed *archiater*), a noble, or chief physician. Zeuss, *Gramm. Celt.* p. 827. The office of Archi-synagogus certainly implied jurisdiction over others, and perhaps we may therefore infer, that the old Irish language would have expressed the title of Archbishop, by *úasal-* (not *ard-*) *epscop* = Angl. Sax., *héah biscop*; but there is nothing of jurisdiction implied in the term 'noble, or chief physician.'

Colgan's argument for the early age of Cogitosus. But there is also another consideration. Cogitosus does not assert that the bishop appointed by St. Brigid was Archbishop of Leinster in either sense of the word. He says expressly that he was 'archbishop of the bishops of Ireland;' that is, an eminent bishop amongst the bishops of Ireland, as St. Brigid was an eminent abbess amongst the abbesses of the Scots. This seems decisive of the question. Cogitosus could not have asserted that the Bishop of Kildare was Archbishop or Primate of all Ireland in the modern sense of the title. He meant only that the individual whom Brigid had appointed her bishop was so remarkable for learning or sanctity that he was regarded as the chief among the bishops of Ireland.

It is curious to observe how Colgan labours to restrict the words of Cogitosus to Leinster; doubtless because he felt that it would be very inconvenient to maintain that the Bishop of Kildare in St. Brigid's time had an archiepiscopal jurisdiction over all Ireland. Hence he tells us in one place that Cogitosus, '*speaking of the Church of Kildare*,'[1] says, that this bishop was pre-eminent as 'archbishop of the Irish bishops, and Brigid as the abbess who was venerated by all the Scots.' Cogitosus, however, was not speaking of the Church of Kildare, but of 'the whole island of Ireland.'[2] The influence of the episcopal and

---

[1] *Kildare.* 'Et in Prologo loquens de ecclesia Kildariensi ait, quam semper Archiepiscopus Hiberniensium episcoporum, et abbatissa &c. felici successione et ritu perpetuo dominantur.'—*Triad.Thaum.*, p. 524, col. 2. It is clear that *dominantur* must signify here *pre-eminence*, not *rule* or jurisdiction.

[2] *Ireland.* 'Amborum meritis,

virginal chair extended, he says, throughout all Ireland. The bishop and abbess of Kildare continued to enjoy their pre-eminence 'in a happy succession and by an enduring ordinance,' down to his own time.

In another place Colgan, quoting the same words, 'archbishop of the Irish bishops,'[1] says, 'the meaning is, not that the Kildare bishop was archbishop of all the Irish, but only of the Leinster bishops.' But Cogitosus says very expressly that he was *archbishop of the Irish bishops*, nay, 'head and chief of all bishops,' not making the smallest allusion to Leinster. And is it not therefore evident that this writer, by the word Archbishop, or *Ard*-bishop, meant only a high or eminent bishop, and not a metropolitan with archiepiscopal jurisdiction in the modern sense of the word?

Cogitosus further tells us (as we have seen) that the jurisdiction *(parochia)* of the monastery *(not of the bishop)* was 'extended throughout the whole Hibernian land, from sea to sea.' This surely cannot mean Leinster only. And it will be remembered that Bede, in the passage already quoted, speaks of the jurisdiction of the

---

says Cogitosus, 'sua cathedra episcopalis et puellaris, ... in tota Hiberniensi insula inolevit. Quam semper, &c.'—*Ibid.* p. 518. It may be said that the word *quam*, in this passage, may refer to *cathedra* instead of to the nearer substantive *insula*; and that we must not accuse Colgan of dishonesty for preferring the former construction, which better suited his theory. But even if we adopt this interpretation, the 'cathedra' of Brigid, or the monastery of Kildare, not the province of Leinster, will be the extent of this archbishop's jurisdiction: and the difficulty of an archbishop in Kildare, without any authority out of his own city, recurs.

[1] *Bishops.* Tr. Thaum., p. 525, col. 1, note 7.

abbey of Hi[1], not of the bishop, and notices it as a remarkable peculiarity that even the bishops were subject to this authority.[2]

11. Cogitosus does not expressly name the anchorite who, as he tells us, was selected by St. Brigid to undertake 'with her' the spiritual care of her churches, as her bishop. It is evident, however, from the subsequent part of the narrative, that Condlaed, who is afterwards mentioned, is assumed to have been the bishop contemporary with St. Brigid. His tomb and that of St. Brigid were placed, highly decorated with pendent crowns of gold, silver, and gems, one on the right and the other on the left of the high altar of the cathedral[3]; and we may therefore safely infer that this Condlaed was the same who had been chosen by her as her peculiar bishop, and who is generally regarded as first Bishop of Kildare. In two of the other lives of Brigid, which Colgan has published, that attributed to St. Ultan, and that attributed to Animosus, 'the bishop[4] and prophet of God, who dwelt in the south of the plain of Liffey,' and

<small>St. Brigid's first Bishop in Kildare.</small>

---

[1] *Hi.* Dr. Reeves (*Adamnan*, Add. Note D., p. 258, *sq.*) has clearly shewn that the modern name *Iona*, now given to this island, is a strange mistake, arising from the change of *u* into *n* in the old adjective form *Ioua insula*, taken from the genitive *Io* or *Ia* of the name *I* or *Hi*; Iovus, Iova, Iovum, of or belonging to Hi.

[2] *Authority.* Bede uses the word *provincia* to denote the jurisdiction of the monastery. See Reeves, *Adamnan*, p. 65, n. and p. 336 n.

[3] *Cathedral.* Cogitosus, cap. 35. Colgan, *Tr. Th.*, p. 523.

[4] *Bishop.* 'Conlianus episcopus et propheta Dei, qui habitabat in dextra Liffii campi, venit in curru ad S. Brigidam,' &c. *Vit.* 3tia (seu *Ultani*), c. 51. Colgan, *Triad. Thaum.* p. 532. 'Conlianus Episcopus sanctus et propheta Dei, qui habebat cellam in australi parte Campi Liffii, venit in curru ad S. Brigidam, et commoratus est apud eam aliquot diebus; quem beata Brigida primum episcopum elegit iu sua civitate Kildara.' *Vit.* 4ta (seu *Animosi*) lib. ii., c. 19. Colgan, *ib.*, p. 552.

was by her elected first bishop in her city, or monastery, of Kildare, is named *Conlianus*. This, however, is to be regarded only as a Latinized form of the Celtic name *Connlead*, or *Condlaed*, under which he is best known in the Irish annals and martyrologies; and which was perhaps an epithet descriptive of his merits or virtues, and not his real name. The metrical martyrology of Aengus the Culdee, written at the close of the eighth century, and still extant in MS., thus records his death at the 3rd of May[1]:

  ' Bás Condlaid cain aige.'
  ' The death of Condlaid, beautiful pillar.'

And the scholium or gloss on this passage, which is probably not later than the eleventh century, tells us that Condlaed is for *Cundail-Aedh*, that is ' Aedh the wise.'[2] If this be so the bishop's original name must have been Aedh, or Hugh, and the title of Cundail, ' the wise,' was given him as expressing his ecclesiastical learning and eminence.

<small>Various names given to him.</small>

The same scholiast (both in the Bodleian and Dublin MS.) adds that the original name of Bishop Condlaed was Ronchend, and that he was the same as S. Mochonna of Daire. This latter statement is probably incorrect[3], occasioned by the great number of places in Ireland that

---

[1] *May.* The year of his death was A.D. 519, according to the Four Masters; more correctly 520, as O'Flaherty has dated the record of it in the annals of Tighernach.

[2] *The wise.* The Martyrology of Aengus in the Brussells MS. has the gloss, ' *i.e.* sapiens' over the word *Cundail.* But this gloss is not given either in the Bodleian or Dublin MS. of that work.

[3] *Incorrect.* See Colgan, *Actt.*

were called Doire or Daire, an oak or oakwood, of which Kill-dara, or Kildare[1], the church of the oak, was one of the most famous.

This variety of names, given to St. Brigid's first bishop, may partly account for the very great confusion which exists in the names of the early bishops in the see of Kildare: a confusion[2] which has no doubt been considerably increased by the absence of diocesan jurisdiction, and local episcopal successions in the early ages of the Church in Ireland. Our ecclesiastical biographers and historians, overlooking this fact, or anxious to conceal it, and finding the names of several bishops in the same place, took for granted that they must have presided in succession to each other; forgetting that, during the early period of which we are speaking, the Irish bishops had no regular succession or jurisdiction, and that there were frequently two or more contemporaneous bishops in the same place.

Confusion in the lists of early bishops of Kildare.

SS., ad 8 *Mart.*, p. 565, and the statement is not repeated by Michael O'Clery in the *Martyrology of Donegal*, although he mentions *Ronchend* as the original name of bishop Condlaed.

[1] *Kildare.* Derry is another instance: the original name is *Daire*, an oak or oak wood, rendered *roboretum* by Adamnan and others. The genitive case of *Daire* is *Dara*; whence *Cill-dara* (Kildare), 'the church of the oak.' *Ath-dara*, (Adare) 'the ford of the oak,' &c. See Colgan, *loc. cit.*, p. 566, note 3, 4; and Reeves, *Adamnan*, p. 160, n. Kildare is translated *Cella Roboris*, in the Life of S. Brigid, attributed to St. Ultan, cap. 47. (Colgan, *Tr.*

Th., p. 531, and note (23) p. 543.) In the 'Vita quarta,' attributed to Animosus, we read that Kildare had its name from an antient oak. 'Illa jam cella Scotice dicitur *Kill-dara*, Latine vero sonat Cella Quercûs. Quercus enim altissima ibi erat, quam multum S. Brigida diligebat, et benedixit eam, cujus stipes adhuc manet.'—Lib. ii. cap. 3. Colgan, *ibid.*, p. 550.

[2] *Confusion.* See Ware's *Bishops*, p. 386, *sq.* The list of early bishops of Kildare, in the 'Red book of the Earl of Kildare,' (Cotton, *Fasti*, part v., p. 222) is manifestly of no authority, and only adds to the confusion. See Colgan *Tr. Th.*, pp. 628 and 565, note.

Subjection of the first Bishop of Kildare to St. Brigid.

12. It will also be observed that Animosus, in the passage just quoted from his life of St. Brigid, tells us expressly that Condlaed was elected *by her*, to be first bishop 'in her city,' or monastic community[1] (Kildare), not to be bishop of a see or territorial district called Kildare. And this language clearly indicates the power claimed by the monastic superior, although in this case a female, over the bishop. The 'city' was hers, not his. He received from her his election or nomination to his episcopal office, and was therefore bound to exercise that office, subject to her jurisdiction, as bishop in her city, Kildare; for that name, signifying 'the Church of the Oak,' was then given, not to a diocese, but to the monastic establishment of St. Brigid only.

Legend of Conlead's vestments.

If we are to credit a legend told by Cogitosus, Brigid would seem to have exercised a right of property over that which belonged to her bishop. 'She followed,' says her biographer, 'the example of the most blessed Job, and never suffered the needy to pass her without a gift; for she gave to the poor the transmarine and foreign vestments[2] of Bishop Condlaed, of glorious light, which he was accustomed to use when offering the holy mysteries at the altars, on

---

[1] *Community.* So the word *Civitas* frequently signifies. See *Book of Hymns of the Antient Church of Ireland*, p. 136, note.

[2] *Vestments.* 'Nam vestimenta transmarina et peregrina Episcopi Conlaith, decorati luminis, quibus in solempnitatibus Domini et vigiliis Apostolorum, sacra in altaribus offerens mysteria utebatur, pauperibus largita est.' The biographer then tells us that when next the bishop required his vestments, vestments exactly similar were miraculously conveyed to St. Brigid, in a chariot of two wheels, sent from Christ Himself. *Cogitosus*, cap. 29, *ap.* Colgan, *Tr. Th.*, p. 522.

the festivals of our Lord, and the vigils of the Apostles.'

The germ of the same story is also found in the Irish metrical Life of St. Brigid, attributed to St. Brogan, and composed, as Colgan would persuade us, about A.D. 525. This author, however, says nothing of her having given the vestments to the poor, but only that she had blessed them. His words[1] are : —

> ' How many miracles she wrought,
> No man can fully tell;
> She blessed the vestments of Condlaed,
> Which he had brought from Leatha.' [2]

Perhaps the word translated ' she blessed ' may have been intended to imply that she consecrated them by giving them to the poor; for the next stanza speaks of their restoration : —

> ' When they were required by her,
> Her Son[3] rendered the event propitious;
> He brought those variegated garments,
> Carrying them in a two-wheeled chariot.'

We learn however incidentally, from this anecdote, that Condlaed had been abroad, and had brought, either from Italy or from Brittany, for the word used in the metrical life may signify either, vestments composed of some variegated[4]

---

[1] *Words.* Colgan, *Tr. Th.*, p. 517 (stanzas 41, 42.)

[2] *Leatha.* Colgan translates this word *Italia* ; but it is often used for Letavia, or Armorica. See Irish Nennius, *Addit. Note*, XI. p. xix. Here, however, it most probably signifies Italy or Latium.

[3] *Her Son.* The author of this hymn had already told us (stanza 2) that ' Brigid was the mother of the Lord of heaven.' This, with other attributes of the B. V. Mary, having been strangely assigned to her by the Irish. See *Book of Hymns of the Antient Ch. of Ireland*, p. 64.

[4] *Variegated.* So they are described in both accounts. Cogitosus

Anecdote of St. Condlaed's death.

texture, which were regarded in that age as peculiarly magnificent, and reserved exclusively for use on the greater festivals.

13. Another curious fact in the history of the bishop, which confirms to a certain extent that just related, at least so far as his travelling propensity is concerned, has been preserved by the author of the Scholia[1] on the 'Martyrology of Aengus,' already quoted. This anecdote, as it will throw some additional light upon the relative position in which Condlaed and his patroness were supposed to stand towards each other, may be here related.

After telling us that his name Condlaed signified 'Aedh, the wise,' as above noticed, our author proceeds:—' He was bishop of Kildare, and wild dogs [or wolves] devoured him, who followed Condlaed, by the side of Liamhan[2], in the plain

---

says, speaking of the restored vestments, 'similia per omnia vestimenta prioribus, tam texturis quam coloribus,' c. 29. In the ' Book of Durrow,' a MS. of the Gospels, said to be the autograph of St. Columba, and now in the Library of Trin. Coll. Dublin, there is a curious figure of an ecclesiastic in a variegated chasuble, the texture of which is represented as composed of squares of different colours, not unlike the modern Scottish plaid.

[1] *Scholia.* Colgan has frequently quoted these Scholia or Annotations on the ' Martyrology of Aengus,' under the title of *Aengusius Auctus,* and he attributes their composition to Cathald or Charles Maguire, who died A.D. 1498. Colgan, *Tr. Th.,* pp. 608, 623, *et al. passim*; *Actt. SS.* p. 57. It is probable that Maguire may have been the transcriber of a valuable copy of the work which Colgan had seen or was in possession of. But it is certain that the annotations themselves were in existence before Maguire was born. The MS. from which the quotations cited in the text are taken, was written at the close of the 14th century—about 100 years before Maguire; and there is another beautiful copy, written in the middle of the 13th century, preserved in the Bodleian Library (Laud, 610). We cannot, therefore, be very far from the truth if we attribute this valuable and most curious collection of legends to a compiler who flourished in the 11th or beginning of the 12th century, but who evidently drew his materials from much more antient sources.

[2] *Liamhan.* Or *Dun Liamhna,* now Dunlavan, a town in the

of Leinster.'¹ He adds : — 'This Condlaed was Brigid's principal artist, and the reason why he was killed by dogs was, that he had set out for Rome², in opposition to Brigid's command; wherefore Brigid prayed that he might come to a sudden death on the way, and this was fulfilled.'³

We may hope, for the sake of St. Brigid's Christianity, that this latter part of the story is not exactly true. But whether the remainder of the legend be founded on fact or not, it shews very clearly that, in the times of the Scholiast, it was taken for granted that the bishop in Kildare was subject to St. Brigid or her successor, and liable to the most extreme punishment from the Almighty Himself for disobeying her commands. There is nothing, however, at all improbable in the anecdote, setting aside the implied miracle. Condlaed, as we have already learned, had previously visited the continent of Europe, and brought from thence certain ecclesiastical vestments for use on the higher festivals, so that his desire to visit Rome was not unnatural; and he may have intended there to procure a new

---

county of Wicklow, and a prebend in St. Patrick's Cathedral, Dublin. This place was antiently one of the forts or residences of the kings of Leinster.

¹ *Leinster.* Here follows the genealogy of Condlaed, which we omit, as unnecessary for our present purpose. It may be observed, however, that Brigid and her bishop were both of the race of Ugaine Mór (*Hugonius magnus* as O'Flaherty calls him), king of Ireland A.M. 3619, although of different branches of that family.

² *Rome.* This tends to prove that by *Leatha*, in the passage just quoted from St. Brogan's metrical Life of Brigid, Latium in Italy, not Letavia, or Brittany, is intended.

³ *Fulfilled.* See the *Martyrol. of Aengus* (3 Maii), and the Scholia in the *Leabhar Breac*, a MS. in the Library of the Royal Irish Academy, Dublin, which is the copy of the Scholia here always quoted.

set of pontifical vestments for the more solemn celebration of Divine service. But this design the stern severity of his patroness discountenanced: and if he was 'eaten by wolves' on his journey, such an event would inevitably be attributed to his having disobeyed the commands or wishes of St. Brigid.

<small>Condlaed St. Brigid's chief artist.</small> 14. It will also be observed that, in the foregoing legend, Condlaed is said to have been 'Brigid's principal artist.'[1] The word denotes an artificer in gold, silver, and other metals, and we know that the antient Irish ecclesiastics of the highest rank did not consider it beneath their dignity to work as artificers in the manufacture of shrines, reliquaries, bells, pastoral staffs, croziers, covers for sacred books, and other ornaments of the Church and its ministers. The ecclesiastics of that period seem to have been in fact the only artists; and several beautiful specimens[2] of their work are still preserved, chiefly belonging to the century or two centuries before the English invasion of Ireland; for almost all the older monuments of this kind, especially if formed of the precious metals, appear to have been destroyed or melted by the Danes.

Condlaed's artistic skill and tastes, therefore, may have formed a strong motive with him for

---

[1] *Artist.* Compare the curious list of St. Patrick's household, Four Masters A.D. 448, in which he is given *two* artists. O'Donnell, in his *Life of S. Columba*, lib. i., c. 99, mentions a famous artist named Conla. (*Tr. Thaum*, p. 405.) But he is not to be confounded with Condlaed of Kildare.

[2] *Specimens.* See Petrie, *Round Towers*, p. 201. Trans. R. Irish Acad., vol. xx.

Multiplication of Bishops.

wishing to visit Rome, even in opposition to the commands of St. Brigid.

15. From the foregoing facts and anecdotes, no doubt can remain in the mind of any unprejudiced reader, that the normal state of episcopacy in Ireland was as we have described, non-diocesan, each bishop acting independently, without any archiepiscopal jurisdiction, and either entirely independent or subject only to the abbat of his monastery, or in the spirit of clanship to his chieftain. *The great number of independent bishops in the antient Irish Church.*

The consequence of this system was necessarily a great multiplication[1] of bishops. There was no restraint upon their being consecrated. Every man of eminence for piety or learning was advanced to the order of a bishop, as a sort of *degree*, or mark of distinction. Many of these lived as solitaries or in monasteries. Many of them established schools for the practice of the religious life, and the cultivation of sacred learning, having no diocese, or fixed episcopal duties; and many[2] of them, influenced by missionary zeal, went forth to the Continent, to Great Britain, or to other then heathen lands, to preach the gospel of Christ to the Gentiles.

---

[1] *Multiplication.* That there was a tendency to multiply bishops in early times on the continent of Europe and in the East, as well as in Ireland, is evident from the many canons of Councils made to restrict the practice. One of the earliest enactments of this kind is that of the Council of Laodicea, *circ.* A.D. 372, can. 16, prohibiting the consecration of bishops for villages, or places where there were no towns.

[2] *Many.* Of these Mabillon says, 'Fatendum est tamen ejusmodi episcopos plurimum Ecclesiæ tum Gallicanæ, tum Germanicæ profuisse: tametsi nonnulli (ut fit) per speciem Evangelii prædicandi, et nomine et officio abusi sunt suo.' *Actt. SS. O. S. B., iii., Præf.*, p.xiii., n. 34.

It is, therefore, an undoubted fact, that the number of bishops in Ireland was very great in early times, in proportion to the population, as well as absolutely; although we are not bound to believe that St. Patrick[1] consecrated 'with his own hand' three hundred and fifty bishops, founded seven hundred churches, and ordained five thousand priests. These figures, however, shew very curiously the ideas of the authors of such a legend, as to the number of bishops and priests which they deemed necessary for seven hundred churches.

Neither are we bound to believe that when St. Columba went from his monastery of Hi, in 590, to attend the synod of Drumcheatt, near Dungiven, in the county of Derry, he was attended[2] by twenty bishops, two score priests, fifty deacons, and thirty students preparing for holy orders. But these numbers could scarcely have been invented, if they had not seemed to the writer who invented them probable, or such as would have been deemed probable by others, in the times for

---

[1] *St. Patrick.* Nennius, c. 5. Jocelin. *Vit. Patricii*, c. 185, ap. Colgan, *Tr. Thaum.* p. 106. The author of the *Tripartite Life*, lib. iii., c. 97, makes the number 370 bishops, 5000 priests; *innumerable* clerks of the inferior orders ('clericorum inferioris ordinis numerum sine numero'), and 700 places of worship of all kinds,—'sacras ædes, sedes episcopales, monasteria, ecclesias, sacella, promiscue connumerando, fundavit septingenta.' Colgan, *ib.*, p. 167. The Four Masters make the number 700 churches, 700 bishops, and 3000 priests; *O'Donovan's Transl*, at A.D. 493, p. 157. Dr. Petrie has published, from the Irish MS. called the *Leabhar breac*, an antient poem attributed to Aileran, or Eleran, who died A.D. 664, at a very advanced age, in which Patrick is said to have consecrated 350 bishops, 300 priests, and 700 churches. *Hist. and Antiq. of Tara Hill*, p. 100 (Trans. Roy. Irish Academy, vol. xviii.). See also Ussher, *Britt. Eccl. Antt*, c. xvii. (Works, vol. vi., p. 518).

[2] *Attended.* See the antient poem quoted by Dr. Reeves, *Eccl. Antiq. of Down and Connor*, p. 132.

which he wrote. No person would now venture to assert that an abbat, himself only a priest, was *attended*, as a part of his retinue, by twenty bishops, forty priests, and fifty deacons.

16. Mochta[1], abbat of Lughmagh, or Louth, is said to have been a disciple of St. Patrick. He was by birth a Briton, who had travelled to Ireland. The Irish martyrologies, and some other authorities, call him a bishop. But he is not so styled by Adamnan, nor by the biographers of St. Patrick; and the Martyrology of Christ's Church Cathedral, Dublin, speaks of him as a 'confessor'[2] only. Be this, however, as it may, a curious poem[3] in the Irish language, which is still preserved, tells us that such was the wealth of St. Mochta's monastery, that he was able to support there, without requiring them to work for their livelihood, engaged altogether in the pursuit of learning, three hundred priests, and one hundred bishops, with sixty, or, according to another reading, eighty singers; and that these numbers constituted the ordinary monastic 'family,' or household of the monastery.

The monastic family of St. Mochta of Louth.

---

[1] *Mochta.* See Reeve's *Adamnan*, p. 6. Colgan, *Actt. SS.* ad 24 *Mart.*

[2] *Confessor.* 'Et in Hybernia Sancti Mocthei Confessoris.' *Obits and Martyr. of Chr. Church* (19 Aug.), p. 147. In the list of St. Patrick's household, given in the Tripartite Life (iii., c. 98, *Triad. Thaum.*, p. 167), and by the Four Masters (A.D. 448), Mochta is called the presbyter, or Archi-presbyter of Patrick. There was also an epistle attributed to him, but no longer extant, in which he thus describes himself, 'Maucteus peccator, presbyter, Patricii discipulus, &c.' Colgan, *Actt. SS.* p. 735. Ussher, *Primord*, (Works, vi., p. 416.)

[3] *Poem.* The antient poem alluded to occurs in the additions to the Martyrology of Aengus; (see *Obits and Mart. of Chr. Church*, loc. cit.), and is quoted in the Mart. of Donegal (at 19 Aug.); also by the Four Masters at A.D. 534 (p. 178); and by Colgan, *Actt. SS.* p. 734.

It has been suggested[1], indeed, that these figures may represent only the total number of bishops, priests, and singers who had emanated from the monastery, or had received their education there during the long life of St. Mochta, who is believed to have reached the age of more than a century.[2] But the antient poem in which the statement occurs gives these numbers to prove that the monastery was not poor, inasmuch as it sustained so many ecclesiastics, devoted to learning only, as the family or household of the abbat, without requiring them to work for their bread. The original words, as they have been printed by Colgan himself[3], with a literal translation, are as follow:—

' Nir bo bochta muinnter Mochta, Lughmaigh lis ;
  Tri ced sagart, um ced nespog, maille fris,
  Tri fichit seanoir salmach, a theglach rioghda remend ;
  Gan ar, gan buain, gan tioradh, gan gniomhradh, acht madh legend.

' Not poor was the family of Mochta, of Louth's fort !
  Three hundred priests, and an hundred bishops along with him,
  Threescore singing elders[4], composed his royal noble[5] household.

---

[1] *Suggested.* Colgan, *Actt. SS.* p. 731, note 8, says, ' Nonnullis forte nimis excessivus hic numerus 100 episcoporum et 300 presbyterorum, ex una schola prodeuntium, videri posset ; sed si rem penitius considerent, non est hic ambigendi locus; ex vetustissimi dierum magistri discipulis, successive ejus celeberrimam scholam frequentantibus, facile tantus numerus exurgere posset.' It is remarkable that the Martyrology of Donegal, as well as the Four Masters, in quoting this poem, omit the lines, which mention the 100 bishops and 300 priests.

[2] *A century.* Even Colgan rejects the fable that Mochta lived 300 years. *Loc. cit.*, p. 734.

[3] *Himself.* One or two obvious typographical errors in Colgan's text have been corrected ; as *dochta* for *bochta*, &c.

[4] *Elders.* Instead of *Seanoir*, ' elders,' the Scholiast on Aengus reads *Searclann*, ' youths,' which is better.

[5] *Noble.* Or magnificent, so Colgan

They ploughed not, they reaped not, they dried not corn, they laboured not, save at learning only.'

It is quite clear, therefore, that the author[1] of these lines intended to represent the monastic 'family' or household of St. Mochta as ordinarily consisting of an hundred bishops, three hundred priests, and sixty singing men, living together, engaged in ecclesiastical studies only. And therefore such numbers must have appeared to him, and to those for whom he wrote, if in some degree exaggerated for the honour of the saint, to have been at least within the limits of possibility. It was not deemed absolutely absurd that an hundred bishops[2] should be found living together in the household of a famous monastery.

17. There is abundant evidence, indeed, to show that two or more contemporary bishops frequently lived together, during the early period

Groups of contemporary bishops living to-

---

renders the word *remend* here. But we may perhaps translate it more correctly 'enumeration,'— thus, 'composed his household—a royal enumeration.'

[1] *Author.* Colgan's copy of the Scholiast on Aengus *loc. cit.*, p. 734, attributed this poem to St. Columcille. But in the Dublin MS. it is anonymous.

[2] *An hundred bishops.* This great number of bishops, which created no difficulty to the author of the legend, or to the Scholiast of Aengus, who has preserved it, was a serious puzzle to Colgan. Notwithstanding his attempt to solve it by spreading the hundred bishops over a century, another difficulty remained. In his mind a bishop necessarily implied an episcopal see; and hence he asks, (*ubi supra*, p. 731), 'Sed ubi, inquis, tot sedes episcopales in an-

gusto regno, in quo nec quadraginta hodie reperiuntur?' He answers, by asserting that Ireland was then more rich and prosperous than now : full of towns and cities, where every town, every village, every great monastery had its proper bishop. ' Respondeo, Regnum illud eo ævo longè florentius extitisse, longè pluribus civitatibus, oppidis, vicis et divitiis abundasse ; et singula pæne oppida, monasteria celebriora, et aliquando vicos, proprios habuisse episcopos, ut liquido constat legenti acta nostrorum sanctorum, et præsertim S. Patricii,' etc. This, however, is an admission that there were bishops without sees, and that the 100 bishops of Louth were contemporary ; for otherwise, if we scatter them through 100 years and among even 40 sees, the difficulty will cease to exist.

of which we speak, in the same town, church, or monastery. The antient Calendars, or Martyrologies, for example, frequently assign to the same day the festivals of such bishops. The number is almost always seven, which may perhaps be connected with the fact that seven churches are found together in many parts of Ireland.

Thus the Martyrology of Donegal mentions the following groups of seven bishops, at the respective days here given:—

Jan. 15. The seven bishops of Drom-arbelaigh, who are said to have been brothers, sons of Finn, or Fincrittan.

May 28. The seven bishops of Teach-na-ccomarce, in Tirconnell, near Lough Foyle.

July 21. The seven bishops of Tamhnach Buadha[1], said to have been also the sons of one father.

Aug. 23. The seven bishops of Aelmhagh, at Domhnach mór.

Oct. 3. The seven bishops of Cluan Cua, or Cluan Caa, said to have been brothers, the sons of one father.

Nov. 1. The seven bishops of Cill-tidil.

But this list is completely eclipsed by the 141 groups of seven bishops of various churches and places in Ireland, who are invoked in the Irish Litany[2], attributed to Aengus Cele De, or the Culdee, and probably composed in the ninth century.

---

[1] *Tamhnach Buadha.* Or Tamnach Buithe, as in the Litany of Aengus.

[2] *Litany.* This curious work has never been printed. It has been frequently quoted and referred to by Colgan, who makes no doubt of its authenticity. See especially *Actt. SS.,* p. 535, note 11; and Ward, *Vit. S. Rumoldi,* p. 206. The original is preserved in the *Leabhar Breac,* fol. 11, a., and in a fragment of the Book of Leinster, now in the College of St. Isidore, at Rome.

It is to be remarked also that some places in Ireland still retain the names given them from the number of bishops, who formerly lived there together: as, *Tulach na nespoic*, the hill of the bishops; *Rath na nespoic*, the fort of the bishops; *Disert na nespoic*, the desert or retreat of the bishops; *Domhnach na nespoic*, the church of the bishops, &c.

That these were considered to have been contemporaries is evident, not only from their being grouped together in the Irish Calendar for religious commemoration on the same day, but also from some of the groups being described as the sons of the same father. It may be said, indeed, that even if this were so, it is not necessary to suppose them to have lived together in the same place. All that is implied in the notices of them that have been quoted is, that they were buried in the same burial-place, and their memories especially honoured on the same day, and in the same church.

But in every instance these groups of bishops are said to have been *of*, not *in*, their respective churches; and when burial only is intended, this latter form of expression is always employed.

18. There is, however, an anecdote on record relative to one of these groups of bishops, which puts it beyond all doubt that they at least were contemporaries, and living together, not buried together, in the same church.

The seven bishops of Cluain-emain.

The story occurs in the curious life of St. Forannan, which Colgan[1] has translated from

---

[1] *Colgan.* Actt. SS. p. 336 *sq.*

the original Irish, and published at Feb. 15th. Forannan is represented as having been a relative and disciple of St. Columba; and Colgan has remarked, that the author must have compiled his work from ancient and trustworthy materials, because he appears to have himself lived after the year 1200; and although he mentions by name a great number of persons and places, he has not fallen into a single anachronism or inconsistency.[1]

Forannan is said to have accompanied St. Columba to the synod of Drumcheatt, of which we have already spoken.[2] Immediately after the business of the synod was concluded, our author tells us that Columba proceeded to the barony of Carbery, county of Sligo, for the purpose of founding a church at Drumcliffe. He stopped at Easdara, now Ballysadare, where he was met by a large concourse of ecclesiastics, male and female, of all ranks. Our author professes to enumerate only those who were descended from Cumaine, daughter of Dalbronach, and sister of Brogsech, the mother of St. Brigid. He mentions on the whole, about thirty bishops and saints, including females. Among the names which are given at length, but which it is not to our present purpose to quote, we find mention of 'the seven bishops of Cluain-Hemain,' or Cluain-emain, now Clonown[3], near

---

[1] *Inconsistency.* Colgan, *l. c.*, p. 338, note 1.
[2] *Spoken.* Sect. 15, *supra.*
[3] *Clonown.* See O'Donovan, *Hy Many*, p. 79. Four Masters, A.D. 1089.

Athlone on the Shannon. It is evident, therefore, that these bishops must have been regarded as living, and living together, when they are represented as having attended to do honour to Columcille on this occasion. The genealogy of the saints in the Book of Lecan represents them as brethren, the sons of the same mother; and they are invoked as the seven bishops of Cluain-emain[1], in the Litany of Aengus.

The fact that Aengus was able to enumerate no less than 141 places in Ireland where there were, or had been, *seven* contemporary bishops, seems to indicate the existence of an institution, founded upon the mystical *seven* of the Apocalypse. The institution itself continued, perhaps, for a short time only; and its object and practical operation are now forgotten. The circumstance that many, if not all, these groups of seven bishops were brothers or near relatives, added no doubt to the mystery, in the eyes of a clannish people, and in a church whose institutions were all so deeply tinged with the spirit of clanship and hereditary succession.

The establishment of seven bishops in various places, an institution of the Irish Church.

We can only now conjecture that the places in which seven bishops had established themselves were intended to be centres of instruction and de-

Its probable object and use.

---

[1] *Cluain-emain.* Colgan, who is greatly puzzled by this story, suggests that they were called bishops of Cluain-emain, not because they were bishops of that see, but because they were afterwards buried there, or because they had been monks there before they were bishops, *loc. cit.*, p. 339, note 28. But this is exceedingly forced and unnatural. If Colgan could have brought himself to acknowledge the non-diocesan episcopacy of the early Irish Church, he would have had no more difficulty in understanding how seven bishops might live together, than in understanding how seven priests might live together.

votion to the surrounding tribes; that the offices of the Church were there celebrated with peculiar pomp and solemnity, kept up, in all probability, without intermission, day and night[1]; hence the people flocked to these centres of religion, certain to find there at all times the teaching, the consolation, and the aids to devotion, which were best adapted to their wants and circumstances.

Such an institution must be viewed in connection with the missionary duties of the Church at that period. It was an institution temporary in its nature, but well adapted to a wild and imaginative people, fond of mystery and symbolism, easily attracted by external pomp and ceremony.

The missionary position of the early Irish Church explains some seeming irregularities.

19. The Irish Church, it should be remembered, was planted in a heathen land, and for some centuries continued to be surrounded on all sides by a very gross form of heathenism, derived partly from the aboriginal superstitions and idolatry of the people, and partly, at least in later times, from the pagan rites and doctrines of the Danes or Norsemen, who had established themselves in the country. The consecration of bishops without sees was therefore a matter of necessity; nor was it irregular that bishops should be so consecrated, whose duties were essentially missionary; the abundance of the harvest led very naturally to a

---

[1] *Day and night.* St. Bernard tells us that St. Columbanus established this, as he did other Irish customs, in his monastery of Luxeuil: 'ita ut ne momentum quidem diei ac noctis vacaret a laudibus,' *Vit. S. Malachiæ*, c. 6. But this enactment is not to be found in the Rule of St. Columbanus as we now have it.

readiness which later ages have thought laxity, in the multiplication of labourers, and every one who was deemed qualified by his piety or learning to spread Christianity among the savage Picts, or heathen Saxons of Great Britain, was, as a natural consequence, deemed qualified to receive episcopal consecration. At home the Church was struggling against a lawless and savage Paganism, in the midst of which neither life nor property was secure ; and against a state of society in which a Christian life was impossible, except in a community exclusively Christian. Hence the monastic character impressed upon Irish Christianity from its first introduction into the island. A cœnobitic association (not always rigidly confined to one sex), seemed the natural and almost the only means of mutual protection. Such societies were therefore formed in many places, and became centres of civilisation, schools of learning, examples of Christian piety, charity, and devotion. But these establishments were necessarily isolated, and often distant from each other. They were, therefore, compelled to provide, each within itself, the means of obtaining for their inmates all the rites of the Church, those which could be administered by priests, and those of which the proper minister was a bishop only. Hence, the monastic bishop of the Scotic religious houses. The abbat, or superior, may have been a presbyter only, or a layman, or, as in the case of St. Brigid, and her dependent abbesses, even a woman. But a bishop was always connected with the society, although without diocese or jurisdiction, and bound like other inmates of the monastery to render an absolute obedience to his monastic superior.

The Bishops of the Clans.

Afterwards, when one of the petty kings or chieftains embraced Christianity, he provided a bishop, sometimes more than one bishop, and other clergy, for the benefit of his clan. The district which owed allegiance to the chieftain, and was inhabited by his followers, became the proper field of labour to his bishops and clergy, and this was the first approach made to a diocesan or territorial jurisdiction in the Church of Ireland.[1] Thus, the bishoprick of Cill-mhic-Duach (now Kilmacduagh), is the antient territory inhabited by the clan of the Ui-Fiachrach Aidhne; the diocese of Enach-Duin (Annadown), was co-extensive with Iar-Connaught, or West Connaught, the seigniory of the O'Flahertys[2]; the diocese of Cill-Finnabrach (now Kilfenora), was the tribe-land of the Corca-Modruaidh, or Corcomroe; the present diocese of Ossory very nearly represents the antient territory of the Ossraighe; and Corca-Laidhe, the country of the O'Driscolls, or the Dairinne, is identical with the diocese of Ros-Ailithre, or Ross, now united to the see of Cork.

---

[1] *Ireland.* On the early episcopal divisions of Ireland, see Reeves, *Eccl. Hist. of Down and Connor*, pp. 126—127.

[2] *The O'Flaherty's.* See Rod. O'Flaherty's *West Conraught*, edited by Mr. Hardiman, for the Irish Archæological Society, p. 1. He says 'Its Cathedrall (for every Irish seigniory had its own, whose diocess runned with the seigniory's bounds) was Enagh-dun,' &c.

Emigration of Irish Bishops.

20. At the close of the eighth century[1] parties of Icelandic, Danish, and other Norse adventurers appeared for the first time on the coasts of Ireland. The churches and monasteries had then amassed some wealth, and were supposed to have amassed much more wealth than they really possessed. The plunder of these establishments, therefore, was the first object of the pirates. Many of them were burned to the ground. A great number of bishops and priests were consequently thrown upon the world, without a home and without their ordinary duties. Many of these emigrated in search of employment to England, and to the continent. Ignorant of diocesan or metropolitical jurisdiction at home, they had no idea that they were violating all ecclesiastical order, when they exercised their functions, without any reference to the local bishops, abroad. They had left Ireland without letters commendatory to foreign bishops; they brought with them no certificate of orders, no evidence to prove that they had themselves been canonically consecrated or ordained. They administered the Sacraments, consecrated churches, conferred Holy Orders and Confirmation, and heard confessions, wherever they went, without any regard to parochial or diocesan regulations, or the decrees of Councils; and it is to be feared that some of them, forced by their necessities, may have given good grounds for the accusation of simony that was frequently made against them.

The Danish invasions of Ireland, and their consequences.

[1] *Eighth century.* The Irish Annals give A.D. 795 as the exact date.

Severe laws against the Episcopi vagi from Ireland.

21. A knowledge of the peculiar position of episcopacy in Ireland at this period, throws great light upon the conduct of these wandering[1] ecclesiastics, and explains the reason of the severe laws that were passed by some Synods and Councils in England, and on the continent against them.

Council of Chalons-sur-Saone, 813.

For example, a provincial council of bishops and abbats, held under Charlemagne, at Chalons-sur-Saone, in 813, declares the orders conferred by these Scotic bishops to be null and void[2],

---

[1] *Wandering.* That there were also bishops without dioceses on the continent, at this period, who were not Irish, is evident from Can. 14, of the *Concilium Vermeriense,* as it is called, a synod held under King Pepin, A.D. 752 or 753, in the royal mansion of Vermerie, diocess of Soissons. 'Ut ab episcopis ambulantibus per patrias ordinatio presbyterorum non fiat: si autem boni sunt illi presbyteri, iterum consecrentur.' Richard, in his *Analyse des Conciles,* shocked at this recognition of a reiteration of Orders, suggests, 'On ne croyoit pas sans doute que ces évêques ambulans eussent reçu l'ordination épiscopale, et qu'ils fussent véritablement évêques.' But the title of this canon is 'Ut ab episcopis vagis presbyteri non ordinentur.' If they were not really bishops, that would have been a better reason for declaring their ordinations void, than their being *episcopi ambulantes* or *vagi.* But this 'Council,' which seems rather to have been a sort of local Parliament, at which secular lords were present, promulgated very unsound principles as to the dissolution of marriage; and we need not, therefore, wonder if it was also ignorant of the law of the Church against repeating ordination; *Concil. Vermeriense,* c. xiv. (Hardouin, *Concil.,* tom. iii., 1992). The Council of all the bishops of Gaul, assembled by King Pepin, July 11, 755, at his royal palace of Verneuil, on the Oise, decreed that all wandering bishops who had no dioceses (episcopi vagantes, qui parochias non habent), should be incapable of exercising any function without permission of the bishop of the diocese, on pain of suspension from their office; and that all clerks or laics who take part with such bishops be excommunicated. The reason alleged for this severity is 'nec scimus ordinationem eorum qualiter fuit.' *Concil. Vernense (seu Vernorense),* c. xiii. (Hardouin, *ib.* 1997.) It is not said, however, that these *episcopi vagantes* were Irish; and as the date of this council is prior to the Danish invasion of Ireland, the probability is that there were other wandering bishops, and other bishops without sees, against whom these enactments were made, besides the Irish, and before the Irish began to visit the continent.

[2] *Void.* See *Concil. Cabilonens. II.,* can. 43. 'Sunt in quibusdam locis Scoti, qui se dicunt episcopos esse, et multos negligentes, absque licentia dominorum suorum, sive magistrorum, presbyteros et diaconos ordinant: quorum ordinationem, quia plerumque in Simoniacam incidit hæresim, et multis erroribus sub-

INTROD.] *against Bishops without Dioceses.* 41

expressing a doubt as to the validity of their episcopacy, and accusing them of simoniacally admitting unfit persons and serfs to the orders of priest and deacon, without license or permission from the lords and masters of the persons so ordained.[1] The title of the canon which pronounces this sentence is, 'On the nullity of the ordinations conferred by the *Scoti,* who call themselves bishops.'

In England, a synod was convened under Cenwulf or Kenulph, King of the Mercians, and Wulfred, Archbishop of Canterbury, which met at Cealcythe[2], on the 27th of July, 816. By the fifth canon of this assembly, no person of Scotic race, 'de genere Scotorum,'[3] is permitted in any diocese to exercise the sacred ministry; and it is declared unlawful for the clergy to receive any assistance from these Scotic ecclesiastics, either in baptisms or in the celebration of the mass, or in administering the Eucharist

Council of Cealcythe, 816.

---

jacet, modis omnibus irritam fieri debere omnes uno consensu decrevimus.' Hardouin, *Concil.,* tom. iv., 1039.

[1] *Ordained.* There were severe laws against the ordination of a slave or freedman without his master's consent. See Bingham, *Antiq.,* book iv., ch. 4, s. 2; and Gratiani *Decretum,* part I., *Dist.* liv.

[2] *Cealcythe.* It is not ascertained where this place was; Chalk (in Kent), Chelsea, and Chulcheth (in Lancashire), have been suggested by different authors.

[3] *Scotorum.* It will be borne in mind that the name of Scotia was not generally given to the present Scotland until the 12th century. It was in 1098 that Eadgar assumed the title of King of Scotland, or *Scotia.* But Ireland still continued to retain the name to a much later period. See Fleming, *Collectanea Sacra,* p. 284. Therefore we must always understand Ireland when we meet with the words Scotia or Scoti in any author who flourished before the twelfth century. In later writers, when Ireland is intended, it is frequently distinguished as Scotia-*vetus, ulterior, major,* or Scotia *insula:* but this is not always the case, and we are frequently left to determine from the context only, whether the Irish or the British Scotia is intended.

to the people.[1] The reasons given for this severe sentence, are: first, because it was uncertain whether or by whom the Scotic bishops were ordained; and, secondly, because they scrupled not to enter other dioceses without the consent of the diocesan. A third reason is added, which is deserving of notice, because it evidently alludes to the absence of metropolitical jurisdiction in the Irish[2] Church:—'We know it to be enjoined in the canons that no bishop or presbyter venture to intrude upon the parish of another without the .consent of his own bishop. So much the more should we refuse to receive the

---

[1] *People.* It seems that even so late as the later half of the twelfth century, there were pseudo-bishops, pretending to be Irish, travelling about in England, and performing episcopal functions. They are mentioned in a circular letter addressed to the bishops of his province, by Richard, Archbishop of Canterbury, which is preserved amongst the works of Peter of Blois; they are called 'quidam pseudo-episcopi Hibernienses, aut Scoticæ linguæ simulantes barbariem,' and it is said of them, 'Quum enim gratiam sacræ unctionis nunquam acceperint, celebrant ordines, ecclesias dedicant, altaria consecrant, benedicunt abbates, et sic victum et vestitum misere mendicantes, sacramenta nostræ redemptionis miserabilem et lacrimabilem convertunt in questum.'—*Pet. Blesens. Epist.* liii. But these seem to have been actually impostors; possibly, however, they may have been real bishops, driven from Ireland by the Norman invaders under Henry II.; in that case, however, they would have had no occasion to *feign* the Irish language, and would not have been described as 'Scoticæ linguæ *simulantes* barbariem.' In that age forged bulls, and other similiar frauds were common. The dies or matrices for manufacturing the leaden seals of such bulls have been found in the ruins of some of the Anglo-Norman abbeys of Ireland; and there may have been also pseudo-episcopi and others going about to vend such wares. But why did they *pretend* to be Irish? Was their trade advantaged by an attempt to speak the 'barbarous' tongue of Ireland?

[2] *Irish.* It is strange that Johnson, in his notes on this Canon, makes the absurd mistake of confounding the Scoti here spoken of with the modern Scotch. *English Canons*, part i., 302 (*Anglo-Cath. Library*). He says, 'It is most reasonable to understand this canon of the Scots of North Britain.' But in the year 816 the Scots of North Britain were not so called. Whereas, we know, from Bede, Adamnan, and other authorities, that the Irish were then ordinarily called *Scoti*, and Ireland *Scotia*, by every one.

sacred ministrations from foreign nations, amongst whom no rank[1] is given to metropolitans, nor honour to other [bishops].'

From this passage we may evidently conclude that the supposed peculiarity of the Irish Church with respect to episcopal jurisdiction was then well known in England, seeing it is made an objection to the ministry of an Irish bishop travelling, or seeking employment elsewhere, that in his own country there were no dioceses, properly so called, no regular episcopal or archiepiscopal jurisdiction, and no limit or canonical restraint upon the consecration of bishops. And we know this to have been the case, from the native records of Irish Christianity. The jurisdiction of a bishop attached to a monastery depended upon the will of his abbat to whom he owed allegiance; and so far as the functions peculiar to his order were concerned, extended probably over the cells or minor religious houses attached to the principal monastery, as at Hi, Kildare and other places. The jurisdiction of a

No diocesan or metropolitical jurisdiction in Ireland.

[1] *No rank.* 'Interdictum est: ut nullus permittatur *de genere Scotorum* in alicujus diœcesi sacrum sibi ministerium usurpare: neque ei consentire liceat ex sacro ordine aliquod attingere, vel ab eis accipere in baptismo, aut in celebratione missarum, vel etiam Eucharistiam populo præbere: quia incertum est nobis, unde, et an ab aliquo ordinentur. Scimus quomodo in canonibus præcipitur, ut nullus episcoporum [vel] presbyterorum invadere tentaverit alius parochiam, nisi cum consensu proprii episcopi. Tanto magis respuendum est ab alienis nationibus sacra ministeria percipere, cum quibus nullus ordo metropolitanis, nec honor aliis habeatur.' *Conc. Celichyth.*,can. 5.(Hardouin,*Concil.*, tom. iv., 1220.) The meaning is this: the canons prohibit any priest or bishop from entering the parish or diocese of another without his own bishop's or metropolitan's consent; how then can we receive the ministry of those who, in their own country, acknowledge neither metropolitical nor diocesan jurisdiction? and, therefore, can bring no authorisation or consent from their own bishops?

bishop who was connected with a chieftain or
'king,' came nearer to the ordinary notion of a
diocesan superintendence, and, as we have already
observed, extended over the whole territory or
district of the clan. This was particularly the
case with Armagh, and hence some writers have
spoken of the See of Armagh, as if it was an
exception[1] to the general rule. But this, as we
shall have occasion to shew hereafter, was not
the case. The antient *primacy* of Armagh
differed essentially from the modern notion of
archiepiscopal or metropolitical jurisdiction.

Bishops without sees not peculiar to Ireland.

22. Nor was the Irish system so entirely
without example in other parts of Christendom,
as has been generally assumed.

That it should be found in North Britain, the
modern Scotland, is not wonderful. All the
religious and ecclesiastical institutions of Scotland[2] were derived from the parent Scotia; her

[1] *An exception.* Thus Lanigan, referring to the Canon of the Synod of *Cealcythe*, above quoted, says that it alluded ' it seems, to the Irish system, according to which there was no regular metropolitical see except the primatical one of Armagh.' *Eccl. Hist.*, vol. iii., p. 276, note 31.

[2] *Scotland.* Hector Boethius, lib. x. (quoted by Spelman, *Concil.*, tom. i., p. 342), speaking of Kenneth, King of Scotland, A.D. 840—855, tells us that he transferred the principal bishopric of the Picts from Abernethy to *Cill-Righmonaigh*, the Church of St. Rule or St. Regulus, changed that name to St. Andrew's, and ordained that the bishops of St. Andrew's should thenceforward be the chief bishops of Scotland; for (he adds) the kingdom had not as yet been divided into dioceses. ' Pontificiam sedem dudum Pictorum ab Abernethi oppido, eo ferro et igne deleto, ad *Templum Reguli* transtulit. Exinde huic oppido Sancti Andreæ ædes nomen est factum, eosque qui illuc per pluscula inde tempora sacrum gessere magistratum, maximos Scotorum episcopos appellârunt. Nondum enim Scotorum regnum, uti nunc, in diocœses divisum erat: sed quivis episcoporum, quos ea ætate vitæ sanctimonia cunctis reverendos fecerat, quocunque fuisset loco sine discrimine pontificia munera obibat.' This passage very exactly describes the ancient Irish episcopal system, which continued in both countries (as it did also in some other places), until the close of the eleventh century. From

not peculiar to Ireland.

principal churches and monasteries were founded by Irish saints, and bear the names of Irish saints to this day. But we have evidence also to prove that bishops without sees existed in very early times on the Continent of Europe, as well as in the East, and were not objected to as irregular. In the Council of Mâcon, A.D. 585, three bishops were present and subscribed the Acts, who had no sees.[1] And more than two centuries before that, the first Council of Antioch, in the year 341, summoned by Constantius to give greater solemnity to the consecration of the magnificent church which Constantine had begun ten years before at Antioch, makes mention of bishops without sees[2], or bishops without duties, as the original term seems to imply (ἐπίσκοποι σκολάζοντες), and enacts rules for their government, but without prohibiting the consecration of such bishops, and without appearing to regard them as at all irregular in themselves.

Council of Mâcon, A.D. 585.

Council of Antioch, A.D. 341.

Among the monks of Edessa in the fourth century, we read of two, Barses[3] and Eulogius, mentioned by Sozomen[4] in his 'Ecclesiastical

Monks of Edessa.

---

that period historians appear to have laboured to conceal and suppress all traces of it, and even to our own times Keith and Spottiswood, in Scotland, Colgan, Ware, Harris, and Lanigan in Ireland, assume the existence of regular diocesan successions in all the principal sees of both countries, contrary to the testimony of all authentic history.

[1] *Sees.* Concil. Matiscon. Hardouin, tom. iii., 466.

[2] *Without sees.* Concil. Antioch., (A.D. 341), can. 19. They were called

also *Episcopi Vagantes* (as in the Council of Verneuil; see above, p. 40, note 1), and *Vacantes.* In the Council of Lyons, so late as 1449, they are spoken of as 'Episcopi *Portatiles.*' Mart. and Durand. Anecd., tom. iv., 377, n. 4.

[3] *Barses.* Another reading calls him *Sarses.*

[4] *Sozomen. Hist. Eccl.,* lib. vi., cap. 34. ι.άρσης τε καὶ Εὐλογίος, οἳ καὶ ἐπισκόπω ἄμψω ὕστερον ἐγενίσθεν, οὐ πόλεως τινὸς, ἀλλὰ τιμῆς ἕνεκεν, ἀνταμοιβῆς ὥσπερ τινῶν αὐτοῖς πεπολιτευμένων, χειροτονηθέντες ἐν τοῖς

History,' who were bishops without sees, and who had been consecrated in exact accordance with the Irish custom, as a mark of honour. 'In Edessa,' says this historian, 'and in the cities around it, were at that time very celebrated *philosophers*,' (for Sozomen ordinarily uses this title to denote monks,) 'Julian, and Ephræm Syrus, the author, (of whom we have already spoken, in the reign of Constantius,) Barses also, and Eulogius, who were both afterwards bishops, not of any city, but as an honourable distinction in recognition of their great merit, consecrated in their own monasteries.' He adds that Lazarus, whom he had mentioned just before, was a bishop of the same kind [1]; that is to say, a bishop without a see. This Lazarus, it appears, was the bishop of the monks called *Boscoi*, from their peculiar discipline, or *philosophy*, as Sozomen[2] calls it, of which they were the first inventors. They had no houses, but lived on the mountains; they ate no bread, flesh, or any cooked or prepared food; they drank no wine; they worshipped God in the open air, according to the rites of the Church, in psalms and hymns; and when the hour of feeding came, like beasts at

The monks called Boscoi.

ἰδίοις μοναστηρίοις. Valesius, in his note on this passage, tells us that Barses was bishop of Edessa, under which title St. Basil addressed two epistles to him. But even if St. Basil's correspondent was the same Barses, which is not certain, he may have been at first consecrated a bishop without a see, as Sozomen says, and afterwards made bishop of Edessa, and so Valesius suggests.

Be this, however, as it may, the foregoing passage proves that there was nothing strange or uncommon in this kind of consecration, as a sort of honorary degree, τιμῆς ἕνεκεν, in the time of Sozomen.

[1] *Same kind.* Ὅν τρόπον καὶ Λάζαρος ὁ δηλωθείς.

[2] *Sozomen*, lib. vi., c. 33. Τούτους δὲ καὶ Βοσκοὺς ἀπεκάλουν, ἰναγκος τῆς τοιαύτης φιλοσοφίας ἄρξαντες.

pasture, each taking a sickle, they spread themselves over the mountains, eating whatever herbs they could find. 'Such,' says our author, 'was the nature of their philosophy;'[1] and yet this singular society had their peculiar bishop.

23. The case of bishops without sees, consecrated as missionaries to the heathen, need not be here mentioned; for that is a custom which still exists, and has never been deemed irregular. Thus St. Swidbert, one of the twelve missionaries who accompanied St. Willibrord to Friesland A.D. 690, was a bishop without a see.[2] And the case was the same with St. Winfrid (A.D. 715), better known by his foreign name of Boniface.[3] St. Amand, as his prose biographer informs us, was consecrated a bishop (without a see) for the office of preaching, according to the custom of the time,'[4] that is to say, of the seventh century; and Milo[5], the author of his Metrical Life, expresses this still more explicitly:—

_{Missionary bishops without sees.}

> 'Nec sedem propriam suscepit pontificalem,
> Sed veluti Paulus populus aggressit Eoos,
> Sic iste occiduas partes transmissus adivit,
> Gentibus et sparsis sparsit pia verba salutis.'

On the whole, it is impossible to doubt that bishops without sees existed both in the east and in the west in very early times, and were not

---

[1] *Philosophy.* Καὶ οἱ μὲν ὧδε ἐφιλοσόφουν. *Sozom. ibid.*

[2] *See.* 'Nulli sedi addictus.' Mabillon, *Annal. O. S. B.*, lib. xix., n. 66, tom. ii., p. 32.

[3] *Boniface. Ibid.*, lib. xx., n. 56, p. 68.

[4] *Time.* 'In officium prædicandi ordinatur episcopus, sicut mos illius temporis exigebat.'—*Vit. S. Amandi, per Phil. Harmeng.*, c. ii., n. 20. (Bolland. *Actt. SS. ad 6 Feb.*, p. 861, D.)

[5] *Milo. Ibid.*, p. 878, D.

deemed uncanonical or irregular. Ecclesiastical writers have been unwilling to acknowledge this, and have endeavoured as much as possible to conceal the fact. But further research, especially among the unpublished records of Christian antiquity, would doubtless prove the existence of bishops without diocesan jurisdiction, perhaps from the very beginning of Christianity, to an extent much greater than is generally supposed. In Ireland this custom continued and prevailed to a later period than elsewhere. For Ireland was never included[1] within the bounds of the Roman empire, and consequently did not receive the decrees of the eastern and western Councils summoned under the authority of the emperors, in which bishops without sees were discouraged or prohibited, and the metropolitical and diocesan jurisdiction finally established.

These considerations, when impartially reviewed, go far to explain the seeming irregularities of which the early church in Ireland was accused, and which, no doubt, were real irregularities, when judged by the standard to which ecclesiastics living in and since the twelfth century have been accustomed to appeal.

Monastic bishops

24. There are traces also in several places out

---

[1] *Included*. The ancient Romans never invaded Ireland. The Christian Emperors scarcely knew of its existence. Pope Adrian, in the 12th century, first claimed ownership, on the authority of the pretended donation of Constantine, because it was an *island*, and gave Ireland as a bribe to the King of England. See O'Callaghan's *Macariæ Excidium* (edited for the Irish Archæological Society,) note 62, p. 242, *sq*. William of Newbury (quoted by the Abbé Mac Geoghegan, *Hist. de l'Irlande*, tom. i., p. 440), says of Ireland 'Nunquam externæ subjacuit ditioni.'

of Ireland of the existence of monastic bishops similar to those whom Bede regarded as peculiar to the Scotic Church, living in the monasteries, and restrained in the exercise of their episcopal functions by their vow of obedience to their abbat.

living under the rule of an abbat, in England, and on the continent.

In the synod of Hereford, held under Archbishop Theodore in 673, the canons of which are preserved by Bede[1] himself, it is enacted 'that bishops who were monks should not go about from place to place, or from monastery to monastery, unless sent by their abbat; but should continue in the same obedience which they had promised at their conversion.'

The Synod of Hereford, 673.

In some respects, no doubt, these bishops were in a different position from the old monastic

The monk-bishop of the

---

[1] *Bede. Hist. Eccl.*, lib. iv. c. 5. 'Ut episcopi monachi non migrent de loco ad locum, hoc est, de monasterio ad monasterium, nisi per demissionem proprii abbatis; sed in ea permaneant obedientia, quam tempore suæ conversionis promiserunt.' This is the reading of Spelman, *Concil.*, tom. i. p. 153; and of Hardouin, *Concil.*, tom. iii. 1016. But Smith and other editors of Bede, with many MSS., read 'Ut *ipsi* monachi non migrent,' &c. This reading, however, although modern controversies have led to its very general adoption, seems to destroy the whole force and meaning of the canon. Why '*ipsi* monachi'? Smith, in his note on this passage, says 'Mira fuit hic *Editorum* ignorantia dicam vel oscitantia? qui legerunt *episcopi*, unde absurdissimam dederint eruditis controversiam, ac si in *hac* etiam ecclesia, sicut in *Hiiense* traditur, episcopi abbatibus obedientiam debeant.' But why is it so very absurd to suppose that the discipline which existed at Hi might also have been found elsewhere? Is it not more absurd to suppose a formal canon made to prohibit 'monks themselves' from migrating to other monasteries, without the leave of their abbats, and enacting that they must continue in the same obedience which they had promised when they became monks? But read 'episcopi monachi' and this is explained. Nothing could be more natural than that a monk who had been raised to the episcopal order should believe himself thereby relieved from monastic obedience, and at liberty, in his episcopal character, to visit other monasteries without the leave of his abbat. The above remark of Dr. Smith is a curious instance of the prejudice which has led learned men to ignore, if not to suppress, the various allusions to the monastic bishop to be met with in antient documents.

Anglo-Saxons not exactly similar to the monastic bishop of Ireland.

bishops of the Irish Church, because the monasteries to which they belonged were, in most places, under the jurisdiction of diocesan bishops. But the very canon we have quoted proves the existence of bishops, who were also monks, and the necessity that was felt for a stringent enactment to confine them within their monasteries, to check the possibility of their interfering with the diocesan bishops, and to bind them to continue under the same strict obedience to their abbats which they had promised when they took upon them the monastic vows.

Such bishops may probably have felt that the obligations of their episcopacy required them to visit other places in the exercise of their peculiar functions, and so loosened the tie of obedience to their monastic superior; but the object of the Church at that time evidently was to strengthen the diocesan jurisdiction of the secular bishops. It was therefore enacted that the monk-bishop should return to his monastic obedience, confine himself to his monastery, and abandon all attempts to exercise his episcopal functions, except so far as he was commanded or permitted to do so by his abbat and the bishop of the diocese. The monk-bishop of the Anglo-Saxon monasteries was not there *ex officio*. He was not chosen as in the Scotic or Irish monasteries, to minister as a bishop to the inmates of the house. His services, in fact, were not needed, because there existed a regular diocesan episcopacy outside and around the monastery. He was either a bishop, who had for some reason been deposed from his see, or who had voluntarily abandoned the duties of his episcopal office for the sake of ascetic retirement and devotion. So far, then, the cases are not strictly parallel; and the canon of Hereford is evidence only of the desire of the Latin party, under the guidance of Theodorus of Canterbury, to check all tendency to assimilation with the Scotic usages.

25. But on the continent of Europe we find some remarkable cases more nearly parallel with the Irish custom, and indicating the existence of an antient discipline which continued in full force in Ireland long after it had been suppressed elsewhere. *The monastic bishops on the continent of Europe.*

The abbey of St. Denis near Paris appears to have preserved the custom of having a bishop of its own from a very early period. *The abbey of St. Denis, near Paris.*

The following anecdote occurs in a curious tract[1], 'On the virtues and miracles of Macarius the Areopagite, Dionysius, and his companions,' written by a monk of St. Denis, whose name is unknown, but who appears to have flourished in the reign of Charles the Bald; the middle of the ninth century. 'About the same time,'[2] says

---

[1] *Tract.* 'De virtutibus et miraculis Macarii Areopagitæ, Dionysii sociorumque ejus,' published by Mabillon, *Acta SS. Ord. S. Benedicti,* tom. iv. p. 311, *sq.*

[2] *Time.* 'Eodem fere tempore quidam incola vici, qui beatorum martyrum veneratione magnifice insignis habetur, post horam nonam Dominici diei annonam excutere ausus est. Inde purgare eam cum aggressus esset, furcillæ qua id satagebat sinistra ejus manus adhæsit tam valide, ut nullus digitorum saltem emoveri aliquo posset conamine. Cerneres miserum opus quod cœperat dissimulare avidius velle, idque divinam non sinere ultionem. Postera die accessit ad Heribertum Episcopum (moris quippe ei fuit ecclesiæ aliquamdiu episcopos habere); eique peccata sua confessus est. Jubet

this writer, meaning the time of King Pepin (who died in 768), 'a certain inhabitant of the town which was held in such great veneration on account of the blessed martyrs, was so irreverent as to shake out his corn after the ninth hour of the Lord's day. And afterwards when he attempted to cleanse it, his left hand stuck so strongly to the fork with which he endeavoured to do so, that he was unable, do what he would, to extricate his fingers. The next day he went to Bishop Heribert (for it was the custom of that church for some time to have bishops) and confessed his sins to him.' The story goes on to say that the bishop summoned the brethren, to pray for the man in the crypt of St. Denis, and his hand was set free by the intercession of the saint. The neighbours were seized with great fear, and many were deterred from attempting similar labours on the Lord's day.

In this story it is incidentally stated, that it was for some time (*aliquamdiu*) the custom of the Church of St. Denis to have bishops of its own; and the language seems also to imply that this custom had ceased[1] to exist at the time when this author wrote, for otherwise he would

---

Episcopus furcillam utrinque præcidi, evocatisque fratribus ut pro eo Dominum precarentur obtinet. Sic una cryptam Beati Dionysii ingredientes, pro eo cum fratres devote orarent, sanctorum meritis sparsis digitis resoluta manus amissum plene recipit officium.'—*Mabillon, ibid.* p. 313.

[1] *Had ceased.* This remark is made by Mabillon, who says in his note on the passage: 'Hinc patet, nonnullis monasteriis a jure communi exemtis proprios fuisse Episcopos.' And in another place he says, 'Ex his porro anonymi verbis intelligimus, jam ipsius tempore desiisse *morem* illum habendi episcopum loci proprium, ut verba auctoris expendenti conspicuum fiet.' *Præfat. in* tom. iii. p. 14.

not perhaps have used the past tense 'moris quippe ei *fuit* ecclesiæ *aliquamdiu* episcopos habere.'

But the abbey appears to have had a bishop of its own from a very early period, if not from its original foundation. Pope Stephen, in 757, the year of his death, gave a charter to the celebrated Abbat St. Fulrad, sanctioning the election of a bishop by the abbat or brethren of St. Denis, and defining the bishop's duty to be to take the pastoral care of all religious houses founded by St. Fulrad, in connection with the parent monastery of St. Denis, and to preach and teach therein: exempting him from the interference of any diocesan bishops, and placing him under the immediate jurisdiction of the Holy See.

This charter has been published in a mutilated form in the editions of the Councils, omitting all that related to the monastic bishop, a fact which seems to shew a desire of suppressing[1] or keeping out of view the supposed irregularity of a bishop without a diocese, who was subject to the abbat of his monastery. But Mabillon found the original in the archives of St. Denis,

---

[1] *Suppressing.* So Mabillon plainly intimates: 'Hæc clausula de proprio episcopo,' (he says,) 'quæ in editis conciliorum libris deest, invenitur in veterrimis scriptis exemplaribus nonnullis, habetque auctoritatem a libro primo miraculorum S. Dionysii, ubi legitur morem ejus aliquamdiu fuisse ecclesiæ episcopum habere, qualis fuit Heribertus episcopus ibidem laudatus. Verum hac de re disputent alii quantum lubet; historica facta notare nobis incumbit, non jus eorum asserere.'—*Annal. Bened.*, lib. xxiii. n. 26. But it is only fair to the editors of the Councils to say, that the mutilation appears to have taken place in the MSS. from which they copied.

and has printed it in full in his life of St. Fulrad.[1]

The charter contains internal evidence of the antiquity of the custom of a special monastic bishop in this monastery. It recites[2] that Landeric or Landri, Bishop of Paris, with the approbation of his canons and suffragans, and at the request of Clovis II., son of Dagobert, had consented to exempt from his own jurisdiction and that of his successors the abbey of St. Denis, and all the clergy *of whatsoever order* who served within its precincts. St. Landri (for he was afterwards regarded as a saint) became Bishop of Paris about A.D. 650 and Clovis died in 656. Therefore the abbey must have had its monastic bishop a full century before the charter of Pope Stephen, and evidently also long before the exemption granted by St. Landri.

Charter of Hadrian I., A.D. 786.

And this appears further from a subsequent charter[3] of Pope Hadrian I., dated A.D. 786, in which he confirms the privilege conceded by his predecessor Stephen, in these words: 'Where-

---

[1] *St. Fulrad.* Acta SS. O. S. B., tom. iv. p. 305.

[2] *Recites.* 'Et quoniam ad preces Chludovii, filii Dagoberti regis, dominus Landericus Parisiacæ urbis episcopus, a sua et omnium successorum potestate deinceps, cum consilio suorum canonicorum et fratrum suorum co-episcoporum regionis illius, cœnobium vestrum et omnes ad eum servientes clericos quorumcumque ordinum in procinctu vestri monasterii absolvit; nos etiam idem, et habere vobis episcopum per singulare privilegium concedimus, qui de vobis ab abbate vel a fratribus in monasterio vestro electus, et a fratribus nostris episcopis de illa regione consecratus, illa vestra monasteria a vobis edificata provideat, et vice nostri nominis ubi et ubi fuerint regat, et prædicationi tam in ipso vestro monasterio quam in sibi subjacentibus deserviat.'—*Acta SS. O. S. B., ibid.*

[3] *Charter.* This letter is addressed to Maginarius, Abbat of St. Denis, the immediate successor of St. Fulrad. After reciting the former grant of Pope Stephen, it proceeds: 'Quapropter auctoritate beati Petri Apostolorum

INTROD.] *of the Abbey of St. Denis.* 55

fore relying on the authority of the blessed Peter, Prince of the Apostles, we enact and declare in the aforesaid venerable monastery, that it be altogether lawful to have a bishop there, *as from antient times and up to this present there hath been;* by whose preaching the people, who come daily with devout intentions from various countries to the sacred precincts of the monastery of the said martyr of Christ, may be rendered worthy to receive the salvation of their souls.'

These words plainly declare that the privilege of electing a bishop[1] of their own was not for the first time conferred upon the abbat and monks of St. Denis by Pope Stephen, but must have existed long before. The words 'from antient times and up to this present,' *(a priscis temporibus et usque hactenus,)* could scarcely have been used in reference to the short period which had elapsed since the date of Pope Stephen's death.

Here, then, in the great French abbey of St. Denis we find an exact parallel with the Irish or Scotic usage, which so greatly startled the

principis fulti, in jam dicto venerabili monasterio statuentes promulgamus, ut penitus liceat ibidem habere episcopum, sicut a priscis temporibus, et usque hactenus fuit ; per cujus prædicationem populus, qui a diversis regionibus devota mente quotidie ad sancta ejusdem martyris Christi monasterii limina convenerit, remedium consequi mereatur animarum.' Hardouin, *Concil. III.*, 2021 D. This document has been given without mutilation in the collections of Councils.

[1] *Bishop.* Mabillon has found the names of two of these monastic bishops of St. Denis, besides *Heribert*, the bishop mentioned by the author of the tract on the miracles of the abbey, viz. : *Turnoald*, who is styled 'bishop and warden of the church of St. Denis' (episcopus et custos basilicæ S. Dionysii), in a charter of King Chilperic (A.D. 716—720) : and *Gotofredus episcopus*, whose name occurs in a list of the monks of St. Denis, published by D'Achery *(Spicil. III.*, p. 333, fol. edit.), at the end of a letter of agreement between the abbeys of S. Denis and of Rheims in 838. *Acta SS. O. S. B.*, tom. iv. p. 306.

venerable Bede: the only difference being this, that the antient custom of a bishop, resident in the monastery, was kept up at St. Denis, after the establishment of an external diocesan episcopacy, which rendered it necessary to procure an express recognition from the Pope, in order to protect the monastic bishop from the interference and jealousy of the diocesan and his suffragans; and also, no doubt, to enable the Court of Rome without difficulty to suppress the monastic bishop whenever it was found convenient to do so.

The Abbey of St. Martin, at Tours. 26. Nor was this a solitary instance. The same custom existed in the celebrated monastery of St. Martin, at Tours; and a confirmation[1] of the privilege was obtained from Pope Hadrian I., expressed in nearly the same words as those already quoted from the charter granted by the same pontiff to the abbey of St. Denis. The usage was retained longer at St. Martin's than at St. Denis. At St. Martin's the jealousy of the diocesan bishops, and especially the refusal of the canons to receive with proper respect the Papal legates, caused Pope Urban II.[2] to abolish

---

[1] *Confirmation.* This document is printed by Papirius Masson, in his book *De Pontificibus Romanis*; and more correctly by Rad. Monsniere, in his *Defensio jurium ecclesiæ S. Martini*, cap. ii., quoted by Mabillon, *Pref.* ad tom. iii. *Acta SS. O. S. B.*, p. xiii.

[2] *Urban II.* 'Viguit aliquamdiu in utroque monasterio usus propriorum episcoporum; diutius quidem in Martiniano quam in Dionysiano, nimirum ad pontificatum usque Urbani II., qui Turonos ad limina S. Martini profectus, sublato proprio episcopo, Martinianam basilicam jussit *Romano specialiter adhærere pontifici*, anno Dominicæ Incarnationis, MXCVI., ad componendas scilicet querelas episcoporum Gallicanorum, præcipue vero Legatorum ecclesiæ Romanæ, quos Martiniani canones debito cum honore suscipere recusabant.'—*Mabillon*, ibid. The docu-

the monastic bishop, in the year 1096, and to annex the Church of St. Martin specially to the Roman Pontiff. In the abbey of St. Denis, as we have seen, the custom appears to have been abandoned in the beginning of the ninth[1] century.

As in Ireland, the bishop was sometimes also abbat. This was the case with Wicterbus, Bishop and Abbat of St. Martin's of Tours, who died[2] A.D. 756. At his death, however, the two offices were divided. Andegarius, or Audegarius[3], succeeded him as bishop, and Wlfard, or Gulfard, as abbat.

The abbat sometimes a bishop.

27. The monastery of Lobes, or Laubes, in Belgium, seems also to have been one of those in which the monastic bishop and abbat-bishop existed for some time. Ursmar, its first abbat, who died A.D. 713, was a bishop; as also Theodulfus, fourth abbat; Franco, twelfth abbat; and Stephen, thirteenth abbat. It is not quite certain that these last were strictly confined to the

The abbey of Laubes.

---

ments are given by Monsniere; *loc. cit.*, cap. iii.; and see the *Epistola ad Clerum Turonensem*, Hardouin, *Concil.*, tom. vi. 1642, in which the words quoted by Mabillon occur : 'Denique quoniam in quibusdam suæ ecclesiæ privilegiis proprium eis habere episcopum concessum est, ejus vice nos Romano eos sancimus specialiter adhærere Pontifici, et graviores eorum causas ex ejus pendere judicio.' And the same words nearly are repeated in the next epistle, *Ad Canonicos S. Martini Turonensis*,' *ib.*, 1643.

[1] *Ninth.* See above p. 52. Monsniere has found the names of ten bishops of the monastery of St. Martin; viz. *Cent.* viii. Amaraldus,

Nicetius, Paternus; to whom Mabillon adds, Wicterbus and Andegarius; *Cent.* ix. Benignus, Desiderius, Wichardus; *Cent.* x. Maximus, Julianus. Besides Philippus and Lucianus, whose date is uncertain.— Mabillon, *ibid.* p. 14.

[2] *Died.* Annal. Masciacens. *ap.* Labbæum Bibl. Novæ. tom. ii., p. 736, quoted by Mabillon, *Annal. Benedict.* lib. xxiii. n. 23.

[3] *Audegarius.* He is said to have been of English descent, his father, Betto, having been a merchant at Marseilles. He died 15 Kal. Feb. 790.—Annal. Masciascens. *ap.* Labbæum, *loc. cit.*, and Mabillon, *Acta SS. O. S. B.*, *Præf. ad* tom. iii. p. 14.

monastery. But the case of Ursmar seems to have been peculiar, from the difficulty it occasioned after a lapse of nearly 300 years to one of his successors, Fulcuin, nineteenth abbat, by whom a history of the abbey[1] was compiled. This writer tells us that he had often searched into the question how Ursmar came to be a bishop. The fact itself was attested by all the antient records of the abbey, but without any mention of the place or time of his consecration, nor by whom he was consecrated; and the older monks gave different explanations[2] of the circumstance: some saying that Ursmar was ordained a bishop that he might preach with more effect to the neighbouring barbarians; and others that it belonged to the dignity of the place, that is of the abbey itself, as being of royal foundation, and in the neighbourhood of the royal palace, that it should be committed only to the charge of a bishop, and accordingly (our author says) many of Ursmar's successors were of episcopal dignity.

This latter opinion seems to have been nearer the truth, although not exactly true. Ermin,

---

[1] *Abbey.* The work of Fulcuin (ob. 990), is entitled 'Gesta abbatum Lobiensium,' and is published by D'Achery, *Spicil.*, tom. ii. p. 730.

[2] *Explanations.* Fulcuin, *Gestt.* c. 3 (*D'Achery, l. c.*, p. 732); 'Varia de hoc est seniorum nostrorum relatio, dicentibus quibusdam, quod prædicandi gratiâ, ut competebat tunc rudimentis novellæ fidei, ad compescendos superfluos ritus gentis barbaricæ episcopus fuerit ordinatus; quod factum de S. Amando legimus. Quibusdam dignitatem hanc loco tribuentibus; quod videlicet locus Regius, Regiâ munificentiâ constructus, Regio, ut dictum est, palatio contiguus, scilicet Liptinis, nulli committeretur, nisi prius ordinatus esset episcopus; quam dignitatem et in plerisque successorum ejus durasse, in subsequentibus dicemus.' See also Mabillon, *Acta SS. O. S. B.*, tom. iii. p. 241.

the immediate successor of Ursmar, does not appear to have been a bishop; but it is remarkable that there were in Ermin's time bishops in the monastery, who, we are expressly told, took a part in the government of the house. 'They were,' says Fulcuin[1], ' co-operators or successors, governors of the place, and co-abbats' with Ermin. Our author names these co-abbats; and it is curious that one of them was Irish, and is placed first on the list: 'The holy Abel, *a Scot by race;* the holy Wlgis, a bishop, and the Lord Amulguin, also a bishop.'

The fact that there was in the abbey a *co-abbat*, in high authority, who was a Scot (that is, an Irishman), is worthy of note, as proving that the Irish Church was not deemed irregular at that time in the monasteries of Europe, and that the Scots were not then rejected or excommunicated in consequence of any peculiar national usages. Whether Abel, the Scot, as he is afterwards[2] called by our author, was a bishop at the time when he was in office under Ermin,

Irish ecclesiastics connected with some foreign abbeys.

---

[1] *Fulcuin.* Gestt. Abb. Lobiens., c. 5 (*D'Achery, ib.*, p. 731) : ' Habuit etiam [Erminus] et co-operatores sive successores ejusdem loci gubernatores, et co-abbates, sanctum utique Abel, Scottum genere, et sanctum Wlgisum episcopum, et Dominum Amulguinum æque episcopum ; qui utrum sibi vicissim successerint, an sancto Erminospirituali- bus occupato rebus locum in commune tractaverint, nihil certi reliquit antiquitas.' From these words it is evident that our author was doubtful as to the nature of the *co-abbacy* of which he speaks, whether it meant that when Ermin was absent on spiritual duties, the three whom he names took the office of abbat in succession, or exercised it in conjunction. A knowledge of the Irish customs would have explained at once the position of these bishops.

[2] *Afterwards.* Fulcuin, c. 7 : ' Nos collatis undecunque numeris, hunc eundem Abel et nostrum fuisse, et Scottum, et episcopum, facile ratione probavimus.' Cf. Mabillon, *Acta SS. O. S. B.*, tom. iii. p. 531 *sq.*

Saltzburgh.

in the monastery, is not certain; but Fulcuin tells us that he was afterwards bishop of Rheims, where he remained, however, only for a short time, and then returned to monastic life.

28. The city of Saltzburgh, anciently called Juvavia[1], appears to have also had some connection with Irish ecclesiastics in the eighth century. Its great Benedictine monastery, dedicated to St. Peter, was founded by St. Rudbert, or Rupert[2], who died 718. With this monastery Rudbert connected an episcopal see, of which he was himself the first bishop, having been, before he devoted himself to missionary labour, bishop of Worms. It does not appear certain that he was a monk; but for many years after his death the abbat of his monastery was either bishop, or the superior of the bishop, after the Irish custom. This appears from the list of the successors to St. Rudbert, which is annexed to the most antient form of his life, published by Canisius, and reprinted by Mabillon.[3] In this list, although they are all called 'successors of St. Rudbert,' yet three of them are termed abbats only, and not bishops. The list[4] is as follows: —

---

[1] *Juvavia.* So called from the river Juvar or Uvar; the name of the river was afterwards changed to *Saltz* or *Saltza,* from which the town takes its present name.—Mabillon, *Acta SS. O. S. B.,* tom. iii. p. 328, n. 9.

[2] *Rupert.* He is also called Hordbert, Ruodbert, Rodbert, &c. There is scarcely any medieval name which occurs under so many varieties of spelling as that now so common under the form of *Robert.*

[3] *Mabillon.* Canisius, *Antiq. Lect.,* tom. ii. Mabillon, *Acta SS. O. S. B.,* tom. iii. p. 325. Canisius (tom. vi.) has edited three other *Lives,* and a fifth is printed by the Bollandists at the 27th of March. These are all founded upon that first-mentioned.

[4] *List.* Mabillon, *l. c.,* p. 331.

1. Vitalis, bishop, immediate successor of St. Rudbert.
2. Anzologus, abbat.
3. Savolus, abbat.
4. Ezzius, abbat.
5. Flobargisus, bishop.
6. Joannes, bishop.
7. Virgilius, abbat, and afterwards Bishop of Saltzburgh.

Mabillon[1] was of opinion that the three names set down in this list as abbats only, ought not to be counted among the successors of St. Rudbert, and he cites an antient poetical account *of the bishops*, by an author of the ninth or beginning of the tenth century, in which these names are omitted. Mabillon's difficulty was occasioned by his having overlooked the fact, that the monastic usages, afterwards deemed peculiar to Ireland, were at that time common enough in several European monasteries. Anzologus, Savolus, and Ezzius were abbats only, and not bishops; but nevertheless, if Irish customs were observed in the monastery, they would have been also reckoned as *successors* of St. Rudbert; the abbat was St. Rudbert's successor whether he was also a bishop or not; and the bishops who were not abbats were, in some degree at least, subject to the jurisdiction of the abbat. This supposition will account for their introduction into the list of St. Rudbert's successors, and will account also for the omission of their names by the author of the poetical catalogue *of the bishops*, whose object did not require him to notice those successors of St. Rudbert who were abbats only.

[1] *Mabillon.* Annal. Ord. S. Bened., *tom.* ii. p. 51.

Irish descent frequently claimed for foreign ecclesiastics.

29. It is also worthy of notice (as shewing that there was then no such great discrepancy in the usages in question between the Irish and continental monasteries), that the foreign authors of monastic biographies seem anxious rather than otherwise to claim an Irish descent for their heroes, and often make that claim where there are no real grounds for it.

For example, in the case before us, one of the biographies of St. Rudbert, published by Canisius[1], expressly asserts that saint to have been 'of the royal family of the Franks, and *of the dukes of Scotia*,' quoting for this statement the 'antient history' which Mabillon supposes to be the antient Life by him reprinted. But in that Life no mention of *the dukes of Scotia* is to be found, and consequently Mabillon rejects the words as an interpolation.[2] It is quite as probable, however, that they may have been omitted by some transcribers of the antient Life, puzzled to understand how Rudbert could have been sprung both from the royal family of France and also from the chieftains of Ireland; and this is indeed a statement not very easily explained.

Our author, however, goes on to say that Rudbert was baptized in Ireland *by St. Patrick*, and received there his ecclesiastical education; after which, with his brother Trudbert and his

---

[1] *Canisius.* Ant. Lectt., tom. vi. p. 1107, c. i. 'Ex regali prosapia Francorum, ducumque Scotiæ originem duxisse antiqua tradit historia.' This Life is also printed, from Canisius, by Colgan, *Actt. SS. Hiberniæ*, p. 756.

[2] *Interpolation.* Acta SS. O. S. B., *ubi supra*, p. 326.

not accused of Irregularity.

sister or niece Erentrudis, or Erndruda[1], he went abroad and devoted himself to the conversion of the heathen. But this part of the story is manifestly untenable; for the year 497 is the latest date which can be assigned to the death of St. Patrick; whereas St. Rudbert (according to Mabillon) lived to 718. He would, therefore, have been more than two hundred years old at the time of his death[2], if he had been baptized in Ireland by St. Patrick. Still this very legend, incredible as it is, could scarcely have been invented, if the connection with Ireland[3], which it attributes to St. Rudbert, had not been regarded as adding, rather than otherwise, to his saintly reputation.

Vitalis, the immediate successor of Rudbert, is also said to have been an Irishman[4]; but it is not to our present purpose to discuss the question whether he was or not. It is enough to remark

---

[1] *Erndruda.* These names are not Irish, although Rudbert, as Colgan suggests, may possibly be a continental form of the Irish Robhartach or Ropartach, the name which is now Rafferty and Robert. *Actt. SS. Hib.*, p. 761, note 2.

[2] *Death.* Colgan (*ibid.*, note 6) attempts to solve this difficulty by suggesting that the St. Patrick here intended, was not the great St. Patrick, but a Patrick junior, nephew of the Apostle, who is said to have written a life of his uncle. But this is mere trifling.—See Lanigan, vol. iii., p. 163, and Andr. Brunneri, *Annal. Boiorum*, lib. v. c. 1 (Colgan *ib.*, p. 764).

[3] *Ireland.* See also Dom Joseph Mezger's 'Historia Salisbergensis, seu Vitæ Episcoporum et Archiepiscoporum Salisbergensium,' *Salisb.*, 1692, fol., lib. I. c. ii., where he discusses the question of the place of St. Rudbert's birth, and decides against Ireland with some hesitation; for he adds, 'Illud facile crediderim, in majoribus Ruperti maritatam esse regum Francorum, ducumque Scotiæ, id est Hiberniæ, nobilitatem; ipsum proinde tam ex regali prosapia Francorum, quam ducali Hibernorum originem duxisse, ut antiqua tradit historia,' p. 80. Colgan, in his account of St. Alto (9 Feb.), mentions several other Irishmen, or reputed Irishmen, who were connected with the monasteries of Bavaria, at the same period.—*Actt. SS.*, pp. 301—2.

[4] *Irishman.* His life is published by Canisius, *Ant. Lectt.*, tom. vi.

64   *Virgil of Saltzburgh.*   [INTROD.

that, however that question be decided, the fact that an Irish descent was claimed, although groundlessly, for two of their antient worthies, clearly shews that the monks of Saltzburgh were without any prejudices against Irish episcopacy, or monachism, and did not regard the Irish Church as meriting any censure for the existence of peculiar or irregular usages.

<small>Virgil, bishop of Saltzburgh, an Irishman.</small>

30. One of the Saltzburgh abbats, Virgil, the last in the foregoing list, was indeed an Irishman by birth; another proof that the Church of Ireland was, at that time, under no ban for irregularity. His history, which illustrates our subject in many ways, will require to be somewhat more fully dwelt upon.

The Four Masters[1] in their 'Annals of Ireland,' at their year 784 (which is really A.D. 789), tell us that he had been abbat[2] of Achadh-bo, now Aghaboe, in the Queen's County, and that he died in Germany in the thirtieth year of his episcopacy. They give him also the title of 'the Geometer,' evidently because he was one of the earliest Christian writers by whom was pro-

---

and Colgan intended to have given it at Oct. 20, but did not live to do so.—*Actt. SS. Hib.*, p. 769. All that is known of him has been collected by the Bollandists, in the volume recently published (1853) at Oct. 20. And the question of his Irish descent is there discussed and decided in the negative, p. 931, E. I believe rightly.

[1] *Four Masters.* 'Fergel an geometer abb Achaidh boo decc, san Germainne, san 30 bliadhain na eapscopoid.' 'Fergel, the geometer,

abbat of Achadh-bo, died in Germany, in the 30th year of his episcopacy.' According to Mabillon, he was consecrated 17 Kal. Jun., 756 or 757, and died 4 Kal. Dec., 780, not 789, as the Irish annals have it. See Dr. O'Conor's account of him, in his notes to the Annals of Ulster.—*Rer. Hib. Scriptt.*, tom. iv. p. 172 *sq.*

[2] *Abbat.* The *Ann. Ult.* give his obit at 788 (=789) as 'Fergill, abbat of Achadh-bo,' without mentioning his having emigrated to the

pounded the theory of the sphericity of the earth and the existence of the antipodes, a speculation which very nearly acquired for its author the reputation of being a heretic.[1] His Irish name was *Fergil*, or *Fergal*.

He appears to have become abbat of St. Peter's monastery, in Saltzburg, soon after his arrival on the continent, and having continued in that office for two years, during which time, we are told, '*he concealed*[2] *his own orders*,' he was consecrated bishop on the death of his predecessor John. His biographer, however, adds that he had brought with him from Ireland a bishop, named Dobda, to perform episcopal functions; and we find the same statement in the list of the successors of St. Rudbert, already quoted, namely, that he brought with him from Ireland ' a bishop of his own,' *proprium episcopum*[3],

<small>His Irish Bishop Dobda.</small>

continent, and hence Dr. Lanigan (*Eccl. Hist.* vol. iii. pp. 202—206) supposes the abbat of Aghaboe and the bishop of Saltzburgh to have been two different persons, fixing the death of the former at 789, and of the latter at 785, which is also the date assigned by Mabillon, *Annales*, tom. ii. p. 274. It is possible that the Four Masters may have been mistaken ; but whether Virgil of Saltzburgh had been originally abbat of Aghaboe or not, is unimportant to our argument. The genealogies of the saints, preserved in the antient Irish records, give the pedigree of a Fergil, or Virgilius, from Laogaire (son of Niall of the Nine Hostages), who was king of Ireland in the times of St. Patrick. But although the number of generations would agree very well with the date of Virgil of Saltzburgh, we cannot be quite certain that this is his pedigree: nevertheless he is therein styled 'Fergil Dergaine,' which looks like an error of transcription for ' Fergil do Germaine,' or Virgil of Germany, and if this were certain, it would settle the question.

[1] *Heretic.* See Dr. O'Conor's *Rerum Hibern. Scriptores, loc. cit.*

[2] *Concealed.* 'Vir itaque Domini, dissimulata ordinatione, ferme duorum annorum spatiis, habuit secum episcopum comitantem de patria, nomine Dobda, ad persolvendum episcopale officium.'—Mabillon,*Acta SS.*, tom. iv. p. 280. Mezger, in his *Hist. Salisb.*, makes no mention of Bishop Dobda, or of Virgil's concealment of his orders.

[3] *Proprium episcopum.* ' Venit vir quidam sapiens et bonus doctor de

F

which is the usual designation of the monastic bishop. In this latter authority the bishop is named *Dordagreus,* or according to another reading, *Dobdagrecus.* This is evidently the Irish *Dubh-da-crioch,* a name very common [1] in Ireland in the eighth and ninth centuries.

The words of the biographer, that Virgil for two years concealed his orders, have been understood [2] as if they signified that he had been a bishop before he left Ireland, and wishing to conceal that fact, brought with him another bishop to perform episcopal duties; but this cannot be so. For our author, immediately after the words referred to, goes on to say that at the instance of the people, and by the persuasion of the bishops of the province, he consented to receive the episcopal unction, and was consecrated [3] a bishop on the 13th of June, 766 or 767. The

---

Hibernia insula, nomine Virgilius, ad prædictum regem [Pippinum] in Francia loco vocato Karisiaco [i.e., *Cressy*].' . . . . 'Qui dissimulata ordinatione ferme duorum annorum spatio, habuit secum proprium episcopum comitantem de patria, nomine *Dordagreum* [*al.* Dobdagrecum] ad persolvendum episcopale officium.'—Mabillon, *Acta SS.,* tom. iii. p. 331.

[1] *Very common.* Thus the Four Masters give the obits of Dubh-da-crioch, Lord of Fotharta, A.D. 733; of Dubh-da-crioch, son of Dubh-da-inber, 718; of Dubh-da-crioch, son of Laidhgnen, 777; of Dubh-da-crioch, son of Maeltuile, abbat of Cill-achaidh, 821. The name signifies 'Dubh of the two countries,' and may have been given to Virgil's bishop from his having settled abroad. If his original name was Dobda, or Dubda, as the life of Virgil (apud Mabillon) has it, he may have received the subsequent appellation of Dubh-da-crioch, after his emigration to the continent.

[2] *Understood.* Ussher quotes Hundius, in whose catalogue of the bishops of Saltzburgh, Virgil is said to have brought with him *a Greek* bishop, named Dobdan. ' Dissimulatâ consecratione, pene duorum annorum spatio, pontificem secum habuit proprium Dobdan nomine Græcum, qui ipsum secutus erat ex patria.' This *Greek* bishop puzzled Ussher; Syllog. Ep. 16. (Works, iv. p. 462.) But Dobdan Græcus is an evident corruption of Dubh-da-crioch.

[3] *Consecrated.* ' Postea ad instantiam populi, necnon assidua coepiscoporum suorum exhortatione inductus, ab ipsis unctionem episcopalem sus-

meaning, therefore, most probably is that he concealed his own orders, namely, his priesthood[1]; and if for this purpose he brought with him from Ireland the bishop Dobda, or Dobdagrecus, it follows that there was nothing uncommon at that time on the continent of Europe in an abbat having 'a bishop of his own;' nor any prejudice at Saltzburg against an Irish monastic bishop.

31. Even in Italy, we find examples of a custom similar to that which prevailed in Ireland. The bishop of Aquino was subject, we are told, to the abbat of Cassino.[2] And again, in the East, in the monastery of Mount Sinai, as we learn from the chronicle of Ademar[3], monk

Monastic bishops subject to their abbats, in Italy and in the East.

cipere consensit, ordinatusque est a provincialibus præsulibus anno nativitatis Domini, 766 [*al.* 767] 17 Kal. Julii.'— Mabillon. *Acta SS.* tom. iv. p. 280. It will be seen that Hundius, as quoted by Ussher *(loc. cit.)*, entirely misrepresents this passage; making Virgil to have concealed his consecration after he had become bishop of Saltzburgh; which is absurd. The original author says, 'dissimulatâ *ordinatione*,' not *consecratione*, as Hundius has it. Fleury understands the words to signify that he remained for two years without consecration, after his nomination to the see of Saltzburgh, causing his Irish bishop Dobda to discharge his episcopal functions *(Hist. Eccles., Livr.* xliv. c. 3); but this can scarcely be reconciled with the statement of the original historian.

[1] *Priesthood.* So Pope Zachary seems to hint, in his letter to Boniface, where he calls him 'Virgilius ille, nescimus si dicatur presbyter.'—

Ussher, *Sylloge, Ep.* xvii. (Works, vol. iv. p. 463.)

[2] *Cassino.* The Benedictines of St. Maur, in their *Nouveau Traité de Diplomatique,* tom. v. p. 445, have quoted the following, from Gattola, *ad Hist. Cassinens. accession.* p. 91 (a work which I have not seen): ' Neque mirum videri debet Aquinensem episcopum subditum Abbati Cassinensi fuisse, cum venerabilis Beda sit autor in *Histor. Anglicana,* lib. 3, cap. 4, omnes Hiberniæ et Scotiæ episcopos subditos abbati S. Columbæ in insula Hyensi fuisse, dum ait, &c.' The author then quotes from Bede the passage already cited, p. 10, n. 2. where, however, it is not said that all the bishops of Ireland and Scotland were subject to the abbat of Hi; but only those of the *province* connected with the monastery.

[3] *Ademar.* His chron. is published by Labbé, *Biblioth. novæ,* tom. ii. p. 175, quoted by Mabillon, *Annal. Ben.,* lib. xxiii. n. 23, p. 179.

of Angoulême, there were 500 monks in the eleventh century living under the government of an abbat, and having their own bishop: 'habentes ibidem proprium episcopum.'

But it is needless to prolong this discussion. The existence of monastic bishops in various places is generally acknowledged[1]; and Ireland is peculiar only in having retained the custom long after it had been suppressed in other parts of Christendom.

The monastic bishop of the Benedictine monasteries.

32. Out of Ireland the monastic-bishop was most generally found in the Benedictine monasteries. In the preface to the first volume of the *Thesaurus novus Anecdotorum*, of Martene and Durand, several monasteries of the Order are mentioned in which the abbats were also bishops. Some of these have been already noticed. The learned authors of the Preface have defended the

---

[1] *Acknowledged.* At the Synod of Attigni, in 765, five monastic bishops were present, viz: Williharius, episcopus de monasterio S. Mauricii; Theodulfus, episcopus de monasterio Laubias; Hippolytus, episcopus de monasterio Logendi [seu Eugendi]; Jacob, episcopus de monasterio Gamundias; Willibaldus, episcopus de monasterio Achistadi.— See Mabillon, *Annal.*, tom. ii. pp. 206—207. Fleury, *Hist. Eccles.*, liv. xliv. c. 21, and *Nouv. Traité de Diplom., ubi supra.* This latter authority says: 'Les Evêques des abbayes exerçoient leur ministère sur toutes les dependances du monastère dont ils étoient les Evêques, corrigeoint et reformoient les abus avec le consentement de l'Abbé auquel ils etoient soumis. Cette soumission n'a rien de surprenant pour ces tems-là [the eighth century], où plusieurs Evêques ordinaires d'Italie, d'Irlande, et d'Ecosse etoient sous la jurisdiction des Abbés de quelques monastères célèbres.' In addition to the abbeys already mentioned, the following also had bishops of their own: the Scotish or Irish abbey of Honaw, or Hohenove, in Alsace; Mabillon, *Annal.*, tom. ii. p. 59. The abbey of Morbach, in Alsace; *ibid.*, pp. 76—703. Eichstadt, in Bavaria (a monastery of Irish foundation), whose bishop, Willibald, has just been mentioned as having been present at the Synod of Attigni. Stavelo, in Ardenne, whose abbat, Aigiluf, having been four years bishop of Cologne, returned to his monastery, 'cujus regimen cum episcopatu retinuerat.' —Mabillon, *ibid.* p. 128.

custom of a monastic bishop, as it existed in such monasteries, by referring it to a general principle laid down in the Rule of St. Benedict. The Rule of St. Benedict, they say[1], enables us to explain the cause and use of this custom: the founder 'was unwilling that the monks should ever leave the monastery, deeming it prejudicial to their souls; and therefore, to take away all necessity for going about to seek for holy orders or confirmation, and lest the occasional presence of a bishop in the abbey for the purpose of holding an ordination should disturb the quiet of the monks, it was arranged that in most monasteries either the abbat or a simple monk should be a bishop.'

From the foregoing facts and instances, therefore, we must conclude that the non-diocesan and monastic bishops were not peculiar to Ireland, nor at first deemed in any way irregular; but it is evident that they gradually disappeared as diocesan and metropolitical jurisdiction gained strength. The councils[2] are full

---

[1] *They say.* 'Jam vero si quis hujus consuetudinis causam rescire voluerit, præcipuam repetendam esse existimamus ex regula S. Benedicti, quæ ægre omnino fert monachos foris monasterium prodire, cap. 66, quia inquit, *omninò non expedit animabus eorum*; igitur ut junioribus præsertim fratribus omnis discurrendi occasio tolleretur ad sacros suscipiendos ordines, ad requirendum Chrisma, neve adventu episcoporum in monasteria ad sacras ordinationes explendas, quies monachorum turbaretur, plerique episcopum ad manum semper in monasteriis, sive abbatem, sive simplicem monachum habere voluerunt.'— Martene et Durand, *Thes. Novus Anecd.*, tom. i. *Præf.*

[2] *Councils.* The second can. of the first general council of Constantinople, although rigidly prohibiting all bishops from exercising their ministry out of their own dioceses, admits nevertheless that there was a more antient discipline, which in some places was still from necessity to be tolerated. 'The churches of God which are among barbarous people may be governed *according*

of enactments for the suppression of this kind of episcopacy, and it was soon branded with the stamp of irregularity. The traces of its existence, therefore, are few and scanty[1]; but there is every reason to suspect that those traces would have been more distinct and numerous than they are, had ecclesiastical records been fairly dealt with, and the more obscure memorials preserved, or transcribed in their integrity.

Bishops consecrated in Ireland by a single bishop and per saltum.

33. But we must now return to Ireland. Besides the accusation of having bishops without dioceses, without jurisdiction, and subject to the authority of the abbats, the Irish Church was censured for permitting bishops to be consecrated by a single bishop, and for allowing consecration *per saltum*, as it is called; that is to say, without requiring the newly consecrated prelate to have previously received the order of priest.

Legend of St. Columba's ordination.

The legend of the ordination of the celebrated St. Columba, or Colum-killè, will illustrate both these irregularities. We have it from the Scholia[2], or Annotations on the Martyrology of Aengus the Culdee, which have been already[3] more than once referred to.

to the custom of the fathers, which is still preserved.' Τὰς δὲ ἐν τοῖς βαρβάροις ἔθνεσιν τοῦ Θεοῦ ἐκκλησίας, οἰκονομεῖσθαι χρὴ κατὰ τὴν κρατήσασαν συνήθειαν τῶν πατέρων. — Bevereg. Pandect. I. p. 87 D. This 'custom of the fathers' was evidently an episcopacy without diocesan jurisdiction.

[1] *Scanty.* Under the year 1085, the Four Masters mention Gilla na naemh Laighen (i. e. Leinster man) bishop of Glandaloch, who became abbat of Würtzburg.—Colgan, *Acta SS.*, pp. 328—321.

[2] *Scholia.* It belongs to the 11th of February (St. Etchen's day), and occurs there in the Bodleian MS. But in the Dublin MS. it has been placed at the end of the month of March, for want of room.

[3] *Already.* See above, p. 20, 24.

The story[1] is this:

Bishop Etchen is venerated in Cluain-fota-Boetain, in Fera-Bile, in the south of Meath[2], and it was to him Colum-killè went to have the order of a bishop conferred upon him. Colum-killè sat under the tree which is on the west side of the church, and asked where the cleric was. 'There he is,' said a certain man, 'in the field where they are ploughing below.' 'I think,' said Colum-killè, 'that it is not meet for us that a ploughman should confer orders on us; but let us test him.' They[3] then approached him, and they first asked him for his ploughshare. He gave it to them immediately, and the oxen continued to plough notwithstanding. 'The cleric is a good man,' said they. 'Let him be tested farther,' said Colum-killè. They then asked him for the outer (or furrow) ox. He gave it to them immediately. Bishop Etchen then commanded a wild ox[4], which was in the wood, to perform the work, which he did immediately. Then Colum-killè went up to the cleric, after having thus tested him, and told him what he came for. 'It shall be done,' said the cleric. The order of a priest was then conferred upon Colum-killè, although it was the order of a bishop he wished to have had conferred upon him. The cleric prayed until the following day. 'I regret,' said Colum-killè, 'that thou hast conferred this order upon me; but I shall never change it whilst I live; for this reason, however, no person[5] shall ever again come to have orders conferred upon him in this church.' And this has been fulfilled, up to this time.

---

[1] *Story.* The original Irish has been printed in the Introd. to the *Book of Obits* and *Martyrology of Christ Church, Dublin,* published for the Irish Archæological Society, 4to, Dublin, 1844, p. liv.

[2] *Meath.* This is the town now called Clonfad, in the barony of Fera-Bile, now Ferbill, County of Westmeath.

[3] *They,* i. e. St. Columba's companions. O'Donnell, in his life of St. Columba, paraphrases this passage thus, as Colgan renders it,—Jubet subinde comitantes se clericos experimento probare, num vera essent quæ de S. Etcheno magnalia ferebantur.' *Vit. S. Columbæ,* lib. i. 47; Colgan, *Triad. Th.,* p. 396; *Acta SS.,* p. 305, n. vii.

[4] *Ox.* So the word *damh* in the original generally signifies, but Colgan's Latin version of O'Donnell translates it, 'a stag,' *cervum. Vit. S. Columbæ, ibid.*

[5] *No person.* Colgan, in his translation of O'Donnell, omits this denuntiation of the church, and says only that St. Columba on this occasion vowed to continue always a presbyter. 'Et cum S. Columba postea in ordinis suscipiendi administratione er-

Inferences from the legend.

This legend seems to have been unknown to Adamnan. It was most probably framed to account for the fact that so eminent a saint as Colum-killè had never risen beyond the rank of a presbyter; and that he had *vowed*, as was believed, never to accept episcopal consecration, or to permit any of his abbats[1] to be bishops. Omitting some few miraculous embellishments, there is nothing improbable or impossible in the story. It is quite in the spirit of the times, and quite consistent with the character of the man. But it is not necessary to our present purpose to assume all the circumstances to be true. We may even concede that the whole is a pure fiction. The author of the legend, however, even in that case, must have aimed at giving some amount of probability to his narrative, and we are therefore entitled to conclude that the circumstances introduced into it were such as he deemed consistent with the ecclesiastical usages of the times in which he himself lived. Let us examine these circumstances.

---

ratum esse, ac Presbyteratum sibi pro Episcopatûs ordine administratum, quæ acta fuerunt, divinæ attribuens dispositioni, noluit prætermisso ordine postea initiari, sed statuit nunquam Pontificalem dignitatem, aut gradum admittere, et in ordine jam suscepto continuo permanere.'—*Tr. Thaum.*, p. 397. But the original Irish of O'Donnell's Life of Columba, preserved in the Bodleian Library, contains the denunciation of the Church, as given above.

[1] *Abbats.* One only of the abbats of Hi, namely Fergna Brit, who was the fourth abbat, (called *Vergnous* in Adamnan,) is spoken of as a bishop. But Dr. Reeves very justly suspects that this is a mistake; as the title is given to him only in the calendar of Marianus O'Gorman, a comparatively late writer, who is followed by the Four Masters (see Reeves' *Adamnan*, p. 372); and we have the much higher testimony of Bede, ' Habere solet ipsa insula rectorem *semper* abbatem presbyterum.' — *Hist. Eccl.* iii. 4. The life of this Fergna is given by Colgan, *Acta SS.*, ad 2 Mart.

INTROD.] *of St. Columba's Ordination.* 73

The bishop St. Etchen was found ploughing, or superintending the ploughing of his land. This is evidence that even down to the age of the author of this legend, (the eleventh or beginning of the twelfth century,) there were bishops in Ireland without any ecclesiastical endowments, who supported themselves by their own labour, as private cultivators of the land, or farmers. But perhaps this circumstance proves nothing more than the primitive simplicity of the times. Although engaged in an employment so humble, St. Etchen was descended from one of the chieftains of Leinster, and his uterine brother[1] was king of Ireland.

<small>Poverty and simplicity of the early bishops.</small>

Again, St. Columba came to be consecrated a bishop; this is all that our author's narrative expressly states. O'Donnell adds[2], that having been deemed worthy of the episcopal dignity, he was *sent* to St. Etchen to be consecrated, by the unanimous vote of the bishops of the country. Why then did not these bishops provide two of their body to assist St. Etchen, and render the consecration canonical? Why did they not give St. Etchen some notice of their wishes? It is

<small>Columba expected episcopal consecration.</small>

---

[1] *Brother.* Briga, the mother of St. Etchen, was, by another husband, the mother of Aedh mac Ainmirech, the king of Ireland, who gave to St. Columba the site of Derry. Bishop Etchen was of noble descent, both on his mother's side and also on that of his father, Maine Eigeas; both his parents were descended from Niathcorb or Messincorb, Milesian ancestor of the kings of Leinster.—See Colgan's Life of St. Etchen, *Acta SS.* (11 Feb.), pp. 304—306.

[2] *Adds.* At least in Colgan's abridged and altered Latin version. *Triad. Thaum.*, p. 396. 'Vir denique Deo plenus jam virtutibus et miraculis clarus ab omnibus episcopali infula dignus judicatus, communi præsulum patriæ consilio missus est ad S. Etchenum episcopum Cluainfodensem, episcopus ordinandus.'— O'Donnell, *Vit. S. Columbæ*, lib. i. c. 47.

evident that this gratuitous addition to the story only increases the difficulties¹ of it. The original author merely says that Columba presented himself to Bishop Etchen, stating that he came 'to have the order of a bishop conferred upon him.' We read nothing of any decree or recommendation from the bishops of the country, or anybody else; we are simply told the purpose for which he came, and that Etchen, recognising his high claims and qualifications for the office, consented without any difficulty to comply with his request.

<small>Bishops consecrated by a single bishop.</small>

It is clear, therefore, that the author of this legend, for we shall assume it to be a pure fiction², believed it to be quite consistent with the ecclesiastical discipline of his times, that an individual should claim episcopal consecration from his personal merits only, without reference to any see or diocese, and that a single bishop might, at his own sole discretion, confer that consecration, without seeking the consent or concurrence of any other bishops. And this is, in fact, the irregularity which, as we have seen, was complained of by St. Anselm³, in the twelfth century, that in Ireland 'bishops, like priests, were ordained by a single bishop.'

<small>Ordination per saltum.</small>

34. We must also admit that St. Columba,

---

¹ *Difficulties.* The bishops who are assumed to have sent Columba to St. Etchen, obviously sanctioned consecration by a single bishop, if not also ordination *per saltum.*

² *Fiction.* Colgan was inclined to believe that this legend was added by Aengus, author of the Martyrology, himself, and not by any later Scholiast; *Acta SS.*, p. 306, note 17. If this be so the story must be as old as the ninth century.

³ *Anselm.* See above, p. 1.

according to this legend, expected to have been consecrated a bishop *per saltum*, without having been previously ordained priest.[1]

It has been suggested that St. Etchen ordained Columba a priest, preparatory to his being consecrated a bishop, omitting the additional rites necessary for the higher order; and that the mistake was no more than this omission of the additional rites.[2] But this is not what the legend tells us. For if this were all that was meant, why did Columba say, as he is reported to have said, '*I regret that thou hast conferred this order upon me*, but I shall never change it whilst I live?' These words evidently mean that the great saint of Hi did not know or believe the priesthood to be a *necessary* step to the order of bishop, and that he expected to have been consecrated a bishop without having received the inferior degree of a priest. He *regrets* that the order of priesthood was conferred upon him, and vows never to rise higher. The story adds, that as a punishment to Bishop Etchen for his mistake, Columba foretold that no person should ever again come to the church of Clonfad to have orders conferred upon him, and that this prediction or anathema, up to the time of the author of the legend, had been fulfilled.

We are entitled, therefore, to infer from this

---

[1] *Priest.* That Columba was already a deacon is certain, from Adamnan ii. 1 (p. 104), 25 (p. 137), ed. Reeves.

[2] *Rites.* See the Rev. P. J. Carew's *Eccl. Hist. of Ireland*, where this mode of solving the difficulty is put very plausibly, pp. 184—185.

story, even supposing it to have no foundation in fact, that in the time of its author, the consecration of bishops by a single bishop, and ordinations *per saltum*, were not considered irregular in the Irish Church.

Columba did not seek consecration as chorepiscopus.

35. Others[1] have suggested that Columba may have sought only consecration as a *chorepiscopus*, and they remind us that by the tenth canon of the council of Antioch (A.D. 341), it was not necessary in such a case to call in the assistance of more than one bishop. But it is not probable that there could have been in Ireland such country bishops or chorepiscopi as were contemplated by the council of Antioch[2]; because there were in Ireland no diocesan or city bishops in the times of which we are speaking, and in all probability no cities in which such bishops could reside; the canon of Antioch related only to those bishops who were ordained without independent jurisdiction, and were wholly subject to the city bishops who required their assistance.[3] It is evident that such a limited episcopal authority as this would not have suited St. Columba, whose object was to go forth as a missionary to the heathen Picts, not to remain in subjection to Bishop Etchen, in the neighbourhood of Clonfad. Nor would such a supposition be consistent with the story,

---

[1] *Others.* Especially Lanigan, *Eccl. Hist.*, vol. ii. p. 128, *sq.*

[2] *Antioch.* Hardouin, *Concil.*, tom. i. 398.— Comp. Bingham, *Antiq.*, book ii. ch. 14.

[3] *Assistance.* There is also good reason to believe that the antient *chorepiscopi*, although enjoying the name, and in part exercising the jurisdiction of bishops, were in reality no more than presbyters. See Morinus, *De Ordinationibus*, part iii. Exercit. iv. p. 40, *sq.* If this be so, Lanigan's solution of the difficulty is worth nothing.

as it is told by our author. For if Columba was to have been ordained chorepiscopus, in subjection to Etchen, his appointment to such an office must have originated with the bishop by whom he was to be ordained. But the legend evidently implies that he was unknown to Bishop Etchen, and Bishop Etchen unknown to him, when he offered himself 'to have the order of a bishop conferred upon him.'

There is no escape, therefore, from the inference that whether this legend be founded in fact, or not, the consecration of bishops by a single bishop, and ordinations *per saltum*, were at least tolerated in the early Church of Ireland.

36. Let us speak first of consecration by a single bishop.

This appears to have been customary, at the period of which we are speaking, in the British as well as in the Irish branch of the Scotic Church: and owing to the paucity[1] of bishops in Great Britain at that time it was sometimes found necessary to bring over a bishop from Ireland when a prelate was to be consecrated. A remarkable instance of this is recorded in the life of St. Kentigern, a contemporary of St. Columba, who is now perhaps better known as the patron saint of Glasgow, under the name of St. Mungo. His biographer, Jocelin[2] of

---

[1] *Paucity.* On the causes of this paucity, see the remarks of Dr. Reeves, *Eccl. Antiq. of Down and Connor*, pp. 125—126.

[2] *Jocelin.* Vit. Kentigerni, cap. xi. (Pinkerton, *Vit. Antiq.*, p. 223.) The words are—'Accitoque uno episcopo de Hybernia, more Brito-

Furnes, tells us that when he was chosen to the episcopal office, a bishop was sent for from Ireland, 'according to the custom[2] of the Britons and Scots of that time,' to consecrate him; meaning by the Britons, the North Britons of the modern Scotland, and by the Scots, the Irish Christians. The form of the ordination consisted in the unction of the head only, by pouring on it the sacred chrism; the invocation of the Holy Ghost; the benediction; and the imposition of hands by the consecrating prelate: and this rite performed by a single bishop, our author tells us, the foolish Britons pretended to have received by tradition from the Apostles; never-

num et Scotorum tunc temporis, in pontificem consecrari fecerunt. Mos inolevit in Britannia, in consecratione pontificum, tantummodo capita eorum sacri crismatis infusione perungere, cum invocatione Sancti Spiritus, et benedictione, et manus impositione: quem ritum dicebant insipientes se suscepisse divinæ legis institutionem et Apostolorum traditionem. Sacri vero canones sanctificant, ut nullus episcopus consecretur absque tribus ad minus episcopis; uno videlicet consecratore, qui sacramentales benedictiones et orationes ad singula insignia pontificalia super sacrandum dicat et duo alii cum eo manus imponant; testes existant; textum evangeliorum cervici illius impositam teneant.'

[2] *Custom.* In a Synod attributed to St. Patrick, the canons of which were published by Ware, Spelman, and in 1835 reprinted by Villanueva, there is the following enactment, (cap. xvi.) entitled, *De falsis episcopis*—' Qui non secundum Apostolum electus est ab altero episcopo, est damnandus, et deinde ad reliquam plebem declinandus et degradandus.' This appears to refer to those who, without having received any episcopal consecration, pretended to be bishops; the word *electus*, from the reference to ' the Apostle,' appears to signify *consecrated* or *ordained*; and if so, the canon must be understood to condemn as false bishops those only who were not consecrated by at least one bishop; the passage alluded to is probably 2 Tim. i. 6. Dr. Villanueva suggests that confirmation by the metropolitan is intended *(Opusc. S. Patr.,* p. 127); but if so such a canon could not have been made in Ireland in the age of St. Patrick, or for some centuries later; and the words 'electus ab altero episcopo,' seem an odd way of expressing confirmed or approved by the metropolitan. We shall see presently that there was, even in the language of the general Councils, a confusion between the election and consecration of bishops. The confusion, however, was verbal only.

theless, he admits the validity of the episcopal consecrations so performed, and excuses their irregularity by the insular position of the Irish and British Churches, placed almost beyond the limits of the world, and surrounded by a hostile heathenism; which rendered pardonable, he says, their ignorance of the canons.[1]

But the custom may not perhaps exhibit such ignorance of the canons as is supposed. It is not certain that the canons which required the assistance of more than one bishop at the consecration of another were applicable, or intended to be applied, to a church under the circumstances of the Church of Ireland. On the continent of Europe the Christian Empire, both in the East and in the West, was divided into episcopal provinces and dioceses based upon the antient civil divisions; and the canonical regulations in question were closely connected with the institution of metropolitical and diocesan jurisdiction. In Ireland, where there were no metropolitans, no dioceses, and no fixed or legally recognized civil divisions of the country, these canonical rules were inapplicable and therefore were disregarded.

37. The first canon of the antient ecclesiasti- *Canonical rule for consecration of bishops.*

---

[1] *Canons.* 'Sed licet consecratio Britonibus assueta sacris canonibus minus consona videatur, non tamen vim aut effectum Divini misterii, aut episcopalis ministerii omittere comprobatur. Sed quia insulani, quasi extra orbem positi, emergentibus paganorum infestationibus canonum erant ignari, ecclesiastica censura ipsis condescendens excusationem illorum in hac parte admittit.'—Vit. Kentig., *ibid.* Jocelin, the compiler of this Life of Kentigern, flourished about the middle of the twelfth century.

cal rules commonly called 'the canons of the Apostles,' does indeed enjoin that 'a bishop shall be ordained by two or three bishops,' and makes no allusion to the metropolitan. But all the other conciliar legislation on the subject makes three, not two bishops, the minimum necessary for canonical consecration, and assumes the existence of metropolitans having jurisdiction over their suffragan bishops. The famous canon[1] of the first Nicene council enacts that a bishop shall be ordained ' by all the bishops of the province, or at the least by three, the remainder giving their consent in writing ; and that the confirmation rest with the metropolitan.' The third council of Carthage[2] (A.D. 397) declares that ' not less than three shall be sufficient, and that they must be deputed by the metropolitan.' All such legislation evidently assumes the existence of metropolitical and diocesan jurisdiction.

<small>Meaning of canon iv. of first Nicene council.</small> There is, however, some reason to doubt whether the canon of the council of Nicæa was originally intended to regulate the *consecration* of bishops. The second council[3] of Nicæa interprets it of the *election* of bishops only. This is also the opinion of Balsamon, and of almost all the Greek canonists, as well as of our own Beveridge[4],

---

[1] *Canon.* Concil. Nicen. I., c. 4.
[2] *Carthage.* Conc. Carth. III., can. 39, 'Forma antiqua servabitur, ut non minus quam tres sufficiant, qui fuerint a metropolitano directi ad ordinandum episcopum.' See also *Conc. Arelat.* II. (A.D. 452 *al.* 443), can. 5—6.

[3] *Council.* Con. Nicen. II. (A.D. 787), can. 3.
[4] *Beveridge.* See the notes of Beveridge on Can. Apostt. 1. and Can. Nicen. 4, in his *Pandectæ Canonum.*, tom. ii. part pp. 2, 11 and

and it is remarkable that the word used by the Nicene fathers to denote the act for which three bishops were necessary is not the word employed in the so-called canon of the Apostles. Both words may signify *election*[1] or *appointment*, although that used in the Apostolic canon more frequently denotes *consecration* or *ordination*. And hence the Greek canonists, Balsamon and Zonaras, in their commentary on the Apostolic canon, although they both interpret *cheirotonia* of consecration, tell us nevertheless that some understood it to speak of the election (περὶ ψήφου) of bishops. And so Aristenus[2] seems to interpret it of election, using the very same word (ψηφίζεσθαι) which the others employ to distinguish election from consecration, and referring to the 13th canon of the council of Carthage[3], and the 19th of the council of Antioch[4], both which speak unequivocally of the election of bishops only, and evidently so interpret the Nicene canon.

38. It is not absolutely certain, therefore, that these canons, as originally understood, did condemn the Irish practice; and it is absolutely

---

[1] *Election*. The Canon of the Apostles has χειροτονέω, the Nicene canon καθίστημι: see *Suicer, Thesaur.* v. χειροτονέω. Bever. *Pandect. l. c.*, p. 9. But there can be no doubt that χειροτονέω generally signifies consecration or ordination, and is so used. Act xiv. 23.

[2] *Aristenus*. Bever. *Pandect.*, tom. i., p. 1.

[3] *Carthage.* Bever. *Ibid.*, p. 529.

[4] *Antioch.* Bever. *Ibid.*, p. 449. It seems evident that the first Apostolic canon speaks only of ordination, and the Nicene canon only of election. Balsamon's arguments appear quite conclusive; for if both (he says) meant ordination or both election, they would be inconsistent with each other: and in Can. Apost. 2, where the same word χειροτονέω is used, there cannot be a doubt that the *ordination* of a priest or deacon is intended.—Bever. *Pandect.*, tom. ii., part 2, p. 10.

Validity of consecration by a single bishop. certain that consecration by a single bishop, although subsequently held to be irregular or uncanonical, was never regarded as invalid.[1] The rule, now universally followed in the Church, has, doubtless, many advantages as a security against fraudulent or false consecrations; but it was never held to be absolutely necessary for the validity of episcopal consecration. A remarkable decision of Pope Gregory the Great upon this subject is recorded by Bede.[2] Augustine of Canterbury, in the year 597, finding himself pressed by many difficulties, proposed to St. Gregory a series of questions, upon which he requested the Pope's opinion and advice. The sixth question was this: 'Whether a bishop may be ordained without the presence of other bishops, if the distance between them be so great that the bishops cannot easily come together?' To this Gregory replied, 'In the Church of England, where thou art now the only bishop[3], thou canst not otherwise ordain a bishop except without other bishops, unless some bishops should

---

[1] *Invalid.* See Bever. *Not. ad Can. Apostl.* 1. Van Espen. *Jus Canon. Univers.*, tom. i., part 1, tit. xv., c. 1. Bingham *Eccl. Antiq.*, book ii., ch. 11, sect. 5.

[2] *Bede.* Hist. Eccl., lib. i., c. 27. 'Sexta Interrogatio Augustini. Si longinquitas itineris magna interjaceat, ut episcopi non facile valeant convenire, an debeat sine aliorum episcoporum præsentia episcopus ordinari? *Respondit Gregorius.* Et quidem in Anglorum ecclesia, in qua adhuc solus tu episcopus inveniris, ordinare episcopum non aliter nisi sine episcopis potes: nisi aliqui de Gallis episcopi veniunt, qui in ordinatione episcopi testes assistant.' Some editors of Gregory's works have the reading, 'non aliter nisi cum episcopis potes:' but this makes no good sense, and Beveridge has shown the other reading to be genuine.—*Pandect.*, tom. ii., part 2, p. 12.

[3] *The only bishop.* The Roman party under Augustine affected to regard the British and Irish prelates as no bishops, in consequence of their differences about the tonsure, Easter, &c.

come from Gaul to assist as witnesses in the ordination of a bishop.' The Pope then goes on to recommend that this be not done without necessity, and that when the number of bishops in England, by God's help, is increased, the rule of requiring three or four bishops to assist at consecrations be observed: but he evidently admits the validity of the consecration by a single bishop in the supposed case of necessity, the necessity, however, having been created altogether by his own and Augustine's exclusiveness, in refusing to hold communion with the Scotic bishops.

But it may very well be doubted whether it was possible for the Irish Church, prior to the sixth century, to have ever heard of, much less received, the canons which made the presence of at least three bishops necessary at the consecration of a bishop. They were all canons of the Greek Church; and the canons of the Greek Church, notwithstanding the exertions of Pope Leo I. and his successors in the See of Rome, were practically unknown in the west until they were translated into Latin by Dionysius Exiguus, in the beginning of the sixth century.[1] The practice of the Irish or Scotic Churches in regard to Easter proves that they had not received, if they had ever heard of the Nicene decision[2] upon that subject; and there is, therefore, no difficulty

The Nicene canons of discipline unknown in Ireland.

---

[1] *Century.* Dionysius must have died before A.D. 556. See *Cave.* 1, p. 513.

[2] *Decision.* The Nicene decision, however, seems to have been no more than this, that the Church should continue to take the time of Easter from the patriarch of Alexandria. No decree or rule for determining Easter is now to be found in the canons of the Council.

84   Consecrations per saltum   [INTROD.

in supposing them equally ignorant of the rule which prohibited consecration by a single bishop only.

In no view of the subject, therefore, is there the smallest ground for asserting that the peculiar practice of the antient Scotic churches, of which we are speaking, in any degree invalidated their episcopacy[1], for it is admitted by all that the validity of consecrations by a single bishop was never doubted in the Church, even by those who condemned them as irregular.

Ordination per saltum.   39. We may now speak of the other custom, of ordination *per saltum*, as it is technically called, or ordination to the higher orders, without passing through the inferior degrees.

There is no evidence that this was a *custom* of the Irish or Scotic Church. The legend of the ordination of St. Columba seems to be the only instance of any such irregularity having been practised; and that story may possibly be misunderstood, or it may only prove the ignorance of its author. Be this, however, as it may, a legend of this kind seems too slight a foundation upon

---

[1] *Episcopacy.* The learned Benedictine Bernard Mareschal, in his 'Concordia SS. Patrum Eccl. Græcæ atque Latinæ,' *Aug. Vind.*, 1769, p. xxxiv., asserts the validity, as well as the primitive antiquity of these consecrations, and argues that the Apostolic canons cannot have proceeded from the Apostles, in consequence of their insisting upon the opposite practice. His words are, 'Ex modo adductis iterum demonstratur Constitutiones istas Apostolis falso adscribi: et ex eo præcipue id demonstratur, quia duo hic, vel tres episcopi requiruntur ad alterius episcopi consecrationem, quando Apostolorum ævo, et illis etiam vita functis, ab uno episcopo alterius episcopi consecratio peragebatur. Cum igitur hujusmodi consecrationes per unum episcopum peractæ probarentur ab ecclesia, consequens est, Constitutiones tunc temporis non extitisse, aut auctoritate caruisse; ideoque ut Apostolorum opus non admittebantur.'

which to build the accusation of an habitual irregularity against the whole Church of Ireland. Nor do either Anselm or Lanfranc in their letters, which have been already quoted[1], nor even St. Bernard, mention this among the ecclesiastical evils of which they complain. They censure the laxity which seems to have prevailed in reference to divorce and marriage within the prohibited degrees. They speak of the custom of consecrating bishops by a single bishop, and of bishops without sees or fixed jurisdiction; but they say not a word of ordinations *per saltum*.

Such consecrations, however, were never regarded in the Church Catholic as invalid, nor were they peculiar to the Irish Church. St. Cyprian[2], in his epistle to Antonianus, which, if it be genuine, must be dated A.D. 252, writes in defence of Cornelius, Bishop of Rome, that 'he did not on a sudden arrive at the episcopate, but having been promoted through all ecclesiastical offices, and having constantly deserved well of the Lord in Divine services, mounted to the highest sacerdotal degree by all the steps of religion;' in other words, he had passed through all the inferior degrees of holy orders before he was consecrated a bishop. When this is put forth as a matter of praise, and in a panegyric

Not invalid, nor peculiar to the Irish Church.

---

[1] *Quoted.* See above, pp. 1, 2.
[2] *Cyprian.* Ep. 55 (*Ed. Fell. Oxon.*). 'Non iste ad episcopatum subito pervenit, sed per omnia ecclesiastica officia promotus, et in divinis administrationibus Dominum sæpe promeritus, ad sacerdotii sublime fastigium, cunctis religionis gradibus ascendit.' Baluze (in whose edition of Cyprian's works this Epist. is numbered 52) says that it was omitted in *eleven* of the antient MSS. which he had collated. Its genuineness is, therefore, somewhat doubtful.

upon an eminent bishop, it is manifest that there must have been many bishops at that time who had 'mounted to the highest sacerdotal degree,' without having been ordained to the inferior orders.

Pope Leo the Great, also, in the middle of the fifth century, writing to the Bishops of Mauritania, censures certain irregular ordinations, and particularly the consecration to the episcopal office of some mere laymen, who had never been ordained to the priesthood. He decides that bigamists who had been ordained to any holy function, whether bishops, priests, or deacons, should be deposed; meaning, by bigamists, not those who had two wives at the same time, but those who had married a second time, after the death of their first wives, and even those who had married widows. But with respect to those who had been raised to the episcopal order, without having passed through the inferior degrees of the ministry, he permits them to retain their office, and extends this indulgence[1] even to some who, after their consecration, had been converted from the Donatist and Novatian heresies, provided

---

[1] *Indulgence.* Ceillier (*Hist. des Auteurs Eccl.*, tom. xiv., p. 375) thus sums up the decision of S. Leo: 'Quant aux Laïcs qui avoient été élevés à l'Episcopat, sans avoir auparavant passés par les divers dégrés du ministère Ecclesiastique, Saint Leon leur permet de demeurer dans leur dignités, même à un Maxime, qui avoit été Donatiste, sans toutefois que cette dispense dût tirer à conséquence, au préjudice des Décrets du saint Siége, et de ceux qu'il avoit déjà fait lui-même sur ce sujet. Il accorde la même grace à Donat de Salicine, qui s'étoit converti de l'hérésie des Novatiens, de même que Maxime: mais il veut que l'un et l'autre donne leur profession de foi par écrit.'—*Vid.* Leonis M. Opp. Epist. i. (*Ed. Quesnell, Paris,* 1675, 4to.)

they made in writing a full and orthodox confession of their faith.

But it is not necessary for our purpose to collect all the instances that might be adduced of the recognition of ordinations *per saltum* in antient times. The great Athanasius was only a deacon when he was consecrated Bishop of Alexandria, and the same thing is said of Agapetus I. (A.D. 535) and of Vigilius (A.D. 538), Bishops of Rome.[1]

If, therefore, such ordinations occasionally occurred in the Irish Church, the irregularity was by no means peculiar to Ireland at the early period of which we are speaking; and there is no evidence that the practice was general, or that it prevailed in later times.

40. The monastic character impressed upon Irish Christianity, from the circumstances of the country at the period when it received the faith, has already been noticed. And if it be true that St. Patrick, as his biographers all say, was the nephew and disciple of St. Martin of Tours, another explanation of the fact will be added to that already derived from the state and constitution of society in Ireland in the fifth century. St. Martin of Tours was the great patron of Monasticism in the west, the founder of the first monastery[2] in the Gallican Church. It was natural, therefore, that his disciple Patrick

Monastic character of Irish Christianity.

---

[1] *Rome.* The authorities are quoted by Bingham (*Antiq.* Book ii., ch. 10, sects. 4—7), who has given several other examples.

[2] *First Monastery.* Locociagum, now Liguge, near Poitiers. — See Montalembert, *Les Moines d'Occident.*, tom. 1, p. 214.

should follow the predilection of his master, and zealously aim at establishing, in the church he had founded in Ireland, the monastic Christianity which was then so much lauded in Gaul.

The monastic Christianity of Ireland not altogether from St. Patrick.

It is, however, far from certain that the monastic ascendancy in Ireland owed its origin to the institutions of St. Patrick. There is reason to suspect that the connection of the bishops with the religious houses, and their subjection to the jurisdiction of the abbats, had its origin at a somewhat later time.

Catalogue of the three orders of Irish saints.

41. There is extant a curious document first published by Ussher[1], which was probably drawn up by some author who flourished not later than

---

[1] *Ussher.* Works, vol. vi., p. 477. See Reeves, *Adamnan,* p. 334, *n.* As there may be frequent occasion to refer to this document, a translation of it from Ussher's copy is here inserted. The title is 'Incipit Catalogus Sanctorum Hiberniæ secundum diversa tempora;' and the tract then proceeds thus:—

'THE FIRST ORDER [*primus ordo*] of Catholic saints was in the time of Patrick; and then they were all bishops, famous and holy [*clari et sancti*], and full of the Holy Ghost; 350 in number, founders of churches. They had one head [*caput*], Christ, and one chief [*ducem*], Patrick; they observed [*sufferebant*] one mass, one celebration, one tonsure from ear to ear. They celebrated one Easter, on the fourteenth moon after the vernal equinox, and what was excommunicated by one Church, all excommunicated. They rejected not the services and society of women: [*mulierum administrationem et societatem non respuebant:* or according to another MS., "they excluded from the churches neither laymen nor women," *nec laicos nec fœminas de ecclesiis repellebant*]; because founded on the Rock Christ, they feared not the blast of temptation [*quia super petram Christum fundati, ventum tentationis non timebant*]. This order of saints continued for four reigns [*per quaterna duravit regna*]; that is, during the time of Laoghaire, and Oilioll Molt, and Lugaidh son of Laoghaire, and Tuathal. All these bishops were sprung from the Romans, and Franks, and Britons, and Scots.

'THE SECOND ORDER was of Catholic Presbyters. For in this order there were few bishops and many presbyters, in number 300. They had one head, our Lord; they celebrated different masses, and had different rules, one Easter on the fourteenth moon after the equinox, one tonsure from ear to ear; they refused the services of women, separating them from the monasteries [*abnegabant mulierum administrationem, separantes eas a monasteriis*]. This order has hitherto lasted for four reigns [*per quaterna adhuc regna duravit*]; that is, from the latter years of Tuathal, and during the whole of King Diarmait's reign, the middle of the eighth century. In this valuable paper (which we shall henceforth refer to

and that of the two grandsons of Muredach, and of Aedh son of Ainmire. They received a mass from bishop David, and Gillas [*al.* Gildas] and Docus, the Britons. Whose names are these: two Finians; two Brendans; Jarlath of Tuam; Comgall; Coemgen; Ciaran; Columba; Cainech; Eoghan mac Laisre; Lugeus; Ludeus; Moditeus; Cormac; Colman; Nessan; Laisrean; Barrindeus; Coeman; Ceran; Coman; [Endeus; Ædeus; Byrchinus;]' (Ussher gives these three names within brackets) 'and many others.

'THE THIRD ORDER of Saints was of this sort [*erat talis*]. They were holy presbyters, and a few bishops; one hundred in number; who dwelt in desert places, and lived on herbs and water, and the alms [of the faithful]; they shunned private property [*propria contemnebant*. According to another MS. "they despised all earthly things, and wholly avoided all whispering and backbiting"—*omnia terrena contemnebant, et omnem susurrationem et detractionem penitus evitabant*]; and they had different rules and masses, and different tonsures (for some had the crown, and others the hair), and a different Paschal festival [*diversam solemnitatem paschalem*]. For some celebrated the Resurrection on the fourteenth moon, or sixteenth [according to another MS. " on the fourteenth moon, others on the thirteenth;" *alii xiii. celebrabant*—but in the black letter numerals xiii. and xui. might very easily be confounded], 'with hard intentions:' [*cum duris intentionibus.* Mr. King, *Primer*, &c., p. 62, translates this, "persevered in calculating it by the sixteenth." Perhaps for *duris* we should read *diversis.*] These lived during four reigns [*per quaterna regna vixerunt*]; that is, the reigns of Aedh Allain (who, in consequence of his evil devices [*pro cogitatione mala*],

reigned but three years), and of Domhnall, and during the joint reigns [*per mixta tempora*] of the sons of Maelcoba, and of Aedh Slaine; and continued to that great mortality [A.D. 666]. These are their names: Petran, Bishop; Ultan, bishop; Colman, bishop; Murgeus, bishop; Aedan, bishop: Loman [*al.* Lomprian], bishop; Senach, bishop. These are bishops, and many others. But these are presbyters: Fechin, presbyter; Airendan, Failan, Coman, Commian, Colman, Ernan, Cronan; and very many others, presbyters.

'The first Order was most holy [*sanctissimus*]; the second Order very holy [*sanctior*]; the third Order holy [*sanctus*]. The first burns [*ardescit*] like the sun, the second like the moon, the third like the stars.'

Archbishop Ussher adds, that in the second and more modern copy of this catalogue which he had before him, this concluding clause, or ἀνακεφαλαίωσις (as he calls it), was given more diffusely thus:—

'Note, that the first order was most holy [*sanctissimus*]; the second holy of holies [*sanctus sanctorum*]; the third holy [*sanctus*]. The first glows like the sun in the heat of brilliancy [*in fervore claritatis, calescit*; perhaps we should read *charitatis.*] The second is pale as the moon [*sicut luna pallescit*]. The third shines like Aurora [*sicut aurora splendescit*]. These three orders St. Patrick understood, taught by an oracle from above, when in that prophetic vision he saw all Ireland filled with a flame of fire; then he saw the mountains only burning, and afterwards lights [*lucernas*] burning in the valleys.'

This alludes to the vision seen by St. Patrick, as recorded by Jocelin, *Vit. Patr.*, c. 175 (Colgan. *Triad. Thaum.*, p. 103).

as the 'Catalogue') the saints of the Irish Church are divided into three classes or orders. The first, who were the founders of the churches, are expressly said to have been all bishops; the second and third orders were for the most part priests, although some few of them were bishops. The first order, who continued for about a century[1] after the coming of St. Patrick, took him for their leader or model, and followed his institutions. 'They rejected not,' we are told, 'the services and society of women,' or, according to another reading, 'they excluded not laymen and women from their churches.' But the second class, of whom St. Finnian of Clonard and St. Columba of Hy may be regarded as the types, 'refused the services of women, and separated them from their monasteries.' The third class dwelt in desert places, as solitaries or hermits, refusing to have any private property; living on the alms of the faithful, and despising all earthly things.

If this statement be worthy of credit, it would seem that the more rigid monastic system was introduced by the second order of saints, and not by those who adopted the discipline of St. Patrick.

It is not, however, to be inferred that the first order of saints had no monasteries: but only that their ministry was not exclusively restricted to the monasteries, and that they did not rigidly reject the services of women[2] in their monas-

---

[1] *Century.* To the latter end of the reign of King Tuathal Maolgarbh, A.D. 533—544.

[2] *Women.* See the curious story told by Jocelyn, c. 102, of Lupita, the sister of St. Patrick, living in

teries. It is remarkable that this is spoken of as an evidence of their superior holiness — 'quia super petram, Christum, fundati, ventum tentationis non timebant.'

42. Dr. Lanigan explains the rule made by the second order of saints, for a more rigid exclusion of women from the monasteries, by telling us that some such regulation became 'necessary, after the monasteries or colleges became crowded with young students.'[1] It is quite true

Exclusion of women from serving in the monasteries.

the same house with her nephew, St. Mel: 'Ut ejus verbo et exemplo proficere posset in exercitio Divini obsequii. Evoluto vero aliquanto tempore, cum sanctus sacerdos juxta morem mediâ nocte surgeret ad confitendum Domino, sancta illa femina solebat se ad soporandum collocare, pellibusque cooperire, in sancti præsulis lecto.' *Triad. Thaum.*, p. 89. The Tripartite Life, speaking of the scandal which arose on this occasion, attributes the malicious story altogether to the fact of the bishop and his aunt residing in the same house ; taking no notice of the other cause assigned for it. 'Habitabant ambo in una domo, quod fuit sinistræ suspicionis fundamentum præcipuum vel unicum.' Lib. ii., c. 29. *Tr. Thaum.*, p. 133.

Students. Lanigan ii., p. 20. Comp. the curious story of St. Mugint (Book of Hymns, p. 97), which seems to show that some such rule was advisable. There is a legend told in the Scholia to the Dublin copy of the Martyrology of Aengus, which scarcely bears translation. It relates to St. Scuthin, said to have been a disciple of St. David of Menevia, a contemporary of the Columbas, Brendans, and Kierans, and therefore belonging to the second order of saints, although his name is not mentioned in any of our copies of the catalogue. Colgan slurs the legend over in general terms, which however clearly show that he was acquainted with it. *Actt. SS.* pp. 9, 10. The practice was a very antient one, and is censured by St. Cyprian. (See Mosheim, *De rebus Christianor. ante Constant.* p. 598.) We may perhaps venture to give an abridgment of the legend, under the protection of a dead language : 'Scuthinus, ut prælium sibi majus fiat, duas pulcherrimas virgines, lecti sui participes omnibus noctibus fecit. De qua re quæstio fuit, et venit Brendanus ad inquirendum utrum contra leges pudicitiæ aliquid committeretur. Scuthinus ait, Hac nocte lectuli mei Brendanus periculum faciat. Consentiens Brendanus lectum ascendit. Virgines in lectum sese Brendano introducunt. Ille autem tali contubernio inflammatus, dormire non potuit.' His companions scoff at him, advising him to cast himself into a tub of water, which they admit Scuthin was often compelled to do. Brendan retired, admitting that Scuthin had attained a higher degree of sanctity than he ; but he seems to have been satisfied by the mere testimony of the parties themselves that there was no violation of morality in the matter ; and Scuthin (as Colgan tells us) had by these means acquired such angelic and ethereal purity, that his body became spiritualized, and he was able to walk on the surface of the sea without sinking. The existence of that the monasteries of the second order of saints were also colleges, in which young men were trained for the ecclesiastical and missionary life. But the regulation in question seems to have had in view something more. The comparison instituted in the Catalogue between the first order of saints, who 'feared not the blast of temptation,' and the second order, who it seems did fear the danger, implies evidently that the regulation had reference to the 'saints' themselves. And it is on this account apparently that the first order are described as like the sun, and most holy; the second, like the moon, and holy in an inferior degree only. This language does not give us the idea that the safety of the 'young students' was the sole object of the regulation in question.

Taking the words strictly, 'abnegabant mulierum administrationem,' 'they rejected the ministrations of women,' we may perhaps infer that the prohibition at first extended only to the employment of women as servants, or attendants, in permanent connection with the monasteries; and that the greater strictness which excluded women[1] from the monastic churches, and forbad

---

this dangerous practice, if it were at all common, would be a better reason for the rule 'abnegabant mulierum administrationem' than that given by Lanigan. Perhaps the difference between the two orders of saints may have been in reality this; that the first order admitted this singular test, 'ventum tentationis non timentes,' and the second order prohibited it; Scuthin alone having been ambitious enough to aim at rivalling in this respect the 'Ordo sanctissimus.'

[1] *Women.* See some examples of this strictness in Ussher, Primord., p. 942, *sq.* (Works, vi. p. 510). The story told of St. Enda or Enna of Aran, that he refused to see his sister, S. Fanche, and her companions, when she visited him in his foreign monastery to induce him to return to Ireland, has evidently been dressed up in the ideas prevalent at the period when his biography was written. He erected a tent for her 'in solo monasterii,' and cover-

a monk so much as to look upon the face or form of even his nearest female relative, was the growth of a later time.

43. St. Patrick and his followers, the first order of saints, in their efforts to evangelise the country, adopted the plan of consecrating and sending forth a great number of bishops, without fixed sees, some of whom became the founders of monasteries; some obtained land and other privileges from the chieftains or petty kings, and built towns or cities, the germ of future episcopal sees and dioceses; others again were content to exercise their ministry in monasteries, subject to the jurisdiction of the abbats. *The first order employed the ministry of bishops.*

The second order, on the contrary, employed for the most part the ministry of priests only. Their plan was to establish monastic schools or colleges for the dissemination of ecclesiastical learning, and for the instruction of students in what they regarded as catholic and orthodox faith. *The second order that of priests.*

And it will be observed, that throughout the whole of this Catalogue there is not the smallest allusion to diocesan or archiepiscopal jurisdiction. Not a word is said of a primacy in Armagh, or of any peculiar authority vested in the successors of St. Patrick, except this, that the first order, having their one Head, Christ, followed Patrick as their leader or guide: retained, in the celebration of their Mass, the Liturgy introduced

ing his own face also with a veil, so that neither could see the other, they conversed together.—*Vit. S. Endei* (Colgan. *Actt. SS.* 21 Mart).

by him; adopted the same tonsure and the same Easter which he had taught; and were so far united in discipline, that what one of their churches excommunicated, all excommunicated.

<small>Nature of the primacy recognised in Armagh by the first order of saints.</small>

In such a system, which it is plain did not include all Ireland, in the age of our author, the recognised successors of Patrick would naturally exercise a moral influence, amounting to a practical jurisdiction over the churches so united together. In any disputed question the successor of Patrick would naturally be the interpreter of his institutions, and the referee as to the real meaning of the traditions received from him. Those whose principle it was to follow Patrick, under Christ the one Head, as their guide or teacher, would necessarily, after the death of Patrick, look up to his legitimate successor as his representative, the depository of his doctrine, and therefore practically their guide, as Patrick was. But this did not amount to a primatial jurisdiction in the see of St. Patrick as such, in the modern sense of the term. The excommunication pronounced by the Church of Armagh was indeed obeyed and submitted to by the first order of saints; but Armagh was equally bound to obey the excommunication pronounced by any other church of the confederacy. There was no special jurisdiction in Armagh. The rule of this first order of saints was simply this, that what one of their churches excommunicated, whether that church was Armagh or any other, all were bound to excommunicate.

The second Order of Saints.

The second order of saints connected with Menevia and the Church of Wales.

The second order of saints do not appear to have had any connection with Armagh, or the institutions of St. Patrick. They acknowledged our Lord as their 'one Head;' they had one tonsure from ear to ear, similar to that which Patrick had introduced. They had one Easter, the fourteenth moon after the equinox. In these respects they agreed with the Patrician saints; but they celebrated different masses, and had different monastic rules. They had received a Mass, or Liturgy, from David, the celebrated bishop of Menevia, now called from him St. David's, another (for that seems to be the meaning) from Gilla or Gildas, and another from Docus, the Britons.[1] This order was therefore connected not with Armagh, but with Menevia and the Church of Wales. This order was also connected with the Columban Church of North Britain, Cumberland, Northumberland, and Durham. From this order proceeded that great stream[2] of Irish missionaries, who went forth to evangelise Europe, at the end of the sixth, and during some following centuries. From them the Venerable Bede must have derived his information respecting the Scotic or Irish Churches. From them must have been obtained all the information respecting Ireland which is to be found in the writings of continental authors.

---

[1] *Britons.* See what Dr. Lanigan has said on the history of these three Welsh saints. *Eccl. Hist.* i., p. 469 sq. ii., p. 19, note (59).

[2] *Stream.* 'Quid Hiberniam memorem (says Heric of Auxerre) contempto pelagi discrimine pene totam cum grege philosophorum ad littora nostra migrantem?' — *Epist. ad. Carol. Calvum.* ap. Duchesne, Hist. Fr. ii., p. 471. We have seen that the word *philosopher* was often employed to signify *a monk.* See above, p. 46.

Silence of Bede and the continental Irish missionaries on the History of St. Patrick.

44. And it is remarkable that in the writings of Bede we find no mention of St. Patrick or of Armagh. He speaks only of Columba, and the presbyters or bishops of the second order of saints. Adamnan also, the biographer of Columba, although he once incidentally mentions St. Patrick[1], is silent as to Armagh. The continental missionaries of the sixth and following centuries seem to have carried with them to Europe no traditions of Armagh or of Patrick.

This remarkable silence has appeared to some unaccountable, and even inconsistent with the existence of St. Patrick.[2] But the explanation of it is obvious; the Irish saints of the second order were connected with the British Church, and not with the Church of St. Patrick. They were disposed to emigration, and their religious zeal carried them to the Picts of North Britain, and to the barbarous nations of the continent of Europe, to win souls to Christ. There was no reason why they should say anything to their converts about Armagh, or the successors of St. Patrick. They were in all probability more anxious to connect the churches and monasteries which they had founded on the continent with Rome and the successors of St. Peter, from whom more effectual support might be obtained. But that they did not altogether ignore St. Patrick,

---

[1] *St. Patrick.* 'Nam quidam proselytus Brito, homo sanctus, sancti Patricii discipulus, Maucteus nomine,' &c.—Adamnan. *Præf.* 2 (ed. Reeves, p. 6).

[2] *St. Patrick.* The argument is put very strongly in some valuable papers, entitled *Palladius restitutus*, by the late Hon. A. Herbert; published (without his name) in the Brit. Magazine, vol. xxv. (1844).

is evident from the great collection of canons, from which D'Achery[1] has published extracts, in which Patrick and the synods said to have been held by him in Ireland are frequently referred to. This collection has been preserved in continental libraries only, and was evidently compiled in one of the continental monasteries connected with Ireland. A note at the end of the MS. states that the compiler, or perhaps only the transcriber, was a cleric named Arbedoc, who had the assistance or permission of the abbat Haelhucar. These names, if they have been correctly transcribed, do not seem to be Irish. But this only strengthens the argument that the Irish missionaries did not abstain from all mention of St Patrick, in their efforts to instruct their European converts.

45. The saints of the third order were hermits and solitaries. They were isolated from each other, and seem to have lived without any direct recognition of episcopal or abbatial authority. They had different monastic rules; different liturgies; different tonsures; different Easters. It is not said from whence they derived their liturgies; neither is it said, as it is said of the two other orders, that they recognised Christ as their 'one Head.' This omission

The saints of the third order.

---

[1] *D'Achery.* Spicil. tom. i. p. 491, sq. D'Achery was of opinion that this collection was made before the eighth century. He had two MSS. of it; one from which he mainly copied, belonging to the Abbey of Corbey, the other to the Library of St. Germain. He does not, however, tell us the age of these MSS. See Ceillier, *Hist. des Auteurs Ecclés.* tom. xvi. p. 574. We have seen also that in the continental lives of St. Rupert or Rudpert, and others, St. Patrick is not ignored.

may have been accidental, and of no significance; but it cannot be without significance that they are not said to have followed the teaching of St. Patrick.

<small>History of particular saints, of the second order.</small>

46. The two saints, Finnen, or Finnian (viz. Finnian of Cluain-Eraird, now Clonard, County of Meath; and Finnian, or Finnbarr of Magh Bile, now Moville, on the banks of Lough Foyle, County of Donegal), are given in the catalogue as the first in the list of saints of the second order.

<small>St. Finnian of Clonard.</small>

The former, St. Finnian of Clonard, was the master of a celebrated school, which is said to have produced three thousand disciples. Thus the hymn *ad laudes*, in the Office of St. Finnian, printed at Paris, 1620, and reprinted by *Colgan*[1], says,—

> ' Trium virorum millium
> Sorte fit Doctor humilis;
> Verbi his fudit fluvium
> Ut fons emanans rivulis.'

And although we may reasonably doubt the authenticity of so large a number, it is certain that the school of Clonard was the *alma mater* of many eminent ecclesiastics. In the Martyrology of Donegal[2], and by the Four Masters[3], this St. Finnian is called ' Tutor (*oidhe*, or foster-father), of the saints of Ireland.' The Latin author of his life tells us particularly that the celebrated saints who were called the twelve apostles of

---

[1] *Colgan.* Actt. SS. Hib. p. 401. (= 549), at which year they tell us
[2] *Donegal.* At Dec. 12. that he died.
[3] *Four Masters.* At A.D. 548

Ireland, together with many others[1], were of his disciples.

We read also[2] that, after having been initiated in ecclesiastical learning by St. Fortchern of Trim (if this be not an anachronism), and afterwards by St. Caiman, of Dair-inis, an island in the bay of Wexford, Finnian passed over to Kill-muine, or Menevia[3], afterwards called St. David's and became the associate or disciple of the three eminent saints, David, Cathmael, and Gildas.

Cathmael was the original baptismal name of the Welsh Saint Cadoc[4], or Cattwg, as we learn

His early education.

---

[1] *Others.* Colgan has enumerated 32 eminent saints who were educated in his school.—*Actt. SS.* p. 405. *App.* c. 3. See also Reeves Adamnan, p. 195, note *b*. The twelve apostles of Ireland were the following: 1. Ciaran, or Kieran, bishop and abbat of Saighir, (now Seir-Kieran, King's Co.). 2. Ciaran or Kieran, abbat of Clomnacnois. 3. Columcille of Hy. 4. Brendan, bishop and abbat of Clonfert. 5. Brendan, bishop and abbat of Birr (now Parsonstown, King's Co.). 6. Columba, abbat of Tirdaglas. 7. Molaise or Laisre, abbat of Damhinis, now Devenish-island, in Loch Erne. 8. Cainnech, abbat of A-chadh-bo, Queen's Co. 9. Ruadan, or Rodan, abbat of Lorrha, Co. Tipperary. 10. Mobi Clairenech, or the flat-faced, abbat of Glasnaoidhen (now Glasnevin, near Dublin). 11. Senell, abbat of Cluain-inis in Loch Erne; and 12. Nannath, or Nennith, abbat and bishop of Inismuige-samh, now Inis-mac-Saint, in Loch Erne.

[2] *Also.* Vit. S. Finniani, c. 4. Colgan, *Actt. SS.*, p. 393.

[3] *Menevia.* In Welsh *Hen-meneu*, translated *Vetus rubus.* Muine, in Irish, and meneu, in Welsh, signify a bramble bush.

[4] *St. Cadoc.* Vita S. Cadoci, ed. *W. J. Rees*, 'Lives of Cambro-British Saints,' pp. 25—27. This legend represents the name as given by Divine command. A voice came at night to the saint's father, predicting that a holy hermit would arrive on the following day to baptize the child, 'nomenque ejus Catmail vocabitur.' A fountain springs up miraculously, and in its water the child is baptized by the hermit, who is said to have been an Irishman, by name Meuthi; 'Postquam autem beatus Meuthi, cum solum saltantem conspexit, alacriori gaudens animo maturius eundem in ipso sacro fonte baptizavit, atque pro precepto angelico nomen ei *Cathmail* imposuit.' The Irish hermit here called Meuthi, is evidently the same who in other authorities is termed *Tathai*, and *Thaddeus*; Colgan, *Actt. SS.* p. 158, c. 2. The Life of S. Tatheus, published by W. J. Rees, 'Lives of Cambro-British Saints,' p. 255, expressly identifies him with the tutor of Cadoc. Ussher places the school of Tathai at the year 469 (*Ind. Chr.* and

H 2

from his life; there cannot, therefore, be a doubt that the three Welsh preceptors of St. Finnian were the same as the three, David, Gildas, and Docus[1], (or Cadocus), from whom the Irish saints of the second order are said in the catalogue to have received their masses or liturgies.[2]

His pilgrimage to Rome prevented by an Angel.   When about to leave his Welsh associates, St. Finnian, we are told, resolved upon a pilgrimage to Rome, but was warned by an angel to proceed rather to his own country, where God would receive his intention as equivalent to the pilgrimage he had meditated, and grant him the same merits as if he had visited Rome. And accordingly he set out for Ireland, ' to gather together there,' as his Latin biographer[3] tells us, ' a people acceptable to the Lord.'

In another Life, extant in manuscript, in the

Works, vol. v. p. 116), quoting the authority of John of Timnuth.

[1] *Docus.* The Annals of Ulster, at the year 473, mention the death of *Doccus*, a British bishop and abbat: ' Quies Docci episcopi sancti Britonum abbatis.' But this can scarcely be the Docus from whom the second order of saints derived their Mass; for the second order are expressly said to have flourished from the close of the reign of Tuathal Maelgarbh (ob. 544), to that of Aodh, son of Ainmire (ob. 599).

[2] *Liturgies.* It is remarkable that St. Cannech or Canice of Kilkenny is said to have been educated by St Doc or Docus, in Wales. ' Perrexit trans mare in Britanniam, ad virum sapientem et religiosissimum, Doc [*al.* Docum], legitque apud illum sedule, et bonos mores didicit, et erat valde humilis et obediens.' *Vit. S. Cannechi*, p. 3 (Dubl. 1853). This Life was privately printed (100 copies only) by the Marquis of Ormonde, from a MS. preserved in the Burgundian Library, Brussels, collated with another in Abp. Marsh's Library, Dublin.

[3] *Biographer.* 'Ut ibi populum Deo acceptabilem acquireret.' *Vit. S. Finniani*, c. xi.—xi. Colgan, *Actt. SS.* p. 394. The Latin Life, published by Colgan, consists of two parts. The first is evidently older than the other, and ends with the words, ' Hæc de primo libro vitæ ejus excerpta sunt,' shewing that it is only an extract from a larger work. The second part consists entirely of legends of miracles, and was written after the Catalogue of the Three Orders of Saints, which it quotes. It begins ' Igitur Finnianus optimus sanctorum secundi ordinis, abbas, volens multiplicare cultum Dei altissimi, &c.'

Irish language, the same story is told more briefly, but with a particular circumstance of some interest, which is omitted in the Latin. After relating the miraculous defeat of an invading party of Saxons[1] (St. Finnian with a stroke of his *baculus* or pastoral staff having caused a mountain to fall upon them), the Irish author[2] proceeds: 'After this, a desire seized Finnian to go to Rome, when he had completed his education. But an angel of God came to him, and said unto him, "What would be given to thee at Rome," says he, "shall be given to thee here. Arise, and renew sound doctrine and faith in Ireland after Patrick."'

This must mean the doctrine and faith which had become corrupted since St. Patrick's time. It is so understood in the office of St. Finnian, reprinted[3] by Colgan, where we read that 'when he was meditating a pilgrimage to Rome, he was persuaded by an angel to return to Ireland, *to restore the faith which had fallen into neglect after the death of St. Patrick.*' We shall see

The Faith corrupted in Finnian's time.

---

[1] *Saxons.* The story is told in the Latin Life, c. 8. Colgan, *loc. cit.*

[2] *Irish Author.* There is a good copy of the Irish Life in the Book of Lismore, a MS. in the possession of the Duke of Devonshire. The Latin author, as printed by Colgan, although he evidently made use of the Irish, of which he frequently adopts the order and often the very expressions, omits all allusion to the coruption of the faith in Ireland, since St. Patrick's time.

[3] *Reprinted.* Colgan, *Actt. SS.* p. 401. This Office, with the Offices of Patrick, Columcille, Brigid, &c., was originaly printed at Paris in 1620, under the editorship of Thomas Messingham. The following are the passages above alluded to:—In 2do Nocturno. Lect. vi. 'Tandem Romam meditanti in Hiberniam reditum Angelus Domini suasit, ad fidem post B. Patricii obitum neglectam restaurandam, &c.' Finnian is also evidently alluded to as a reformer in the 'Hymnus in utrisque vesperis.'

'Refulsit sol justitiæ,
Quæ prius fuit sub nubilo.
Cleri contubernia
Reformantur divinitus,' &c.
—Colg. *ib.*, p. 400.

reason presently to accept this as the real meaning of our author.

<small>Finnian of Maghbile.</small>

47. The second of the two saints Finnian mentioned in the Catalogue among the saints of the second order, is believed to have been St. Finnian, or Finnbarr, of Maghbile. Colgan has maintained the identity of this ecclesiastic with the Frigidian or Fridian, who was bishop of Lucca, in Tuscany, in the sixth century. There cannot be a doubt that the traditions of the church of Lucca support this conclusion; and Colgan has printed two lives, one taken from the Office of St. Fridian, as used in the church of Lucca, the other from a MS. preserved in the Carthusian abbey at Cologne. Both these are, in fact, lives of St. Finnian of Maghbile, with an addition which makes him, after the completion of his labours in Ireland, to have become Bishop of Lucca in Italy. But we are not now concerned with this question.[1] The second of the two lives mentioned above states that Finnian, or Fridian, having made a pilgrimage to Rome, to visit the tombs of the Apostles, remained there three months, having been honourably received by Pope Pelagius.[2] In that time, being of an

---

[1] *Question.* See *Book of Hymns of the Irish Church*, p. 98, *sq.* Lanigan, vol. ii. p. 27. It seems impossible to reconcile the chronology with the opinion that Fridian of Lucca and Finnian of Maghbile are identical.

[2] *Pelagius.* The first Pelagius died 560. But as he was always in bad odour with the western bishops, and even with the bishops of Italy, who virtually denied him their allegiance, it is probable that our author meant Pelagius II., whose times, however, 578—590, do not synchronize with the early part of St. Finnian's life. Tighernach, and the Annals of Ulster, give the death of Finnian at 588 or 589. This entry is found in both Annals, in these words, 'Quies Uinniani episcopi nepotis Fiatach.' Dr. O'Conor was

ardent mind, 'ut erat ardentis ingenii,' he committed to memory the ecclesiastical and apostolical customs. He then returned to his own country, having received the pontifical benediction, carrying with him certain relics given him by the Pope, and the Decrees, which in his biographer's time were still called 'the Canons[1] of St. Fridian.' He brought with him also the Gospels, which that country (says our author) had not yet fully received; to which [meaning apparently the particular copy] God gave such great virtue, that if any one swore falsely by them, he was punished with death or madness in the same year.[2]

It is curious that the native legends, also, speak of St. Finnian as having *first* brought the Gospels to Ireland.

Said to have first brought the Gospels to Ireland.

unable to read the contractions of the original, and has printed the name *Uinniani* in Tighernach *Mani*, and in Ann. Ult. *Umaniain* : (Rer. Hib. Script. ii. p. 154; iv. p. 28). But *Uinnian*, is the same as Finnian, and it is evident that Finnian of Maghbile is intended, for he was of the Dal Fiatach, or descendants of Fiatach Finn, King of Ireland. See *Book of Hymns, loc. cit.*

[1] *Canons.* In the great collection of Irish Canons, transcribed by 'Arbedoc clericus, Haelchuchar [? *Maelchuchar*] Abbate dispensante,' from which D'Achery has published some extracts, we find one (*lib.* 28, c. 7) attributed to *Vinniavus*, an evident mistake for *Vinnianus*, i.e. *Finnianus*. D'Achery, *Spicil.* I. p. 497. It is greatly to be regretted that the learned Benedictine did not publish this Collection of Canons without abridgement. The single canon attributed to Finnian, relates to the punishment of a Clerk who was guilty of theft. We must not, however, be too sure that the book alluded to in the Life of St. Fridian, under the name of *St. Fridian's Canon* or *Canons*, was a collection of canons in the present signification of the word. For the name of a *Canon* was sometimes given to a copy of the Gospels, or to the New Testament. The Book of Armagh, which contains several ecclesiastical writings, together with the whole of the New Testament, is very commonly called 'The Canon of Patrick.'

[2] *Year.* Colgan, *Actt. SS.* p. 638, cap. 3 : 'Evangelia quoque, quæ terra illa nondum plene susceperat, quibus nimirum Deus tantam virtutem concessit, quod si quis per ea juraverit [perhaps we should read *perjuraverit*], morte vel amentia in eodem anno divina ultione mulctetur.'

The stanza in which he is described in the Metrical Calendar of Aengus, the Culdee, is very obscure[1], and puzzles our best Irish scholars. But the Gloss in the Dublin MS. of it explains the words to mean that he brought over the sea, or from foreign parts, the Gospel : ' quod est lex nova,' adding, in the Irish[2] language, ' that it was he who first brought the Gospel to Ireland.'

This passage has greatly perplexed our historians. The Martyrology of Cashel[3] explains it to mean 'the law of Moses and the Gospel.' The Brussels copy[4] of the Calendar of Aengus omits the gloss above quoted, but gives in its stead the following note : ' It was Finnian of Maghbile that first brought the law of Moses into Ireland, *if this be true* [si verum] : or it is to the Gospel is given the name of the Law, for it was he who brought into Ireland, as they say, the whole Gospel in one volume, if indeed this also be true [si verum hoc ipsum].' A more recent hand adds, as a gloss on the word Gospel,

---

[1] *Obscure.* Felire of Aeng. at 10th Sept. ' Clii dergoir co nglaine, Co riacht tar sal side.' Mr. Curry translates this ' Body of red gold with purity, which reached across the sea hither.' The Gloss explains ' purity' to signify the Gospel. Colgan has paraphrased the lines thus (*Actt. SS.* p. 643) :
' Roma aureus et præfulgidus,
Qui contulit libros legis ultra mare.'
But this is remote indeed from the original.
[2] *Irish.* ' Arise thuc soscela in Erinn artus.' ' For it was he who first brought the Gospel to Erinn.'
[3] *Cashel.* As quoted by Colgan,

Actt. SS. p. 643, col. 1.: ' Finnianus Fionn [*id est* albus] de Magbile; ipse est qui primo legem Moysaicam [id est Vetus Testamentum] et totum Evangelium in Hiberniam portavit.' So that Colgan would get over the difficulty by making the word *Gospel* to signify the whole canon of the Old and New Testament, which Finnian was the first to bring into Ireland. The words within brackets contain the interpretation suggested by Colgan.
[4] *Brussels Copy.* Mr. Curry's transcript, p. 287 (*Orig. MS.* p. 29). Both notes occur in the MS. of Aengus preserved at St. Isidore's, in Rome.

'correctum la Cirine,' 'corrected by St. Jerome,' which suggests another mode of meeting the difficulty. Finnian was not the first to bring the Gospel to Ireland, but the first to bring to Ireland St. Jerome's translation of the Gospel.[1]

48. The author of the Life of Finnian preserved in the Cologne MS., in the passage already quoted, seems to mix together two stories: one, that the Irish had never fully received the Gospel until St. Finnian brought it to them; the other, that what he brought over from Rome was a particular copy of the Gospels, possessed of miraculous virtues. *St. Finnian's copy of the Gospels celebrated in Irish legends.*

That Finnian was the owner of a remarkable copy of the Gospels, of which he was particularly careful, appears incidentally from an anecdote related in the Life of St. Fintan[2], of Dunflesk. *Anecdote of St. Fintan of Dunflesk.*

It appears that Fintan once asked St. Finnian for a loan of his volume of the Gospels, that he might read it, but his request was peremptorily refused. Fintan was at that time a pupil of St. Comgall, of Bangor, and complained to his master, who told him to be faithful[3], and that perhaps he should soon have that very copy of the Gospels. The next night Maghbile was plundered by pirates, who, with other spoils, carried off the precious volume. St. Fintan was praying under a large tree on the sea shore, near to the place where the pirates had

---

[1] *Gospel.* It will be observed also that this Scholiast shews a desire to discredit the whole story, by adding ' Si verum' and ' si verum hoc ipsum.'

[2] *Fintan.* Colgan, *Actt. SS.* at 3 Jan., c. 5 (p. 11).
[3] *Faithful.* ' Si fidelis fueris forsitan in primo [meaning perhaps at the hour of Prime] illud ipsum evangelium habebis.'—*Ibid.*

landed, and he heard them, when preparing for their departure, consulting about plundering St. Comgall's abbey also ; but lo, a sudden storm arose, the tree was blown down upon the ships, which were all destroyed, and the pirates drowned. But their spoil, with the book of the Gospels, was found upon the shore, and thus St. Fintan obtained his desire.

St. Columba's transcript of Finnian's Gospels.

The well-known story of St. Columba's transcript of the book of the Gospels, which he had borrowed from St. Finnian, is another example of the jealousy with which Finnian guarded his rights to the exclusive possession of the sacred volume. Columba worked night and day to make a copy of the book for his own use without the knowledge of its owner. Finnian claimed the transcript as his property, because it was made surreptitiously, and because the original was his; and the case was brought before the Supreme Court of Diarmait, King of Ireland, who decided against Columba[1], with the curious *rann*, or oracular saying, that as the cow is the owner of her calf, so the book is the owner of any transcript made from it.

These legends are quoted, not that we would attach any importance to them as true stories, but because they shew that St. Finnian was popularly believed to be, in some peculiar sense,

---

[1] *Columba.* See Colgan, *Actt. SS.*, p. 644, *sq.* Reeves, *Adamnan*, p. 248. Four Masters, 555. The box called the *Cathach* (Reeves *ubi supra*) now contains a Psalter. This MS. may possibly be as old as St. Columba's time, but there is no evidence that it was the MS. to which the legend relates. The box received the name of *Cathach*, or battle book, because it was carried in battle. Reeves, *ib.* pp. 249, 250, 319.

INTROD.] *Second Order of Saints Reformers.* 107

the possessor of the Gospels, or of some remarkable copy of the Gospels. It is evident that when such tales were told, books must have been rare and highly valued in Ireland; and it is probable that, in some parts of the country at least, St. Finnian's Codex, if it was really a copy of the Gospels[1], may have been regarded as the first complete copy that ever was brought into Ireland, and that it was held in extraordinary veneration accordingly.

49. But the legends give us also this important information, that both the Finnians were believed to have returned to Ireland after their foreign education, for the purpose of effecting a reformation in the decaying faith and morals of the country. In other words, the second order of saints represented by the two Finnians, were a body of missionaries and reformers, whose object it was to undermine the paganism which still prevailed in Ireland, as well as to correct the errors which had crept into the faith and practice of professing Christians since the death of St. Patrick. *A reformation of religion in Ireland the object of the second Order of Saints.*

And that there was such a period of declension, there is abundant evidence. Anmchad, or Animosus, author of the Life of St. Brigid, must have flourished in the tenth century.[2] He was probably the Anmchad, bishop of Kildare, whose *Evidence of a real declension of faith.*

---

[1] *Gospels.* There is no doubt that the word *Evangelium* was used with considerable laxity; and it is not impossible that the *Gospel*, brought into Ireland for the first time by St. Finnian, may have been *a Missal.* See Reeves, *Adamnan,* p. 325, note. The saints of the second order are said to have had different Missals.

[2] *Century.* 'Post annum 823 et ante 1097,' is the decision of Colgan *Tr. Thaum.,* p. 564, note 4.

death is recorded by the Four Masters A.D. 980, or more correctly 981. At all events, he must have lived after the age of the second order of saints, and therefore after the period of apostasy, or partial apostasy, which they laboured to correct. And he has taken care to put into the mouth of St. Brigid, in conjunction with St. Patrick, a prophecy of that apostasy. He tells the story thus :[1]

<small>St. Brigid's prophecy of it.</small>

'She had gone with St. Patrick to the North of Ireland. One day St. Patrick was preaching to the people of the country; but Brigid fell asleep during the sermon. When St. Patrick was done preaching, he said to her, "Holy virgin, why didst thou sleep at the word of God?" Brigid fell on her knees and asked pardon, saying, "Spare me, Father; spare me, holy Lord; for during that time I saw a dream." The holy pontiff said to her, "Tell it us, my daughter." The holy virgin said, "I, thy handmaid, saw four ploughs ploughing the whole of Ireland; and sowers were sowing seed; and straightway the seed sprang up, and began to ripen: and rivers of new milk filled the furrows. And those sowers were clad in white garments. After this I saw other ploughs, and they that ploughed were black; and they upturned the good crop, and cut it with their ploughshares, and sowed tares; and muddy waters filled the furrows."

'And the bishop said unto the virgin, "O, blessed virgin, thou hast seen a true and wondrous vision. This is the interpretation of it. We are the good ploughers, for we open the hearts of men with the four ploughs of the Gospels; and we sow the word of God; and from us flow rivers of the milk of Christian faith. But at the end of the world[2] there shall come

---

[1] *Thus.* Vita (quarta) S. Brigidæ, cap. 27, *Ap.* Colgan, *ibid.*, p. 553.
[2] *World.* 'In fine seculi.' Perhaps this may signify 'at the end of a century;' but the other is the more general meaning of the phrase. M. L. Tachet de Barneval maintains that it has here the former signification. 'Non pas,' he says, 'à la fin du monde, mais à la fin du siècle même où il [S. Patrice] avait apporté l'Evangile à l'Irlande.'— *Histoire Légendaire de l'Irlande*, p. 126. A similar prophecy is attributed

evil teachers, conspiring with evil men, who shall overturn our doctrine, and seduce almost all men."
'Then those who were there with St. Patrick and St. Brigid blessed God.'

50. The testimony of the abbess Hildegardis may also be cited, although she lived near to the close of the twelfth century.[1] Nevertheless she is a witness to the tradition being prevalent in her times, that the Irish Church of the sixth and seventh centuries was troubled with serious evils. In her Life of St. Disibod, or Disen, abbat of Disemberg, in the diocese of Mayence, she thus speaks of the state of Ireland about the year 620, when her hero was living as a bishop in that his native country.[2]

Testimony of Hildegardis.

'At the time when the holy man was thus governing his people with words and examples, a huge schism, and great scandals prevailed in all that country (i. e. Ireland). Some rejected the Old and New Testament, and denied Christ; others embraced heresies; very many went over to Judaism; some relapsed into Paganism; some desired to live, not as becomes men, but like beasts, in a base manner; others, in fine, although, from outward decency, they observed some appearance of morality, in reality cared for nothing good. To these gross errors, to this Babylonish confusion, Disibod opposed himself with manly and unbroken courage, bearing patiently many calumnies and injuries, and desiring rather to lose his life, than connive at such vile and nefarious doings. But when he had for some years patiently endured these evils, not without bodily danger, and nevertheless was unable to eradicate them, he was at length wearied out, and, with many tears, poured forth this prayer to the Lord: "Almighty God,

Corruption of the Irish Church in the times of St. Disibod.

---

to St. Patrick, which we shall have occasion to notice elsewhere.
[1] *Century.* She died 17 Sept. 1180.

[2] *Country.* Vita S. Disibodi, cap 6, *ap. Surium* (8 *Julii*), tom. iv. p. 141.

who comest to judge the quick and the dead, and to search out the deeds of men, what use am I, wearing myself out in this nation, which not only cannot endure thy righteousness, but is also tearing itself to pieces with rabid bites."'

Disibod, for this reason, made up his mind to quit Ireland, and to go forth as a missionary to other lands. He had been a bishop for some years in his own country; and in Disemberg, the monastery he afterwards founded abroad, he was an *episcopus regionarius*, an abbat-bishop without jurisdiction out of his abbey.

The foregoing statement, however, is most probably exaggerated. It is not possible to believe that any great number of the Irish people in the seventh century could have gone over to Judaism[1]; but these words are a curious commentary on the whole passage, and enable us to estimate the value of such language. In the middle of the twelfth century, controversies and public discussions between Christians and learned Jews were very common on the Continent of Europe; and Hildegardis, wishing to describe the most schismatical state of things in Ireland which she could conceive, may very naturally have adopted the ideas and language of her own time and country, and assumed that a large number of the Irish people became converts to Judaism. This mistake, however, ought not to invalidate her testimony

---

[1] *Judaism.* The original words are: 'Plerisque ad Judaismum se conferentibus.' There is also mention of a Jewish heresy in the Life of St. David, of Menevia:. 'Judæorum (inquit) et Hæreticorum malitia his diebus in Christianos nimis invaluit.'—*Vit. S. David.* cap. 21: Colgan. *Actt. SS.* p. 428. But this perhaps only proves that the author of St. David's life lived at the same time as Hildegardis.

to the fact, confirmed as it is by native authorities, that the Irish Church in the sixth and seventh centuries had in a great degree corrupted the faith.

51. An express and very distinct confirmation of this fact is to be found in the Life of the Gildas[1], from whom the saints of the second order are said to have received a Mass, or Liturgy. Ainmire, King of Ireland (A.D. 568—571), first cousin of the celebrated St. Columkille[2], is said to have sent for Gildas, 'promising that he would obey him in all his doctrines, if he would come and restore ecclesiastical order in Ireland, because almost all the inhabitants of that island had abandoned the Catholic faith.' Our author proceeds, 'When Gildas heard this, armed with heavenly weapons, he went to Ireland to preach Christ.' He was presented to King Ainmire, who offered him many gifts, and prayed him to remain in the kingdom, ' to restore ecclesiastical order in the country, because all, from the highest to the lowest, had lost the Catholic faith.'

Corruption of the faith in the times of Gildas.

---

[1] *Gildas.* Colgan, *Actt. SS.* p. 183, cap. 10. He is commonly called Gildas Badonicus, from the Battle of Bath, fought at the time of his birth, about A.D. 520. It should be observed that *Gildas,* in Irish *Giolla De,* 'Servant of God,' was not a name but a title; a sort of ecclesiastical degree, given by the schools of Ireland. There were therefore necessarily several who had a right to this title, and were distinguished from each other by being called *Sapiens, Badonicus, Albanicus,* &c. We are not now concerned with the question whether or not Gildas Badonicus, ' cognomento Sapiens,' was the same as Albanicus or not.—See Cave I. 538, and *Lanigan* I. 476, 482. Colgan makes a palpable mistake about Gildas Albanicus, whom he supposes to have been contemporary with St. Patrick; and he also attributes to him the writings of Giolla-Caemain, who lived in the 11th Century.

[2] *Columkille.* See Reeves' *Adamnan*; *Geneal. Tables,* No. xv, and Append. A. to this Introd. Tab. II.

112 Gildas a Reformer in Ireland [INTROD.

His reformation in Ireland.

Gildas, we are told, accepted this mission. 'He made a circuit of all Ireland, restored the churches, taught all the clergy to worship the Holy Trinity in the Catholic faith; healed the people who had been wounded by the bites of heretics; cast far away heretical frauds, with their authors.'

How far this statement is to be credited.

We are not perhaps bound to accept the language of this description as in every respect to be relied upon. The Annals and other native records give no countenance to the assertion that almost all the inhabitants of Ireland had abandoned the Catholic faith. Nevertheless we cannot reject it as wholly without foundation. It is supported, directly and indirectly, by the whole history of the period. The coming of Gildas into Ireland is especially commemorated in the Welsh Annals, and the date of his death is entered in the Annals[1] of Ireland. It is evident, therefore, that he was regarded as having had some special mission in Ireland; and we have seen from independent sources that, making allowance for some exaggeration, there is reason to receive as substantially true, the statement made in his life, that the Irish Church was at that time in a state of declension, and that serious errors of some kind had crept in. Colgan, Ussher, and Lanigan[2], all very high authorities, deny this statement altogether, which is certainly going too far. Colgan's refutation of it is singularly

---

[1] *Annals.* A.D. 565, 'Navigatio Gildæ in Hibernia,' A.D. 570, 'Gildas Britonum sapientissimus obiit,' *Annales Cambriæ.* A.D. 570, 'Itea Culana Credil et Gillas quieverunt,' *Tigern.* A.D. 569, 'Gildas obiit,' *Ann Ult.* A.D. 559, 'Quies Gildais episcopi,' *Ann. Inisf.* (*Bodl*).

[2] *Lanigan. Eccl. Hist.* i. p. 488, note (168).

INTROD.] *Objections of Colgan and Ussher.* 113

weak and inconclusive. He gives us a list[1] of ecclesiastics from A.D. 496 to 594, and he argues that the Church which, in that hundred years, had produced so many eminent men, cannot fairly be said to have been in a state of decay or apostasy. But he forgets that almost all the saints and doctors he enumerates were the missionaries of the second order, or their disciples, who had laboured to counteract the evil. His argument, therefore, does not prove that the evil did not exist, but only that most active and successful measures were adopted to counteract it.

Colgan's attempt to refute it.

Ussher's argument[2] is open to nearly the same objection. He convicts, indeed, the author of the Life of exaggeration. We cannot believe, he reasons, what this author tells us, that Gildas preached not only throughout all Ireland, but also 'through the whole region of the Angli and of foreign nations, instructing them by his example and speech.'[3] Why, then, should we believe, on the testimony of such a writer, that Ireland had apostatized, and was re-converted by Gildas to the Catholic faith? No doubt these are exaggerated statements. And it is quite true that if we had this fact on the sole testimony of the author of this life, we might perhaps be justified in disbelieving it; but, as we have seen, the fact is attested by independent and native witnesses.

Archbishop Ussher's argument.

Again Ussher says, that, according to the tes-

[1] *List. Actt. SS.* p. 189, note 13.
[2] *Argument. Primordia*, p. 907, sq. (*Works*, vol. VI. p. 471.)
[3] *Speech.* 'Omnem denique regionem Hibernensium, et Anglorum, et exterarum nationum suo instruxit exemplo et erudivit sermone,' c. 10. Colgan, *Actt. SS.* p. 183.

I

timony of this very biographer, it was in Ireland that Gildas had received the completion of his ecclesiastical education, which had been begun in the school of the Welsh saint Iltutus. After having learnt all that this doctor could teach him, 'he took leave of his master and fellow-scholars, and went over to *Ire*, that he might learn and investigate the opinions of other doctors in philosophy and sacred literature.'[1] Assuming *Ire* to mean Ireland in this passage, Ussher proceeds to show that there were in Ireland celebrated schools of learning. He enumerates the schools of Finnian, at Clonard; of Brendan, at Ross; of Ciaran, at Clonmacnois, &c. But he forgot that these were the very saints of the second order who are represented as having received their rule and Mass from this very Gildas. It is not possible, therefore, that they could also have been his masters. The inference is, that the author of the Life, when he represented Gildas as having gone to *Ire* for instruction, was guilty of an anachronism; if, indeed, he meant Ireland by *Ire*; which perhaps he did, although in no other passage of his work does he give the island that unusual name, but always speaks of Hibernia and Hibernienses.

Tendency to foreign pilgrimage in the second order of saints

52. On the other hand we have seen that the saints of the second order are represented as having gone, in the first instance, to Wales and other

---

[1] *Literature.* 'Valedicens pio Magistro venerandisque condiscipulis *Iren* perrexit; ut et aliorum Doctorum sententias, in philosophicis atque Divinis literis, investigator curiosus enquireret,' c. 6.—Colgan, *ib.* p. 182.

countries to look for the ecclesiastical education which the state of Ireland denied them at home. There they received an impulse which gave them a tendency to quit their own country and go forth as missionaries abroad. And many of them, in fact, did go abroad, and became the founders of flourishing churches on the continent of Europe and elsewhere, in which their names are, to this day, held in religious veneration and honour. That efforts were made to counteract this tendency may be inferred from the legends, one of which has been quoted[1], in which angels are represented as promising the same spiritual advantages to those who labour at home as might have been expected, according to the opinions of the age, from a pilgrimage to Rome.

Another curious anecdote from which the same conclusion may be drawn, is recorded in the antient Latin Life of St. Aedan, or Moedhog[2], of Ferns : —

Legend of St. Molua.

'A certain holy man named Molua came to St. Moedhog, saying, "I wish to go in pilgrimage to Rome." The bishop said to him, " Thou shalt not have my permission." Molua answered, " Verily, if I see not Rome, I shall soon die." Then St. Moedhog took him up with him into his chariot, and they were not seen by their companions until the following

---

[1] *Quoted.* See p. 100, supra.

[2] *Moedhog.* This alias is puzzling to an English reader. The Irish had two ways of expressing devotion to a particular saint. The first was by using the diminutive of his name. The second was by prefixing to his name the pronoun *mo*, my. Sometimes, as in the present case, both were combined. *Aedh* was this bishop's original name: the Latin diminutive form of this was *Aedanus*; the Irish diminutive was *Aedh-og* ; to which if we prefix *mo*, we have *Mo-aedh-og*, or *Moedhog*, or as it is pronounced *Mogue* ; the name by which he is now generally known. It is a curious circumstance that in the Diocese of Ferns the peasantry who are of English descent call their children *Aedan* or *Edan*; those of Irish descent call their children *Mogue* to this day.

day. And it seemed to St. Molua that they had been at Rome on that night, and that he had there paid his vows at the shrines of the Apostles. On the morning of the following day, the saints returned to the city of Ferns. And the aged saint said to the blessed Molua, "Dost thou still wish to go to Rome?" He answered, "Why should I wish it? Have I not paid my vows there yesterday and last night? But I am ashamed to return so soon to my monastery." Straightway the bishop went with him, and sent him forth to his own place, telling that he had been at Rome (perhibens [i. e. Episcopus] eum fuisse Romæ).

'The mystery of this affair the Lord alone knoweth; but we know that this holy man was well acquainted with Rome, as if he had been there a long time.'[1]

The Molua of which this legend was told was St. Molua of Clonfert-Molua, now Clonfertmulloe, *alias* Kyle, in the Queen's County; and it is remarkable that St. Moedhog was his junior, but is represented in the story as his senior and as exercising authority over him, in virtue of the episcopal character, Molua having been a presbyter only. It appears also that before St. Moedhog was consecrated a bishop, Molua had been his confessor.[2]

The Case of Saint Canice.

The Life of St. Cannech, or Canice, of Kilkenny, tells us a story of similar import. When he had completed his education with St. Docus, in Wales, he made up his mind first to visit Rome, and then to return to Ireland, to convert his own people from heathenism to the Lord.

---

[1] *Time.* Vit. S. Moedoci, cap. 42. Colgan, *Actt. SS.* p. 213. From the concluding words of the above extract, Colgan infers that the author of this life was either himself a contemporary of St. Molua, or transcribed the narrative of a contemporary.

[2] *Confessor.* Vit. S. Moedoci, c. 20 and 54. Moedhog died A.D. 632; S. Molua A.D. 608 or 609. *Ann. Ult.* and *Tighern.*

INTROD.] *the Tendency to foreign Pilgrimage.* 117

Accordingly, after having been ordained priest, he went to Italy. There, however, he obtained from a certain king a grant of land, and built a monastery; and forgetting poor Ireland, promised the king to make that place his tomb. But an angel appeared to him and rebuked him, telling him that the place of his resurrection was in Ireland. The saint then, in obedience to the command of the angel, set out for Ireland; but, to save his promise, left a toe of his right foot to be buried in Italy.[1]

Many other instances might be quoted[2] from the Lives of the Irish Saints of this period; but to do so at any length would carry us too far from our immediate object. It must suffice to observe that the tendency to foreign travel, and the efforts obviously made to counteract it, are fully explained by the alleged existence of social and ecclesiastical disorder at home.

In a word, the second order of saints were reformers, and missionaries at home and abroad.

---

[1] *Italy. Vita S. Cannechi*, fol. 4, 5 (Dubl. 1853); Marquis of Ormonde's edit.

[2] *Quoted.* There is another instance in the Life of St. Comgall of Bangor (Fleming. *Collect.* p. 395, cap. 13). St. Comgall had resolved to leave Ireland and travel to Britain; but the saints of Ireland persuaded him to remain in his own country. 'Post hæc B. Comgallus totam deserere Hiberniam, et pro Christo peregrinare in Britanniam voluit, et ibi manere; sed Deo concedente, precibus et flebili rogatu *S. Lugidi* episcopi, consecratoris sui, et aliorum sanctorum victus, retentus est in Hibernia,' &c. So also St. Fanchea is represented as having gone to visit her brother St. Enda, in his foreign monastery, for the purpose of persuading him to return to Ireland. 'Ut talenta sibi a Deo data cum populo terræ suæ nativæ condivideret.'—*Vit. S. Endei*, c. 9; ap. Colgan, *Actt. SS.* p. 706. To mention one instance more; St. Molagga, when in attendance on St. David of Menevia, was commanded by an angel to return to Ireland; 'ab angelo monitus est ut in Hiberniam revertatur.'—*Vit. S. Molaggæ*, c. 16; Colgan, *ib.* p. 147.

Those who remained at home established monastic schools for the instruction of the clergy and people. Those who went abroad were founders of monasteries and bishoprics, anchorites, scholars, and teachers in schools of learning, pilgrims visiting the holy places of Christianity; but all were engaged, in different ways, and according to their different tastes and capabilities, in the same work of propagating amongst the heathen the faith of Christ.

Nature of the evils then prevalent in the Irish Church.

53. It is to be regretted that we have not more detailed information as to the exact nature of the alleged apostasy, or disorganization of the Irish Church, which Gildas was sent for to correct. Hildegardis, in the passage just quoted, speaks of it as infidelity; a disbelief in the Holy Scriptures; a denial of Christ; a return to paganism; a corruption of morals and of decency.

Druidism.

But there is evidence that Druidism and its attendant superstitions were in existence in the times of the second order of saints, and that a belief in the efficacy of such pagan rites still lingered amongst the people, and was countenanced even by some who made the highest profession of Christianity.

Anecdote of St. Columba.

Adamnan[1] tells the following story when speaking of St. Columba's wonderful vocal powers. The saint was sitting with a few of the brethren outside of the fortress of King Brude, on the banks of Loch Ness. They began to sing the evening psalms, according to their custom, when some

[1] *Adamnan.* Lib. i. 37 (Reeves, p. 73).

Magi or Druids came around them, and endeavoured, apparently by making loud noises, to prevent the sound of their psalmody being heard by the people of the neighbourhood. But Columba, with a voice which drowned the outcry of the Druids, began to intone the psalm, *Eructavit cor meum verbum bonum,* ' My heart is inditing a good matter.' The sound, says the biographer, was like thunder in the air, and struck the king and the people with inexpressible awe.

This proves that the national Druidism was then in hostility to Christianity. But this was in a country and amongst a people still heathen, and to whom the effects of St. Patrick's preaching had not penetrated. We find mention, however, of Druids and Druidical charms in the court of the King of Ireland at the same period. [Druidical rites practised in the court of the King of Ireland.]

In the account of the battle of Cuil-dreimhne, given by the annalist Tighernach, we read that Fraechan, son of Tenius[1], who in another authority[2] is called ' the Druid of King Diarmait,' made ' the Druidical *airbhe* between the two hosts;' and that Tuatan, a distant relative[3] of St. Columba, ' put the Druidical *airbhe*[4] over his head,' whatever that may mean, and was the only man of Columba's side who was slain in the battle. [Battle of Cuil-dreimhne.]

---

[1] *Tenius.* ' Mac Teniusan.' Tigh. A.D. 561; and Four Masters A.D. 555. But Teniusan seems the genitive case. In the Dublin copy of the Ann. Ult. (A.D. 560) he is called ' Mac Temnan.'

[2] *Authority.* See the account of this battle first published by Dr. Petrie from the *Leabhar Buidhe*

Lecan. Hist. of Tara Hill, p. 123 (*Trans. R. Irish Acad.,* vol. xviii.).

[3] *Relative.* His descent is given as fifth inclusive from Eoghan, son of Niall the great.

[4] *Airbhe.* This word is not explained. It has been supposed to mean an incantation of some sort; but if so it is not easy to understand

The annalist quotes the poetical prayer which Columba addressed to the Almighty on this occasion, to which the victory of his party is ascribed.[1] In this poem, which is apparently of the nature of an incantation, Columba alludes[2] to the magical arts of his adversaries; he complains of the mist which encircled the army; he speaks of the enemy as 'the host which went round the carn,' probably because they had marched round some carn of stones as a Druidical ceremony; and he adds,

> 'My Druid,— may he be on my side!
> Is the Son of God, and Truth with Purity.'

O'Donnell represents St. Finnian of Maghbile as engaged in prayer on the side of King Diarmait. But Columba's prayers being more powerful, the two saints came to a compromise; and Finnian, to stop the slaughter of his party, consented to cease praying, and permit Columba to obtain the victory.[3]

This story is founded upon a strange idea of God, which indeed pervades many of the bio-

---

how Tuatan could have 'put it over his head,' unless we assume that to have been a figurative mode of saying that he disregarded it. Dr. O'Conor (*Rer. Hib. Scriptt.*, ii. p. 142) completely mistakes the meaning, and translates *in airbhe ndruad* 'expulsio Druidarum,' as if the word was *inarbhadh*. See Dr. O'Donovan's note: Four Masters, *loc. cit.* O'Donnell, or rather, perhaps his translator Colgan, suppresses here all mention of the Druidical ceremony, and tells us that Tuatan lost his life by imprudently crossing the *river*, which separated the two armies; 'qui fluvium, utrasque copias dividentem, temere trajiceret.' *Vit. S. Columbæ*, ii. 3 (Colgan. *Tr. Th.*, p. 409).

[1] *Ascribed.* 'Victores erant per orationem Coluimcille, dicentis,' &c. —*Tigern. loc. cit.*

[2] *Alludes.* See the transl. of it given by Dr. Petrie, *Tara Hill*, *loc. cit.* Dr. O'Conor has entirely mistaken and mistranslated this antient poem.

[3] *Victory.* O'Donnell, *Vit. S. Columbæ*, *loc. cit.*

graphies of the Irish saints, as if the intercession of different individuals, differing in degree of power, had each, although on opposite sides, a sort of necessary influence[1] upon the Almighty. If Finnian were on the side of Diarmait, and the other particulars of the story were true, he was directly sanctioning the Druidical practices of the king; nevertheless his prayers are represented as having to a certain extent prevailed.

There is also other evidence that such practices were tolerated at the court of Diarmait. After that king had given his celebrated decision against Columba, in the matter of St. Finnian's book, a story[2] which has been already alluded to, he endeavoured to prevent Columba from joining his own clan in the North of Ireland. Columba, however, escaped from the royal palace of Tara, and took his

[1] *Influence.* A very extraordinary story is told in the Life of St. Finnian of Clonard, for which even Colgan thought it necessary to apologize, in which two saints, by making the sign of the cross, reversed each the miracle wrought by the other. St. Ruadan or Rodan of Lorrha, had a tree called *Tylia*, in his cell, from which dropped a wonderful fluid, upon which his monks lived. St. Finnian, of Clonard, at the instance of the saints of Ireland, as having been their master, went to St. Rodan, to ask him to permit his monks to live as the other monks of Ireland did; 'ut communem vitam cum aliis haberet.' When St. Finnian arrived at Lorrha, he made the sign of the cross upon the miraculous tree, and its virtue was immediately destroyed. There was therefore nothing for the usual dinner of the house. St. Rodan hearing this, ordered the servant to bring up a vessel full of water from the well. He signed the water with the sign of the cross, and it was instantly converted into the same nutritious and wondrous fluid which had distilled from the tree. When set before the guests, however, St. Finnian signed it with the sign of the cross, and it again became mere water. The contest ended by St. Rodan consenting to allow his monks to live as the other monks of Ireland did: 'ut similem cum aliis vivendi modum haberet.' — *Vita Finniani* (23 Feb.). Colgan. *Actt. SS.* p. 395, c. 25.

[2] *Story.* See above, p. 106, and Reeves, *Adamnan*, p. 247, note B, where the history of the causes which led to the battle is fully given.

122   Existence of Druidism in Ireland   [INTROD.

St. Columba's Lorica, or protecting Hymn.

way alone across the mountains, sending his followers by another road. During his solitary journey he is said to have composed a poem[1], which is still extant, and, if not genuine, is undoubtedly of great antiquity. In this production he expresses his conviction that his life is in the hands of God, that King Diarmait cannot touch him if God has predetermined his deliverance; and he concludes by an evident allusion to the influence of pagan superstitions in the court of Tara; declaring that he put no trust in any such vanities, but depended only on the protection of the true God. His words[2] are worth quoting: —

> 'Our fate depends not on sneezing,
> Nor on a bird perched on a twig;
> Nor on the root of a knotted tree,
> Nor on the noise of clapping hands.
> Better is HE in whom we trust,
> The FATHER, the ONE, and the SON.'

And in another stanza,

> 'I adore not the voice of birds,
> Nor sneezing, nor lots in this world;
> Nor a boy, nor chance, nor woman:
> My Druid is CHRIST, the SON of GOD,
> CHRIST, Son of Mary, the Great Abbat,
> The FATHER, the SON, and HOLY GHOST,' &c.

---

[1] *A poem.* This poem has been printed, with a translation by Dr. O'Donovan, in the Miscellany of the Irish Archæological Society, Dublin, 1846.

[2] *Words.* Since the poem was published by the Irish Archæological Society, some progress has been made in our knowledge of old Irish, and therefore a new translation of the stanzas quoted has been here given. But as this is not the place for any philological discussion, the reader must be content with a reference to the *Irish Version of Nennius*, p. 144, note.

We have here an enumeration of the principal omens and methods of divination in use amongst the antient pagans, some of them not even yet wholly forgotten. And it is evident that King Diarmait, feeling himself perhaps the weaker party in the contest with his Northern cousins[1], had recourse to the spells and incantations of the old religion, notwithstanding his profession of Christianity.

It appears incidentally that Diarmait was in ill odour with the Church. He was not disposed to recognize the right of sanctuary, at that time claimed by the 'saints' of Ireland, and was in this way brought into collision with St. Columba[2]; as also with St. Ruadan, or Rodan, of Lorrha, in the county of Tipperary. This latter saint is said to have denounced the palace of Tara[3], in which Diarmait and his predecessors had always hitherto held their court. And in consequence of this denunciation no subsequent King of Ireland had the courage to make Tara his residence.

54. It is not easy to vindicate the second order of saints and their disciples from the charge of attributing to their own hymns, poems, shrines, and reliquaries, as well as to *The saints of the second order not free from a belief in the power of charms and incantations.*

---

[1] *Cousins.* The battle of Cuildreimhne was in part a contest between the Southern Hy Niell, of whom Diarmiad was the chief, and the Northern Hy Niell, represented by the two clans of the Cinel Conaill and Cinel Eoghan.—See Reeves, *Adamnan*, p. 251. The genealogical tables in the appendix to this Introduction, will shew the reader at a glance the relationship between the clans engaged in this contest.

[2] *St. Columba.* Four Masters, at A.D. 555.

[3] *Tara.* Petrie *On Tara Hill*, p. 125, *sq. Vita S. Rodani, ap.* Bolland, *Actt. SS.* 15 Apr.

their denunciations of wrath and imprecations, the same sort of magical powers which the Druids claimed for their prophecies, charms, and incantations. The hymn attributed to St. Columba, from which we have just quoted some stanzas, is said to have possessed the virtue[1] of protecting whoever repeated it on a journey from all the dangers of the road. The *lorica*[2] of Gildas — the same Gildas no doubt who was sent for by King Ainmire to reform the Irish Church — is said to have been composed for the express purpose of protecting the person who recites it from the influence of demons. And so also the *lorica* or Irish Hymn of St. Patrick, first published by Dr. Petrie, was believed to have had the power of protecting those who devoutly recited it, from all imminent dangers, whether bodily or spiritual.[3]

Lorica of Gildas.

Lorica of St. Patrick.

The "Cathach" or battle-book of St. Columba.

The very book, transcribed surreptitiously from St. Finnian's MS., which formed, in part at least, the cause of quarrel between Columba and King Diarmait, was supposed to possess magical virtues. It was termed the *cathach*, 'præliator' or battle-book, and was subsequently enclosed in an ornamented silver case, to which in later times the same powers were ascribed

---

[1] *Virtue.* Irish Archæol. Miscell., p. 6.

[2] *Lorica.* This was the name (in Irish *Luirech*) given to these compositions, because they were regarded as a breastplate or corslet, to protect from spiritual foes. The Lorica of Gildas was first published by Mr. Stokes, for the Irish Archæol. and Celtic Society; *Irish Glosses*, p. 136, *sq.*—See also *Book of Hymns*, p. 33.

[3] *Spiritual.* So says the Tripartite Life of St. Patrick, a composition originally compiled, as Colgan thinks, in the 6th century, but in its present interpolated form of the 9th or 10th. *Trias Thaum.* p. 126. Petrie, *On Tara*, p. 55.

that were no doubt originally believed to be inherent in the book. Its virtue consisted in this: that if it were sent rightwise, that is in a direction from right to left, round the army of the Cinel Conaill (the clan descended from Columba's ancestor Conall Gulban) that army was certain to return victorious from battle. But it must have been carried round the army on the breast of some Coarb, that is successor of some bishop or abbat, who was to the best of his power free from mortal sin.[1]

55. There is a very curious story told by O'Donnell in his life of Columba, and also in an Irish life of that saint. It appears that one of Columba's followers, named Odhran, a Briton by birth as Adamnan tells us, consented to a voluntary death, in order that he might deliver the island of Hy from Druidical influences by being the first of the Christians to be there interred. The story seems at first sight to intimate that Odhran or Oran was buried alive. This, however, is not expressly said; but only that he gave up the ghost, immediately after having expressed his willingness to die for the good of the community.[2] Adamnan's narrative

Consecration of Hy by the voluntary death and burial of Odhran.

---

[1] *Sin.* See the passage quoted from Keating's History by Dr. Reeves, *Adamnan*, pp. 249, 250, and note M, where some other reliquaries are mentioned, to which similar powers were ascribed. The *Cathach*, or battle crozier, of St. Grellan is noticed by Dr. O'Donovan, *Tribes and Customs of Hy Many*, p. 81.

[2] *Community.* Another curious story of a voluntary death is told in the Life of St. Enna or Endeus of the Aran islands. Enna succeeded his father as chieftain of his clan; and, at the head of his followers, he came to the hermitage of St. Fanche (who was his sister) singing a song of victory over the recent slaughter of his enemies. The virgin remonstrated with him on the ungodly life he was leading; he answered 'Give me to wife that royal girl

implies that the death was a natural one: he mentions no previous consent on Oran's part; but only that Columba in an ecstatic vision saw the soul of the religious Briton carried by angels to heaven; the angels contending by the way against the powers of evil, meaning no doubt the demons who had hitherto possessed the island. 'I give thanks,' said Columba to one of his monks, who had observed his ecstasy, 'I give thanks to Christ and to this His soldier, because the victorious angels have carried to the joys of our heavenly country the soul of this pilgrim, who was the first of our society to die in this island. But,' he adds, 'reveal not, I pray thee, this sacrament to any one during my life.'[1] There was, therefore, even in Adamnan's account of the matter, a *sacrament*, or mystery, in the death and burial of Oran, and we have seen how that mystery has been

you are educating, and I will do as you wish.' St. Fanche, asking some delay before she gave answer, went to the girl, and offered her her choice to become the wife of the chieftain, or else, as she expressed it, 'to love Him whom I love—quem amo velis amare.' The girl answered 'I will love whom thou lovest.' St. Fanche said, 'Come then with me into my chamber, and rest there awhile—ut ibi parum quiescas.' The girl went, and when she lay down upon the bed immediately expired: 'in lecto se ibi ponens expiravit, atque animam suam Deo sponso, quem optaverat, dedit.' Enna was then brought in to view the corpse; and the exhortations addressed to him on the occasion by St. Fanche, were the means of his conversion to Christianity.—*Vit. S. Endei* (24 Mart.), Colgan, *Actt. SS.* p. 705.

A very similar story is told of St. Patrick and the daughters of King Laoghaire, *Jocel.* c. 58: *Trip.* ii. 45. But whatever corruptions of religion such legends may represent, we must attribute them, not perhaps to the saints themselves of whom they are told, but to the biographers who have recorded them. They belong therefore in all probability to a period subsequent to that in which the second order of saints flourished.

[1] *My life.* Adamnan, *lib.* iii., cap. 6; edit. Reeves, p. 203, and the authorities there cited, O'Donnell, ii. 12 (*Triad. Th.* p. 411). *Irish Nennius, Add. Notes*, p. xxv.; Innes, *Civil and Eccl. Hist of Scotland*, p. 192.

interpreted by O'Donnell and other native biographers of Columba.

56. It would seem, therefore, that the Second Order of Saints in Ireland were unable to divest themselves altogether of the old superstitions of their race and country: they were content to eradicate the grosser practices of idolatrous worship; but they took the course adopted by other missionaries of the period, and not without example even in our own day, of engrafting their own faith upon the antient objects of pagan veneration, dedicating to a saint the pillar stone or sacred fountain, and claiming for their own sacred books and reliquaries the same virtues which the Druids by their incantations pretended to give to rings, and stones, and talismans.

The Christian faith engrafted on the antient objects of Pagan veneration.

St. Patrick indeed, if we may credit the compilers of his life, overthrew, wherever he found them, the pillar stones which seem to have formed the principal objects of worship with the pagan Irish. Thus the idol of King Laoghaire, which stood in Magh Sleacht, a plain in the County of Cavan, with its twelve brazen subordinate idols which surrounded it, was destroyed, of course miraculously, by St. Patrick: who simply raised his pastoral staff, called the Baculus Jesu, but without touching the idol, which seems to have been a massive stone pillar. Immediately, it fell with its head towards Tara, and the surrounding brazen idols were swallowed up by the earth.

St. Patrick overturned pillar stones.

Cromdubh Sunday.

This idol[1], commonly called *Crom-cruach*, is supposed to have been also termed *Crom-dubh*, 'the black stooping stone;' and under this latter appellation to have given rise to the name of *Domhnach Crom-duibh*, i.e. Cromdubh Sunday or *Cromduff* Sunday, by which the last Sunday[2] in summer, or the Sunday next before All Saints day, is commonly known in Ireland. If this be so, we have an instance of the adaptation of a heathen festival to a Christian observance: for the eve of Samhain, that is, of November 1st, the first day of winter, was the festival[3] of Cromcruach, the day on which King Tighernmas and his people held the great assembly in honour of the idol, in which he and a large proportion of his subjects were slain. Hence it is probable, that finding it impossible to abolish altogether the observance of the old festival, the ecclesiastics

---

[1] *Idol.* This idol, in the Tripartite Life, ii. 31, is called *Cromcruach*, a word which seems to signify the bent or stooping mound; by *Jocelin*, c. 56, the same idol is called *Ceancroithi*, which he interprets *caput omnium deorum*. The third Life, c. 46 (Colgan, *Tr. Th.* p. 25), gives to this idol the name of *Cennerbhe*. It is probable that this word is wrongly transcribed, and that it is really the same as Jocelin's *Ceancroithi*. Keating calls this idol *Crom-cruadh*, (*Reign of Tighernmas*).

[2] *Sunday.* O'Flaherty says that it was the Sunday next before the Kalends of *August*; but this is a mistake for *November*. He also suggests that this Sunday was so called in memory of the destruction of the idol (*Ogyg.*, p. 199). But the coincidence of the day with the antient pagan festival destroys this hypothesis. Dr. O'Donovan (F. M. at A.D. 1117) says that the Sunday got this name from a chieftain named *Crom-dubh*, who was converted by St. Patrick; but he gives no authority for the existence of any such person, and he was probably misled by Colgan, who translates the *Domhnach Cromm-duibh* of the Four Masters, 'in festo S. Crumdubii.' *Tr Th.*, p. 508 (at the year 1117). But there was no such saint, and Colgan had no authority for translating *Domhnach* by *festival*: he was compelled to do so however when he made *Crom-dubh* a saint, for he was well aware that Sundays were not dedicated to saints, a fact overlooked by Dr. O'Donovan in his note (p. 1004) on this passage of the Four Masters.

[3] *Festival.* See Four Masters A.M. 3656, p. 43, and A.D. 1117; *Ann. Ult.* 117. O'Conor, *Rer. Hib. Scriptt.*, tom. i. Proleg. pt. i. p. xxii.

attempted to transfer it to the Sunday before, and thus to substitute a Christian solemnity for the pagan orgies. Even at the present day All-hallows eve is observed in many parts of Ireland with sports, and now unmeaning rites, which are however most probably remnants of the antient idolatrous worship.

We read also that when St. Patrick visited Cashel, the royal residence of the Kings of Munster, all the idols of the country fell down before him, as Dagon before the ark : and then Aengus, King of Munster, was converted to Christianity with his people. But it is remarkable that here also an attempt seems to have been made to conciliate the old superstitions: for we are told that there was a stone there, at which or near which the king was baptized, which was thenceforth called *Leach-Phadruic*, or Patrick's stone.[1] The Leach-Phadruic (St.Patrick's Stone) at Cashel.

But to pursue this subject would carry us too far from our present purpose. It must suffice to mention the antient stone dedicated to an idol called *Cermand Celstach* (or *Kermand Kelstach*[2]), which in pagan times was covered with plates of gold, and was preserved (doubtless without the gold) inside the porch of the cathedral of Clogher, up to the times of Cathal Maguire, who has recorded the fact, and who died A.D. 1498.[3] From this stone the town of Clogher is said to have taken its name, *cloch-oir*, ' stone of gold.'[4] The idol-stone of Clogher.

---

[1] *Patrick's stone.* Jocelin, c. 74; Vit. Trip. iii. c. 29.
[2] *Kermand Kelstach.* This name is not explained. Colgan writes it *Cermand Clestach* (perhaps an error of the press), *Actt. SS.*, p. 740.
[3] *Died A.D.* 1498. See Four Masters in anno.
[4] *Stone of gold.* This etymology is more than doubtful. Irish authorities always write the name *Clochar*, not *Cloch-oir*; and there were other

The bards, or poets, in general favoured by the clergy.

57. The bards, or poets, appear to have inherited many of the offices, and to have assumed several of the pretended powers of the antient pagan Druids. Many, if not all of them, in the sixth century, professed Christianity. Dubhtach[1], who is called chief poet of Ireland, in the reign of King Laoghaire, was one of the first of St. Patrick's converts in the court of that monarch. And his conversion was followed by that of Fiac, his disciple, who afterwards became a bishop, and is the reputed author of a hymn[2] in praise of St. Patrick, which however bears internal evidence of a somewhat later date. St. Columba, if we may judge from the number of poems ascribed to him, was himself a bard. The Book of Rights[3], a composition which is evidently bardic, has been attributed to St. Benin, or Benignus, one of the early successors of St. Patrick in the chair of Armagh.

---

places called *Clochar* in Ireland, which word signifies 'a stony place,' or, as others think, an assembly or congregation; for it is so glossed in the Brussels MS. of the Felire of Aengus (Aug. 15). The etymology, however, from Cloch-oir, stone of gold, has the authority of the Calendar of Cashel, (Colgan, *loc. cit.*), and of the Scholia attributed to Cathal Maguire on the Felire of Aengus; these scholia do not exist in the Dublin or Brussels copies of the Felire. The quotation given by Colgan (*ib.*) is as follows : ' Item oppidum *Cloch-ar* appellari a *cloch-oir*, id est Lapide aureo, nempe auro et argento cœlato, qui asservatur ad dextram ingredientis ecclesiæ; et quem Gentiles auro obtegebant, quia in eo colebant summum partium Aquilonalium idolum, *Cermand Clestach* nuncupatum.' O'Flaherty quotes these words, as from the Scholia of Maguire, *Ogyg.* p. 197.

[1] *Dubhtach.* Vita 2da. c. 38 (*Tr. Th.*, p. 15); Jocelin, c. 44 (*ib.* p. 74); *Vita Tripart.* i. 61 (*ib.* p. 126). Some poems attributed to him are still extant: Ware, *Writers of Ireland* by Harris, p. 6; O'Reilly, *Irish Writers* (Iberno Celtic Society), p. xxvi; Book of Rights, p. 235.

[2] *Hymn.* See *Book of Hymns of the Antient Irish Church*, p. 287 *sq.*, where the history of Fiac and the authenticity of his poem is discussed.

[3] *Book of Rights.* This book has been printed with a translation and notes by Dr. O'Donovan (Celtic Society, Dublin, 1847).

It is evident, therefore, that the Bardic order was not regarded as essentially hostile to Christianity. Nevertheless, there is evidence that, in the times of which we speak, some of those called bards or poets had adopted opinions hostile to the Church; and that their power and exactions had become intolerable to the whole nation.

The following story is told in the life[1] of St. Colman, first Bishop of Dromore, a production of perhaps the eleventh century:—

'St. Colman was one day preaching to the people in a wood, when some shamefaced bards came up and impudently begged of him some gift. The man of God said, "I have nothing now to give you," says he, "except the word of God." Then one of them answered, "Keep the word of God for thyself; but give us something else." The saint said, "Thou hast rejected what is better, and foolishly chosen what is worse." Then the bard, tempting the man of God, said, "Cast this great tree down to the earth." The holy man said, "If thou wilt profit in faith, thou shalt see the power of God." Having said so, he knelt for a short time in prayer, and straightway the tree fell to the ground. But the son of unbelief was not changed; he persevered in his obstinacy, and blaspheming said, "This is not wonderful, for old oak trees fall every day, but if thou canst only set it up again, then I will acknowledge it to be a miracle." Without delay the tree was immediately raised again, by Divine power, as if it had never fallen.

'These bards, hardened in infidelity, like a second Dathan and Abiram, were then swallowed up by the earth. Seeing this, all present bowed their knees before the man of God, and glorified the Lord God in him.'

St. Colman flourished about A.D. 500. He

[1] *Life*. Published by the Bollandists, at 7 June. The original of the passage here quoted is given by Dr. Reeves, *Adamnan*, p. 80, note. See Acta SS. Junii, tom. ii. p. 27, cap. 2, sect. 10.

belonged properly to the first order of saints, and it may be said, that the 'shamefaced bards,' of whose infidelity the legend speaks, may have been some who had never received Christianity; their opinions, therefore, cannot be any evidence of the apostacy of the Irish Church, or of the dying out of the seed of faith planted by St. Patrick. And this is quite true. But we can scarcely be required to receive the story as an historical event which actually occurred in St. Colman's time. It must be understood rather as representing what the author of the life deemed probable, or likely to have occurred. We take it, therefore, as evidence that the sentiments put into the mouths of the bards by that author were the sentiments which they were known to have entertained in his own times.

In this point of view the anecdote leads to the suspicion that, in the age of the second order of saints, the influence of the bards was sometimes exerted against Christianity. There were no doubt amongst them many who were Christians, and employed their poetical talents on the side of the Church. But, so far as they aimed at exercising the power formerly exerted by the Druids, the superstitions of paganism would appear at first sight more favourable to their interests than the pure doctrines of Christianity: and hence it may be conjectured that in the century after St. Patrick they had succeeded in undermining the faith of many, and that they were themselves as a body arrayed in hostility to the Church.

58. This suggestion, however, it must be admitted, is not fully borne out by our extant records. It is true that in the sixth century attempts were made to suppress the order of bards, or to banish them from Ireland. But in the accounts we have of the motives which dictated those attempts no charge of apostacy, infidelity, or heresy, is brought against the order. King Aedh, or Aidus, who reigned from 572 to 599, son of the King Ainmire, by whom Gildas is said to have been invited into Ireland, was the last sovereign who attempted the extinction or banishment of the bards. This was one of the measures which he proposed to the celebrated Convention of Drumceat[1]; his reasons for proposing it are given in full by our antient Irish authorities, and a good summary of them will be found in 'Keating's History[2] of Ireland,' as also in Colgan's Latin version of 'O'Donnell's Life[3] of St. Columba.' The following is a literal translation of Keating's narrative:—

Attempts made to suppress the Bardic order.

Convention of Drumceat.

---

[1] *Drumceat.* For the exact situation of this place see Reeves, *Adamnan*, p. 37, note *b*. It is remarkable that the Four Masters, in their annals, make no mention of this assembly.

[2] *History.* Keating's History is a work which has been greatly underrated in consequence of the very ignorant and absurd translation by Mr. Dermot O'Connor, in which it has hitherto appeared before the English public. In 1857 a new and much better translation, by Mr. John O'Mahony, was published at New York. But this, although creditable, is also faulty; and it is much to be regretted that the translator has made it the vehicle of objectionable political opinions. The original Irish text of Keating requires to be collated with good copies, and his authorities to be carefully compared with the original MSS., most of which are still accessible. The publication of the work so edited would be a valuable addition to Irish historical literature.

[3] *Life.* Lib. iii. c. 2. ap. Colgan, *Triad. Thaum.*, p. 430. For the

Keating's account of its object.

'It was by Aedh, son of Ainmire, was convoked the convention of Drum-ceat, at which were assembled, as we are told, the nobles and ecclesiastics of Ireland. He had three principal reasons for calling this assembly. The first, with which alone we are now concerned, was to banish the bards out of Ireland, on account of their numbers, and the unreasonableness and exorbitancy of their demands. For the train of attendants upon an *Ollamh*[1] was thirty in number. Fifteen men constituted the train of an *Anrot*, that is, of the person who was next in learning to the Ollamh. At that time almost a third of the men of Ireland belonged to the Bardic order[2]; and from Samhain to Belltaine[3] they used to quarter[4] themselves on the people of Ireland. But according to Aedh's judgment this was too heavy a burden upon Ireland; and therefore he undertook to banish them out of the whole kingdom. He had also another reason for banishing them, because they had made a demand for the golden brooch that was in his mantle. For this was a notable jewel which every king left after him to the king who was his successor; and it was in consequence of their demanding this brooch so covetously, that Aedh had resolved to banish them, and actually did expel them to Dalriada of Ulster.'[5]

---

antient MS. authorities on the history of the Convention of Drumceat, see Reeves, *Adamnan*, p. 79, note *c*.

[1] *Ollamh.* This word, pron. *Ollav*, is explained a doctor, professor, teacher of any art. It was the name of a sort of *Degree*, or title given to a poet of high attainments. See O'Curry's Lectures, p. 239 *sq*.

[2] *Order.* The original word is *Fileadacht*, bardism; from *filedh*, a bard, poet, antiquary, or genealogist. See O'Curry's Lectures, p. 2, and append. No. 1. O'Flaherty adopts *philosophus* as most nearly equivalent to the *filedh* or *fili* of the Irish. *Ogyg.* p. 215.

[3] *Belltaine.* i.e. from 1 Nov. to 1 May. These were the two great heathen festivals of Ireland, which are not altogether without observance even to the present day. *Samhain* was the first day of winter; *Belltaine* the first day of summer. The names are supposed to have been derived from pagan deities.

[4] *Quarter.* The original word is *coinn-mhiodh*, from which the English gave the name of *Coyne* or *Coyney* to this species of oppression. Harris (Ware's Antiq. p. 77) makes a great mistake in supposing the word to be derived from the English *coin*. It signifies the billeting of soldiers; an exaction of food and 'entertainment,' not of coin or money.

[5] *Ulster.* Besides his measure for the banishment of the bards, King Aedh brought before the assembly at Drumceat two other questions, viz.: whether the Dalriadans of Scotland, as being a colony of the Dalriadans of Ulster, were not liable to pay tribute to the king of Ireland; and also whether Scanlan, chieftain of Ossory, was not liable to tribute also. The kings of Ulster, partly from their sympathy with

Our author then goes on to mention some other instances of attempts made to expel the bards, which we need not stop to notice, as the narrative contains nothing to our present purpose. It will be seen, however, that the account we have quoted makes no accusation against the order of any corruptions of Christianity, although it is almost certain that erroneous opinions were maintained, at least by some of them. The main cause which induced the king to desire their expulsion was a political one—namely, the great numbers of their retainers, their intolerable exactions, and, especially, their claim to the right of billeting themselves and their followers, upon the peasantry and nobles, for the winter half of the year. If there be any truth in the statement that one-third of the whole population of the country was connected with the Bardic order, the exercise of such a privilege was a burden intolerable indeed.

59. It is clear that the saints of the second order were not in favour of the king's proposal to banish or suppress the bards. Columcille, and the clergy who were with him, resisted that proposal at the Convention of Drumceat, and advocated the more moderate measure of limiting their numbers and curtailing their privileges. *The bards protected by the "Saints," and a compromise agreed to.*

the Dalriadans, and partly from their jealousy of the supreme king of Ireland, took part with the bards against Aedh; and St. Columba appears to have been against him on all the three questions brought before the meeting. Although he declined to adjudicate on the Dalriadic question, which was decided in favour of Aedh, Columba, if his biographers are to be depended upon, seems to have contrived to render this decision practically null.

The compromise that was agreed to was that certain lands should be set apart for the endowment of the Bardic order. Each king and chieftain was to maintain an ollamh attached to his court, and the ollamhs, out of the lands assigned to them, were to maintain the inferior members of the order, as well as their own special retinue. The ollamhs were bound also to open schools and give instruction in history, antiquities, and all other branches of learning then known in Ireland. This prudent measure relieved the people from the oppressive claim of *Coyney*, or billeting, and had an obvious tendency to diminish the number of retainers attached to each ollamh.[1]

It promoted also the views of the clergy, by requiring the ollamhs to open schools, in which no doubt the influence of the 'saints of the second order' soon became predominant, and the infidel or heretical teachers of the day were effectually discountenanced. O'Donnell[2] defends the conduct of St. Columba in thus resisting the destruction of the Bardic order, by explaining at some length the various duties which they had inherited from the antient Magi, or Druids, of pagan Ireland. They were antiquarians or historians, he says, as well as poets; it was their duty to record the deeds of the kings, chieftains, and heroes; to describe their battles and victories; to register the

Duties of the Bardic order.

---

[1] *Ollamh.* See Keating, under the reign of Aedh, son of Ainmire, in continuation of the passage just quoted.

[2] *O'Donnell.* Vit. Columbæ, lib. iii. cap. 2.; ap. Colgan. *Triad. Thaum.* p. 430.

genealogies and privileges of noble families, together with the bounds and limits of their lands or territories. These were useful and important functions, and although the bards were guilty of promoting great dissensions amongst their respective clans, by extravagant panegyrics and equally extravagant lampoons, Columba was of opinion that a reformation of the abuse might be obtained without an entire extirpation of the order[1], which would have deprived the country of their really useful services as historiographers and instructors.

60. There seems to have been a party hostile to the clergy in the very court of King Aedh. His queen[2], we are told, instigated her eldest son, Conall, to insult Columba and his attendant clerics. The young man caused some of his followers to fling mud upon the clergy as they entered the assembly of Drumceat. Columba, we are told, rang his bells, and solemnly cursed[3] the prince, who was thenceforward stricken with fits of idiotcy or insanity[4], and

---

[1] *Order.* Even so late as the 12th century the Anglo-Irish, in their Statutes of Kilkenny, denounced the bards, under the name of 'Rimers.' See Hardiman's *Stat.of Kilkenny*,p.55, published in vol. II. of 'Tracts relating to Ireland' (Irish Archæol. Soc.). Shakespeare also makes frequent allusion to the Irish Rhymers. See a paper by the author of this work,in the 'Proceedings of Royal Irish Academy.'

[2] *Queen.* So says Keating. But O'Donnell attributes the instigation to the king himself. Vit. Columbæ, lib. iii. c. 5. The antient authorities support Keating.

[3] *Cursed.* This word is not too

strong. O'Donnell says: 'Provocatus Christi famulus, jussis prius sociis cuncta sua tintinnabula pariter in dirum, et imprecationis, et appellati justi Judicis signum, pulsare ; Conaldum quem jam audierat tantæ improbitatis incensorem,maledictione feriit; et ex tunc regni exspem et mentis impotem, qualis mox evasit, futurum prædixit.'—*Ibid.*

[4] *Insanity.* Hence the bards gave Conall the nick-name of Conall Clugach, or Conall the mad ; and several Bardic fictions were written on his insanity.—See Colgan, *Tr. Th.*, p. 452, col. 2, note 5. *Book of Hymns*, p. 88 *sq.*

excluded from the succession to the crown. His mother also and her waiting maid were transformed into two herons; condemned to stand for ever, watching for their prey, at the ford of the river near Drumceat.

On the other hand, Domhnall, a younger son of King Aedh, then a mere boy, rose up to meet Columba, kissed him with reverence on both cheeks, and resigned to him his own seat. For these marks of respect he received the saint's benediction, who prophesied that he should live to reign over Ireland; that he should survive all his brothers, never fall into the hands of his enemies, and die in a good old age, of a natural death, in his own house, and on his own bed, surrounded by his relatives and friends.[1] This latter blessing very rarely fell to the lot of an Irish king in those days.

The Amhra Coluimcille, or Elegy on St. Columba.

61. In return for the services conferred upon the Bardic order on this occasion by St. Columba, the chief poet or ollamh of Ireland composed a poem in his praise. This poem is supposed to be the same which is entitled *Amhra Coluimcille*, 'The Elegy or Panegyric on Colum-cille,' and is still extant. It is in a very antient dialect of the Irish language[2], and is in all probability genuine. Its author, Eochaidh Dallan, or the blind, called also Eochaidh Forgaill, and Dallan Forgaill, from his mother Forchell, was descended

---

[1] *Friends.* Adamnan, lib. i. c. 10; ed. Reeves, pp. 36, 37.

[2] *Language.* Even in Colgan's time there were few Irish scholars capable of reading it; he calls it a work, 'hodiè paucis, usque peritissimis penetrabile.'—*Actt. SS.* p. 204, note 12.

from Colla Uais, monarch of Ireland in the fourth century, and is said to have been uncle [1], or, more probably, first cousin of St. Moedhog of Ferns. He was, therefore, young at the Convention of Drumceat, although recognised as the chief poet, and head of the antiquaries and historians of Ireland. He is honoured as a saint in the Irish calendar on the 29th of January [2], a fact which proves that the profession of Bardism was not regarded as necessarily inconsistent with the highest Christian honours.

Great virtues were ascribed to the mere recitation of the *Ambra Coluimcille*. This superstition appears to have existed even in the times of Adamnan [3], who speaks of certain poems in the Scotish language in praise of Columba, and in commemoration of his name, the repetition of which was efficacious to deliver even ungodly murderers from the hands of their enemies. There can scarcely be a doubt that this is spoken of the *Ambra Coluimcille*.

Virtues connected with the repetition of it.

If in the days of Adamnan such a story was believed, it seems more than probable that this kind of superstition was tolerated, if not encouraged, by the saints of the second order; who may have thought themselves justified in the attempt to avail themselves in this way of the influence of

---

[1] *Uncle.* See Colgan, *ib.* note 8.
[2] *January.* Colgan has published a life of him on that day, *ib.* p. 203. His name, however, does not occur in the antient metrical calendar of Aengus; but only in the more recent calendars of Tamlaght, Marian O'Gorman, and Donegal.

[3] *Adamnan.* Vit. Columbæ, lib. i. c. 1 (Reeves, p. 17). O'Donnell, who, of course, amplifies all this, understands Adamnan to speak of the *Ambra Coluimcille* in this passage.—Vit. S. Columbæ, iii. c. 67 (Colgan, *Tr. Th.*, p. 444).

Hymn in praise of St. Finnian.

the bards to undermine the Druids with their own weapons.

In the Life of St. Finnian[1] of Clonard, we have the following story:—

'Another time, also, there came a bard[2], named Geman, to St. Finnian, having with him a magnificent poem, in which many of the virtues of the saint were celebrated; and for this poem he demanded not gold or silver, or any worldly substance, but only fertility of produce in his lands. The worshipper of the Trinity answered him and said, "Sing over water the hymn which thou hast composed, and sprinkle thy lands with that water." When the bard had done this, his land became fertile, even to the present day.'

Legends like this savour a good deal of the magical ideas of Paganism; and it would be easy to quote many other instances of the existence of similar superstition in antient times. It continues indeed in Ireland to the present day, and is by no means peculiar to Ireland. We have alluded to it here only to show that the bards of the sixth century, the age of the second order of Irish saints, were not as a body under the ban of the Church.

Pelagianism prevalent in Britain in the age of St. David.

62. The Life of St. David, of Menevia, speaks of Pelagianism[3] as a prevalent heresy in his time in Britannia. He is represented as having attended a synod at a place called Brevi[4], or Brefi, in Cardiganshire, which however appears

---

[1] *Finnian.* Colgan. *Actt. SS.* (23 Feb.) p. 395, cap. 5.

[2] *A bard.* 'Carminator nomine Gemanus.' This Gemanus was a Christian, and one of St. Columba's instructors, if he be the same as the *Gemmanus* mentioned by Adamnan ii. c. 25 (Reeves, p. 137, note *d*.)

[3] *Pelagianism.* Vit. S. David. cap. 23, ap. Colgan. *Actt. SS.* (1 Mart.), pp. 428-9.

[4] *Brevi.* So says Giraldus Cambrensis, *Vita S. David.* Lect. viii. (ap. H. Wharton. Angliam Sacr. ii. p. 638), and comp. Rees, Welsh Saints, p. 192, note.

to have partaken more of the nature of a parliament, inasmuch as the kings, princes, and lay nobles of the country, as well as bishops[1] and other ecclesiastics, were present. To this synod David preached, and the result was the entire abandonment of the heresy, and an unanimous vote of the assembly that David should be archbishop of the province. Being thus clothed with the highest ecclesiastical jurisdiction, he shortly after summoned another synod, in which certain canons were regularly drawn up, and imposed upon all the churches under his obedience by a mandate under his own hand. These synods are dated by Ussher[2] A.D. 529.

There is no evidence, however, that Ireland was at this time infected with Pelagianism, or that Gildas was sent for to oppose that heresy in particular. It is true that about a century later, when Tomene, or Tommian, MacRonain was Bishop of Armagh, a letter appears to have been addressed by him and some other bishops and clergy to the Bishop of Rome, on the subject of Easter. The letter itself no longer exists; but Bede[3] has preserved a fragment of the answer

No evidence of Pelagianism in Ireland at this period.

Letter of the Roman clergy to Tomene of Armagh A.D. 640.

---

[1] *Bishops.* The life published by Colgan says 118 bishops; a number which, however incredible, Colgan endeavours to reconcile with possibility by the, for him, remarkable admission, that in Britain as well as in Ireland there were at that time more bishops than episcopal sees; and he adds, ' Tunc enim non erat Diocesium districtus ita limitati et restricti sicut modo, et multi erant episcopi titulares, quibus nullæ erant dioceses determinatæ vel subjectæ.'—

Ibid. p. 432, note 27. This is the very peculiarity of the Irish or Scotic Church, which he elsewhere ignores and even denies; but which forces itself upon us in almost every page of our ecclesiastical history.

[2] *Ussher.* Index Chron. in anno.

[3] *Bede.* Hist. Eccl. ii. 19. Ussher has also republished the extracts given by Bede; *Sylloge Epist.* ix. (Works iv. p. 427). See also his *Goteschalci et Predestin. controversiæ Hist.* (Works iv. p. 1 *sq.*).

to it, which the Roman clergy, in the vacancy of the see, addressed to their Irish brethren. Pope Severinus had shortly before died, and his successor, John, had been elected, but not consecrated. The letter is in the name of Hilary, archdeacon, guardian[1] during the vacancy of the holy Apostolic see; John, the deacon, Bishop of Rome elect, 'in Dei nomine electus;' John, the *primicerius*, also a guardian of the see; and John, 'servus Dei,' i.e., most probably, the representative of the regular or monastic clergy, *counsellor* (conciliarius ejusdem sedis). This enables us to date this document exactly; for Pope Severinus died on the 1st August 640, and his successor, John IV., was consecrated on the 24th December following. The letter was therefore written in the interval.

<small>Attributes Pelagianism to the Irish.</small> In reference to the Pelagianism attributed to the Irish in this document, the Roman clergy say[2], 'And this also we have learned, that the poison of the Pelagian heresy has of late revived amongst you.' These words seem to imply that this was not the first time that Ireland had been infected with Pelagianism, and also that the Roman clergy had heard of its revival, not from the communication made to the late Pope by Tomene and his associates, but from some other source of information.

This inference, however, so far as the use of the word 'revive' is concerned, cannot be abso-

---

[1] *Guardian*: i.e. apparently guardian of the temporalities.

[2] *Say.* 'Et hoc quoque cognovimus, quod virus Pelagianæ hereseos apud vos denuo reviviscit.'—*Bede, ib.*

lutely relied on. The heresy may have been spoken of as reviving in Ireland, after having been effectually crushed elsewhere, without our being compelled of necessity to conclude that it had ever before existed in Ireland. And the context does not support the conclusion: for the authors of the letter go on to speak of Pelagianism as having been condemned, and for two hundred years suppressed and buried elsewhere; and they therefore exhort the Irish clergy 'not to permit the ashes of those whose weapons are burned everywhere else to revive amongst them.'[1] Still it is evident that the Roman clergy believed the Pelagian heresy to have shown itself again at that time in Ireland. Of this, however, we find no evidence elsewhere. The evils of the Church of Ireland, spoken of in the documents we have quoted, and especially in the Life of Gildas, are not described as Pelagianism, or any other heresy properly so called, but as a disorganisation of discipline, a dissolution of morals, a partial apostacy from the faith, a return to the superstitions of paganism.

63. And this view of the subject is supported by the fragments which have come down to us, of the conciliar legislation and canons attributed to Gildas during his missionary labours in Ireland. The following are given in the collection of Irish canons, already spoken of, from which D'Achery has published extracts[2]:— *Irish conciliar legislation attributed to Gildas.*

---

[1] *Amongst them.* 'Ne quorum arma combusta sunt, apud vos eorum cineres suscitentur.'—*Ibid.*

[2] *Extracts.* Spicileg. vol. i. p. 493 sq. (folio ed.)

'Priests and bishops have a terrible Judge, to whom, and not to us, it appertains to judge them, both in this world and in the next. It is better that we should not judge our fellow bishops and our fellow abbats, as well as our fellow subjects.'—Lib. i. c. i. 15.

'Abstinence from bodily food is useless without charity.' [This canon goes on to censure extravagant abstinence from food: urging that from the heart are the issues of life, and that our first object should be to have a clean heart before God. Extreme asceticism generates spiritual pride, &c.]—Lib. xii. c. 5.

'Truth has charms for a wise man, no matter from whose mouth it proceeds.'—Lib. xxii. c. 1.

'We should fear how we withdraw ourselves from our princes [i.e. from our bishops or abbats] for light faults: for Aaron, when he blamed Moses on account of his Ethiopian wife, was punished in the leprosy of Miriam.'—Lib. xxxvi. c. 5.

'Let every one continue in the calling wherein he was called: so that neither a superior (primarius) should change his condition without the assent of his subjects: nor a subject be moved to a higher place without the counsel of his elder.'—*Ib.* c. 31.

'If a monk has any superabundance of secular goods, it should be accounted luxury and riches; but what he is compelled to have by necessity, and not of self-seeking, that he may not fall through want, should not be considered in him as wrong.'—Lib. xxxviii. c. 5.

'An abbat who is lax ought not to prohibit his monk from seeking a stricter rule.'—*Ib.* c. 6.

[Monks flying from a lax to a more perfect discipline, and whose abbat is irreligious or immoral, and unfit to be admitted to the table of the saints, may be received even without the knowledge of their abbat. But those whose abbat is not excluded from the table of the saints, ought not to be received. How much more those who come from holy abbats, whose only fault is that they possess cattle, and ride in chariots, either from the custom of the country, or because of infirmity.] 'For these things are less injurious, if they are possessed in humility and patience, than labouring at the plough, and driving stakes into the earth with presumption and pride.' 'When the ship is wrecked let him swim who can swim.'—*Ib.* c. 7.

Lib. i. c. 6 relates to the Tonsure. [It is very obscure, and the text corrupt. For our present purpose it will suffice to mention the subject of it.]

Lib. lxiv. c. 8 [professes to be an extract from the Epistles of Gildas. It is entitled 'Of them who think themselves righteous, but are not.']

These canons, it will be seen, relate all to ecclesiastical order and discipline, or to morality, not to heresy. But until the whole of this collection is revised, by a careful collation of the MSS., and published without mutilation, we cannot rely much upon its testimony. D'Achery may have omitted many things that to him seemed of no interest, but which would be most important in reference to the question now before us. So far as they go, however, the canons attributed to Gildas in this document confirm the opinion that heretical doctrines, properly so called, were not the class of errors to which his reforms were directed.

Martene[1] found another MS. of the Irish canons in Rouen, and has printed some extracts, selecting canons which D'Achery had overlooked, or which perhaps were not to be found in his manuscripts. The Rouen MS. appears to have belonged to the monastery of Fiscan, in Normandy, and is supposed by Martene to have been written in the eleventh century. From this codex he has published twenty penitential canons[2] attributed to Gildas. They make no

---

[1] *Martene*. Thesaur. Nov. Anecd., tom. iv. p. 1. There is a MS. containing apparently another copy of this collection of Canons (which I have seen since this sheet was in the printer's hands), in the Vallicellian Library in Rome.

[2] *Canons*. Ibid. col. 7.

mention of Pelagianism, or any other heresy; they are occupied for the most part in defining the duration and manner of the penance to be imposed on gross offenders, and especially ecclesiastics; and if the offences described are to be taken as in any degree an index of the moral state of Ireland at the time, the words of the abbess Hildegardis are fully borne out, that crimes were then common which made men resemble beasts, rather than rational and moral beings.

Conclusion. On the whole, we may safely conclude from the foregoing authorities that a state of disorganisation, a relaxation of discipline, and very probably some erroneous if not heretical opinions were prevalent in Ireland in the age when the second order of saints is said to have flourished. And there is reason to suspect that our imperfect information, as to the nature of those opinions, arises mainly from the fact that documents have been suppressed, and those that have not been suppressed mutilated, or altered, under the mistaken idea that a concealment of such scandals was necessary, for the glory of God and of His Church, or for the honour of the country.

The second order of saints called Catholic Presbyters. 64. That the saints of the second order were believed to have had for their mission the correction of some sort of heretical doctrines, is intimated perhaps by the author of the Catalogue, when he calls them 'the second order of *Catholic* Presbyters'—Catholicorum Presbyterorum. And that some distinction of this kind was introduced by them, or their followers, in assuming the title of Catholic, appears also from the language used by the biographer of St. Moedhog, when describing the ordination of that prelate as chief bishop to the King of Leinster. After mentioning the offerings and land which King Brandubh gave to St. Moedhog, and the monastery built at Ferns, which became the burial-place of the saint himself as well as of Brandubh and his successors, our author proceeds: 'Then a great city arose there in honour of St. Moedhog, which was called by the same name, viz., Ferns; and a great synod having been afterwards summoned in the territory of Leinster, King Brandubh, with the laity and clergy, decreed, that the archbishopric of all the men of Leinster should for ever be in the city and see of St. Moedhog. Then was St. Moedhog consecrated archbishop by *many Catholics*.'[1]

We have already mentioned the 'twelve apostles of Ireland,' disciples of St. Finnian of Clonard. It is not quite clear why they were given that name. St. Patrick, the great apostle of Ireland, was not of their number. They were all of the second order of saints. Only one amongst them, viz., St. Columba of Hi, appears to have gone forth to preach to a heathen land. All the rest seem to have settled in Ireland.[2] They were, therefore, apostles to the Irish only

---

[1] *Catholics.* 'Et tunc Sanctus Moedog a multis Catholicis consecratus est archiepiscopus.' *Vit. S. Moedoci* (31 Jan.), cap. 28; Colgan, *Actt. SS.*, p. 211. See the remarks already made on the use of the word *Archbishop* in this passage: *supra*, p. 14 *sq.*
[2] *Ireland.* See the list of them given above, p. 99, note 1.

And if so, the Irish must have been regarded as having almost relapsed into their original paganism.

Why so called.

But it is probable that there may have been another reason for the title. The 'twelve apostles of Ireland' appear to have formed themselves into a kind of corporation, and to have exercised a sort of jurisdiction or superintendence over the other ecclesiastics or 'saints' of their times. They were especially jealous of the right of sanctuary which they claimed for their churches. It was in consequence of a violation of this right, that Columba instigated the war with King Diarmait, and that Tara was denounced 'by St. Ruadan of Lorrha, the twelve apostles of Ireland, and all the other saints of Ireland.'[1] Domhnall, King of Ireland in 636, is represented as sending for the twelve apostles, 'in order to bless and consecrate' the banquet of Dun-na-ngedh, and avert the curse[2] pronounced upon it by Bishop Erc of Slaine. This is indeed an anachronism, as Dr. O'Donovan has shown; but it may possibly mean that the successors[3] of the original twelve, in their respective Churches, were still regarded as the 'apostles' of Erinn. At all events, it is an instance of the popular belief in a sort of jurisdiction or supremacy resident in the 'twelve apostles.'

---

[1] *Ireland.* Banquet of Dun-na-ngedh and battle of Magh Rath, p. 5 (Irish Arch. Soc., 1842).

[2] *Curse.* Ib. p. 27.

[3] *Successors.* Ib. Note B. p. 327. The story of the miraculous tree of St. Ruadan of Lorrha, which he consented to give up, on the remonstrance of the saints of Ireland made through St. Finnian of Clonard, may have some connection with this subject. See above, p. 121, note 1.

In this case, however, we are told that they were not able to avert the malediction, because the feast had been already tasted, and the penalty already incurred, before they were called upon to undo the evil.

65. There are some other peculiarities in the Irish episcopal and monastic system, which appear to have had their origin in the laws which regulated the tenure of land, and the relation between chieftain and clansman, or vassal, in ancient Ireland. The land granted in fee to St. Patrick, or any other ecclesiastic, by its original owner, conveyed to the clerical society of which it became the endowment, all the rights of a chieftain or head of a clan; and these rights, like the rights of the secular chieftains, descended in hereditary succession. The comarb, or co-arb, that is to say, the heir or successor of the original saint who was the founder of the religious society, whether bishop or abbat, became the inheritor of his spiritual and official influence in religious matters. The descendants in blood, or 'founder's kin,' were inheritors of the temporal rights of property and chieftainship, although bound to exercise those rights in subjection or subordination to the ecclesiastical co-arb.

Laws regulating the tenure of land.

Rights of chieftainry transferred to the ecclesiastical landlord.

The curious history[1] of the foundation of the bishopric of Ath-Truim, now Trim, in the County of Meath, will illustrate this. It is told

Foundation of the bishopric of Trim.

---

[1] *History.* Lib. Ardmach. fol. 14. This document will be given in the original, with a translation, in the Appendix B. to this Introduction.

in the antient notes on the Life of St. Patrick, preserved in the Book of Armagh[1], a manuscript of the ninth century.

St. Patrick had landed at the mouth of the Boyne, and proceeded up the country, leaving his nephew and disciple, Lomman, to take care of the boat in which he had sailed, with directions to wait for him forty days. At the end of that time, his master not having returned, Lomman waited forty days more, and then proceeded up the river to a place called Ath-Truim, or 'the ford of Trim.'[2] There he presented himself at the house of Fedlimid, or Phelim, son of Laogaire[3], King of Ireland. He was hospitably received, as a matter of course. The next morning Fortchern, the son of Fedlimid, overheard Lomman reciting the Gospel, and was so struck with what he heard, that he embraced Christianity, and was baptised. Lomman, it appears, was a Briton, or Welshman, son of Gollit[4]; and Fortchern's mother was of the same country: finding her son with the strangers, she rejoiced when she perceived that they were

---

[1] *Armagh.* This valuable MS., by the liberality of his Grace the Lord Primate of Ireland, is now in the library of Trin. Coll. Dublin. It will shortly be published by Dr. Reeves, with such notes and illustrations as he alone is capable of compiling. The attempted publication of a portion of it, many years ago, by Sir Wm. Betham, in his 'Irish Antiquarian Researches,' is so full of errors as to be quite useless.

[2] *Trim.* The word Truim, genitive of Drom or Drum, signifies a long low hill: *dorsum.*

[3] *Laogaire.* Pronounced *Leary*, was son of Niall of the nine hostages, and was King of Ireland, according to O'Flaherty's Chronology, A.D. 428 to 463. *Ogyg.*, p. 429. See Geneal. Tables, Append. A. to this Introduction, p. 252.

[4] *Gollit.* Perhaps Goliath. Darerca, sister of St. Patrick, is said to have been his mother. See Colgan's conjectures on the name Gollit, *Actt. SS.*, p. 262, n. 13.

British, and she also became a Christian. She forthwith communicated with her husband Fedlimid, whose mother Scothnoe, having been also British, he was able to address Lomman in the Welsh language. The result was that the whole family were converted to Christ, and Fedlimid dedicated to Lomman and Patrick, and to Fortchern, his son, who appears to have become at once an ecclesiastic, all his territory and possessions at Trim, together with all his substance, and *his clan* or *progenies*.

After this Fedlimid crossed the Boyne, and settled in the district called by our author *Cloin Lagen*, or the plain of Leinster. Lomman and Fortchern remained at Trim until St. Patrick returned to them, when they built a church, which was founded, we are told, two and twenty years before the Church of Armagh.

66. It is impossible to doubt that this story was told with a purpose, and that it was intended to prop up certain pretensions of the Church of Armagh. But it may have been founded in fact: there is nothing impossible in it; and the original form of it makes no mention of the miracles with which the later biographers of St. Patrick have adorned it. Our present concern with it, however, is only to call attention to the manner in which Fedlimid is said to have made over his property for the endowment of the Church, which no doubt was in accordance with the practice of the age in which the author of the legend lived. It will

The patriarchal rights of chieftain conferred with the lands upon the ecclesiastical successors.

be observed that he gave to the ecclesiastics and to his son, as being of their society, not only his lands and their appurtenances, but also his clan or 'progenies,' that is to say, his patriarchal rights, as a chieftain, over his followers.

<small>Death of Lomman.</small>
The story goes on to say, that after some years, Lomman, finding his end approaching, set off to visit his brother Broccaide, who was abbat, or bishop of Imleach-Each, in the barony of Costello, County of Mayo. There Lomman died; and in his last moments, calling Fortchern, insisted upon his undertaking the government of the Church of Trim, as its bishop. To this Fortchern objected. If he became bishop the ecclesiastical and civil chieftainship would be combined in his person, and he feared lest it should seem as if he was taking back to himself the gift which his father had made to the Church. However, he was compelled to yield to the earnest injunctions of his master, and immediately after set out for Trim. The journey, we are told, occupied three days; and Fortchern, still retaining his scruples, lost no time, after he had reached home, in resigning his office, to which one Cathlaid, a pilgrim, was forthwith appointed.

<small>His successors chieftains as well as bishops.</small>
Our author then proceeds to give us the twofold line of succession which was kept up in this Church to his own times. And it is remarkable that he calls both lines the *progenies* or clan of Fedlimid, implying that the bishops, as well as the lay chieftains, were all of the same family. So that Fortchern's scruple seems to have had

reference to himself, as chieftain by hereditary right, and not to the other branches of the family, who could lay no such claim to the chieftainry.

The bishops, who are styled ' ecclesiastica progenies Fedelmtheo,' *the ecclesiastical clan or descendants of Fedlimid,*— are then enumerated.[1]

'And these,'[2] says our author, 'were all bishops and princes (or chieftains) venerating St. Patrick and his successors.' In other words, they belonged to the first order of saints, and gave allegiance to the Church of Armagh; and we may infer incidentally that this was not then universally done, or else it would not have been here so particularly mentioned in especial praise of these bishops.

It will be noticed that Cathlaid, the pilgrim to whom Fortchern resigned the Church, is not mentioned in the list. From which we may conclude, either that he is to be identified with 'Aedh the great,' whose name immediately follows that of Fortchern, or else that he was not a bishop[3], but only an abbat, who governed the house as co-arb, Fortchern continuing to reside

Cathlaid the pilgrim.

---

[1] *Enumerated.* See the names, Append. B, p. 261.

[2] *These.* "Hii omnes episcopi fuerunt et principes venerantes Sanctum Patricium et successores ejus.' Lib. Ardm., fol. 14. The word *princeps* is frequently applied to a bishop or abbat in the Collection of Irish canons, published by D'Achery, and already frequently quoted. *Spicil.* i. p. 495 (ex libr. xviii. c. 6), p. 499 (ex libr. xxxvi.).

[3] *Bishop.* Colgan calls him 'Episcopum natione Britannum,' but without any authority. *Actt. SS.*, p. 365, col. i. Even Jocelin, whose words he cites, calls him simply *peregrinus*, but adds 'genere Britanno.' The Book of Armagh has *peregrinus* only. His being called a *pilgrim*, or as Colgan understands it, a Briton, militates against identifying him with ' Aedh the great,' whom the Irish genealogies represent as the nephew of Fortchern. See Append. A. Table III., p. 252.

there, in subjection to the abbat, to perform episcopal offices.

We learn, from another authority[1], that Aedh the great and Aedh the less were brothers, and the sons of Fergus, Fortchern's younger brother. Ossan[2] was also a descendant of Laoghaire, son of Niall. Of the other names in the list nothing is at present known; but it is more than probable that further research may prove them also to have been of the same family.

An ecclesiastical, as well as a lay succession, both of the founder's kin.

The lay descendants of Fedlimid, 'plebilis progenies ejus,' are also given in this document.[3] There was therefore a twofold line of succession, the ecclesiastical and the lay *progenies*, both connected in blood with the original founder, or donor of the lands; those of the lay line succeeding each other in hereditary descent, from father to son.

Tendency of this system to throw the ecclesiastical succession into lay hands.

In Hi, as Dr. Reeves has shown, there was no lineal or lay succession, as at Trim, Armagh, and other places, although the early abbats, with scarcely an exception, were all of a branch of the Tirconnell family.[4] But the tendency of the system was obviously to throw the ecclesiastical succession into the hands of the lay succession, and so to defeat the object of the founder by transferring the endowment to the laity; and this is what we find to have actually taken

---

[1] *Authority.* The *Sanctilog. Geneal.* Book of Lecan.
[2] *Ossan.* See Martyrol. of Donegal (at 17 Feb.).
[3] *Document.* See App. B. p. 261.
[4] *Family.* See Dr. Reeves's Genealogical Table of the Abbats of Hi, and his valuable remarks, in his additional note N, on the constitution of the Irish Monasteries.—*Adamnan,* p. 334 *sq.*

place. The successors of St. Comgall at Bangor, the successors of St. Patrick at Armagh, were for many generations lineal descendants of the family from which the original endowment in land had been derived; and especially in the case of Armagh, there was no small confusion between the temporal and spiritual successions, giving good grounds, as we shall see hereafter, for the complaint made by St. Bernard, that the spiritual authority and influence had passed into the hands of mere laymen[1], although some of them may perhaps have made a sort of compromise, by taking the tonsure, and a minor degree of holy orders.

67. It will be necessary here to explain some terms which will be of frequent occurrence in the following pages.

We have already had occasion more than once to employ the word *comharb*, or *comarb*, pronounced nearly as if written *co-arb*. This word properly signifies co-heir, or inheritor; co-heir or inheritor of the same lands[2] or territory which belonged

Explanation of terms: Comarb or Co-arb.

---

[1] *Laymen.* Bernard. Vit. S. Malachiæ, c. 7, and see also what Giraldus Cambrensis has said of the *Abbates laici* of Ireland and Wales. *Itiner. Cambriæ*, ii. 4.

[2] *Lands.* The word is explained by Colgan: 'Vox autem Hibernica *Comhorba*, vel radicitus *Comh-fhorba*, a qua desumitur, derivata videtur a *Comh*, id est, *con* vel *simul*; et *forba*, id est, terra, ager districtus: ut ex vocis origine Comhorbanus idem sit quod conterraneus, ejusdem terræ, vel ejusdem districtus.'—*Trias. Thaum.*, p. 630. The word is frequently written *Corbe*, by Ussher and others. But it is always a

dissyllable in the Irish pronunciation, which is more nearly represented by *co-arb*. Ussher is quite wrong in his explanation of the word *Corbe*. Original of Corbes, &c.—Works xi. p. 430. His notion that Corbe, or Comharba, is a corruption of Chorepiscopus, is absurd. The word is used to denote a secular, as well as an ecclesiastical, heir or successor. In the Brehon Law MS. (H. 3, 18, fol. 10 b., Trin. Coll. Dubl.), we have rules laid down for the division of secular property among the heirs of chieftains, *comarbus cenn*: and the word *comarba* is used to the original founder of a church or monastery; co-heir also of his ecclesiastical or spiritual dignity, as well as of his temporal rights.

Bishops and Abbats called Co-arbs of the founder of their sees or abbeys.

In the absence of diocesan territorial designations this term was employed in Irish Church history to designate the bishops or abbats who were the successors or inheritors of the spiritual and temporal privileges of some eminent saint or founder. Thus the co-arb of Patrick was the bishop or abbat of Armagh: the co-arb of Columcille was the abbat of Hi: the co-arb of Barré was the bishop or abbat of Cork. But this language has led many readers and writers of Irish history into great mistakes. Patrick had co-arbs at Trim as well as at Armagh: Columcille had co-arbs at Derry, at Durrow, and at Swords, as well as in Hi: and there is nothing in the title itself to show whether the co-arb was a bishop or only a presbyter abbat, or even a layman: indeed, the successor of Patrick is as often designated abbat of Armagh as co-arb; and, on the other hand, the bishop of Rome himself is frequently called co-arb of Peter, and sometimes also abbat of Rome[1], showing how completely the abbatial and co-arban authority, implying as

---

throughout to signify secular heirs. The etymology suggested by Colgan is wrong. The Celtic *arbe, orbe, orpi* occurs in the signification of an heir, and is cognate with the German *erbe*, and Gothic *arbja*. In the old language the *m* is never aspirated: it is *com-arbe, com-arba, com-arbus*; not *comh*. From the same root comes *indarbad* (with the negative *ind*), *exilium, expulsio*. See Stokes, *Irish Glosses*, p. 93. The word properly signifies a co-heir, a joint inheritor. The ecclesiastical successor of Patrick was *joint heir* or *com-arbe* with him.

[1] *Rome.* Thus, in the Scholia on the Martyrology of Aengus, the gloss on the name of S. Gregory the Great (19 March) is *i. abb. Romæ*, 'abbat of Rome.'

it did in Ireland the rank of a feudal lord of the soil, and chieftain over the inhabitants of the soil, swallowed up, as it were, and obscured the accident of a co-existing episcopal or sacerdotal character, in the co-arb, or spiritual chieftain.

The foregoing remarks will also explain the use of the term *Ard-comarb*, or chief co-arb, which we meet with in some passages of the annals[1] to denote the co-arb of a saint's principal church: thus the ard-co-arb of Patrick would be his successor in Armagh, not in Trim, or any minor foundation; the ard-co-arb of Columcille would be the abbat of Hi, not of Durrow, Swords, or Derry.

The annals of Ulster, which are written in a curious mixture of Irish and Latin, commonly employ the word *hæres*, and occasionally also *princeps*[2], to translate the Irish term *comarba*, or *co-arb*; and it is remarkable that the term *princeps* is generally used as the title given to the temporal chieftains, who are called *principes* and *capitanei suæ nationis*: the princes or chiefs of their races or clans[3].

This is conclusive evidence that the ecclesiastical *co-arb*, or *heir* of the saint who had originally obtained the grant of land, was regarded

---

[1] *Annals.* See the references given by Mr. King, 'Early Hist. of Primacy of Armagh,' p. 16.

[2] *Princeps.* See Dr. O'Donovan's note, *Four Masters*, A.D. 752, p. 356. In the Ann. Ult., at 742, Affrica, whom the Four Masters call *ban-abb*, or abbess, is styled *Dominatrix* of Kildare.

[3] *Clans.* The Irish word *Clann* signifies *children*, or descendants. The tribe being all descended from some common ancestor, the chieftain, as the representative of that ancestor, was regarded as the common Father of the *Clann*; and they as his children.

as entitled to the civil or temporal principality, with all the rights primarily belonging to the *princeps* or chieftain from whom the grant of land had emanated ; and as the co-arb was elected by the community over whom he presided, and the chieftain, under certain restrictions, by the clan, there was an obvious tendency, as has been already remarked, to throw the spiritual succession into the family who were successors in blood of the founder.

<small>Exaction of tribute by the Comarb of saints.</small>

Hence we find the co-arbs of saints holding 'visitations' of the territories belonging to them, for the purpose of exacting taxes and tribute, after the manner of the secular chieftains: and what was still more unclerical, two co-arbs sometimes made war upon each other, with slaughter on both sides. Thus in the year 763, the annals of Ulster and those of Tighernach and Clonmacnois tell us, but the fact is suppressed by the Four Masters[1], that a battle took place at Arggamain, or Ardgamain, between the *family*, or monastic society of Clonmacnois, and the *family* of Durrow, that is to say, between the co-arb of St. Ciaran of Clonmacnois, and the co-arb of St. Columba of Durrow; who mustered their retainers and fought it out like secular chieftains. The victory was gained by Breasal Mac Murrough and the *family* of Clonmacnois; two hundred men of the *family* of Durrow having been killed on the other side, with Diarmaid Dubh Mac Donnell,

---

[1] *Four Masters.* The Four Masters lived after the Reformation, and therefore they often suppress facts of this kind which might have caused scandal at a time when many were too glad to seize upon the materials for scandal against the antient state of the Church.

and Diglach Mac Duibhliss; but it is not said whether these were secular chieftains or ecclesiastics connected with the contending monasteries, neither are we told the cause of the quarrel.[1]

68. The *family* (in Irish, *muinntir*) of a monastery comprehended, ordinarily, the monks or religious inmates, but sometimes included also those who were subject to the jurisdiction of the abbey, or who lived as vassals, serfs, or clansmen, on the territories of the co-arb. In some cases the *family* included also those who were so connected with the minor or more recently founded religious houses that were under the rule of the co-arb, or subject to the principal monastery. Thus the abbat of Hi, or co-arb of Columba, in that island, was the common head of the monasteries of Durrow, Kells, Swords, Drumcliff, and other houses in Ireland, founded by Columba, as well as of the parent monastery of Hi; and the *muinntir Coluim-cille*, or family of Colum-kille, was composed of the congregations, or inmates and dependants of all those monasteries.[2] The families, therefore, of such monasteries as Clonmacnois and Durrow might muster a very respectable body of fighting men. In general, however, the *family* meant only the monks or religious of the house.[3]

The family of a church or monastery

---

[1] *Quarrel.* The words of the Ulster Annals are these: 'Bellum Arggamain, inter familiam Cluana mac cunois et Dermaighi, ubi cecidit Diarmait Dubh mac Domhnaill et Dighlach mac Duibhliss, et cc. viri de familia Dermaighi; Bresal mac Murchadha victor exstetit, cum familia Cluana.' Tighernach records the same battle at A.D. 764, and calls it *Cath-argain*, 'a battle of plunder between the families of Cluanmicnois and Darmagh, ubi cecidit Diarmait mac Domhnaill.'

[2] *Monasteries.* See Reeves, *Adamnan*, p. 162, note x. and p. 342.

[3] *House.* Thus, when we read in the Ann. Ult., A.D. 748, that the family of Hi were drowned, 'Dimersio familiæ Iæ,' we must necessarily understand the inmates of the monastery of the Island only.

160   *Termon Lands—Erenachs.*   [INTROD.

Termon-lands.

The Church lands called Termon-lands, in Ireland, had their name in all probability from the *Termini,* pillar-stones, or crosses set up to mark their boundaries, within which there was a right of sanctuary, and a freedom from the taxes and tributes of secular chieftains. Nevertheless their inhabitants paid rent and other taxes to the Church, bishop, or monastery to which the land belonged.[1] But this was probably an institution of a period much later than the times of which we have been speaking.

Erenachs or Herenachs.

69. The Erenachs, Herenachs, or in the correct Irish orthography *Airchinneachs,* in the primitive age of the Irish Church before the settlement of dioceses in the twelfth century, were most probably the stewards whose duty it was to superintend the lands and farms, and to collect the rents or other tributes paid by tenants. That *Erenach* was another name for corbe or co-arb, and that it was a corruption of the word *Archidiaconus,* or of the word *Ethnarch,* are opinions which, although countenanced by Ussher and Ware, are wholly untenable. Neither Ussher nor Ware had any knowledge of the Irish language; they were compelled to depend upon 'poor scholars' of no great learning or intelligence for everything that they quoted from the annals and other Irish records. In a question of this kind, therefore, their authority is very small. It is probable that the erenach was in every case himself a tenant of land under the

---

[1] *Belonged.* See Ussher, Origin of Corbes, Herenachs, and Termon-lands. Works xi. p. 421 *sq.*

co-arb; that he held his land in fee, under the tenure of performing certain duties; and there is no doubt that the office was hereditary, which would be the natural result of the sort of tenure of which we speak. The duties of the office were to super- *His Duties.* intend the farmers or tenants of the Church, or monastery, and perhaps also to distribute amongst the poor the alms or hospitality of the co-arb[1] and his *familia*.

In the more recent history of the Irish Church, *Modification of his duties* after the establishment of archiepiscopal and *after the establishment of* diocesan jurisdiction, the offices of co-arb and *ment of* erenach underwent necessarily very considerable *dioceses.* modification. The lands and jurisdiction of the co-arb were transferred to the bishop: and the duties of the erenach were dispensed with, or transferred to the rural dean, or archdeacon. This circumstance has been the cause of great confusion to our historians; even Ussher, Ware, and Lanigan, led away by their preconceived opinions as to the existence of diocesan succession from the age of St. Patrick, were unable to realise to themselves the strange state of society indicated by our antient records, and the still more strange state of the Church, when bishops were without dioceses or territorial jurisdiction. Hence it is that these eminent writers took the

---

[1] *Co-arb.* Colgan (*loc. cit.*) thus describes the duties of the Erenach: 'Omnium colonorum certi districtûs præpositus seu præfectus, suoque familiæ princeps et caput habebatur.' See also Mr. King's 'Memoir Introductory to the Early History of the Primacy of Armagh,' pp. 18, 19. A work well worthy of being reprinted in a form more accessible to general readers, as well as more worthy of the remarkable learning and research displayed in its pages.

modern state of the Church, since the establishment of dioceses, as the model of what they conceived was or ought to have been the state of the Church in the days of Patrick and Columb-kille, and thus they have confounded the antient Corbes with Chorepiscopi, and Erenachs with Archdeacons.

The Erenach not an archdeacon.

Even Colgan, influenced by the same prejudices, fell into the same mistakes. He tells us that the etymology of the word *Airchinneach* was to him doubtful[1]; but that if it were a corruption of *Archidiaconus* it would rather have been written *Airchidneach*. And it is a remarkable example of the secret influence of a prejudice over a mind led by the most honest intentions, that although (as he admits) there is no instance of the occurrence of the word in this form in any Irish authority[2], nevertheless in his Annals of Armagh extracted from the Four Masters, which follow on the same page, Colgan uniformly writes the word *Airchidneach*, and explains it *Archdeacon*.[3]

Etymology of the word.

He suggests also two other etymologies; one from the Greek *Ethnarch*, and the other from the Irish[4] *ar*, super, and *ceann*, caput. These

---

[1] *Doubtful.* Colgan, *Tr. Th.*, p. 293. 'Vox *Airchindeach* dubiæ mihi est originis et etymologicæ significationis. Waræus, *de Scriptor. Hib.* tradit per eum Archidiaconum significari. Quod si verum sit *Airchidneach* potius scribi deberet.'—See also *ibid.* p. 631.

[2] *Authority.* We find *Airchinneach* and *Airchindeach* (*nn* and *nd* being equivalent in Irish orthography): but never *Airchidneach*.

[3] *Archdeacon.* See his annals, under the years 980, 1015, 1039,

1061, 1069, 1103, 1108. In all which places the Four Masters write *Airchinneach*.

[4] *Irish.* The Greek etymology is wholly untenable. The antient Glossary, called Cormac's (recently published, Williams and Norgate, London), p. 4, explains *ar*, by *uasal*, noble; and suggests also that the first syllable of the word may be from the Greek ἀρχος: so that *Archinnech* would signify 'chief, or noble head.' But this is mere trifling. Colgan's Irish ety-

both give the signification of a præfect, a superior, *præpositus*: and this signification, he remarks, is more in accordance with the ordinary use of the word, and with the duties which were assigned to the office.

Those duties he then explains with great accuracy. 'Whatever[1] be the origin of the name,' he says, 'the airchinneach was the head præpositus, or supreme prefect of the ecclesiastical territory and of the family (or monastic body) inhabiting that territory.' In another place[2] he gives the same account of the office at somewhat greater length:—'The Erenach (in Irish, Airchinneach) signified a person who was appointed to exercise some power or authority over all those who held lands and farms belonging to the Church; he held therefore a principality amongst such tenants: subject, however, to the bishop in the same way as the comharb was; with this

---

mology (*ar*, over, and *ceann*, a head) is no doubt the true one, as is evident from the corresponding Welsh *Arbennig*, where, as Zeuss has remarked (Gram. Celt. p. 191) the initial of the second syllable is aspirated from *p*, as the initial of the second syllable in the Irish *Airchinnech* is aspirated from *c*. This shows that the first syllable is the preposition *ar*, or *air*, the original form of which was *ari* or *are*, and therefore causes aspiration in the first letter of the following word. That *Airchinneach* is not from *Archdeacon*, is evident from the secular use of the term, both in Irish and Welsh, to denote a *chieftain* or leader: and as an adjective to signify *chief* or *principal*. —See Irish Nennius, p. 170, note. And so in Welsh, *Arbennig milwyr*, a leader of soldiers: *y tair Gwyl ar-*

bennig, the three principal festivals; i.e. Christmas, Easter, and Pentecost. It should also be mentioned that in Irish the word is sometimes spelt *Oirchinnech*, Ann.Ult. A.D. 604. *Airdcennach*, a form which occurs in the Dictionaries of O'Brien and O'Reilly, is certainly incorrect, although it seems to be in use in Scotland. We have no authority for it in Irish.

[1] *Whatever.* 'Cujuscunque sit originis, usus obtinuit ut eo nomine appelletur Caput, Præpositus, vel supremus Præfectus territorii Ecclesiastici, et familiæ illud inhabitantis.' And just before 'cum per eam (vocem) videamus denotari præfectum familiæ ecclesiasticum prædium vel territorium inhabitantis.'—*Ibid.*

[2] *Place.* Colgan, *Tr. Th.*, p. 631.

amongst other differences, that they alone were called comharbs who presided over the district originally belonging to some celebrated and antient monastery, or at least to some episcopal see; whereas they were called Airchinneachs who held the chief place in the manner explained over the other tenants of the lands or farms of some Church, whether a monastery or not: and from time immemorial they were mere laymen: so that it is doubtful whether in their origin the dignity or office of airchinneach was annexed to the clerical or monastic state.'[1] After repeating what he had said before as to the various proposed etymologies of the name, he adds, 'They were wont to exercise continual hospitality by some special, and as it were hereditary obligation or inclination; but this may perhaps have originated in this, that the first persons who held the office of airchinneach were archdeacons of the poor, having the care of hospitality: which care, after the primitive times of the Church, may have passed into the hands of mere laymen.'

The offices of Co-arb and Erenach both had reference to the land.

70. No doubt Colgan had mainly in view the position which the comharbs or co-arbs and erenachs occupied in relation to the bishops, at the beginning of the eleventh century, when the necessity of diocesan and archiepiscopal jurisdiction began to be felt. But making allowance for this, his description of the offices of the co-arb and erenach is sufficiently correct. It will be

---

[1] *State.* How this agrees with the opinion that the Airchinneach was an Archdeacon, Colgan does not explain.

seen that both offices had reference to the landed property with which the monastery, or collegiate or cathedral church, was originally endowed. The co-arb inheriting the general rights of chieftainship derived from the donor of the lands; together with the spiritual authority and influence of the first abbat or bishop, who had received the grant, and by whom the ecclesiastical or monastic institutions of the place were first organised. The erenach or airchinneach being himself a tenant, with a delegated jurisdiction over the other tenants, held lands or farms under the co-arb, with the tenure of discharging certain duties. And it is evident, as already remarked, that, in some places at least, the office of erenach was hereditary[1], a custom however which seems to have been peculiar in a great measure to the North of Ireland.

As the antient annals of Tighernach and annals of Ulster give the Latin name of *hæres* to the co-arb, so they usually give the name of *princeps*[2] to the airchinneach. The Four Masters, living at a time when these names, with the offices they indicated, were becoming obsolete, and confounded with more modern ecclesiastical titles, their use of these terms cannot be depended

---

[1] *Hereditary.* See King, 'Early Hist. of the Primacy,' p. 19, who mentions the names of several families in which the office of erenach was hereditary, all belonging to the counties of Donegal and Derry.

[2] *Princeps.* The Life of St. Moedhog gives the name of '*Comes* Lageniæ' and '*Comes* Saranus' to Saran Saobhderg, by whose instigation Brandubh, king of Leinster, was murdered. But the annals of Tighernach and Ulster call the same individual ' Airchinneach of Seanbotha-sen,' i. e. of Temple shambo, Co. Wexford.—Vit. S. Moedhog. (31 Jan.) c. 37-8. Tigern. A.D. 605, Ult. 604.

upon. They frequently confound the co-arb and bishop, as well as the abbat and airchinneach.

71. There is, however, another officer, chiefly to be found in the monasteries, who is termed by the older annalists, and also by the Latin biographers of the saints, *Œconomus*.[1] The Irish name of this officer was *Fertighis*, which literally signifies 'House-man,' and denotes a steward, a purveyor, one whose duty it was to look after the domestic or internal affairs of the monastery, to superintend the labour of the monks, and to see that the house was supplied with fuel and all other necessaries.

The œconomus and the abbat are often found in opposition to each other. We have a record in the annals of Ulster (A.D. 782) of an actual battle[2] between Cathal, the abbat, and Fianachtach, or Finatty, the *œconomus* of Ferns. And the rule of St. Columbanus[3] in one place seems to hint that the abbat and œconomus had separate jurisdictions, inclining strongly to support the authority of the œconomus. 'If a monk,' says the rule, 'desires anything which the œconomus prohibits, although the abbat orders it, he must do penance for five days.'

---

[1] *Œconomus*. Sometimes also called *famulus* and *custos* monasterii.—See Reeves, *Adamnan*, pp. 46, n. and 365. The *equonimus* of the Ann. Ult. is only a variety of spelling. The Four Masters frequently call this officer *prior*. In general, however, they translate the œconomus or equonimus of the Ann. Ult. by *fertighis*.

[2] *Battle*. 'Bellum *hi Fernae moer* inter abbatem et economum, i.e. Cathal et Fianachtach.' This is, of course, passed over in silence by the Four Masters for a reason already explained.

[3] *St. Columbanus*. 'Si quis voluerit aliquid et prohibet œconomus et jubet abbas, quinque dies.'—*Reg. S. Columbani*, c. 12 (Fleming, Collect. p. 377).

The œconomus, however, sometimes abused his power, and persecuted a youthful saint, to whom he had taken a dislike in consequence of the saint preferring study or devotion to manual labour; or for some other capricious reason.

Thus, in the Life of St. Moedhog of Ferns: The saint was in the monastery of St. David at Kill-muine. The œconomus found him reading in his cell, and attacked him angrily, saying, 'Go off, idle fellow, after the other brethren, and fetch faggots from the wood.' This œconomus, says the biographer, hated the saint without a cause. Moedhog, without a murmur, obeyed the rough command, and went off, leaving his book open out of doors. The œconomus gave him two unbroken oxen, without yoke or harness, to draw his cart; this was done from malice. But the oxen became miraculously tame, and drew the cart as if they had been properly harnessed, making a short cut across a deep bog, as if it had been a hard road. On his return, notwithstanding that it had rained heavily in the interval, St. Moedhog found his book perfectly dry. These miracles opened the eyes of St. David to the malice of his œconomus, who nevertheless persisted in his enmity to the disciple.

St. Moedhog persecuted by the Œconomus of St. David's.

He went so far at length as to plot against St. Moedhog's life. He employed a man to accompany the saint to the wood, and to kill him as he was stooping to lift the logs. The man raised his axe to slay the holy youth, but was straightway paralysed, and unable to move his arms. St. David, hearing this, ran half dressed to the wood, and returned with Moedhog to the monastery. He then called the œconomus before him, and sharply reproved him. But Moedhog said to David his master, 'Father, chide him not, for God will chide him for us: he shall shortly die, and no man shall know his grave.' And this prophecy, says our author[1], was speedily fulfilled.

A similar anecdote of St. Finnian of Clonard.

A similar story is told in the Life of St. Finnian of Cluain-iraird, or Clonard; he was also in St. David's monastery: when the œconomus, for St. David seems to have been unfortunate in his stewards, commanded Finnian to go immediately to the wood, and bring home timber. St. Finnian remonstrated, saying that he had neither tools for cutting wood, nor means of drawing it, and moreover that he knew not the way. But receiving only another angry and more peremptory command, he obeyed; and aided by angelic guidance, he returned sooner than the other monks, and with a more ample supply of timber.[2]

And of St. Canice.

The same story is also told of St. Cannech, or Canice, of Kilkenny. He was a student in Britain or Wales, in the monastery of the wise and religious Doc or Docus. The steward, who is in one place called *famulus*, and immediately after *æquonomus*, took a dislike to the youth for no other reason but because he saw him to be a

---

[1] *Author.* Vit. S. Moedoci (31 Jan.) c. 11-18; Colgan, *Actt. SS.*, p. 209.

[2] *Timber.* Vit. S. Finniani, c. 5; Colgan, *Ibid.* p. 393.

favourite of the abbat. One day Cannech was sitting reading, when the œconomus came in and angrily reproved him, saying, 'The whole family (tota familia) is gone across the sea with oxen and waggons to bring home necessary goods, go thou after them.' The saint arose to obey. The steward gave him two untamed oxen (this seems to have been a favourite mode of annoying a young monk), but they immediately became gentle and manageable. When Cannech reached the sea-shore, he found the tide was full, and the strand impassable. But the water miraculously divided itself into two parts, so that St. Cannech passed over dry shod, and returned again the same way with his loaded waggon. The abbat seeing this, feared greatly, praised his obedient disciple, and reproved the œconomus.[1]

These stories, which exhibit a singular amount of sameness and want of invention, prove nevertheless, that the office of the œconomus, or *Fertighis*, was to see to the supply of the house with necessaries. It appears also that he was invested with authority over the monks, to make them labour for the service of the community. He was therefore naturally an unpopular officer. We can scarcely help thinking, that the biographer who inserted such a story into his Life of a Saint must at one time have smarted himself under the discipline of some strict œconomus, and sought in this way to reform the whole body of monastic stewards.

<small>Office of the Œconomus.</small>

[1] *Œconomus.* Vit. S. Cannechi, p. 3 (Dublin, 1853, privately printed by the Marquis of Ormonde).

The Maor of Armagh.

72. We find mention, in connection with the *familia* of Armagh, of an officer called *maor*, who appears to have been the keeper of certain sacred relics, such as the bell, and book, and crozier of Armagh, and who, in later times at least, held lands from the see, under the tenure of producing these relics when required. As we shall probably have occasion to speak of this officer elsewhere, it may be enough here to say, that in the Annals of Ulster[1], A.D. 928 [al. 929], we have the following notice of one of these stewards :—

| Tuathal mac Oencain scripa [*sic*] et episcopus Doimliac et Lusca et moer muinnteri Patraicc o sleibh fadhes, heu immatura ætate quievit. | Tuathal, son of Oencan, scribe and Bishop of Duleek and of Lusk, and *moer* of the family of Patrick from the mountain on the south. Alas! immatura ætate quievit. |

And again, in the same annals[2], A.D. 813 :—

| Feidlimidh abbas Cillemoinni et moer bregh o Phatraic, ancorita precipuus, scribaque optimus, feliciter vitam finivit. | Feidlimidh, Abbat of Cillemoinni[3], and *moer* of Bregia, from Patrick, chief anchorite, and excellent scribe, ended his life happily. |

From these brief entries we learn that there were *maors* or keepers for the co-arbs of Patrick in different places, where the *family* of Armagh had churches or landed property; and that these keepers were, sometimes at least, ecclesiastics of

---

[1] *Ulster.* The same entry occurs in the Four Masters, A.D. 927.
[2] *Annals.* See also Four Masters, A.D. 809.
[3] *Cillemoinni.* Now Kilmoone, Co. Meath.

INTROD.] *Ecclesiastical Tenure of Land.* 171

the highest order. Besides their more sacred duties of guarding the precious treasures of the Church, Dr. O'Donovan thinks that they may have also been the collectors of dues, or tribute, payable to the Church or bishop, in the district to which they were appointed.

73. On the whole, it appears that the endowments in land, which were granted to the antient Church by the chieftains who were first converted to Christianity, carried with them the temporal rights and principalities originally belonging to the owners of the soil; and that these rights and principalities were vested, not in bishops as such, but in the co-arbs or ecclesiastical successors of those saints, to whom the grants of land were originally made. It is easy to see, therefore, that in the districts where such lands were so granted, a succession of co-arbs would necessarily be kept up. It did not follow that these co-arbs were always bishops, or even priests; in the case of Kildare the co-arbs were always females; and there is an instance on record, although in a different sense, of a female co-arb of St. Patrick at Armagh. But it is evident that the abbat or co-arb, and not the bishop as such, inherited the rights of chieftainship and property, and was therefore the important personage in the ecclesiastical community. Hence we have in the annals a nearer approach to a correct list of the abbats and co-arbs, than to a correct list of the bishops. The bishop, or bishops, for there were often more than one

Rights conveyed in the ecclesiastical tenure of Land.

bishop connected with the monastery, or with what afterwards became the episcopal see, were in subjection to the co-arb abbat, and did not necessarily succeed to each other, according to our modern notions of an episcopal succession. There were frequent breaks[1] in the series. The presence of a pilgrim or travelling bishop, who remained for a time in the monastery, would be enough to supply the wants of the community for that time, by giving the episcopal benedictions; and it was not until he had left them that the monastic 'family' would feel it necessary to provide themselves with another.

<small>Difficulty of the attempt to make out a regular succession of bishops.</small>

Considerable difficulty has therefore been created by the attempt to make out a regular succession of bishops in Armagh and elsewhere. The truth is, that there was no such thing. The names handed down to us as successors of Patrick are many of them called abbats, some are called bishops as well as abbats, some are styled bishops only, and some co-arbs of St. Patrick. But there is nothing in this last title to indicate whether the personage so designated was a bishop, a priest, or a layman.

<small>Ancient Lists of the Co-arbs of Patrick.</small>

74. Four antient lists of the co-arbs of St. Patrick have been preserved. They all bear internal evidence of having been drawn up at the close of the eleventh, or beginning of the twelfth century, when archiepiscopal and diocesan jurisdiction was introduced; and it is probable

---

[1] *Breaks.* See Reeves, Eccl. Ant. of Down and Connor, p. 136.

that their authors were influenced by a wish to establish a claim to a regular episcopal succession, at least at Armagh, and thus to escape so far the reproach of irregularity which the Roman party amongst the Norsemen and English of that period had brought against the Irish Church.

These lists differ considerably, as might be expected, from each other. They differ also from the list which may be gathered from the Irish Annals. But they are not on that account the less valuable. They are here given exactly as they are found in the original authorities, and it will be observed that they all terminate about the same period; and are in fact lists of the co-arbs or successors of St. Patrick, abbatial as well as episcopal, who flourished before the establishment of metropolitical and diocesan jurisdiction in the twelfth century.

The first list is that which has been printed by Colgan, as from the Psaltair or Psalter of Cashel. But there can scarcely be a doubt that the true Psalter of Cashel did not exist in his time, and that his real authority was the 'Psalter[1] of Mac Richard,' now in the Bodleian Library, a manuscript transcribed in 1454, by John O'Clery, who tells us that he copied for Mac Richard Butler all such portions of the old Psaltair of Cashel as were then legible.

On the opening of the two pages, fol. 114 b,

<small>The first List from the Psalter of Mac Richard Butler.</small>

---

[1] *Psalter.* This MS. is marked Laud. 610. The word *Psalter* was used by the Irish to denote a collection of historical, religious, and miscellaneous documents, as necessary to an historian or man of learning as the Psalter is to an ecclesiastic.

and 115 a, of this MS. are six columns (three on each page), which were intended to exhibit contemporary lists of the Roman emperors, the popes of Rome, the kings of Ireland (these last occupying the third column of fol. 114 b, and the first of fol. 115 a); as also the co-arbs of Patrick, and the kings of Cashel, which fill the two remaining columns of this latter page.

The title prefixed by Colgan[1] to this list of the Armagh prelates, is 'Catalogus Primatum, seu Archiepiscoporum Metropolis Ardmachanæ, cum annis quibus sederunt, ex Psalterio Casselensi.'

It is needless to say that this title is entirely his own, and has no authority from the MS., where the list is headed simply *Do Comarbaibh Patraic*, 'Of the Co-arbs of Patrick.'

We shall now give it exactly as it is found in the Bodleian MS., with the numbers which signify the duration of each prelate's incumbency. The only liberty[2] taken with the original is that of prefixing a number to each name, for the convenience of reference.

1. Patraic.		6. Cormac	xv.
2. Sechnaill	vi.	7. Dubtach	xvi.
3. Senpatraic	x.	8. Ailill	xiii.
4. Binen	x.	9. Ailill	x.
5. Jarlaithe	xviii.	10. Duach	.

---

[1] *Colgan.* Tr. Th, p. 292.

[2] *Liberty.* Colgan has Latinized the names: but we have preserved the Irish forms exactly as in the original. It has not been thought worth while to mark Colgan's deviations from the original orthography of the names. But he sometimes differs in the years assigned to each prelate's incumbency. Thus in No. 2, he has xvi. instead of vi. In No. 22, vii. for viii. No. 31, xiii. for xiiii. No. 40, xxix. for xxxix. These are probably mere errors of the press.

INTROD.] *from the Psalter of Mac Richard.* 175

11. Fiachraig	.	31. Mac Loingse	. .	xiiii.
12. Fedilmed	xx.	32. Artri	. . . .	ii.
13. Caerlan	x.	33. Eogan Manistrech		viii.
14. Eochaig	.	34. Forannan	. .	xiiii.
15. Senach	.	35. Dermait	. . .	iiii.
16. Mac Laisre	.	36. Fethgna	. .	xxii.
17. Tomine	xxxv.	37. Anmere	. . .	i.
18. Segine	xxvii.	38. Cathasach	. . .	iiii.
19. Flann Febla	xxvii.	39. Maelcoba	. . .	v.
20. Suibne	xv.	40. Maelbrigde Mac Tornan	. . .	xxxix.
21. Congus	xx.			
22. Celepetair	viii.	41. Joseph	. . .	ix.
23. Ferdacrich	x.	42. Maelpatraic	. .	i.
24. Foennelach	iii.	43. Cathassach	. .	xx.
25. Dubdalethe	xv.	44. Muiredach	. .	ix.
26. Airechtach	i.	45. Dubdalethe Mac Cellaig	. . .	xxxiii.
27. Cudinisc	iiii.			
28. Connmach	xiiii.	46. Murecan	. . .	iii.
29. Torbach	i.	47. Maelmaire	. .	xix.
30. Nuadu	iii.			

Colgan adds five more prelates to the list, whose names do not occur in the Bodleian MS., viz.—

48. Almagadius	xxx.	51. Moel-isa	. . .	xxvii.
49. Dubdaletha	xii.	52. Domnaldus	. . .	
50. Cumascacius	iii.			

He remarks that the number of years of the incumbency of this last prelate is not given, and therefore he infers[1] that the author of the list must have written it during the lifetime of that Domnald, before the year 1105, in which he died, and after the year 1091, in which he suc-

---

[1] *Infers.* 'Videtur authoris hujus Catalogi scripsisse ante annum 1105, quo obiit Domnaldus, quem ultimum in eo nominat, et cujus tanquam adhuc viventis annos regiminis non determinat.'—*Tr. Th.*, p. 292.

ceeded to the bishopric. In any case, it is evident that the list (which even in its shortest form is carried down to A.D. 1021, the date of Maelmaire's death) could not have formed a part of the Psalter of Cashel, composed by the king and bishop Cormac Mac Cullenain, who died A.D. 908.

It will be observed that the number of years of St. Patrick's episcopacy is not given[1], probably because there was some uncertainty as to the beginning of his settling at Armagh, and also because the two or perhaps four immediately following him were bishops along with him at Armagh before his death. The years of incumbency are also wanting, after the names of Nos. 10, 14, 15, and 16, probably because the author was not certain as to the exact duration of their prelacy.

The five names added to the list by Colgan, or perhaps by his transcriber, for he himself evidently believed them to have been in the original, were probably taken from the second list, of which we shall now speak.

Second List of the Co-arbs of Patrick.

75. The second antient list is preserved in the *Leabhar Breac*[2], or speckled book of the Mac Egans, a MS. of the latter end of the fourteenth, or beginning of the fifteenth century.

---

[1] *Given.* The fourth list gives the number of years from the arrival of St. Patrick in Ireland to his death. See p. 180, *infra*.

[2] *Leabhar Breac.* This MS. is now in the Library of the Royal Irish Academy, Dublin. Its proper Irish name is *Leabhar mór Dúna Doighre*, or great book of Dun Doighre, a fort near Athlone, which was the antient residence of the Mac Egans. It got the name of *Leabhar Breac*, or speckled book, from the colour of its binding. See *O'Curry's Lectures*, p. 352.

This List[1] is headed 'Do Chomarbaib Patraic inso,' i.e. 'Of the Co-arbs of Patrick here;' it is in the Irish language, with sometimes a few words of Latin; and besides the years of each prelate's incumbency (omitted in Nos. 3 and 28), it has several curious remarks on the personal history of some of the individuals of the series. It is scarcely necessary to encumber these pages with the original; but the following translation is strictly literal: a few notes are added; and the liberty has been taken of prefixing, as before, a number to each name, to facilitate reference :—

1. Patrick, cxx^{mo}. etatis sue quievit.[2]
2. Sechnall, xiii.
3. Benen, son of Sescnen, Patrick's psalm-singer. He was of the Cianachta Glinne Gaimen, of the race of Taidg, son of Cian of Cashel.
4. Hiarlathi, son of Log[3], xiiii.
5. Corbmac, xv. annis.
6. Dubthach, xxiiii.
7. Fiachra, xx. annis.
8. Cairellan, x. annis.
9. Eochaid, x. annis.
10. Senach, annis xv.
11. Mac Laisre, xiiii.
12. Tomine, xxxv. annis.
13. Segine, xxvi. annis.
14. Flann Febla, son of Scannal; he was the pupil[4] of Berchan, son of Mican : xxvii. annis.
15. Suibne in Sui[5], xv. annis.
16. Congus, xx. annis.
17. Cele-Petair, viii. annis.
18. Fer-da-crioch, x. annis.
19. Foendelach, vi. annis.
20. Dubdalethi, xviii.

---

[1] *List.* Leabhar Breac, fol. 98, b. b. [or by another pagination, fol. 108, b. b.]. This List was first published (in English) by Mr. King ; *Primacy of Armagh*, p. 112.

[2] *Quievit.* The Irish annals always use this word to express the entering into rest of a saint or ecclesiastic. They sometimes also use *pausavit*, and *pausatio*. These words are never applied to laymen, however exalted. For this reason, the word 'quievit,' as in some sort technical, has been here retained.

[3] *Log.* In the original, 'Hiarlathi mac Loga,' but Loga seems to be the genitive case.

[4] *Pupil.* The original word *Dalta* signifies foster-son; a person brought up, supported, and educated by another.

[5] *In Sui* : i. e. the sage.

21. Oirechtach, i. anno.
22. Cudinisc, iiii. annis.
23. Condmach, xiii. annis.
24. Torbach, uno anno.
25. Nuada, iii. annis.
26. Mac Lonsig, xiii.
27. Artri, duobus annis.
28. Eogan mainestrech, m̄ buti meic Bronaig.[1]
29. Forandan, xiiii. annis.
30. Dermait, iiii. annis.
31. Fethgna, xxv. annis.
32. Ainmire, uno anno.
33. Cathussach, iiii. annis.
34. Maelcaba, v. annis.
35. Maelbrigte mac Dornain[2], xxxix annis.
36. Iosep, annis ix.
37. Maelpatraic, anno uno.
38. Cathassach, xx. annis.
39. Muiredach mac Fergusa[3], ix. annis.
40. Dubdalethi mac Cellaig[4], xxxiii.
41. Muirecan, iii. annis.
42. Maelmuire, xiii. annis.
43. Amalgaid, xxix. annis.
44. Dubdalethi, ii. annis.
45. Cummascach, iii. annis.
46. Moelissu, xxvii. annis.
47. Domnall, viii. annis.

Third List of the Co-arbs of Patrick.

76. The third List occurs in the *Leabhar buidhé Lecain*, or 'Yellow Book[5] of Lecan,' a MS. written about A.D. 1390, and now preserved in the library of Trinity College, Dublin. This list contains very little more than the names and duration of the incumbencies, but is continued to Gilla, or Gelasius, who died 1174. The same liberty has been taken as before, of prefixing a number to each prelate's name, for the convenience of reference. The years of incumbency are omitted in Nos. 8, 12, 13, 25, 36, 49, 50, 51, and 58.

---

[1] *Bronaig.* These words have been left untranslated, because, as Mr. King has justly remarked, there is in them an error of transcription. We should read 'Eoghan mainestrech-buti mac Bronaig;' i. e. 'Eoghan [or Owen] of Monasterboice, son of Bronach.'

[2] *Mac Dornain*: i. e. son of Dornan.
[3] *Mac Fergusa*: i.e. son of Fergus.
[4] *Mac Cellaig*: i. e. son of Cellach or Kelly: the Irish C is always pronounced as K.
[5] *Yellow Book.* For an account of this MS. see O'Curry's Lectures, p. 190.

INTROD.] *from the Yellow Book of Lecan.*

1. Patraic, xxii.
2. Sechnall, xiii.
3. Sen-Patraic, x.
4. Benen, x.
5. Iarlaithe, xiiii.
6. Patraic, iiii.
7. Cormac, xii.
8, 9, 10. Cormac [1] and Dubtach, xiiii., and Ailill xiii.
11. Ailill, x.
12. Duach.
13. Fiachra.
14. Feidlim, xx.
15. Cairellan, x.
16. Eochad, xv.
17. Senach, xii.
18. Mac Laisre, xiiii.
19. Tomine, xxxv.
20. Segine, xxiiii.
21. Flann Febla, xxiiii.
22. Suibni, xii.
23. Congus, xx.
24. Celi-Pedair, vii.
25. Ferdacrich.
26. Foendelach, x.
27. Dubdalethi, xviii.
28. Airechtach, i.
29. Cudinisc, iiii.
30. Connmach, xvi.
31. Torbach, i.
32. Nuada, iii.
33. Mac Loingsi, xvii.
34. Arti, ii.
35. Eogan mainistrech, viii.
36. Forandan.
37. Dermait, iiii.
38. Fethgna, xxii.
39. Ainmire, i.
40. Cathusach, vii.
41. Maelcoba, v.
42. Maelbrigde, xxix.
43. Iosep. ix.
44. Maelpatraic, i.
45. Cathusach mac Fergusa, xx.
46. Muiredach mac Fergusa, ix.
47. Dubdalethi mac Cellaig, xxxviii.
48. Muirecan mac Eathach [2], xix.
49. Maelmuire.
50. Amalgaid.
51. Dubdalethi.
52. Cumascach, iii.
53. Maelissa, xxvii.
54. Domnall, xiiii.
55. Cellach, xxvii.
56. Muircertach, iii.
57. Maelmuadoc, h. mongair.[3]
58. Gilla mac Liac meic Diarmada meic Ruaidri.[4]

77. The fourth List is the most antient and valuable of them all, and has been now for the first Fourth List.

---

[1] *Cormac.* This is obscure. In the MS. it is written thus:
xiii   7 xiii
' Cormac   7 Dubtach,   7 Ailill.'
Where the character 7, is the usual Irish contraction for *ocus* or *agus*, ' and.'

[2] *Mac Eathach*: i.e. son of Eochadh.
[3] *h. mongair*: i.e. grandson of Mongar, written in full *hua Mongair*, or *O Mongair.*
[4] *Ruaidri*: i.e. Gilla, son of Liac, son of Diarmait, son of Rory.

time published. It is preserved in the Book of Leinster[1], compiled or written by Finn Mac Gormain, who was Bishop of Kildare from 1148 to 1160. This list is entitled *Comarbada Patraic*, 'The Comarbs of Patrick.' A number has been prefixed to each name, as before. This list gives some curious genealogical and topographical information, which renders it very interesting and important.

1. Patraic; lxiiii. from the coming of Patrick into Erinn to his death.
2. Sechnall, son of Restitut, xiii.
3. Sen-Patraic, ii.
4. Binnen, son of Sescnen, x.
5. Iarlaithe, son of Tren, xiiii., of Cluain-Fiacla.[2]
6. Cormac, xii. Primus abbas de Chlainn-Chernaigh.[3]
7. Dubthach, xiii.
8. Ailill, xiii., primus. } Both Ailills were of Druim-
9. Ailill, x., secundus. } chád, in Hi Bresail.
10. Duach, xii., of Ui Tuirtri.
11. Fiachra, x., son of Colman, son of Eogan, of Enuch Senmáil.
12. Feidilmid, xv., grandson of Faelan of Domnuch-nemaind.
13. Caurlan, iiii., of Domnuch-mic-hu-garba, of the Ui Nialláin.
14. Eochaid, son of Diarmait, iii., of Dumnuch-rig-druing.
15. Senach-garb[4], xiii., of Cluain-hu-mic-Gricci, of the Ui Nialláin [i.e. the smith[5] who was in [holy] orders of Cill-mór].
16. Mac Laisre, xviii.

---

[1] *Leinster*. A MS. in Trin. Coll. Dublin, H. 2, 18, fol. 21 b. col. 3. See O'Curry's Lectures, p. 186.

[2] *Cluain-Fiacla*. Now Clonfeacle.

[3] *De Chlainn Chernaigh*: i. e. of the Clann Cernaigh or Kearney.

[4] *Senach-garb*, or Senach the rough.

[5] *Smith*. It is doubtful whether the note within brackets was intended to belong to No. 15 or to No. 16. It is written in the MS. as if it was meant to be a sort of gloss on No. 16. But this question will be considered elsewhere.

17. Tommine, lxxxiii.
18. Segini, xxvii., son of Bresal, of Acudh-Chlaidib.
19. Forannán, i.
20. Fland Febla, xxvi., son of Scanlan, grandson of Fingin.
21. Suibne, xv., son of Crunmael, son of Ronan of the Ui Nialláin.
22. Congus Scribnid [1], xx. Unde Torad penne Congusa; i.e. grandson of Dasluaig, son of Ainmire of Cuil-Athgoirt.
23. Cele-Petair, viii., of Druim Chetna in Ui Bresail.
24. Ferdachrich, x.
25. Cudinisc, iiii., son of Concas, grandson of Cathbath, son of Eochad.
26. Dubdalethi, son of Sinach, xviii.
27. Airectach, grandson of Faelan, of the Ui Bresail, i. year.
20. Faennelach, iii., son of Moenach-Mannacta. It was he who was killed by Dubdalethi at Ros-bodba; unde dicitur:—

Faendelach aness, isé a less, Teclaim sluaig; Dubdalethi mac Siniag, do fail Corigaib atuaid.	Faendelach, from the south, he would do well To collect an army; Dubdalethi, son of Sinach, he is With kings from the north.

29. Condmach, xiii., son of Dubdalethi. This was the son in succession to his father, ut prophetavit [2] Bec-mac-de.
30. Artri, ii. It was he who suffered martyrdom from O'Niall, and from Suibni, son of Sairnech.
31. Eogan Manistrech, viii. Eogan, son of Anbtech, Comarb of Patrick, and of Finnian, and of Buite, spiritual director of Niall Glundub.[3] Here are three Airchinnechs, who took the abbacy by force, who are not commemorated in the Mass; viz. Fland-roi, son of Cumascach, son of Conchobair, who died in the chariot; and Gormgal, son of Indnotach.
32. Forannan, xvii., son of Murgel; i.e. Murgel[4] was the name of his mother

---

[1] *Congus Scribnid*: i. e. Congus the Scribe. The words that follow signify ' Hence [the saying: or hence the poem beginning] The fruit of Congus's pen,' alluding to his having been a scribe. Over the word Dasluaig is the gloss ' i. mensa,' which I am unable to explain.

[2] *Prophetavit*. The meaning is, this was the son who succeeded his father, as predicted by the poet and prophet Bec-mac-de.

[3] *Glundub*. This is a mistake for Niall Cailne.

[4] *Murgel*. This last clause is in Latin, 'i. Murgel nomen matris ejus.'

33. Dermait, grandson of Tigernan. It was by him the linen cloth was placed between the spears at the cross of Ardachad[1], and the ridge of leeks and parsneps, so that they rotted by the greatness of his power.

34. Fechgna, xxii.; i.e. Figlech[2], son of Nechtan: of the Clann Eochadh.

35. Ainmere, i. year; grandson of Faelan. He was sovereign of the Nialláin, and of the priesthood of Armagh.

36. Maelcoba, v. years, son of Crundmal, of the family of Cill mór.

37. Cathassach, son of Rabartach, iiii., grandson of Moinach, of the Clann Suibne. He died in his pilgrimage in the island of[3] . . .

38. Maelbrigti, son of Tornan, xxxix., comarb of Patraic and of Colum-cille, of the Clann . . . ; i.e. of the O . . .

39. Joseph, ix., son of Fathach, of the Clann . . . . -gaeta of the Dalriattai.

40. Maelpatraic, i. year, son of Mailtuile.

41. Cathassach, xx., son of Doligen.

42. Muridach, son of Fergus, ix., of Glinn-arind in Sliabh . . .

43. Dubdalethi, son of Cellah, xxxiii. Deolaid, daughter of Mailtuile, son of . . . . of Mis-cain-dega, was the mother of Dubdalethi.

44. Murican, iii., son of Ciaracan, of Both-Domnaig.

45. Maelmaire, xix., son of Eochocan.

46. Amalgaid, xxix.

47. Dubdalethi, xii.

48. Cummascach, iii.

49. Domnall, xiiii.

50. Cellach.[4]

51. Maelmoedóc, grandson of Morgar.

52. Gillamacliac, i.e. Mac-ind-fhirdana.[5]

53. The bishop Hua Muiredach.

---

[1] *Ardachad,* now Ardagh. This passage is very obscure.

[2] *Figlech.* This word signifies *vigils*: meaning that this prelate was called 'Fechgna of the Vigils.'

[3] *Island of* . . . The MS. is illegible here, and also in the places marked by dots, Nos. 38, 39, 42. and 43.

[4] *Cellach.* Here the original list stops. The remaining names are added in another hand.

[5] *Mac-ind-fhirdana.* These words signify 'Son of the poet.'

54. Gilla-chomdad Hua Carain.
55. Tomaltach, son of Aedh, son of Toirdelbach Hui Chonchobair.

The historical and genealogical information given in the foregoing list is of great value to the student of Irish Church history, in which the bishops of Armagh have played so important a part. At present it is only necessary to note, that the years of each prelate's incumbency appear to have been added after the list of names was written; they are, however, in a hand coeval with the list itself, if not in the original hand. They are written over the lines, at the places where they are inserted above, which will explain the circumstance that they sometimes interrupt the sense.

78. The same MS. (the Book of Leinster) contains a curious list of the kings of Ireland since Christianity, in which are inserted, in the briefest form of annals, notices of the principal battles and other events of each king's reign, and, in particular, the deaths of the bishops and abbats of Armagh.[1] It will be worth while to extract from this list, under each king's reign, the ecclesiastical events which illustrate the subject of this work.

Annals of ecclesiastical events, from the Book of Leinster.

The tract is entitled *Incipit do flaithesaib ocus amseraib h-Erenn iar creitim.* 'Here begins, Of the reigns and times of Erinn since Christianity.' Some of the entries or events recorded in this

---
[1] *Armagh.* The dates of the earlier kings will be found in the Appendix A, Table VI. p. 256. The reader will observe the ancient and more simple orthography of the names in the following Annals.

document are in Latin. They are here given in that language without translation. The Irish entries are translated into English.

LAOEGAIRE, SON OF NIALL.

xxx. annos regnum Hibernie post adventum Patricii tenuit.
Ardmacha fundata est.
Secundinus et senex Patricius quieverunt.

AILIOLL MOLT, SON OF DATHI.

Quies Benigni sancti episcopi.
Quies Iarlathi tertii episcopi.

LUGAID, SON OF LAOEGAIRE.

Patricii scotorum episcopi,
Cormac primus abbas,
Quies Ibari episcopi.

MURCHERTACH, SON OF ERC.

Dubthach abbat of Ardmacha quievit.
Dormitatio S. Brigitae.
Ailioll abbat of Ardmacha.
Quies Colmain McDuach.

TUATHAL MAELGARB.

Quies Ailbe Imlecha.[1]
Ailiol[2] [ii.] abbat of Ardmacha.
Nem episcopus.

DIARMAIT, SON OF CERBHAILL.

Duach abbat of Ardmacha.
Ciaran mac-int-saer.
Colum mac Crimthaind.
Fiachra abbat of Ardmacha.

DOMNALL ET FERGUS DUO FILII MEIC ERCA.

Quies Brenaind Birr. ccc$^{mo.}$ anno ætatis suæ [dlxxx.[3]].

---

[1] *Imlecha.* The *Quies*, or rest, i.e. death, of Ailbe, of Imleach [Emly].

[2] *Ailiol.* Over this name is the number ii. (added above in brackets), which indicates that he was the second of the name.

[3] *Dlxxx.* This number is written over the line; it denotes A.D. 580.

BAETAN AND EOCHAID.

[No ecclesiastical events are recorded under this reign.]

AIMIRE, SON OF SETNA.

[No ecclesiastical events recorded.]

BAETAN, SON OF NINNIDH.

Ite Cluana-Oenu, h. Loigsi.
Gillas sapiens quievit.

AED, SON OF AINMIRE.

Daig son of Cairell quievit.
The great convention of Drum-Ceatt.
Feidlimid abbat of Ardmacha moritur.
Eochu abbat of Ardmacha.
Grigorius Papa.
David of Cill-muine.
Quies Coluim-cille et Baithine.

COLMAN RIMID, ET AED SLAINE.

Quies Comgaill Benchoir.
Fintan of Cluan Eidnech.
Quies Cainnig.

AED UARIDNACH.

Senach abbat of Ardmacha
Vel hic Grigorius.

MAELCOBA.

[No ecclesiastical events recorded.]

SUBNE MENN.

Mac Lasre abbat of Ardmacha.

DOMHNALL, SON OF AED.

Mochuta of Rathin quievit.
Molasse of Leth-glinn quievit.

CELLACH AND CONALL CAEL, SONS OF MAELCOBA.

Fursu quievit.

BLAITHMAC ET DIARMAIT.

Fechin of Fobar, Manchan of Leith, Aineran of Indecna quieverunt.
Then was the Buidh Coneill [the yellow pestilence].
Synodus Constantinopolitana.

SECHNASACH, SON OF BLAITHMAC.
Navigatio Columbani episcopi cum reliquiis sanctorum to Inis-bo-finn.

CENDFAELAD, SON OF CRUNDMAEL.
Prima combustio Airdmacha.

FINNACTA FLEDACH.
Adomnanus captivos duxit ad Hiberniam.

LOINGSECH, SON OF OENGUS.
Moling of Luachra.
Esuries maxima in Hibernia ut homo hominem comederet.

CONGAL OF CENN MAGAIR.
[No ecclesiastical events recorded.]

FERGALL, SON OF MAELDUIN.
[No ecclesiastical events.]

FOGARTACH, SON OF NIALL.
[No ecclesiastical events.]

CINAED, SON OF IRGALACH.
[No ecclesiastical events.]

FLAITHBERTACH, SON OF LONSECH.
He died [1] at Ardmacha.
Subne abbat of Ardmacha moritur.

AED ALLAIN, SON OF FERGALL.
[No ecclesiastical events.]

DOMNALL, SON OF MURCHAD.
Quies Fidmuine [2] [i. h. Suanaig].
Cucumne.

NIALL FROSSACH, SON OF FERGAL.
Ferdachrich, abbat of Ardmacha.

---

[1] *Died.* The Four Masters add, 'having resigned his kingdom for a monastic life,' A.D. 729.

[2] *Fidmuine.* The words in brackets occur as a gloss over the name, and signify that he was the grandson of Suanach. The Four Masters call him 'Fidhairle Hua Suanaigh,' A.D. 758.

DONDCHAD, SON OF DOMNALL.
Dubdaleth, abbat of Ardmacha.

AED ORDNIDE.
Condmach, Torbach, Toictech, Nuado, abbats of Ardmacha quieverunt.

CONCHOBAR, SON OF DONDCHAD.
Eogan Manistrech of Ard-macha.

MAELSECHLAINN, SON OF MAELRUANAID.
Forannan et Diarmait duo abbates Airdmacha quieverunt.

AED FINDLIATH.
Fethgna abbat of Ardmacha.

FLANN, SON OF MAELSECHLAINN.
Ainmeri et Maelcoba abbates Airdmacha quieverunt.
Battle of Belach-mugna by the Leinster-men against the Munster-men, in quo cecidit Cormac, son of Culenan.

NIALL GLULDUBH.
[No ecclesiastical events.]

DONDCHAD, SON OF FLANN.
Maelbrigte, son of Tornan, et Joseph, et Maelpatraic, tres abbates quieverunt.

CONGALACH, SON OF MAELMITHIG.
[No ecclesiastical events.]

DOMNALL, GRANDSON OF NIALL.
Muredach abbas Airdmacha moritur.

MAELSECHLAINN, SON OF DOMNALL.
Dubdaleithe comarb of Patrick.

BRIAN, SON OF CENNETIGH.
[No ecclesiastical events.]

MAELSECHLAINN, SON OF DOMNALL [restored].
Maelmaire, comarb of Patrick.

INTERREGNUM OF TWO YEARS.
Amalgaid comarb of Patrick.

TAIRDELBACH, GRANDSON OF BRIAN.
Dubdalethi, comarb of Patrick.

MUIRCHERTACH, GRANDSON OF BRIAN.
Maelisu, comarb of Patrick.

INTERREGNUM OF SIX YEARS.
Cellach comarb of Patrick.
Mael-isu, grandson of Ainmire, chief senior [ardsenoir] of Erinn, quievit.
Synod of Cenannus [Kells], ubi Johannes Cardinalis præsidens interfuit. Millessimo c$^{mo.}$ l$^{mo.}$ secundo celebratum fuit istud nobile concilium.

MUIRCHERTACH, SON OF NIALL.
Domnall, grandson of Londgan, Archbishop [ardespoc] of Munster, quievit.
Synod at Bri-mac-Taidc.

RUADRI,[1] SON OF TAIRDELBACH, GRANDSON OF CONCHOBAIR.
The Saxons came into Erinn; and Erinn was full of wounds from them.
Gilla mac Liac, comarb of Patrick.
The Saxons came into Erinn. Erinn was wounded by them.
Domhnall, grandson of Brian, King of Tuadmuman [Thomond], quievit.

These short Annals, never before published, will be found to fix the dates of several bishops and ecclesiastics of Armagh, and appear to have been written before the use of the Christian era became general in Ireland.

Having placed on record these important documents, we may now conclude this Introduction by some remarks on the existence of Christianity in Ireland, before the mission of St. Patrick, and on the history of some natives of Ireland who appear

---

[1] *Ruadri.* This last paragraph is in a hand later than the rest of the MS.

to have embraced Christianity independently, or prior to that event.

79. Ireland, unlike Spain, and other countries, makes no claim to the honour of having received Christianity from the preaching of one of the original apostles.[1] The traditions which have been handed down to us are, in themselves, by no means improbable. They amount to this, that isolated and accidental visits to the island made by Christian men in the third or fourth century, some of them perhaps merchants, some ascetics, or ecclesiastics, had raised up here and there, principally it would seem in the south or south-east, some few Christian families, separated from each other, and probably ignorant of each other's existence.

Origin of Christianity in Ireland.

Some natives of Ireland also, who had emigrated to the Continent before the coming of St. Patrick, appear to have there become imbued with Christian doctrine, and notwithstanding the great difficulty in that age of intercourse with so inaccessible a land, may have produced some preparatory influence on their friends at home. But the fact that there were Irishmen on the Continent in that early period who were believers in Christ, does not necessarily prove that they had received their Christianity in their native country, or that there was any Christianity in Ireland at the time.

Irish Christians before St. Patrick.

From a passage in the writings of St. Jerome,

Pelagius or Cælestius.

---

[1] *Apostles.* The story that St. James, the son of Zebedee and brother of St. John, had preached in Ireland, is not found in any Irish authority, and probably originated in the similitude between Hiberia and Hibernia. — *Lanigan*, vol. i. p. 3.

said to be of Irish birth. some have inferred that the celebrated heretic Pelagius was of Irish birth; others suppose that Jerome alluded not to Pelagius, but to Cælestius, the follower of Pelagius. He names neither, and the words are certainly very obscure.[1] 'The devil,' he says, 'although silent himself, barks through a huge and corpulent Alpine dog, who can do more mischief with his claws than with his teeth: for[2] he is by descent of the Scotic nation, the next country to the British; and like another Cerberus, according to the fables of the poets, must be struck down with a spiritual club, that he may be silenced for ever with his master Pluto.'[3]

The corpulent Scot censured by St. Jerome. In another place St. Jerome speaks also of a Scot, or at least of one in some way connected with the Scots, a man corpulent in his person, and so far apparently to be identified with the 'Alpine dog' of the foregoing passage. This man, who is not named, is described as having written against Jerome's Commentary on the Epistle to the Ephesians, in the spirit of an

---

[1] *Obscure.* Hieron. *Comm. in Jerem.*, lib. iii., *Præf.* 'Ipseque mutus latrat per Albinum [*al.* Alpinum] canem, grandem et corpulentum, et qui calcibus magis possit sævire, quam dentibus. Habet enim progeniem Scoticæ gentis, de Britannorum vicinia: qui juxta fabulas poetarum, instar Cerberi, spirituali percutiendus est clava, ut æterno cum suo magistro Plutone silentio conticescat.' It seems plain, from the context, that *Ipse*, in the beginning of this sentence, must refer to *diabolus*, not to Pelagius. The word Albinum, or Alpinum, is obscure. The former reading is preferred by Vallarsius, and understood by him as alluding to Albion or Alba, the modern Scotland. But the name of Scotia, in S. Jerome's time, was applied exclusively to Ireland.

[2] *For.* The vis consequentiæ here is not very apparent. *Enim* is, perhaps, to be referred to Albinum or Alpinum.

[3] *Pluto.* Ussher reasons that St. Jerome here distinguishes between Cerberus and Pluto: meaning by the latter Pelagius, who remained in retirement himself, whilst he propagated his opinions by means of Cerberus, i.e. Cælestius his barking disciple.—*Britt. Eccl. Antiq.*, c. 8 (Works, v. p. 255). But all this is weak, and hangs on the assumption that 'Ipse mutus latrat' signifies Pelagius.

INTROD.] *spoken of as a Scot by St. Jerome.* 191

'unlearned calumniator,' as did also his 'præcursor Grunnius,' by which nickname Ruffinus[1] is supposed to be intended. It is stated also that the same 'calumniator' had objected to the books against Jovinian, that in them virginity was preferred to marriage, marriage to digamy, digamy to polygamy.[2] To this latter objection Jerome replies: 'But this most stupid fellow, overloaded with the porridge of the Scots, does not recollect that in that very work we had said, I condemn not digamists, nor yet trigamists, nay, not even octogamists, if that could be,'[3] &c. The Scotic calumniator therefore must have been either Pelagius or Cælestius: probably the former, from the allusion to his great stature.[4]

---

[1] *Ruffinus.* This is probable, because Ruffinus had formerly made the same objection to the Comm. on Ephes., that in it Jerome had transcribed passages from Origen (see *Ultima responsio,* commonly cited as lib. iii. *contra Ruffinum,* cap. 11): and also because Jerome goes on to say, that he had answered this Grunnius in two books (evidently alluding to the two books *contra Ruffinum*), in which he had refuted not only what Grunnius had alleged, but also what had since been advanced by the present calumniator. 'Quod non videns præcursor ejus Grunnius, olim nisus est carpere. Cui duobus responsi libris, ubi quæ iste quasi sua profert, et alio jam calumniante, purgata sunt.'—*Comm. in Jerem. Prolog.*

[2] *Polygamy.* The reader will recollect that by digamy and polygamy are here meant, not the marriage with two or more wives all living; but a marriage with a second or third wife after the death of the former.

[3] *Could be.* 'Ut nuper indoctus calumniator erupit, qui Commentarios meos in epistolam Pauli ad Ephesios reprehendendos putat,' &c. . . . 'Nec recordatur stolidissimus et Scotorum pultibus prægravatus, nos in ipso dixisse opere: Non damno digamos, immo nec trigamos, et si fieri possit, octogamos,' &c.

[4] *Stature.* In another place also, Jerome alludes to the great stature of Pelagius, saying that he had the shoulders of Milo. 'Tu ipse qui Catoniana nobis inflaris superbia, et Milonis humeris intumescis,' &c.— *Dial. contra Pelagianos* i. n. 28. So also Paulus Orosius calls Pelagius *a Goliath*: 'Stat etiam immanissimus superbia Goliat, carnali potentia tumidus, omnia per se posse confidens.' — *Liber Apologet. contra Pelag.* (Bibl. PP. Lugdun. vi. p. 449, c.). And again, addressing Pelagius: 'Sed tibi specialis inde portandi operis fortasse fiducia est, quod balneis epulisque nutritus, latos humeros gestas robustamque cervicem: præferens etiam in fronte pinguedinem,' &c.—*Ibid.,* p. 457, c.

St. Augustine has called Cælestius a man of acute genius[1], and always speaks of Pelagius as one whom he greatly loved, a man of holy and most Christian life[2], it may seem extraordinary therefore that St. Jerome should have intended to speak of either of them in such terms as he has employed. But these are not the only passages in his works from which it appears that St. Jerome occasionally suffered himself to be carried away by the heat of controversy.

Learned men, however, have generally supposed that Cælestius, not Pelagius, was the opponent to whom St. Jerome applies the opprobrious terms of 'Alpine dog,' 'fattened on Scotic porridge;' &c. And their reason is this:—Pelagius, as we learn from St. Augustine[3], and others, was called 'the Briton,' to distinguish him from Pelagius of Tarentum, and therefore, it is inferred, was of Welsh[4] descent, and not a Scot or Irishman.

---

[1] *Acute genius.* 'Homine acerrimi ingenii.'—*Contra duas Epistolas Pelagianorum*, lib. ii. n. 5.

[2] *Life.* 'Egregie Christianus.' —*De Peccator. meritis et remiss.* iii. n. 6.

[3] *Augustine.* 'Pelagium, quem credimus, ut ab illo distingueretur qui Pelagius Tarenti dicitur, Britonem cognominatum, quod ut servum Dei dilexeris, novimus.'—*Epist.* 186 (Paulino episcopo), tom. ii. 663, ed. Bened.

[4] *Welsh.* This is, in fact, the whole ground of the opinion so generally received, that Cælestius was an Irishman. Ussher and others appear to have reasoned thus: St. Jerome must be understood to speak either of Pelagius or Cælestius: he cannot mean Pelagius, because Pelagius was a Briton. Therefore, he must mean Cælestius. Therefore, Cælestius was a Scot, i. e. an Irishman. It seemed also some confirmation of this, that the Irish name Cellach, although generally Latinized *Celsus*, is sometimes made *Cælestius*; not with any reference to its signification, but simply as a remote imitation of the sound. It is remarkable that Ware and Harris, although they could not have been ignorant of Ussher's opinion, have omitted Cælestius, as well as Pelagius, in their list of Irish writers. Gennadius, who flourished at the close of the fifth century, in his book, *De viris illustr.*, c. 44, tells us that Cælestius, when a youth in his

INTROD.] *as a Theologian in St. Jerome's Time.* 193

Possibly, however, in that age the name of Briton in popular use may have included the Scots.

Be this however as it may, for the object of this work prohibits our enlarging upon such questions, it must suffice to observe that St. Jerome, in the foregoing extracts, manifestly speaks of a Scot, or Irishman, who was a professor of Christianity, and engaged in the controversies of that day. This is unquestionable evidence that there was at least one Irishman, on the continent of Europe, at that early period, who was a Christian. It does not necessarily follow that he had received the faith in his native country, neither does it affect our argument whether we identify him with Cælestius, Pelagius, or anybody else, whose name is known in history. *An Irishman, whether Pelagius or some other, distinguished as a theologian in St. Jerome's time.*

80. St. Beatus, Biat, or Bie, apostle of Switzerland, first bishop of Lausanne, is said to have been a Scot, but on scarcely any evidence except that he was the companion of St. Mansuetus, or *SS. Beatus and Mansuetus said to be Irish.*

---

monastery, and before he had adopted the Pelagian errors, had written some excellent letters to his parents. It is not said that the parents were in Ireland, or that Cælestius was an Irishman, much less that his monastery was in Ireland. Nevertheless, Dr. O'Conor infers, from this mention of the monastery, that the monastic institute existed, *in Ireland,* a whole century before St. Patrick: (*Rer. Hibern. Scriptt.* I. Proleg. i., p. lxxviii.). Ussher concludes that the parents of Cælestius must have been Christians (as if he could not have written to his parents, even though they had been Pagans), *Primord.,* c. xvi.

(Works vi. p. 340); and Dr. Petrie argues, that if he wrote letters to his parents, the parents must have been able to read them, and, therefore, there was a knowledge of letters *in Ireland* before the age of St. Patrick (Essay on Tara, Trans. R. Irish Acad. xviii. p. 47). But none of these inferences follow from the premises, even though we admit that the parents of Cælestius were in Ireland, except the last; and that is valid only on the assumption—which, as we have seen, is more than doubtful—that Cælestius was of Irish birth, and his parents resident in Ireland.

O

Mansuy, first bishop of Toul in Lorraine. They have been both set down as disciples of St. Peter; and if so, must have flourished in the Apostolic age. Mansuetus is expressly said to have been an Irishman, by his poetical biographer Adso[1]:—

'Insula Christicolas gestabat Hibernia gentes,
Unde genus traxit, et satus inde fuit.'

'Hibernia's soil was rich in Christian grace;
There Mansuy saw the light, there lived his noble race.'

But it is impossible to suppose Ireland to have been full of Christians in the first century, and therefore we must conclude that Adso, who died A.D. 994, attributed to the Ireland of the Apostolic age what was true of it in his own. Calmet[2], in his 'Dissertation on the Bishops of Toul,' seems to have proved, that St. Mansuy was sent from Rome to Toul about the middle of the fourth century. If he was sent from Rome, this may explain[3] the mistake that he was a disciple of St. Peter, for it was a common idiom to say 'sent from St. Peter,' to signify 'sent from Rome.' But however this may be, St. Mansuetus, which may possibly be the translation of his Celtic name, was in all probability an Irishman, distinguished as an eminent

---

[1] *Adso.* Quoted by Ussher, *Primord.*, p. 750; Calmet, Hist. Eccl. et Civ. de Lorraine, tom. i., Preuves, p. 86. Mansuetus is said to be 'nobili Scotorum genere oriundus.'— *Actt. Tullensium Episcopor.*, ap. Martene et Durand. Thes. Nov. iii. p. 991.

[2] *Calmet.* Dissert. sur les Evesques de Toul., pref. to vol. i. of the Hist. Eccl. et Civ. de Lorraine, p. xxvii. sq.

[3] *Explain.* This remark has been made by Dr. Lanigan, *Eccl. Hist.* i. p. 5.

Christian missionary about a century before St. Patrick.

Eliphius, and his brother Eucharius, with their sisters, were also connected with Lorraine, and are said to have suffered martyrdom at or near Toul, under Julian the Apostate. But we cannot place much reliance on the statement that they were the children of a king of Scotia.[1] Their names are not Irish. Rupertus Tuitiensis, who flourished in the beginning of the twelfth century, in his Life of Eliphius[2], gives us to understand that they were natives of Toul, and seems to have been wholly ignorant of the story of their Irish descent. Calmet[3] makes no allusion to it. *Eliphius and Eucharius not Irish.*

Cathaldus of Tarentum, however, has undoubted claims to be considered an Irishman. His biographers, and the traditions of the Church of Tarentum, all agree in the assertion that he was born in Ireland; and his name is evidently Irish. The antient MS. of his Life[4], preserved in the archives of the Church of Tarentum, tells us that he was born just before the death of the emperor Trajan, and Baronius[5], in his notes to the Roman Martyrology, dates him accordingly A.D. 166 circiter. The truth, however, slips out in the Life[6] just referred to, where we read that Cathaldus, before he left Ireland, was a public teacher *Cathaldus of Tarentum an Irishman.*

---

[1] *Scotia.* The only authority for this is Peter Merss, or Merssæus, who says, 'Eliphius filius regis Scotiæ.'—Quoted by Ussher, *Primord.*, p. 784.

[2] *Eliphius.* Ap. Surium, 16 Oct., tom. v. p. 884.

[3] *Calmet.* Ubi supr. *Liv.* v., where he treats fully of St. Eliphius. —Lanigan i. pp. 6-8.

[4] *Life.* Published by Colgan, *Actt. SS. Hibern.* p. 545.

[5] *Baronius.* Mart. Rom. ad 10 Maii.

[6] *The Life* : cap. 4 (Colgan, *loc. cit.*, p. 546).

in the school of Lismore. But the school of Lismore did not exist in the second century. Its foundation by St. Mochuda, otherwise Carthag, is variously dated by the Irish annalists, between the years[1] 630 and 636. It is certain therefore, if Cathald was a scholar or a teacher at Lismore, that he could not have left Ireland much before the middle of the seventh century. He belonged therefore to the second order of Irish Saints, who were wont, as we have seen[2], to devote themselves to missionary work abroad. At all events we cannot refer to him with any certainty, as an instance of a Christian Irishman, before the times of St. Patrick.

The poet Sedulius claimed as an Irishman. The Christian poet Sedulius has also been claimed as an Irishman. He flourished in Italy, it is said, about the end of the fourth and beginning of the fifth century.[3] His works were collected by Turcius Rufus Asterius, who was consul in 494; from which circumstance, Ussher, Ware, and others conclude that he must have lived to about that year. Be this as it may, it cannot be said that this Sedulius owed his Christianity to the preaching of St. Patrick. There can be no doubt that Trithemius and other authors believed him to have been a native of Ireland; and his name, in its Irish

---

[1] *Years.* Ussher, *Ind. Chron.* A.D. 630: Four Mast. 631: Ann. Clonmacnois, 632: Ann. Ult. 635: Tigh. 636. See Colgan, *ubi supr.* p. 560, who refutes unanswerably the early date attributed to S. Cathald. Conf. Ware, *Opusc. S. Patricii*, p. 105.

[2] *Seen.* Vid. supra, p. 114. sq.

[3] *Century.* Cave gives his *floruit* 434: Ware (*Winters of Ireland*, ed. Harris, p. 7), 490: Ussher, *Primord.*, p. 777, and *Ind. Chron.*, circ. 494. Colgan supposes him to have been distinguished as a writer before 395, and to have died shortly before 450. *Actt. SS.*, p. 324.

form *Siudhul,* or *Siadhal,* is of common occurrence.[1]

From the foregoing examples, without entering into any discussion of some other alleged instances, which are, to say the least, doubtful, it is evident that there were Irish Christians on the continent of Europe before the mission of St. Patrick, some of whom had attained to considerable literary and ecclesiastical eminence.

Irish Christians on the continent of Europe before St. Patrick.

It does not follow, as we have already observed, that these Irishmen had received the faith of the Gospel in their native land before they had emigrated to the continent; but there is nevertheless evidence sufficient to show that there were Christians[2], isolated indeed, and not formed into canonically disciplined Churches, but still Christians, and even perhaps Christian ecclesiastics, in Ireland, before the coming of St. Patrick.

---

[1] *Occurrence.* It has been doubted whether Sedulius the poet is the same as the 'Sedulius Scotus Hiberniensis' who wrote the commentary on St. Paul's epistles. Some have maintained that Sedulius the commentator did not live until the beginning of the ninth century, and consequently cannot be Sedulius the poet, who certainly flourished in the fifth. But if both were natives of Ireland, this will not affect our argument.

[2] *Christians.* A very curious document, entitled 'Senchas na relec,' or History of Cemeteries, first published by Dr. Petrie, from a MS. in the Library of the Royal Irish Academy, collated with another copy in Trinity Coll. Dublin, claims for Cormac mac Airt, surnamed Ulfada, King of Ireland, A.D. 254, the honour of having renounced idolatry, and states that he was one of three remarkable individuals who had attained to the knowledge of the one true God, in Ireland, before St. Patrick. The following is a translation of the passage alluded to. After speaking of the good government of the country under Cormac, the writer adds—'for Cormac had the faith of the one true God, according to the law' [i. e. apparently the Mosaic law]; 'for he said that he would not adore stones or trees, but that he would adore Him who had made them, and who had power over all the elements: namely, the one powerful God who created the elements: in Him he would believe. And he was the third person in Erinn, who believed, before the coming of

The story of the four Munster bishops and other ecclesiastics, before St. Patrick, apocryphal.

81. The statement that there were four Munster bishops together with several priests and Christian ascetics in Ireland, before St. Patrick, cannot be received with any degree of credit, although it has been adopted by Colgan[1] and countenanced by Ussher.[2] Nevertheless the story, for several reasons, must be noticed here. It has no better authority than the legendary lives of the very Saints who are said to have been the predecessors of St. Patrick, and is not supported, but rather refuted, by the Irish Martyrologies and Annals. 'We have it,' says Colgan, 'from the most antient acts of our Saints, written about a thousand years ago and upwards, that there were in various parts of Ireland not only very many believers in Christ, but also many distinguished for sanctity: as Kieran, Ailbe, Declan, and Ibar, bishops; and also before them, St. Colman, bishop; St. Dima, the teacher of St. Declan; St. Corbre, bishop; St. Mochelloc, St. Bean, St.

Patrick. Conchobhar mac Nessa' [King of Ulster, who died A.D. 48], 'to whom Altus had told concerning the crucifixion of Christ, *was the first*; Morann (surnamed Mac Main), son of Caìrpre Cinn-Cait, was the second person; Cormac was the third; and it is probable that others followed in the same belief.' —*Round Towers* (Trans. R. Irish Acad., vol. xx. p. 100). The 'Altus' here mentioned seems to have been the same who is elsewhere called Conall Cearnach. He was an Irish warrior, who happened to be at Jerusalem at the crucifixion of Christ, and returned to his own country full of indignation at the conduct of the Jews.—See O'Flaherty, *Ogyg.*, p. 283 *sq.* Caìrpre Cinn-Cait (the cat-headed) was the plebeian King of Ireland, A.D. 90, set up after the murder of the nobles by the insurgent peasantry. His son Morann (whose mother's name was Main) became afterwards chief brehon or judge of Ireland, and was celebrated for his legal skill and justice.—*Ogyg.*, p. 300. But these legends cannot be seriously quoted as historical, and they do not appear to ascribe a knowledge of Christianity, properly so called, to the individuals mentioned, but only a renuntiation of idolatry.

[1] Colgan. *Quinta append. ad Acta S. Patr.*, c. 15; *Triad. Thaum.*, p. 250.
[2] Ussher. *Primord.*, c. 16, p. 781, (Works, vi. p. 332).

INTROD.] *in Munster before St. Patrick.* 199

Colman, St. Lactin, St. Mobi, St. Findlug, St. Cuminian, hermits, who flourished in Ireland before St. Patrick and St. Palladius.'

There is no sufficient evidence, however, that the lives here alluded to by Colgan can be older, in their present form, than the end of the eleventh or beginning of the twelfth century[1], But certainly they were compiled from authentic documents, as appears from the knowledge they display of the genealogy, family history, and topography of the country; we are therefore bound to examine the claims of the four bishops who are said in these biographies to have laboured in Ireland before St. Patrick.

82. St. Ciaran, or Kieran[2], as his name is generally written, is called by the author of his Life, 'the first born of the saints of Ireland.' His father was descended from the chieftains of Ossory; his mother was of the race of the Corcalaidhe, of which district he was himself a native, having been born in Cliar island, now Cape Clear island, barony of West Carberry, County of Cork. His principal Church, however, was Saighir, now Seirkieran, a parish in the barony of Ballybritt, King's County. The word *Saighir* is said to

St. Kieran of Saigher.

---

[1] *Twelfth century.* This is also the opinion of the Bollandist Papebrock: 'Verum quod bonâ Colgani veniâ dictum sit : non sunt tam antiqua illa acta quam credi vult ipse, sed ab auctoribus fabulosissimis consarcinata pleraque, nec ulla seculo xii. priora.' — *App. ad Vit. S. Patr.*, § 1, n. 3 (17 Mart., p. 581, c).

[2] *Kieran.* In Irish, as already re-marked, the C is always pronounced hard, as K, even before the vowels e and i : and it is now generally admitted that this was also its antient pronunciation in Latin.

[3] *First born.* 'Hiberniæ sanctorum primogenitus.'—*Vit. S. Kierani*, c. 1 ; Colgan, *Actt. SS.*, p. 458.

have been the name of a well or fountain¹, probably venerated in Pagan times; and a prophecy attributed to St. Patrick is cited as having directed St. Ciaran to the place. This prophecy is the foundation of the chronology which assigns the early date to Ciaran's birth. He was thirty years of age, we are told, before he had heard of the Christian religion; he then went to Rome, where he spent twenty years in ecclesiastical studies: having been ordained a bishop, he was returning to Ireland, when he met St. Patrick, who uttered this *rann*², or prophetical quatrain : —

> 'Saighir the cold! Saighir the cold³!
> Raise a city on its brink.
> At the end of thirty fair years
> We shall meet there, I and thou.'

Patrick was then on his way to Rome, and had not as yet been consecrated a bishop. If, therefore, we suppose the predicted meeting at Saighir to have occurred immediately, or soon after St. Patrick's arrival in Ireland, A.D. 432, Ciaran must have left Rome for his native country thirty years before; and being then, as we have seen, fifty years of age, must have been

---

¹ *Fountain.* It is glossed 'nomen fontis,' in the antient Scholia on the Calendar of Aengus, at March 5th: and see Ussher, Works vi. p. 345.

² *Rann.* This prophecy is given in the Genealogies of Corcalaidhe, published from the Books of Lecan and Ballimote, by Dr. O'Donovan, *Miscell. Celtic Society*, p. 20. It occurs also in the Scholia on Aengus (5 March), translated by Colgan, *Actt. SS.*, p. 471.

³ *The cold.* The Irish word signifying *cold* is *fuair*, which the author of the Life of St. Ciaran, published by Colgan from the Kilkenny MS., evidently took for the name of the fountain: 'adi fontem ... qui vocatur *Fuaran*,' c. 5; Colgan, *ib.* p. 458.

born about 352, or thereabouts.¹ Thus Ciaran was thirty years a bishop in Ireland before St. Patrick, during which time he converted the chieftains of his mother's family, the Corcalaidhe, who are therefore spoken of as the first who 'believed in the Cross,'² and the first who granted a site for the foundation of a Christian place of worship in Ireland. This was Cill-Chiarain, St. Kieran's Church, on Cape Clear island, the ruins of which are still visible, together with a cross, sculptured on an antient pillar stone, near the strand called Srath-Chiarain, or Kieran's Strand, on the island. Cill-Chiarain, therefore, according to this story, was the first Christian church erected in Ireland.

Kieran thirty years a bishop in Ireland before St. Patrick.

He afterwards established a church or monastery at Saighir, on the confines of the boundary between the northern and southern divisions of Ireland, but on the Munster side. He began by occupying a cell, where he lived, we are told, as a hermit, in the midst of a dense wood, and tamed some of the wild animals of the forest for his amusement; but his fame drew disciples: a monastery followed, and then a city³, to which the name of *Saighir* (pronounced *Seir*) was given, from the name of the antient well; and it afterwards became *Seir-kieran*, from the name of the saint.

Foundation of Seir-kieran.

But the early date attributed to St. Ciaran is

The early date attri

---

¹ *Thereabouts.* This is the argument of Ussher, *Primord.*, p. 788 (Works vi. 342 sq.), adopted by Colgan, *loc. cit.*, p. 466.
² *Cross.* See Genealogies of Corcalaidhe, by Dr. O'Donovan (*Celtic Society's Miscell.*), p. 23.
³ *City.* Vit. S. Kierani, c. 6. Colgan, *ib.*

buted to St. Kieran untenable.

inconsistent with several particulars related of him in the very Lives which assert that early date. He was a contemporary[1] of the second St. Ciaran of Clonmac-nois, of St. Brendan of Birr, of St. Brendan of Clonfert, and of St. Ruadan of Lodhra. Nay, he was the disciple of St. Finnian of Clonard, and was accounted one of the twelve apostles of Ireland who were sent forth from that school.[2]

All these celebrated ecclesiastics belonged to the second order of saints, and died in the middle or latter half of the sixth century.[3] It is impossible, therefore, that Ciaran could have been born in 352, if he was the disciple of St. Finnian, who died just two hundred years afterwards. We are told, indeed, by the author of his Life, that he was far advanced in years[4], and a bishop, when he became the disciple of Finnian; and other difficulties are obviated by the assumption that he lived to be three hundred years[5] old. No doubt we must have recourse to some such hypothesis[6], if we believe him to have been a

---

[1] *Contemporary.* Ib. capp. 33, 36.

[2] *School.* Ib. c. 34; Vit. S. Finniani, c. 19; Colgan, *Actt. SS.*, p. 395, and note 24, p. 398. See above p. 99.

[3] *Sixth Century.* Ciaran of Clonmacnois died A.D. 549; Brendan of Birr, A.D. 565 or 571; Brendan of Clonfert, 577; and Finnian of Clonard, 552. The date of S. Ruadan's death is not entered in the Irish Annals; but it must have been after 656, when he cursed Tara.— Petrie *on Tara Hill*, p. 125.

[4] *In years.* ' Cum enim ipse erat senex sapiens et benedictus Pontifex, dignatus est discere sub genu alterius, propter humilitatem suam et amorem sapientiæ.'—*Vit.* c. 34. Colgan, *ib.* p. 463.

[5] *Three hundred Years.* The Mart. of Donegal, p. 65, says 360 years.

[6] *Hypothesis.* Colgan endeavours to reduce this great age, by showing that we need not suppose Ciaran to have lived beyond the year 540, when the School of Clonard was founded. This brings his age down to 192. It may as well be mentioned, that the genealogy of his father Luaigre is preserved in nine descents from his ancestor Aengus

INTROD.] *History of St. Ailbe of Emly.* 203

disciple of St. Finnian in 540, and a bishop in 402. But whether this hypothesis removes all difficulty, is another question. The whole story of his studying at Rome, and his meeting with St. Patrick there, is as apocryphal as the prophecy of the thirty years, on which the chronology of the legend rests.

83. St. Ailbe was the son of Olcu, son of Nais[1], a descendant of Rudraighe, or Rory, King of Ireland. He was born, as the author[2] of his Life tells us, in the territory of Eliach, now called Ely O'Carroll[3], including the baronies of Clonlisk and Ballybritt, in the King's County, in which latter district St. Ciaran erected his monastery and town of Saighir. Ailbe was the illegitimate son of a female slave, whose master, a chieftain of the country, ordered the child to be exposed, and he was left under a rock in the fields. There a man named Lochan, son of Luidir, found the infant, and placed him under the care of some Britons[4] who had settled in the

St. Ailbe of Emly.

of Ossory, who was expelled from his lands, by the Desii, in the reign of Cormac Ulfada (A.D. 254-277). Colgan, *Actt. SS.*, p. 472, cap. 3. If this be so, St Ciaran's father could not have been born much before A.D. 500.

[1] *Nais.* Hence the mistake made in some MSS. of his Life, where his father is called *Olcnais*, instead of Olcu mac Nais, combining the two names.—*Ussher*, Works vi. p. 333. The territory of Ara, including Ara cliach, in the west of the Co. Limerick, and the barony of Ara or Duhara, in the N.W. of the Co. Tipperary, were inhabited by the descendants of Fertlacht, son of

Fergus (King of Ulster in the first century), and grandson of Rudraighe, King of Ireland, A.M. 3845.—See O'Flaherty, *Ogyg.*, p. 274.

[2] *Author.* 'Ex orientali parte regionis Eliach, quæ est in Mumenia [read Mumonia] ortus est.' Quoted by Ussher, *ubi supra*.

[3] *Ely O'Carroll.* See Dr. O'Donovan's notes, p. lxxxiv. (759) and (760) to *Topographical Poems* (Irish Archæol. and Celtic Society), 1862. and *Book of Rights* (Celtic Society), 1847, p. 78, note i.

[4] *Britons.* Could it have been from them that the district was called *Ballybritt*?

country. The Britons gave him the name of Ailbe, because, says our author, he was found *alive*[1] under the rock. After a few years, a Christian priest visited the place. It is possible that the British colony may have had some Christians among them; but the biographer of our saint tells us that this priest had been specially sent[2] into Ireland by the Apostolic see, *many years* before St. Patrick. By this missionary the boy was baptized and instructed; and the next thing we hear of him is, that St. Declan[3], his future friend and fellow-labourer, met him at Rome, where he remained 'many years' under the instruction of Hilary, the bishop. The Bollandists[4] Papebrock and Stilting are of opinion that this was Pope Hilary himself, who presided over the see of Rome from 461 to 467. But the author of St. Ailbe's Life, as Ussher remarks, evidently did not think so; for he represents the bishop Hilary as sending his pupil Ailbe to the Pope[5], and recommending his

---

[1] *Alive.* Ail, is a rock, and beo, living. This etymology is very doubtful.

[2] *Sent.* 'Missus a sede apostolica ad Hiberniam insulam, multis annis ante Patricium, ut fidem Christi ibi seminaret.'—Ussher, *ib.*

[3] *Declan.* Ussher, vi. pp. 342, 343.

[4] *Bollandists.* Papebrock, in *append.*, c. I., *ad Actt. S. Patricii* (*Acta SS.*, tom. ii. Martii, p. 581). Stilting, *De vita S. Albei*, § 2 (*Actt. SS.*, tom. iv. September, p. 28). The same authors suggest that what is said of St. Patrick, in the Acts of St. Ailbe, may refer not to the great Patrick, but to Sen Patrick, his successor in the see of Armagh. But they forgot that Sen Patrick was not properly successor, in the modern sense of the word, for he died before the great St. Patrick. They also suggest that the priest who had baptized St. Ailbe, having been *sent from Rome*, can be no other than Palladius. This requires that we should expunge the '*many years* before Patrick,' spoken of by the biographer. But we may as well also expunge the 'sent from Rome,' which is quite as apocryphal, and is the only reason for supposing that Palladius was intended. Moreover, Palladius was a bishop.

[5] *Pope.* 'Misit illum ad Domi

elevation to the episcopacy. Whatever this biographer's opinion on the subject may be worth, he clearly regarded Hilary and the Pope as two distinct persons. St. Ailbe, if he ever was at Rome, could not have been there in the days of Pope Hilary.

Fifty Irishmen, we are told, who were of course Christians, had followed Ailbe to Rome. The Pope placed them by themselves in a cell, 'dedit eis Papa cellam seorsum,' and made St. Ailbe their president. After remaining at Rome for a year and fifty days, Ailbe set out for Ireland with his fifty companions, amongst whom were twelve of the name of Colman, twelve called Coemgen, or Kevin, twelve Fintans, together with St. Declan and others. *His fifty Irish companions.*

Before settling in Ireland, St. Ailbe preached the Gospel in the apostolic way, 'apostolico more,' to the Gentiles — what Gentiles we are not told. However, a great multitude of them believed, and were baptized. He built a monastery in their country, and left there certain sons of Goll, 'filios Goill,'[1] which may perhaps signify Galli, or Gauls. *His continental missionary labours.*

---

num Papam ut ab eo ordinaretur episcopus.'—Ussher, *ubi supra*.

[1] *Filios Goill.* Ussher, *ubi supra*, p. 346. The Bollandist Papebrock (*Append. ad Vit. S. Patricii*, 17 Mart. p. 581, F.) cites a passage from the Life of St. Ailbe, which, however, he does not give in full: 'A Roma perrexit in fines gentium, et magna pars gentilium credidit . . . deinde venit in civitatem Dolomoir cum episcopus illius civitatis Sampson nomine, corpus Christi offerret,' &c. This must have been Dole [*Dole mór*, the great Dole], in Brittany, of which the Welsh saint, Sampson, son of Caw, was bishop in the sixth century (Rees, *Welsh Saints*, p. 228). It is probable, therefore, that the 'gentiles' spoken of were in Gaul or Brittany. It follows, if this be true, that St. Ailbe's return from Rome cannot be dated much before 524.

He then set sail to Ireland in a very bad ship, 'in navi vilissima,' and reached a port in the northern part of the country, where one of his Colmans built a cell or church, which was called *Cill-ruadh*[1], the red church. The author adds that this was in Dal-aradia (Co. of Down), and that St. Ailbe was a native of the district. But this is evidently a mistake[2], and contradicts what this same biographer had said before, that he was born in Munster. Ailbe then made a circuit of all Ireland, preaching baptism. He converted many, but not all; for God had reserved for St. Patrick the privilege of converting all the Irish to the faith.

St. Ailbe flourished in the sixth century.

Such is the story. But it is not possible to reconcile its chronology with the statement of the Irish authentic annals[3], that St. Ailbe died in 527, or according to another date, 541. If he had been a bishop so long before the mission of St. Patrick, A.D. 432, as to have converted foreign Gentiles, and made a missionary circuit of Ireland, he must have lived to a very advanced age.

St. Declan of Ardmore a contemporary of St. Ailbe.

84. It will be seen from this narrative, that Ailbe and Declan were regarded as contemporaries. They were students in Rome together, and re-

---

[1] *Cill-ruadh.* See Reeves, *Eccl. Antiq. of Down, Connor,* &c., p. 245.

[2] *Mistake.* The cause of the error is obvious. The people of the country of which Ailbe was a native are called ' populus Aradensium, hoc est, illius terræ quæ Ara dicitur,' meaning the barony of Ara or Duharra, in the Co. of Tipperary. The biographer confounded this with Dal-aradia, in the Co. of Down.

—Bolland., *Actt. SS.* ad. 12 Sept., p. 27, F.

[3] *Annals.* The Four Masters give the death of St. Ailbe at 541. In the Annals of Tighernach, and Ulster, and also in the Bodleian Annals of Inisfallen, the ' Pausatio' of St. Ailbe is dated 526 (=527); but the Annals of Ulster give a second date, A.D. 541.

turned to Ireland together in the same company.
Therefore whatever reduction we are compelled
to make in the early age assigned to St. Ailbe,
must also apply to the history of Declan.

Declan was of the tribe of the Desi, or Desii,
descended from Fiacha Suidhe, son of Fedlimidh
Rechtmar (or the Lawgiver), who was King[1] of
Ireland from A.D. 164 to 174. The three sons
of Fiacha Suidhe had been banished from their
original territory, the barony of Deece, County
of Meath, and took possession of the districts in
the County of Waterford, still called Decies, after
the name[2] of their clan. This was about the
year 270.

St. Declan was born in the country of the
Munster Desi[3], of which his father Erc is said
to have been a chieftain. His genealogy, as
given in the Latin Life, makes Erc fifteenth in
descent[4] from Fedlimidh Rechtmar, who died
A.D. 174. This would bring the birth of Declan

Genealogy of St. Declan.

---

[1] *King.* See O'Flaherty, *Ogygia*, p. 306, who translates his name *Fedlimius Legifer.*

[2] *Name.* See O'Donovan, *Book of Rights*, p. 49, note, and p. 184. Also O'Flaherty, *Ogygia*, p. 339. The romantic story of the causes which led to their expulsion from Meath is told by Keating, Reign of Cormac mac Art.

[3] *Desi.* His father is called 'Dux Nandesi,' in the Latin Life of Declan.—Ussher, *Primord.*, p. 782. But *na* is the Irish definite article, and *nandesi* signifies 'the Desi' or Desii.

[4] *Descent.* Vit. S. Declani, cap. i. *Actt. SS.*, Bolland. tom. v. Julii, p. 594). The copyists have made sad havoc of the Irish names, and it is probable that the genealogy has thus been made too long. For example, Lugadh Niadh is split into two, and made Luaghiudh, son of Niut; but the genealogy given in the Irish authorities is evidently as much too short as this is too long: giving only seven or eight descents (see Colgan, *Actt. SS.*, p. 73, col. 2). The Mart. of Donegal is in error in tracing Declan to Eochadh Finn, son of Fedlimidh Rechtmar, instead of to Fiacha Suidhe; for if that were true he would not be of the Desi, to which tribe his whole history shows him to have belonged. The recurrence of the same names in these genealogies is the cause of the confusion.

208 Declan lived in the seventh Century. [INTROD.

to near the middle of the seventh century, which is probably too late.

Baptized by St. Colman of Cloyne. His parents were converted to Christianity in their own country by a certain presbyter named Colman, who afterwards became a bishop. The child was baptized by Colman, who gave him the name of Declan.

It is clear that the Colman here intended must have been the celebrated Munster saint, Colman, son of Lenin, founder of the Church of Cloyne, who died A.D. 600[1]; for otherwise he could scarcely have been named without any patronymic or other title to distinguish him from the great number of Colmans who flourished in that age.

Educated by Dimma. When seven years old, the boy Declan was sent to a holy man who had just returned from abroad to Ireland, which was his native country. This man's name was Dimma, or Dima; he had established himself in a cell in the neighbourhood, and is described as a religious[2] and wise man, proved in the faith of Christ. Besides Declan, Dimma had another pupil named Carbre, son of Colum, who afterwards became a holy and venerable bishop.

This Dimma is believed[3] to have been the

---

[1] A.D. 600. This is the date given by the Four Masters. Ware, who is corrected by Harris, gives 4 Nov. 604, which ought to be 24 Nov. 600.—*Bishops*, p. 573.

[2] *Religious.* 'Qui fuit vir religiosus et sapiens, atque probatus in Christi fide.'—*Vit. Declani*, c. 2, n. 16.

[3] *Believed.* This opinion is supported by the high authority of Michael O'Clery, compiler of the Mart. of Donegal, who says (6 Jan. p. 7), 'I think this is the Dima Dubh, son of Aongus, &c. I think that he is the Dima to whom Declan was sent to be educated.' See also Reeves, *Eccl. Ant. of Down and Connor*, pp. 149, 240, who says that the Annals of Ulster erroneously call him *Dimmaingert*. The error, however, is Dr. O'Conor's. The true reading of the Ann. of Ulster

Dimma Dubh (Dimma the Black), who was afterwards Bishop of Connor, and died 658. He was of the great Munster family of the Dal Cais, and of the clan called Sil-mBlod, or seed of Blod, son of Cas, of the race of Oilioll Olum.[1] He was therefore very likely to have settled originally near the birthplace of St. Declan. But if he lived to 658 his pupil Declan could not possibly have been a bishop in 402.

After remaining some time under the instruction of Dimma, Declan, we are told, set out for Rome. There he met St. Ailbe, and was consecrated a bishop, receiving from the Pope a special commission to return to his own country, and evangelize the Irish people.

Declan consecrated a bishop.

Several Christians, amongst whom was 'the son of the king of the Romans, named Lunanus,'[2] followed him to Ireland, desiring to live with him in pilgrimage. Before quitting Italy, however, Declan met St. Patrick, then on his way to Rome, and of course before his consecration. A firm friendship was cemented between the two saints, and they separated with the kiss of peace. This meeting is dated by Ussher[3] 402; the same year in which Patrick met also St. Ciaran, and, according to the prophecy already noticed (for this date has no better foundation),

His meeting with St. Patrick.

---

is *Dimma niger*. Colgan has collected almost all that is known of him, *Actt. SS.*, 6 Jan.

[1] *Oilioll Olum.* Oilioll Olum was King of Munster, A.D. 237. O'Flaherty, *Ogyg.*, p. 327.

[2] *Lunanus.* Vit. Declan., cap. iii. Who this Lunanus was is not easy to guess.

[3] *Ussher.* Index Chron, in anno,

thirty years before the arrival of St. Patrick in his episcopal character in Ireland.

His cell with seven ascetics near Lismore.

St. Declan, on his return to his native country, devoted himself especially to the conversion of his own tribe, the Desii. He visited also the spot where he was himself born, a place called Maghscethi, near Lismore; and there he established 'a cell,' in which he placed seven men, whom he had been the means of converting to Christianity before he left Ireland: their names, which are all Irish, were Mochellog, Bean, Colman, Lachnin, or Lachtin, Mothey, or more correctly Mobhi, Finnluch, and Caimin. Although Colgan[1], adopting the date of 402, arbitrarily places these saints in the fifth century, there cannot be a doubt that they belong more properly to the middle or latter end of the sixth.[2] But to discuss this question would carry us too far from our immediate object.

His visit to St. David of Menevia.

Declan then made an attempt to convert the king of Cashel, Aengus, son of Natfriach, but was unsuccessful, and soon after paid another visit to Rome. On his return he visited St. David, in his city of Killmuine or Menevia, and remained there forty days, celebrating mass himself daily. At the end of that time, with the kiss of peace and benediction of the most holy bishop St. David, he sailed to Ireland. The year 540 is the most probable

---

[1] *Colgan. Actt. SS.*, ad 7 Mart., p. 511; *Triad. Thaum.*, p. 251.

[2] *Sixth.* See the reasons given by Lanigan, i. p. 27.

date[1] that can be assigned to St. David's consecration, and it seems almost certain that he was alive after the year 560. Colgan[2] says that he lived to 607 or 608. If this be so, and if Declan was a bishop in 402, he must have reached a very advanced age when he visited St. David at Menevia.

On his voyage to Ireland he was miraculously guided to a spot called Ard-na-gcaorach, 'the hill of the sheep,' *altitudo ovium*[3], but to which he afterwards gave the name of Ard-mòr, 'the great hill, or height,' which it still retains; and here he fixed his church and monastery.

His monastery of Ardmore.

Some time after Declan[4] had established himself in Ireland, St. Ailbe, who was then in his own city Imleach Iubhair[5], finding his death approaching, set out to visit his old friend. St. Declan hearing this went forth to meet him, to a place called Druim-luchra, from whence he conducted him with all honour to the monastery of Ardmòr. Ailbe remained there fourteen days, and then returned home to die. This must have been about the year 527, or, if we adopt the later date of St. Ailbe's death, 541; and even assuming this later date, it will be necessary to conclude

Declan survived St. Ailbe of Emly.

---

[1] *Date.* Lanigan i. p. 470; Rees, Welsh Saints, p. 201. In the *Annales Cambriæ*, his death is entered at the year 601. The Life of St. David, attributed to Giraldus Cambrensis, and published by Wharton in the Anglia Sacra, is full of anachronisms, and assumes the truth of the ante-Patrician bishops.

[2] *Colgan.* Actt. SS., p. 432, note 31, Giraldus Cambrensis says that St. David died on *Tuesday*, 1st of March (*Ussher, Prim.*, p. 526). This would indicate the years 600 or 606.

[3] *Altitudo ovium.* Vit. Decl., c. iv. n. 32.

[4] *Declan.* Ibid. c. viii. n. 68.

[5] *Imleach Iubhair.* 'The marsh of the yew tree,' now Emly.

that the visit to St. David in Wales must have taken place either in the very same year, or else soon after the meeting with St. Ailbe. At all events, it follows that Declan survived Ailbe some years, and probably lived to the beginning of the seventh century.

Legend of St. Ultan of Ardbraccan. There is a curious legend told in the Life of Declan which will fully confirm this later date. Ultan[1], we are told, was one of Declan's disciples. A fleet of gentiles appeared on the coast, with the intention of plundering the monastery. The inmates all ran to Declan for protection, who called to his disciple Ultan, and desired him to make the sign of the cross in the direction of the ships. Instantly they all sank like lead into the sea, and the sailors who attempted to swim to shore were turned into great rocks. But Ultan had made the sacred sign with his left hand, and not with his right: his right hand[2] having been at the time otherwise occupied; and hence came the saying used by the Irish when in peril, 'May Ultan's left hand be against it!'

This story is told of Ultan of Ardbraccan in the Scholia on the Metrical Calendar of Aengus the Culdee, which have already been frequently quoted; and an antient poem is there cited, in which it is said that if Ultan had used his right hand on the occasion, instead of his left, no

---

[1] *Ultan.* Vit. S. Declan., c. ix. n. 71.

[2] *Right hand.* 'Occupatus tunc dextra manu, signavit sinistra contra classem.'—*Vit. S. Decl.*, c. ix., n. 79. 'Et adhuc Scoti, videntes et audientes periclum, dicunt, Manus sinistra Ultani contra illud.'—*Ib.* n. 72.

foreign fleet would ever again have effected a landing in Ireland.

It is also stated in the same Scholia[1], and the story is alluded to in the text of Aengus, that St. Ultan took charitable care of the children whose mothers died of the 'yellow' or 'straw-coloured plague,'[2] which was so fatal a scourge in the British Islands about the middle of the seventh century. This gives us his date, and the Annals of Tighernach record his death at A.D. 657. We must therefore suppose Declan to have lived at a much later time than the Life assigns to him, or else St. Ultan must have died at a very advanced age. The latter alternative is adopted by Colgan, on the authority of the Four Masters[3], who assign to him the great age of 180.

St. Ultan was the bishop of the tribe called the Dal Conchubhair, or Connor, a branch of the Desi of Meath. He was therefore of the same clan or family as St. Declan, and it is highly probable

Date of St. Ultan.

Ultan of the same clan as St. Declan.

---

[1] *Scholia*: at 4 Sept. The original Irish of the scholium here alluded to, with a translation, has been printed in the Introd. to the *Book of Obits and Martyrol. of Christ Church*, p. lxxv. The first *yellow plague* in Ireland is dated 534, but it became particularly fatal in 548, and appears to have continued until about 560. There was a second outbreak of the same disease in 656, which continued for several years. See Mr. Wilde's valuable Report on the Tables of Deaths, part v. of *The Census of Ireland*, 1856; a document containing an amount of learning and historical information not commonly found in a *blue book*.

[2] *Plague*. The Life of Declan makes mention of a plague which had spread through Munster, but was particularly fatal at Cashel, in the time of Declan and of King Aongus, son of Natfriach. The dead bodies are described as 'cærulea et flava cadavera,' which seems to identify it with the *Buidhe Chonaill*, or flava ictericia of the sixth century. But Aongus was killed in 489, more than 50 years before the first pestilence. Here, then, is an anachronism which leads to the suspicion that Declan ought to be placed in the seventh century.

[3] *Four Masters*. At A.D. 656. The Annals of Ulster give two dates for his death, 656 and 662. The Calendar of Donegal (at Sept. 4) makes his age 189.

that he was in fact Declan's disciple.¹ It is also expressly stated that St. Declan had visited the district of Meath, which was the original seat of his tribe, and had there founded a monastery², where he left a remarkable copy of the Gospels, which was held in great honour, and believed to possess miraculous powers. Here in all probability he placed St. Ultan.

But it is not necessary to prolong this discussion. It must suffice to observe, that in the Scholia to the Calendar of Aengus³, Declan is expressly said to have been the pupil of St. Moling, who died in 696, according to the Four Masters, or more correctly 697. This is perhaps a mistake. But it shows that the author of the Scholia was not acquainted with the legend that Declan was a precursor of St. Patrick.

St. Ibar of Begery Island. His clan family.

85. It remains now to speak of St. Ibar. He was of the family of Ui Eachach Uladh, the antient inhabitants of the baronies called Iveagh⁴ in the county of Down. They were a tribe of the Oir-

---

¹ *Disciple.* Colgan, *Actt. SS.*, p. 608, maintains that this legend does not refer to St. Ultan of Ardbraccan, and he has assumed that the Ultan who was a disciple of St. Declan was not Ultan of Ardbraccan, but another Ultan, of whom we seem to know nothing, except that his name occurs as 'Ultan of Maghnidh,' in the Irish Calendars at the 14th March. *Cal. of Donegal*, p. 77. The Mart. of Tallaght (Brussells MS.) calls this latter personage 'Ultan h. Aignigh,' or grandson of Aignech. It is a purely arbitrary assumption, as indeed Colgan admits, to make the Ultan of 14 March St. Declan's disciple. The Scholiast on Aongus is surely a much higher authority.

² *Monastery.* Vit. Decl., c. vii. n. 5. The biographer calls this 'Monasterium canonicorum,' thus betraying his own late date.

³ *Aengus.* At 24 July. The Scholiast says: 'Declan, of Ardmore, was the pupil of Moling, and he is [buried] at Teach Moling [now St. Mullin's, Co. Carlow], or else at Lismore.'

⁴ *Iveagh.* This word is a corruption of the ablative form, Uibh Eachach. The name Ui Eochadh Uladh, signifies 'descendants of Eochad of Ulster.' See Reeves, *Eccl. Ant. of Down and Connor*, p. 384, *sq.*

ghialla, or Oriel, situated in the district of Tuath Eochadha, or Eochadh's territory, which was called by the English 'Toaghic' or 'the Toaghie,' and is included in the present barony of Armagh.[1]

The Life of St. Bridgid by Anmchad or Animosus, a composition attributed by Colgan to the latter half of the tenth century, speaks of St. Ibar[2] as ' a sower of the faith in many parts of Ireland, before the most blessed Patrick ;' and if Colgan's conjecture as to the age of the writer be correct, this is the oldest authority in which the fable of ante-Patrician bishops is alluded to. We must therefore be allowed to suspect, either that the passage is an interpolation, or that Animosus should be placed at least a century later than Colgan's date.

Jocelin[3] speaks expressly of Ibar as a disciple of Patrick, and even Colgan[4], notwithstanding the inconsistency, has inserted his name, with that of Ailbe, in the list of St. Patrick's disciples. But it is still more important to observe that the antient author, Tirechan, quoted by Ussher[5] from the book of Armagh, names Ibar as one of the bishops consecrated by St. Patrick ; and when

A disciple of St. Patrick.

---

[1] *Armagh.* See Dr. O'Donovan's note z, *Book of Rights*, p. 148.

[2] *St. Ibar.* 'Sanctus Hibarus episcopus, qui seminator fidei multis in locis in Hibernia fuit ante beatissimum Patricium.'—*Quarta Vit. S. Brig.*, lib. ii. c. 23; Colgan, *Tr. Th.*,p. 553. Ussher quotes these words from an anonymous Life of St. Bridget, *Primordia*, p. 794.

[3] *Jocelin.* 'Injunxit ibi duobus episcopis Albeo et Ibaro discipulis suis.' *Vit. S. Patricii*, c. 83. Colgan, *ib.* p. 84.

[4] *Colgan.* Tr. Th., p. 265.

[5] *Ussher.* Primord., p. 950. Betham's Irish Antiq. Researches, part ii. Append. p. xx.

Date of his death.

to this we add that he is said to have died[1] A.D. 500 or 503, the evidence seems complete against the opinion that he was a bishop in Ireland before A.D. 432. Some authorities[2] add that he died at the advanced age of 303 years. This would make him to have been born A.D. 200. But such a supposition is not necessary to reconcile the chronology, even though we suppose him to have been a bishop in the year 400.

Contest of Ibar with St. Patrick.

A singular story is told by the Scholiast on Aengus, which, if known to the biographers of St. Patrick, has been entirely suppressed by them :—

'This was the bishop Ibar,' says the writer, 'who had the great conflict with Patrick; and it was he that kept the roads full and the houses empty in Ard-Macha. Then the man[3] Patrick became angry with him, so that he said, 'Thou shalt not be in Erinn,' said Patrick. 'But Eri shall be the name of the place where I shall be,' said bishop Ibar. 'For this reason it was named Beg-Eri [little Eri, or little Ireland]; it is an island that is in Ui Cennselaigh[4], and it is out in the sea.'

This seems to indicate a contest for juris-

---

[1] *Died.* Tighernach dates his obit 503; Ann. of Ulster, 489 or 500, and again 503; Four Masters, 500; Ann. of Clonmacnois, 504.

[2] *Authorities.* Tighernach says 303; the Four Masters and the Mart. of Donegal, 304; the Scholiast on Aengus, 333.

[3] *The man Patrick.* This is only an emphatic way of saying Patrick, 'Patrick himself,' 'the very Patrick.'

[4] *Ui Cennselaigh.* The country inhabited by the Ui Cennselaigh, or descendants of Enna Cennselach, who was king of Leinster in the fourth century. Beg-eri, now Begery, or Begrin island, is situated in the bay of Wexford, about two and a half miles from the town.

diction at Armagh; and around Armagh, it should be remembered, was the hereditary district which belonged to Ibar's family. It is remarkable that the story given in the Life of Declan, of the composition made by St. Patrick and the prelates of Munster, in the court of King Aengus at Cashel, represents Ibar as at first strongly dissentient, and very reluctantly at length induced to submit.[1] This narrative is as follows:— *Alleged composition between St. Patrick and the prelates of Munster.*

'The four bishops aforesaid, who were in Ireland before St. Patrick, having been sent from Rome, as he also was, namely, Ailbe, Declan, Kieran, and Ibar, were not of the same mind as St. Patrick, but differed with him; nevertheless, in the end they came to an agreement with him.

'Kieran, indeed, yielded all subjection, and concord, and supremacy[2] to St. Patrick, both when he was present and absent. But Ailbe, seeing that the great men[3] of Ireland were running after Patrick, came to St. Patrick in the city of Cashel, and there, with all humility, accepted him as his master in presence of King Aongus; this, however, had not been his original intention. For those bishops[4] had previously constituted Ailbe their master, and therefore he came to St. Patrick before them, lest they, on his account, should resist Patrick. But Ibar, by no argument, could be induced to agree with St. Patrick, or to be subject to him. For he was unwilling to receive a patron of Ireland from a foreign nation: and Patrick was by birth a Briton, although nurtured in Ireland, having been taken captive in his boyhood. And Ibar and Patrick had at first great conflicts[5] together, but afterwards, at the persuasion of an angel, they made peace, and concord, and fraternity together.

[1] *Submit.* Vit. S. Declan., c. v. n. 39, 40.
[2] *Supremacy.* 'Omnem subjectionem, et concordiam, ac magisterium dedit.'
[3] *Great men.* 'Majores Hiberniæ.'
[4] *Those bishops:* meaning Kieran, Declan, and Ibar.
[5] *Conflicts.* 'Conflictus magnos.' The same word which is used by the Scholiast on Aengus.

'Declan, indeed, was unwilling to resist St. Patrick, because he had before made fraternity with him in Italy: but neither did he think of becoming his subject, inasmuch as he also had the apostolic dignity: but having been at length admonished by an angel, he came to Patrick to do his will. For the angel of the Lord came to St. Declan, and said unto him, "Go now quickly to St. Patrick, and prevent him from cursing thy tribe and thy country, for he is this night in a place which is called Hynneon, in the midst of the plain of Femhin [1], in the northern district of the Desii, and he is fasting in reference to the chieftain of thy tribe; and if he should curse thy tribe, cursed shall it be for ever."

'Then St. Declan, with all haste, in accordance with the bidding of the angel, went forth that very night to the aforesaid place Hynneon (which is in the midst of the plain of Femhin, in the northern district of the Desii), through Mount Gua, i.e. Sliabh Gua [2], across the Suir, and in the morning reached St. Patrick. Then St. Patrick saw St. Declan and his people: and Declan was honourably received by St. Patrick and his people. Then St. Declan humbled himself before St. Patrick, and prayed him not to curse the clan or country of the Desii: and promised submission to his will. And St. Patrick said unto him, "Because thou intercedest for them, I will rather bless them."'

St. Ailbe made Metropolitan of Munster.

The nature of the agreement that was ultimately entered into, by which St. Ailbe was constituted Metropolitan of Munster, is then described. It is remarkable that no mention is made either of Kieran or of Ibar, as having been included. The arrangement was not that which was afterwards sanctioned by Cardinal Paparo,

---

[1] *Femhin.* Magh Femhin, or the plain of Femhin, is a district, comprising that part of the Co. of Tipperary which belongs to the diocese of Lismore, including the present baronies of Iffa and Offa. Hynneon, is the place called Inneoin nan Desi, or Mallagh-inneona, near the town of Clonmell. See Four Masters, A.D. 852 (and Dr. O'Donovan's note), also Book of Rights, p. 92, note.

[2] *Sliabh Gua*: or Sliabh Cua, the antient name of the range of mountains separating the counties of Waterford and Tipperary, and now called Knockmeilidown mountains. See Four Masters, A.M. 3790, and Dr. O'Donovan's note.

in which Cashel, not Emly, was made the archiepiscopal see. We may therefore conclude that the author of St. Declan's Life must have lived at the end of the eleventh, or beginning of the twelfth century, before the ecclesiastical arrangements of the dioceses, as ultimately established, were known. His narrative[1] is as follows :—

' St. Patrick, St. Ailbe, and St. Declan, with many of their holy disciples, during their sojourn in the city of Cashel, with King Aengus, made many regulations for ecclesiastical rule and Christian vigor, and for the further propagation of the Christian faith. Then St. Patrick and King Aengus, with all his people, ordained that the Archbishopric of Munster should be in the city and see of St. Ailbe, who was then by them ordained archbishop for ever. They appointed also to St. Declan the territories which he had converted from paganism to the faith, namely, the Desii; that they should be in the jurisdiction of his bishopric [ut ipsi in parochia episcopatus ejus essent], which is great and glorious ; and that the Irish in other places should be subject to St. Patrick, so that the tribe of the Desii might render all obedience to their patron, St. Declan. Then St. Patrick, the Archpontiff and Patron of all Ireland [archipontifex et patronus totius Hiberniæ] sang to them the following verse in the Scotic tongue, as a kind of oracle, having the force of law. Which verse the family [2] of St. Ailbe, and the family of St. Declan would never suffer to be turned into Latin for their own use, either in metre or rhyme ; to give it, therefore, the greater authority, we shall here quote it in the original and genuine language in which it was pronounced and composed by St. Patrick. Thus, then, the stanza is expressed in the Scotic :—

" Ailbhe umhal, Patruig Mumhan, mo gach rath,
Declan Padruig nanDesi, nanDesi ag Declan go brath."

In these words [3] it was decreed that Ailbe should be the second

---

[1] *Narrative*. Vit. S. Declan., c. vi. n. 47. It will be observed that the diocese here assigned to Declan was the territory of his clan, the Desii. See above, p. 38.

[2] *Family*. This word, signifying the Monastic Society, has been already explained.

[3] *Words*. Ussher, *Prim.*, p. 866 (Works, vi. p. 427, 8), and Colgan,

220   *Origin and Purpose of the Story*   [INTROD.

Patrick and Patron of Munster, and Declan the second Patrick and Patron of the Desii; and that the Desii should be his diocese to the end of the world.

'Then the holy bishops, giving King Aengus their blessing, went forth with the kiss of peace, with spiritual joy, to spread the Divine work.'

Silence of the Lives of St. Patrick as to former bishops in Munster.

86. The Lives of St. Patrick tell us that he laboured *for seven years* in Munster[1], travelling through every part of the province, receiving the homage of kings and chieftains, and making converts to the faith; but they say not a word of any former labourers in the same district, nor of the archiepiscopal jurisdiction said to have been established with the consent of St. Patrick at Emly and Ardmore.

Silence of the Calendar of Aengus.

The antient Calendar of Aengus also, although it commemorates Ciaran, Ailbe, Declan, and Ibar, says not a word of their having preceded St. Patrick as preachers of the faith. And it will be observed that they were all Munster bishops; not all of Munster descent, or belonging to Munster families, but all having their principal churches or monasteries in Munster.

Origin and purpose of the story of bishops before St. Patrick.

It seems perfectly manifest, therefore, that the whole story of bishops sent from Rome to the south of Ireland, before St. Patrick, was invented

Tr. Th., p. 201, have given this extract from the Life of Declan. The Irish verses literally translated signify:
Humble Ailbe is the Patrick of Munster, With all my honour.
Declan is the Patrick of the Desii; The Desii are with Declan for ever.
The copy of Declan's Life used by Ussher and Colgan differs from that printed by the Bollandists, but the differences do not affect our present purpose.

[1] *Munster.* Vit. Trip. iii. c. 54. 'Deserente Patricio Mumoniam in qua septem annis continuis juxta supra dictis laboravit, et veniente ad extremos ejus fines, monstrarunt totius Provinciæ magnates et populi se tanto spiritualis Patris et Apostoli duci desiderio et affectu,' &c.— Colgan, *Tr. Thaum.*, p. 159.

at the beginning of the eleventh (perhaps we should say the twelfth) century, for the purpose of laying the foundation of a claim for the establishment of archiepiscopal jurisdiction in the south. When the question was mooted, to divide the country into dioceses, it became a matter of some importance to the chieftains or 'kings,' as they were called, of Munster and Connaught, to have archbishops of their own. Had the whole island been placed under the metropolitical jurisdiction of Armagh, the kings of Munster and Connaught would frequently have felt much inconvenience, from their bishops being in subjection to a prelate who was necessarily under the influence, and generally himself a clansman, of the great northern family of O'Neill. They laboured, therefore, strenuously to induce the people and the ecclesiastics to clamour for archbishoprics of their own; and hence the story that the south of Ireland had been evangelized before St. Patrick, and that although God had reserved for Patrick the honour of a complete conversion of the Irish, nevertheless the four Munster missionaries had received episcopal consecration at Rome, and had been commissioned to evangelize the country at least thirty years before the mission of St. Patrick.

87. But, although we are compelled to reject this story as unworthy of credit, it cannot be denied that the traditions of Irish Church history speak of isolated congregations of Christians in Ireland before the arrival of Patrick. A curious anec-

Isolated congregations of Christians before St. Patrick.

dote bearing on this subject is told in two of the legendary lives of the apostle — that by Jocelin of Furnes, and that which is generally called the Tripartite[1], from its being divided into three books. We shall quote the story as it is told in this latter authority[2]:—

'After crossing the Shannon, Patrick and his companions came to a place called *Dumha-graidh*, and there he ordained the excellent presbyter Ailbe. He it is who is [commemorated, or buried,] in the Church of Senchua, in the country of the Ui Oiliolla. But when the things necessary for divine service and sacred vessels were wanting, the holy prelate, divinely instructed, pointed out to the presbyter in a certain stone cave of wonderful workmanship, an altar under ground, having on its four corners four chalices of glass; and because of the glass he admonished them to dig very cautiously, saying:—

'Cavendum ne frangantur ore[3] fossuræ'

This story is certainly antient: for it occurs in the Book of Armagh, where, however, no mention is made of the glass chalices, nor of the cave[4], but only that St. Patrick showed Ailbe

---

[1] *Tripartite.* Joceline undoubtedly lived at the close of the twelfth century. The Tripartite life is attributed to St. Evin, a writer of the seventh century. It was originally written in Irish, but is now known only by Colgan's Latin version. An imperfect and apparently abridged copy of the Irish is preserved in the British Museum.

[2] *Authority.* Vit. Tripart., lib. ii. c. 35 (*Triad. Thaum.*, p. 134).

[3] *Ore.* The Irish Tripartite life reads here *oræ*, which is no doubt right. The meaning seems to be, 'beware of breaking the edges of the excavation.'

[4] *Cave.* The words are 'Et venierunt (*sic*) per alveum fluminis Sinnae qui dicitur *Bandea* ad tumulum *Gradi*, in quo loco ordinavit Ailbeum sanctum prespiterum (*sic*), cui indicavit altare mirabile lapideum in monte nepotum Ailello.'—*Book of*

'a wonderful stone altar on (or in) a mountain of the Ui Oiliolla.'[1]

The existence of such an altar, which was known to St. Patrick, most probably from information obtained from the inhabitants, is a curious incidental proof that Christianity existed before his time in this remote district. The cave, if we adopt that part of the story, was probably a rudely constructed chapel, on the side of a mountain, chosen for the sake of concealment, and built up when the few Christians, to whose use it was dedicated, were forced to leave the district. It is possible that the visit of St. Patrick to the place, and the ordination of his disciple Ailbe, were suggested by his knowledge that such an altar existed, and his wish to restore, in a spot so consecrated, the celebration of the sacred mysteries.

The mention of the four glass chalices, which however does not occur in the more antient form of the story, is curious: for it is well known that chalices of glass[2] were in very antient times

---

Armagh, fol. 11. *b a*. It will be observed that the place called in Irish *Dumha-graidh* is here translated *Tumulus-gradi*: the word *Dumha* signifying a mound. Neither this place nor the part of the Shannon called *Bandea* is now known.

[1] *Ui Oiliolla*. The tribe name Ui Oiliolla or Ui Ailiolla, i.e. descendants of Oilioll or Ailioll, is here given to the territory inhabited by the tribe, according to the usual Irish custom. The district is the present barony of Tirerrill, a corruption of Tir-Oiliolla (Land of Oilioll), in the Co. Sligo. This tribe derived their name from Oilioll or Ailioll, son of Eochaidh Muigh-mheadon, king of Connaught, who, in 358, became king of Ireland.—O'Flaherty, *Ogyg*. iii. c. 79, p. 373, 374; and see Appendix A to this Introduction, Table 1, p. 249.

[2] *Glass*. It is known that in the fifth century vessels of glass were used in the Eucharist, but it should be borne in mind that at that time glass was a costly material. In the Life of St. Hilary of Arles, who was a contemporary of St. Patrick (*Actt. SS.*, Bolland. *ad* 5 Maii), we are told that he sold all the treasures of his

employed in the administration of the eucharist, although afterwards prohibited, in consequence of the danger of breakage. The mention of this cave, with its altar and chalices, seems so incidental, and is so entirely devoid of any apparent purpose, that we can scarcely doubt the substantial truth of the legend.

<small>Jocelin's version of the story.</small>

Jocelin represents the newly-ordained priest Ailbe as having complained[1] to St. Patrick that he had not the necessary sacred vessels for the celebration of the divine service; and therefore St. Patrick showed him the altar and its furniture in the subterraneous cave. Jocelin then adds, 'By whom this altar was made, and with its chalices there set up, is as yet unknown to us. Some think that they belonged to the bishop Palladius or to his companions, and were left there after his departure.'[2]

It does not appear from this that Jocelin was acquainted with the story of the four bishops, missionaries in Ireland before Palladius; for otherwise he would in all probability have suggested that this cave and its altar might have been set up by Ciaran, Ailbe, Ibar, or Declan, or some of their disciples.[3] With respect to

---

church for the redemption of captives, 'quousque ad patenas et calices vitreos.' The author of this life, which is also in the collection of Surius, was Honoratus, bishop of Marseilles, 'claruit anno 490.'— Cave, *Hist. Liter.* See also Bona, *Rer. Liturg.*, lib. i. c. 25, n. 1. Baronius, *Ann.*, A.D. 216. Bingham, *Antiq.*, book viii. ch. 6, sect. 21.

[1] *Complained.* 'Ordinatus presbyter conquestus est S. Patricio,

quod sibi deessent necessaria sacerdotali ministerio. Sanctus, divinitus instructus, indicavit presbytero quoddam altare mirandi operis habens in quatuor angulis, quatuor calices vitreos,' &c.—Colgan, *Tr. Th.*, p. 89.

[2] *Departure.* Jocelin (*Vita Sexta*), c. 105, *Triad. Thaum.*, p. 89.

[3] *Disciples.* This is, in fact, what Colgan has suggested. He says, 'Hinc collige fidem Christi fuisse in aliquibus partibus Hiberniæ

INTROD.] *Palladius sent to Christian Scots.* 225

Palladius, as Colgan remarks, we have no record of his having extended his labours to Connaught. There is no reason to suppose that he ever went beyond the province of Leinster. Therefore this altar must have been the remains of the devotion of some antient and isolated congregation of Christians, who were settled for a time before the arrival of Palladius or of Patrick, in the remote district of the Ui Oiliolla.

But conclusive evidence of the existence of some Christianity in Ireland before St. Patrick is derived from the words of Prosper of Aquitaine, who tells us in his Chronicle that Pope Celestine sent Palladius to the Scots, who were already believers in Christ, 'ad Scotos credentes in Christo;' and the same statement is repeated by Bede. We shall have occasion presently to speak

Mission of Palladius.

cultam, ante adventum S. Patricii. Quod aliqui conjiciunt calices istos cum altari fuisse ibi absconditos per Palladium ejusve discipulos, vel per S. Hibarum, vel S. Alveum, vel etiam Kieranum Sagirensem' [but nobody has made this latter suggestion] 'mihi non approbatur tanquam vero simile. Nam Palladius eodem anno quo venit in Hiberniam, inde decessit ; nec legitur ipse, vel ejus discipuli ultra fines Lageniæ uspiam profecti per Hiberniam.' — *Triad. Thaum.*, p. 113, note 120. It is to be observed that the Ailbe, who was ordained a presbyter on this occasion, must be a different person from the St. Ailbe of Emly, of whom we have already spoken, and who is said to have been a bishop in Ireland before Palladius or St. Patrick. We are told that he was of the Church of Senchua, now Shancoe, in the county of Sligo. The Four Masters record the death of 'Ailbe of Senchua-Ua-Oililda,' A.D. 545, and Tigernach at 542. The annals of Tigernach were dated by O'Flaherty : and here he seems to have made a mistake. For the year of Ailbe's death is marked '*Kal.* ii.' i. e. the first of Jan. was on *feria* ii. or Monday. The Sunday letter was, therefore, G, which indicates either the year 540 or 546. Ailbe is called *Cruimther*, the Gaelic form of the word *Presbyter*, by Marianus O'Gorman, and the Mart. of Tallaght, at Jan. 30, but without any mention of Senchua, or any other criterion to identify him with the Ailbe ordained priest by St. Patrick. The Mart. of Donegal (same day) tells us that he was 'son of Ronan, of the race of Conall Gulban, son of Niall.' See Appendix A, Table II., Gen. 88, p. 250.

Q

more at length on the history of Palladius. It must suffice to observe now that his mission obliged him, not so much to preach to the heathen, as to gather together into regularly organised congregations the scattered Christians who were to be found in the country; to supply them as far as possible with clergy; and to provide for them such permanent means of grace as might save them and their children from the danger of relapsing into idolatry.

The spirit of Clanship pervaded the Irish Church. 88. We have said enough to give the reader a general view of the peculiarities of Irish Christianity during the period to which the following pages relate. It will be seen that the spirit of clanship pervaded the antient Church of Ireland, as it did all the other institutions of the country. The genealogical descent of the chieftain from the common ancestor of the clan was his surest title-deed to the possession of his lands, the foundation of his influence and authority. For him, as the visible representative and head of their race, the clan would gladly shed their blood, and sacrifice the most sacred rights and affections of man. And so also the bishop or abbat was the successor, the co-arb or heir, of the honoured saint by whom his church or monastery was founded. In him that saint still lived and spake, as his recognised representative on earth; and when the same individual, as was not unfrequently the case, was at the same time spiritual co-arb and temporal chieftain, the loyalty of his subjects was confirmed by a double bond, the strongest and most indissoluble by which man can be bound to man.

To a clannish people it is not merely a habit, but a matter of necessity, to follow a guide — to be led by a superior and unquestionable authority. They care not for arguments, proofs, or reasons. They ask only to receive a command from a chieftain, whose right to command nobody can dream of questioning. It is not too much to say that this spirit of clanship is the key to Irish history. *Clanship the key to Irish history.*

The measures adopted in the reign of James I. for the abolition of hereditary clanship, were calculated at first sight to abolish great and crying evils. They were a step in the direction of improved civilisation. They would doubtless have been endorsed by the modern science of political economy, had the modern science of political economy been then in existence. They aimed at abolishing the arbitrary exactions[1] of the chieftains, which were intolerably burdensome to the people, and which, to say nothing of their evil moral influence, destroyed all possibility of agricultural and social improvement. But with all these advantages, the destruction of the chieftain's power was productive of new and unexpected evils. The change was too sudden and too violent. Neither chieftains nor people were prepared for it. Very many chieftains were induced — perhaps it would be more true to say *compelled* — to resign to the crown their antient *Abolition of the clans by James I.*

---

[1] *Exactions.* See Ware's *Antiq.*, Orig. Latin, capp. viii. xiii.; Harris's Edit. chap. xi. xii.

rights and territories, receiving back again their lands under a royal patent, in which the power of taxing and exacting *ad libitum* from the clan was abolished, and rents[1] *in money*, payable to the chieftain, substituted in stead; and *money*, it should be remembered, was a variable standard of value, not very generally understood at that time. The chieftain, in fact, became a landlord, and his clansmen tenants. But neither chieftain nor clansmen understood their new position. The clansman, no doubt, felt relief from the oppression, which in disturbed times had become intolerable, of *cosherings, bonaght, coinnmedh*, or coigne, and the rest. But the idea of paying *rent*, subject to ejectment, for a farm which had been held by his ancestors from time immemorial was quite unintelligible to him. He would have infinitely preferred the antient oppressive enactments, although they were to cost him an hundred per cent. more than the new rent. The result was that the chieftain, in his new character of landlord, lost his antient rights, under the Irish Brehon laws, but was unable to recover his new rights under the laws of the English Parliament. It will be remembered, also, that down to the middle of the seventeenth century, not only the

---

[1] *Rents.* Sir John Davis, attorney-general for Ireland, and speaker of the Irish House of Commons in the reign of James I., thus describes the process: 'Where an Irish Lord doth offer to surrender his country, and hold it of the crown, his own proper possessions in demesne are drawn into a *particular*, and his Irish duties, as *coshering, sessings, rents of butter, and oatmeale*, and the like, are reasonably valued, and reduced into certaine summes of money, to be paid in lieu thereof.' — *Discovery of the true causes why Ireland was never subdued.* Lond. 1612, p. 259 *sq.*

populace, but even the gentry, were unable to speak the English language. They were, therefore, not only ignorant of the new law under which they found themselves, but incapable of becoming acquainted with it. No steps were taken to instruct them. It was necessary to support the law by a military force; and hence, as Sir John Davis says, 'the circuits of justice, by which the people were made independent of their Lords, did more terrifie the loose and ydle persons, than the execution of the martial law itself, though the martial were more quick and sodaine.'

It came to pass, therefore, as the natural consequence of this state of things, that the chieftains were suddenly[1] impoverished. They besieged the Lord Deputy and the Court with petitions for relief; and many of them, dissatisfied with their reception at Court, fled to foreign countries, and took military service under foreign powers. Thus the people were left without their accustomed guidance; their head, the representative of their race, the arbitrator of their disputes, the dispenser of their laws, was an absentee. The modern English law courts provided no substitute; their proceedings were conducted in a foreign language; they made no

The chieftains suddenly impoverished.

---

[1] *Suddenly.* 'The greatnesse and power of those Irish Lordes sodainly fell and vanished, insomuch that, wanting means to defray their ordinary charges, they resorted ordinarily to the Lorde Deputy, and petitioned that by license and warrant of the State they might take some aid and contribution of their people; and some of them, being impatient of their domination, fled out of the realme to foreign countries.'—Sir J. Davis, *Discovery* &c., *ibid.*

allowance for the inveterate customs and prejudices of the people; their tone was hostile and contemptuous; and they were therefore not unfrequently the dispensers of injustice: 'summum jus summa injuria.' In short, they were regarded by the people with terror and dislike.

The peasantry laid open to foreign intriguers.

Thus the peasantry, left without their accustomed guides, and exasperated against their new rulers, became the victims of foreign intriguers. The foundation was laid for that tendency to insurrection and to agrarian outrage which has exhibited itself so prominently in Irish history, even to our own times.

Their loyalty to their chiefs unshaken.

But notwithstanding this, there appeared a phenomenon which has puzzled historians, and sorely exasperated political partisans. Whenever a chieftain[1] lifted his finger, he was followed at once by his people. They followed him alike, whether he supported the English crown, or the enemies of the English crown. They followed him even after the period of the Reformation, in opposition to what we might presume to have been their religious prejudices. They fought with their chieftain on the side of Queen Elizabeth, although she had been excommunicated by the see of Rome, and her subjects absolved from their allegiance.[2]

89. And equally disastrous was the result pro-

---

[1] *Chieftain.* A good instance in evidence of what is here said will be found in the story of Balldearg O'Donnell so late as the year 1690, as it is told by Lord Macaulay, *Hist.* *of England,* iii. p. 671 *sq.*

[2] *Allegiance.* See Dr. O'Conor's *Historical Address*, p. 11 *sq.* Columbanus *ad Hibernos*, No. 2.

duced by the measures adopted in reference to the Church. The Danish bishops of Waterford and Dublin in the eleventh century had received consecration from the see of Canterbury, entirely ignoring the Irish Church and the successors of St. Patrick. From that time there have been two Churches in Ireland. The Anglo-Norman settlers ignored also the native bishops; and they did so under the authority of the Court of Rome, in virtue of the donation of Ireland to Henry II. by the celebrated Bull of the only English Pope, Nicholas Breakspeare, better known by his papal title of Adrian IV.

Two hostile Churches in Ireland since the eleventh century.

That document described the Irish as barbarians, and exhorted the King to make known 'the true Christian faith to those ignorant and uncivilised tribes,' as if there had never been any Christianity in the land from whose missionaries half of Europe had received its Christianity. The King was authorised 'to enter the island for the purpose of bringing the people into subjection to law; to exterminate the nurseries of vices from the country,' and especially 'to pay to St. Peter an annual tribute of one penny for every house in the country;' preserving, however, the Pope takes care to add, 'the ecclesiastical rights of that land'—that is to say, his own assumed rights in that land — uninjured and inviolate.[1]

Bull of Pope Adrian IV.

---

[1] *Inviolate.* See Mr. O'Callaghan's remarks on this bull, and the original Latin given by him from the Roman Bullarium.—*Destruction of Cyprus*, p. 242 sq. (published for the Irish Archæological Society).

This commission the English monarch executed by filling the country with needy adventurers, thirsting for spoil, reckless of human life, and looking out greedily for every pretence to confiscate the lands of the Irish chieftains. On these principles, or rather, we should say, for these ends, they governed the country.

At first, indeed, and for a considerable period after the invasion of Henry II., the native chieftains submitted with a good grace to English rule, and generally used their influence in support of the Crown. But at length the licentious outrages of the colonists, together with the unwise policy adopted by the English government, irritated and exasperated the native lords, and produced those bitter feuds and animosities, the effects of which continue to the present day.

<small>Laws to enforce English manners.</small>

The impolitic attempt was made to compel the Irish to adopt English manners, under pretence of bringing the whole nation under English law. Whether or not the advisers of the crown really desired and hoped for this latter result, the measures adopted, as might have easily been foreseen, produced consequences directly the reverse. The two nations became permanently and completely separated. It was assumed that by an act of Parliament, making confiscation or imprisonment the punishment of disobedience, an entire nation could be compelled in a moment to abandon their national habits, their national dress, yea, their native language, and to adopt at once the customs, the dress, and the language of another people. Let it be admitted that the Irishman of that day was a barbarian; his costume uncouth; his national usages and his language barbarous; it did not follow that he was to be deprived of the rights of citizenship and equal law; that he should be denied security for his life and property, and subjected to a treatment which was in its tendency nothing short of extermination. This was indeed to make him a barbarian, and at the same time to punish him for being a barbarian.

Irritated at length beyond endurance, and driven to extremities by injustice and oppression, the Irish chieftains had recourse to arms; the English of the pale, and the colonists in remote parts of Ireland, were attacked, plundered, and massacred. Hence it came to pass that the settlers in Connaught, and the more distant regions of Munster, seeing that their brethren of the pale could give them no support, were forced to conciliate the Irish. They intermarried with the natives, and gradually adopted the manners and customs, the laws, and even the language of the people; in a word, they became, according to the well-known reproach, 'more Irish than the Irish themselves'—'ipsis Hibernis Hiberniores.' *The English settlers more Irish than the Irish themselves.*

90. To check this evil now became the object of the English government; and no better mode of doing so suggested itself, than to enact pains *Statute of Kilkenny, 1367.*

and penalties to compel the degenerate English, who had in fact renounced their allegiance to the crown, to return to obedience. The famous statute enacted in the Parliament held at Kilkenny[1] in 1367 had this for its object. It declared alliances with the Irish by marriage, fostering, gossipred &c. to be high treason. It denounced the old Brehon law as 'wicked and damnable,' and enacted that all who followed it should be accounted traitors.[2]

It is not denied that the statute of Kilkenny contained some good and useful enactments. But its general tendency was to erect a harsh and impassable barrier between the two nations.

Penal enactments against the mere Irish.

The Irishman dwelling within the English pale, who did not adopt the English dress and the English language, was to be punished by confiscation of his land and property, or if he had no land and property, by imprisonment, until he submitted. The English were commanded not to allow an Irishman to graze his cattle upon their lands. It was made penal to present an Irishman to any ecclesiastical benefice; and it was also made penal for any religious house, 'situated amongst the English,' that is to say, within the English pale, 'to receive any Irishman to their profession, but,' it is added, 'they

---

[1] *Kilkenny.* This statute was printed (for the first time) by the Irish Archæological Society, with the very valuable notes of the late James Hardiman. To this work the reader is referred for full information on the period of Irish history here referred to.

[2] *Traitors.* See the extract from Sir John Davis's 'Discoverie of the causes why Ireland never was subdued,' quoted by Mr. Hardiman, *Stat. of Kilkenny*, Pref. p. viii. *sq.*

may receive any Englishman, without taking into consideration whether he be born in England or in Ireland.'

Thus it appears that the Irishman was subjected to these disabilities, and excluded even from the monastic profession, simply because he was of Irish blood; for it will be observed that the native of Ireland who was of English blood was exempted. Nor was any provision made for the relaxation of this prohibition in the case of an Irishman who had conformed to English usages. His Irish blood was his crime. This clearly appears from the exception (the only exception permitted by the statute), in favour of the native of Ireland who was of English descent.

The concluding section of the statute of Kilkenny contains the names of three archbishops and five bishops,[1] who pledge themselves to denounce the spiritual sentence of excommunication against all violators of the act. These prelates all owed their promotion to papal provisions: some of them were consecrated at Avignon, where the papal court was then held; and it is evident that they must have been

Sanctioned by the Bishops and by the Court of Rome.

---

[1] *Bishops.* Stat. of Kilkenny, p. 119. The names are, Thomas [Mynot], Archbishop of Dublin; Thomas [O'Carroll], of Cashel; John [O'Grada], of Tuam; Thomas [Le Reve], of Lismore and Waterford; Thomas [O'Cormacan], of Killaloe; William, Bishop of Ossory, who is not, however, included in the received lists of the prelates of that see; John [Young], of Leighlin; and John [de Swafham], of Cloyne. It is evident from this list that some prelates of Irish surnames, and probably therefore of Irish blood, had succeeded in obtaining the confidence of the Anglo-Irish government. So that we must not infer that all who bore Irish names were necessarily disaffected to the English rule.

consenting parties to the statute, including the clause which protected the monks of the English pale from the possibility of having their devotions contaminated by the presence of a mere Irish brother.

Absence of the Archbishop of Armagh.

The absence of the Archbishop of Armagh and his suffragans from the Kilkenny Parliament may be accounted for by the controversy then at its height between the sees of Dublin and Armagh for precedency. The Archbishop of Armagh at the time was an Englishman, Milo Sweetman, and was nominated to his see by Pope Innocent VI. Most of the other bishops of Ireland were also at that time the nominees of the Court of Rome, and as a matter of course the representatives of its policy. Rome, therefore, must be considered to have been as fully responsible as England for the great political mistake of erecting the unhappy wall of distinction between the native Irish, 'the King's Irish rebels,' as they were called, and the Anglo-Norman colonists of the pale.

We read of no remonstrance or protest having been ever made against this unjust oppression of the natives by the bishops of that day, whether they were present or not at the convention of Kilkenny. It is evident that they were all in the English interest, and that the English interest was supported also by the Court of Rome.

Remonstrance of the Irish chieftains, 1317.

91. But the statute of Kilkenny, of which we are speaking, was only the re-enactment, with more stringent penalties, of a series of older

statutes framed in the same spirit. Fifty years before, the chieftains and nobles of Ireland, headed by Domhnall O'Neill, styling himself 'King of Ulster, and rightful successor to the throne of all Ireland,' addressed a remonstrance[1] to Pope John XXII. against the injustice and outrages of the English colonists. They begin by asserting the great antiquity and original independence of the monarchy of Ireland. They complain that Pope Adrian, acting on the representation, 'false and full of iniquity,' made to him by Henry II., King of England, and blinded by his own 'English prejudices,' as being himself an Englishman, had made over to the English monarch the realm of Ireland; thus bestowing *de facto* upon a sovereign, who for his murder of St. Thomas of Canterbury 'ought rather have been deprived of his own,' a kingdom which '*de jure* the Pope had no right to bestow,' and that this grant was the real source of all the miseries of their country. 'For ever since that time' (they proceed[2] to say), 'when the English, upon occasion of the grant aforesaid, and under the mask of a sort of outward sanctity and religion, made their unprincipled aggression upon the territories of our realm, they have been endeavouring, with all their might, and with every art which perfidy

---

[1] *Remonstrance.* It is preserved in the *Scotichronicon* of Fordun, edited by Hearne, iii. p. 908 *sq.* 8vo, *Oxon.*1722. Mr. King has published an English translation of it in the supplementary volume to his Church History of Ireland, p. 1119.

Domhnall O'Neill died in 1325. See his Genealogy, in Dr. O'Donovan's 'Circuit of Ireland,' p 63 (published by the Irish Archæol. Society, 1841).

[2] *Proceed.* Mr. King's translation is here followed.

could employ, completely to exterminate and utterly to eradicate our people from the country.' And they add, 'We hold it as an undoubted truth, that in consequence of the aforesaid false suggestion[1], and the grant thereupon founded, more than fifty thousand persons of the two nations, from the time when the grant was made to the present date, have perished by the sword, independently of those who have been worn out by famine or destroyed in dungeons.'

The conditions of Adrian's Bull violated.

The remonstrants then proceed to show that Henry II. and the English sovereigns, his successors, had violated the conditions upon which Ireland was granted to them in the papal bull; they had not paid to St. Peter, as they were enjoined to do, a penny annually for every house; they had not enlarged the boundaries of the Irish Church; on the contrary, they had plundered the endowments of the Cathedral Churches, abolished ecclesiastical privileges of every kind, and imprisoned the Irish bishops and prelates. They had barbarised and depraved the people of Ireland, instead of enlightening and civilising them, as Pope Adrian had intended. The remonstrants then go on to specify some gross instances of misrule, arbitrary cruelties, and injustice, perpetrated by the English, and permitted, if not encouraged, by their administration of the law.

Among these instances of oppression, a pro

---

[1] *Suggestion.* Meaning the suggestion made by Henry II. to the Pope as to the barbarous state of Ireland.

minent place is given to the regulation which prohibited the admission of a native Irishman to any of the religious houses of the pale; a regulation which the remonstrants say was made law by the influence of the Anglo-Norman clergy, in 'an iniquitous statute' enacted at Kilkenny, alluding, not to the statute of Kilkenny of 1367, already quoted, but to an older statute, which has never been printed, in which the same enactment was contained. They further say, that 'even before this statute, the preaching friars, and the minors, monks and canons, and other English, were in the habit of observing this practice,'—the practice, namely, of refusing to receive any Irish to the monastic profession; 'and yet,' they add, 'the monasteries for monks and canons, from which in modern times the Irish are thus repulsed, were founded, for the most part, by themselves.'

Exclusion of the Irish from the monastic profession.

The authors of this letter dwell also with natural and just indignation upon the fact that the murder of an Irishman was not punished as a felony[1] by the practice of the English courts of justice. They say, 'It is not merely their lay and secular persons, but even some of the religious among them, who assert the heretical doctrine that it is no more sin to kill an Irishman than to kill a dog, or any other brute

The murder of an Irishman not considered a sin, nor punished as a felony.

---

[1] *Felony.* That this was so, is admitted by Sir J. Davis in his *Discoverie,* &c. ' Lastly ' (he says) 'the mere Irish were not only accounted aliens, but enemies, and altogether out of the protection of the law; so as it was no capital offence to kill them; and this is manifest by many records.'—*Historical Tracts by Sir John Davis,* p. 88 *sq.* London 8vo. 1786.

animal;' and they quote some examples (for which the reader must be referred to the letter itself), showing that this doctrine was not only taught, but fully acted upon by the monks and canons of several abbeys, accusing especially of this abominable tenet the members of the Cistercian and Franciscan orders.

<small>Alliance of the Irish with Bruce, Earl of Carrick.</small>

The chieftains conclude by announcing to the Pope their intention of seeking redress by force of arms from this intolerable tyranny, inviting to their aid and assistance 'Edward de Bruce, the illustrious Earl of Carrick, brother-German of the most illustrious Lord Robert, by the grace of God King of the Scots, and a descendant of some of the most noble of our own ancestors.' And then, after dilating on the merits of Bruce, and the advantages of the proposed alliance with him, they make the following request :—

'May it please thee, therefore, most Holy Father, out of a regard for justice and the public peace, mercifully to sanction our proceedings in relation to our said Lord the King; prohibiting the King of England and our adversaries aforesaid from farther molestation of us. Or, at least, be graciously pleased to enforce for us from them the requirements of justice.'

The Pope does not appear to have given any encouragement to the proposed insurrection, or to have communicated directly with the authors of the remonstrance. He took the intermediate course of writing to King Edward II., a letter still extant,[1] in which he recommends him for his own sake, and for the sake of religion, to redress the evils complained of, if the statements of the complainants should be found to have any foundation in fact. He transmitted also to the King a copy of the remonstrance of the Irish chieftains, together with a copy of the bull of Pope Adrian IV.

The result was what might have been expected. The King referred the matter to his Irish Parliament, and the Irish Parliament returned for answer that the petition of the chieftains could not be granted, without material injury to the King and his government.

92. But this is not the place to enlarge upon the history of these transactions. It must suffice to make here one or two general remarks. In the first place it will be seen that there were two Churches in Ireland separated from each other, without any essential difference of discipline or doctrine, at a period long previous to the Reformation. The Church of the English Pale was at first strongly supported by all the power of the Court of Rome. The Church of the native Irish was discountenanced and ignored by Rome, as well as by England. It consisted of the old Irish clergy and inmates of the monasteries, beyond the limits of the English Pale, who had not adopted the English manners or

Two distinct Churches in Ireland long before the Reformation.

---

[1] *Extant.* It has been published by Peter Lombard, *De Regno Hiberniæ*, Lovan. 1632, p. 260. See also Mac Geoghegan, *Hist. de l'Irlande*, ii. p. 116.

language, and who were therefore dealt with as rebels, and compelled to seek for support from the charity or devotion of the people. Many of these took refuge in foreign countries, or connected themselves with foreign emissaries, hostile to England, at home; but at a subsequent period, when the Anglo-Irish Church had accepted the Reformation, the 'mere Irish' clergy were found to have become practically extinct. Their episcopacy had merged into, or become identified with the episcopacy which was recognised by the law. Missionary bishops and priests, therefore, ordained abroad, were sent into Ireland to support the interests of Rome; and from them is derived a third Church, in close communion with the See of Rome, which has now assumed the forms and dimensions of a national established religion.

Hatred of England not caused by religious differences.

It will be seen also that the deadly hatred of England and of everything English, which has unfortunately for so many centuries rankled in the native Irish heart, was not at first created by any differences in religion. It originated, and had reached its height, at a time when the only difference in religion was that the Established Church of the English Pale was more thoroughly devoted to Rome, and more completely under Papal, or, as we would now say, ultramontane influence, than the antient clergy and bishops of the aboriginal Irish ever were, or could have been.

The Reformation rejected as being English.

It is indeed highly probable that had the Reformation been presented to the Irish people in a Gaelic dress and in the Gaelic language, it would have been accepted without difficulty.

But, unfortunately, the reverse was the case. The Reformation was almost studiously brought into Ireland in ostentatious connection with the Church of the Pale and the English colonists: it was planted on the basis of Puritanism and iconoclastic outrage; and to this day the influence of that unhappy mistake continues to destroy the usefulness and to paralyse the energies of the Irish clergy. The reformed doctrines were regarded by the oppressed and degraded natives of Ireland as essentially English; and accordingly they were rejected without examination, and spurned with the detestation and abhorrence with which the English, and everything coming from England, were, as a matter of course, received.

When the Court of Rome, therefore, quarrelled with the Court of England, and excommunicated the sovereigns of England, all its former complicity with England was forgotten. The fact so prominently put forward in the Remonstrance to Pope John XXII., that the English crown laid claim to the sovereignty of Ireland on the authority of a papal bull, was forgotten. The fact that the Anglo-Irish Church had for almost four centuries been supported by Papal power, and the antient clergy, of Irish descent, and of Irish tongue, banished from their livings, and suffered to become extinct by Papal policy, was forgotten also. The fact that the Pope had *now* become the deadly enemy of England, was enough to turn the scale the other way. The Pope had still great power; that power was sure to be exerted against the English. Ireland, therefore, gave herself to the Pope, in the hope that by the influence of the Papal power, and by the aid of those European nations who were hostile to England, the Anglo-Norman colony in Ireland might at length be extirpated, or at least expelled.

<small>Indirect political evils of the Reformation.</small>

With all the blessings, therefore, which were the essential concomitants of the Reformation, this unfortunate result was an indirect consequence of it. Ireland was thrown open more completely than it ever was before to the intrigues of foreign adventurers. Spain poured in her emissaries; begging friars and foreign priests, or native priests educated abroad, went about as preachers of sedition; the old chieftains, or their successors returned, and stirred up the old spirit of clanship, in the hope of recovering their lands by the expulsion of the English.

The result was insurrection and bloodshed, continued with unrelenting energy through a long series of years; sometimes in the form of local outbreaks; sometimes rising to the dignity of civil war, conducted with a fury which justified, if anything could justify, the demolition of the castles and other strongholds of the chieftains by Cromwell, the compulsory exile of the multitudes who were driven by his policy from their native land, and the final confiscations of William III.

<small>The Penal Laws of</small>

93. It was at this latter period that religious

distrust unfortunately led to the enactment of those unhappy penal laws, whose ill consequences have continued to the present day. It is true that the enlightened principles of modern legislation have done much to check the evil, and to repair the wrong. The legislative union of the three kingdoms; the full concession of equal rights to all; the education of the people; the firm foundation upon which the tenure of land in Ireland, once the source of so much bloodshed, has now been placed—all these things must necessarily in no long time work a cure, which is already far advanced, and of which the generation now living will probably witness the completion. *Cromwell and William III.*

It is worthy of remark, however, that the Union of Great Britain and Ireland, essential as it was to the advance of civilization, and the establishment of a right feeling between the two countries, was nevertheless productive also of indirect evil. It induced many of the landlords to follow the Parliament to London, and to leave the management of their estates to their agents or stewards. The consequences which had resulted from the sudden destruction of the chieftains two centuries before, were reproduced in another form. The people were deprived of the guides to whom they had begun to look up, almost as they had looked up of old to their hereditary chieftains. The people had not lost their clannish feelings. It was impossible for them to do without some guides. The leaders *The Union of Great Britain and Ireland.*

who presented themselves were peculiarly unfitted to become the political guides of the people. They were themselves, for the most part, of the same race as the peasantry. They were naturally infected with all the old hatred of England, which had become the characteristic of the class to which they belonged. They viewed everything through the distorted medium of that unfortunate prejudice. The people were taught to regard themselves as still living in a state of war; the oppressed victims of superior and hostile force.

But this evil also is now greatly diminished. It is quite possible now for an Irish landlord, without any neglect of his parliamentary duties, to spend as much time in his Irish estate as an English landlord spends ordinarily at his property in an English county. The legitimate influence of the nobility and gentry has begun to be felt, and has already in a great measure undermined the trade of political agitation. Let us hope that there may soon be nothing to agitate about; that all classes may soon learn to forget and to forgive what is past, and to thank God for the great blessings that are present; the equal enjoyment by all subjects of the British Crown, without distinction of race or religion, of the inestimable privileges of the British Constitution.

APPENDIX

TO

THE INTRODUCTION

A.

Genealogical Tables of Kings and other Personages mentioned in the foregoing Introduction.

The eminent Irish Antiquary, Roderick O'Flaherty,[1] has endeavoured, with great ingenuity and learning, to reconcile the Irish Bardic traditions and genealogies with the received dates of sacred and profane history. He adopted, indeed, almost all those traditions with implicit faith as true history. No improbability in the narratives created any scruple in his mind; but for this very reason his pages exhibit a faithful transcript of the historical traditions of Ireland, clothed with the most seemly garments of consistency which they are capable of receiving. Firmly persuaded that the pedigrees of the antient Irish families could be traced to the patriarchal age, O'Flaherty has not hesitated to affix to the names of his kings and chieftains the number which indicated, according to the Bardic genealogies, their distance in generations from our first parent Adam.

We are not, however, bound to reject all these traditions as mere fabrications. The later genealogies, especially, are found to harmonise in so remarkable a manner with each other, and with the history, that it is impossible not to receive them as founded upon truth.

The object of the following tables is simply to furnish the

---

[1] *O'Flaherty.* See his 'Ogygia, seu rerum Hibernicarum Chronologia.' 4*to.* Lond., 1685.

reader with an easy mode of seeing at a glance the relationship assumed to exist amongst the personages mentioned in these pages, and to prevent the necessity of frequently interrupting the narrative by explanatory notices of such relationship.

The settlement in Ireland of the Scotic or Gaedhelic colony is assigned by the bards to the year 1000 B.C. It is said to have come from Spain, led by the sons of Golam Miled, i. e. Miles or the Knight. That word having been converted into a proper name, he is usually termed Milesius, and his posterity Milesians. Two of his sons Eber or Heber, and Herimon, having ultimately obtained sovereignty over the rest, divided Ireland between them. Eber took the southern half, and became the ancestor of the great Munster families; Herimon received the northern half, and from him were descended almost all[1] the kings of Ireland, from the middle of the third century to the virtual overthrow of the Irish monarchy in the eleventh century. This arrangement, however, was partly deranged in later times by internal dissensions.

The families and kings of the race of Herimon, descended from Eochaidh Muighmeadhon, through his celebrated son King Niall of the nine hostages, will be found to play the principal part in the history of St. Patrick and his successors, down to the beginning of the eleventh century. The following tables are therefore confined to them. The names of the Kings of Ireland will be followed by the letter K, with the years marking the beginning and the end of their reigns. The names of Saints are printed in Italics, and followed by the day of the month on which they are commemorated in the calendar of the Irish Church, with the years of their deaths. O'Flaherty's generation numbers are prefixed to each name, for the convenience of reference, and because they show very clearly the parallel lines of the genealogies according to his chronology.

---

[1] *Almost all.* From the reign of Cormac Ulfhada, A.D. 254, to that of Brian Boromha, A.D. 1002, there were but three exceptions to this rule, viz. Brian, himself, and Crimthan, A.D. 365, who were both of the race of Eber, and Coelbad of the race of Hir, A.D. 357. Ith, the paternal uncle of Golam or Milesius, had also descendants from whom some kings were chosen, but the last king of this line was Lugadh MacCon, A.D. 250. There were also several kings of the posterity of Hir, son of Milesius, the last of whom was Coelbad, above mentioned.

TABLE I.

General View of the Lines of Kings descended from Eochaidh Muighmeadhoin, of the Race of Herimon.

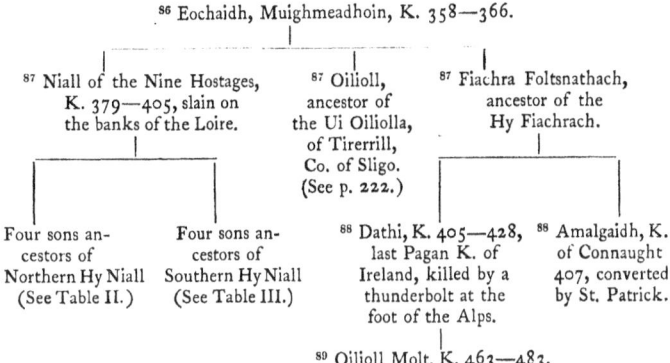

⁸⁶ Eochaidh, Muighmeadhoin, K. 358—366.

⁸⁷ Niall of the Nine Hostages, K. 379—405, slain on the banks of the Loire.

⁸⁷ Oilioll, ancestor of the Ui Oiliolla, of Tirerrill, Co. of Sligo. (See p. 222.)

⁸⁷ Fiachra Foltsnathach, ancestor of the Hy Fiachrach.

Four sons ancestors of Northern Hy Niall (See Table II.)

Four sons ancestors of Southern Hy Niall (See Table III.)

⁸⁸ Dathi, K. 405—428, last Pagan K. of Ireland, killed by a thunderbolt at the foot of the Alps.

⁸⁸ Amalgaidh, K. of Connaught 407, converted by St. Patrick.

⁸⁹ Oilioll Molt. K. 463—483. Last king of this line.

Between the Kings Eochaidh Muighmeadhoin and Niall of the Nine Hostages succeeded Crimthan (K. 366—379), descended from Oilioll Olum, king of Munster A.D. 237, of the race of Eber. Crimthan was the only king of Ireland of the Munster race, from this period to Brian Boromha, A.D. 1002. (See Table VI.)

It will be seen from Table II., that two lines of Irish Kings, both belonging to the Northern Hy Niall, were connected with the Kings of Scotland: Erc or Erca, daughter of Loarnmòr, was successively married to two grandsons of Niall of the Nine Hostages. To mark this relationship, her two sons (Muirchertach, offspring of her first husband, and Sedna of her second), from whom the two lines of Irish Kings were descended, are each styled 'Mac Erca,' son of Erc; the other sons of the same fathers not being sons of Erc, and therefore not connected with the Kings of Scotland.

TABLE II.
The Northern Hy Niall.

Mac, prefixed to Irish surnames, signifies *son of*. *Ua*, now generally written O', signifies *grandson, great grandson*, or any later descendant. *Hy* is the plural of *Ua*, or *O*, and is more correctly written *Ui*; The plural form denotes, therefore, the *clan*, or the whole body of the descendants. *Cinel*, signifies race, family; *Siol*, seed, offspring; *Dal*, tribe, race (*lit*. part, portion, applied to the land). These are all names given to the clan or tribe.

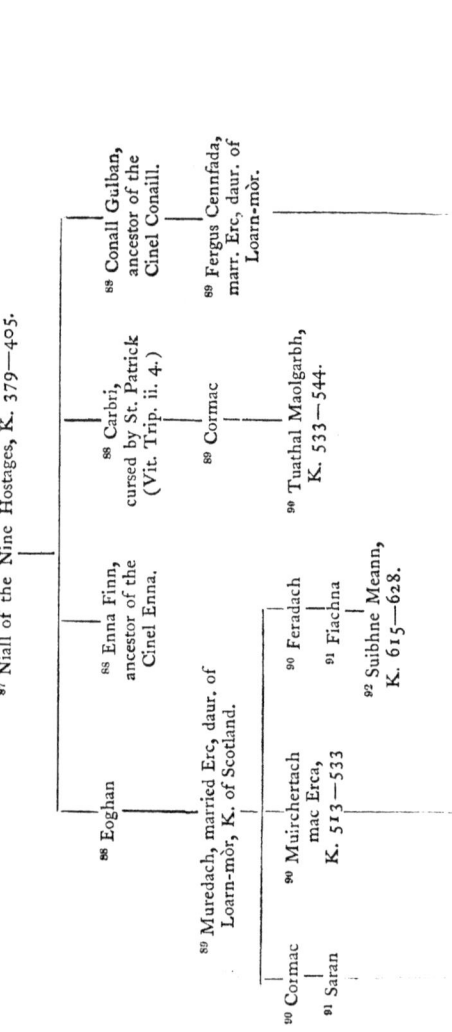

[INTROD.] *Genealogical Tables.* 251

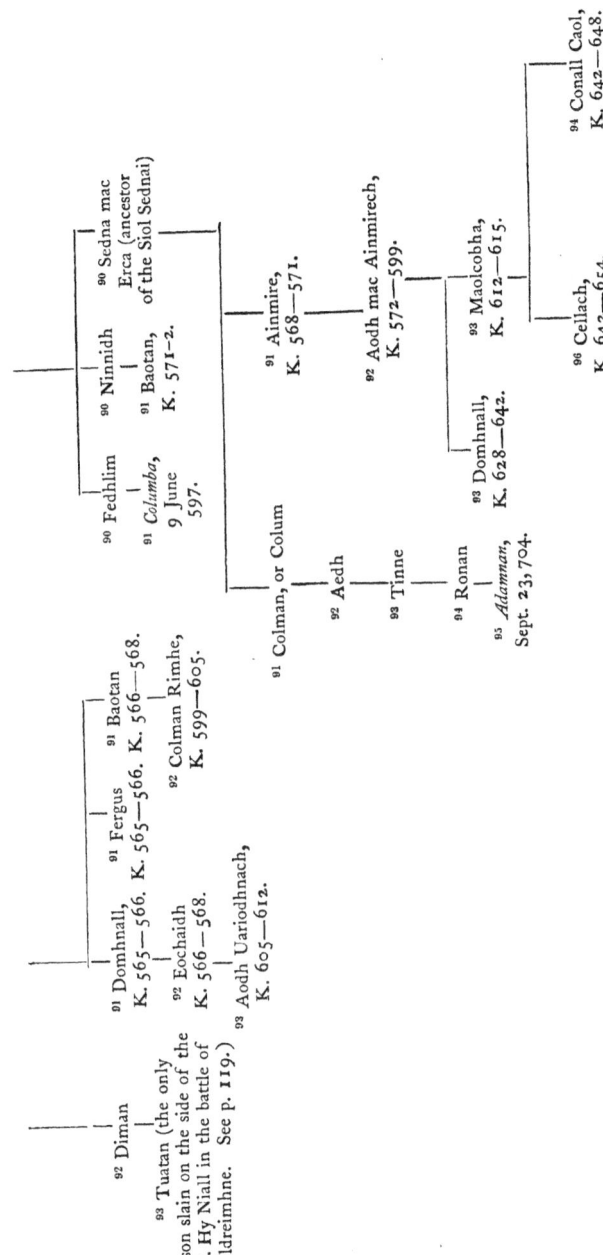

TABLE III.
Southern Hy Niall.

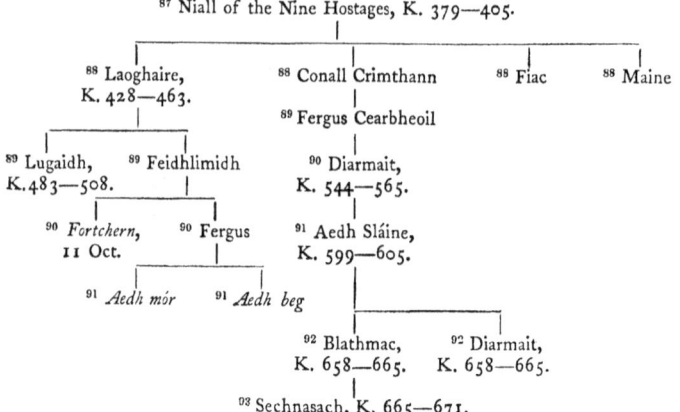

TABLE IV.
Shewing the Relationship between St. Brigid and St. Columba.

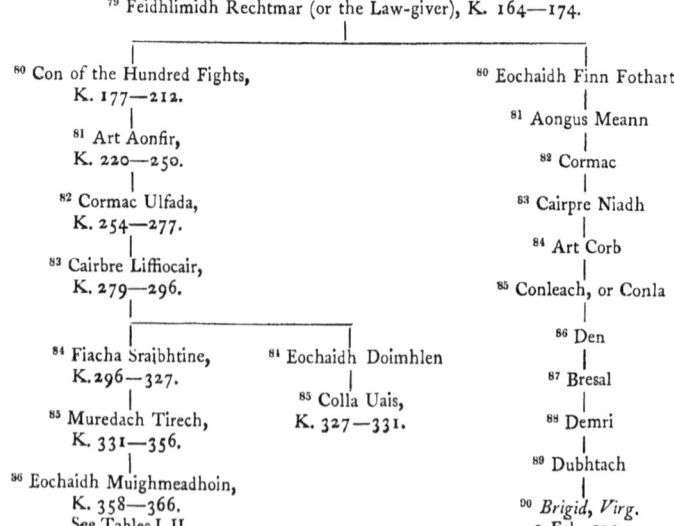

INTROD.] *Genealogical Tables.* 253

TABLE V.

Shewing the Relationship between the Families of St. Brigid and of her first Bishop Conlaedh.

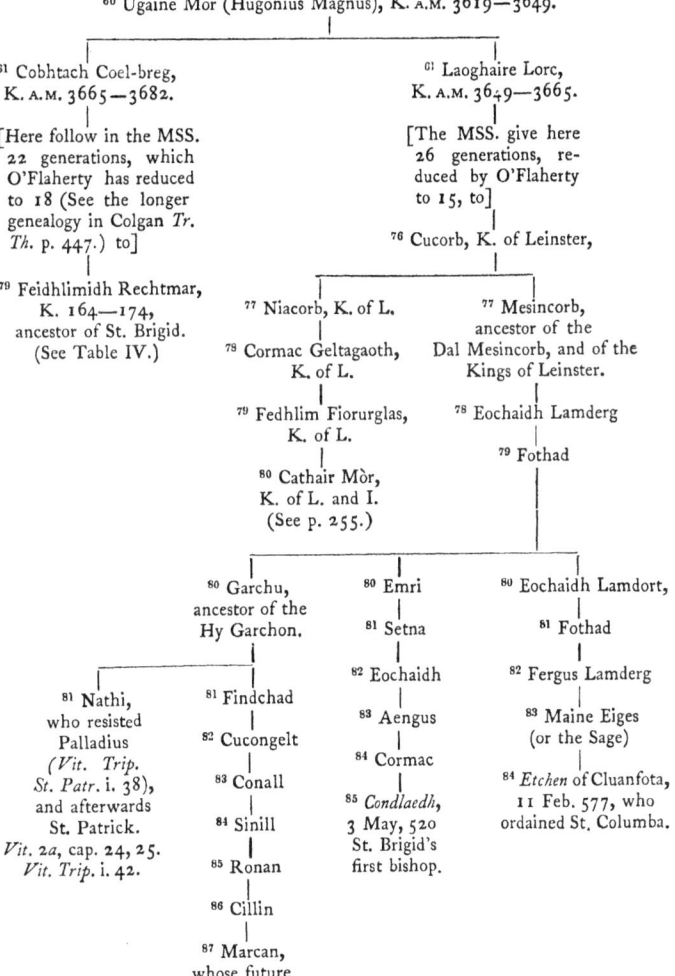

⁶⁰ Ugaine Mór (Hugonius Magnus), K. A.M. 3619—3649.

⁶¹ Cobhtach Coel-breg, K. A.M. 3665—3682.

[Here follow in the MSS. 22 generations, which O'Flaherty has reduced to 18 (See the longer genealogy in Colgan *Tr. Th.* p. 447.) to]

⁷⁶ Feidhlimidh Rechtmar, K. 164—174, ancestor of St. Brigid. (See Table IV.)

⁶¹ Laoghaire Lorc, K. A.M. 3649—3665.

[The MSS. give here 26 generations, reduced by O'Flaherty to 15, to]

⁷⁶ Cucorb, K. of Leinster,

⁷⁷ Niacorb, K. of L.

⁷⁸ Cormac Geltagaoth, K. of L.

⁷⁹ Fedhlim Fiorurglas, K. of L.

⁸⁰ Cathair Mòr, K. of L. and I. (See p. 255.)

⁷⁷ Mesincorb, ancestor of the Dal Mesincorb, and of the Kings of Leinster.

⁷⁸ Eochaidh Lamderg

⁷⁹ Fothad

⁸⁰ Garchu, ancestor of the Hy Garchon.

⁸¹ Nathi, who resisted Palladius (*Vit. Trip. St. Patr.* i. 38), and afterwards St. Patrick. *Vit.* 2a, cap. 24, 25. *Vit. Trip.* i. 42.

⁸¹ Findchad

⁸² Cucongelt

⁸³ Conall

⁸⁴ Sinill

⁸⁵ Ronan

⁸⁶ Cillin

⁸⁷ Marcan, whose future eminence was foretold by St. Patrick. *Vit. Trip.* iii. 17.

⁸⁰ Emri

⁸¹ Setna

⁸² Eochaidh

⁸³ Aengus

⁸⁴ Cormac

⁸⁵ *Condlaedh,* 3 May, 520 St. Brigid's first bishop.

⁸⁰ Eochaidh Lamdort,

⁸¹ Fothad

⁸² Fergus Lamderg

⁸³ Maine Eiges (or the Sage)

⁸⁴ *Etchen* of Cluanfota, 11 Feb. 577, who ordained St. Columba.

These families separated from their common ancestor at a very early period. There is some discrepancy in the number of generations, owing principally to the attempt made by the bards to place the arrival of the Scots or Milesians in the reign of Solomon, son of David. It would not be consistent with our present purpose to discuss this subject, nor will it be necessary to give in detail the long list of obscure names, some of which from their similarity were probably repeated and others omitted by antient transcribers. We have given, in the foregoing Table, the lines of descent in an abbreviated form, with O'Flaherty's dates, and generation numbers.

It is evident that the genealogies of Conlaedh and of Etchen in this table must be deficient in some generations. They represent Conlaedh as five generations, or a century and a half older than St. Bridgid; and Etchen as seven generations, or more than two centuries older than St. Columba, whom he ordained. There cannot, however, be a doubt that, making allowance for the omission of some descents, the genealogies are in the main correct. The Book of Lecan (*fol.* 95, *b*) tells us that 'Bishop Conlaedh, of Cill-dara,' was descended from Emri, son of Fothad; and that 'Bishop Etchen, son of Maine Eiges, of Cluan-Fota-Baedain-Aba,' was descended from Fergus Lamderg, son of another Fothad, but in neither case are the intermediate steps of the descent given. These difficulties seem to have been mainly caused by O'Flaherty's corrections of the MS. authorities.

It is impossible, however, that Nathi, son of Garchu, can have been contemporary with Palladius and St. Patrick, if we suppose him to have lived six generations (at the lowest computation, 180 years) before Marcan, who, although in infancy, was also contemporary with St. Patrick. But the Nathi, mentioned in the Lives of St. Patrick, although there called 'Son of Garchu,' may not have been literally his *son*, but a great-grandson, or some later descendant of the same name.

The genealogy of Marcan is taken from the Book of Lecan (*fol.* 95 *b*), and is evidently quite consistent with the history. It has been given in the present Table, because there may be occasion hereafter to refer to it.

It may be added, in further evidence of error in the genealogy of St. Etchen, that Brig, or Briga, his mother, is represented as descended[1] from Cathair mòr, monarch of Ireland (who was also of the family of Cucorb, King of Leinster), according to the following pedigree :—

```
        80 Cathair Mòr, K. 174—177.
                 |
            81 Fiac
                 |
         82 Bresail Belach
                 |
            83 Labradh
                 |
         84 Enna Cennselach
                 |
          85 Crimhthann
                 |
            86 Cobtach
                 |
             87 Brig
```

This makes her three generations *younger than her son Etchen*, and shows that there must be an omission of at least that number of descents in his pedigree. This Brig, after the death of her first husband, Maine-eiges, was married to Ainmire, King of Ireland (Table II., No. 91), and became the mother of his son, Aedh mac Ainmirech. It will be seen that the generation numbers make her four generations older than her second husband : so that there is probably a defect of some descents in his pedigree also. But it would be foreign to our present purpose to point out the causes of these errors, or the manner in which they may, with most probability, be corrected.

TABLE VI.

The Kings of Ireland mentioned in the foregoing Tables, in their Chronological Order.

The Kings whose names are marked with an asterisk in the following list belonged to families which did not come within the scope of the preceding Tables, but they are nevertheless inserted in their proper chronological places, in order that the reader may have before him, without any break, a complete list of the Irish Kings to whose reigns there may be some reference in the present volume.

---

[1] *Descended.* See Colgan's pedigree of Etchen, taken from his copies of the Sanctilog. Genealog.—*Actt. SS.* p. 306, notes 3, 4, 5; and for the pedigree of Briga, note 9, *ibid.*

Appendix A.

Began to reign.	Table and Gen. No.	Names of Kings.
A.D.		
164	IV. 79	Feidhlimidh Rechtmar
174	V. 80	Cathair Mòr
177	IV. 80	Con of the Hundred Fights
212	82	*Conaire Mac Moghlamha (race of Herimon, Ernai of Munster)
220	IV. 81	Art Aonfir
250	82	*Lugadh Mac Con (race of Ith)
253	82	*Fergus Duibhdeadach, i.e. of the Black Teeth (race of Herimon Ernai of Ulster, clan Dal-fiatach)
254	IV. 82	Cormac Ulfada
277	84	*Eochaidh Gonnat
279	IV. 83	Cairbre Liffiocair
297	IV. 84	Fiacha Sraibhtine
327	IV. 85	Colla Uais
331	IV. 85	Muredach Tirech
357	86	*Coelbad (race of Hir, Clan-Rudraighe)
358	I. 86	Eochaidh Muighmeadhoin
366	87	*Crimthann, of the race of Eber (see p. 249)
379	I. 87	Niall of the Nine Hostages
405	I. 88	Dathi mac Fiachrach
428	III. 88	Laoghaire mac Néill
463	I. 89	Oilioll Molt mac Dathi
483	III. 89	Lugaidh mac Laoghaire
508		Interregnum
513	II. 90	Muirchertach mac Erca
533	II. 90	Tuathal Maolgarbh
544	III. 90	Diarmait mac Fergusa Cearbheoil
565	II. 91	Domhnall and Fergus } sons of Muirchertach mac Erca *(joint kings)*
566	II. 91 / II. 92	Baotan, son of Muirchertach mac Erca, and Eochaidh, son of Domhnall, } *(joint kings)*
568	II. 91	Ainmire, son of Sedna, son of Fergus Cennfada
571	II. 91	Baotan mac Ninnedhai
572	II. 92	Aodh mac Ainmirech
599	III. 91 / II. 92	Aodh Sláine, and Colman Rimhe, } *(joint kings)*
605	II. 92	Aodh Uariodhnach
612	II. 93	Maolcobha, surnamed the Cleric, son of Aodh mac Ainmirech
615	II. 92	Suibhne Meann
628	II. 93	Domhnall, son of Aodh mac Ainmirech
642	II. 94 / II. 94	Cellach and Conall Caol, } sons of Maolcobha *(joint kings)*
654	II. 94	Conall Caol, sole king, after the death of Cellach
658	III. 92 / III. 92	Blathmac and Diarmait, } sons of Aodh Sláine *(joint kings)*. Died in the great pestilence of 665
665	III. 93	Sechnasach, son of Blathmac

INTROD.] *Foundation of Trim.* 257

B.

History of the Foundation and Endowment of the Church of Trim, from the Book of Armagh, fol. 16 *a. b.*

Incipiunt alia pauca serotinis temporibus inuenta, suisque locis narranda, curiossitate heredum dilegentiaque sanctitatis quæ in honorem et laudem Domini, atque in amabilem *Patricii* memoriam, usque in hodiernam diem congregantur.

Quando autem *Patricius* cum sua sancta nauigatione ad Hiberniam peruenit sanctum *Lommanum* in hostio *Boindeo* nauim custodire reliquit xl. diebus et xl. noctibus, ac deinde alium quadragensimum, post oboedentiam Patricio mansit ; de-

Here begin some few other things discovered at later times, and to be narrated in their proper places, by the care and holy diligence of the heirs [*comarbs*], which are collected to the honour and praise of the Lord, and in loving memory of Patrick, even to the present day.

But when Patrick, with his holy companions in voyage, had arrived in Ireland, he left holy *Lomman* in the mouth of the Boind [1] to guard the ship, forty days and forty nights ; and then he remained another period of forty [2], after having

---

[1] *Boind.* The river Boyne: *Boindeo* is the Celtic genitive: nom. *Boinn,* or *Boind.* It will be observed that the spelling of the original MSS., as being characteristic of the Irish school, has been carefully preserved ; as in *curiossitate, dilegentia, quadragensimum,* &c.—See Reeves, *Adamnan,* p. xvi. *Pref.* The proper names, usually written *Loman, Trim,* &c., are in this MS. written with the double *m*, indicating the strong emphasis of the antient Celtic pronuntiation.

[2] *Period of forty.* 'Alium quadragensimum.' The Tripartite Life strangely takes this to mean that S. Lomman was left to take care of the ships during Lent: but the true meaning is evidently that here given, viz.: that Patrick desired him to remain, 40 days and 40 nights : but he remained another 40 days, and 40 nights. So Jocelin understands it (c. 51). In other words, finding his master did not return at the end of the first 40 days, he waited 40 days more, and then went up the river to Ath-Truimm, or the ford of Trim, where he safely arrived 'under the guidance of the Lord.' Jocelin makes a great miracle of this, and adds, that he ascended the river not only against the stream, but in the face of a strong contrary wind : 'O signum hactenus inauditum et incompertum ! Navis nemine

S

inde secundum imperium sui magistri in sua naui contrario flumine usque ad uadum *Truimm* in hostio *Areis Feidilmedo* filii *Loiguiri*, domino gubernante, peruenit.

Mane autem facto *Foirtchernn* filius *Fedeilmtheo* invenit [eum] euanguelium recitantem et ammiratus euanguelium et doctrinam eius confestim credidit, et aperto fonte in illo loco a *Lommano* in Christo babtitzatus est, et mansit cum illo donec mater eius quaerere eum peruenit, et laeta facta est in conspectu eius, quia Brittonissa erat. At illa simi-

obeyed [1] Patrick : then, according to the command of his master, he arrived, under the guidance of the Lord, against the stream, as far as the ford of *Trimm* [2], at the door of *Aras Feidilmedo* [3] [the house of Feidilmidh], son of Loigaire. And when it was morning, *Foirtchernn*, son of *Feidilmith*, found him reciting the Gospel, and, wondering at the Gospel and his doctrine, straightway believed; and there being an open fountain [4] in that place, he was baptized in Christ by *Lomman*. And he stayed with him until his mother came to seek him, and she rejoiced at the sight of him, for she was [5] a British wo-

---

gubernante, contra fluvium et ventum ad votum viri Dei velificavit,' &c. This is a good specimen of the manner in which such writers as Jocelin manufactured miracles from the statements of more antient authors. The original, it will be seen, says nothing of opposing winds, or of the ship sailing without guidance against the stream. There is nothing of the miraculous necessarily implied in the narrative. It is not even necessary to suppose the river to have been then more navigable than it is now; for the light boats of the period might easily have been carried over the shoals and rapids.—Cf. Ussher, *Brit. Eccl. Antiq.*, p. 853 (Works vi., 413).

[1] *Having obeyed.* This seems evidently the meaning: Ussher, misreading the contraction in the MS., has, ' propter obedientiam,' which makes no sense. Jocelin (l.c.) adds some nonsense about Lomman having remained in the hope of martyrdom, which has no foundation in the original.

[2] *Ford of Trimm.* ' Vadum Truimm'

is a translation of the Irish name *Ath-Truimm* (*Ath*, vadum, a ford), now Trim. See p. 150, note 2.

[3] *Aras Feidilmedo.* ' Aras ' is an old Irish word, signifying a house or dwelling: the genitive *Areis* in the text was mistaken by Ussher for *Arcis*, which luckily makes no great difference of sense: he has also changed *Feidilmedo* into *Feidilmedi*, not perceiving that the former was the Celtic genitive. Another form of the genitive, *Fedeilmtheo*, occurs in the next line. Feidilmith, or Feidhlimith, was the son of Loiguire, or Laoghaire, who was King of Ireland, A.D. 428—463.—O'Flaherty, *Ogyg.*, p. 429. See Table III., p. 252.

[4] *Fountain.* We might perhaps translate, ' And a fountain having been opened by Lomman, he was baptized,' &c. Jocelin of course makes the opening of the fountain a miracle.

[5] *For she was.* The meaning probably is, ' She rejoiced at finding her son among strangers who were Britons, because she was herself British.'

INTROD.] *Foundation of Trim.* 259

liter credidit, et iterum reuersa est in domum suam et nuntiauit marito suo omnia quæ accederant illi et filio suo. At uero *Fedelmidius* laetificabatur in aduentu clerici, quia de Brittonibus matrem habuit, i. filiam regis Brittonum, i. *Scothnoe.*

Salutauit autem *Fedelmidius Lommanum* lingua Brittannica interrogans eum secundum ordinem de fide et genere. Respondit ei, Ego sum *Lommanus* Britto Christianus alumpnus Patricii episcopi, qui missus est a Domino babtitzare populos Hibernensium et conuertere ad fidem Christi, qui me missit huc secundum uoluntatem Dei. Statimque credidit *Fedelmidius* cum omni familia sua, et immolauit illi et sancto *Patricio* regionem suam cum possesione sua et cum omnibus substantiis suis et cum omni progenie sua. Hæc omnia immolauit *Patricio* et *Lommano,* et *Foirtcherno* filio suo usque in diem iudicii.

Migrauit autem Fedelmid trans amnem *Boindeo,* et mansit *hi Cloin Lagen,* et mansit

man. And she also believed in like manner, and returned back to her house, and told to her husband all things that had happened unto herself and unto her son. But *Feidilmidh* rejoiced at the coming of the cleric, for his mother was of the Britons, viz., daughter of the King of the Britons, viz., *Scothnoe.*[1]

And *Feidilmidh* saluted *Lomman* in the British tongue, asking him in order concerning his faith and family. He answered him, 'I am *Lomman,* a Briton, a Christian, the disciple of Bishop *Patrick,* who is sent by the Lord to baptize the tribes of the Irish, and to convert them to the faith of Christ: who hath sent me hither, according to the will of God.' And forthwith *Feidilmidh* believed, with all his family, and he devoted[2] to him and to holy *Patrick* his territory, with his possessions, and with all his substances, and with all his race. All these he devoted to *Patrick* and *Lomman,* and to *Foirtchernn* his son, unto the the day of judgment.

But *Feidilmidh* passed across the river of Boind, and remained at *Cloin Lagen,* and

---

[1] *Scothnoe.* Ussher reads *Scothnoesa,* taking *sa* from the first syllable of the following word, by an error of transcription. The Tripartite Life makes *Scoth* the mother of Fortchernn, instead of his grand-mother, and drops the syllable *noe.*

[2] *Devoted.* The word *immolavit* in the original signifies, he *dedicated, offered up* as a free gift, as a sacrifice is offered to God. — See Reeves, *Adamnan,* p. 435.

Lomman cum *Foirtcherno* in uado *Truimm*, usque dum peruenit *Patricius* ad illos et aedificauit aeclesiam cum illis xxii. anno antequam fundata esset aeclesia Alti Machæ.

Progenies autem *Lommani* de Brittonibus, i. filius Gollit. Germana autem *Patricii* mater ejus : germani autem Lommani hii sunt :—

Episcopus *Manis*, hi *forgnidiu la ciurcniu*.

Broccaide in *Imbliuch* equorum apud *Ciarrige Connact*.

Broccanus imbrechmig apud nepotes *Dorthim*.

Mugenóg, hi *Cill Dumi Gluinn* in deisciurt *Breg*.

Lomman remained with *Foirtchernn* at the ford of *Trimm*, until Patrick came to them, and built a church with them, the twenty-second year before the church of Armagh [1] was founded.

Now the race [2] of *Lomman* of the Britons *was this*: he was the son of Gollit. And the sister of Patrick was his mother; and the brothers of *Lomman* are these :—

Bishop *Manis* [3], in *Forgnidhe* in the district of the *Cuircne*.

Broccaide [4] in Imliuch of horses, in Ciarrighe of Connacht.

Brocan in *Brechmigh* [5] among the *Ui Dorthim*.

Mugenóg [6] in *Cill Dumigluinn*, in the east of *Bregia*.

---

[1] *Armagh*. The Latin *Altum Macha*, a literal translation of the Irish name *Ard-macha*, establishes beyond all doubt the true signification and etymology of the name, 'height' or 'high place of Macha.' Ussher has printed this document only thus far.

[2] *Race*. The original word *progenies* denotes race, family, genealogical descent. *Feidlimidh* is said above to have dedicated to Patrick all his territory and possessions, with his *progenies*, i.e. race, posterity, his clan.

[3] *Manis*, or Munis, as Colgan calls him (*Actt. SS.*, 6 Feb.). The following words are Irish. *Forgnidiu* and *Ciurniu* are ablative forms : *Lit.* 'he was bishop among the Forgnidians who are in the district of the Cuircnians.' The parish is now Forgney, Co. of Longford, diocese of Meath. For the boundaries of the district of the Cuircne, see O'Donovan, *Book of Rights*, p. 181, *n.*, and *Martyr. Doneg.*, at 18 Dec.

[4] *Broccaide*. His church was at Imliuch or Imleach Each, 'Emlagh (or the Marsh) of the horses.' It is situated in the barony of Costello, Co. of Mayo. Four Mast., A.D. 757, and O'Donovan's note. *Book of Rights*, p. 100, note f; *Mart. of Donegal*, at 9 July.

[5] *Brechmigh*. Generally written Bregh-magh, or Magh-bregh, the great plain of Bregia or Bregmagia (as the name is usually Latinized), in Meath. *Book of Rights*, p. 11, note. *Nepotes*, in the text, is the word usually employed to translate the Irish *Ui* (plural of *Ua* or *O*) descendants, posterity. The *Ui Dorthim*, more correctly *Ui Dortain* or *Ui Tortain*, were a tribe seated near Ardbraccan in the Co. of Meath. *Ibid*, p. 151, *n*.

[6] *Mugenog*, or Mogenog. His church was called Cill Dumhagluinn, in the same district of Bregia.—*Mart. Doneg.*, 26 Dec. It is now called Kilglin, and is situated

Foundation of Trim.

Hæc autem progenies Patricii propria est consanguinitate et gratia, fide et babtismate et doctrina, et omnia quæ adepti sunt de terra, de regionibus, aeclessiis, et omnibus oblationibus propriis sancto Patricio in sempiternum obtullerunt.

Post aliquantum autem tempus adpropinquante *Lommani* exitu, perrexit cum alumpno suo *Foirtchernno* ad fratrem suum *Broccidium* fratrem salutandum perrexerunt autem ipse et alumpnus eius *Foirtchernn*.

Commendauitque sanctam aeclesiam suam sancto *Patricio* et *Foirtcherno* ; sed recussauit *Foirtchernn* tenere hereditatem patris sui quam obtulit Deo et *Patricio*, nisi *Lommanus* dixit non accipies benedictionem meam nisi acciperis principatum aeclesiæ meae. Tenuit autem post obitum magistri sui principatum .iii. diebus, usque dum peruenit ad uadum *Truimm*, ac deinde statim *Cathlaido* peregrino distribuit suam aeclesiam.

Hae sunt autem oblationes

Now this is the proper race of Patrick by consanguinity and by grace, by faith and baptism and doctrine. And all that they had acquired of land, of territories, of churches, and of all special oblations, they offered to holy Patrick for ever.

But after some time, when *Lomman's* death was approaching, he went [1] with his disciple *Fortchernn* to his brother *Broccaide* : and they went to salute his brother, himself and his disciple *Fortchernn*.

And he committed his holy church to holy *Patrick*, and to *Fortchernn*. But *Fortchernn* refused to hold the heritage of his father, which he had offered to God and to *Patrick* : until *Lomman* said, 'Thou shalt not have my blessing unless thou accept the chieftainship of my church.' He held the chieftainship however for three days *only* after the death of his master, until he arrived at the ford of *Trimm*, and then he straightway gave his church to *Cathlaid* the pilgrim.[2]

These are the offerings of

---

within the parish of Balfeighan, Co. of Meath. — Four Mast., at 834, and O'Donovan's note.

[1] *He went*. His object evidently was to die at his brother's church ; and according to a very antient custom he designated his disciple Fortchernn his successor.

[2] *Pilgrim*. So the word *peregrinus* signifies in Adamnan (see the *Glossary* in Reeves' *Adamnan*). The typographical errors in Colgan's *Trias Thaum*. have made great confusion in the name of this pilgrim. There can be no doubt that *Cathlaid* is the correct form of the name.

Fedelmedo filii Loiguiri sancto Patricio et Lommano et Foirtcherno, id est —
 Uadum *Truimm* in finibus *Loiguiri Breg.*
 Imgæ in finibus *Loiguiri Midi.*
 Hæc est ecclesiastica progenies *Fedelmtheo.*
Fortchernus,
Aed magnus,
Aed parvus,
Conall,
Baitán,
Ossan,
Cummene,
Sarán.
 Hii omnes episcopi fuerunt et principes, uenerantes sanctum Patricium et successores eius.
 Plebilis autem progenies eius hæc est :—
Fergus filius *Fedelmtheo.*
Feradach filius *Fergosso.*
Cronán filius *Feradig.*
Sarán filius *Cronáin.*
Failán filius *Saráin.*
Failgnad filius *Failáin.*
Forfáilid filius *Failgnaith.*
Segene filius *Forfáilto.*
Sechnassach filius *Ségeni.*

Feidilmidh, son of Loiguire, to holy Patrick and to Foirtchernn, that is —
 The ford of *Trimm,* in the territories of *Loiguiri* of *Bregia.*
 Imgæ, in the territories of *Loiguire* of *Meath.*[1]
 This is the ecclesiastical race of *Feidilmidh.*
Fortcherrn,
Aodh the great,
Aodh the little,
Conall,
Baitán,
Ossan[2],
Cummene,
Sarán.
 These were all bishops and chiefs, venerating holy Patrick and his successors.
 But his lay[3] race is this : —

Fergus son of *Fedilmidh.*
Feradach son of *Fergus.*
Cronán son of *Feradach.*
Sarán son of *Cronán.*
Fáilán son of *Saran.*
Failgnad son of *Fáilán.*
Forfáilid son of *Failgnad.*
Segene son of *Forfáilid.*
Sechnassach son of *Segene.*

---

[1] *Meath.* The two districts inhabited by the Cinel Laoghaire are here distinguished; the Cinel Laoghaire Bregh, in Bregia; and the Cinel Laoghaire Midhe, in Meath. Trim is described as in the former district; and *Imgæ* (which has not been identified) in the latter.

[2] *Ossan.* See *Mart. Dungal.* ad 17 Feb.

[3] *Lay.* The word *Lay* seems the best representation of *plebilis,* here; *plebilis* being formed from *plebs,* as *Laicus* is from λαὸς.

ST. PATRICK

APOSTLE OF IRELAND

A Memoir of his Life and Mission

' Le peuple monastique des temps barbares, le peuple missionaire, et destiné à porter la lumière de la foi et de la science dans les ténèbres croissantes de l'Occident, c'est le peuple irlandais, dont on connait mieux les malheurs que les services, et dont on n'a pas assez étudié l'étonnante vocation.'

OZANAM (*La Civilisation Chrétienne chez les Francs, ch.* 4).

ST. PATRICK
APOSTLE OF IRELAND.

A Memoir of his Life and Mission.

CHAPTER I.

The antient Church of Britain; and the Mission of Palladius to the Scots believing in Christ.

HRISTIANITY had followed the course of Roman civilisation into Britain, and it is probable that there were believers in Christ among the native tribes of Britannia before the end of the second century. That may be the meaning of the celebrated passage of Tertullian[1], which does not, however, assert the existence of a regularly organised British Church at this early period. We are not bound to credit the fable

<small>Christianity established in the British provinces at an early period.</small>

---

[1] *Tertullian.* 'Britannorum inaccessa Romanis loca Christo vero subdita.' *Contr. Judæos,* c. 7. written A.D. 208. Comp. Euseb. De *Præpar. Evang.* lib. iii. c. 1,

of the British king Lucius, in the year 180, nor the still more apocryphal story of Donald, King of the Albanian Scots in 202, who are both said to have, of their own accord, solicited the Roman Pontiff to send them Christian instruction and baptism.[1]

The colony of Scots in Britain under Cairbre Riada.

It was about the middle of the third century, according to Irish tradition, that Cairbre Righfada[2] (or Riada, as his name is pronounced) established the colony of Scots on the northwest coast of Albanian Britain, in connexion with the head-quarters of his clan on the adjacent shores of the present county of Antrim, in Ireland. Both tribes, as well as the regions they inhabited in both countries, received from his name the appellation of Dal-riada[3], 'the

---

[1] *Baptism.* 'Hic [sc. Eleutherus] accepit epistolam a Lucio Britanniæ rege ut Christianus efficeretur, per ejus mandatum.' So says the Liber Pontificalis: and see Bede I. 4. Lucius is therefore assigned to the middle of the second century. There was a chieftain of Glamorganshire whose native name was Lleurwg, surnamed Lleufer Mawr, 'the Great Luminary,' which title may have been latinized Lucius. Rees, *Welsh Saints*, p. 82, sq. Irish version of Nennius, *Add. Notes.* No. VIII. p. xiii. The other story of Donald king of Scots, who is represented as having made a similar application to Pope Victor I., is totally without foundation. There never was such a king, nor were there any Scots in North Britain, A.D. 202, to have a king. The legend is no more than a repetition of the fable of King Lucius: and appears to have no higher authority than Hector Boece. See Innes, *Civil and Eccles. Hist. of Scotland* (Spalding Club), p. 14.

[2] *Cairbre Righfada,* i.e. Carbry of the long arm. The surname Righfada is pronounced and often written Riada, the *gh* and *f* being both quiescent. He was one of three named Cairbre, sons of Conaire Mac Moghlamha, King of Ireland, A.D. 212—222. (See App. to Introd. table VI. p. 256, *supra.*) Bede calls this chietain *Reuda* (*Hist. Eccl.* I. 1.) See the valuable Dissertation on the history of this tribe in Reeves's *Eccl. Antiq. of Down and Connor*, p. 318, sq., and the Genealogical Table of Dalriadic chieftains of both countries, showing the descent of the principal Highland families from their Irish or Scotic ancestors, in the same author's edition of *Adamnan's Life of Columba*, p. 438.

[3] *Dalriada.* The Irish word *Dal*, as Bede (I. 1.) has explained it, signifies a part, or portion, 'a quo videlicet duce [sc. Reuda] usque hodie Dalreudini vocantur, nam lingua eorum *Daal* partem significat.'

Tribe, or Tribe-land of Riada.' In Ireland, the territory still retains the name in the corrupted form of *The Route*, and in Scotland a record of the historical fact may be found in the name of *Argyle*[1], which is properly *Airer Gaedhil*, or region of the Gaedhil—that is to say, of the Irish. The geographical position of this territory, which appears to have included the islands on the coast, is thus described by the venerable Bede: —'There is a very large gulf of the sea,' he says, 'which antiently divided the nation of the Britons from the Picts, and which breaks from the west a long way into the land, where to this day stands the well-fortified city of the Britons, called Alcluith. The Scots, we have mentioned, arriving on the north side of this bay, made themselves a home there: *sibi locum patriæ fecerunt.*'

The city of Alcluith was the western fortification of the wall, or entrenchment, originally thrown up by Agricola between the Clyde and the Forth, and repaired or restored, with additional forts, in the reign of Antonine. This wall, ditch, or series of fortresses, formed the northern boundary of the Roman power in Britain; and the district included between it and the wall of Adrian, or Severus, in Northumberland, running from Car-

The city Alcluith.

---

[1] *Argyle*, called by the Irish *Airer Dalriatai*, and *Airer Gaedhil*; the district, or territory of the Dalriadans, or of the Gael. Airiur, or Airer, signifies *finis, regio, margo.* See Reeves's *Adamnan*, p. 395, note, m. The district of Dalriada, in Ireland, is not to be confounded with the neighbouring region of Dalaraide, which has its name from a different chieftain. See Reeves's *Eccl. Hist. of Down and Connor,* p. 334, sq. The one is Dal-Riada, the other Dal-Araide.

lisle to Tynemouth, and still called the Pict's wall, formed the debateable ground so long contested with the Picts and Scots, until by the victories of Theodosius, at the end of the fourth century, it became the fifth Roman province of Britain, under the name of Valentia.

British martyrs in the Diocletian persecution.

In the early part of the fourth century, the British Church contributed to the ranks of the noble army of martyrs[1] in the Dioclesian persecution, and soon afterwards, on the restoration of liberty of conscience under Constantine, we find bishops established in the chief cities of the Roman provinces. Eborius of York, Restitutus of London, and Adelfius, probably of Caerleon upon Usk[2], subscribed the Acts of the Council or Synod of Arles, in 314, and it is evident, from many authorities, which may be seen collected by Ussher and Stillingfleet[3], that an organised Christian Church existed in the Roman provinces of Britain very early in the century of which we are speaking.

---

[1] *Martyrs.* St. Alban at Verulam, (22 June). SS. Aaron and Julius at Caerleon upon Usk, with others, (1 July). *Bede* I. 7.

[2] *Caerleon upon Usk.* The subscription of this latter prelate is given thus in the printed editions of the Councils: 'Adelfius Episcopus de civitate Colonia Londinensium,' for which some would read *Colonia Lindum*, i.e. Lincoln: Lappenberg I. 50. (Thorpe's Transl.) Ussher suggests *Colchester*, which was *Caer Colun*, in Nennius: *Works*, v. 82. 236. But the Irish Nennius gives the name of Caer *Lonin*-oper-uisc to Caerleon on Usk, which name may have been easily corrupted into Colonia *Londinensium*, Colonia being the equivalent of *Caer*. This conjecture derives some support from the tradition that York, London, and Caerleon on Usk were the original archbishoprics of Britain. Ussher, *Antiq.* cap. v. *Works* v. p. 101. Irish Nennius, p. 28. Add. Notes. No. 1. Stillingfleet is in favour of Caerleon on Usk (*Antiq.* ch. 2. *Works* vol. iii. 48), as on that supposition the three Roman provinces were represented at the Synod by these three bishops. Some give to this Synod of Arles the date 326 or 328. Spelman, *Concil.* I. 43.

[3] *Stillingfleet.* Ussher, *Antiq.* capp. vii. viii. (*Works*, vol. v.) Stillingfleet, *Antiq.* ch. iii. (*Works*, vol. iii.)

But the withdrawal of the Roman power, at the beginning of the fifth century, seems to have prepared the way for many evils. The civilisation introduced by the Romans was in a great measure destroyed by the ravages[1] of the Picts and Scots, and, before the middle of the century, the Pelagian heresy had made considerable progress in Christian Britain. St. Germain, Bishop of Auxerre, was twice sent over to counteract this evil. On the former of these missions, with which alone we are here concerned, he was attended by St. Lupus, Bishop of Troyes, and other ecclesiastics of inferior rank. Two different, but not, perhaps, inconsistent accounts of this event, both from coeval authorities, are handed down to us. Constantius of Lyons, the biographer and contemporary[2] of St. Germain, tells us that the rapid spread of Pelagianism occasioned a deputation from the British to the Gallican bishops, praying for aid to defend the Catholic faith, and that a numerous synod[3], summoned for the purpose, commissioned Germanus and Lupus to undertake the confutation of the heretics.

This mission is usually dated A.D. 429, the consulship of Florentius and Dionysius at Rome.

---

[1] *Ravages.* Bede I. c. xi. xii.

[2] *Contemporary.* Father Peter Bosch, the Bollandist, says:—' Constantii labores anno Christi circiter 473, hoc est quinto tantum aut sexto supra vigesimum ab obitu S. Germani, &c. . . . Diu ergo cum sancto, de quo scribit, ejusque æqualibus vixisse debuit.' *Actt. SS. Julii*, vii. p. 191, D.

[3] *Synod.* ' Eodem tempore ex Britanniis directa legatio, Gallicanis episcopis nuntiavit, Pelagianam perversitatem in locis suis late populos occupavisse: et quam primum fidei Catholicæ debere succurri. Ob quam causam synodus numerosa collecta est:' &c. *Ibid.* p. 211, E.

Under that year another contemporary authority, St. Prosper of Aquitaine, in his Chronicle[1], without any mention of the intervention of the Gallican bishops, attributes the mission of Germanus to the Pope Celestinus. 'Agricola, a Pelagian,' he says, 'son of Severianus, a Pelagian bishop, corrupted the churches of Britannia by insinuation of his doctrine; but by the instrumentality [or negotiation] of the deacon Palladius— *ad actionem Palladii diaconi*—Pope Celestinus sends Germanus, Bishop of Auxerre, in his own stead —*vice sua*—to displace the heretics and direct the Britons to the Catholic faith.' And in the year next but one following, the same Chronicle tells us that, during the consulship of Bassus and Antiochus, the year in which the general council of Ephesus condemned Nestorius, or A.D. 431, 'Palladius was consecrated by Pope Celestine, and sent to the Scots believing in Christ, as their first bishop, 'Ad Scotos in Christum credentes ordinatur a Papa Celestino Palladius, et primus episcopus mittitur.'

Sanctioned by Pope Celestine.

Mission of Palladius to the Scots, A.D. 431.

Negotiation of Palladius for St. Germain at Rome.

We must speak of these passages separately. If Palladius was a disciple of St. Germain, and also a deacon, as is commonly said, of the

---

[1] *Chronicle.* St. Prosper is supposed to have been born A.D. 402, and lived to about 463. *Ceillier*, xiv. p. 518, sq. There are two editions of the Chronicle of Prosper, one corrupt and interpolated: published by Pet. Pithou, Paris, 1588, and again by Labbé, *Bibl. Nov. MSS.* (Paris, 1657), tom. i. p. 56. This edition of the Chronicle does not contain the passages here quoted, which occur only in the edition usually annexed to the Chronicle of Eusebius continued by St. Jerome; it will be found in the new edit. of the *Lectiones Antiquæ* of Canisius, i. p. 264, in the *Bibl. Patrum, Lugd.* 1677, tom. viii. and in the works of St. Jerome. From this last reprint of it, it is here quoted; edit. Vallarsii. tom. viii. See Cave, *Scriptores*, I. p. 347, Oxon. 1740.

CHAP. I.]   *the Papal Sanction.*   271

Church of Rome, it is not impossible[1] that, at his instance or suggestion, Pope Celestine, after the two bishops of Auxerre and Troyes had been selected by the Gallican synod, may have given to the senior of them an additional commission to act in his name. Prosper has mentioned St. Germain only, because St. Germain only, as head of the mission, had received this further authority to represent especially the Roman bishop; and Constantius, the biographer of St. Germain, if he was[2] acquainted with this fact, did not perhaps think it of sufficient importance to be particularly noticed in his account of the matter. Germain and Lupus were primarily sent by the Gallican bishops. The fact that Germain had received also the sanction of Celestine, was not, in the fifth century, regarded as a circumstance of such moment as to require special notice. There is, therefore, no actual inconsistency between the two narratives. *Papal sanction of St. Germain's mission not mentioned by his biographers.*

But here we are met by another difficulty. The venerable Bede[3] had certainly the Chronicle of Prosper before him. He states, almost in the words of the Chronicle, that Pelagianism had been introduced into Britain by Agricola, son of the Pelagian bishop, Severianus. He states also, *nor by Bede.*

---

[1] *Impossible.* This mode of reconciling the two authorities is suggested by Baronius, ad an. 429, n. 10, but it does not explain the silence of Constantius.

[2] *If he was.* Heric of Auxerre (*circ.* 880), author of a metrical life of St. Germain, is equally silent about Celestine's commission: so are the anonymous authors of the Acts of St. Lupus. (*Actt. SS.* ad 29 Junii, p. 69, sq.) This silence can only arise from the fact having been unknown, or from its having been deemed of no such consequence as to require to be mentioned.

[3] *Bede.* Hist. Eccl. i. c. 17.

almost in the words of the Chronicle, that Palladius was sent by Celestine, Bishop of Rome, to be the first bishop of the Scots who were believers in Christ; but he says not a word of the statement for which the Chronicle is our only authority, that St. Germain had been constituted by Celestine the legate or representative of the Bishop of Rome.

The Roman mission of St. Germain alluded to by Prosper elsewhere.

This statement, therefore, it may be said, was not in the copies of Prosper's Chronicle which existed in the time of Bede, and the story of St. Germain having gone to Britain, as the representative of Pope Celestine, is an interpolation[1] of later times. But, on the other hand, Bede may have had before him the mutilated text of the Chronicle. It does not necessarily follow that the copy cited by Bede must have been the genuine work of Prosper, and that all other texts are corrupt. The fact of the Roman mission of Germanus is otherwise authenticated, however we may agree to explain the silence of Bede, and of the biographers. In another work, whose authenticity is undoubted, Prosper[2] alludes very dis-

---

[1] *Interpolation.* See what Stillingfleet has said on this subject, *Antiq.* ch. iv. (*Works* III. p. 117, sq.)

[2] *Prosper.* See the book, *Contra Collatorem* (i.e. against the 13th *Collatio* of John Cassian), published with the works of St. Augustine, tom. x. part ii. Append. p. 196. (*Ed. Bened.*) The passage referred to is as follows : ' Wherefore also the Pontiff Celestine of venerable memory, to whom the Lord gave many gifts of His grace for the protection of the Catholic Church, knowing that for those who are already condemned the remedy to be applied is not a further judicial enquiry but only repentance, commanded Cælestius, who demanded a further hearing in a matter already settled, to be driven from the borders of all Italy. . . . . . and with no less zealous care he delivered the Britannias from the same disease, when he drove even from that secret place of Ocean some enemies of Grace, who were settling in the soil of their origin ; and by ordaining a bishop for the Scots,

tinctly to something which Pope Celestine had done to extirpate Pelagianism in Britain. He does not tell us so distinctly what that something was. He appears rather to take for granted that the fact to which he alluded was well and generally known. 'Whilst the Pope,' he says, 'laboured to keep the Roman island Catholic, he made also the barbarous island Christian, by ordaining a bishop for the Scots.'

The book against Cassian in which this allusion occurs must have been written after the death of Celestine, and soon after the consecration of his successor Sixtus[1] or Xistus. The allusion is evidently to the mission of St. Germain. The terms in which the deliverance from heresy of the British provinces is spoken of agree very well with the account we have of the proceedings of St. Germain in that mission. But Stillingfleet[2] objects that, if this event had been intended, and if Celestine had made St. Germain his vicar for the suppression of Pelagianism in Britain, the names of such eminent prelates as Germanus and Lupus could scarcely have been omitted by St. Prosper. This argument, however, is certainly not strong. The object of Prosper was to show the zeal of the Popes in suppressing the Pelagian heresy. It was not necessary for him to name the instruments employed in the work.

Prosper's book against Cassian.

whilst he laboured to keep the Roman island Catholic, made also the barbarous island Christian.'
[1] *Sixtus.* The author says that St. Augustine wrote, 'Ad beatissimum quoque apostolicæ sedis tunc presbyterum Sixtum, nunc vero Pontificem, &c.' *Loc. cit.* Sixtus was consecrated 7 Aug. 432, and died 440.
[2] *Stillingfleet.* Loc. cit. (*Works* III. p. 115.)

The very eminence of Germanus and Lupus would have rather been a reason for suppressing their names, when the object was to give as much credit and prominence as possible to the Pope, who had given his authority to their mission[1], and thereby made it his own. But, as we have already said, the words must mean that Celestine did *something* which had the effect of banishing the propagators of Pelagianism out of the British provinces. What was this something? If Germanus was known or believed to have received any sort of legatine authority from the Roman See, that would be quite enough to justify the words of our author, that Celestine had delivered the Britannian provinces; and if Celestine did not commission Germanus, we know not what else he did to rescue Britain from the plague of Pelagianism.

Success of St. Germain in Britain.

The success of Germanus and his followers, according to all the extant histories, was rapid and decisive. The favourers of the heresy were unpopular. At a public discussion, although they came with great display of wealth[2], attended

---

[1] *Mission.* Stillingfleet speaks throughout as if Lupus, as well as Germanus, had been commissioned by the Pope. One of his arguments, taken from the fact that Lupus was the brother of Vincent of Lerins, is built upon this mistake. 'It is very unlikely,' he says, that Celestine 'should pitch upon one of that society [of Lerins] most suspected for semipelagianism, and whose brother appeared so early and warmly in it.' (*Loc. cit.* p. 119.) But who ever said that Celestine 'pitched upon Lupus?' The Chronicle of Prosper says not one word of Lupus, or of his connexion with the mission. The same oversight is committed by Lappenberg, who says, 'the orthodox, through the intervention of Palladius, who afterwards became the first Scottish bishop, prevailed on the Pope Celestinus to send hither Germanus, bishop of Auxerre, and Lupus, bishop of Troyes, &c.' (*Thorpe's Transl.* I. 65.)

[2] *Wealth.* 'Procedunt conspicui divitiis, veste fulgentes, circumdati assentatione multorum.' *Bede* I. c. 17.

by numerous flatterers, they were completely silenced. The people applauded their defeat by shouts, and could scarcely be restrained from violence.[1] The popularity of St. Germain was attested by his having soon after been accepted as leader of the British troops, in a celebrated battle against the Saxons[2] and Picts. His assumption of such an office may seem inconsistent with the ecclesiastical character of the bishop. But the army was his former profession, and the victory was gained in a manner truly ecclesiastical. The story is told by the contemporary authority of Constantius, and is not in itself improbable. The attendant priests, by intoning *Halleluiah* in a voice of thunder, taken up by the soldiers, and re-echoed by the surrounding hills, so terrified the barbarous enemy, that the Britons remained masters of the field without a blow.[3]

All this was done in less than a year, and St. Germain immediately after returned to France. There was, therefore, time for the success of the mission to have been known to Prosper; so that he may be excused for attributing to Celestine the honour of having made 'the Roman island' Catholic. Hence the text of the Chronicle, in

His popularity.

---

[1] *Violence.* 'Populus arbiter vix manus continet, judicium tamen clamore testatur.' *Bede*, ibid.

[2] *Saxons.* As the year 430, which is usually fixed as the date of the Halleluiah Victory (See Ussher, *Index Chron.*), seems too early for a battle with Saxons, Father Innes suggests that Constantius may have written here *Saxons*, instead of *Scots*, by a natural mistake. *Civ. and Eccl.*

Hist. of Scotland, p. 49. But Ussher's solution seems preferable, for he shows that occasional inroads were made by the Saxons, before the arrival of Hengist. *Antiquit.* c. xi. (*Works*, v. p. 385), and cf. Lappenberg (Thorpe's Transl.) I. 63, *note*.

[3] *A blow.* See the account of this battle, Constantius (lib. i. c. vi. 51). *Actt. SS. Julii.* tom. vii. 213. Bede I. 20.

which the Pope is said to have sent Germanus *vice sua* into Britain, receives confirmation from this indirect allusion to the fact made by the same author in another work, when he was writing with a different object.

<small>No reason to doubt the Roman mission of St. Germain.</small> On the whole, there seems no valid ground for doubting that, in addition to his appointment by the Gallican synod, St. Germain may have been armed with a commission from Rome. There is nothing inconsistent with the ecclesiastical usages of the time in the fact itself, and the authority of Prosper is sufficient to give it credit.

<small>Palladius not a deacon or archdeacon of Rome.</small> The mention of Palladius, as the person by whose intervention the sanction of Rome was obtained, together with his being called a deacon in the Chronicle, seems the only foundation of the opinion that he was a deacon in the Church of Rome. With this hint to begin with, however, some modern manufacturers of history have gone farther, and made him an archdeacon[1] or deacon to Pope Celestine; nay, cardinal and apostolic nuncio.

<small>More probably St. Germain's deacon.</small> But it is nowhere said that Palladius was of Rome, or a deacon of Rome, much less that he was deacon to Pope Celestine. All this is unauthorised assumption and fancy. It seems much more natural to interpret the words of Prosper's Chronicle[2] as signifying that Palladius

---

[1] *Archdeacon.* Ralph of Chester, in his Polychronicon, makes him deacon *of Rome*; Probus and Jocelin, in their lives of St. Patrick, call him *arckdeacon of the Pope*; and Leslie declares him to have been a *Cardinal and Nuntio apostolical.* See the references in Ussher, *Primord.* cap. xvi. (Works vi. 357.)

[2] *Chronicle.* The words of the Chronicle are these : ' Agricola Pelagianus, Severiani episcopi Pela-

was St. Germain's deacon: 'at the negotiation of the deacon Palladius, Pope Celestine sends Germanus in his own stead.' In this there is nothing unusual, or strange. When Germanus was nominated by the Gallican bishops, he sent his deacon to Rome, to negotiate a further special mission from the apostolical patriarch[1] of the imperial city. He most probably felt that, as representative of the Bishop of Rome, his influence in a Roman province would be vastly increased, and his deacon was the proper officer, according to the usages of that age[2], by whose intervention the negotiation with Rome would naturally have been conducted. Equally without foundation is the supposition that Palladius was influenced, during his negotiations at Rome, by some special zeal for the welfare of Great Britain. That may or may not have been so. He was zealous, no doubt, for the success of his master's mission, and he succeeded in obtaining for his master's mission the recognition of the Roman bishop. This is all that we can legitimately infer from the brief words of the Chronicler, 'ad actionem Palladii.' Nevertheless, the supposed interest[3], manifested by Palladius in

giani filius, ecclesias Britanniæ dogmatis sui insinuatione corrupit, sed ad actionem Palladii diaconi Papa Celestinus Germanum Antissiodorensem episcopum vice sua mittit, ut deturbatis hæreticis Britannos ad Catholicam fidem dirigat.'

[1] *Patriarch.* The word *Papa* was at that time the title of all bishops, and signified simply 'Father!' See the letters of Sidonius Apollinaris, in which the bishops, his correspondents, are all styled *Papa.*

[2] *Age.* See Bingham, *On the Antient Duties of the Deacons,* Book ii. chap. 20.

[3] *Interest.* Palladius, says Father Innes, 'had a particular zeal for the Britons.' *Civ. and Eccl. Hist.* p. 50. This is one of those presumptions which so often bias the minds of writers of history: neither Prosper

the spiritual welfare of the British churches, has given birth to the assertion that he was himself a native[1] of the island. The Chronicle makes no mention of the place of his birth, and there is literally no reason for calling him a Briton, except the surmise just mentioned. If we are to determine his birthplace by conjecture, conjecture would seem rather to point towards Gaul, not only from his connection with Germanus of Auxerre, but also because we find that the Palladian family, at that time, had risen to eminence in the Gallican episcopacy, and probably, also, in the legal profession. Simplicius[2],

nor any other antient writer has told us that Palladius had any particular zeal *for the Britons*. He may have had a particular zeal against the Pelagian heresy: but that is all that we can fairly infer, and even that inference perhaps is not perfectly warranted. He successfully negotiated a certain business at Rome. This is all that Prosper really says.

[1] *A native.* See Innes, *Civil and Eccl. Hist. of Scotland*, p. 52. Ussher quotes a MS. work of William of Malmesbury, *De antiquitate Glastoniensis ecclesiæ*, in which Palladius is said to have been a Briton. Trithemius calls him a Greek, author of the Life of St. Chrysostom, in which he is followed by Bale and others. But for this there is no authority, except the identity of name. For this and some other still more unfounded opinions, see Ussher, *loc. cit.* The Lessons of the Breviary of Aberdeen make him an Egyptian. ' Palladius pontifex egregius ex egiptiaca gente illustris [read *illustribus*] ortus natalibus, &c.' *Brev. Aberd. (Propr. SS.)* ad 6 Julii, fol. xxiv. b. This opinion originated in the assumption that the Palladius of whom we are treating was the author of the *Historia Lausiaca*,

of which there is no probability, nor any evidence; Fordun, *Scoti-Chronicon*, tom. i. lib. iii. c. 8, p. 112. (Edit. Goodall, *Edinb.* 1759.) The Bollandist, Father J. B. Solliere, who compiled the Acts of St. Palladius (*Actt. SS. Julii*, tom. ii. p. 286, sq.) maintains that he was an Italian, assuming that Prosper in the Chronicle had styled him a deacon of the Roman church: ' Et sane cum synchronus nullus de Palladio usquam meminerit, excepto solo Prospero: is vero patriam ejus nullo modo attigerit, *Romanæ ecclesiæ diaconum* dumtaxat (non archidiaconum, archiepiscopum aut cardinalem) asserens, id unum reliquit probabilissime supponendum, non monachum aliquem orientalem, multo minus Britonem, sed *clericum Italum* fuisse sanctum nostrum Palladium.' *Ibid.* p. 288. But it is not true that Prosper has called him a deacon *of the Roman Church.*

[2] *Simplicius.* He was elected to the see of Bourges whilst still a layman. On the vacancy occasioned by the death of his father Eulodius, who was his immediate predecessor, the candidates for the see were so numerous and turbulent, that the citizens

CHAP. I.]   *Probably a Native of Gaul.*   279

who was elected Archbishop of Bourges in 472, had been married to a lady of this family, the daughter of Palladius, a former prelate of the same see, who became archbishop, A.D. 377, and seems to have lived beyond 451. He was probably the Palladius whose name appears in this latter year subscribed to the synodical epistle of the Gallican bishops, addressed to Pope Leo I[1], on the question then mooted as to the jurisdiction of the Churches of Arles and Vienne. Some have made a second archbishop of the name, distinguishing the Palladius of 451, who subscribed the synodical epistle, from the Palla-

The Palladian family eminent in Gaul.

of Bourges deputed the celebrated Sidonius Apollinaris, then but recently promoted to the see of Arverni (now Clermont in Auvergne), to nominate their Archbishop, binding themselves by oath to acquiesce in his selection. His correspondence with the bishops of the province on this subject is still extant, and also the speech in which he announced to the people of Bourges his choice of Simplicius, and his reasons for the selection. In this discourse he mentions incidentally the wife of Simplicius: 'His wife,' he says, 'descends from the family of the Palladii, who have filled their chairs both of letters and of altars, with the applause of their order. And inasmuch as the person of the matron' [she was probably present] 'requires that she should be mentioned in a becoming manner as well as briefly, I would strongly affirm that that woman worthily represents the priesthood of both, whether we regard her birth and education, or her after life when chosen as a wife :' in other words she was worthy of the priesthood both of her father, who had been Archbishop of Bourges, and of her husband, now chosen to the same

dignity. The original words are as follow : ' Uxor illi de Palladiorum stirpe descendit, qui aut literarum, aut altarium cathedras cum sui ordinis laude tenuerunt. Sane quia persona matronæ verecundam succinctamque sui exigit mentionem, constanter adstruxerim, respondere illam feminam sacerdotii utriusque, vel ubi educata crevit, vel ubi electa migravit.' From this it appears that the Palladian family had distinguished itself in the fifth century (Sidonius wrote these words in 472),both in literature and in the church : and possibly the words *altarium cathedras* may contain an allusion to Palladius the first bishop of the Scots, as well as to Palladius the Archbishop of Bourges : for the authors of the Gallia Christiana (vol. ii. p. 7) tell us that there was no other bishop of the name in that age. See the Works of Sidonius Apollinaris, lib. vii. epist. 9. *Biblioth. Patrum, Lugdun.*, 1677, tom. vi. p. 1111. 12.

[1] *Pope Leo I.* See the Letter of Pope Leo: Epist. 50 (Opp. ed. Quesnel, *Ludg.* 1700),tom. i. p. 271, and the Epistola Synodica Episcoporum Gallorum, ib. p. 288.

280   *Palladius a Gallican Missionary.*   [CHAP. I.

Palladius probably of Gaul.

dius who became archbishop in 377. But this opinion is not adopted by the authors of the Gallia Christiana.¹ There is another circumstance, also, not the less valuable because it is told incidentally in the lives of St. Patrick, which seems to point to Gaul as the country of Palladius, first bishop of the Scoti. After his death, his disciples, Augustine and Benedict, we are told, went, on their return home, to a place called Ebmoria, or Eboria², where they made a report of their master's decease. Conjecture has been busy in the attempt to discover the modern name and exact position of this place. All, however, agree that it must have been in France.³ If so, France was probably the country from which Palladius and his companions came; and the mission to Ireland, of which he was the head, although sanctioned by the see of Rome, was in reality projected and sent forth by the Gallican Church.

Sent to the Scots of Ireland.

The question of the country or birthplace of

---

¹ *Gallia Christiana.* It is advocated however by Tillemont, *Mémoires*, tom. xvi. pp. 239, 751.

² *Eboria.* This name is written *Ebmoria* in the Book of Armagh: *Euboria*, by Probus: *Eboria*, by the authors of the second and fourth lives. Colgan has suggested that it may mean *Bologna*, assuming *Eboria* to be an error of the scribe for *Bononia*. But he prefers *Liege*, which was in the country of the *Eburones* mentioned by Cæsar (*Bell. Gall.* ii. 4. vi. 31), and may have been called Eboria or Eburia. *Tr. Th.*, p. 11, n. 34, p. 254. Lanigan suggests *Ebro-*

ica, or *Evreux*, the capital of the people called by Cæsar (ib. iii. 17) *Aulerci Eburovices*, *Eccl. Hist.* i. p. 196, sq. *Eborolacum*, or *Ebrolium*, now *Évreuil*, in Auverne, is mentioned by Sidonius Apollinaris, lib. iii. epist. 5 *Hypatio*, (*Biblioth. Patrum*, vi. p. 1089.) But these are mere conjectures.

³ *France.* The opinion of the Bollandists, that *Eporedia* or *Ivrea*, in Piedmont, was intended, is unworthy of notice. See Lanigan, i. p. 197. Eboria must have been somewhere near the coast from which St. Patrick embarked for Britain.

Palladius, however, is of minor consequence. A more important enquiry is — who were the Scots to whom he was sent? This cannot now be doubtful.[1] In the age of Prosper, as everybody now knows, the inhabitants of Ireland were the only Scoti; but, even if this were otherwise, the words of Prosper settle the question. 'Pope Celestine,' he says, in a passage already quoted, 'whilst he laboured to keep the Roman island Catholic, made the barbarous island Christian.' As the modern Scotland can, with no propriety, be called an island, there cannot be a doubt that Prosper believed Palladius to have been sent to the Scots of Ireland.[2]

It has been said, that as Palladius was sent to the Scots, who were already believers in Christ, and as Ireland was not at that time Christian, the North British Scots must have been intended.[3] But if we are to receive as history the story of Pope Victor, and the imaginary King Donald, the Albanian Scots had been converted to Christ in the third century; and just before the times of

Not to the Albanian Scots.

---

[1] *Doubtful.* See Colgan's dissertation on this subject, Append. V. ad Acta S. Patr. cap. 14. (*Tr. Th.* p. 245, sq.) Dr. Reeves's *Adamnan*; Lanigan, *Eccl. Hist. of Ireland.* Innes, *Civil and Eccl. Hist. of Scotland.* In fact this question is now decided, and at rest.

[2] *Ireland.* Solliere says (speaking of the words of Prosper, just quoted), 'Insula barbara, ab insula Britannica Romana sejuncta et contradistincta non potest non esse Hibernia.' *Actt. SS. loc. cit.* p. 288, E. It is curious that Baronius evidently leans to the opinion that Palladius was sent to North Britain. *Annal.* A.D. 429 n. 4.

[3] *Intended.* This, Solliere says, is the Achillean argument of the modern Scotch writers: 'Hic rei totius nodus, is ferme Scotorum Achilles est, verum si recte expendatur, ipsis æque ac Hibernis solvendus: cum necdum satis constet per id tempus magis credentem fuisse gentem unam quam alteram, &c.' *Acta SS. Ibid.*

Palladius, St. Ninian, as we are told by the author of his life, had divided the country into parishes or dioceses.[1] If so, how could Palladius have been the *first* bishop? Did Pope Celestine so entirely forget the labours of his predecessors, Victor and Damasus, as to suppose that he was himself the first to send a bishop to the Scoti? Did he forget that Ninian was a bishop, sent also, as is alleged, from Rome? Or, if he regarded Ninian as sent to the Picts, and not to the Scots, can we believe that the Scots, christianised in the days of Pope Victor, unlike the rest of the Christian world, were without bishops[2] for upwards of two centuries, until Palladius went over, ' ad Scotos credentes in Christo primus episcopus?'

Ireland the only Scotia in the fifth century.
This question, once debated with extraordinary heat by the Scotch and Irish writers of the 17th century, may now be discussed more calmly. Whoever reads the works of Bede and Adamnan will not need to be informed that, even in their times, *Scotia* meant no country but Ireland, and *Scoti* no people but the inhabitants of Ireland. In the former half of the fifth century, the tribes

---

[1] *Dioceses.* Aildredi Vit. S. Niniani, c. vi.: ' Cœpit deinde sacer Pontifex ordinare Presbyteros, consecrare episcopos, *etc.* totam terram per certas parochias dividere.' Pinkerton *Vit. Ant. Sanctorum*, p.11. St. Ninian is supposed to have died A.D. 430 or 432, the very date of the mission of Palladius. Ussher, *Ind. Chron.* A.D. 432.

[2] *Without bishops.* This latter alternative is adopted by Buchanan and many Scotch writers. Fordun, to meet the difficulty, asserts that the antient Scotish church was ministered to by priests and monks only. Abp. Spottiswood's Hist. vol. i. p. 13. (Bannatyne Club, Edinb. 1850). Ussher, *Antiqq.* c. 16. (Works, vi. p. 354.) And see what Innes has said on this subject, (*Civ. and Eccl. Hist.* p. 59, sq.) in reference to the use made of this supposed absence of bishops, in the Presbyterian controversy.

of Scoti, who had some time before settled in the islands and western coasts of Argyle, were not known or regarded as a people distinct from the Scoti of Ireland. They had no kings[1] or chieftains of their own, they had no fixed seats in the country to which they had migrated; it was impossible that they could have been specially designated by the name of Scoti. The Scots, who appeared in alliance with the Picts in their inroads upon the Roman provinces of Britain, were not exclusively those who had taken up an abode in Argyleshire, but tribes who came direct from Ireland to the assistance of their kinsmen. The name of Scots was naturally given to all. The distinction between those Scoti who had seized habitations in the islands and wilds of the western coast north of Britain, and those Scoti who had come over as reinforcements direct from Ireland, was not, perhaps, so much as noticed by the Roman colonists who had to repel their incursions. Thus the poet Claudian[2], in one of his panegyrics, speaking of the victory of Theodosius over the Picts and Scots, A.D. 398, represents Thule as warm with Pictish blood, and icy Erinn[3], weeping over her heaps of slaughtered Scots:—

---

[1] *Kings.* The year 502 is the date assigned by the Irish annals for the settlement of King Fergus mór mac Eirc, and the Dalriadan tribe in North Britain, or rather for his death there, and the commencement of the Dynasty founded by him.

See Reeves's *Eccl. Hist. of Down and Connor*, p. 319, sq.

[2] *Claudian.* De quarto consulatu Honorii. *Paneg.* v. 82.

[3] *Icy Erinn.* The Romans believed Ireland to be a country of perpetual ice and snow: as if they took *Hibernia*

―― Incaluit Pictorum sanguine Thule,
Scotorum cumulos flevit glacialis Ierne,

assuming evidently that the Scots all came from Ierne or Erinn, without any allusion to those who had made themselves a home in Britain.

Palladius not sent to oppose the Pelagian heresy.

There is not the slightest authority for the assertion, hazarded by some modern Scotch writers[1], that Palladius was sent to the Scots to oppose the Pelagian heresy. Not a single antient author has made this statement. And, in fact, it is certain that Palladius was not sent to refute Pelagianism, because there was no Pelagianism, either in Alba or in Erinn, in the fifth century, for Palladius to refute.

Scattered Christians in Ireland.

We must, therefore, conclude that the believing Scots to whom Palladius was sent were the Scots of Ireland. Although the island was still Pagan, in reference to the large majority of its inhabitants, there is good reason to believe that many scattered individuals, and probably some isolated congregations, were to be found there, at this early period, who were 'believers in Christ;' and such congregations, or individual

---

to signify wintry. Bede was better informed :—' Hibernia autem et latitudine sui status, et salubritate ac serenitate aerum, multum Britanniæ præstat, ita ut raro ibi nix plusquam triduana remaneat.' Lib. i. c. 1.

[1] *Writers*. Buchanan, *Rer. Scot.* lib. v. Even Archbishop Spottiswood has adopted this opinion. *Hist.* i. p. 12. See Lanigan, *Hist.* i. p. 47. Ware also was misled by the bold assertions of the Scotch, and attributes to the mission of

Palladius the double object of preaching Christianity and subverting the Pelagianism, then, as he says, beginning to sprout *in Ireland* : —' A Celestino missus tum ad fidem Christianam propagandam tum ad Pelagianam hæresim, tunc apud Hibernos pullulantem, extirpandam.' *De Script. Hibern.* lib. ii. c. 1. But how could the Pelagian heresy be in Ireland at that time, when the island was Pagan? and is there a shadow of authority for such a statement?

believers, greatly needed the unity[1] which a bishop alone could give them.

The fable of four bishops and several priests in Ireland, before the preaching of St. Patrick, is indeed the only difficulty in the way of receiving in their plain and obvious meaning the words of Prosper, that Palladius was *the first* bishop sent to the Irish Scots. Even Ussher was disposed to give credit to that fable[2], and suggested that *primus* episcopus may mean chief or principal bishop. Others have conjectured that Palladius was called 'primus episcopus,' because he was the first bishop sent by Celestine, St. Patrick being the second[3]; and others again would cut the knot by maintaining that the word *primus* is an erroneous reading, omitted[4] in some copies of the Chronicle.

Palladius first bishop of the Scoti.

But the reader whose mind is unbiassed by theories of an antient church in Scotland, and of ante-Patrician bishops in Ireland, will have no difficulty in receiving the statement of Prosper in its literal sense, that Palladius was the first bishop sent from Rome to the scattered believers among the Scots; and that the Scots to whom he was sent were the inhabitants of Ireland is evident, not only for the reasons already stated, but also from the historical fact that it was to Ireland he went. Let us examine the

Went to Ireland.

---

[1] *Unity.* See above Introd. sect. 87, p. 221.
[2] *Fable.* See Introd. sect. 81—85, p. 198, sq. *supra.*
[3] *Second.* Innes, *Civ. and Eccl. Hist.* p. 54.
[4] *Omitted.* Ussher's *Antiquitt.* c. xvi. (Works vi. p. 354).

traditions which he has left behind him in the two countries.

<small>He landed in the county of Wicklow.</small>

The Irish authorities tell us that, having received his mission from Pope Celestine, he went at once to Ireland, and landed in the region of the Hy Garchon, that is to say, in the country inhabited by the descendants of Garchu[1], a chieftain whose genealogy is known. The particular district is called by the scholiast on Fiacc's Hymn, *Fortuatha Laighen,* or the ' Stranger Tribes[2] of Leinster,' a region which seems to have included the celebrated valley of Glendaloch[3], extending probably to the sea. A scholiast[4] on the Martyrology of Aengus informs us that the territory of Hy Garchon, or Ui Garchon, was in the *Fotharta* of Leinster, which some have inter-

---

[1] *Garchu.* The genitive of Garchu is Garchon. Hy or Ui Garchon signifies descendants of Garchu. His genealogy is given in the Append. to the Introd. Table V. p. 253, *supra.*

[2] *Stranger Tribes.* The Scholia on Fiacc's Hymn, (original Irish, in the MS. at St. Isidore's Convent, Rome) has *i fortuathib Laighen,* which Colgan renders, 'in extremis Lageniæ finibus,' or 'the lower districts of Leinster.' *Tr Th.* p. 5 : ' Venit ergo Palladius in Hiberniam : et appulit in regione de Hi Garrchon in extremis Lageniæ finibus, &c.' But the word *Fortuatha* certainly means ' Stranger tribes' not belonging to the race or clan of the chieftain. There were *Fortuatha* in Munster, (*Book of Rights,* p. 78, with Dr. O'Donovan's note) in Aileach, Co. of Derry (*ib.* p. 120.) in Ulidia (*ib.* p. 172.)

[3] *Glendaloch.* A life of St. Coemhgen, or Kevin, quoted by Ussher,*Primord.* p. 956 (Works, vi. p. 525), speaking of Glendaloch, says, ' ipsaque civitas est in oriente Laginensium in regione quæ dicitur *Fortuatha.*' Who the 'stranger tribes' were who gave name to this district is doubtful. The O'Tooles were driven from their original seats in Kildare, and settled in this region of the Co. of Wicklow, in the 12th, or beginning of the 13th century. But the name of Fortuatha Laighen was given to the district long before that time. See Dr. O'Donovan's note. *B. of Rights,* pp. 207, 210. *Topograph. Poems,* pp. xlvii. (367), lv. (450).

[4] *Scholiast.* The Scholia on the Felire of Aengus, at August 18th, tell us that St. Ernin, son of Cresine, was of Rathnoi,*in uib Garchon i Fothartaibh Laighen,* ' in Ui Garchon in the Fotharta of Leinster.' And the same words occur in the gloss on the name of St. Ernin in the Calendar of Marian O'Gorman, (18 Aug). See Reeves, *Adamnan,* p. 25, note i.

preted to signify the barony of Forth[1] in the county of Wexford. But as the same authority speaks of the Church of Rathnoi, now Rathnew, near the town of Wicklow, as situated in Hy Garchon, and in the *Fotharta* of Leinster, it is evident that the same district must be intended by both names. We may, therefore, conjecture that it received the former name, *Fortuatha*, or ' stranger tribes,' from the *Fotharta*, or family of Eochadh Finn Fothart[2], who settled there, having been driven from their original seat near Tara, county of Meath, about the middle of the third century. It is well known that this tribe gave name to several districts, still from them called *Forths*[3], in different parts of the south-east of Ireland.

Palladius, therefore, according to the Irish tradition preserved in these authorities, must have landed on some part of the strand where the town of Wicklow now stands, and then proceeded into the interior of the country.

Of his subsequent history some antient narratives are extant, the source of all that is to be found on the subject, in the Lives of St. Patrick, the Historia of Nennius, and other records. These we must now examine.

Antient narratives of his subsequent history.

1. The first of them occurs in the Life of St. First Document.

---

[1] *Forth*. See Lanigan, *Eccl. Hist.* i. p. 40.

[2] *Eochadh Finn Fothart*. He was son of Felimidh the Lawgiver, King of Ireland, A.D. 164—174, and brother of Con of the Hundred Fights.

See Introd. Append. Table IV. p. 252, *super*.

[3] *Forths*. See O'Flaherty, *Ogyg.* p. 324, 325. O'Donovan, *Book of Rights*, p. 221, *n*.

Patrick, written, as there is reason to think, not later than A.D. 700, and preserved in the Book of Armagh, a MS. of the early part of the 9th century. The words of this author[1] are as follows:—

'Palladius was ordained and sent to convert this island, lying under wintry cold, but God hindered him, for no man can receive anything from earth unless it be given him from heaven; for neither did those fierce and savage men receive his doctrine readily, nor did he himself wish to spend time in a land not his own, but he returned to him who sent him. On his return hence, however, after his first passage of the sea, having commenced his land journey, he died in the territories of the Britons.

'Therefore, when the death of Palladius in the Britains was heard of (for the disciples of Palladius, viz. Augustinus and Benedictus and the rest, on their return, brought the news of it to Ebmoria), then Patrick and those who were with him,' &c.

The very words of this narrative are appropriated by the author of the Second Life of St. Patrick in Colgan's Collection, and also by Probus, author of the Fifth Life, with no material alteration except that they changed 'territories of *the Britons*' into 'territories *of the Picts*.'[2]

---

[1] *Author*. Maccuthenius, as Ussher erroneously calls him (see p. 314 *n*.) The original is as follows: 'Certe enim erat quod Palladius archidiaconus Papæ Celestini urbis Romæ episcopi qui tunc tenebat sedem apostolicam quadragensimus quintus a Sancto Petro apostolo ille Palladius ordinatus et missus fuerat ad hanc insolam sub brumali rigore [? frigore] possitam convertendam. Sed prohibuit illum [Deus?], quia nemo potest accipere quicquam de terra nisi datum ei fuerit de cælo. Nam neque hii feri et immites homines facile receperunt doctrinam ejus, neque et ipse voluit transegere tempus in terra non sua, sed reversus ad eum qui misit illum. Revertente vero eo hinc et primo mari transito cœptoque terrarum itenere Britonum finibus vita factus' [read *functus*]. B. *of Armagh*, fol. 2, a, a. For the age of the Book of Armagh see Dean Graves's valuable paper in the Proceedings of the Royal Irish Academy, iii. 316. The evidence goes to show that this curious MS was transcribed A.D. 807.

[2] *Picts*. The *Vita Secunda* says

CHAP. I.]   *of Palladius.*   289

11. Equal in antiquity to this is the following passage in the 'Annotations of Tirechan,' on the Life of St. Patrick, also preserved[1] in the Book of Armagh. From this we learn the remarkable fact that Palladius was called by another name, *Patrick* :—

<small>Second Document. Annotations of Tirechan.</small>

'Palladius the bishop is first sent, who by another name was called Patricius, who suffered martyrdom among the Scots, as antient saints relate. Then Patricius the Second is sent by the angel of God, named Victor, and by Pope Celestine. In whom all Hibernia believed, and who baptised almost the whole of it.'

By the Scots in this passage, it is needless to say, the Irish Scots must be intended.

111. Another antient version of the story, which contains some additional particulars, occurs in the Scholia on Fiacc's Hymn, published by Colgan as the First Life in his collection of the Biographies of St. Patrick. The original Irish of these Scholia is preserved in the copy of the Book of Hymns now in the convent of St. Isidore at Rome, a MS. of the 11th or 12th century; but the author of the Scholia flourished, no doubt, at an earlier period.

<small>Third Document. Scholiast on Fiacc.</small>

After recording the arrival of Palladius in

'in Pictavorum (meaning Pictorum) finibus defunctus est,' cap. 23. (*Tr. Th.* p. 13.) Probus (lib. i. c. 24) says ' Cumque aggressus Palladius mare transmeasset, et ad fines *Pictorum* pervenisset, ibidem vita decessit.' *Tr. Th.* p. 48.

[1] *Preserved.* The original words are ' Paladius episcopus primo mittitur, qui Patricius alio nomine appellabatur, qui martyrium passus est apud Scottos, ut tradunt sancti antiqui. Deinde Patricius secundus ab anguelo Dei Victor nomine, et a Celestino Papa mittitur. Cui Hibernia tota credidit, qui eam pene totam babtizavit.' *Lib. Armach.* fol. 16, *a. a.* Tirechan flourished about the close of the 7th century : as he was a disciple of St. Ultan, who died, according to the annals of Tighernach, A.D. 657. Colgan, *Tr. Th.* p. 217.

U

the country of the Hy Garchon, in the words to which we have already referred[1], this author says :—

'He [Palladius] founded there some churches, viz., *Teach-na-Roman*, or the House of the Romans, *Killfine*, and others. Nevertheless, he was not well received by the people, but was forced to go round the coast of Ireland towards the north, until driven by a great tempest he reached the extreme part of *Modhaidh* towards the south, where he founded the church of Fordun, and *Pledi* is his name there.'

Discrepancies of these accounts.

These accounts are certainly at variance with each other, and give rise to the suspicion that the truth has been tampered with. In one version of the story Palladius is represented as having gone to the country of the Britons, on his way back to Pope Celestine, and as having there died. We are not told what part of the country of the Britons he had reached, or in what particular place he died. Nothing is said of a storm[2], or of his

---

[1] *Referred.* See note 2, p. 286. Colgan, *Tr. Th.* p. 5, col. 1. The words are: 'Non fuit bene ab illis exceptus, sed coactus circuire oras Hiberniæ versus aquilonem, donec tandem tempestate magnâ pulsus, venerit ad extremam partem Modhaidh versus austrum; ubi fundavit ecclesiam Fordun; et Pledi est nomen ejus ibi.' It is much to be regretted that the original Irish of this passage in the MS. at St. Isidore's in Rome, is now almost illegible. It seems, however, to have contained a more particular account of the course sailed than Colgan's version has preserved. After mentioning the great storm, the words *co roact co cend airter descertach* are visible: 'So that he reached *Cenn airthir* southwards.' It does not appear what place was intended, but Cenn-airthir may possibly have been the antient name of the headland now called Kinnaird Head, the N.E. coast of Aberdeenshire. *Cenn airthir* signifies 'Eastern head.'

[2] *Storm.* Nennius (cap. 55, *Mon. Hist. Brit.* p. 71) mentions the storm, although his account agrees in other respects even verbally with document No. 1: 'Missus est Palladius episcopus primitus a Cœlestino Papa Romano ad Scottos in Christum convertendos, qui prohibitus est a Deo per quasdam tempestates, quia nemo potest quicquam accipere in terra nisi de cœlo datum illi fuerit. Et profectus est ille Palladius de Hibernia, pervenitque ad Britanniam, et ibi defunctus est in terra Pictorum.' The land of the Picts therefore was regarded by this author as a part of Britannia. The Irish version of Nennius (p. 106) has only these words, 'Pledius was driven from Erin and went and

having been driven from his course. The story implies that he crossed the sea in the usual way, and met with no disaster, until he had commenced his land journey. If his object had been to go by the shortest route to Rome, he would naturally have sailed from the shores of Wicklow to the opposite coast of Wales. It is probable, however, that such a route may have at that period been dangerous or impracticable, and that in travelling to Rome it was necessary to make for the Roman provinces in North Britain. Subsequent writers, although evidently building on this antient biography in the Book of Armagh, make Palladius to have gone much more northward, and to have died in the region of the Picts. They appear to have so interpreted the antient narrative, although that narrative speaks of the territory of the Britons only, not of the Picts. It did not occur to them to explain why Palladius had travelled so far north if his object had been merely to return to Pope Celestine who had sent him.

The other story, however, as given by Fiacc's Scholiast, meets this difficulty. On leaving Hy Garchon in Wicklow, Palladius sailed northwards along the coast of Ireland, but was driven by a great storm still further north, towards the Orkneys, perhaps through Pentland Firth, and was unable to land, or, at least, effected no permanent

served God in Fordun, in Mairne.' No mention is made of his death, nor of any connexion between that event and the mission of St. Patrick by Pope Celestine.

landing, until he had got down to the shores of Kincardineshire. However extraordinary, this was certainly not impossible. The light boats or coracles of that age were frequently driven to considerable distances. It will be observed that in this version of the story nothing is said of an intention on the part of Palladius to return to Rome in despair. He is represented as having been still intent upon prosecuting the object of his mission. He sailed along the coast of Ireland with that object in view, and when he found himself driven from Ireland to the region of the Picts, he lost no time in establishing a Christian Church amongst that people.

The narrative of Tirechan (No. II.) entirely ignores the voyage of Pailadius to the Britons or Picts, and represents him as having suffered martyrdom amongst the Scoti, the people to whom he was sent in Ireland. No mention is made of his companions, or of churches founded by him, in either of the two earlier versions of his story. The existence of these churches is recorded for the first time in the document No. III. preserved by the Scholiast[1] on Fiacc's hymn; but it is remarkable that Probus, the author of the fifth Life in Colgan's collection, although he can scarcely have been ignorant of the tradition, makes no mention of the churches of Hy Gar-

---

[1] *Scholiast.* The age of this Scholiast is a subject of controversy. He seems to have collected legends of different dates, and to have lived himself before the 11th century. See the Irish Book of Hymns (publ. by the Irish Archæol. and Celtic Soc.), p. 299, *sq.*

CHAP. I.]   *History of Palladius.*   293

chon, or of Fordun. This looks as if he had deliberately rejected that part of the legend.¹

IV. The author of the 'Vita Secunda,' after quoting, as we have seen, the narrative of the Book of Armagh, which we have called Document No. I., goes on to transcribe into his work another account of the acts of Palladius, in which the churches are mentioned as then actually existing and well known. This account differs in many respects from the former versions of the story, and may, therefore, be regarded as an independent authority. Colgan's opinion that the author of the second Life flourished in the middle of the sixth century, is founded on an argument² singularly weak and inconclusive. But we shall, probably, not err very much, if we assume that author to have written about A.D. 900. His information was probably derived from some now lost acts of Palladius, of still higher antiquity; and the narrative alluded to, which we may call Document No. IV., is probably not later than the eighth

Fourth Document.
Vita Secunda.

---

¹ *Legend.* The author of the Vita Tertia has also omitted the story of the churches, and follows essentially the narrative No. I, concluding by the statement 'Sed ille mortuus est in regione Britonum.' cap. 26. Tr. Th. p. 23.

² *An argument.* The argument is that this author speaks of Loarne, bishop of Brettan, now Bright, near Downpatrick, as being alive when he wrote. Loarne was a disciple of St. Patrick, and could not have lived beyond the middle of the 6th century. Therefore the words are 'Sed hodie civitatula est quæ dicitur Inreathan, [read *in Breathan*] ubi est episcopus Loarne, &c.' cap. 31, 'where bishop Loarne is.' But this phrase signifies that Loarne was buried there, and therefore proves that Loarne was then dead : the very reverse of the conclusion which Colgan derives from it. The same argument would prove this author to have been contemporary with the companions of Palladius, for he says, speaking of the Church of Domhnach Arda, 'in which are the holy men of the family of Palladius, Sylvester, and Salonius.' Abundant instances of this way of speaking may be found in the Martyrology of Donegal and other authorities.

century. It stands isolated in our author's work; being inconsistent in some respects with the account which immediately precedes it, and having no connection with what follows. The words are these :—

'For[1] the most blessed Pope Cælestine ordained bishop an archdeacon of the Roman Church, named Palladius, and sent him into the island of Hibernia, after having committed to him the relics of the blessed Peter and Paul, and other saints, and having also given him the volumes of the Old and New Testaments. Palladius, entering the land of the Scots[2], arrived at the territory of the men of Leinster, where Nathi Mac Garrchon[3] was chief, who was opposed to him. Others, however, whom the divine mercy had disposed towards the worship of God, having been baptised in the name of the sacred Trinity, the blessed Palladius built three churches in the same district. One, which is called *Cellfine*, in which even to the present day, he left his books which he had received from St. Cælestine, and the box of Relics of the blessed Peter and Paul and other saints, and the tablets on which he used to write, which in Scotish are called from his name *Pall-ere* [or *Pallad-ere*], that is, the Burden of Palladius, and are held in veneration. Another, viz., *Tech na Roman* [the House of the Romans]; and the third *Domnach ardec* [or *Domnach Aracha*], in which are [buried] the holy men of the family[4] of Palladius,

---

[1] *For.* 'Nam beatissimus Papa, &c.' Colgan, *Tr. Th.* page 13. *Vit. Secunda,* cap. 24. The *nam* in this passage has no connexion with what precedes; the words immediately preceding record the death of Palladius: 'in Pictavorum finibus defunctus est;' then follows, '*nam* beatissimus papa . . . Palladium episcopum ordinavit.' Nothing can show more clearly that our author transcribed this document from some antient source, and inserted it without considering its connection with the preceding matter in his narrative.

[2] *Scots.* It will be observed that what is here called 'terram Scotorum,' was just before termed 'Hiberniam insulam.'

[3] *Nathi Mac Garrchon.* It has already been observed (see p. 254), that the *Mac* is here used to signify a more remote descendant than *Son* in the literal sense of the word. See the genealogy of Garchu, ancestor of the tribe or clan Hy Garchon, in the Appendix to the Introduction, Table V.

[4] *Family,* i.e. of his attendants — the clergy who accompanied him; See above, Introd. p. 159.

Sylvester and Salonius, who are honoured there. After a short time, Palladius died in the plain of Girgin, in a place which is called *Forddun*. But others say that he was crowned with martyrdom there.'[1]

The new facts recorded in this narrative are that the Pope, on giving Palladius his commission, presented him with certain relics of Peter, Paul, and other saints, together with copies of the Old and New Testaments; that Nathi, chief of the Hy Garchon, who is not mentioned in the former accounts, opposed him on his landing in Wicklow; that, nevertheless, he baptised several of the inhabitants, and built or founded three churches; in one of these, *Cell-fine*[2], he deposited the relics, together with the copies of the Old and New Testaments, given him by the Pope, and the tablets on which he was wont to write. In another of these churches, called *Domhnach Arda*[3], his companions, Silvester and Solinus, were buried, and their memory afterwards held in honour. No mention is made of the cause of his leaving Ireland, nor of the adventures which carried him to North Britain. But it is said that he died *in*

<small>New facts recorded in the Fourth Document.</small>

---

[1] *There.* The origin of this opinion seems to have been derived from the words of Tirechan, ' qui martyrium passus est apud *Scottos*.' And if the writer interpreted this word to mean the Albanian Scots, he must have lived at a later period than that which we have assigned to him.

[2] *Cell-fine.* This name seems to signify ' Church of the tribe' or ' people.' In the Vita Quarta, attributed to St. Aileran, it is called Ecclesia *Finte*: this is most probably a mistake, although Colgan says that it is for *Fin-tech*, i.e. Ædes Fine, or house of the tribe. If so the word Ecclesia would be redundant, *Tr. Th.* p. 49, note 17. It is now unknown.

[3] *Domhnach Arda.* Variously written *Domhnach Ardec, D. Ardacha, D. Airte.* The name D. Arda signifies Church of the high place. D. Ardacha, Church of the high field. The other forms are probably mere errors of transcription. This church is supposed to be the same as the present Donard, in the County of Wicklow, near Dunlavin.

Campo Girgin, or Magh-Girgin¹, the country of the Picts, at a place called *Fordun*. It is not said that he built a church there, and the fact that he suffered martyrdom there is stated to have been the opinion of some only.

Fifth Document. Vita Quarta.

v. The Fourth Life in Colgan's collection is attributed by him to St. Aileran or Eleran, without any apparent reason, except that St. Aileran was reputed to have written a Life of St. Patrick, and that the Fourth Life, in Colgan's judgment, was compiled about the middle of the seventh century, when St. Aileran² was alive. Therefore, this Fourth Life is by St. Aileran. However, it is certainly antient, and cannot well be referred to a period much later than the close of the eighth or beginning of the ninth century. The traditions it has preserved of the history of Palladius may be quoted as a fifth antient document. After mentioning the consecration of Palladius, and his mission to Ireland by Pope Celestine, this author³ proceeds:—

'Therefore when Palladius arrived there in the territory of

---

[1] *Magh-Girgin.* The antient name of the Mernis or Mearnes (old spelling Moerne). The story of the Picts who emigrated from Ireland after receiving their wives from the Milesians, (Book of Lecan, fol. 141 *a*.) names Magh-Cirgin as the district of North Britain in which they settled. *Irish Nennius*, p. lxxi. Fordun is said to be 'in Mairne.' (*Ibid.* p. 106). The Scholiast on Fiacc says that Fordun was 'in the extreme part of Modhaidh towards the south,' so that Magh Girgin, 'the plain of Girgin,' Moerne, Mairne, and Modaidh, were probably all names for the region of the Picts, now Kincardineshire, in which the church of Fordoun stood. In this district was settled in later times an Irish tribe, called the *Eoghanacht* of Magh Girgin, from their ancestor Eoghan mòr, son of Oilioll Oluim. O'Flaherty, *Ogyg.* p. 328.

[2] *St. Aileran.* His death is recorded in the Irish Annals, 29 Dec. 664.

[3] *This author.* Cap. 28. Colgan, *Tr. Th.* p. 38.

the Lagenians[1], he began to preach the word of God. But, inasmuch as Almighty God had not predestined the Hibernian people to be brought by him from the error of heathenism to the faith of the Holy and Undivided Trinity, he remained there only a few days. Nevertheless, a few did believe through him. And in the same district he founded three churches—*in eodem pago tres ecclesias constituit*—one which is called *Ecclesia Finte*, in which, even to the present day, are preserved his books, which he had received from Celestine, and a box with the relics of the blessed Apostles Peter and Paul and other saints; and the tablets on which he used to write, which are called from his name in Scottish, Pallad-ir, i.e., the burden of Palladius, and are held in great veneration. Another church was built by the disciples of Palladius, and is called the House of the Romans, *Domus Romanorum*. The third is the church which is called *Dominica Arda*, in which are [buried] holy men of the companions of Palladius, viz., Silvester and Solinus, whose relics after some time were carried to the island of Boethin, and are there held in merited honour. But St. Palladius seeing that he could not do much good there, wishing to return to Rome, migrated to the Lord in the region of the Picts. Others, however, say that he was crowned with martyrdom in Hibernia.'

The writer of this account has added to the information given us in the other documents that the sojourn of Palladius in Ireland was only 'for a few days;'[2] that the church called 'House of the Romans' was built by the disciples of Palladius, not by Palladius himself; and that the relics of his companions Sylvester and Solinus, after having remained for some time at Domhnach Arda, were translated to *Inis-Boethin*, or the island of St. Boethin, and were there venerated in the time of the writer.

Additional particulars in the Fifth Document.

This place was situated within the townland of Inishboheen, or Inishboyne, to which it has

Inis-Boethin, where.

---

[1] *Lagenians.* Lageniensium, the men of Leinster.

[2] *Days.* 'Paucis ibi diebus permansit.'

given its name, in the parish of Dunganstown, barony of Arklow, county of Wicklow. It was burned, according to the Annals of Ulster[1], in the year 774: and there is no record of the relics having escaped. Our author therefore most probably wrote before the church was burnt, if the relics were there in his time. Boethin, the saint from whom the church took its name, is supposed to have flourished about the close of the sixth[2] and beginning of the seventh century. The exact date of his obit has not been preserved in the Irish Annals.

The martyrdom of Palladius by the Irish, which Tirechan had recorded as a certain fact, is mentioned by this author as the opinion of some only. He says nothing of the storm, or of the foundation of a church among the Picts; and attributes the abandonment of the mission to Palladius having despaired of success. But if 'in a few days' Palladius had succeeded in baptising some of the natives, as well as laying the foundation of three churches, and was nevertheless dissatisfied with the results of his mission, his expectations of success must have been sanguine indeed.

<small>Scotch traditions about Palladius.</small>

The Scotch or North British traditions respecting Palladius are comparatively modern and

---

[1] *Annals of Ulster*: or A.D. 770, according to the Four Masters.

[2] *Sixth.* So says Colgan, *Tr. Th.* p. 18, note 33. His Festival occurs (22 May) in the most antient Irish calendar, the *Felire of Aengus.* His mother is said to have been the daughter of Ronan son of Colman, King of Leinster. Ronan's death is variously dated in the annals 610, 619, 623, and 624. Boethin may therefore have lived to near the close of the seventh century.

unauthentic. They can scarcely be traced to a higher authority than the Scotichronicon of John of Fordun[1], who flourished in the fourteenth century. The Breviary of Aberdeen, printed at Edinburgh 1509 and 1510, contains the oldest known calendar which marks the 6th of July as the festival of St. Palladius; it is there given as a lesser[2] festival, although he is styled 'Apostle of the Scots.' His relics (or supposed relics) were disinterred at Fordun, and placed in a silver shrine[3], by William Schewes, Archbishop of St. Andrews, so late as 1494, where they continued to be venerated until the Reformation.[4] In the Lessons for his Day given in the Breviary of Aberdeen, Palladius is said to have been an Egyptian by birth, and to have died not at Fordun, but 'at Langforgund[5] in the Mearnes.' This is a remarkable proof how vague the traditions of Scotland were respecting Palladius, even so late as the beginning of the sixteenth century. The traditions followed by Archbishop Schewes, which fixed Fordun as the death place of the saint, were ignored in the neighbouring diocese of Aberdeen,

---

[1] *John of Fordun.* See Innes, *Civ. & Eccl. Hist. of Scotland*, p. 59.

[2] *Lesser.* 'Palladii episcopi et confessoris apostoli Scotorum, minus.' *Brev. Aberd.* (*Prop. SS.*) *Prid. non. Julii.* This Breviary has been beautifully reprinted, London, 1854.

[3] *Shrine.* Hector Boece, *Scot. Hist.* vii. fol. 128 b. (quoted by Ussher, *Antiq.* c. xv., *Works*, vi. p. 211.)

[4] *Reformation.* Archbishop Spottiswode tells us that the silver shrine 'was taken up at the demolishing of the churches, by a gentleman of good rank, who dwelt near that place. The people of the country, observing the decay which followed in that family not many years after, ascribed the same to the violation of Palladius's grave.' *Hist. of the Church of Scotland*, i. p. 13. (Bannatyne Club), 1850.

[5] *Langforgund.* *Brev. Aberd.* (*Prop. SS. Pars Æst.*) Lect. vi. fol. xxv. b. 'Tandem beatus Palladius, variis per eundem miraculis Divinitus ostensis, annorum plenus apud Langforgund in Mernis in pace requiescit beata.'

and not without evidence of carelessness or mistake; for it happens that Langforgund is a parish not in the Mearns, but in the east of Perthshire, in Gowry, a little to the west of Dundee, on the north of the Firth of Tay, in another diocese and at a considerable distance from Fordun.

Discrepancies between the Irish and Scotch traditions.

The Scotch traditions make no mention of the visit of Palladius to Ireland, or of the supposed connection of his mission with that of St. Patrick. They represent him also as having laboured among the Picts for many years[1] after the establishment of his church at Fordun. Whereas the Irish writers are unanimous that his life, after his consecration, was short, and that he died before Pope Celestine, who had time after receiving the news of his death to nominate his successor. But Palladius was consecrated, as Prosper expressly states, in the consulship of Bassus and Antiochus, or A.D. 431, and Pope Celestine died in July 432. It was impossible, therefore, that he could have lived at Fordun more than a few months or weeks, so that the traditions of the two countries are here directly contradictory and opposite.

The Calendar and Lessons of the Aberdeen Breviary at variance.

It is to be observed, also, that the Calendar prefixed to the Breviary of Aberdeen is at variance with the Lessons given in the same Breviary for the festival of Palladius. In the Calendar, Palladius is called 'Apostolus Scotorum,' implying that by him the Scots were converted to Christianity.

---

[1] *Many years.* Abp. Spottiswode says 23, I know not on what authority: but he has not a word of Ireland: *ubi supra.*

CHAP. I.] *Companions of Palladius.* 301

This ignores the story of the conversion of Scotland under Pope Victor in 203. But this story is nevertheless adopted[1] in the Lessons, where the statement of John of Fordun is repeated that before the coming of Palladius the Scots had received the faith in the time of Pope Victor, and since that time had had priests and monks only (not bishops) as teachers of doctrine and ministers of the sacraments amongst them.

The Irish authorities have preserved the names of four missionaries of inferior rank who had accompanied Palladius from Rome. Sylvester and Solinus are said to have been left behind in Ireland, and their relics, as we have seen, continued to be honoured there for centuries. Augustinus and Benedictus, with others whose names are not given, are represented as having followed Palladius into Britain, but upon his death they returned to their homes, and are said to have brought the news of that event not to Rome, but to Ebmoria, or Eboria[2], to St. Patrick.

Companions of Palladius according to Irish tradition.

The Scotch traditions state that Palladius brought with him several companions[3] from Rome, but name none. They mention, however,

His converts and disciples in Scotland.

---

[1] *Adopted.* Lectio iv. fol. 24 b. 'Ante quorum adventum Scotorum gens præfata, per Marcum et Dionisium viros religiosos Christi, in magnam partem habebant fidem, Romano presidente imperio Victore hujus nominis primo, qui pro Christi nomine durum subiit martyrium, habentes fidei doctores et sacramentorum ministros presbiteros et monachos, primitive ecclesie solummodo sequentes ritum et consuetudinem, de cujus historii testimonio sequitur carmen; Christi transactis tribus annis atque ducentis Scocia catholicam cepit inire fidem Roma Victore primo Papa residente, Principe Severo martyr et occubuit.'

[2] *Eboria.* See above p. 280, note 2.

[3] *Companions.* 'Secumque acceptis monachis nonnullis aliisque pluribus viris vite approbatissimis, &c. *Brev. Aberd.* (*Propr. SS.*) Lect. iii. (*Pars Æstiv.*) fol. xxiv. b.

two of his disciples or converts, Servanus and Tervanus, or Ternanus, both natives of Scotland. Servanus was converted in mature life, consecrated by Palladius, and sent as a bishop to the Orkneys.[1] He is said to have been the tutor of the celebrated Kentigern[2], or St. Mungo. Ternanus was baptised by Palladius in infancy, and afterwards by the same Palladius consecrated archbishop[3] of the Picts. If this be true, the Life of Palladius after he had settled among the British Picts

---

[1] *Orkneys.* Fordun, and the Lessons of the Breviary of Aberdeen, represent Servanus as having been consecrated to assist Palladius in his episcopal duties : 'Et quia tante genti mysteria pastoralia solus impendere non sufficiebat, beatum Servanum, ut in vinea Domini secum operaretur doctrina ecclesiastica sufficienter imbutum, et per eundem in episcopum ordinatum, in omni Scotorum gente suum constituit suffroganeum.' *Brev. Aberd. (Propr. SS.* 1 Jul.) *Pars Æstiv.* p. xvi. b. No mention is made of the Orkneys. His mission there rests on the authority of modern writers, Johannes Major, Polydore Vergil, and Hector Boetius. In fact, Servanus or St. Serf, belongs to the century after Palladius. Ussher, *Primord.* p. 672, *sq.* (*Works* vi. 212, *sq.*) Lanigan, *Eccl. Hist.* ii. 167. On the 12th June, S. Ternanus or Tervanus is commemorated in the Scotch Calendar : and it is curious that the name of *Torannan* occurs at the same day, in the Irish Calendar. The Mart. of Donegal, p. 167, supposes this Torannan to have been an Irishman and Abbot of Bangor in Ireland. But the Scholiast on the Mart. of Aengus gives two opinions about him, one of which oddly enough identifies him with Palladius: In the text he is called 'Torannan, the far famed voyager,' and the Scholiast adds 'viz. Palladius, who was sent from the successor (Comarb)

of Peter to Erinn before Patrick to preach to them. He was not received in Erinn, whereupon he went into Albain ; et sepultus est in *Liconio.* Or Torannan is the same as Mothoren of Tulach Foirtgern in Ui Felmedhu and of Drumcliabh in Cairpri.' Whatever may be thought of the claims of Servanus and Ternanus to be deemed disciples of Palladius, it is evident that the legend which speaks of one as bishop 'in omni Scotorum gente,' and of the other as bishop of the Picts, must have been invented before episcopal sees were established in Scotland. The Lessons in the Aberdeen Breviary on 12 June, represent St. Ternan as having visited Pope Gregory in Rome, who gave him a Bell. See also the *Registrum Episcopatus Aberdon.* published by the Spalding Club. Append. to Pref. No. 1, p. lxxxvi. note. St. Gregory the Great died A.D. 602. St. Irchard, a disciple of St. Ternan, is commemorated 10 Kal. Sept. (or 20 Aug.) : and according to the Lessons in the *Brev. Aberd.,* he was consecrated by St. Gregory, and sent back to Kincardineshire his native country.

[2] *Kentigern.* See *Vita Kentigerni,* cap. 4. (Pinkerton, p. 206.)

[3] *Archbishop.* So says Hector Boetius, 'Tervanum, quem infantem lustrico laverat fonte Pictorum archiepiscopum constituit.' *Scot.*

requires a much longer duration than either the Irish or Scotch writers have assigned to it.

It seems probable that the Irish biographers of St. Patrick felt themselves compelled to shorten the life of Palladius in order to make room for the new commission to succeed him, which they assume to have been given to St. Patrick by Pope Celestine. This is the great difficulty in the history of both missionaries. It is not possible that Palladius could have effected all that he is said to have effected in Ireland 'in a few days.' It is even less possible that he could have effected all that he is said to have effected amongst the Picts, if there was time to make known his death and to have his successor appointed at Rome, within a year[1] from his consecration. There is reason to believe, therefore, that national vanity and national prejudice have corrupted this part of the history. Facts which were true of Palladius only have been transferred to St. Patrick, and the acts or legends of both saints mingled together in utter confusion. The martyrdom of Palladius in Ireland, as recorded by Tirechan, would diminish the difficulty. But it would leave no room for his ministry in Scotland, and it is rendered suspicious by that writer's anxiety to quote for it the authority of 'antient saints,' who are anonymous. Subsequent biographers repeat the story as a doubtful opinion, or transfer the

The short life of Palladius inconsistent with his history.

Hist. lib. i. fol. 128 b. (Quoted by Ussher, *Works*, vi. p. 212).
[1] *Within a year.* Dr. Lanigan in his *Ecclesiastical History of Ireland* (vol. 1. p. 201) has put this difficulty very strongly.

guilt of the martyrdom to the Scots or Picts of North Britain.

It was probably with a view to meet the objection from the shortness of the time that some writers have attributed the foundation of the churches in Wicklow to the disciples of Palladius rather than to Palladius himself. But this part of his history presents less difficulty, and is more easily reconciled with the short time allotted to his ministry in Ireland, than the account of his actions in Scotland. He was sent to the Irish Scoti, who were already believers in Christ. Although the pagan natives of the country rejected him, these Christian Scoti would necessarily receive him with joy. It would take no great length of time to form them into regular churches. The material fabrics were probably of wood;[1] and he left behind him experienced clergy to complete and perpetuate the ecclesiastical organisation of the congregations. The later collections of biographical legends could scarcely have named these churches if they had not continued to exist in their times, and if popular tradition had not attributed their foundation to the mission of Palladius.

---

[1] *Wood.* So the Four Masters expressly tell us, A.D. 430. Joceline makes the same statement, cap. 25. *Tr. Th.*, p. 70. Wooden churches were usual in Ireland down to the beginning of the twelfth century. St. Malachy's design of building a stone oratory at Bangor was resisted as *a novelty*; 'Scoti sumus non Galli,' were the words used by his opponent, as St. Bernard tells us. And Bede, speaking of the Church built by St. Aidan in Lindisfarne, says that it was 'more Scotorum, non de lapide, sed de robore secto,' iii. 25. But we must not infer that there were no stone churches in Ireland, for the remains of many of very great antiquity are still extant. See *Life of St. Malachy*, by Rev. J. O'Hanlon, p. 146 sq.

Palladius called also Patrick.

The fact recorded by Tirechan, that Palladius was also called Patrick, is of great importance. It may have been the cause of much of the confusion. There is no difficulty or improbability in the fact itself. Palladius may have been the name of his family, and Patricius his baptismal name[1], or a title given him from his rank. It is remarkable, however, that on the sixteenth of March, the day before the Irish St. Patrick's day, we have in the Roman Martyrology the name of a Patrick, bishop, who was commemorated at Arverni, or Clermont, the very country to which, as we have seen, there is reason to think Palladius belonged. The words are, 'Arvernis depositio S. Patricii episcopi.' It is not said that he was bishop of Auvergne, but only that his *depositio*, that is to say, his death, was on that day commemorated there. Baronius, therefore, need not have expressed surprise[2] at being unable to find his name among the bishops of Clermont. If he was the Palladius or Patricius who was first bishop of the Scots, and whose family was in high reputation in Auvergne, there is no difficulty in supposing that his *depositio* may have been recorded in the Calendar of Clermont.

If this be so, it is probable that Palladius died

Palladius called also Patrick.

Commemorated at Clermont.

Coincidence of his day with that of St. Patrick.

---

[1] *Name.* Patricius was a name in common use at that time, as also *Patricia* for a female. We are not under the necessity of supposing it to be a title indicating Patrician rank. Gibbon (*Decline and Fall*, viii. p. 300, ed. Milman and Smith) says, 'The meanest subjects of the Roman empire' [at the close of the 5th century] 'assumed the *illustrious* name of *Patricius*, which, by the conversion of Ireland, has been communicated to a whole nation.'

[2] *Surprise.* 'Miratus sum hunc non recenseri in tabulis Democharis inter episcopos Arvernenses.' *Not. ad Martyrol. Rom.* in loco.

on the 16th of March, and by a curious coincidence the 17th of March was afterwards dedicated to the memory of the more celebrated St. Patrick. To this coincidence there may be allusion in the following lines which occur in the Hymn of St. Fiacc:—

> Intan conhualai Patraic adella in Patraic naile
> Ismalle connubcabsat dochum n-Isu meicc Maire.

which may be thus translated,

> When Patrick died[1] he went to the other Patrick,
> And both ascended together to JESUS, Son of Mary.

In other words, Patrick after his death went in the Calendar to the day next after the festival of the other Patrick; the other Patrick met him, on the day after his own festival, and both ascended together to heaven.[2]

Great number of Patricks a cause of confusion.

The great number of Patricks who are mentioned in this period of Irish history is a source

---

[1] *Died.* Lit. 'was wailed for.'

[2] *To heaven.* A curious anecdote, which may illustrate this, is told in the Life of St. Gertrude, abbess of Nivelles in Brabant, who died on Sunday 18 March (the day after St. Patrick's day), A.D. 658. Feeling her end approaching she sent a friar to an Irish monk named Ultan, who was then at the neighbouring monastery of Fossæ. 'Go,' she said, 'to the pilgrim Ultan, and say to him, The Virgin Gertrude hath sent me to ask thee on what day she shall depart this life, for she says that she feareth greatly, although at the same time she rejoiceth.' The friar delivered the message, and Ultan answered, 'This is the 16th of the Kalends of April: and to-morrow, during the solemnities of Mass, that handmaiden of God and virgin of Christ, Gertrude, shall depart from the body. Tell her to fear not, nor be troubled at her decease, for blessed Patrick the bishop, with the elect angels of God, are ready to receive her with great glory.' *Actt. SS. ord. S. Bened.* tom. ii. p. 447. Here the idea seems to have been that Patrick, on the morning after his Festival, came down with the angels to accompany the soul of St. Gertrude to heaven. In Fiacc's Hymn Patrick's soul is represented as going to the other Patrick, or Palladius, who had come to meet him, on the day after his festival, and both ascended together to heaven. The Ultan mentioned in this story is not St. Ultan of Ardbraccan (see p. 212), but another Ultan (whose festival is May 1), brother of SS. Faolan and Fursa. See *Calendar of Donegal*, p. 117.

of much embarrassment. The author of the Tripartite Life tells the following childish story[1]:

'Once upon a time, when St. Patrick was in the Tyrrhene [Mediterranean?] Sea, he came to a place in which there were three other Patricks. They were in a solitary cave, between a mountain and the sea, and he asked their permission to remain with them. They answered that they would not permit this unless he would consent to draw water from an adjacent fountain, for there was in that place a beast which did much injury to men. Patrick, however, consented, and went to the fountain; and the beast seeing him, gave signs of joy, by his gestures, and became to him quite tame and gentle. After this Patrick drew the water, and brought it home with blessing,' &c.

Colgan[2] suggests that one of these Patricks may have been Patrick of Auvergne, and another, Patrick of Nola[3], whose feast is on the 17th of March. But it is absurd to treat such a fable as history. It can only prove, if indeed it proves so much, that the name of Patrick was then common; and this certainly seems to have been the case. There is said to have been a Patrick junior, a supposed nephew of the great saint, to whom Colgan attributes the authorship of the Life which he has placed second in his collection. And there was also an older Patrick, called Sen-Patrick, or Senior Patrick, of whom we shall say more presently.

Henry of Saltrey, in his History[4] of the celebrated Purgatory[5] of St. Patrick in Lough Derg, Palladius known by the name of Patrick to a late period.

[1] *Story.* Septima vita, lib. i. c. 34, Colgan, *Tr. Th.*, p. 122.
[2] *Colgan.* Ibid. p. 171, not. 16.
[3] *Patrick of Nola.* Mentioned in the Catal. SS. Italiæ of Ferrarius. But Ughelli supposes him to be the Irish St. Patrick. Bolland, *Actt. SS.* Martii, tom. ii. p. 506.
[4] *History.* Published by Colgan, ib. p. 274.
[5] *Purgatory.* It should be borne in mind that this 'Purgatory' had nothing to do with the Purgatory of a future life, a mistake into which Harris seems to have fallen, *Bishops*, p. 25. It was a cave or series of

attributes that institution to 'the Great Patrick the second from the first'—*Magnus Sanctus Patricius qui a primo est secundus*—the first being evidently the Patrick who is more generally known by the name of Palladius. The story of the Purgatory was not invented until the beginning of the twelfth century. This allusion to the first Patrick is therefore evidence that the memory of the Palladian Patrick was preserved under that name to a late period; and another opinion, mentioned in the Polychronicon[1] of Ralph of Chester, which attributes the institution of the Purgatory to an abbot Patrick, who lived about 850, and who quitted Ireland 'because he was unable to convert the Irish,' is apparently a transfer of a part of the story of Palladius Patricius to a different Patricius of a much later age.

The Acts of Palladius transferred to St. Patrick.

It appears then that Palladius continued to be known in Ireland by the name of Patrick until about the period of the English invasion. It was natural that some confusion should arise from this circumstance, and it will assist very materially to clear up the difficulties and contradictions in the early history of Patrick the Apostle, if we can disentangle[2] from the story

caves, in which living pilgrims were made to do penance, to atone for the sins of their previous life.

[1] *Polychronicon.* Quoted by Ussher's *Primord.* p. 896.

[2] *Disentangle.* This observation has been made by Dr. Petrie: having quoted a passage from the book of Lecan, this author says, 'The passage, however, is of great importance, as tending to show that the acts of at least two distinguished preachers in Ireland may have been blended together, and thus furnishing a sufficient explanation of the apparent chronological and other contradictions in which the lives of our Saint abound.' *Essay on Tara Hill.* (Trans.

of his early life, those particulars which belong in reality to the Palladian Patrick.

The words of Prosper that Pope Celestine made 'the barbarous island Christian,' by nominating a bishop for the Scots, have sometimes been interpreted as a too sanguine anticipation of the success of Palladius. But their meaning is probably no more than this, that by the formal nomination of a bishop for them, the *Scoti credentes in Christo* were recognised as a Christian nation. Be this, however, as it may, it seems evident that Prosper can have had no knowledge of more than one bishop sent by Celestine to the Scots. If he had known of the second Patricius, the fact would have greatly strengthened his argument, and could scarcely have been omitted by him; and if Pope Celestine, immediately before his death, had consecrated a second bishop for Ireland, it is almost impossible that Prosper could have been ignorant of it.

Prosper knew nothing of the second Patrick.

R. Irish Acad. vol. xviii. p. 88). The same view has also been ably developed by the late Hon. A. Herbert, in an Essay called *Palladius Restitutus*, published in the *Brit. Mag.* 1844. This very learned and acute writer, however, was strongly prejudiced against the history of St. Patrick, which he believed to be a forgery of the Columban age. He had never seen Dr. Reeves's edition of Adamnan, which was not published until after his death, and he was ignorant also (as he admits) of the writings of Dr. Lanigan. The Irish unpublished authorities were of course wholly unknown to him. Sir Wm. Betham (*Irish Antiq. Researches*, p. 266) appears to have also inferred from a perusal of the Book of Armagh, that the acts of two different missionaries were, as he states, 'so jumbled together as to render it impossible to separate them.' But his learning was defective, and he drew the singular conclusion that one of these missionaries lived at a much earlier period than that usually assigned to St. Patrick, and that the other was Palladius, who was identical with the Patrick who is now venerated as the apostle of Ireland. Mr. Herbert has ably exposed the absurdity of this theory in his 'Animadversions upon the Bethamian St. Patrick.' *British Magazine*, xxiv. (1843), p. 597.

But his words are express, 'ordinato Scotis episcopo,' by the ordination of a bishop for the Scots, the barbarous island was made Christian. Why did he not say by ordaining *two* bishops, for the Scots, if he had known that two had been ordained? The suspicion therefore arises that the Roman mission[1] of the second Patrick, and most probably also his continental travels and his connexion with St. Germain of Auxerre, are facts in his biography which belong in reality to the history of Palladius.

The Roman Mission of St. Patrick not mentioned in his Confession.

This suspicion is strongly confirmed by other considerations. The autobiography, first published by Sir James Ware, under the name of 'The Confession of Patrick,' contains not a word of a mission from Pope Celestine. Of this curious tract we shall have occasion to speak more at length presently. It must suffice to observe here, that one object of the writer was to defend himself from the charge of presumption in having undertaken such a work as the conversion of the Irish, rude and unlearned as he was. Had he received a regular commission from the see of Rome, that fact alone would have been an unanswerable reply. But he makes no mention of Pope Celestine, or of Rome, and rests his defence altogether on the Divine call which he believed himself to have received for the work. He fully admits his

---

[1] *Roman mission.* Tillemont, speaking of the short period between the mission of Palladius and the death of Pope Celestine, observes: 'et je croy que sur cela seul il est impossible de croire que S. Patrice a esté ordonné par S. Celestin.' Mémoires, *Hist. Eccl.* tom. xvi. p. 784.

want of education, his rudeness, and ignorance of languages. He says[1] :—

'Wherefore, I thought of writing long ago, but hesitated until now, for I was afraid of falling upon the language of men [i. e. I was afraid of attempting to write in the language of the civilized world], because I have not read like others who have been well imbued with sacred learning, and have never changed their studies from infancy, but have added more and more to perfection; for my speech and language has been changed to another tongue.'

It is not possible that an ecclesiastic, who had been regularly educated in the schools of St. Germain and St. Martin, could have thus spoken of himself, and nevertheless it is thus that he speaks of himself throughout the whole of the 'Confession.' The same remark may be made also on 'the Epistle to Coroticus,' or ' to the Christian Subjects of Coroticus,' as some copies[2] call it. It makes no allusion to a mission from Rome, or to the foreign education of the author. He speaks of himself throughout as unlearned, ' indoctus,' and alludes to his want of skill or knowledge 'imperitia mea.' The rude Latinity[3] of this tract, as well as of the Confessio, is confirmatory of

Nor his ecclesiastical Education on the Continent.

---

[1] *Says.* ' Quapropter ollim cogitavi scribere, sed et usque nunc hessitavi : timui enim ne incederem in linguam hominum : quia non dedici, sicut cæteri, qui optime itaque jure et sacras literas utroque pari modo jure conbiberunt, et sermones eorum ex infantia nunquam motarunt, &c.' *Lib. Ardmach.* fol. 22, b. *a.*

[2] *Copies.* It was first published by Sir James Ware, from the Cotton MS. (*Opusc. S. Patr.* p. 24), under the title of ' S. Patricii ad Coroticum epistola :' then by the Bollandists, from a MS. at Treves, under the title of 'Epistola ad Christianos Corotici tyranni subditos.' (*Actt. SS.* 17 March) : by Dr. Villanueva, from the Bollandists, ' *S. Patricii Synodi et opuscula*, p. 240, and by Dr. O'Conor, *Rer. Hib. Scriptt.* i., Proleg. i. 117, from the Cotton MS.

[3] *Rude Latinity.* Bollandus suggests that St. Patrick, by his long residence among the barbarian Irish, may have lost the purity of the Latin tongue, which he had learned in his youth. *Comm. præv. ad Vit. S. Patr.* sect. 3.

the author's defective education, and a collateral evidence of the authenticity of both. Whether genuine or not, these documents were written before the Roman mission from Pope Celestine, and the connexion with St. Germain had been transferred from the acts of Palladius to the second Patrick.

The Hymn of St. Sechnall is also silent.

The Hymn of St. Sechnall, or Secundinus, in praise of St. Patrick, is supposed to have been written during his lifetime[1], and contains nothing which can be deemed very inconsistent with that opinion. The author is said to have been the disciple of Patrick, his nephew, the son of his sister, and his successor, or rather a contemporaneous bishop with him, in the see of Armagh. But this hymn, although its object was to celebrate the praises of St. Patrick, makes no mention of his mission from Rome, or of his ecclesiastical education on the continent. His apostleship and call to teach barbarous nations is expressly derived from God Himself, without any mention of a commission from Pope Celestine. He is described[2] as 'constant in the fear of God, immoveable in faith, one upon whom as a second Peter the Church is built, who obtained from God the apostleship of the Church, to the injury of which Church the gates of hell prevail not. The Lord chose him to teach barbarous nations, and to fish with the nets of doctrine,' &c.

---

[1] *Lifetime.* See *Book of Hymns of the Irish Church*, (publ. by the Irish Archæolog. and Celtic Soc.) p. 41.
[2] *Described.* Ibid. p. 12.

'Constans in Dei timore et fide immobilis
Super quem ædificatur ut Petrus ecclesia,
Cujusque apostolatum a Deo sortitus est,
In cujus portæ adversus[1] inferni non prævalent.
Dominus illum elegit ut doceret barbaros
Nationes, ut piscaret per doctrinæ retia,' &c.

It is very unlikely that St. Patrick's mission from the see of Rome would have been omitted in this description of his apostleship, if it had been known to the writer.

The Hymn of St. Fiacc is purely biographical. The author, who was bishop of Sletty,[2] is said to have been a disciple and contemporary of Patrick. But it is impossible for many reasons to attribute to the Hymn so high an antiquity. It contains an allusion to the desolation of Tara,[3] and consequently must have been written after the middle of the sixth century. The object of the writer was to record the principal events of St. Patrick's life. Nevertheless there occurs in this work no allusion to the Roman mission of St. Patrick. He is said to have undertaken the conversion of the Irish, in consequence of the admonition of an angel, and of a vision in which he seemed to himself to hear the voices of the youths of Ireland from the wood of Fochlut,[4] like the man of Macedonia[5] in the history of St. Paul, calling upon him to come and help them. There is not a word of a commission from Pope Celestine.

The Hymn of St. Fiacc is silent as to a Mission from Rome.

---

[1] *Adversus.* This word must here be taken as a substantive in the accusative plural.
[2] *Sletty.* See above, *Introd.* p. 14. Irish Book of Hymns, p. 287.
[3] *Tara.* Colgan meets this difficulty by supposing St. Fiacc to have spoken by the Spirit of Prophecy. *Triad. Thaum.* p. 4.
[4] *Fochlut.* In the district of Hy Fiachrach, county of Mayo. See O'Donovan, *Tribes and Customs of Hy Fiachrach,* p. 463 n.
[5] *Macedonia.* Acts xvi. 9.

But mentions his ecclesiastical education under St. Germain.

This Hymn, however, contains an express statement[1] that Patrick had studied 'the canons' under St. Germain, and alludes distinctly to his travels across all the Alps, his living, with St. Germain, 'in the south of Italy,' and his sojourn among the islands of the Torrian, or Tyrrene sea, meaning perhaps the Mediterranean. It is evident, therefore, that this part of the history of Palladius had begun to be transferred to the second Patricius in the interval between the publication of the former works, and the composition of St. Fiacc's Hymn. But it is a fact of great significance that in none of the extant writings, possessing the smallest claim to be considered contemporary with St. Patrick, is his mission from Rome so much as alluded to; whilst the writings attributed to Patrick himself equally ignore his ecclesiastical education under St. Germain, and represent him as lamenting his rudeness, his rusticity, and his ignorance of the learned languages.

The Life of St. Patrick in the Book of Armagh ignores the Roman mission.

The antient Life[2] preserved in the Book of

---

[1] *Express statement.* Colgan, *Tr. Th.*, p. 1. 'He went across all Alps, beyond the sea, happy was the journey. He remained with Germain, southwards in the south of Leatha. He dwelt in the isles of the Torrian Sea, as I record: He read the Canons with Germain, as histories relate.' Here Leatha probably means *Latium* or Italy, not Letavia or Armorica; if so the author has fallen into the geographical error of placing the see of St. Germain in Italy. There can be but little doubt that these facts, for which the author quotes 'histories,' are a part of the lost or suppressed history of Palladius.

[2] *The antient life.* Dr. Petrie is of opinion, following Ussher, that the summary of chapters of the Life of Patrick, fol. 20 a, of the Book of Armagh, belongs to the first book of this antient life, having been misplaced by the error of the transcriber. If so, the following note, which occurs at the end of this summary, makes known to us the name of the compiler of this antient collection of traditions. 'Hæc pauca de Sancti Patricii peritia et virtutibus *Muirchu Maccumachtheni*, dictante A iduo Slebtiensis civitatis episcopo, conscripsit.' Aedh, bishop of Sletty, is probably the anchorite who died 698 (*Four M.*), so that *Maccuthenius*, as Ussher erroneously calls him, must have written

CHAP. I.] *Roman Mission of St. Patrick.* 315

Armagh unfortunately wants the first leaf. We cannot, therefore, say with absolute certainty that it did not contain a notice of St. Patrick's mission from Celestine. But the story told in what still remains of this venerable record is scarcely consistent with such a notice. It represents Patrick as having seen an angelic vision, in which the same angel who had frequently before appeared to him, when he was a captive in Ireland, was again seen by him. The angel announced that the time was come when he was to go forth to fish[1] with evangelic net, amid the fierce and barbarous nations whom God had sent him to teach; and that the sons and daughters of the wood of Fochlut were calling for him to come and save them. He was then apparently in France[2], with St. Germain, and immediately set out 'to the work for which he was before pre-

about the close of the seventh century, and of course collected legends of a much older date. The summary of St. Patrick's life, which is ascribed to him, does not altogether agree with the Life with which the book of Armagh begins, but the conjecture that Maccumachtheni was the compiler of that life, is nevertheless probably true; and it is quite clear that the summary distinctly ignores the Roman mission of St. Patrick. It states that St. Patrick desired to visit the Apostolic see and there to learn wisdom, but that meeting with St. Germain in Gaul, *he went no further*. Two of the headings of consecutive sections are as follow : — ' De etate ejus quando iens videre sedem apostolicam voluit discere sapientiam. — De inventione sancti Germani in Galliis, et ideo non exivit ultra.' See Petrie *On Tara Hill*, pp. 109—

111. The complaints of Maccumachtheni, as to the great uncertainty of the facts of St. Patrick's life, quoted by Dr. Petrie, are worthy of consideration, and will be noticed hereafter.

[1] *To fish.* In this expression we recognise the lines just quoted from the Hymn of St. Sechnall, which the author of this Life must therefore have had before him.:—' uisitauit [angelus] dicens ei addesse tempus ut ueniret et æuanguelico rete nationes feras et barbaras ad quas docendas misserat illum Deus ut piscaret ; ibique ei dictum est in uissione uocant te filii et filiæ silvæ Foclite, etc.' *Lib. Ardm.* fol. 2. a. a.

[2] *In France.* So Probus (i. 21, 22) understands the antient life, adopting its words, although not without interpolations. *Colgan, Tr. Th.,* p. 48.

pared, namely, the work of the Gospel.' St. Germain sent with him an aged priest named Segetius[1], to be a witness and companion of his labours, because Germain had not yet raised Patrick to the Pontifical order, inasmuch as[2] it was certain that Palladius had been already ordained and sent by Pope Celestine to convert the Irish.

He is not said to have been sent to Pope Celestine.

Here it is not said that Germanus sent Patrick to Celestine, although this is what the later biographers[3] have made this passage say. On the contrary, the narrative expressly asserts that Patrick went forth to the work 'for which he had been prepared,' not being at the time a bishop; and that Segetius, an aged presbyter, was sent with him by St. Germain as his companion and adviser in his mission. In short, he is represented to have received his commission as a missionary priest from St. Germain, and he had actually set out for the scene of his future labours when the news of the death of Palladius reached him. Augustine and Benedict, the disciples of

Commissioned by St. Germain.

---

[1] *Segetius.* The name is written Segestius, Segitius, Segerus, Sergecius. Heric of Auxerre, (*Miracula S. Germani*, c. 2) says, 'ineptumque ducens [Germanus] robustissimum agricolam in Dominicæ *segetis* torpere cultura ad S. Cælestinum ... per Segetium presbyterum suum eum direxit.' Bolland. Actt. SS. Julii vii. p. 259 B. This play upon the word proves that Heric read Segetius.

[2] *Inasmuch as.* Here follows the passage already quoted above, p. 288, and here we see the force of the word *enim*, with which that passage begins. It gives the reason why Patrick had not been previously consecrated a bishop, and Probus (i. 24) paraphrases it thus, 'Necdum tamen vir Domini Patricius ad pontificalem gradum fuerat promotus: quod ideo nimirum distulerat, quia sciebat quod Palladius, &c.' *Tr. Th.*, p. 48. Compare this with the original, 'Quia nec adhuc a sancto domino Germano in pontificali gradu ordinatus est; certe enim erat quod Palladius, &c.' *Book of Armagh*, fol. 2, a. a.

[3] *Later biographers.* See Vit. Trip. i. c. 35. (*Tr. Th.*, p. 122).

CHAP. I.] *and Consecration of St. Patrick.* 317

Palladius, on their return home, met Patrick at *Ebmoria,* and communicated to him the news of their master's death. Patrick[1] then, with those who were with him, went a little out of their way—'declinaverunt iter'—to a wondrous man, and chief bishop, Amathorex (or, as he is called in the same paragraph, Mathorex), who dwelt in a neighbouring place, and there Patrick was consecrated a bishop. His companions Auxilius, Iserninus, and some others of inferior rank, were ordained the same day.

There is here no mention of Pope Celestine, or of a mission from Rome; nor is there any difficulty in the story, considered as the genuine history of Patrick, and not of Palladius, except for the name of his consecrator. The Scholiast on Fiacc's Hymn says expressly that Amatorex was bishop of Auxerre, confounding him most probably with St. Amator, the predecessor of St. Germain in that see. But Amator[2] of Auxerre died A.D. 418, and therefore could not have been the consecrator of St. Patrick, in 431, or 432.

The bishop Amatorex is not spoken of as re-

St. Patrick consecrated by Amatorex, a Gallican bishop.

---

[1] *Patrick.* 'Patricius, et qui cum eo erant, declinauerunt iter ad quendam mirabilem hominem summum aepiscopum Amathorege nomine, in propinquo loco habitantem; ibique Sanctus Patricius, sciens quæ euentura erant, ibi episcopalem gradum ab Mathorege sancto episcopo accepit. Etiam Auxilius, Iserninusque et cæteri inferioris gradus eodem die quo sanctus Patricius ordinati sunt.' *Lib. Ardmach.* fol. 2. a. b.

[2] *Amator.* See Colgan, *Tr. Th.,* p. 9. *not.* 34. The Gaulic termination *rex,* or *rix,* has sadly puzzled transcribers. Thus the Tripartite Life tells us that Patrick was consecrated by Pope Celestine in presence of S. Germain and Amatus *King* of the Romans, (i. 39): and Nennius mixes up the two statements, that St. Germain sent Patrick with Segetius to Amatheus *the King*; 'ad Amatheum Regem in propinquo habitantem,' and also that he was consecrated a bishop 'by Matheus *the King*, and by a holy bishop,' *cap.* 55.

siding in his see, but as dwelling, probably as an accidental sojourner, in a place near Ebmoria, wherever that was; and the language implies that Patrick was consecrated by a single bishop only. It was not unusual at that time that a bishop should be without a see, and the incursions of the Goths, with other political troubles of the day, may sufficiently account, even without reference to any such custom, for a bishop being found in retirement or concealment in an obscure village. The story, therefore, is not discredited by our being unable satisfactorily to identify the bishop Mathorex or Amathorex[1] with any Gallican bishop whose name is now known in history.

Said to have accompanied St. Germain to Britain.

The Scholiast on Fiacc's Hymn tells us that St. Patrick accompanied St. Germain to Great Britain in 429 to suppress the Pelagian heresy. If this have any real foundation in fact[2] it is more likely to have been true of Palladius than of the second Patrick. It would be natural that Germain should have taken with him[3] his archdeacon, who had so recently procured at Rome the Papal authority for the British mission. This,

---

[1] *Amathorex.* Lanigan suggests Amandus of Bordeaux, vol. i. p. 200, but this is only conjecture. Our lists of the Gallican bishops of the time are so imperfect that we can neither wonder at the difficulty nor expect very easily to remove it.

[2] *In fact.* See *Tr. Th.*, p. 5, note 10 K. And see Colgan's remarks, *ib.* p. 96, not. 24. Comp. Lanigan, i. 180.

[3] *With him.* Heric of Auxerre (a writer of the ninth century), in his prose life, or *Miracula S. Germani,* speaks of one *Michomeris* who had followed Germain from Ireland, ' qui sanctum virum (Germanum *sc.*), de Hibernia fuerat prosecutus.' These words have been made to intimate that St. Germain had been in Ireland, but without probability; see the Bollandist father Bosch, *Comm. præv. in S. German.* num. 74, (*Actt. SS.* tom. vii. p. 200) Heric, *Miracula,*

CHAP. I.] *Connexion with St. Germain.* 319

however, is certain, that the chronology of St. Germain's life is plainly inconsistent with the statement, that St. Patrick continued studying theology under that prelate's superintendence for a period of thirty years.¹ Although originally intended for the law, and having received a legal education at Rome, St. Germain was an officer in the army up to the very day on which he was ordained.² It was therefore impossible that Patrick could have been his disciple prior to that event, which took place in 418, the year of St. Amator's death.

St. Patrick's thirty years' study impossible.

---

num. 7 (p. 256 ibid.), and the remarks of Papebroch, at April 30, p. 776.
¹ *Thirty years.* See Colgan's elaborate note on this difficulty, *Tr. Th.* p. 30, not. 18. He supposes that Patrick went first to St. Germain, in the south of Italy, Germain being then a secular man. This he says was A.D. 395, when St. Patrick was twenty-three years of age, and St. Germain was studying law at Rome. St. Gemrain may have then assisted him in his studies, as St. Fiacc intimates: num. 5. In 398 or 399, Patrick went to St. Martin of Tours, with whom he remained four years, or to about 402 or 403; he then went to Rome, where he met St. Kieran of Seir-Kieran (see above p. 200,) exactly thirty years before his mission to Ireland by Pope Celestine. In 404 he went to the Hermits with the naked feet—spent with them eight years (Probus, i. 15). This brings us to 412, in which year he went to the island of the Tyrrhene Sea, where he had the adventure with the beast, the guardian of the fountain, there he remained nine years, (ib. i. 16), or rather seven (*Vit. Trip.* i. c. 34). St. Germain was then Bishop, and St. Patrick continued with him from thenceforth to the time when Celestine sent him to Ireland. So that the thirty years of Patrick's studying with Germain is to be counted from A.D. 395 or thereabouts, although some nineteen or twenty years of that time were spent with St. Martin, and in the islands of the Mediterranean, and not with St. Germain. It is evident from this how insuperable are the difficulties of any attempt to reconcile the interpolated lives with the facts of history. Colgan assumes throughout that St. Martin died in 402 or 403, Ussher, *Ind. Chron.* gives 401 as the date of St. Martin's death. Others say 412. But 397, which is most generally received, would be wholly inconsistent with the story of St. Patrick's spending four years under his instruction. *Mem. de Trevoux*, A.D. 1795, p. 1238, 1269.
² *Ordained.* The circumstances of his ordination are curious, and prove that in the Gallican church of the fifth century there were violations of ecclesiastical rules quite as great as those which have been objected to the primitive church of Ireland. 'Il n'y a rien de plus surprennant,' says Tillemont, 'que cette vocation de S. Germain, ni qui paroisse plus contraire aux règles de

His connexion with St. Germain transferred to him from Palladius.

We infer that the whole story of Patrick's connexion with St. Germain and mission from Celestine should be regarded as a fragment of the lost history of Palladius, transferred to the second and more celebrated Patrick, by those who undertook to interpolate the authentic records of his Life. The object of these interpolaters was evidently to exalt their hero. They could not rest satisfied with the simple and humble position in which his own writings, his Confession, and his Letter to Coroticus, had placed him. They could not concede to Palladius the honour of a direct mission from Rome, without claiming for Patrick a similar honour; they could not be content that their own Patrick should be regarded as an unlearned, a rude, and uneducated man, even though

---

l'Eglise.' *Hist. Eccl.* tom. xv. p. 10. In his early life Germain had been greatly addicted to the pleasures of the chase, and was in the habit of hanging his trophies on an antient tree, which was probably in some way connected with the still remaining paganism of the country. St. Amator remonstrated in vain, and at length, in the absence of Germain, had the tree cut down and burned. Germain on his return home was furious; *ferocem* is the term employed by Constantius. He went so far as to threaten the bishop's life, although he was then himself by profession a Christian. But the long-sighted Amator discerned in him the seeds of future eminence, and resolved to secure for the Church the services of so great a man. Finding his own end approaching, he saw, or thought he saw, a vision in which Germain was divinely pointed out as his successor in the see of Auxerre. Germain was then an officer of the state in some military capacity. It is difficult to avoid the suspicion that he may have been privy to Amator's design. The bishop, however, when his measures were taken, assembled the people in the Cathedral. Germain was there under arms, and probably with some of his soldiers. The bishop called upon all to lay aside their arms, in reverence for the sacred services of the place: and ordered the ostiarii to close the doors of the church. He then, surrounded by a band of ecclesiastics and nobles, laid violent hands on Germain, and calling upon the name of the Lord, gave him the clerical tonsure and habit: 'glomerata secum turba clericorum atque nobilium, injiciens manus Germanum apprehendit: et invocato nomine Domini, cæsariem ejus capiti detrahens, habitu religionis, rejectis secularibus ornamentis, cum promotionis honore induit.' *Constant. Vita S. Germani*, lib. i. c. 1. (*Actt. SS.* Junii. vii. p. 203. A.)

CHAP. I.]   *true only of Palladius.*   321

he had so described himself. The biography of Palladius, 'alio nomine Patricius,' supplied them with the means of effecting their object, and gave to the interpolated story the appearance of antient support.

It will be desirable to make the reader acquainted with some of the versions of the history which have been given by these interpolaters:—

The Scholiast[1] on Fiacc's Hymn, for example, who is probably one of the oldest of them, tells us that 'when St. Patrick had received the angelic vision, calling him to go to Ireland, he applied to St. Germain for advice. St. Germain said to him, "Go to the successor of St. Peter, namely, Celestine, that he may ordain thee, for this office belongs to him." Patrick, therefore, went to him; but Celestine gave him no honor, because he had already sent Palladius to Ireland.' After this repulse, Patrick, says our author, went away to the islands of the Mediterranean Sea, received the Staff of Jesus in one of those islands, and returned again to St. Germain, who sent him a second time to the Pope, accompanied by the presbyter Segetius. Celestine, by this time, had heard of the death of Palladius, and no longer made any difficulty in complying with the request of St. Germain. Patrick was therefore consecrated[2] in presence of Pope Celestine, and of Theodosius the emperor, by Amatorex, bishop of Auxerre. Celestine lived only a

Story of the Roman mission of Patrick as told by Fiacc's Scholiast.

---

[1] *Scholiast.* Colgan, *Tr. Th.*, p. 5, not. 13 *n*.

[2] *Consecrated.* 'Tunc ordinatus est Patricius in conspectu Cælestini et

week after the ordination of Patrick, who arrived in Ireland the first year of Pope Sixtus, after having received also the sanction of that pontiff, together with some relics of Peter and Paul, and many books.

In these last words it would seem that a clause has been taken from the acts of Palladius, and it is obvious also that the antient narrative is the foundation of this story, interpolated so far as was necessary to make way for the Roman mission of St. Patrick. The interpolater, however, did not perceive how impossible it was that all these transactions could have taken place in the short time allotted to them, to say nothing of the other chronological difficulties[1] of his narrative.

Discrepancies of the later biographers.
The discrepancies of the later Lives in the endeavour to introduce the Roman mission into the original story are still more instructive.

Narrative of the Vita Tertia.
One biographer[2] tells us that after spending four years with St. Martin at Tours, and nine in an island called *Tamerensis*, to which Martin sent him, Patrick wished to visit Rome, as being the head of all churches. St. Germain approved

---

Theodosii Junioris, Regis mundi. Amatorex Autissiodorensis episcopus est qui eum ordinavit. Et Cælestinus non vixit nisi una septimana postquam ordinatus est Patricius, ut ferunt. Sixtus vero ei successit, in cujus primo anno Patricius venit ad Hiberniam : et ipse perhumaniter tractavit Patricium, et dedit ipsi partem reliquiarum Petri et Pauli et libros multos.' *Ibid.* n. 14 *o.*

[1] *Difficulties.* The character of the Eastern emperor Theodosius II.

for piety and devotion is evidently the reason why he is made to have been present on this occasion, although there is no probability that he was ever at Rome. If Amatorex was bishop of Auxerre at this time, during the lifetime of St. Germain, as this author's narrative implies, were there two coexisting bishops there, or of what see was Germain bishop?

[2] *One biographer.* Vita Tertia, cap. 22—27. *Tr. Th.*, p. 22—3.

CHAP. I.]   *Accounts of the Roman Mission.*   323

of this, and sent with him Segetius, as a witness, 'ut testem haberet idoneum.' Patrick on his way to Rome met with a hermit, 'dwelling in a certain place,' who gave him the Staff of Jesus. Then Patrick went out of his way, 'declinavit iter,' to a certain wonderful man, a chief bishop, named Amator, from whom he received the degree of a bishop. He then went to Rome, and was well received by Celestine. There he heard the voice of an angel, commanding him to go to Ireland. He refused, saying, 'I will not go until I salute the Lord.' The angel took him to Mount Arnon, on a rock in the Tyrrhene Sea[1], in a city called Capua. There Patrick saluted the Lord, like Moses. Meanwhile, the news of the death of Palladius arrived, and Celestine commanded Patrick to go to Ireland.

Another version[2] of the story is this: Patrick receives the angelic vision whilst with Germain, who sends him forth, with Segetius, not having as yet consecrated him a bishop, in consequence of the previous mission of Palladius. But upon the news of this missionary's death, St. Germain sends Patrick to Rome for the apostolic licence. Patrick sails through the Tyrrhene Sea, receives the Staff of Jesus 'from a certain youth in a certain island who had given a lodging to Christ.'

Narrative of the Vita Quarta.

---

[1] *Tyrrhene Sea.* The author gives the name of this sea first in Irish and then in Latin, ' *Ar muir Lethe,* supra petram maris Tyrreni.' The Irish words signify ' on the sea of Letha,' or Latium. *Ibid.* p. 23, cap. 25.

[2] *Another version.* Vita Quarta, c. 27, sq. *Ibid.* p. 38.

Patrick spake with the Lord on the mount, who commanded him to go to Ireland. He then goes to Rome, is well received by Pope Celestine, who gives him the relics of saints and sends him to Ireland. Nothing is said in this narrative of his ordination; but the author, after stating that Patrick, on receiving the apostolic licence, set out for Ireland, inserts into his history, out of its regular order, the story told in the Book of Armagh, that Augustine and Benedict met him in Euboria, told him of the death of Palladius; and Patrick then went out of his way to the holy and venerable bishop named Amatorex, by whom he was consecrated.

Here we have the strongest evidence of interpolation. The writer had before him two different and inconsistent documents, which he incorporated into his narrative, without perceiving their inconsistency.

The version of the story given by Probus. The story as told by Probus[1] is still more complicated. After spending four years with St. Martin, who gave him the clerical tonsure, an angel commanded Patrick to pass some time with 'the people of God,' that is, as our author explains it, with the hermits and solitaries who were barefoot—'eremitas et solitarios nudis pedibus.' Patrick remained with these hermits eight years. The angel appeared to him again, and commanded him to go to some islanders, who dwelt in an island 'between the mountains and the sea.' Here he remained nine years, and

---

[1] *Probus.* Lib. i. c. 14 sq. *Ibid.* p. 48.

here occurred his adventure with the beast which guarded the fountain.[1] The angel now appeared the third time and said to him, 'Go to St. Senior, a bishop, who is in Mount Hermon, on the south side of the ocean, and his city is fortified with seven walls.' Here Patrick was ordained priest, and here he heard the voice of the children[2] in Ireland, calling him to come and save them. The angel commanded him to go to Ireland. Patrick refused, saying, 'I cannot go, because bad men dwell there.' The angel said, 'Go.' Patrick said, 'I cannot, unless I see the Lord.' Patrick then went forth with nine men, and saw the Lord. The Lord said unto him, 'Come unto my right hand.' Patrick went to the Lord's right hand. The Lord said unto him, 'Go thou to Ireland, and preach therein the word of eternal life.' Patrick answered, 'I ask of Thee three petitions—that the men of Ireland be rich in gold and silver—that I may be their patron—and that after this life I may sit on Thy right hand in heaven.' The Lord said to him, 'Patrick, thou shalt have what thou hast asked, and, moreover, whosoever shall commemorate[3] thee by day or by night, shall not

---

[1] *Fountain.* See this story quoted from the Tripartite Life, p. 307, supra.

[2] *Children.* Here the miracle is magnified in the true spirit of legendary exaggeration: the children cried out from their mothers' womb. 'Audivit in visione voces puerorum de sinu et de ventre matrum, &c.'

[3] *Commemorate.* Alluding to the recitation of the Hymn of Patrick, as Colgan observes. *Ibid.* p. 62, not. 20. Comp. Petrie, *Tara Hill*, p. 56. *Book of Hymns*, p. 22—33.— The great quantity of gold and silver ornaments found in Ireland, numerous specimens of which may be seen in the Museum of the Royal Irish Academy, may perhaps explain St. Patrick's first petition.

perish everlastingly.' Patrick then went to Ireland, but the inhabitants refused to listen to him. He, therefore, poured forth this prayer, ' O Lord Jesu Christ, who didst guide my path through the Gauls and Italy unto these islands, lead me, I beseech Thee, to the Holy See of the Roman Church, that I may thence receive authority to preach thy word with faithfulness, and that the people of the Hiberni may by me be made Christians.' He then set out for Rome, and on his way spent some time with St. Germain, in all obedience, charity, and chastity. The angel now again admonished him that the time was come when he should return to Ireland, to convert the fierce and barbarous inhabitants to the faith of Christ. He therefore set forth, and Germain sent with him Segetius, the presbyter. Patrick[1] had not yet been promoted to the episcopal order, because Palladius had been sent to convert the Irish. But when the death of Palladius was communicated to him by Augustine and Benedict at Euboria, Patrick and his companions went out of their way to 'a man of wondrous sanctity, a chief bishop, named Amator, dwelling in a neighbouring place,' and by him St. Patrick was consecrated a bishop. Then the venerable prelate, Patrick, quickly got on board a ship, and proceeded to Britain, from whence with all speed, after a prosperous journey,

---

[1] *Patrick.* This part of the story is told by our author in the very words of the Book of Armagh, with some little paraphrase. The author must have had the life given in the Book of Armagh before him, and therefore must have deliberately interpolated the more antient story.

' he reached our sea in the name of the Holy Trinity.'

This narrative is curiously lame, and is followed by two different and contradictory statements: first, that he went to Rome and returned with the apostolic benediction; secondly, that he was on his way to Rome when he heard of the death of Palladius, and that then he received consecration from Amator, in some part of Gaul, but did not actually reach Rome. It is also very remarkable that this differs from all other versions of the story, in making St. Patrick to have commenced his ministry in Ireland, without the sanction of the Holy See, whilst still a presbyter. A ray of truth has here broken out through clouds of fable, and no greater proof can be desired that the Roman mission was a modern addition to the facts of history.

The story told by Joceline represents St. Patrick, after his second captivity in Ireland, as at home with his parents, that is to say, in Britain. There the angel appeared to him, and there he heard the children of the Irish, from their mothers' wombs, calling to him to come and save them. Notwithstanding the opposition[1] of his father and mother, who, according to this author, were still alive (another story represents them to have been murdered when he was taken

The story as told by Joceline.

---

[1] *Opposition.* 'Utroque parente renitente.' That the author supposed him to be in Great Britain is evident from the words which he puts into the mouth of the angel, 'ut patriam parentesque deserens Galliam peteret, &c.' *Sexta Vita.* c. 21, 22. *Tr. Th.* p. 69.

captive some years before), Patrick placed himself
under the tuition of St. Germain, and afterwards
under that of St. Martin. But St. Martin was
commanded by an angel to go to the island *Tamarensis*[1], and Patrick returned to St. Germain,
with whom he remained some days. St. Martin,
who in a former account is said to have given St.
Patrick the clerical tonsure only, is here represented as having given him the monastic habit
and rules. Patrick was tempted to break his rule
by a strong desire for flesh meat, but miraculously
overcame the temptation, and the flesh was converted into fish. He then resolved to visit Rome.
St. Germain approved of his doing so and appointed Segetius to accompany him. On his
way he stopped at an island in the Tyrrhene Sea,
where he found a certain solitary, who gave him
the Staff of Jesus. In the same island he found
also some apparently young men, with others in
decrepit old age: upon enquiry he was told that
those who had retained their youth and vigour
were the fathers of the seemingly older men.
They had been in the habit of receiving in hospitality every traveller who passed that way.
One night a pilgrim came with a staff in his
hand. He was received as usual with all kindness. In the morning he announced himself to
be Jesus Christ, and left behind him the Staff,

---

[1] *Tamarensis.* The story told in the *Vita Tertia* is that Patrick went to the insula Tamarensis at the command of St. Martin. Here we read that St. Martin himself went there, leaving Patrick to return to St. Germain.

desiring that it should be safely preserved, and delivered to a certain pilgrim named Patrick[1], who after a long time should come there. After this Christ ascended into heaven. But the good people of the island continued in the enjoyment of youth: whilst their sons, who had not merited the favour of such a miracle, grew old like other men. Patrick then went to Rome, where he was consecrated a bishop by Celestine himself, and sent into Ireland to succeed Palladius.

Here it will be seen that our author cuts away, without mercy, all that he found in the older narratives about the bishop Amatorex, and the consecration of Patrick before the Emperor Theodosius. He felt, doubtless, that many difficulties were obviated by making Pope Celestine perform the ceremony himself. He adds that *after* Patrick had been thus consecrated a bishop, the angel appeared to him, and commanded him to set out at once for Ireland. Patrick objected, until he could first behold and salute the Lord. The angel therefore transported him to Mount Morion, near to the Tyrrhene Sea, by the city of Capua, where, like Moses, he saw the Lord. In the story as told by Probus, it was here that Patrick was ordained priest, before he went forth the first time, without a commission from Rome, to Ireland.

Discrepancy with former accounts.

---

[1] *Patrick.* The author of this ridiculous story forgot to reconcile it with the antient Irish tradition that Patrick did not receive that name until he was commissioned by Celestine. For the history of the Staff of Jesus, which was long preserved at Armagh and Dublin, and was publicly burned at the Reformation, see *Obits and Martyrol. of Christ's Church, Introd.* p. viii. sq.

The story as given in the Tripartite Life.

The Tripartite Life, as it is translated by Colgan, tells the story thus[1]: Patrick was amongst his relations after his third captivity. They urged him strongly to give up all further missionary labours: but whenever he fell asleep, he saw Ireland in vision, and heard the voices of the youths in the wood Fochlut, calling upon him to go and help them. He resolved, however, first to visit Rome. He therefore passed the Iccian Sea[2] to France, and crossing the Alps to the south of Italy, he found there[3] St. Germain, with whom he read the ecclesiastical canons, like Paul at the feet of Gamaliel. After this[4] he went to Tours to St. Martin to receive the monastic tonsure. Having overcome his temptation to eat flesh, which was miraculously converted into fish, he went to the island Arelatensis, where he pursued his ecclesiastical education under St. Germain. He was thirty years old when he came to St. Germain, and continued thirty years under instruction with him. When he was sixty[5] years of age the angel Victor appeared to him and commanded him to go to Ireland: Patrick immediately resolved to visit Rome, to obtain the apostolic authority for his mission. Germain approved of this, and sent

---

[1] *Thus.* Vita Septima, seu Tripartita, i. c. 30 *sq.*

[2] *Iccian Sea*, i.e. the English channel; see Irish Nennius, p. 31.

[3] *Found there.* This is the same geographical error as to the situation of Auxerre which occurs also in Fiacc's hymn, see p. 314, note [1].

[4] *After this.* St. Martin died 412, and St. Germain continued in the secular state until 418. So that this author's chronology is here as much at fault as his geography.

[5] *Sixty.* Here the MS. of the original Irish in the British Museum recommences after a gap of some pages.

with him Segetius, who was his own vicar in spirituals. Patrick then with nine companions embarked to cross the Tyrrhene Sea, and landed on an island, in which he found what seemed a new house. In it was a young married couple and a decrepit old woman unable to walk, who went about on all fours. The young man, who was the master of the house, on being asked, said that this aged woman was his daughter's grand-daughter, and that her mother, still more feeble and decrepit, was alive: that Christ under the form[1] of a pilgrim had visited them, very many years before, with a staff in His hand, and had left the staff, as in the former story. St. Patrick refused to receive the staff until it was given to him by the Lord Jesus Himself. Having remained three days in the island with these remarkable people, he went to a mountain in the neighbourhood, called Hermon, in which our Lord appeared to him and commanded him to prepare himself for the conversion of Ireland, giving him[2] the Staff of Jesus. On his arrival at Rome, Pope Celestine received him with favour, and, when the death of Palladius was announced, committed to him the

---

[1] *Under the form.* Here it would seem that Colgan has endeavoured to lessen the absurdities of the original; for the Irish text says that our Lord had visited them during His sojourn amongst men, so that they had retained their youth for 400 years. It was scarcely worth while to commit this little piece of dishonesty. The discrepancies in these legends are curious: and possibly worthy of being more closely investigated. The aged people here are women; in the story as told by Joceline they are men.

[2] *Giving him.* The Irish text here adds the three petitions of St. Patrick, as given before from Joceline. These Colgan, in his translation, has suppressed. But he had given them before in the Vita Sexta: what purpose therefore was served by their suppression here?

conversion of the Irish, which he knew had been promised to St. Patrick by an angelic oracle. Then Pope Celestine himself, in presence of St. Germain, and of Amatus King of the Romans, consecrated him bishop, and gave him the name of Patricius. Auxilius, Iserninus, and some others of his companions, were consecrated[1] at the same time. Three bodies of Psalmodists sang praises to God on this occasion: the heavenly choir; the choir of the Romans; and the voice of the Irish children of the wood Fochlut, who sang, 'Hibernienses omnes rogamus te S. Patrici, ut venias, et ambules inter nos, et liberes nos.'

The original narrative interpolated.

On comparing these narratives no unprejudiced mind can doubt that the writers of these collections allowed themselves the utmost licence in dealing with their authorities. The original narrative of the Book of Armagh was interpolated to impose upon an uncritical and credulous people the fables of the ecclesiastical education of St. Patrick under St. Germain, his monastic tonsure under St. Martin, and his mission from Pope Celestine. No antient or trustworthy authority has countenanced these statements, in reference to the second Patrick. Palladius Patricius was undoubtedly commissioned by Pope Celestine. Palladius was undoubtedly closely connected with St. Germain. But we have no evidence that the same things were true of

---

[1] *Consecrated.* 'Consecrati sunt.' But we are not necessarily to understand by this word episcopal consecration.

Patrick the Apostle of Ireland. The great discrepancies in the several versions of the story prove it to be legend and not history. Modern writers, prejudiced in favour of the legend, in order to prop up what they wished to retain of the story, have been compelled to interpolate the original narrative like the old legendary biographers. No man could be more thoroughly honest, or more perfectly ready to express his honest convictions, than Dr. Lanigan. But he was pledged by his education and prejudices to uphold the Roman mission[1], and with it the ecclesiastical education of St. Patrick. He has therefore maintained that Patrick was sent to Rome by St. Germain, not for the purpose of being consecrated a bishop for the Scoti, but to obtain authority to accompany, in an inferior capacity, the mission to Ireland of which Palladius was the chief. He asserts without hesitation, notwithstanding the contrary assertion of Fiacc's Scholiast, 'there can be no doubt' that bearing the recommendation of so great a saint as Germain, Patrick 'must have been' well received[2] at Rome. Accordingly he adds with as much confidence as if he himself was an original

Modern interpolations of the narrative.

---

[1] *Roman mission.* It is a pity that this question should ever have been in any way connected with the controversies between the Churches of England and Rome. So far as those controversies are concerned, we are no more affected by the Roman mission of St. Patrick, (if the fact could be proved) than we are by the Roman mission of St. Germain or of Palladius. The fact that missionaries were sent out with the sanction of Rome, no more proves the modern Papal claim to universal supremacy than the fact of a bishop being now sent to the interior of Africa with the sanction of Canterbury, would prove the universal supremacy of the Primate of England.

[2] *Well received.* Lanigan, *Eccl. Hist.* i., p. 184.

witness of the fact, that Patrick was 'appointed principal assistant to Palladius: a situation which, although it entitled him to be raised to the episcopacy in case of the death of Palladius, was not equivalent to episcopal institution.' He says again, 'I have no doubt[1] that the Pope's intention was that in case of the demise of Palladius St. Patrick should succeed him.' All this, however, we should bear in mind, is mere fiction, without the slightest support from any antient authority. The fiction indeed is better adapted to sustain the ordeal of modern criticism, and is in itself perhaps more probable, than the stories which antient credulity was content to swallow. But it is as purely fiction, and in reality as truly legend, as the silly tales we have just quoted from more antient interpolaters. The difficulties which have given birth to these fictions, modern as well as antient, have been created altogether by the attempt to maintain, without any evidence from original documents, that Patrick had received a complete ecclesiastical education in the best schools of the Gallican church, and that he was regularly commissioned by the Roman Pontiff to take the place of Palladius as bishop of the Scots in Ireland.

<small>How much of the story is historical, and likely to be true.</small> The historical fact is probably no more than this, that Patrick (if this be not a fragment of the history of Palladius) was at Auxerre, when he believed himself to have seen a vision, calling upon

---

[1] *No doubt.* Ibid. p. 192.

him to preach the Word of God to the Irish: he set out immediately, attended by the experienced presbyter Segetius, whom St. Germain (if that be true) had appointed to accompany him: and it is possible that he may have received episcopal consecration from some Gallican bishop named Matorex or Amatorex, before he set sail for Great Britain. If these be the facts it must follow that he was a missionary to Ireland, not from Rome, but from St. Germain and the Church of Gaul. One authority identifies his consecrator with the celebrated Amator of Auxerre. But if it were so, we must suppose St. Patrick to have been consecrated a bishop whilst his supposed tutor St. Germain was still a layman, and to have begun his labours in Ireland before Palladius, fourteen years at least before the date[1] usually assigned to his mission.

It can scarcely be doubted, however, that some of the legends which have been interpolated into this more simple story, preserve curious fragments of forgotten geography, which lead to the suspicion of their possible authenticity. They belong in all probability to the first or Palladian Patrick, and are remnants of his lost or suppressed acts. His connexion with St. Germain is an historical fact. He may have been

<small>Fragments of forgotten geography.</small>

---

[1] *Date.* This is on the supposition that Amator died and was succeeded in the see of Auxerre by Germain in 418. Probus, as we have seen, preserves a tradition that Patrick had been in Ireland as a missionary before Palladius. This may be a fragment of truth, especially as it has been worked into the narrative with much clumsiness.

ordained[1], not indeed consecrated a bishop, but ordained perhaps deacon, by Amator or Amatorex of Auxerre: and we first read of him as *the deacon* Palladius. He may have been originally a disciple of St. Martin, and may have gone at the advice of his master to the island of Lerins[2], in the Mediterranean Sea, where St. Honorat had then recently founded a celebrated religious society. But this is mere conjecture.

Story of St. Senior at Mount Hermon.

With respect to the story of Patrick having been ordained *priest*, by a bishop St. Senior, near Mount Hermon, who dwelt in a city fortified with seven walls, this is most probably another fragment of the life of Palladius. Colgan[3] suggests that the real name of this prelate was Senator, not Senior, and that he may have been the Senator, a friend of St. Germain, who dwelt in Italy, and who is mentioned by Constantius.[4] Constantius indeed calls him 'a presbyter' only; but that title was often indifferently given to bishops and priests. Palladius may have received

---

[1] *Ordained.* Amator of Auxerre died 1 May, 418, according to the best authorities.

[2] *Lerins.* This island, or rather, group of two islands, is not far from the coast opposite Cannes. One of the islands is now called St. Marguerite, the other St. Honorat. The names Aralenensis, Arelanensis, Tamarensis, are all probably corruptions of *Lerinensis*. The name Tamarensis presents the greatest difficulty, but may have been taken from the name of Cap de Camerat, a headland in the neighbourhood. Colgan, (following Ussher, *Ind. Chron.* A.D. 409,) suggests that Tamarensis may be intended for *Camargue*, a name given to the Delta at the mouth of the Rhone: which was antiently Caprensis, or Capraria. *Tr. Th.* p. 30, not. 19, 20. The Bollandists (ad 17 Mart. p. 528), have suggested Lerins, with much greater probability. It is curious that St. Lupus, who accompanied Germanus to Britain, spent some time in the monastic society of Lerins, about A.D. 417. *Actt. SS.*, Julii vii. p. 62. B. 72. F.

[3] Colgan. *Tr. Th.*, p. 62, not. 17.

[4] *Constantius.* Vit. S. German. ii. cap. 1. n. 6. (*Actt. SS.*, Julii vii. p. 217 B.) Lanigan suggests that *Senior* may not be a proper name, but only an assertion of the bishop's age.

priest's orders from this prelate preparatory to his being consecrated at Rome first bishop of the Scots. Mount Hermon, Arnon, Morion, as it is variously called, is described as being on 'the south side of the ocean,' '*ar muir Letha*,' i.e. on the sea of Letha, 'on a rock in the Tyrrhene sea,' 'in the city of Capua,' and 'near the city of Capua.' It is not easy to guess[1] what place is intended by these descriptions. Capua is not on the sea, and cannot be recognized as being 'on the south side of the ocean,' even though we should understand by the ocean the Mediterranean sea. It is impossible that Mount Arnon or Hermon can have been at the same time 'on a rock in the Tyrrene sea' and also 'in the city of Capua,' as the author of Vita Tertia tells us it was. The description of it as a city surrounded by seven walls, and its being on the south side of the ocean, has led Dr. Lanigan to conjecture that the celebrated Mount St. Michael[2], in the bay of Cancale near Avranches, may be intended.

---

[1] *Guess.* Colgan would read *Caieta* for Capua, and the Mount, or *Arx*, Orlond, for Mount Hermon. *Tr. Th.* p. 31, note 25, 26. The author of Vita Tertia seems to have combined three not very reconcileable descriptions of the place when he describes it first in Irish *ar muir Letha*, then as 'supra petram maris Tyrreni;' and lastly as 'in civitate quæ vocatur Capua.' *Letha*, for Letavia, frequently signifies Armorica, but is sometimes used for *Latium*. On the whole there is here confusion apparently inextricable, owing most probably to antient errors of transcription. The Irish Tripartite life places Mount Hermon near the island where Patrick met the married couple endowed with perpetual youth, and where he received 'the Staff of Jesus.'

[2] *Mount St. Michael.* Lanigan, *Eccl. Hist.* i. p. 166. The Celtic derivation of the word Hermon, from *her* great, and *maen* rock, adopted by Lanigan from Bullet, is untenable. Autbert, Bishop of Avranches, in 708, built on this isolated rock the Church of St. Michael, which afterwards became the famous Benedictine Abbey; see Mabillon, *Actt. SS., O.S.B. Secul.* iii. part i. 75; also *Annal.* ii. 19.

It seems difficult to avoid suspecting, from the contradictory accounts given of the geographical position of the place, that two different stories may have been mixed together: one relating to the ordination of Palladius near Capua; the other to the ordination of Patrick 'on the south side of the ocean,' *ar muir Letha*, on the sea of Armorica.[1]

One or two other anecdotes, which we may suspect to have been taken from the lost acts of Palladius, may be here noticed for the reader's consideration.

Story of St. Patrick's landing in Ireland.

St. Patrick, on his arrival in Ireland, after having been consecrated a bishop, landed, we are told, at Inbher Dea[2], the mouth of a river in the county of Wicklow, in the district of Hy Garrchon; he was repulsed by the chieftain Nathi Hua Garrchon, and compelled to return to his ships, after which he sailed northwards.

Identical with the adventures ascribed to Palladius.

This story is in almost every particular identical with the adventures which, as we have already seen, the Irish traditions attribute to Palladius. It

---

[1] *Armorica.* It must be admitted that this description applies very well to Mount St. Michael; but we have no record of that place having ever borne a name resembling Hermon, Arnon, or Morion. The natives called it *Tumba*, from its resemblance to a Roman tomb: and it is usually known by the name of *St. Michael in monte Tumba*. It is called also *S. Michael in periculo maris*, from the danger of crossing to it at an unfavourable state of the tide. See Mabillon, *Actt. SS., ubi supr.* 76. 'Hic locus *Tumba* vocitatur ab incolis.'

[2] *Inbher Dea.* Keating (in the reign of Laoghaire) writes this *Inbher Degaid*, the Inver (river's mouth) of *Degad*, which seems to be a man's name; see Colgan, *Tr. Th.* p. 109, note 29. The other authorities all read Inbher Deæ or Dea, and Ostium Deæ, Dee, Dea, or Deac. It is the antient name given to the mouth of the Vartry river, on the strand near the town of Wicklow. The Danes seem to have made a settlement there in 835. (See O'Donovan, *Four Masters*, at A.D. 835 and 430). It may have been a better harbour for ships in antient times than it is at present.

attributed to St. Patrick.

is not reasonable to suppose that both missionaries should have done exactly the same things; that both should land at the same place, both be driven off by the same chieftain, and both turn to the north of the island; with this difference only, that Palladius is driven (according to some accounts), by a storm, round the northern coast of Scotland to the region of the Picts; and Patrick lands safely in Dal-aradia, where his ministry is at once successful. It can scarcely be doubted that the foregoing account belongs to Palladius, and not to Patrick, who, we may readily believe, went at once to Ulster, to visit the place with which, as we shall see, he was formerly acquainted, and where he probably expected to be well received.

This conjecture is confirmed by observing the fragmentary nature of the early lives of St. Patrick. They are made up from passages culled out of more antient biographies. These passages are often inserted out of their chronological order, and not unfrequently we find in the same author two or more different, sometimes inconsistent, accounts of the same event. *Fragmentary structure of the Lives.*

We have eight[1] antient records of the Life of St. Patrick. Of these, four make no mention of the landing-place of Palladius in Leinster, and not one of them particularises *Inbher Dea* as the port at which he landed, although, all say in *Analysis of the accounts given of the landing place of St. Patrick.*

---

[1] *Eight*, i.e. eight more important records, viz., the seven lives published by Colgan, and the collection in the Book of Armagh, which we may hope soon to see published, by Dr. Reeves. There are also some Lives, in the Irish language, of which we need not here speak.

general terms, that he landed in Hy Garrchon, in the territory of the Leinster men, or in the province of Leinster. Inbher Dea is first-named when mention is made of the landing of St. Patrick; but, two of the Lives[1], in speaking of Patrick's landing-place, say that it was 'the port of *the same river*, Dea,' meaning evidently the same at which Palladius had landed, although no mention of this port or river had occurred in the previous portion of their narratives. This is a clear proof that Inbher Dea had been mentioned as the landing-place of Palladius, in the documents copied by these writers, and was omitted by them or their transcribers, perhaps to avoid making both missionaries land at the same place. Keating[2] is the only writer who expressly states that Palladius landed at Inbher Dea, or Inbher Degaid, as he calls it: and it is remarkable that he is entirely silent as to the landing place of St. Patrick.

<small>Patch-work composition of the second Life.</small> The second Life, in Colgan's Collection, taken from a MS. in the monastery of St. Hubert in Ardennes, is evidently old, and has transcribed considerable passages from the Life in the Book of Armagh.[3] It affords a remarkable evidence of the patch-work manner of compilation adopted

---

[1] *The Lives.* Viz.: the *Vita Secunda* in its *first* account of the landing of Patrick, c. 25; and the Tripartite, i. c. 41. This latter authority probably copied the earlier life without consideration.

[2] *Keating.* He is too modern to be himself of any authority; but he may have copied antient documents now lost.

[3] *Book of Armagh.* The fact that this writer had the Book of Armagh before him is a sufficient refutation of Colgan's too easy credulity in supposing him to be 'Patrick junior, or one of St. Patrick's disciples.' He cannot have lived earlier than the eighth century.

in these biographies, by putting together different narratives of the same event. Thus, this writer gives us first (c. 23) from the Book of Armagh, with only some verbal alterations, the account of Palladius already quoted[1], in which no mention is made even of the county or district in which that missionary landed in Ireland. Then follows (c. 24) another account[2] in which Palladius is said to have arrived in the district of the Lagenians, where Nathi Mac Garrchon opposed him. We have also (c. 25) an account of the arrival of St. Patrick 'at the mouth of *the same river*, i.e. Deac'[3] as he calls it (although, as already remarked, no such river had been mentioned before) where he was opposed by ' the same unrighteous chieftain, Nathi, who had before resisted Palladius.' This is evidently out of its place, for it is immediately followed (c. 26) by the story[4] from the Book of Armagh, of Patrick having heard in Euboria of the death of Palladius, and of his having gone out of his way to be consecrated by Amatorex. Then follows (c. 27), also from the Book of Armagh, the story of the Druids of King Laoghaire, at Tara, predicting the coming of Patrick, and the overthrow of idolatry; and then (c. 28), we have the account, taken again from the Book of Armagh, of the arrival of Patrick in the country of the Lagenians, at *Ostium Dea*,

---

[1] *Quoted.* See above p. 288. Document I. *Vita Secunda*, c. 23. *Tr. Th.* p. 13.

[2] *Account.* Given above, p. 294, Document IV.

[3] *Deac.* This may possibly be a typographical error for *Deae*; unless *Deac* be the Celtic genitive.

[4] *Story.* See p. 288, Document I.

his resolution not to remain there, and his sailing to the north of Ireland.

The Scholiast on Fiacc tells the story of Palladius only.

It is also worthy of note that the Scholiast on Fiacc's hymn records the landing in Wicklow, the repulse by the natives, and the journey towards the north, as the story of Palladius only. He says not a word of the place at which Patrick landed. But, on the other hand, the Book of Armagh, Probus, and Joceline, have transferred the substance of these adventures to Patrick, without any notice of the landing-place of Palladius. The author of the third Life has also attributed the same adventures to Patrick, and says only of Palladius (c. 26), that the inhabitants of the island rejected him—'habitatores hujus insulæ non receperunt ejus doctrinam.' We can scarcely desire a more conclusive proof that the legend originally belonged to Palladius, and was transferred to St. Patrick.

Additional particulars in the later Lives.

That part of this story which describes St. Patrick as having been also rejected by the same people who had rejected Palladius is embellished in the later Lives by additional particulars which are instructive. The third Life (c. 28), followed by Joceline and the Tripartite, tells us, that when Patrick arrived at Inbher Dea, he begged a supply of fish from the inhabitants, but was rudely refused; whereupon he cursed the river, which, although formerly abounding with fish, immediately became barren. He then (c. 29) disembarked at a place which this writer

CHAP. I.] *of Palladius and St. Patrick.* 343

calls *Anat-cailtrin,* and Joceline[1] *Aonach Taillten;* there again the people repulsed him violently, 'cum magna vi repulerunt eum;' immediately the sea covered their land, which became a useless swamp for ever. Thus, according to the authors of these legends, the first visit of this messenger of the Gospel of peace to the future scene of his labours was marked by acts of implacable and permanent vengeance on the rude and ignorant inhabitants.

Probus is the only biographer who has assigned a different reason and a different date to the rejection of St. Patrick by the men of Wicklow. According to this author[2], as we have already seen, Patrick went originally to Ireland as a priest, and commenced his labours there without any commission from Rome. Attributing his want of success to this defect, he resolved to abandon his work, and seek for authority from the Holy See: on his return, after having obtained episcopal consecration, he lands in the region of the Cuolenni[3], in Wicklow, but reflecting that it was his duty to attempt first the conversion of his old master Milchu, with whom he had

A different story told by Probus.

---

[1] *Joceline.* Aonach Taillten, now Telltown, in the county of Meath, is a very long way from the sea, and cannot be the place intended. Ussher thought that some place on the shore near Bray was meant. See Colgan, *Tr. Th.,* p. 31, n. 29. The story of the inundation of Anat-cailtrin is omitted in the Tripartite Life. Anat-cailtrin is not now known under that name.

[2] *Author.* Lib. i. c. 19. See above, p. 325, *sq.*

[3] *Cuolenni.* Not *Evoleni,* as in Probus, which is an error of transcription, although it is followed by Ussher. The territory of Cualann was coextensive with the present barony of Rathdown, in the north of the county of Wicklow. See O'Donovan, *Book of Rights,* p. 13 *n.* The name remains in that of *Glencullen,* a valley near Bray. The old name of the 'Sugar Loaf' Mountain, in the same district, was *Sliabh-Cualann.*

been in servitude in Dal-aradia, he sails to the north. No mention is made of his having received any repulse from the natives of Wicklow; and it is worth noting, that this explanation of his motives for sailing northward is given in the Book of Armagh, whose words Probus has borrowed, and by all those biographers[1] who have suppressed the story of his rejection in Wicklow. These discrepancies are an additional confirmation of the suspicion that all this account of the landing in Wicklow belongs to Palladius, rather than to Patrick.

Sinell and Dichu both said to be the first converts of Patrick in Ireland.

To this we may add another circumstance which gives rise to the same suspicion. The author of the second Life, in that account of St. Patrick's landing at Inbher Dea (cap. 25), which he has not taken from the Book of Armagh, tells us that notwithstanding the resistance of the ungodly Nathi, another chieftain of the same family, Sinell son of Finncadh, believed, and was the first native[2] of Ireland baptised by St. Patrick. The very same author, however, in another passage[3] tells us that Dichu, a chieftain of the Dal-fiatach, dwelling near Sabhall, now Saul, in the county of Down, was the first who believed from St. Patrick's preaching: 'primus Scotorum[4] per Patricium

---

[1] *Biographers.* See *Vita Secunda,* c. 28, (which is, however, the Book of Armagh.) *Vit.* 4*ta.* c. 31.

[2] *First native.* 'Primus ex gente Scotorum baptisatus est.' The same statement is repeated by the *Tripartite Life,* Part i. c. 42.

[3] *Passage.* See *Vit.* 2*da.* cap. 29. The whole passage, with the exception of the statement that Dichu was the first convert, is taken from the Book of Armagh.

[4] *Primus Scotorum.* Probus, (lib.i.c. 28.) makes the same statement. 'Credidit ergo homo ille primus omnium insulanorum, cum omni domo et familiâ suâ.' *Tr.Th.*,p. 53, (wrongly numbered 49.)

confessus est.' These statements are directly contradictory. But we read that notwithstanding the short sojourn made by Palladius in Leinster, some of the natives were baptised by him[1]: possibly, therefore, the foregoing contradiction may be reconciled by supposing Sinell to have been the first fruits of the teaching not of Patrick but of Palladius. Sinell was of the race of the kings of Leinster, of the clan Hy Garrchon: his genealogy is known[2]: he was a cousin of the Nathi Ua Garrchon who resisted Palladius, and there is nothing inconsistent with the Chronology in supposing him to have been converted to Christianity by that bishop.

Sinell perhaps converted by Palladius.

[1] *Baptised by him.* See above p. 294, Document IV.

[2] *Known.* See Geneal. Table V. No. 84, p. 253 supra. Colgan has confounded this chieftain with St. Sinchell of Cill-achaidh-droma-foda (now Killeigh, King's County), who was surnamed *Senex*, or the *elder*, and died A.D. 548. (*Tr.Th.*, p. 18, note 34. *Four Masters*, p. 187). Our author calls Sinell 'son of Findchad,' although he was in reality great grandson of Findchad. This is very common with Irish writers, and is a source of confusion in our history. It means only that he was of the immediate descendants of Findchad in the direct line, and of the family called Mac Findchadha. In the list of St. Patrick's household, (*Four Masters*, A.D. 448) Sinell is said to have been Patrick's *bell-ringer*: and in another authority, quoted by Dr. O'Donovan in his note (*ibid.*) he is called St. Patrick's Ostiarius, or *Doorkeeper*. But this list is not antient, nor of any authority, and the name of Sinell or Sinchell occurs so frequently in Irish history, that no inference can be drawn from the document. The insertion of the name in the list was probably suggested by the very story we are considering. This renders unnecessary the violent explanations of the difficulty suggested by Colgan, that Sinell was Patrick's first convert in Ireland absolutely, and Dichu his first convert in Ulster; or that Dichu was the first who became a monk. 'Quæ sic sunt intelligenda, quod Dichu sit primus in Ultonia, Sinellus vero primus absolute conversus in Hibernia.' *Tr. Th.* p. 18, *n.* 35.

CHAPTER II.

The History and Acts of St. Patrick Apostle of Ireland, and Founder of the see of Armagh. His Writings. His early History as gathered from his Writings. Date of his Mission.

St. Patrick's Confession.

THE Confession[1] of St. Patrick has been already spoken of. It is older than any of the extant biographies of the Saint, for they almost all quote and adopt its words; a copy of it was transcribed at the end of the 8th or very early in the 9th century into the collection called the Book of Armagh. This copy professes to have been taken from the autograph of St. Patrick, for that seems to be the meaning of the colophon, 'Thus

---

[1] *Confession.* This work was first printed by Sir James Ware (*S. Patricio ascripta Opuscula*, Lond. 1656), from four MSS., viz. the Book of Armagh, a MS. in the Cottonian Library, and two in the library of Salisbury Cathedral, which are now in the Bodleian. The Bollandists printed it in 1668, from a MS. of the Abbey of St. Vaast, at Noialle, *Actt. SS.*, Mart. tom. iii. p. 533). Dr. O'Conor reprinted it from the Cotton MS. in 1814, (*Rer. Hibern. Scriptt. tom. i. Proleg. I.* p. cvii.) Sir Wm. Betham gave very inaccurately the text of the Book of Armagh, with a most faulty English version, in his *Irish Antiq. Researches*, part ii. Dubl. 1827. Dr. Villanueva reprinted it from the text of the Bollandists with various readings and notes, *Opusc. S. Patricii*, p. 184, Dublin, 1835: and a new edition of it may soon be expected in the forthcoming publication of the Book of Armagh by Dr. Reeves. A well executed English translation appeared, *Dublin*, 1853, by Rev. Thomas Olden: and an inaccurate one by an excellent Roman Catholic clergyman, *Dublin*, 1859. The confession of St. Patrick was unknown to Colgan, whose *Trias Thaumaturga* was printed in 1647, nine years before the publication of Ware's *Opuscula S. Patricii*; at least he knew it only from Ussher's quotations, which are taken from the Book of Armagh.

far the volume which Patrick wrote with his own hand.'—*Huc usque volumen quod Patricius manu conscripsit sua.* It was certainly transcribed from a MS. which even in the year 800 was beginning to become obscure, and of whose obscurities the transcriber more than once complains. It possesses, therefore, no mean external evidence of authenticity.

Although this Tract is not free from supersti- *Its claim to authen-* tion, it contains none of the ridiculous miracles *ticity.* which the later biographers of St. Patrick delighted to record, and which are to be found in abundance even in the more antient collections preserved in the Book of Armagh. It is altogether such an account of himself as a missionary of that age, circumstanced as St. Patrick was, might be expected to compose. Its Latinity is rude and archaic; it quotes the ante-Hieronymian Vulgate; and contains nothing inconsistent with the century in which it professes to have been written. If it be a forgery it is not easy to imagine with what purpose it could have been forged.[1]

The copy of the Confession in the Book of *The Armagh* Armagh is much shorter than the copies found *copy of the Confession.* in later MSS., and the suspicion arises that the tract may have been interpolated after the date

---

[1] *Forged.* The genuineness of this work and of the Epistola ad Coroticum, is admitted by Ussher, Ware, Cave, Spelman, Tillemont, Mabillon, D'Achery, Martene, Du Cange, Bollandus, Dupin, O'Conor, Lanigan, Villanueva, and others, 'a quorum judicio' to use the words of Dr. O'Conor, 'absque validissimis in contrarium argumentis, temerarii esset, et prorsus insani discedere.' *Rer. Hib. Scriptt.* Vol. i. Proleg. i. p. cv.

of the original or autograph copy from which that in the Book of Armagh was transcribed. This is a circumstance of some importance. If we are to regard the passages not found in the Book of Armagh as interpolations, it is evident that we cannot draw from them the same inferences as if they were the undoubted words of the author. Nevertheless these interpolations, as we may call them for convenience' sake, are of a high antiquity. They are written in the same rude dialect of Latin, and exhibit internal evidence of having proceeded from the same pen as the rest of the work. The difficulty is to explain why they are omitted in the Armagh copy, which professes to have been transcribed from the author's autograph. It is possible that they may have formed the substance of a second part, which copyists took upon themselves to incorporate with the first. If it be maintained that the scribe of the Book of Armagh has designedly abridged[1] his original, he must have done so either because it contained passages which he was unable to read, or because he had other copies of the work in which the omitted paragraphs were to him plain and

---

[1] *Abridged.* Dean Graves is of opinion that the Armagh copy is an abridgment, and avowedly an abridgment, of the original work. There occur in the margin in several places, the letter *z*, (meaning as he thinks, the initial of the Greek word ζητεῖτε,) and in other places the letter *d*, for *deest*. The words *incertus liber*, signifying that the original was difficult or obscure, are also of frequent occurrence in the margin. The Book of Armagh is full of Greek letters; which renders the above explanation of the *z* the more probable. In some places also we find *et cetera*, or *et reliqua*, as if the writer left out portions of the narrative which were well-known, or of which he had other copies.

obvious. The omitted passages, however, are of considerable length, and if put together would probably very nearly equal in bulk the whole text of the Confession as it appears in the Book of Armagh. Until further examination of the extant MSS. has thrown more light on the subject, it would be rash to reject altogether the evidence of these interpolations.

The Epistle to Coroticus does not occur in the Book of Armagh. Perhaps it was not found in the autograph book of St. Patrick from which the Confession was transcribed into that Codex. Its Latinity is apparently of the same age, and from the same pen, as the *Confessio*. It quotes the old Latin version of the Bible, and there seems no internal evidence against the supposition that Patrick may have been its author. The Epistle to Coroticus.

Nevertheless, the learned Casimir Oudin[1] opposes strongly the authenticity of these documents. His main objection is the rude and barbarous Latinity, which in his opinion was affected to impose on uncritical and simple readers. He adds that it is difficult to believe the Roman pontiffs '*so stupid*' as to send forth missionaries to instruct others who were themselves barbarous and incapable of writing pure Oudin's objections.

---

[1] *Oudin.* De Scriptoribus Eccl. tom. i. col. 1167. 'Verum quisquis opuscula ista attente legerit, et ad stylum seculi v. apertum et purum ex plurimis scriptoribus tum Gallis tum Italis, attenta mente respexerit : statim barbariem hanc agnoscet consulto, ab eo qui ista supposuit, excogitatam esse, quo simplicioribus ac minus apertarum narium viris, imponeret. Quis enim credat ita stupidos fuisse Romanos Pontifices, ut ad prædicationem Evangelii promovendam, viros indoctos seculo Ecclesiæ quinto, ac latinitate barbaros mitterent ? Jam si Patricius homo eruditus ac seculo v. clarus, quis credat scripsisse stylo semilatino ac barbaro ?'

Latin. 'Who can believe,' he says, 'if Patrick was a man of learning and celebrity in the fifth century, that he could have written in a half Latin and barbarous style?'

But this is one of the strongest arguments in favour of the authenticity of these writings. The Patrick of the Confessio and of the Epistle about Coroticus does not so much as pretend to any learning, and says not a word of having been commissioned by the Bishop of Rome. He makes no claim to primacy or archiepiscopal jurisdiction in Ireland. He says nothing of Armagh, or any other episcopal see in that country. He calls himself in general terms a bishop in Ireland, deriving his commission directly from God himself;—'Hiberione constitutus episcopus, certissime reor, a Deo accepi quod sum.'[1]

Oudin's argument retorted.

May we not, therefore, retort the argument? It is impossible to conceive with what purpose these Tracts could have been forged or attributed to Patrick, and a barbarous style of language purposely assumed, if that missionary was believed to have been a man of learning and celebrity, sent with a commission from Rome to exercise archiepiscopal jurisdiction in Ireland. It must at least be admitted that if they are forgeries they were forged before these things came to be asserted or popularly believed of the great St. Patrick.

---

[1] *Quod sum.* Or according to another reading, 'Hiberione constitutum episcopum me esse fateor. Certissime reor a Deo accepi quod sum.' *Epist. ad Coroticum.* Opusc. Villanueva, p 240.

These Tracts the Basis of the Lives. 351

Assuming, then, the genuineness of these writings, we shall proceed to gather from them such particulars as they may be found to contain of the life, opinions, and actions of St. Patrick; noticing, whenever it may seem necessary, the additional information supplied by the Lives and other later authorities. This, at least, is certain, that the biographical outline of the acts of St. Patrick, given in these documents, has been made the basis of all the Lives now extant. That outline is as it were the skeleton which the biographers have clothed with miracle and legend.

These Tracts are the basis of all St. Patrick's Lives.

Both these works are written in the style of *Epistles*, and were antiently known by that name. The Confession is frequently cited in the Lives as 'from the Book of Epistles of Patrick.' In some MSS. the Confessio is entitled[1] *Epistolarum Liber* I., and the Letter about Coroticus, or to the subjects of Coroticus, *Epistolarum Liber* II.

The author was advanced in life and had laboured for some years in Ireland when he wrote these Tracts. The Confession is a defence of himself against some undefined and not very clearly stated charges of presumption in under-

Both written when he was advanced in life.

---

[1] *Entitled.* So in the Cotton MS. according to Dr. O'Conor. *Rer. Hib. Scriptt. loc. cit.* p. cxvii. The Confessio, in Colgan's Vita 4ta, cap. 1 and 4, is cited 'ex libris Epistolarum:' cap. 16, 'ex libro quem de vita et conversatione sua ipse composuit.' The second Life, cap. 4, quotes the Confession, 'ex libro episcopi,' and cap. 11, 'ex libris episcopi.' The third Life, cap. 4, 'in libro episcopi,' and cap. 11, 'in libris suarum Epistolarum.' The Tripartite, lib. i. c. 19, 'ex libro Epistolarum ipsius.' The Book of Armagh contains the Confession only, but speaks in the plural, as if the scribe had intended to give more: 'Incipiunt Libri Sancti Patricii Episcopi.'

taking his mission, and of incompetency for the work. In answer, he appeals to his own history, and alludes, with great modesty and humility, to the success of his labours as a proof that his ministry was recognised by God himself. The Epistle is a denunciation of a chieftain Coroticus, who appears from his name to have been a petty sovereign of Cardiganshire. He is supposed [1] to have been the Caredig, or Ceredig, son of Cynedda, who flourished in the fifth century, and who gave his name to the county of Cardigan, called by the Welsh Caredigiawn. Be this, however, as it may, the Caradoc spoken of in the Epistle, although a nominal professor of Christianity, is represented to have landed in Ireland, at the head of his followers, committing every kind of outrage. Amongst other victims he put to death some neophytes on the very day after their baptism, whilst the symbol of their faith was wet upon their foreheads, and they were still clad in their white baptismal vestments.[2] Others he carried off prisoners to sell as slaves; and when Patrick remonstrated by letter, sending a holy presbyter and some clergy, to implore that some of the plunder and the baptised captives might be

---

[1] *Supposed.* See *Welsh Saints*, by Rev. Rice Rees, p. 135. Caredig, son of Cynedda Uledig, is said to have expelled the Gwyddyl or Irish from South Wales, and afterwards to have taken possession of the country. See his genealogy from the Welsh records, *Hist. and Antiq. of the Co. of Cardigan*, by S. R. Meyrick. *Introd.* p. 18. Lond. 4to. 1808.

[2] *Baptismal vestments.* 'Postera die qua chrismati Neophyti in veste candida, dum [fides] flagrabat in fronte ipsorum, crudeliter trucidati atque mactati [sunt] gladio a supradictis. Et misi epistolam, cum sancto Presbytero, quem ego ex infantiâ docui, cum clericis, ut nobis aliquid indulgeretur de præda, vel de captivis baptizatis quos ceperunt. [Sed] cachinos fecerunt de illis.' *Villanueva, Opusc.* p. 241.

CHAP. II.] *His own Account of his Family.* 353

restored, the lawless chieftain dismissed the venerable embassy with scoffs and ridicule.

The author styles himself in both these Tracts *Patricius*, and in both, at the very commencement of the epistolary style which he adopts, acknowledges himself to be unlearned—'indoctus' — and rustic or rude — 'rusticissimus'— in other words, brought up in the country as an uneducated man.

He admits his want of learning.

In the Confession he tells us that he was the son of Calpurnius a deacon, who was the son of Potitus a priest[1], the son of Odissus. Upon this hint the biographers have constructed a genealogy, tracing him up to Britus or Britannus, the ancestor of the Britanni. The names are none of them Celtic, and the genealogy proves only that the antient tradition regarded him as a native of Great Britain. The biographers tell us also, but without any authority from the Confession[2], that his mother's name was Conches, or Conchessa, daughter of Ecba-

His account of his parents and family.

---

[1] *A priest.* 'Patrem habui Calpornium diaconem, filium quondam Potiti presbyteri.' *Ware, Opusc.* p. 1. The Tripartite Life (i. 1.) reverses this, making Calpurnius the priest and Potitus the deacon. The Book of Armagh adds, in the margin, but in the handwriting of the original scribe, 'filii Odissi,' a name which is possibly meant for *Photius.* See Colgan, *Tr. Th. Append. V. ad vit. S. Patricii*, cap. 3, p. 224. The Scholiast on Fiacc gives the genealogy thus: 'Patrick mac Calpuirn, mᶜ Potit, mᶜ Odissi, mᶜ Gorend, mᶜ Mencruid, mᶜ Ota, mᶜ Muric, mᶜ Leo, mᶜ Maximi, mᶜ Hencriti, mᶜ Ferin, mᶜ Bruti, a quo sunt Bretani nominati.' *S. Isidore MS. (Rome).*

This genealogy being evidently too short, several generations have been added by later writers. (See Ussher, *Antiqq.* c. 17, *Works*, vi. p. 378.) In the Hymn of Fiacc three generations are given, and Odissus is said to have been also a deacon, *Mac Calpuirn, mac Otide, ho deochain Odisse.* Tr.Th. p. 1. i.e. 'He was son of Calpuirn, son of Potitus, and grandson of the deacon Odissus.'

[2] *From the Confession.* At least not from our present copies; but the author of Vita Quarta, cap. 1. quotes the Confession for the statement that his mother's name was Conchessa. This is perhaps the Latin *Concessa*, or *Conquesta.*

A A

tius, or, as some authorities call him, Ochmus[1], a Frank. She is said to have been a sister, or a sister's daughter, of St. Martin of Tours; but for this there is no real evidence.[2]

In the Epistle against Coroticus Patrick tells us that he was of a respectable family[3], according to the flesh, his father having been a Decurio, and that he gave up his nobility for the good of others when he devoted himself to the missionary life. There is no inconsistency in this. His father, although in deacon's orders, may also have held the civil office of a decurio, which conferred of itself a certain amount of temporal rank and nobility.[4] And the fact that Calpurnius is said to have held that office may perhaps tend

---

[1] *Ochmus.* Ochmus and Ecbatius, or Ecbasius, are in fact, the same, the *b* being interchanged with *m*. The antient tract 'On the mothers of the saints of Ireland,' attributed to Aengus the Culdee (9th cent.), gives a different name to the mother of Patrick, and makes her a Briton, not a Frank. It begins thus: 'Ondbahum or Gondbaum of the Britons was the mother of Patrick and his five sisters, viz.: Lupait and Tigris, and Darerca and Ricend,' [the fifth is omitted]. 'Others say that Concheass was the name of his mother, and she was the sister of Martin. Or Cochmais daughter of Ochmus was his mother.' *Book of Lecan*, fol. 43, a, a. The name of Ondbahum or Gondbaum is not alluded to by Colgan, or any of the biographers: the Franks were then Pagan and not likely to give the Latin name of *Concessa* to a daughter. Gondbaum seems Frankish, not British, and probably signifies 'Battle-tree.' *Gond* is battle, and *bahum*, or *baum*, is the Teutonic word for a tree, of which our English *beam* and *boom* are descendants. *Gondebaud* occurs in French history as the name of one of the sons of Gondiochus, King of the Burgundians in the fifth century.

[2] *Evidence.* The oldest authority for this seems to be the Scholiast on Fiacc's Hymn, who says, '*ocus ba siur side cobnesta do Martain*;' i. e. 'She was near sister to Martin.' *S. Isidore MS.* (*Rome*). This shews that the Irish word *siur*, sister, often signifies a more distant relative, and hence Jocelin translates it *consanguinea*, and Colgan's version of the Tripartite 'soror seu cognata.' *Sister* in the literal sense was not thought tenable. The other lives say nothing of this supposed relationship.

[3] *Respectable family.* 'Ingenuus sum secundum carnem; nam Decurione patre nascor.' *Villanueva*, p. 243.

[4] *Nobility.* See Dr. Villanueva's note, p. 252. The office of a decurio was that of a magistrate and counsellor in the Roman colonies. In later times the clergy were exempted by law from these offices; but in the times here spoken of, and

to shew that he belonged to one of the Roman provinces of Great Britain rather than to Bretagne Armorique. It is a mistake to suppose that a decurio was necessarily a military officer.

The Confession goes on to say that his father was of the village, or *vicus*, called Bonavem Taberniæ, and had there a farm or small property, from whence he himself (Patrick) was taken captive.[1] It is strange that these words have been so generally understood to signify that he was *born*[2] at Bonavem Taberniæ, wherever that place may have been; whereas it seems very clear that our author says only that it was from thence he was carried away captive: (ubi ego capturam dedi.)

The Hymn of Fiacc tells us expressly that ' Patrick was born at Nemthur ; ' and the question arises, where were these places? At all events, there is no inconsistency between the two statements, even though we suppose Nemthur

Bonavem Taberniæ not said to have been the birth-place of St. Patrick.

in the remote colony to which the father of St. Patrick belonged, there is no difficulty in believing him to have been at the same time a deacon and a decurio, especially as he is represented as having had some landed property in the colony. See Bingham, *Antiq.* book iv. c. 4, sect. 4. In the times of St. Ambrose and St. Augustin, the question of exempting the clergy from such secular services was strenuously mooted; see *Tillemont, Hist. Eccl.* x. p. 206. Dr. Lanigan says, (i. p. 125) ' I believe it would be difficult for the sticklers for St. Patrick's birth in North Britain to find a Curia or Decurions in Kilpatrick, or any place near it, in the fourth century.' But if Kilpatrick was in a Roman colony, there must have been the usual magistrates of a Roman colony in the district.

[1] *Captive.* ' Qui [*sc.* pater ejus] fuit vico Bannavem Taberniæ, villulam enim prope habuit, ubi ego capturam dedi.' *Book of Armagh,* fol. 22, *a a*. The reading ' Villulam Enon,' given by Ware, is not countenanced by the Book of Armagh, or by the MS. of St. Vedast, as published by the Bollandists.

[2] *Born.* This mistake is at the foundation of all that Dr. Lanigan has said in favour of Bologne-sur-mer having been the birth-place of the saint. *Eccl. Hist.* i. p. 92, *sq.* But the same mistake is made by some of the older biographers. See *Vita* 2*da*, c. 1. *Vita* 3*tia*, c. 1. *Probus,* lib. i. c. 1.

and Bonavem Taberniæ to be different and in different countries; for, as we have said, the Confessio does not mention the latter as the place of his birth, but only as the place from which he was carried captive to Ireland.

Nemthur his birthplace.

The question does not seem of sufficient importance to the object of this work to be allowed to occupy much space. The Scholiast[1] on Fiacc's Hymn understood by Nemthur the fort of Alcluaid, now Dumbarton, on the Firth of Clyde. And the Irish tradition undoubtedly favours this opinion. In the Confession St. Patrick speaks of the Britanniæ (in the plural number[2]) as his country, and the country of his parents or relations. For instance, having mentioned his escape from captivity in Ireland, he says, 'Again after a few years I was in the Britanniæ[3] with my parents (cum parentibus meis), who received me as a son, and earnestly (ex fide)

---

[1] *Scholiast.* His words are '*Nemthur*, i.e. it is a city, in North Britain, viz., Alcluada.' Dr. Lanigan's criticism that the *m* in *Nem-thur* ought to be aspirated and pronounced *b*, *v*, or *p*, is untenable, and only proves his ignorance of the Celtic language. *Eccl. Hist.* i. p. 101. This sort of aspiration occurs in the modern Celtic only.

[2] *Plural number.* And therefore denoting the Roman Britanniæ or provinces of Great Britain.

[3] *Britanniæ.* 'In Britanniis,' so Ware, p. 9, and the Book of Armagh: Villanueva reads, 'in Britanniâ,' p. 194, following the text published by the Bollandists, p. 535, (ad 17 Mart.). There is another passage, which, however, does not occur in the Book of Armagh, in which Patrick says, speaking of the virgins who had devoted themselves to Christ, 'Wherefore, however I might have been able and willing to leave them and go into the Britanniæ, as to my country and relatives (parentes), and not only so but also to the Galliæ, to visit my brethren, and to see the face of the saints of my Lord; God knows how greatly I wished it,' etc. *Villanueva*, c. 19, p. 203. *Ware*, p. 17. This seems to imply that he had spiritual brethren in the monasteries of Gaul. But it clearly distinguishes between the Britanniæ, which is spoken of as his country, and the Galliæ; in the former he had his relatives or parents (parentes), in the latter his monastic brethren and the Lord's saints.

besought me, that then at least, after the so great tribulations which I had endured, I should never again leave them.'

The second and third Lives, compiled after the patchwork fashion of which we have already spoken, assign to St. Patrick two birthplaces, evidently copied from two different documents. He was born, they tell us, in Nemthur, and, immediately afterwards[1], he was born 'in Campo Taburne,' or 'in Campo Taburniæ,' as if they meant to translate so the Bonavem Taberniæ of the Confessio. The word *Bonavem*, however, can scarcely be made to signify *Campus*, or a plain. If it be of Celtic origin, as it seems to be, it might possibly be translated *river's mouth*.[2] The only way of reconciling these statements is by supposing that Bonavem Taberniæ and Nemthur were different names for the same place; or that Nemthur was a fort or town, as one of the biographers tells us it was, in *the region* of Bonavem Taberniæ. Of such a *region*, however, we have no information. It is not called a *region* in the Confession, but a town, village, or

---

[1] *Afterwards*. 'Natus est igitur in illo oppido Nemthor nomine . . . Patricius natus est in campo Taburne.' *Vit.* 2*da*, cap. 1. 'Natus est igitur Patricius in illo oppido Nemthor nomine . . . . . Patricius natus est in campo Taburniæ.' *Vit.* 3*tia*, cap. 1. The fourth Life makes Nemthor a town *in* the Campus Taberniæ, c. 1. Probus tells us that Patrick was born 'in Britanniis;' that his father was 'de vico Bannave Tiburniæ regionis, haud procul a mari occidentali:' he adds that having investigated the matter he had ascertained (indubitanter comperimus) the Vicus Bannave to have been in Nentria, or Neutria, 'in quâ olim gigantes habitasse dicuntur.' This Lanigan tells us is Neustria. But Jocelin, and the Tripartite did not understand it so: and it is not easy to see how Neustria could be *in Britanniis*. Jocelin renders the mare occidentale of Probus, by mare Hibernicum.

[2] *River's mouth*. This interpretation has been suggested by Lanigan, vol. i. p. 93.

vicus. Some of the biographers say that the place had its name of *Tabernæ* or *Taberniæ* from the tabernacles or tents of an antient Roman camp¹ which was formerly there. This cannot possibly be so; for Tabernæ signifies booths or shops, not tabernacles or tents. Lanigan's conjecture, that Bononia Tarvannæ, or Tarabannæ, was intended, and that the place so designated is now Boulogne-sur-mer², however ingenious, is contrary to all the antient traditions on the subject.

The Epistle to Coroticus does not say that he was a native of Ireland.

A passage in the Epistle to Coroticus has been understood as if it asserted that St. Patrick was a native of Ireland³, an assertion which would be in contradiction to all other authorities. But the text of this passage is so corrupt that no inference can fairly be drawn from it. The MSS. read *Yberia* and *Hiberia*. 'Hibernia' seems to have been substituted by the editors. In every other place the author of these Tracts gives the name of *Hiberio* to Ireland; and *Hiberia* may be a mistake for *Hiberio*. But even admitting that this is so, and that Ireland is intended, the words from which the inference is drawn appear to have been applied to those of whom he was writing, not to himself.

---

¹ *Roman camp.* See *Vita 2a*, c. 1. *Vita 3a*, c. 1. *Vita 4a*, c. i. *Jocelin*, c. 1.

² *Boulogne-sur-mer.* Lanigan, i. p. 93, *sq.*, supports this theory with very great plausibility and learning.

³ *Ireland.* Ussher has quoted several modern authors, (among the rest Baronius) who supposed Patrick to have been born in Ireland. *Antiqq.* c. 17. (Works, vi. p. 377.) But this mistake arose from a confusion of which it is strange to find Baronius a victim: 'In Scotia natale S. Patricii,' in the antient Calendars, denoted not the day of his birth, but the day and place of his death, as Ussher has shewn.

The Church[1], he says, weeps and wails over her sons, and over her daughters whom the sword has not yet slain but who are exiled and carried away to far off lands, where sin openly prevails and shamelessly abounds. There Christian freemen are reduced to slavery, and that by the most unworthy, most infamous, and apostate Picts. Therefore with sorrow and sadness I will cry out, O most beauteous and well beloved brethren — my sons whom I have begotten in Christ — I cannot tell what to do with you! I am not worthy to give help to God[2] or men. The unrighteousness of the unrighteous hath prevailed over us. We are become[3] as aliens. Perchance they believe not that we have received one baptism, that we have one God our Father. With them it is a crime that we are born in Iberia, but it is said[4], Have ye not one God? Why do ye wrong one to another? Wherefore I grieve for you, I grieve, my well beloved, for myself; but at the same time (*iterum*) I rejoice within myself that I have not laboured in vain, and that my pilgrimage has not been in vain; and yet there hath come to pass this so horrible and unspeakable outrage.

It is clear that in this passage, the author is not speaking of himself, but of those who were sold as slaves to the apostate Picts. He speaks in their name, and in the plural number, making himself as one of them. The general meaning seems to be, that the captives were treated as aliens or strangers; the pirates by whom they were carried

---

[1] *The Church.* Ware, *Opusc.* p. 28, whose text gives the best sense, and is here followed.

[2] *To God.* Meaning perhaps, 'in the sight of God or men.' The MS. followed by the Bollandists, omits *Deo*: 'non sum dignus hominibus subvenire.'

[3] *We are become.* The Bollandists omit the words, ' Quasi extranei facti sumus.' *Villanueva*, c. 9, p. 245.

[4] *It is said.* Actt. vii. 26. Here the two sets of MSS. differ widely. Ware reads, 'Indignum est illis, *Hibernia* nati sumus, sicut ait, Nonne unum Deum habetis, &c.' The Bollandists read, ' Indignum est illis quod de *Hibernia* nati sumus: sic enim aiunt,' omitting the quotation 'nonne unum Deum,' &c. Although they print Hibernia, they tell us that their MS. reads *Yberia*, and that they had omitted the quotation, *Nonne unum Deum*, &c., because they could make no sense of it, and suspected that some words had been lost. They add,'Ex quibus alius conjectando felicior commodum sensum exsculpat; putamus nos verba aliquot excidisse,' p. 540.

off professed indeed Christianity, but they forgot that their captives were also baptised believers in Christ; they made no scruple of imputing to them their Iberian or Irish birth as a crime. If Coroticus had at that time succeeded in banishing the Gwyddil or Irish settlers from South Wales, and in the frenzy of victory had pursued them to Ireland, it is not unnatural that his followers should regard every native of Ireland as an enemy, and treat him as such.

St. Patrick's family connected with Armorica.

It appears, however, from an antient tradition, although it is not distinctly alluded to in the Confession or in the Epistle, that St. Patrick's family had either come originally from Armoric Britanny, or was closely connected with that country. The Scholiast on Fiacc preserves the following legend[1], which is given as a note on the words of Fiacc's Hymn ' He was six years[2] in slavery :'

'This was the cause of the servitude of Patrick ; his father was Calpuirnn ; Conches daughter of Ochmuis was his mother and [the mother] of his five sisters, namely Lupait, and Tigris, and Liamain, and Darerca, and the name of the fifth was Cinnenum. His brother was Sannan. They all went from the Britons of Alcluaid, across the Iccian sea, southwards, on a journey[3] to the Britons who are on the Sea of Icht, namely, the Britons of Letha[4], because they had brethren [i.e.

---

[1] *Legend.* This narrative is translated from the original Irish, preserved in the copy of the Book of Hymns belonging to the College of St. Isidore at Rome, which by the great kindness of the Superior, the author was permitted to transcribe in March 1862. Colgan gives a Latin version of it, *Tr. Th.* p. 4.

[2] *Six years.* The Scholiast explains the six years thus, ' i.e. six years after the similitude of the lesser jubilee of the Jews.'

[3] *On a journey.* In Irish ' for turus.' Colgan understands this to mean a journey for a commercial purpose : ' negotii causa.' *Turus* generally signifies a religious pilgrimage. The *muir nIcht* or Iccian Sea, is the English Channel. Ussher, *Antiquitt.* c. 17, (Works, vi. p. 381).

[4] *Britons of Letha.* ' Co Bretnaib

CHAP. II.]   *Bretagne or Armorica.*   361

relatives] there at that time. Now the mother of these children, namely, Conches, was of the Franks, and she was a near relative [*siur*, sister] to Martin. At that time came seven sons of Sectmaide[1] King of Britain, in ships from the Britons; and they made great plunder on the Britons, viz., the Britons of Armuric Letha, where Patrick with his family was, and they wounded Calpuirnn there, and carried off Patrick and Lupait with them to Ireland. And they sold Lupait in Conaille Muirthemne[2], and Patrick in the north of Dal-araidhe.

If this story[3] be true, Bonavem Taberniæ, where, as St. Patrick himself tells us, he was taken captive, must have been in Armoric Britain; and if Nemthur, the place which Fiacc mentions as his birthplace, was another name for Alcluaid or Dumbarton, the whole is at least consistent.

Leteoc.' *Leteoc* is the adjective formed from *Letha*, or Letavia. *Irish Nennius*, p. 69, and *Add. notes.* No. XI. p. xix.

[1] *Sectmaide.* This word (from *sect* seven,) may be the Latin *Septimius*. The word is written *Factmudius* in Colgan's translation of these Scholia; and we meet with it in the Lives under the transformations of *Rectmitius, Fectmagius, Sectmatius*, &c. There seems no clue to the real name or history of the chieftain who was intended. Keating and other Irish authors suppose the celebrated Niall of the nine hostages to have been the leader of the expedition in which Patrick was captured. See Lanigan, who favours the same opinion, i. p. 137. O'Flaherty, *Ogyg.* p. 393, *sq*. Ussher, *Antiquitt.* c. 15, (Works, vi. p. 115). But Sechtmadius could not have been intended as a name for King Niall.

[2] *Conaille Muirthemne.* These were the tribe or people inhabiting that part of the present Co. of Louth, extending from the Cuailgne, or Cooley, mountains to the Boyne. See Colgan's note, *Tr. Th.*, p. 8, n. 16.

Dal-araidhe is a district in the east of Ulster, which takes its name from Fiacha Araidhe, King of Ulster A.D. 236. It extended from Newry, Co. of Down, to Sliabh Mis, (now Slemish) in the Co. of Antrim. See O'Donovan, *Book of Rights*, p. 21, n. s. and p. 23, *n.* x; also Dr. Reeves's account of Dal-aradia, *Eccl. Hist. of Down and Connor*, p. 334.

[3] *This story.* It is not worth while to examine the alterations made in this story by the biographers. The second, third, and fourth Lives make Patrick to have been captured near Alcluaid, by a fleet of Irish pirates: Probus and the Tripartite, repeat the Armoric story nearly as given in Fiacc's Scholiast, except that they make his mother to have been killed as well as his father. Probus (lib. i. c. 12) mentions a brother of Patrick named *Ructi*, who was carried off with him and a sister. The Tripartite (lib. i. c. 16) makes no mention of his brother, but says that his two sisters *Lupita* and *Tigris* were carried off: and both sold in Louth; Patrick being ignorant of his sisters' captivity, and they of his.

Patrick's own account of his captivity.

His own narrative, as given in the Confessio, is this[1]:—

> I, Patrick, a sinner, the rudest and least of all the faithful, and the most despicable among most men, had for my father Calpornius a deacon, son of the late (*quondam*) Potitus a presbyter, who was of the town (*e vico*) Bonavem Taberniæ; for he had a farm (*villulam*) in the neighbourhood, where I was taken captive. I was then nearly sixteen years old. I knew not the true God, and I was carried in captivity to *Hiberio*, with many thousands of men, according to our deserts, because we had gone back from God, and had not kept His commandments, and were not obedient to our priests, who used to warn us for our salvation (*nostram salutem admonebant*). And the Lord brought upon us the wrath of His displeasure, and scattered us among many nations, even unto the ends of the earth[2], where now my littleness is seen amongst aliens. And there the Lord opened the sense of my unbelief, that even, though late, I should remember my sins, and be converted with my whole heart unto the Lord my God, who had regard unto my lowliness, and had compassion on my youth and on my ignorance, and preserved me, before I knew him, and before I could understand or distinguish between good and evil, and protected me, and comforted me, as a Father would a son.

There is here no historical fact except that he was taken captive at *Bonavem Taberniæ*, when he was sixteen years of age. He says nothing of his birthplace, he says nothing of the murder of his father and mother, nor of the country from whence the pirates by whom he was captured came. He asserts only in general terms that he was carried to *Hiberio*[3], the name he always gives to Ireland, with 'many thousands of men.'[4]

---

[1] *Is this.* Sir James Ware's text is followed collated with the Book of Armagh.

[2] *Ends of the earth.* This passage of the Confession is evidently the origin of the absurd story that Patrick was of Jewish descent. See *Vita 4ta,* c. 1.

[3] *Hiberio.* See O'Flaherty, *Ogyg.* p. 22.

[4] *Thousands of men.* The Book of Armagh reads, 'cum tt milia

His various Names.

The Hymn of Fiacc tells us that the baptismal name of St. Patrick given him by his parents was *Succat*: and the Scholiast adds that the word is British[1], signifying 'god of war,' or 'strong in war.' We are told also that his masters during his servitude in Ireland gave him the name of *Codraige*[2], or as some of the Lives have it *Quadriga*; and that St. Germain gave him the name of *Magonius*, written *Maun* by some transcribers of Nennius. But these childish stories, and the still more childish etymologies[3] proposed in explanation of these names, are unworthy of notice.

His original name Succat.

Why he took the name of Patrick does not appear. We read indeed that he received this name from Pope Celestine, at his consecration.

Why called Patrick.

hominum.' Ware makes the contraction tt, signify *tot*, and corrects *milia* to *millibus*: the ungrammatical reading *milia* is probably a confusion of some numeral letters, which the scribe was unable to read: perhaps the original was 'cum turba vili hominum.'

[1] *British.* The words of the Scholiast are ' *Succat*, i.e. in old British; *Deus belli, vel fortis belli* in Latin; for *Su* in British is *fortis* or *Deus*; *Cat* is *bellum*.' *St. Isidore MS. (Rome).* Perhaps the word *Su* is a dialectic form of *du*, now in Welsh *Duw*, the *d* made *s*. Lanigan says ' This was an odd name for the son of a Calphurnius and the grandson of a Potitus,' i. p. 140, meaning perhaps that it was odd for a Christian deacon to call his son God of war, or Strong in war—but many things of this kind survived from Pagan customs without being much noticed. Was it not just as odd that Palladius should bear a name derived from a pagan goddess ?

[2] *Codraige.* I was once of opinion that this word was only a Celtic pronunciation of the word Patrick, or Padruic, the *c* being substituted for *p* according to a well known law of the language. *Proceedings Royal Irish Acad.* vol. vi. p. 292. My opinion has been shaken by finding that such eminent philologists as Mr. W. Stokes and Dr. Siegfried do not agree with me.

[3] *Etymologies.* The Scholiast on Fiacc, in a mixture of Irish and Latin, gives the story thus: ' Multa Patricius habuit nomina ad similitudinem Romanorum nobilium; i.e. *Succat* was his original name given him in baptism by his parents. *Codriga* was his name when in slavery in Erinn. *Mogonius*, i. e *magis agens quam ceteri monachi*, was his name when he was learning under Germain: *Patricius* was his name at his degrees [holy orders] and it was Celestine the Comarb of Peter who gave it to him.' *S. Isidore MS.* Comp. *Nennius*, c. 54, 55.

But the story of his mission from Pope Celestine is, as we have seen, open to much question. All that is now certain is that he bore the name of Patrick at the advanced period of his Life when the Confessio and the Epistle to Coroticus were written, and that by this name he is known as the 'Apostle of Ireland.' He may have had originally a British name *Succat*, and also a Roman name *Patricius*.[1] This, perhaps, was not uncommon among the colonists who lived in contact with the barbarous tribes at the extremities of the Roman empire,

His brothers and sisters.

Nothing is said in the Confession about his brothers and sisters. But Irish tradition has preserved the names of several of his sisters as well as of his sisters' sons. His sister Liamain, or Limania, is said to have married one Restitutus, or Rechtitutus, a Longobard, or as others call him Mac Ua Baird, ' son of O'Baird,' or ' of the Bard's descendant.' By him, we are told, she had seven sons[2]: the eldest of whom, Sechnall or Secundinus, was Bishop of Armagh, and author of a Hymn in praise of St. Patrick, of which we have already spoken. There must

---

[1] *Patricius.* Tirechan seems to have taken Patricius as a translation of *Succat.* But perhaps a line has been omitted in the MS. 'Inveni quatuor nomina in libro scripta Patricio apud Ultanum ... *Magonus* qui est clarus ; *Succetus* qui est Patricius : *Cothirthiac* quia servivit .iiii. domibus magorum.' Book of Armagh, *fol.* 9. *a. b.* This supposes the last name to be compounded of *Cathair* four, and *tech* a house.

[2] *Seven sons.* Their names were Sechnall, bishop ; Nechtan, bishop ; Dabonna, priest ; Mogornan, priest; Darigoc, or Rioc, bishop ; Ausille, [Auxilius] bishop ; and Lugna, priest. *Sanctil. Geneal.* (Book of Lecan, fol. 49, *a b*). Colgan has collected almost all that can be said of the brethren and sisters of St. Patrick ; *Append.* V. c. 4. *Tr. Th.*, p. 224. See also Ussher, *Antiquitt.* c. 17. (*Works*, vi. p. 381.)

have been some foundation in truth for these traditions, although treated with contempt by many writers. This has been curiously confirmed by Dr. Petrie's discovery of a tombstone of unquestionable antiquity, on the island called *Inis an ghoill craibhtigh*, 'the Island of the Religious or Devout Foreigner,' now Inchaguile, in Loch Corrib, county of Galway. This tombstone[1], in characters which may with almost certainty be regarded as not later than the beginning of the sixth century, bears the following inscription :

| LIE LUGNAEDON MACCLMENUE | *The stone of Lugnaed Son of Limania.* |

where it will be observed that LUGNAEDON is the Celtic genitive of *Lugnad* or *Lugna*, the name given to the youngest of the seven sons of Liamain or Limania.[2]

It is quite true, as Tillemont has remarked, that all we know concerning the sisters of St. Patrick is derived from the fabulous lives[3], and

Credibility of their history.

---

[1] *Tombstone.* See Petrie, *Eccl. Architect. of Ireland*, p. 162, *sq.* (*Trans. R. I. Acad.* vol. xx.) The author has given an accurate fac-simile of the inscription, p. 164, where see his very valuable remarks upon this discovery, and upon the character of the ruined church near which the stone lies.

[2] *Limania.* The name on the stone is *Lmenue* (genitive of Liamain), for *Limenue*; perhaps there was originally attached to the foot of the L, a small *i*, which is now obliterated. Lugnad was probably born on the continent, and the island in which he resided, and died, was therefore called the Island of the religious *foreigner*. For the history of his father, see *Irish Book of Hymns*, p. 34, *sq.*

[3] *Fabulous lives.* Tillemont, *Hist. Eccl.* tom. xvi. p. 470, and see also Lanigan, i. c. 3, sect. 18, p. 125. Both these writers refer to a passage in the Epist. to Coroticus, where St. Patrick, as they say 'has plainly told us,'—nous assure lui-même— that none of his relations were with him in Ireland.—But the words do not necessarily mean more than that, when he devoted himself to the conversion of the Irish, he separated himself from his own family: and he

is therefore suspicious. It is also quite true that there is great confusion as to the names of these sisters[1] and of their sons. No doubt their history is full of fable and all sorts of blunders. But Dr. Petrie's discovery shews that we ought to use great caution in dogmatically rejecting as fable all that we find even in the midst of the most silly legend. The facts are doubtless overlaid with childish stories: but let us beware lest, if we cast out the rubbish without sifting, we should cast out also precious stones which have long lain concealed in the mass.

His condition in his captivity. Of his condition and adventures during his captivity in Ireland St. Patrick gives us an interesting account in the Confessio: premising that he did so for the sake of making known God's grace and everlasting consolation[2], to spread the knowledge of God's Name; as well as to leave it on record after his death to his

---

might have said this even though his sisters had afterwards followed him to Ireland. 'Numquid sine Deo, vel secundum carnem Hiberionem veni? Quis me compulit? Alligatus sum spiritu ut non videam aliquem de cognatione meâ.' *Villanueva*, p. 243. The allusion is evidently to Gen. xii. 1.

[1] *Sisters.* The confusion is probably greatly increased by the loose use of the word *Siur*, or sister, by Irish writers. It is applied to nieces, cousins, and often to sisters in religion. Errors of transcription of proper names abound in all Irish MSS., and add to the confusion. But it is clear from the dates assigned to their deaths, that some of those who are said to have been sisters of St. Patrick belonged to the sixth or following century. *Lanigan,* i. 127.

[2] *Consolation.* This is one of those passages which the scribe of the B. of Armagh has marked as obscure in the original MS., writing in the margin the words 'Incertus liber.' The text is ' In mensura itaque fidei Trinitatis oportet distinguere sine reprehensione periculi notum facere donum Dei et consolationem æternam sine timore fiducialiter Dei nomen ubique expandere, ut etiam post obitum meum ex a Gallias [*read* extra Gallias] relinquere fratribus, et filiis meis quos in Domino baptizavi.' Fol. 23, *a a.* Ware reads, 'post obitum meum Gallicis relinquere fratribus;' the Bollandists omit the word *Gallicis*, but otherwise follow Ware.

brethren out of Gaul, and to his sons whom he had baptised in the Lord. He was employed when he came to *Hiberio*, as he always calls Ireland, in tending cattle daily; but was every day frequent in prayer[1]: thus, he says, the love and fear of God and faith increased so much, and the spirit of prayer so grew upon him, that often in a single day he would say an hundred prayers[2], and in the night almost as many, so that he frequently arose to prayer in the woods and mountains before daylight, in snow and frost and rain : 'and I felt no evil,' he adds, 'nor was there any laziness (*pigritia*) in me, because, as I now see, the Spirit was burning within me.'

One night, as he tells us, he heard in a dream a voice saying to him, 'Thy fasting is well: thou shalt soon return to thy country.' He waited some time, and again had a dream, in which the same voice told him that the ship was ready, but was distant two hundred miles.[3] Although he had never been to the place, and knew nothing of the inhabitants, he fled from his master, with whom he had been in slavery for six years[4]; 'and

His escape from captivity, and return to his native country.

---

[1] *Prayer.* This is a clear proof that when he said, 'Deum verum ignorabam,' he is not to be understood too literally. Tillemont's remark is just: 'non qu'il ne fust Chrétien, comme cela paroist assez par la suite, mais parcequ'il n'avoit pas encore cette foi animée de la charité qu'il l'eust dû avoir, &c.' *Mem. Eccl.* xvi. p. 456.

[2] *Prayers.* Or collects; *orationes.*

[3] *Two hundred miles.* In the B. of Armagh 'cc. milia passus.' If the ordinary miles of five to a league be meant, he must have travelled from Dal-aradia to the S.W. coast of Ireland. But the number is probably exaggerated by errors of transcription. Lanigan, on the strength of this passage, makes our saint travel from Dal-aradia to Bantry bay. *Eccl. Hist.* i. p. 146, note (42). The Scholiast on Fiacc (n. 9) makes the distance ' 60 miles, or as others say, a hundred,' shewing that the MSS. even then had various readings.

[4] *Six years.* There is nothing here of the nonsense that it was the

I went,' he adds, 'in the power of the Lord, who directed my way for good[1], and I feared nothing until I arrived at that ship.' The captain of the ship, however, roughly refused him a passage, and Patrick was about to return to the hut[2] where he dwelt, first offering up a prayer, as was his wont. His prayer was not finished, when one of the sailors called to him, saying, 'Come back quickly, for these men call thee.' He returned, and they said to him, 'Come, for we receive thee in faith, make friends with us how thou wilt:' meaning, perhaps, that they were willing to receive him without passage money, in the faith that in some other way he might find the means of remunerating them. What follows is very obscure[3], but seems to signify that he was surprised to hear them speak of faith, seeing they

---

custom of the pagan natives of the country to manumit their slaves, at the end of six years, after the manner of the Jubilee of the Jews. See above, p. 360. *n.* 2.

[1] *For good.* ' Dirigebat ad bonum.' *Ware* and *B. of Armagh*. The Bollandists read, 'Veni ad *Benum*,' which they suppose to mean the Boyne. But the other reading is preferable. The Boyne is always *Boindus*. The Scholiast on Fiacc makes the mouth of the Boyne the place where Patrick embarked, *Tr. Th.*, p. 4. n. 9.

[2] *Hut.* ' Ad tuguriolum ubi hospitabam :' ' to the hut where I used to dwell '—in other words, he was about to return to his master; so Tillemont understands it, perhaps rightly, 'ainsi il retourna en priant à sa cabane, au hazard d'estre maltraité de son maistre,' *ubi supra*, p. 457. Or it might mean that he returned to the cabin where he had been received as a guest by some peasant in the neighbourhood of the port.

[3] *Obscure.* The *Book of Armagh* reads, ' Et in illa die itaque reppuli sugere mammellas eorum propter timorem Dei. Sed verumtamen ab illis speravi venire in fidem Jesu Christi quia Gentes erant, et ob hoc obtinui cum illis.' Fol. 23, *a. b.* Ware reads, ' Et in illa die repuli fugere, propter timorem Dei. Veruntamen speravi ab illis, ut mihi dicerent, Veni in fide Jesu Christi, quia gentes erant,' p. 7. The Bollandists have ' Et in illa die debui surgere in navem eorum propter Deum. Veruntamen [*the editor adds* non] speravi ab illis ut mihi dicerent, Veni in fide Christi, quia Gentiles erant. Et hoc obtinui cum illis, et protinus navigavimus.' *Villan.* p. 191.

were Pagans, but went with them the more readily in consequence of their having used that word, hoping that they might come over to the faith of Jesus Christ.

They were three days at sea, and afterwards twenty-eight days wandering in a desert[1], until their provisions ran short. No doubt, Patrick had been speaking to them of the power of God, of the efficacy of prayer, and of trust in God's Providence. The leader of the party therefore said to him, 'What sayest thou, Christian? Thy God is great and all powerful. Why then canst thou not pray to Him for us? for we perish with hunger, and we can find here no inhabitants.' Patrick answered, 'Turn ye in faith to my Lord God, to whom nothing is impossible, and He will send you food, and ye shall be satisfied, for He has abundance everywhere.' And so it was, for a herd of swine soon after appeared, many of which they killed. Patrick and his

[1] *Desert.* Lanigan argues that three days would be about the time usually taken for sailing from Bantry Bay to some port on the coast of Armoric Britain : and appeals to the lessons of a Breviary printed at Rheims in 1612 (reprinted by Colgan, *Tr. Th.*, p. 194), where it is said that Patrick was sold by a certain Irishman, to merchants of Gaul, who carried him to Treguier ; 'ad Trecorensem minoris Britanniæ civitatem.' But such an authority is too modern to be of any value. The existence in Britanny of a waste which took twenty-seven days to cross, is accounted for by the ravages of the Franks and Saxons on the coasts of Armorica. *Eccl. Hist.* i. 150, 152. Tillemont, who thinks that the three days' voyage carried our saint to the north of Scotland, accounts for the existence of a waste there by the ravages of the Picts and Scots. *Mem. Eccles.* xvi. p. 457. The lesson in the Rheims Breviary alludes to the story of St. Kienan told by the Scholiast on Fiacc, *Tr. Th.*, p. 4, n. 9. When Patrick had fled from his master he came to the south bank of the Boyne; there a man named Kienan seized him and sold him to some sailors ; but repenting of this deed, he soon after procured his liberation. At a subsequent period Kienan was baptized by Patrick, and founded the church or monastery of Daimhliac-Kienain, now Duleek, in the county of Meath. See *Mart. of Donegal,* at 24 Nov.

companions were relieved from their hunger, and remained in that place for two nights. 'After this,' he says, 'they gave great thanks to God, and I was honoured in their eyes.'

They found also some wild honey, and gave Patrick a portion of it, but because one of them had said, 'This is an offering; thank God,'[1] Patrick would not taste of it, fearing lest it had been offered to an idol.

<small>His night-mare and the invocation of Elias.</small>
The same night an event occurred which, he says, he could never forget, 'cujus memor ero quamdiu fuero in hoc corpore.' He had a night-mare, which he believed to be a temptation of Satan. He felt as if a great stone had fallen upon him; he was unable to move a limb: and he says, 'how it came into my mind to call out *Helias* I know not, but at that moment I saw the sun rising in the heavens, and whilst I cried out *Helias! Helias!* with all my might, lo, the brightness of the sun fell upon me and straightway removed all the weight. And I am persuaded that I was relieved by Christ my Lord, and that His Spirit then cried out for me. And I trust it may be so in the day of my trouble, for the Lord saith in the Gospel[2], "It is not ye that speak, but the Spirit of your Father which speaketh in you."'

It is strange that this curious anecdote should

---

[1] *Thank God.* 'Et unus ex illis dixit, Immolatitium est, Deo gratias.' *B. of Armagh*, fol. 23, *b. a.* Patrick probably thought that this Gentile must have meant one of his own gods, and therefore would not eat of the honey. 1 Cor. viii. 10 — 28, and cf. 1 Sam. xiv. 26.

[2] *Gospel.* St. Matt. x. 20.

have been taken as a proof that St. Patrick prac- *Not an invocation of saints.* tised the invocation of saints.[1] If this was an invocation of a saint, and if it was the custom of the time to invoke saints, and more particularly to invoke Helias as a saint, why did St. Patrick say, 'I know not how it came into my mind to call upon Helias?' Do not these words very clearly prove that to invoke saints, or at least to invoke Helias, was a somewhat unusual thing in St. Patrick's time?

It has been suggested, from the allusion to the sun, which immediately follows the mention of Helias, that it was not Helias the prophet, whom Patrick invoked, but *Helios*, the Sun[2]; and this would certainly account for his saying, 'I know not how it came into my mind to do so;' but the still greater difficulty will remain, how a Christian could have invoked the Sun.

The true reading of this passage is probably *Eli, not Elias, the true reading.* not Elias, or Helias, or the Sun, but *Eli*, 'my God;' which the copyists, not being able to understand, made *Helias*. We have an instance of the use of this Hebrew Name of God, shewing that it was not unknown to the Irish, in the Hymn

---

[1] *Invocation of saints.* Dr. Lanigan was weak enough to say, 'This will, I believe, be admitted to be a sufficient proof, that St. Patrick considered the invocation of saints as commendable and salutary,' i. p. 155. So far from being a sufficient proof, this is no proof at all; if Patrick called upon Elias, he speaks of it as an unusual thing. Elias is regarded by the Church as still living, and was never invoked as a saint. The festival of Elias on Mount Carmel, which occurs in the present Roman Breviary (July 20), cannot be older than the 14th or 15th century: although in the Greek church it probably dates from the 10th century. See Baillet, *Vies des Saints*, tom. i. p. 179, *sq. Paris*, 1739.

[2] *The Sun.* King's *Church History of Ireland*, vol. i. p. 48.

of St. Hilary in praise of Christ, which has been published by Muratori from the Irish Antiphonary of Bangor, and which occurs also in the Irish Book of Hymns.[1] The lines are these:—

'Tu Dei de corde Verbum, Tu Via, Tu Veritas,
Jesse Virga Tu vocaris, Te Leonem legimus,
Dextra Patris, Mons, et Agnus, Angularis Tu lapis,
Sponsus idem, EL, Columba, Flamma, Pastor, Janua.'

These verses contain an enumeration of the Titles of Christ: the Word in the Bosom of the Father, the Way, the Truth, the Rod of Jesse, the Lion of Judah, the Right Hand of the Father, the Mount, the Lamb, the Corner Stone, the Bridegroom, EL, the Dove, the Flame, the Pastor, the Door.

It is therefore not improbable that Patrick may have known the word EL as a name of God[2] or of Christ, and in his distress may have cried out ELI, ELI. His knowledge of the Gospels[3] would of itself have made him acquainted with the exclamation 'Eli, Eli,' without supposing him to have had any oriental learning; especially as we find that the name was applied to Christ, in the antient Hymn just quoted.[4]

---

[1] *Book of Hymns.* See 'Hymnus S. Hilarii in Laudem Christi,' *Book of Hymns*, p. 152, and note; where *El* is shown to be the true reading. Muratori reads *vel*. This hymn is attributed to St. Hilary of Poictiers, and therefore probably came from the Gallican church. But it is not published in the Benedictine Ed. of St. Hilary's works.

[2] *Name of God.* Comp. the Hymn of Hildebert, Bishop of Le Mans, (12th century), published by Ussher, *De Symbolis*, (Works, vii. p. 339) It begins

Alpha et Ω, magne Deus,
Eli, Eli, Deus meus, &c.

[3] *Gospels.* St. Matt. xxvii. 46. St. Mark xv. 34.

[4] *Quoted.* If we reject this expla-

CHAP. II.] *St. Patrick's Master in Dalaradia.* 373

In confirmation of this conjecture it is remarkable that both in the second and third Lives[1] Patrick is represented as having cried out *Eli,* not Elias. It is true the biographers, and even Colgan, evidently understood the word to signify Elias, overlooking its real meaning as an invocation of God, sanctioned by our Lord Himself in the Gospel. But the text of the Confessio from which they copied must have had *Eli,* not Elias.

Patrick in the Confessio speaks but once of the master whom he served in his captivity. 'I took to flight,' he says, ' and left the man with whom I had been for six years.'[2] He does not name ' the man,' nor mention his rank or situation in life. But these omissions are amply supplied by later writers. His name, we are told,

St. Patrick's master in Ireland.

---

nation, and adhere to the reading which makes Patrick call upon the prophet Elias, we may suppose him to have done so influenced by the antient belief of the Church, that Elias was to come literally, in person, according to the prophecy of Malachi, and restore all things, before the great and terrible Day of the second coming of the Lord. He may therefore, with this prophecy in mind, have called out, as he says, without knowing why, Helias, Helias. And his mention of the sun immediately afterwards may have had reference to the prophecy of the Sun of Righteousness, which occurs in the same chapter of Malachi, just before the prediction of the coming of Elias. (Mal. iv. 5, 6, and ver. 2.)

[1] *Lives.* In the second Life the words are retained in the Irish language, c. 20, ' ro guidh Eli dia indarput uadh.' ' He prayed Eli to expel it [i.e. the stone] from him.'

The Irish writer apparently understood Eli to mean Elias, and so Colgan translates it. *Tr. Th.,* p. 17, n. 22. The third Life (c. 17), says ' Tum Patricius vocavit Eli, in adjutorium suum trinâ voce ; venitque Eli et eliberavit eum.' It is probable, therefore, that the MSS. of the Confession, which these writers had before them, read *Eli,* and they interpreted it *Helias,* falling into a very natural mistake. Probus says nothing of the invocation of Helias, but tells us that Patrick when he awoke signed himself with the sign of the cross, and then called three times upon Christ the true Sun.—' Et cum trinâ voce Christum Solem verum invocasset, statim ortus est ei Sol, &c.' Lib. i. c. 8. (*Tr. Th.,* p. 51.)

[2] *Six years.* ' Conversus sum in fugam, et intermissi hominem cum [quo] fueram vi. annis.' *Ware, Opusc. S. Patricii.* p. 6.

was Miliuc, Michul or Milchu[1]: his tribe or family[2] was the Dal-Buain, clan or descendants of Buan of Dalaradia; the Scholiast on Fiacc tells us that he was '*King* of North Dalaradia and that he dwelt in Arcuil,' a valley in the north of Dalaradia near Mount Mis, now Slemish. This is now called the valley of the Braid, from the river Braighde or Braid[3] which flows through it, and the spot where St. Patrick had the dream or vision, which induced him to fly from his master, is marked by the ruins of an antient church called Sciric or Skiric Arcaile, now Skerry[4], on a basaltic hill, where, according to the tradition mentioned by Fiacc, the angel Victor appeared to St. Patrick and left the impression of his feet. The later biographers represent Milchu as a savage tyrant, deeply rooted in Paganism, and Tirechan calls him a *magus*[5], or Druid. But there is nothing of all this in the Confessio.

His second captivity apocryphal.

Patrick at the time when he escaped from Milchu was twenty-two years of age; for he

---

[1] *Milchu.* The Hymn of Fiacc, (st. 4) calls Patrick ' gniad Milchon,' *slave of Milchu.* The Scholiast, on the word Milchon, says ' Genitivum est hic. Michul m^c hui Buain ri tuaiscirt Dalaraide.' The translation of this is:—' Milchon is here the genitive. Michul MacHyBuain, was king of North Dalaradia.' *S. Isidore MS. (Rome).*

[2] *Family.* ' Dal-Buanica familia,' says Colgan, 'olim in Ultonia celebris, licet hodie ignota et extincta.' From this tribe descended the celebrated St. Maccarthen of Clogher, and many other saints. *Actt. SS.* p. 740, *sq.*

[3] *Braid.* See Reeves, *Eccl. Ant. of Down and Connor*, p. 83, 345.

[4] *Skerry.* Schol. on Fiacc, quoted by Reeves, *ib.* Vit. Trip. i. 22. The word *Sciric* signifies rocky. It is worthy of note, that St. Patrick, in the Confession, speaks only of a dream. The apparition of an angel is the embellishment of later writers. The allusion to this tradition seems fatal to the claim of Fiacc's poem to antiquity.

[5] *Magus.* Ussher, *Primord.* p. 829. (Works, vi. p. 387.) Probus, (i. 22) calls him ' quendam gentilem immitem regem.' Jocelin, ' regulus paganissimus,' c. 13.

tells us that he was sixteen when he was taken captive, and spent six years in slavery. He remained with the sailors, who had given him a passage after his escape from Milchu, sixty days or two months. Probus and others have understood this of a second captivity: and there is certainly some obscurity[1] in the MSS. Patrick very probably regarded his sojourn with the sailors as a second captivity—that in Ireland with Milchu being the first. The Book of Armagh seems to say that of the sixty days twenty-eight were passed in the desert, and ten after the drove of swine had supplied them with food. Perhaps the remainder of his time with them was spent under compulsion, and so was a real captivity:

'On that sixtieth night' (he says) 'the Lord delivered me from their hands. And even on our road He provided us with food and fire, and dry weather (*siccitatem*), until on the tenth[2] day we arrived at men' [i.e. at human habitations]: ' having travelled, as I have said, above eight and twenty days through a desert; and the very night when we arrived at men, we had no more food.'

---

[1] *Obscurity*. The Book of Armagh, as its text stands, is here corrupt and unintelligible. 'Multos adhuc capturam dedi ea nocte prima itaque mansi cum illis: responsum autem divinum audivi duobus autem mensibus eris cum illis, quod ita factum est.' But the text printed by the Bollandists has evidently introduced violent alterations to mend this confusion, first by transposing the passage mentioned above; and then by reading ' Et iterum post annos [non] multos adhuc in capturam decidi : nocte vero prima mansi cum illis. Responsum autem, &c.' This is one of the passages marked by ≈ in the margin of the Book of Armagh. See above p.

348, note 1. The summary of St. Patrick's acts, by Muirchu Maccumachtheni, evidently took for granted that the captivity of sixty days was a *second* captivity : and so it was if the captivity under Miliuc in Ireland was the first. Two of the headings of chapters in the summary of Maccumachtheni, (Book of Armagh, fol. 20, b.) are as follows : ' De navigio ejus cum gentibus, et vexatione diserti, cibo sibi gentilibus divinitus delato ;' and ' De secunda captura quam senis decies diebus ab inimicis pertulerat.'

[2] *Tenth*. Ware, (p. 9,) and the Bollandists read *fourteenth*. (Villanueva, p. 193.)

This passage has been transposed and placed *before* the mention of the sixty days in the copy of the Confessio printed by the Bollandists. But if we adhere to the text of the Book of Armagh, as we now have it, there is no mention of a second captivity[1] except in the sense that has been explained: the meaning seems to be that he was sixty days altogether in the hands of the mariners with whom he had sailed from Ireland.

His return to his family. He proceeds to tell us that 'after a few years' he was with his parents in the Britanniæ; 'post paucos annos in Britanniis eram cum parentibus meis.' But we are not obliged to understand the word *parents* of his father and mother; there is therefore no necessary contradiction between this passage and the legend that his father and mother had been killed long before. Still we must remember that the murder of his father and mother is not recorded in the Confession, and that the Scholiast[2] on Fiacc mentions his father as having been wounded only, not killed, and says nothing of his mother.

---

[1] *Second captivity.* Still less of a third, which rests altogether on the authority of Probus, and of which Ussher says, 'non parum mihi suspecta est.' *Works,* vi. p. 390. Of the other stories here interpolated by Probus, of Patrick having converted the mariners and their countrymen, and of his travels on the continent of Europe, there is not a word in the Confession. It is evident that the chronology of the Confession leaves no time for his four years with St. Martin, forty with St. Germain, and sojourn in the islands of the Tyrrhene sea. Even Lanigan admits 'it is exceedingly difficult, and I believe impossible, to arrange correctly either as to chronological order or topographical accuracy, the succeeding transactions of his life, until near the time of his mission,' i. p. 161. The reason of the difficulty is obvious. Almost all those transactions are groundless fictions, or facts transferred from the acts of Palladius to Patrick.

[2] *Scholiast.* The passage is quoted above p. 361.

His parents, he tells us, received him as a son, and earnestly besought[1] him not to expose himself to fresh dangers, but to remain with them for the rest of his life.

Patrick, however, felt constrained to devote himself to the conversion of the Irish, amongst whom he had spent so many years of his youth, and whose language he had doubtless acquired. He says nothing of Palladius. He says nothing of Rome, or of having been commissioned by Pope Celestine. He attributes his Irish apostleship altogether to an inward call, which he regarded as a Divine command. He tells us that he had a dream, which he thus describes :—

His call to convert the Irish.

'And there,' he says [namely in the Britanniæ, with his parents] 'in the dead of night[2], I saw a man[3] coming to me as if from *Hiberio*, whose name was *Victoricus*, bearing innumerable epistles. And he gave me one of them, and I read the beginning of it, which contained *the words*, 'The voice of the Irish,' *Vox Hiberionacum*. And whilst I was repeating the beginning of the epistle, I imagined that I heard in my mind (in mente), the voice of those who were near the wood of *Foclut*, which is near the Western Sea. And thus they cried : 'We pray thee, holy youth, to come, and henceforth walk amongst us.' And I was greatly pricked in heart, and could read no more; and so I awoke. Thanks be to God, that after very many years the Lord granted unto them the blessing for which they cried : (præstitit illis Dominus secundum clamorem illorum).'

---

[1] *Besought.* 'Qui me ut filium susciperunt(*sic*) et ex fide rogaverunt me, ut vel modo ego, post tantas tribulationes quas ego pertuli, nusquam ab illis discederem.' *Book of Armagh,* fol. 23, b. b.

[2] *Dead of night.* 'In sinu noctis,' *Book of Armagh.* 'In visu nocte,'

Ware, p. 9. 'In visu de nocte,' *Villanueva,* p. 194.

[3] *A man.* Not an angel, as the Lives all have it. The name of *Victor,* given by the legend writers to St. Patrick's guardian angel, has evidently been derived from this passage.

> 'Again on another night, I know not, God knoweth, whether it was within me or near me, I heard distinctly words which I could not understand, except that at the end of what was said, there was uttered, 'He who gave His Life for thee, is He who speaketh in thee.' And so I awoke rejoicing. And again I saw in myself one praying, and I was as it were within my body, and I heard him, that is to say, upon my inner man, and he prayed there mightily with groanings. And meanwhile I was in a trance (*stupebam*), and marvelled, and thought who it could be who thus prayed within me. But at the end of the prayer, he became so changed (*efficiatus est*) that he seemed to be a bishop.[1] And so I awoke, and recollected the apostle's words, The Spirit helpeth the infirmity of our prayer. For we know not what to pray for as we ought, but the Spirit Himself maketh intercession for us, with groanings that cannot be uttered, which cannot be expressed in words. And again[2], The Lord our advocate intercedeth for us.'

There is nothing in all this which is not quite consistent with the feelings of an enthusiastic mind, filled with the holy ambition of converting to Christ the barbarous nation amongst whom he had been in captivity. There is no incredible or absurd miracle. He believed, no doubt, that his call was supernatural, and that he had seen visions and dreamt dreams. But other well-meaning and excellent men, in all ages of the Church, have in like manner imagined themselves to have had visions of this kind, and to have been the recipients of immediate revelations.

Another Vision.

He then goes on to describe another vision,

---

[1] *A bishop.* 'Sed ad postremum orationis, sic efficiatus est ut sit episcopus.' *Book of Armagh.* Ware and the Bollandists read, perhaps rightly, 'Sic effatus est ut sit Spiritus,' that He was the Holy Ghost. The contractions *eps.* and *sps.* were easily confounded in the MSS.

[2] *Again.* The texts alluded to are Heb. viii. 26, and perhaps 1 John ii. 1.

CHAP. II.]   *His Intention opposed.*   379

which decided him to persevere in his intention of going to Ireland; he says:

'I saw in a vision of the night, there was a writing[1] opposite to my face without honour. And then I heard an answer unto me: We have seen unfortunately the face of one designated without a name. He did not say, thou hast unfortunately seen, but, we have unfortunately seen; as if He had included Himself, as He said, He that toucheth you toucheth the apple of mine eye [Zech. ii. 8.]. Therefore I give thanks to Him who hath comforted me in all things and did not hinder me from the journey I had resolved upon, nor from my labour which I had dedicated to my Lord Christ. But on the contrary, I felt no small power from Him, and my faith was proved before God and men. Wherefore, I boldly say, my conscience reproves me not here nor hereafter.'

This seems to allude to the circumstance that his design of returning to Ireland was opposed by his relatives, and that he was compelled to go 'without honour' and 'without a name.' But the voice, which he regarded as a Divine oracle, having used the plural number, Patrick, for the reason stated, considered the vision as an approbation of his design, and immediately devoted himself to the missionary life. The obscurities of the passage are mainly due to errors of transcription in the manuscripts.

We have already remarked that Patrick must have written the Confession towards the close of his life, and after he had seen much fruit from his labours. The following passages from the

The Confession written at the close of his life.

---

[1] *Writing.* It is difficult to understand or translate this. The original words are, 'Vidi in visu noctis scriptum erat contra faciem meam sine honore. Et inter hæc audivi responsum dicentem [*sic*] mihi, male audivimus [Ware and Bolland. read *vidimus*] faciem designati nudato nomine, &c. *Book of Armagh*, fol. 24, a.a. Ware, p. 11.

Armagh text of the work will enable the reader to judge for himself:—

'I am greatly a debtor to God, who hath vouchsafed me such great grace, that many people by my means should be born again to God: and that clergy should be ordained every where for them, for the people who had lately come to the faith; for the Lord hath taken them from the ends of the earth, as He had promised of old by His prophets: 'The Gentiles shall come unto Thee from the ends of the earth, and shall say, Surely our fathers have inherited lies, vanity, and there is no profit in them.' [Jer. xvi. 19]. And again, 'I have given thee as a light to the Gentiles that thou mayest be for salvation, even unto the end of the earth.' [Is. xlix. 6.] And there I desire to wait for the promise of Him who never faileth: as He promiseth in the Gospel, 'They shall come from the East and from the West, and shall sit down with Abraham, and Isaac, and Jacob' [Matt. viii. 11]: as we believe that believers shall come from the whole world.'

Again he says:—

'Whence comes it that in *Hiberio*, those who never had any knowledge of God, and up to the present time worshipped only idols and abominations (*idula et inmunda*): how are they lately become the people of the Lord, and are called the sons of God? The sons of Scots[1] and daughters of chieftains (*regulorum*) appear now as monks and virgins of Christ.'

This passage[2] is one of the most remarkable evidences of the antiquity of the Tract. It must have been written when the very name of

---

[1] *Scots.* The Book of Armagh reads *Sanctorum,* (fol. 24, b. a.); but the context favours the reading *Scottorum.* 'Sanctorum' is an evident mistake. This passage, it has been said, proves that all the inhabitants of Ireland were not at that time called Scots, (*Lanigan*, vol. i. p. 235) because the author elsewhere uses the term Hiberionaces, when speaking of the whole nation. It may be added, that he speaks of the 'filii Scottorum and filiæ regulorum,' as belonging to the nobility or higher ranks of the people: and in fact the kings and chieftains were almost all of the Scotic or Milesian race.

[2] *This passage.* See Ware, p. 16. *Book of Armagh,* fol 24, b.a.

Scots, and of reguli, or chieftains, was almost synonymous with pagans. It must have been written after Patrick had made many converts, and after the monastic life had been established by him in Ireland. But it is immediately followed by a passage in which the author is made to say,

'Especially one blessed Scottish lady, *una benedicta Scotta*, of noble birth and of great beauty, who was adult, and whom I baptised.'

We know not who the lady here alluded to was.[1] She came, however, we are told, of her own accord to Patrick and his followers, saying that she had received a message from God, commanding her to remain a virgin of Christ, that she might be nearer to God. Others also had done the same, even at the cost of enduring persecution from their parents or relations. But nothing of all this is to be found in the Book of Armagh.

Patrick concludes the Confession thus:—

'But I pray those who believe and fear God, whosoever may condescend to look into or receive this writing (scripturam) which Patrick the sinner, although unlearned, wrote in *Hiberio*,

---

[1] *Was.* See Dr. Villanueva's note, (20) p. 234. It is very probable that the mention of this noble lady in the Confessio is the foundation of what we read in the Lives, about St. Cethuberis, Cechtumbria, Cectamaria, or Ethembria, (for she is variously described by all these names), who, as Jocelin (c. 79) tells us, was 'the first of all the Irish virgins to receive the veil from St. Patrick.' Her name, in whatever form we take it, is not Irish. S. Cinne or K'nnia has also been suggested. She was at least a 'nobilis Scotta,' being the daughter of Eochaidh, prince of the Oirghialla, who lived near Clogher. But neither of these saints is mentioned in the Irish genealogies. The name of Cinne occurs in the later calendars at Feb. 1, but the Martyrol. of Tallaght has 'Cinni sacerdotis,' instead of Cinne 'virginis,' on that day. Colgan has collected all that the Lives of St. Patrick say of her, at Feb. 1. *Actt. SS.* p. 234.

if I have done or established any little thing according to God's will, that no man ever say that my ignorance did it, but think ye and let it be verily believed that it was the gift of God.'[1]

Tillemont's judgment on the Confession.

Tillemont knew the Confessio only from the copy printed by the Bollandists: he was not aware of the shorter form of its text which is preserved in the Book of Armagh, and therefore could pass no judgment on the authenticity of what we have called the interpolated passages. But his judgment upon the work as he had it, in its more complete form, is just, and may be here quoted. 'It was written,' he says[2], 'to give glory to God for the great grace which the author had received, and to assure the people of his mission, whom he addressed, that it was indeed God Himself who had sent him to preach to them the Gospel; to strengthen their faith, and to make known to all the world that the desire of preaching the Gospel, and of having a part in its promises, was the sole motive which had induced him to go to Ireland. He had long intended to write, but had always deferred

---

[1] *Gift of God.* The text is so corrupt that some licence has been taken in the attempt to translate it. The words are ' Sed precor credentibus et timentibus Deum, quicumque dignatus fuerit inspicere vel recipere hanc scripturam quam Patricius peccator, indoctus scilicet, *Hiberione* conscripsit, ut nemo umquam dicat quod mea ignorantia, si aliquid pusillum egi vel demonstraverim secundum [Dei placitum], sed arbitramini et verissime credatur quod donum Dei fuisset. Et hæc est Confessio mea antequam moriar.' *Book of Armagh,* fol. 24 b.a. The words within brackets are added by Ware, and occur also in the Bollandist copy. Opposite to the word ' secundum,' where there is a manifest defect, occurs the letter z in the margin of the B. of Armagh, which as we have already mentioned, marks always something which the scribe found to be difficult or obscure in the original. See p. 348, note. By ' mea ignorantia,' he means himself. It is the same sort of phrase as ' humilitas mea,' ' pusillitas mea,' &c.

[2] *He says.* Tillemont, Mem. Eccl. (*S. Patrice*), xvi. p. 463. (Art. vi.)

doing so, fearing lest what he wrote should be ill received amongst men, because he had not learned to write well, and what he had learned of Latin was still further corrupted by intermixture with the Irish language.[1] It must be admitted that the Latin of this Tract is very bad, insomuch that there are many places where it is difficult to make out the sense, even after every allowance for the mistakes of transcribers. But on the whole this work is full of good sense, and even of intellect and fire, and, what is better, it is full of piety. The saint exhibits throughout the greatest humility, without, however, lowering the dignity of his ministry. He had also a great desire of martyrdom, even though his body were destined to be eaten[2] by birds and beasts. In a word, we see in the Tract much of the character of St. Paul. The author was undoubtedly well read in the Scriptures.'

In the Epistle on the outrages of Coroticus, Patrick claims and exercises the highest spiritual function of the episcopal office by cutting off an unworthy member from the communion of the Church. His first remonstrance with the robber chieftain was treated with contempt; and the deputation of clergy who brought it to Coroticus

The Epistle on Coroticus.

---

[1] *Irish language.* This is the interpretation which the Bollandists have put upon the passage here referred to. St. Patrick says nothing of the Irish language, but the words 'Nam sermo et lingua nostra translata est in linguam alienam,' may possibly bear that meaning. See above, p. 311.

[2] *Eaten.* The passage referred to occurs sect. 23, (Villanueva, p. 208); but it is not in the *Book of Armagh*.

was dismissed with ridicule and insult.[1] Patrick therefore wrote 'with his own hand'[2] the Epistle, which we still possess, to be given and sent to the soldiers of Coroticus :—

'Soldiers' (he says), 'whom I no longer call my fellow citizens, or citizens of the Roman saints, but fellow citizens of the devils, in consequence of their evil deeds; who live in death, after the hostile rite of the barbarians; associates of the Scots and Apostate Picts; desirous of glutting themselves with the blood of innocent Christians, multitudes of whom I have begotten in God and confirmed in Christ.'

This remarkable passage must have been written whilst the alliance between the Picts and still pagan Scots of Argyleshire and Ireland was in existence: and it is remarkable that the Picts are spoken of as *apostate*, implying that they had been at least once nominally Christian.[3] After enlarging on the enormity of the crimes of Coroticus, and denouncing in the language of Holy Scripture the judgments of God against him and his followers, the Epistle concludes thus :—

'Thus shall sinners and the ungodly perish from the face of the Lord; but the righteous in great joy shall feast with Christ, and shall judge the heathen, and rule over ungodly kings for ever and ever. Amen.

'I testify before God and His holy angels, that it shall be so as my ignorance[4] has said; these are not my words, but the

---

[1] *Insult.* See above, p. 352. This 'first epistle,' as he expressly calls it, no longer exists.

[2] *Own hand.* 'Et manu mea scripsi atque condidi verba ista, &c.' *Villanueva*, p. 241.

[3] *Christian.* This is an undesigned confirmation of the tradition that the Picts were partially converted to Christianity by the labours of SS. Ninian and Palladius before the time of Patrick.

[4] *Ignorance,* or unskilfulness, 'mea imperitia,' meaning, 'I myself.' This

words of God, of Apostles, of Prophets, who never lie, which I have translated into Latin: they who believe shall be saved, but whoso believeth not shall be damned. God hath spoken. I therefore earnestly request of everyone, whosoever as a willing servant of God may become the bearer of this Letter, that it be not withheld from any one, but rather that it be read before all the people[1], and in the presence of Coroticus himself. May God inspire them to return to a better mind towards Him, that even though late, they may repent of their impious deeds. They have been murderers of the brethren of the Lord: but let them repent, and set free the baptised captive women whom they have heretofore carried off; so shall God count them worthy of life, and they shall be made whole here and for ever. Peace[2] to the Father, to the Son, and to the Holy Ghost. Amen.'

'Such,' says Tillemont[3], 'is the account we have of St. Patrick in the original pieces which bear his name, and to which we believe the most entire faith may be given. He speaks always in his Confession as in charge of the whole Church of Ireland; he styles himself Bishop of Ireland[4] in his Epistle about Coroticus. This may give some ground for supposing that he was then the only bishop there, and that if he established other bishops there, it was not until afterwards. In fact, he speaks in his Confession[5]

Tillemont's Judgment.

is an instance of the same manner of speaking which has been mentioned above, p. 382, n.[1].

[1] *People.* As this letter is expressly said to have been originally written in Latin, we may infer that the people to whom it was to be read must have understood Latin. The followers of Coroticus were therefore Roman citizens of the provinces of Britannia, the colonists, or descendants of the colonists, who had settled there under the Roman rule.

[2] *Peace.* ' Pax Patri, et Filio, et Spiritui Sancto.' This seems a singular doxology: perhaps the author meant *gloria*; or else we must take it as a prayer that Coroticus on his repentance may have the peace of God.

[3] *Tillemont.* Mem. Eccl. xvi. p. 465.

[4] *Of Ireland.* Or rather, 'in Ireland.' *Hiberione constitutus episcopus.*

[5] *Confession.* 'An quando ordinavit ubique Dominus clericos per modicitatem meam, &c.' Sect. 22. *Villanueva*, p. 206. This passage is not in the B. of Armagh.

of the *clerics* whom he had ordained, but not of *bishops*. Nevertheless, he may have included bishops under the name of clerics: and indeed the existence of bishops who ruled under him would not hinder his being the principal bishop, and in some sense bishop of this whole Church.'

In the Epistle against Coroticus, says the same author[1], 'we see his tender love of his people: and his grief for the Christians who had been slain, whilst at the same time he rejoices that they shall reign with the Prophets, the Apostles, and the Martyrs.' The passage[2] alluded to occurs in immediate continuation of a paragraph already quoted:—

> 'Thanks be to God, O ye believers and baptised, ye have gone from this world to paradise. I behold you — you have begun to migrate to where there shall be no night, nor sorrow, nor death any more: but ye shall exult like calves let loose[3], and ye shall trample on the ungodly, and they shall be as ashes under your feet. Therefore shall ye reign with apostles and prophets and martyrs; and ye shall receive everlasting kingdoms, as He testifieth saying, They shall come from the east and from the west, and shall sit down with Abraham, and Isaac, and Jacob in the kingdom of heaven. Without are dogs, and sorcerers, and murderers, and liars, and perjurers, their portion is in the lake of eternal fire.'

The Confession irreconcilable with the mission from Rome. We have already more than once spoken of the silence of the Confession on the two subjects of St. Patrick's mission from Rome, and his ecclesiastical education in the schools of St. Germain and St. Martin on the Continent of

---

[1] *Author.* Ibid. p. 463.
[2] *Passage.* Villanueva, sect. 9, p. 245. See above, p. 359.
[3] *Let loose.* 'Exultabitis sicut vituli resoluti.' Ware reads 'Sicut vituli ex vinculis resoluti.' *Opusc.* p. 29.

Europe. It is impossible to believe that a writer, whose object it was to defend himself against those who questioned his qualifications and authority, could have failed to have urged these unanswerable arguments, if he had indeed received any such education, or was the bearer of any such commission from the chief Bishop of the Latin Church. And this argument is valid even though the Confession be rejected as a forgery. For the author of the forgery, writing in the name of Patricius, evidently wrote without any design to prop up the Roman mission or the continental education of St. Patrick.

Assuming, however, the genuineness of the Confession, its testimony is undoubtedly inconsistent with the commission from Celestine ; and this of itself may sufficiently account for the circumstance that there now remain to us only a few scattered copies[1] of it, notwithstanding that its authenticity was admitted by the biographers of St. Patrick, who have quoted it as his, and, as we have already remarked, made it the basis of their histories of him.

When the story of his mission from Rome became an essential part of his history, this authentic account of his life, which did not countenance that story, and which contained no extravagant miracles, fell at once into oblivion or disrepute ; the Lives, full of wondrous tales and exciting legends, cast it into the shade,

---

[1] *Scattered copies.* This circumstance has been urged as an argument against the Confession, by Mr. Herbert, *Brit. Mag.* xxiv. p. 608.

although it was universally received as the genuine composition of St. Patrick, and a copy of it, believed to be his autograph, preserved at Armagh to the beginning of the ninth century.

It should be borne in mind also, that this Treatise and the Epistle on Coroticus are not merely silent on the subjects alluded to, but give an opposite testimony. The author speaks of himself in express terms in both these tracts as rude and unlearned; he rests the authority of his Mission altogether on dreams and visions: in fact, on an immediate revelation which he believed himself to have received, and which conveyed to him a direct commission, similar to that of the Apostles, from the Almighty Himself.

Doctrine of the Confession.

It remains now to say a few words on the doctrine put forth in the Confession. For this it will suffice to quote a sort of creed or statement of the Author's faith which we find near the beginning of the Tract. It is not expressed in the technical language of a formal creed or symbol. He aimed evidently at employing as much as possible the language of Holy Scripture : for the Confessio was addressed to his converts, whom he had instructed in the letter of the Scriptures, and upon whose ears the words of Holy Writ fell with an authority from which there was no appeal.

The Creed of St. Patrick.

This Creed, as we may call it for convenience' sake, is contained in the following passage, which occurs in continuation of the paragraph already quoted, where we have the account of his capture at Bonavem Taberniæ.[1]

'Wherefore I am not able, nor would it be right to be silent on such great benefits and such great grace which [God] hath vouchsafed unto me in the land of my captivity: for this is our recompense[2] [to Him] that after we have been corrected and brought to know God, we should exalt and confess His wondrous works before every nation which is under the whole heaven: that there is none other God, nor ever was, nor shall be hereafter, except God the Father unbegotten, without beginning, from whom is all beginning, upholding all things (as we have said); and His Son Jesus Christ, whom we acknowledge to have been always with the Father, before the beginning of the world, spiritually with the Father, in an ineffable manner begotten, before all beginning; and by Him were made things visible and invisible; and being made man, and, having overcome death, He was received into heaven unto the Father. And [the Father] hath given unto Him all power, above every name, of things in heaven and things in earth and things under the earth, that every tongue should confess that Jesus Christ is Lord and God. Whom we believe, and we look for His coming, who is soon about to be the Judge of quick and dead, who will render unto every man according to his works, and hath poured into us abundantly the gift of the Holy Ghost, and the pledge of immortality (pignus immortalitatis), who maketh the faithful and obedient to become the sons of God the Father, and joint heirs with Christ[3], Whom we confess and worship (quem confitemur et adoramus) one God in the Trinity of the sacred Name. For He Himself hath said by the Prophet[4], Call upon Me in the day of thy tribulation and I will deliver thee, and thou shalt magnify Me. And again He saith[5], It is honourable to reveal and to confess the works of God.'

---

[1] *Taberniæ.* See above, p. 362. *Book of Armagh*, fol. 22, *a. b.*
[2] *Recompense.* 'Hæc est retributio nostra,' i.e. the only recompense we can render to Him: the only way in which we can make any return for His benefits. *Olden's Translation*, p. 44.
[3] *With Christ.* 'Coheredes Christi.' Omitted in the Bollandist copy.
[4] *Prophet.* Jer. xxix. 13.
[5] *He saith.* Tobit, xii. 7.

Its antiquity.

This confession of faith is certainly not Homoousian[1]; neither can we absolutely conclude that its author had seen the Creed of Nicæa. It omits so much which might have been expected from a theologian of the fifth century, that it is scarcely fair perhaps to regard it as a creed. It makes no mention of the resurrection of the body, nor of our Lord's descent into hell. It does not even mention our Lord's burial, which is supposed to include and contain the article of the descent into hell in those antient creeds where that article is wanting. It seems evidently to have been written before the Macedonian controversy. There is no allusion to Pelagianism or to any of the great heresies of the day. It contains, however, as far as it goes, a statement of St. Patrick's doctrine. He attributes the creation of all things to the Son. He teaches his disciples that the second Person of the Trinity poureth into us abundantly the Gift of the Holy Ghost, 'the pledge of immortality.'[2] It is the Holy Ghost who maketh us sons of God the Father and joint heirs[3] with Christ: it is the Holy Ghost whom we worship with the Father and the Son, One God, in the Trinity of the sacred Name, or

---

[1] *Homoousian.* After the words 'visible and invisible,' the Bollandist editor inserts 'qui Filium Sibi consubstantialem genuit,' but for this he admits that he had no authority from the MS. he professes to follow. He merely observes that these or similar words are required by the context: 'Hæc aut similia verba in MS. Atrebatensi desiderari contextus indicat,' p. 534, note *d*. But if such liberties are taken with the sources of history, no sound conclusions can be deduced.

[2] *Immortality.* Alluding no doubt to Eph. i. 14. Comp. 2 Cor. i. 22. v. 5.

[3] *Joint heirs.* Rom. viii. 17.

CHAP. II.] *Date of the Author.* 391

perhaps the meaning may be, under the sacred Name of Trinity.¹

There is but little in the two Tracts we have been considering to lead us to any decisive conclusion as to the date of the author, or the precise year when he commenced his missionary labours amongst the Irish. *Date of St. Patrick's Mission.*

The Epistle about Coroticus must have been written whilst the Franks were still pagan, and therefore before the adoption of a nominal Christianity by Clovis and his subjects in 496. St. Patrick reasons with Coroticus that it was the custom of Roman and Gallican Christians to raise large sums of money for the redemption of baptised captives from the Franks and other Pagans; whereas, he says, Coroticus, although professing Christianity, slew or sold to heathen nations his Christian captives; handing over the members of Christ to the abominations of the heathen.² *As inferred from the Epistle about Coroticus.*

When this was written, Patrick had been many years a bishop in Ireland. The messenger sent by him to Coroticus to demand the restoration of the captives was a venerable priest, whom he had himself, as he tells us, instructed from infancy, 'quem ego ex infantia docui.' He says also that he had begotten in God and confirmed in Christ

---

¹ *Trinity.* The synod of Alexandria, A.D. 317, is said to have first used the term Trinity, in its strict theological signification. See Suicer, *Thesaur.* in voce Τριας.

² *The heathen.* The words are 'Consuetudo Romanorum et Gallorum Christianorum, mittunt viros sanctos idoneos ad Francos, et cæteras gentes cum tot mil. solidorum ad redimendos captivos baptizatos. Tu toties interficis, et vendis illos genti exteræ ignoranti Deum, quasi in lupanar tradis membra Christi.' *Ware,* p. 28.

innumerable Christians in Ireland. The letter was therefore written near the close of his ministry. If he had brought up *from infancy* one who was then a priest and fit to be put at the head of a delicate mission, we cannot assign less than 30 or 40 years to his previous episcopal labours in Ireland. Therefore, taking some year between 480 and 490 as the approximate date of the Epistle, we may assume A.D. 440 to 450, or at latest 460, as the limits within which must be found the year of the consecration of St. Patrick and of his arrival as a missionary in Ireland.[1]

As deduced from the Confession. The Confession, as we have it in the Book of Armagh, contains nothing to aid us in this enquiry. But one of the passages, found in the other copies, informs us, that a fault, which he had committed at the age of 15, was brought forward, and objected to him by his friends, 30 years afterwards, with a view to prevent his being consecrated a bishop, and to obstruct his design of devoting himself to the Irish mission. If this be true, he must have been 45 years of age at his consecration; and A.D. 395 to 415 will be the limits of the date of his birth.[2] In another passage, which is also one of those omitted in the Armagh copy, he is made to say that he began his ministry among the Irish whilst as yet a young man.[3] This, if we can credit Probus[4],

---

[1] *In Ireland.* This is the reasoning of Tillemont. *Mem. Eccl. S. Patrice*, note, iii. p. 783.

[2] *Birth*; i.e. assuming 440 to 460, as the extremes within which we must place the date of his consecration, as above.

[3] *Young man.* 'Vos scitis et Deus qualiter apud vos conversatus sum a juventute mea.' *Ware*, p. 18.

[4] *Probus.* Lib. i. c. 19. *Tr. Th.* p. 52. See above, p. 326.

was whilst he was still only a priest, and consequently before he was forty-five years old.

The Irish annals, with singular unanimity, give A.D. 432 as the date of his consecration and arrival as a bishop in Ireland. But this date is in fact the story of his being commissioned by Pope Celestine, and with that story must fall to the ground. The year 432 is the year of the death of Pope Celestine; the latest year in which a commission from Celestine could have been received by St. Patrick. He was then, we are told, sixty years of age; he laboured in Ireland sixty years more, and died, 'after the similitude of Moses,' at the age of 120. He was therefore born A.D. 372 and died A.D. 492, or 493. These are the dates adopted by Archbishop Ussher. But the very mention of the similitude to Moses[1], and the division of Patrick's life into four equal periods of thirty[2] years, are enough to render these dates very suspicious.

The annals, whose authority was paramount with Ussher, all take for granted the Roman mission of St. Patrick, and are therefore compelled to make A.D. 432 the date of his consecration.

The dates given in the Irish Annals are founded on the Roman Mission.

---

[1] *Moses.* Nennius, c. 60, (Haviniæ, 1758, p. 101). Ussher, *Primord.*, p. 887. (Works, vi. 450).

[2] *Thirty.* The periods of sixty and thirty pervade Irish Hagiography. We have seen above, p. 200, that Patrick being then thirty years of age, met St. Kieran at Rome, and predicted that they should meet again, after thirty years, in Ireland. He predicted also that St. Brigid should survive him thirty years. Ussher, *Primord.*, p. 883. (Works, vi. p. 446). See also Reeves, *Adamnan*, p. 6, note ᵐ. The four periods of Patrick's life are thirty years in servitude in Ireland and study on the continent; thirty in his journeyings and studies in the islands of the Tyrrhene sea; thirty in missionary labours in Ireland; and thirty in monastic retirement. *Ussher ib.* p. 449. The story that he lived to the age of 120 is as old as the collections in the Book of Armagh.

But there are traces, in other extant records, of a different chronology and of an earlier tradition.

The Irish version of Nennius[1] says expressly that when Palladius was sent to Ireland, Patrick was a captive with Miliuc or Milchu in Dalaradia. If this be true, since he was two or three and twenty when he escaped from captivity, and assuming that his escape could not have been later than the mission of Palladius, Patrick must have been born not later than 410. This coincides with the period already determined by a comparison of the Epistle and the Confession; but is entirely at variance with the received chronology of his Life.

The curious Tract[2] in the Irish language, quoted by Ussher and O'Flaherty, 'On the Synchronisms of the Kings and provincial Kings of Ireland and Scotland,' tells us that the battle of Ocha, in which King Oilioll Molt was slain, happened exactly forty-three years[3] after the coming of Patrick to Ireland, meaning of course his coming as a missionary. This would make Patrick's arrival about eight years after the death of Celestine, and is consequently inconsistent with the story of the Roman mission. For the battle of Ocha, according to the Annals of Ulster, was

---

[1] *Nennius.* Irish Nennius, p. 107.
[2] *Tract.* Book of Lecan, fol. 23, *a, a.* Ussher says of this work, 'Qui lingua Hibernica tum monarcharum et provincialium Hiberniæ principum tum Albaniæ regum synchronismos delineavit, non novitius author, &c.' *Works,* vi. 145. O'Flaherty, *Ogyg.,* p. 427.
[3] *Forty-three years.* The words are, 'iii. bliadhan ar .xl. ó thanic Patraic i nErinn co cath Ocha hi torcair Ailioll Molt.' O'Flaherty says that the writer is in error, and that we ought to read fifty-one years. But this is only saying that we must adhere to the story of Patrick's mission from Pope Celestine. Ocha was a place in the Co. of Meath, near Tara hill.

fought A.D. 482 or 483, and therefore counting 43 years back, A.D. 439 or 440 would be the date of Patrick's coming. It is remarkable that this is the same date which we have deduced independently from the Epistle on Coroticus.

Again, in the Annotations of Tirechan[1] preserved in the Book of Armagh, we have the following chronological note:—

'From the Passion of Christ to the death of Patrick are in all 436 years. But Loiguire reigned two or five years after the death of Patrick. And the total duration of his reign was, as we think, 36 years.'

Here the death of Patrick is dated 436 from the Passion, or 469 from the Nativity of Christ. And it is said that Loiguire, or Laoghaire, reigned either two or five years after Patrick's death, that is to A.D. 471 or 474. If, therefore, Laoghaire reigned 36 years, as Tirechan says he believed, he must have begun to reign, according to Tirechan, A.D. 435 or 438, both which dates are inconsistent with the Roman mission; especially if it be true that Patrick arrived in Ireland in the fourth year of King Laoghaire. On that hypothesis the date of his coming will be 439 or 442, a result curiously in accordance with the foregoing conclusions derived from very different data.

in Tirechan;

---

[1] *Tirechan.* B. of Armagh, fol. 9. a. b. 'A passione autem Christi colleguntur anni .cccxxxui. usque ad mortem Patricii. Duobus autem vel u. annis regnavit Loiguire post mortem Patricii. Omnis autem regni illius tempus .xxxui. ut putamus.' This passage is a curious undesigned proof that Tirechan copied from early documents in which it was uncertain whether the numeral letters were ii. or u. But the date which he assigns to the death of Patrick is inconsistent with the history of Patrick the apostle: and approaches more nearly to the date at which the death of Sen-Patrick is recorded in the annals. This, however, does not affect the calculation of the beginning of King Laoghaire's reign.

in the poem of Gilla-Caemhain;

The valuable Chronological Poem, by Gilla-Caemhain[1], an Irish bard and historian of the eleventh century, supplies abundant evidence of the existence of a chronology inconsistent with the mission from Celestine; but to examine or state this evidence would occupy too much space here. It must suffice to mention that this writer counts 162 years from the advent of St. Patrick to the death of Pope Gregory[2] the Great. Gregory the Great, as is well known, died March 12, 604; therefore the advent of Patrick, according to Gilla-Caemhain, must be dated 442.

in the 'Chronology of the Kings.'

Once more, there is a very curious tract preserved in the Book of Lecan[3], entitled 'On the Kingdom of Ireland and the Chronology of its Kings from the reign of Laoghaire son of Niall

---

[1] *Gilla Caemhain.* The work here alluded to has been published by Dr. O'Conor, in the original Irish, with a Latin version. *Rer. Hib. Scriptt.* i. Proleg. ii. p. xxxi. *sq.* The author died 1074. Gilla or Gildas, which signifies *servant*, was often prefixed, as in this case, to the names of saints, to form a Christian name. See O'Donovan,*Topogr.Poems*, Introd. p. 55.

[2] *Pope Gregory.* The particular numbers are, from the advent to the death of Patrick 58; from that event to the death of Brigid 30; from that to the death of King Tuathal Maolgarbh 21; to the death of King Diarmait Mac Carroll 20; and to the death of Pope Gregory 33; in all 162. Dr. O'Conor in his notes labours hard to correct the numbers given in the text of this poem, in order to reconcile its Chronology with the story of the mission from Pope Celestine. But he forgot that although the numbers are almost always written in the MSS. of the poem in numeral letters, they must have been read in words, and these words must be consistent with the metre and prosody of the lines in which they occur. Dr. O'Conor's corrections will not always stand this test; and the conclusion is inevitable, even after making due allowance for errors of transcription, that the chronology of Gilla-Caemhain, be it right or wrong, does not square with the Roman mission.

[3] *Book of Lecan.* Fol. 306,*a.* 'Do flathis Ereand, ocus dia naimsearaib na rig,ó flaithis Loegaire mec Neill, co haimsir Ruaidri mec Thairrdealbaig hi Conchobuir.' This is an enlarged copy of the older form of the same Tract in the Book of Leinster, mentioned p. 183, from which the annals of ecclesiastical events, printed p. 184 *sq.*, were extracted.

to the time of Roderick son of Torlough O'Conor.' This tract tells us that Laoghaire reigned thirty years, and his successor Oilioll Molt, twenty. But this latter chieftain, as we have seen, was killed at the battle of Ocha in 482, or 483; therefore 432 or 433 must have been the first year of King Laoghaire Mac Neill, according to this authority. And if Patrick arrived in Ireland in the fourth year of Laoghaire, the date of his coming will be 436 or 437, four or five years after the death of Pope Celestine.

To meet this difficulty O'Flaherty asserts that Laoghaire reigned in reality thirty-five years, counted as thirty only in the series of Christian kings, because during the first five years of his reign he was a pagan. Therefore, the fourth year of his reign was 432, the year in which Patrick received Pope Celestine's commission. The authority upon which O'Flaherty relies for this statement is the following passage, with which the tract just referred to begins. We shall give it in the original mixture of Irish and Latin, with a literal translation : —

O'Flaherty's explanation.

' Ro gob tra Laegairi mac Neill noigiallaigh rigi tricha annis.

Regnum Hiberniæ post adventum Patricii tenuit.

Ardmacha fundata est.

Secundinus (i. Sechnall) et senex Patricius in pace dormierunt.'

Now Laegairi, son of Niall of the nine hostages, held the kingdom thirty years.

He retained the kingdom of Ireland after the coming of Patrick.

Armagh was founded.

Secundinus (i. e. Sechnall) and Old Patrick slept in peace.

Dates of King Laoghaire's Reign.

Here it will be observed that the length of King Laoghaire's reign is first stated in Irish to have been thirty years; and then in Latin he is said to have reigned after the coming of Patrick, but the number of years is not given. This suggests a suspicion that the figures marking this latter number may have been suppressed, and that this antient document has been tampered with.

O'Flaherty[1] quotes it most unfairly; he says:—

'Thirty years are usually assigned to him [i.e. to Laoghaire], but those thirty years are to be counted from the time when he embraced Christianity, as in the Book of Lecan is thus explained in Latin: *Triginta annis regnum Hiberniæ post adventum Patricii tenuit.*'

But these words are not to be found *in Latin* in the Book of Lecan; the Book of Lecan does not say that Laoghaire reigned thirty years after the coming of Patrick; but only that Laoghaire 'reigned after the coming of Patrick.' The thirty years are mentioned in the Irish, not in the Latin words of this document, and were certainly meant to include the whole duration[2]

---

[1] *O'Flaherty.* His words are, *Ogyg.* p. 429, 'Huic triginta annos plerique tribuunt; illi vero triginta accipiendi sunt, ex quo Jesu Christi familiæ nomen dedit, ut in codice Lecano ita Latine explicatur, *Triginta annis,* &c.'

[2] *Whole duration.* It is curious that Dr. Petrie, although he quotes both the Irish and Latin words of the Book of Lecan, omits inadvertently the two words 'Regnum Hiberniæ,' in the Latin part of the quotation, and thus continues the confusion. *On Tara Hill,* p. 87. The copy of this Tract in the Book of Leinster, (see p. 184, supra) seems to support O'Flaherty's view. It states apparently that Laoghaire reigned thirty years after the coming of Patrick. But the meaning is nevertheless, that thirty years were the entire duration of his reign, and that he continued to reign after the advent of Patrick, the number of years being omitted. This would place the advent of Patrick in the first year of King Laoghaire: and such is the testimony of the annals of Ulster, in which the death of Laoghaire is dated 462, or thirty years after 432, the death of Pope Celestine.

CHAP. II.] *the Papal Mission.* 399

of Laoghaire's reign, not merely the portion of it which followed his supposed conversion to Christianity.

But enough has been said to establish the fact that a Chronology existed before the period of the Irish Annalists[1] which was entirely inconsistent with the story of a mission from Pope Celestine, and which placed the arrival of St. Patrick from eight to ten years after the death of that Pontiff. This older Chronology is confirmed by the evidence of the Confession and of the Epistle about Coroticus; evidence the more important because it was undesigned, being derived, not from any express statement of a date, but from a comparison of passages written evidently without the most remote intention of fixing the year or century in which the author flourished. *The older Chronology inconsistent with the Roman Mission.*

We may now proceed to consider the particulars recorded of St. Patrick's missionary labours in Ireland, and his success in converting to Christianity the rude and barbarous tribes whom he found in the country.

[1] *Irish Annalists.* Tighernach, the earliest of them, died in 1088.

CHAPTER III.

The Missionary Labours of St. Patrick in Ireland. His interview with King Laoghaire. His Irish Hymn. His Adventures in Connaught. Festival of his Baptism. Story of King Laoghaire's Daughters. Foundation of Armagh. His supposed Revision of the Pagan Laws. His Canons. His Death.

Legends inserted into the Acts of St. Patrick with a special purpose.

IT would be inconsistent with the purpose of these pages to record minutely all the adventures and acts attributed to St. Patrick by his biographers. Many of those adventures were evidently invented to pay a compliment to certain tribes or clans by ascribing the conversion of their ancestors to the preaching of St. Patrick. Others were intended to claim for certain churches or monasteries the honour of having been by him founded: and others, again, were framed with the object of supporting the pretensions of the see of Armagh to the possession of lands or jurisdiction in various parts of Ireland.

Such stories, however, although we cannot regard them as history, frequently possess an interest of another kind. They are precious records of antient topography; they illustrate the manners and customs of the times when

CHAP. III.] *Obscurity of St. Patrick's Acts.* 401

they were invented, and often preserve curious information as to the origin of Church property or jurisdiction, and the laws regulating the tenure of land.

We have already pointed out some of the difficulties with which the attempt to make Patrick a regularly educated missionary from Rome has encumbered the chronology of his life. Those difficulties have been greatly increased by the introduction of the legends to which we have alluded; and it is now, perhaps, impossible to separate completely the true from the fictitious in his history.

Muirchu Maccumachtheni, one of the earliest authors whose collection of the Acts of St. Patrick has come down to us, admits in strong and somewhat inflated language the hopeless obscurity of the materials he undertook to arrange. His Preface or Dedication is addressed to Aedh, or Aidus, anchorite and bishop of Sletty in the 7th century, at whose suggestion, as he tells us, he compiled the work.[1] This Preface, written in a

The complaint of Maccumachtheni.

---

[1] *The work.* See above, p. 314, note 2. The original words, of which a translation is attempted above, are these :—' Quoniam quidem, mi domine Aido [Irish vocative of *Aedh*], multi conati sunt ordinare narrationem, utique istam, secundum quod patres eorum, et qui ministri ab initio fuerunt sermonis tradiderunt illis, sed propter difficillimum narrationis opus, diversasque opiniones et plurimorum plurimas suspiciones, numquam ad unum certumque historiæ tramitem pervenierunt. Ideo ni fallor iuxta hoc nostrorum proverbium, ut deducuntur pueri in ambiteathrum(*sic*),in hoc periculossum et profundum narrationis sanctæ pylagus, turgentibus proterve gurgitum aggeribus inter acutissimos carubdes per ignota æquora insitos, a nullis adhuc lintribus, excepto tantum uno patris mei Cognito si, expertum atque occupatum, ingenioli mei puerilem remi cymbam deduxi. Sed ne magnum de parvo videar finguere, pauca hæc de multis sancti Patricii gestis, parva peritia, incertis auctoribus, memoria labili, attrito sensu, vili sermone, sed affectu pissimo, caritatis etiam sanctitatis tuæ et auctoritatis imperio oboedens, carptim gravatimque explicare aggrediar.' *Book of Armagh,* fol. 20, *a.a.*

D D

strain obviously copied from the introductory verses of St. Luke's Gospel, is as follows:—

'Forasmuch as many, my lord Aidus, have taken in hand to set forth in order a narration, namely this, according to what their fathers, and they who from the beginning were ministers of the Word, have delivered unto them; but by reason of the very great difficulty of the narrative and the diverse opinions and numerous doubts of very many persons, have never arrived at any one certain track of history; therefore (if I be not mistaken, according to this proverb of our countrymen, Like boys[1] brought down into the amphitheatre) I have brought down the boyish row-boat of my poor capacity into this dangerous and deep ocean of sacred narrative, with wildly-swelling mounds of billows, lying in unknown seas between most dangerous whirlpools,—an ocean never attempted or occupied by any barks, save only that of my father Cogitosus.[2] But lest I should seem to make a small matter great, with little skill, from uncertain authors, with frail memory, with obliterated meaning and barbarous language, but with a most pious intention, obeying the command of thy belovedness, and sanctity, and authority, I will now attempt, out of many acts of Saint Patrick, to explain these, gathered here and there with difficulty.'

This complaint was made before the close of the seventh century. We need not, therefore, in the nineteenth, affect to be able to clear up what was then so obscure, nor hesitate to confess our inability to do so. In the following account

---

[1] *Boys.* The meaning seems to be, 'If I do not overrate my powers, as boys brought into the arena, who are then found incapable of acting their parts.'

[2] *Cogitosus.* The MS. reads *Cognito si*, in two separate words. Dean Graves, with a critical acuteness that cannot be too highly estimated, suggests the reading *Cogitosi*, as the name of the author's father: an emendation which gives sense and meaning to a passage hitherto quite unintelligible. He has also shewn that our author's Irish surname Maccu-machtheni, signifies 'Filiorum Cogitosi,' the Irish word *Machtheni*, from a root which denotes *think, deliberate*, being the equivalent of the Latin *cogitosus*. His ingenious and very valuable paper, lately read before the Royal Irish Academy, will shortly be printed in the Transactions of that body.

of St. Patrick's labours we shall confine ourselves to some of the leading facts of his history, selecting those which seem most likely to be true, and illustrating them occasionally with such anecdotes as are calculated to exhibit in the most striking manner the character of the man and the nature of his religious teaching.

We have already[1] noticed the accounts given of the rejection of St. Patrick by some tribes of Leinster amongst whom he is said to have landed; and we have suggested some reasons for believing that all such accounts belonged originally to the Acts of Palladius, and were transferred, either ignorantly or with design, to St. Patrick. In further confirmation of this opinion it may be observed that the antient Life by Muirchu Maccumachtheni in the Book of Armagh says nothing of any opposition made to St. Patrick on his arrival, or of his having been violently expelled from the coasts of Leinster. He arrived, this author tells us, at Inbher Dea, in the territory of the Cuolenni[2], and recollecting that he had left his master Milchu without having been redeemed, as a slave, in order to recover his freedom, ought to have been, he resolved to visit[3]

St. Patrick's supposed rejection by the tribes of Leinster.

---

[1] *Already.* See above, p. 338, *sq.*
[2] *Cuolenni.* See above, p. 343, note.
[3] *To visit.* This appears to be the meaning. The honored ship of the saint, our author says, ' In oportunum portum in regiones Coolennorum, in portum apud nos clarum qui vocatur hostium Dee dilata est, ubi vissum est ei nihil perfectius esse quam ut semetipsum primi-tus redemeret, et inde appetens sinistrales fines ad illum hominem gentilem Milcoin apud quem quondam in captivitate fuerat, portansque geminum servitutis pretium, terrenum utique et cœleste ut de captivitate liberaret illum, cui antea captivus servierat.'—*Book of Armagh,* fol. 2, *b.b.* Here we find no mention of its having been the custom of the country to manumit

the place of his captivity, and offer to his former master a double ransom: an earthly one, namely, in money and worldly goods, and a spiritual one, by making known to him the Christian faith and the Gospel way of salvation.

His sojourn in the islands off the coast of Dublin.

Sailing northwards with this view, he stopped at an island on the east—*ad anteriorem insolam*— 'which has since been called by his name.' This was no doubt Inis Patrick, a small island off Skerries on the coast of the County of Dublin, which still bears the name of St. Patrick's Island. The parish to which it belongs is called Holmpatrick. Tirechan tells us that Patrick came also to the islands of *Maccuchor*[1], attended by some Gauls, and by a multitude of holy bishops, presbyters, deacons, exorcists, ostiarii and lectors, and also 'sons whom he ordained;' meaning, perhaps, by this last phrase, students on probation. But this part of the story is no doubt an exaggeration. It is not credible that at this early period of his mission St. Patrick could

---

slaves every seventh year, like the jubilee of the Jews, or of the angel showing him a mass of gold to pay for his redemption. *Schol. on Fiacc*, n. 5, 9. (*Tr. Th.*, p. 4, *b*.) These stories, however, all show that the biographers considered it necessary for the honor of the saint, that he should not be represented as a mere *runaway* slave.

[1] *Maccuchor*. In the MS. *Maccuchor*, more correctly *Maccu Chor*, 'the islands of the sons or descendants of Corr.' The Ui-Chorra, sons of Conall Dearg Ua Chorra, were three noted adventurers, who flourished about the middle of the sixth century. Although they belonged to the West of Ireland, and most probably to the islands of Arann, off the coast of Galway, it is not impossible that in the age of Tirechan, the group of islands, now the Skerries, may have been called from them. A romantic tale is extant, being an account of their voyage into the Atlantic Ocean. Professor O'Curry has given an abstract of it in his Lectures, p. 289, *sq*. A place in Munster, called Aill mic Cuirr, 'Cliff of the Son of Corr,' is mentioned as one of the seats of the King of Cashel. *Book of Rights*, p. 89, 91.

have provided himself with so large a staff of attendants. The statement, however, is worth noting from the mention of the Gauls[1] who accompanied him; which tends to confirm the opinion, already expressed[2], that Patrick had his mission from the Gallican Church.

The islands[3] forming the Skerries' group are low and sandy, easily accessible to light boats or small ships: and offering convenient landing-places. In Patrick's time they were probably uninhabited; and may have been the islands which Tirechan calls 'insulæ Maccu Chor.' Inis Patrick, in its very name, still affords evidence favourable to the tradition that it was visited by St. Patrick. It is possible that he may have sought a temporary refuge there, as offering a harbour safer than the coast, if only from the very fact that it was uninhabited. His object probably was to obtain provisions, of which all the legends represent him to have been in want. We have seen that on his arrival at Inbher Dea, the mouth of the river Vartry, he begged fish[4], and was refused; whereupon the river was smitten 'with the bolt of his malediction:'[5] as the author of the Tri-

Landed at Inis Patrick.

His want of provisions.

---

[1] *Gauls.* 'Venit vero Patricius cum Gallis ad insolas Mac cuchor et insola orientali (*sic*) quæ dicitur insola Patricii.' *Book of Armagh*, fol. 9, *a.b.* Muirchu had called this island 'anterior insola,' with the same meaning. See Reeves, *Adamnan. Glossary*, in *v.* ' *Anterior.*'

[2] *Expressed.* See p. 335, *supra.*

[3] *Islands.* The Second and Third Lives say nothing of these islands: the other Lives in Colgan's collection mention only Inis Patrick.

[4] *Fish.* See above, p. 342.

[5] *Malediction.* 'Jaculo maledictionis flumen illud feriit.' *Vit. Trip.*, i. 41 (p. 123). The Irish text tells this story of *Inbher Domnann*, which is now Malahide. See Reeves' *Adamnan*, p. 31, note *d*: Colgan, *Actt. SS.* p. 304, note 17.

partite life expresses it. At Inis Patrick, the same authority tells us, he was in great distress[1] for food, and sent a party to Inbher n-Ainge (the mouth of the Nanny water), to seek fish, but without success. That river also was punished with the curse of unproductiveness. Let us hope that these examples of vengeance, so common in his story, represent only the mind of the ecclesiastics of a later age, and that his biographers knew not what spirit he was of.

<small>Curses the Nanny Water.</small>

<small>Sails to Dalaradia.</small>

The antient Life in the Book of Armagh goes on to say that Patrick sailed from the island, leaving on his left Bregia and the territory of the Conalnei[2], or descendants of Conall Cearnach; passing by Ulidia[3], the present County of Down, until he arrived at a strait called Brene, and landed at the mouth of a river Slain[4], at the

---

[1] *Distress.* 'Ubi cum fame nimium laborabat, et nulla adesset via, qua refici posset, misit aliquos ex sociis ad ostias fluminis de Inbher Ainge, pro piscibus ibi quærendis,' &c. *Vit. Trip.* i. 44 (p. 124). The river Nanny, as it is now called, flows through the midst of the antient territory of Cianachta-Bregh, and forms the boundary between the Baronies of Upper and Lower Duleck, Co. of Meath. The mouth of the Nanny is distant about nine statute miles from St. Patrick's island.

[2] *Conalnei.* See p. 361, *note.* This district was inhabited by the tribe of Conaille Muirtheimhne, a branch of the Clanna Rudhraighe (Clann-Rury), descended from Conall Cearnach, who was 6th in descent from Rudhraighe, or Rury, King of Ireland, and is fabled to have witnessed our Lord's Crucifixion at Jerusalem. See above, p. 198, *n.*, and O'Flaherty,

Ogyg. pp. 278, 283. For an account of the district inhabited by his descendants, see Dr. O'Donovan's valuable notes, *Book of Rights,* pp. 21, 166.—Bregia, (by Irish writers usually called Magh Bregh, or the Plain of Bregh,) is a district including the counties of Meath, Westmeath, and the northern half of Dublin, with part of Louth. *Ibid.,* p. 11, *n.*

[3] *Ulidia.* See Reeves, *Eccl. Antiq. of Down and Connor,* p. 352.

[4] *Slain.* 'Ad extremum fretum quod est Brene se inmissit, et discenderunt in terram ad hostium Slain ille et qui cum eo erant in navi,' &c. *Book of Armagh,* fol. 2. *b. b.* The 'Fretum Brene' is the 'Balibren' of the Taxation of 1306, now Ballintogher, 'Town of the Causeway.' Reeves' *Down and Connor,* p. 40. The Slain is a small river, now called *Slany,* between the townlands of Ringbane and Ballintogher, about two miles from *Sabhal* or Saul. See

CHAP. III.] *Conversion of Dichu.* 407

S.W. extremity of Strangford Lough; here he hid his boat, and proceeded with his companions to explore the country.

They had not gone far when they met a swineherd. Supposing them to be pirates or robbers, the swineherd ran away and called his master, whose name was Dichu. Dichu was a chieftain of high birth, one of the family of the Dal-Fiatach, descended in a direct line from Fiatach Finn[1], who was King of Ireland A.D. 116. Hearing that pirates had landed on his territories he came out sword in hand to oppose the invaders; but struck with the venerable appearance of St. Patrick, he received him with kindness, took him to his house, listened to his preaching, and finally became a believer in Christ — 'the first[2] of the Scots,' say more than one of the Lives, who confessed the faith under Patrick's ministry.

Conversion of Dichu.

Patrick remained for a few days only with his new convert, being still desirous of visiting the scene of his captivity and attempting the conversion of his former master Milchu. Leaving his boat with Dichu he set out with his companions on foot to the territories of the Cruitheni or Picts[3] of Dalaradia, and reached Sliabh Mis,

Patrick visits his old master Milchu.

a valuable paper (privately printed) by Mr. J. W. Hanna of Downpatrick, entitled, 'An Inquiry into the true landing-place of St. Patrick in Ulster.' And compare what is said of the fountain *Slan*, in Fiacc's Hymn, *Tr. Th.*, p. 2, and page 5, note 19.

[1] *Fiatach Finn.* See O'Flaherty, *Ogyg.*, pp. 142—301.
[2] *First.* See above, p. 344.
[3] *Picts.* They were the descendants of Conall Cearnach, of whom we have already spoken. His first wife Lonnchad was the daughter of Eochaidh Echbeoil of the Picts of

now called Slemish, a basaltic hill of remarkable shape, at the extremity of that district, the scene of his supposed visions and angelic apparitions during his captivity. Here he stood to view the woods where he had so long tended the herds of Milchu, but was astonished at beholding the house of his old master in flames. The legend states that Milchu, instigated by the devil, had set fire to his house and all his substance, casting himself also voluntarily into the fire, lest he should be compelled to submit to the authority and jurisdiction of his former slave.[1]

He denounces the family of Milchu.

As a punishment for this singular mode of shewing his obstinate infidelity, the family of Milchu were denounced by St. Patrick. He predicted that none of the sons of Milchu should sit as a king on the throne of his kingdom, and that his seed should be slaves for ever.[2]

The faith spread in Lecale.

Patrick then retraced his steps to Magh-inis, the antient name of the district, now the barony of Lecale[3], where Dichu resided. There he

---

Scotland. By her he had Irial Glunmor, King of Ulster, whose descendants were therefore called Picts or Cruitheni, until they received the new name of Dal-Aradians, from his descendant Fiacha Araidhe, King of Ulster, A.D. 240. See Reeves, *Down and Connor*, p. 334, *seq.*

[1] *Slave.* 'Ne servo subjectus fieret, et ille sibi dominaret, instinctu diabuli sponte se igni tradidit, et in domu in qua prius habitaverat, rex, congregato ad se omni instrumento substantiæ suæ incensus est.'—*Book of Armagh*, fol. 3, *a.a.*

[2] *For ever.* 'Nemo de filiis ejus sedebit rex super sedem regni ejus a generatione in generationem, insuper et semen ejus serviet in sempiternum.' *Ib.*, fol. 3, *a.b.* Notwithstanding this prediction, we read of Milchu's son Guasacht, who was a bishop in the church of Granard (*Mart. of Donegal*, 24 Jan), and two of his daughters, both named Eimer or Emeria, who were in the neighbouring nunnery of Clon-Bronaigh. *Vit. Trip.*, i. c. 20, ii. c. 30. 136.

[3] *Lecale.* Magh-Inis signifies the island-plain, the district being very nearly surrounded by the sea. Lecale, properly *Leth-Cathail*, signifies the portion or district of Cathal, a

CHAP. III.] *Foundation of Sabhal Patraic.* 409

remained for some time — *diebus multis* — going about in the neighbourhood preaching and teaching; and there 'the faith began to spread.'[1]

We are told in the later Lives that Dichu granted to St. Patrick on this occasion a certain tract of land for the foundation of a church, together with a barn or granary, which having been converted into a place of worship, was afterwards known by the name of *Sabhal Patraic,* 'Patrick's granary,' and became in after times a celebrated monastery. The place still retains the name of Sabhal, or Saul[2], and is situated about two miles N.E. from Downpatrick.

This story, which does not occur in the antient Life, is evidently one of those interpolations, of which we shall have frequent occasion to speak, foisted into the Acts of St. Patrick in later times, for the purpose of doing honour to a monastic establishment.[3] But the account given

<small>Foundation of Sabhal or Saul.</small>

Chieftain who flourished about A.D. 700. See Reeves, *Down and Connor*, p. 201, *sq.*

[1] *Spread.* 'Rursum pervenit in campum Inis ad Dichoin, ibique mansit diebus multis, et circumiit totum campum, et elegit, et amavit, et cœpit fides crescere ibi.' *Book of Armagh*, ibid.

[2] *Saul.* The word *Sabhal*, pronounced nearly as its modern name Saul, signifies a barn, and is Latinized 'Horreum Patricii.' See Reeves' *Down and Connor*, p. 220, *sq.*

[3] *Establishment.* Dr. Lanigan (i. p. 215) quotes a passage from the Confession, in which he says, St. Patrick tells us that 'he made it a rule not to accept of presents, at least of any considerable value.' But the passage referred to says nothing of

the *value* of the presents. It asserts only that he received nothing from his converts in return for baptism or holy orders:—'Forte autem,' he says, stating it as an objection made against him, 'quando baptizavi tot milia hominum, speraverim ab aliquo illorum vel dimidium scriptulæ? Dicite mihi et reddam vobis. Aut quando ordinavit Dominus clericos per modicitatem meam et ministerium, gratis distribui illis. Si poposci ab aliquo illorum vel pretium calceamenti mei, dicite; dicite adversus me, et reddam vobis.' Ware, *Opusc.* p. 19. This is a very different thing from making 'a rule' not to accept grants of land for the establishment of Christianity, and the erection of churches.

of the donation is worthy of notice. The author of the third Life[1] thus describes it: having said that Patrick preached the Word of God to Dichu, he adds :—

'Then Dichu believed in him, the first before all others who did so, and gave him the land on which they were standing. And Dichu asked St. Patrick that the length of the Church should not be turned from west to east, but from north to south, and this request St. Patrick granted. Then Patrick erected in that place the *transverse* Church, which is called even to the present day Sabhul Patrick.'

Orientation of Churches in Ireland.

This is evidence that the usual position of churches in Ireland, when this story was received, must have been east and west—a fact which is curiously confirmed by the celebrated prophecy[2] of St. Patrick's coming, attributed to the Druids of Ireland.

The Druidical Prophecy of St. Patrick.

This prophecy, in a very antient dialect of the Irish language, is preserved by the Scholiast on Fiacc's Hymn. It is so characteristic in many

---

[1] *Third Life.* Cap. 31. The same story is repeated by Joceline, c. 32. The Tripartite Life (i. 47) mentions the donation of land, but says nothing of the *transverse* position of the church. That part of the story may be no more than a sort of apology to explain why St. Patrick permitted such an anomaly. Ussher quotes this story (*Epist.* 49, *ad Seldenum*, now 51, *Works*, xv. p. 175), to show that in St. Patrick's time there was no law prescribing the orientation of Churches. The story can scarcely prove anything as to the practice of St. Patrick, or of his age. Bingham infers that St. Patrick's *usage* was to build churches north and south. *Antiq.*, Book viii. c. 3, sec. 2. The opposite conclusion would, however, be more reasonable.

[2] *Prophecy.* Reeves, *Down and Connor*, p. 221. This prophecy is alluded to by Fiacc, in his *Hymn*, stanza 10; and Muirchu, in the Book of Armagh, speaks of it as obscure in his time: 'verba pro linguæ idiomo [*sic*] non tam manifesta,' although perhaps he only means that they were obscure to those unacquainted with the Irish language, and that they needed translation into Latin, fol. 2, b. See also Petrie, *On Tara*, p. 77, 78.

ways of Irish legend that we shall venture to insert it here:—

> 'Ticfa tailcend
> Tar muir murcend,
> A brat tollcend,
> A crand chromcend,
> A mias in iarthur a thigi,
> Frisgerad a muinter uili
>   Amen, Amen.'

These lines, it will be observed, are in a rude rhyme, having much of the character of an incantation. They may be thus rendered:—

'He comes, He comes, with shaven crown,[1] from off the storm-toss'd sea,
His garment pierced at the neck, with crook-like staff comes he.
Far in his house, at its east end, his cups and patens lie,
His people answer to his voice, Amen, Amen, they cry.
   Amen, Amen.'

It is clear that no Pagan Druids ever wrote these verses, and it is evident also that they were written when the orientation of churches was the rule, and the altar always in the eastern end of the building. The allusion to the shaven tonsure[2], the clerical habit, and the episcopal staff, proves beyond question that this stanza

---

[1] *Shaven crown.* The word *tailcend* is rendered *Lasciciput* [not *Asciciput*, as Dr. Reeves supposed, *Adamnan*, p. 351, *n.*] in the Book of Armagh, which has greatly puzzled the biographers. *Lascivium*, is barber's soap; written also *Lasaverium, Lesavium*, French, *Savonette*; English, *Lather*. 'Lasciciput' is therefore shaven head, and proves that these lines allude to the modern tonsure, or shaving of the head, not to the more antient tonsure, which was only a clipping or shortening of the hair. *Tailcend*, is shaven head, from *tal*, take away, deprive, cut off (French *tailler*), and *cenn*, the head.

[2] *Tonsure.* See Synod. Toletana. (A.D. 633) *can.* 41. Isid. Hispal., *De Off. Eccl.*, ii. 4.—Greg. Turon., *De Gloria Martyrum*, i. 28.

cannot be older than the beginning of the seventh century. And this may possibly be also the age of the legend of Dichu's 'transverse church.' Dr. Reeves has shewn that *Sabhall* was a name given also to a church at Armagh, which seems[1] to have been in like manner built north and south; and he infers with much probability that churches possessing this peculiarity may have been all called *Savals* or Sauls (i. e. Barns), perhaps to indicate their deviation from ecclesiastical propriety.

Patrick goes to Tara at Easter.

To return, however, to St. Patrick. Having laid the foundation of Christianity in Dalaradia, he resolved, we are told, to visit the central parts of Ireland, and to preach Christ in the very citadel of its idolatry. Easter was approaching, and he determined to select that festival as the season most fitting for his purpose. Whether it be true, as the writers of his life all tell us, that this was the first Easter celebrated by him in Ireland, is very doubtful. The adventures[2] assigned to him and his successful preaching in the North, must have taken some considerable time. After leaving Dichu he sailed, we are told, to Inbher Coltpha, the mouth of the

---

[1] *Seems.* The Armagh church is called by different authorities *Damliag an tSabhaill,* 'the Stone Church of the Savall,' the 'Septentrionalis ecclesia,' and the 'Sinistralis ecclesia.' Reeves, *Down and C.* p. 220, 221, and *Churches of Armagh*, p. 15.

[2] *Adventures.* Besides those here mentioned, the biographers record also his meeting with Benen or Benignus; the conversions of Rus, or Ross, brother of Dichu, and of St. Mochaoi, grandson of Patrick's master Milchu, by his daughter Bronach. (See *Mart.Doneg.*,23 June.) Mochaoi became Abbot at Aondruim, or Nendrum (not *Antrim*, as Lanigan supposed, i. p. 217), now island Mahee, or Mochaoi. Reeves,*Ibid.*,p. 187,sq. Patrick was long enough in Lecale to baptise,instruct,and ordain Mochaoi, who was also called Caolàn.

Boyne; and leaving his boats[1] there, proceeded on foot to execute his intention. He arrived in the neighbourhood of Tara on Easter eve, during the celebration of some pagan feast or solemnity which happened to coincide with the Christian Easter, and presented himself before the Pagan monarch. This is the story whose claims to credibility we must now examine.

The hypothesis of the Roman mission of St. Patrick assumes that he arrived in Ireland soon after the death of Pope Celestine. But Celestine died[2], on the 28th or 29th of July 432. Let Patrick, therefore, have made all speed, let us reject the stories of his having stopped at Menevia, Cornwall, or anywhere else on the way, he cannot possibly have arrived at Wicklow harbour earlier than some time in the month of August. The Easter-day of the following year 433 fell upon the 26th of March: there remain just seven months for the conversion of Dalaradia and all the other transactions we have described. It is difficult, therefore, to believe that the Easter-tide, at which Patrick resolved to appear before the court of King

Not the first Easter after his arrival in Ireland.

---

[1] *Boats.* Here (according to the Tripartite Life, i. c. 55) occurred the transaction of which we have already spoken, which led to the foundation of the Church of Trim, and the acquisition of certain lands, with chieftainry, for the See of Armagh, although Armagh was not founded for 22 years after. See above, p. 150, sq. *Introd. App.* B., p. 257. The story was avowedly of late origin: *serotinis temporibus inventa.* The events it records, if true, must have taken some time. Lomman remained 80 days at the mouth of the Boyne, before he ascended the river in search of his master: but we are not to suppose that his adventures all took place before the Easter day at which Patrick is said to have preached to King Laoghaire. There is no mention made of Easter in the story.

[2] *Died.* See Fran. Pagi, *Breviarium Gestorum Pontiff. Rom.* Antv. 1717, vol. i. p. 180.

Laoghaire was the Easter immediately following his arrival in Ireland.

The argument of Dr. O'Conor.

Dr. O'Conor has maintained with much ingenuity and learning[1] that the Feast of Tara was celebrated at the vernal equinox, and that the near coincidence of the Easter of A.D. 433 with that equinox affords a strong confirmation to the date required by the hypothesis of the Roman mission. But the same argument applies with even greater force to the year 441, in which Easter fell on the 23rd of March; and this year is not only more in accordance with the probable date of St. Patrick's arrival which we have deduced from his own writings[2], but will enable us also to allow without difficulty a year or more for his successful preaching in Dalaradia.

The Festival of Tara not the Beltine.

Dr. O'Conor's theory is built upon two gratuitous and unsupported assumptions, namely — that the Festival of Tara, which coincided with St. Patrick's Easter, was the Druidical Festival of Beltine, and that the Druidical festival of Beltine[3] was at that time celebrated, not, as is

---

[1] *Learning.* Dr. O'Conor's dissertations on this subject, *Rer. Hib. Scriptt.*, tom. i. *Epist. Nuncupat.*, p. lxxi. sq. *Stowe, Catal.*, i. p. 32, 33, contain everything that can be said in favour of this view. But, as Dr. Petrie has remarked, Dr. O'Conor's arguments are 'more ingenious than satisfactory, and his references to authorities in support of his conclusions, are such as, on examination, will seldom be found to bear him out in his assertions.' *Tara Hill*, p. 85.

[2] *Writings.* See above, p. 392. *sq.*

[3] *Beltine.* This word is supposed to signify 'lucky fire,' or 'the fire of the god Bel,' or Baal. The former signification is possible; the Celtic word *Bil*, is good, or lucky; *tene*, or *tine*, fire. The other etymology, although more generally received, is untenable. Petrie, *On Tara*, p. 84. The Irish Pagans worshipped the heavenly bodies, hills, pillar stones, wells, &c. There is no evidence of their having had any personal gods, or any knowledge of the Phœnician Baal. This very erroneous etymology of the word Beltine is nevertheless the source of all the theories about the Irish Baal-worship, &c.

generally supposed, on the first of May, but at the vernal equinox. Tradition, however, and all our remaining records make the first of May the Beltine of the Pagan Irish; we have no notice of its having ever been otherwise. The first of May in every part of Ireland, and in all the Gaelic regions of Scotland[1], is still called 'La Beltine,' or 'Beltine's Day,' and the Beltine fires are in many places still kept up in both countries. Dr. O'Conor reconciles this fact to his hypothesis by asserting that the original Druidical festival was transferred in Christian times from the vernal equinox to the first of May. The Christian clergy, he tells us, being unable wholly to extirpate the Pagan observance, changed the time of its celebration to the first of May, lest it should interfere with the holy season of Lent, and the solemnities of Easter. Of this change, however, there is not the smallest evidence. It would probably have been quite as difficult as the total abolition of the festival. Moreover, it is not said, in any of the Lives of St. Patrick, or any other authority, that the festival celebrated by King Laoghaire was the *Beltine*. So that the whole of this theory, however ingenious and plausible, falls to the ground.[2]

On the other hand it is said, in more than one of the Lives of St. Patrick, that the festival celebrated by King Laoghaire on this occasion

The Feis of Tara celebrated in November.

---

[1] *Scotland.* See Armstrong's *Gaelic Dict.*, voce Bealtuine.

[2] *Ground.* See Introd. *Book of Rights*, p. xlviii. *sq.*

was the *Feis Temrach*[1], or Convention of Tara. If so, it was held, according to all the authorities, on *Samhain*, the last day of October or first of November. A poem[2], attributed to the bard Eochaidh O'Flynn, who died A.D. 984, gives the following account of this festival, which is described as having been of the nature of a Parliament or legislative assembly, but partaking also of a religious character:—

> 'The Feis of Tara, every third year,
> To preserve Laws and Rules,
> Was then regularly convened
> By the illustrious Kings of Erinn.
> . . . . .
> Three days before *Samhain*, always,
> Three days after it, it was a goodly custom, &c.'

This poem, Dr. Petrie says, is perhaps the most antient authentic record which describes the nature of these meetings. They are there spoken of as triennial, although other authorities[3] make them septennial; but this is a question with which we are not now concerned. It is enough for us to remark that whether the

---

[1] *Feis Temrach.* So say the *Vita 2da*, c. 34. *Vita 3tia*, c. 37. the Tripartite, i. c. 50; and Joceline, c. 40. This latter authority says that the feast was called *Rach*; but this is no doubt an error either of Joceline himself, or of his copyists. *Feistemrach*, was mistaken for *Festum Rach*. The word *Feis* signifies a feast; and is translated *cœna* by Tighernach and the Ann. of Ulster; *Temrach* is the genitive case of *Temur*, Tara.

[2] *Poem.* Quoted by Keating, in his account of the reign of Ollamh Fodla, who was King of Ireland, according to O'Flaherty, A.M. 3236.

Keating (ed. Haliday), p. 330. O'Mahony's Transl., p. 232. The original Irish is given by Dr. Petrie, *Tara Hill*, p. 31.

[3] *Authorities.* See the *Book of Rights*, p. 7, and Dr. O'Donovan's Introduction, *loc. cit.* Keating attributes the origin of this assembly to an institution of Ollamh Fodla: afterwards remodelled by Tuathal Techtmar, King of Ireland, A.D. 130, who took portions from the five Provinces of Ireland to form the Province of Meath. *O'Mahony's Keating*, p. 298, sq. Petrie, *On Tara*, p. 32, 33.

Nature of the Pagan Festival.

festival was the *Beltine* or the *Samhain* of the Pagan Irish, it never could have coincided with the Christian Easter.

It is true that some of the Lives[1] speak of this festival as if it were an occasional solemnity only, not of periodical celebration; and one authority asserts that at this time King Laoghaire was celebrating his own birthday.[2] If this be so, the feast may possibly have coincided with St. Patrick's Easter, but there will result no data from that circumstance to enable us to determine the year. It is, on the whole, more probable that the coincidence of the Pagan festival with Easter eve, the opposition between the Paschal fire of St. Patrick and the idolatrous fires of the Druids, together with the other manifestly fabulous stories introduced into the legend, are all circumstances created by the imagination of the biographers, which cannot be dealt with as history.[3]

It is probable, also, that the interview of St. Patrick with King Laoghaire, at the Feis of Tara, if it had any foundation in fact, did not take place until a period of his missionary labours very much later than that to which it is usually assigned. Keating[4] does not record this interview until after his account of Patrick's travels in Munster

Patrick's preaching at Tara, not in the first year of his Mission.

---

[1] *Lives.* So *Vita* 4ta, 'In illo anno contigit ut quandam idololatriæ solemnitatem gentiles celebrarunt,' c. 40. Probus has nearly the same words, i. c. 34.

[2] *Birthday.* This is said in the unpublished Irish Life, preserved in the Book of Lismore, a MS. in the possession of the Duke of Devonshire. See O'Donovan, *Book of Rights*, Introd. p. l.

[3] *History.* See Petrie, *Tara Hill*, p. 82.

[4] *Keating.* In the reign of Laoghaire. O'Mahony's Translation, p. 414.

and Connaught, and after the foundation of Armagh. It is, in fact, the last event noticed by him in his Life of King Laoghaire.

If this may be taken as evidence of his having formed an opinion so contrary to the received Chronology, and even to what we may presume to have been his own natural prejudices on the subject, he may have been influenced by the following note, which occurs at A.D. 461, in the Annals of Ulster:—

| 'Laoghaire filius Neill post coenam Temro annis vii. et mensibus vii. et diebus vii. vixit.' | 'Laoghaire son of Niall after the Feis of Tara lived seven years and seven months and seven days.' |

It can scarcely be doubted that by the *Coena Temro*[1] in this passage the author of these Annals meant the celebrated Feis or Feast of Tara at which St. Patrick appeared before Laoghaire; if so, and if A.D. 463 be the true date of Laoghaire's death, the Tara festival must have taken place in the year 455.

The story of the first Easter a mere legend.

The truth appears to be that the period of Easter was fixed upon by the legendary historians in order to support their imaginary parallel between Patrick and Moses; between the delivery of the Israelites from the power of Pharaoh, and the delivery of the Irish from the Egyptian bondage of Paganism. Muirchu Maccumactheni, in his Life of Patrick, labours everywhere to imitate the style of the Scriptures. His preface, as we have seen,

---

[1] *Coena Temro.* See Petrie, *Tara*, p. 82. The genitive case of Temur, or Temair, is *Temro*, or *Temrach*.

is an imitation of the Preface to St. Luke's Gospel. His account of St. Patrick's dealings with Laoghaire is an imitation partly of the Book of Daniel, and partly of the contest between the Magicians of Egypt and Moses. This latter contest took place at the first Passover of the children of Israel; therefore Patrick's contest with the Druids of Tara ought to take place at the first Christian passover or Easter celebrated by him in Ireland. Muirchu introduces the subject in the following words:—

'Now in those days the Passover (*Pascha*) drew near, which Passover was the first that was celebrated to God in our Egypt of this island, as it was of old celebrated in Gessen[1]; and they took counsel where they should celebrate this first Passover amongst the gentiles to whom God had sent him. And after many counsels about this matter were suggested, at length it seemed good to St. Patrick, being divinely inspired, that this great festival of the Lord, which is as it were the head of all festivals, should be celebrated in that very great plain[2] in which the chief Kingdom (*Regnum*) of these nations was, &c.'

Here our author almost gives us notice that he was about to parallel the first Easter of Patrick in Ireland with the first Passover of Moses in the land of Goshen. The story, therefore, that Patrick's interview with King Laoghaire took place at Easter, and at the first Easter celebrated

---

[1] *Gessen.* So the Latin vulgate renders the name, which in the Hebrew, and in our English Bible, is *Goshen*. The *Book of Armagh* has *ingen esseon*, which seems a mistake for *in Gessen.*

[2] *Great plain.* 'Campus maximus.' So our author uniformly calls the Plain of Bregia. 'Ubi erat regnum maximum nationum harum'—here *regnum* is evidently put for the palace or seat of royal authority. *Book of Armagh*, fol. 3, a.b.

in Ireland, is clearly legend; and we need not embarrass ourselves with the Chronological difficulties it may create.

<small>Patrick lights his Paschal fires at Ferta-fer-Feic.</small>

The Legend, however, as we find it, is this:—Having left his ship at Inbher Colptha, the mouth of the river Boyne, Patrick travelled with his companions to the great plain of Bregia, and arrived about nightfall at Ferta-fer-Feic[1], the place now called Slane, in the County of Meath. There he pitched his tent, and began the solemn devotions of Easter-eve. Our author then proceeds, imitating the Book of Daniel:—

> 'Now there happened, in that year, the idolatrous festival, which the Gentiles were wont to observe, with many incantations and magical inventions, and some other superstitions of idolatry; gathering together the kings, satraps[2], dukes, chieftains, and nobles of the people; summoning also the magicians, enchanters, augurs, with the inventors or teachers of every art and gift unto Laoghaire (as unto King Nabcodonossor of old), to Temoria, which was their Babylon, and on the same night on which St. Patrick was celebrating Easter, they were worshipping and exercising themselves in that Gentile festivity.'

It appears that the Pagan festival began by the extinguishing of every fire[3] in the country; and

---

[1] *Ferta-fer-Feic*, i. e. 'the graves of the men of Fiacc.' The Book of Armagh has '*Ferti* Virorum *Feec*, quæ ut fabulæ ferunt fodorunt [*sic*] viri, id est servi, *Feccol Ferchertni*, qui fuerat unus e novim magis profetis Bregg,' fol. 3, *b, a*. See 4 *Mast.* at A.D. 512, and Dr. O'Donovan's note ᵏ.

[2] *Satraps*. Comp. Dan. iii. 3.

[3] *Extinguishing of every fire*. This supposed Pagan rite seems taken from the ceremonies practised in some churches, on Easter-Eve, of blessing new fire, ' Benedictio novi ignis.' In some places the new fire was taken from oil collected from certain lamps of the Church; in other places it was struck from flint or crystal (possibly the crystal may have been used as a burning glass). This custom appears to have prevailed principally in the Gallican Church. But it was also practised at Rome: Martene tells us that one of the rites there enjoined was that all fires

there was a practice among them (it is said) 'made known by proclamation'[1] to all, that whosoever should on that night kindle a fire, before the king's fire had been kindled on the hill of Tara, 'that soul should be cut off from his people.'[2] But Patrick, disregarding this regulation, lighted his Paschal fire on the hill of Slane; and this being seen from Tara, caused astonishment and indignation. The king demanded who it was that was guilty of such presumption. The magi answered:—

'O King[3] live for ever. This fire which we see shall never be extinguished to all eternity, unless we can put it out to-night. Moreover it shall prevail over all the fires of our wonted observance; and he who has kindled it, and the Kingdom he is introducing, shall prevail over us all and over thyself, and shall win away from thee all the men of thy kingdom; and all kingdoms shall fall down before it, and it shall fill all things, and shall reign for ever and ever.'

This is a manifest imitation of Daniel's explanation of Nebuchadnezzar's image:—'In the days of those kingdoms shall the God of Heaven set up a kingdom, which shall never be destroyed, and His kingdom shall not be given over to another people, but it shall break in pieces and destroy all these kingdoms, and itself shall stand for ever.'[4]

---

[1] *Proclamation.* 'Erat quoque should be extinguished and lighted again from the newly kindled fire of the Church:—' Interim autem omnes qui in civitate sunt vel in villis extinguantur ignes, et benedicto igne accendantur.' *De Antiquis Eccl. Ritibus*, tom. iii., lib. iv., c. 24, p. 144, 145.

quidam mos apud illos per edictum omnibus intimatus, &c.' *Book of Armagh*, fol. 3, *b, b.* Comp. Dan. iii. 4.

[2] *People.* 'Periret anima ejus de populo suo.' Exod. xii. 15.

[3] *O King.* See Dan. iii. 9.

[4] *For ever.* Dan. ii. 44 (*Vulgate*).

Patrick's contest with the Magi [CHAP. III.

His interview with King Laoghaire.

Our author proceeds, still imitating the Scripture:—

'Now when King Laoghaire heard these things he was greatly troubled, as Herod[1] was of old, and all the city of Temoria with him; and he answered and said, This shall not be so, but we will now go and see the end of the matter, and we will take and kill the men who are doing such wickedness against our Kingdom.

'Having therefore yoked nine chariots, according to the tradition of their gods, and taking with him those two magi for the contest who were the best of them all, namely, Lucetmael and Lochru, Laoghaire proceeded in the latter part of that night from Tara to Ferti-fer-Fecc, turning the faces of the men and horses to the left, the direction that was most suitable to them.'[2]

The Druids would not permit the king to enter the enclosure in which Patrick's fires were burning, lest by some magical virtue he should be constrained to adopt the new religion. They counselled that Patrick should be sent for, and that no person should rise up at his coming or pay him any respect, lest those who did so should believe on him. Patrick came, and seeing the chariots and horses he entered the assembly intoning the verse, 'Some put their trust in chariots and some in horses, but we will remember the Name of the Lord our God.' One only of the king's attendants disobeyed the injunctions of the magi, and rose up from respect to St. Patrick. This was Ercc filius Dego[3], afterwards

Conversion of Ercc filius Dego.

---

[1] *Herod.* See St. Matt. ii. 3.
[2] *Suitable to them.* The left hand being deemed unlucky.
[3] *Filius Dego*, i.e. Son of Deg, or Decc; *Dego* being the genitive case. His genealogy up to Rudraighe, King of Ireland, in eighteen generations, is preserved.

a bishop, 'whose relics,' says our author, 'are now venerated in the city which is called Slane.'[1] Then follows the contest of Patrick with the magi of King Laoghaire, intended, as we have already said, to imitate the contest of Moses with the magi of Pharaoh. It is unworthy of any attention as history. The magus Lochru begins the contest by blaspheming the Catholic Faith. Patrick fixed his eyes upon him, as Peter upon Simon Magus, and prayed that he might be lifted out and die.[2] Immediately Lochru is lifted up into the air, and falling down again his brains are dashed out upon a stone[3] in sight of all.

Contest of Patrick with the Magi.

The king is furious, and commands his people to seize Patrick. But the saint intones the Psalm, 'Let God arise, let His enemies be scattered; let them also that hate Him flee before Him.' Immediately a thick darkness falls upon the Pagan hosts, with an earthquake; they kill each other; horses and chariots fly over the plain, and at length a few, half dead, escape to the mountain Monduirn. The king and queen remain before Patrick.

---

[1] *Slane.* 'Cujus nunc reliquiæ adorantur in illa civitate, quæ vocatur Slane.' *Book of Armagh,* fol. 4, *a, b.* Probus copies these words, substituting 'venerantur' for 'adorantur,' lib. i., c. 37.

[2] *Die.* 'Hunc autem intuens turvo oculo talia promentem, sanctus Patricius, ut quondam Petrus de Simone, cum quadam potentia et magno clamore confidenter ad Dominum dixit, Domine qui omnia potes, et in tua potestate consistunt, quique me missisti huc, hic impius qui blasfemat nomen tuum elevetur nunc foras, et cito moriatur.' *Book of Armagh,* ibid.

[3] *A stone.* Tirechan tells us that he had himself seen the stone, and that it lay in the south-east boundaries, meaning apparently of the Palace of Tara. 'Et est lapis illius in oris australibus orientalibusque usque in presentem diem, et conspexi illum oculis meis.' *Ibid,* fol. 10. *a, b.*

The queen approaches, and humbly begs the life and pardon of the king. The king forced by fear kneels before the saint; but intending with treachery to kill him, as they were about to separate, recalls St. Patrick. Patrick had with him eight companions, one of whom was a boy. He knew the king's evil purpose, and as he returned and appeared before the king, he and his companions suddenly disappeared, and the gentiles saw only eight deer and a fawn going to the wilderness. The king, sad, terrified, and humbled, set out for Tara about daylight with the few of his attendants who had escaped.

<small>Patrick appears at Tara on Easter Sunday.</small>

The next day was Easter Sunday. It was a very great feast[1] with Laoghaire and his court. In the midst of their festivity, the doors being shut[2], Patrick and five of his companions appeared amongst them. None rose up at his approach except *Dubhtach Macculugil*, or Maccu Lugair, the king's chief bard, who had with him a certain young bard or poet named *Fecc* (or Fiacc), afterwards a wondrous bishop, whose relics[3], in the time of our author, were venerated at Sletty. Dubhtach was the first who believed in God on that day, and it was counted unto him for righteousness.

---

[1] *Feast.* 'Festus enim dies maximus apud eos erat.' *Ibid.*, fol. 4. *b. b.*

[2] *Shut.* 'Coram omnibus nationibus, hostiis claussis, secundum id quod de Christo legitur.' *Ibid.*

[3] *Relics.* 'Apud quem tunc temporis ibi erat quidam adoliscens poeta nomine *Fecc*, qui postea mirabilis episcopus fuit, cujus reliquiæ adorantur *hi Sleibti*. Hic, ut dixi, *Dubhtach*, solus ex gentibus in honorem Sancti Patricii surrexit, et benedixit ei sanctus. Credidit que primus in illa die Deo, et repputatum est ei ad justitiam.' *Ibid.* The Fecc or Fiacc, here mentioned, Bishop of Sletty, is the reputed author of the Hymn in praise of St. Patrick, already so often mentioned.

The Druid or magus Lucetmael pours poison into Patrick's cup. Patrick blesses the cup, and the fluid it contained congeals. He inverts it; and the poisonous drops fall out. The wine again becomes fluid and harmless.[1]

His contest with the Druid Lucetmael.

The Druid then by his incantations covers the plain with snow, but admits his inability to remove the enchantment until the same hour on the morrow. Patrick, saying to the Druid, 'Thou canst do evil, but not good,' blesses the plain, and the snow disappears.

Again Lucetmael brings on a thick darkness, but is unable to remove it. Patrick prays and blesses the plain. Straightway the darkness vanishes, and the sun shines forth, to the admiration and joy of all the beholders.

Some other equally marvellous stories follow, which we need not stop to transcribe. The reader can now judge how much of this narrative deserves to be treated as history. It is reduced apparently to this single fact, that Patrick, at some period of his missionary labours, appeared in the Court of King Laoghaire, and preached Christ before the courtiers of Temoria.

On this occasion Patrick is said to have composed a Hymn[2] in the Irish language, which was

Patrick's Irish Hymn.

---

[1] *Harmless.* This is copied from the well-known legend of St. John and the poisoned cup.

[2] *Hymn.* It is preserved in the Irish Book of Hymns, and was first published by Dr. Petrie, who has added a Latin and English translation, with a valuable grammatical analysis by the late eminent Celtic scholar, Dr. John O'Donovan. *Essay on Tara Hill,* p. 57. Dr. Petrie says that some portions of this Hymn are still remembered by the peasantry, and repeated at bed-time, as a protection from evil. *Ibid.,* p. 69.

celebrated for many ages, and probably did not fall into oblivion until after the English invasion. This Hymn is of the nature of what was called a *Lorica*[1], that is to say, a prayer to protect those who devoutly recite it, from bodily and spiritual dangers. It is undoubtedly of great antiquity, although it may now be difficult, if not impossible, to adduce *proof* in support of the tradition that St. Patrick was its author.[2] The following literal translation of it may be interesting to some readers:—

1. I bind to myself[3] to-day,
    The strong power of an invocation[4] of the Trinity,
    The faith of the Trinity in Unity,
    The Creator of the elements.

2. I bind to myself to-day,
    The power of the Incarnation of Christ, with that of his Baptism,
    The power of the Crucifixion, with that of his Burial,

---

[1] *Lorica.* See above, p. 124.

[2] *Author.* It was called *Feth Fiadha*, 'the instruction of the deer,' because it was said to have been sung by St. Patrick when he and his companions were saved from the vengeance of King Laoghaire, by appearing to the pagan courtiers as deer escaping to the forest. See p. 424, and Petrie, *ib.*, p. 56; also *Festivities of Conan*, edited by Mr. O'Kearney (*Ossian. Soc.*), p. 190, *n*.

[3] *I bind to myself.* The first word of this Hymn, '*Atomriug*,' was mistaken by Dr. Petrie and Dr. O'Donovan, for an obsolete form of the dative of *Temur*, Temoria, or Tara, and was by them translated 'at Tara.' We cannot now regret this error, as to it we owe the publication of this curious poem in the *Essay on Tara*. But it is certainly a mistake, and was acknowledged as such by Dr. O'Donovan before his death. The word is a verb; *ad-dom-riug*, i.e. *ad-riug*, adjungo, with the infixed pronoun *dom*, to me (see Zeuss, *Gramm. Celt.*, p. 336); the verb *riug*, which occurs in the forms *ad-riug*, *con-riug*, signifies to join. The true analysis of this word was first pointed out by Mr. Whitley Stokes1 See an article in the *Saturday Review*, Sept. 5, 1857, p. 225, where a translation of this hymn (from the pen of that eminent scholar) is given.

[4] *Invocation.* Drs. O'Donovan and Petrie translate the original word *togairm*, invoco: but it is a substantive, not a verb: and so also in the next line they render *cretim*, credo, whereas it is *fides*. See Zeuss, p. 88. They were led into these mistakes by the want of a verb in the sentence, resulting from their having translated *Atomriug*, 'at Tara.'

The power of the Resurrection, with the Ascension,
The power of the coming to the Sentence of Judgement.

3. I bind to myself to-day,
   The power of the love of Seraphim,
   In the obedience of Angels,
   In the hope[1] of Resurrection unto reward,
   In the prayers of the noble Fathers,
   In the predictions of the Prophets,
   In the preaching of Apostles,
   In the faith of Confessors,
   In the purity of Holy Virgins,
   In the acts of Righteous Men.

4. I bind to myself to-day,
   The power of Heaven,
   The light of the Sun,
   The whiteness of Snow,
   The force of Fire,
   The flashing of Lightning,
   The velocity of Wind,
   The depth of the Sea,
   The stability of the Earth,
   The hardness of Rocks.

5. I bind to myself to-day,
   The Power of God to guide me[2],
   The Might of God to uphold me,
   The Wisdom of God to teach me,
   The Eye of God to watch over me,
   The Ear of God to hear me,
   The Word of God to give me speech,
   The Hand of God to protect me,
   The Way of God to prevent me,
   The Shield of God to shelter me,
   The Host of God to defend me,
      Against the snares of demons,
      Against the temptations of vices,

---

[1] *Hope.* The word *frescisin* in Dr. Petrie's text ought to be *frescisiu.* See Zeuss, p. 268.

[2] *To guide me.* Lit. 'for my guidance,' and so on in the following lines, 'for my preservation,' 'for my teaching,' &c.

Against the lusts of nature,
Against every man who meditates injury to me,
Whether far or near,
With few or with many.

6. I have set around me all these powers,
Against every hostile savage power,
Directed against my body and my soul,
Against the incantations of false prophets,
Against the black laws of heathenism,
Against the false laws of heresy,
Against the deceits of idolatry,
Against the spells of women, and smiths, and druids,
Against all knowledge which blinds the soul of man.

7. Christ protect me to-day,
Against poison, against burning,
Against drowning, against wound,
That I may receive abundant reward.

8. Christ[1] with me, Christ before me,
Christ behind me, Christ within me,
Christ beneath me, Christ above me,
Christ at my right, Christ at my left,
Christ in the fort,
Christ in the chariot-seat,
Christ in the poop.[2]

9. Christ in the heart of every man who thinks of me,
Christ in the mouth of every man who speaks to me,
Christ in every eye that sees me,
Christ in every ear that hears me.

10. I bind to myself to-day,
The strong power of an invocation of the Trinity,
The faith of the Trinity in Unity,
The Creator of the Elements.

---

[1] *Christ.* i.e. 'May Christ be with me,' 'May Christ be before me,' &c. There is a passage not unlike this in Bishop Andrewes's *Preces Privatæ*, p. 127. (*Anglo-Catholic Library.* Oxford, 1853).

[2] *Poop.* i.e. Christ when I am in the fort (at home). Christ when I am in the chariot-seat (travelling by land); and in the poop (travelling by water). See Stokes, *Irish Glosses* (580), p. 81.

11. Domini est salus,[1]
Domini est salus,
Christi est salus,
Salus tua Domine sit semper nobiscum.

That this Hymn[2] is a composition of great antiquity cannot be questioned. It is written in a very antient dialect of the Irish Celtic. It was evidently composed during the existence of Pagan usages in the country. It makes no allusion to Arianism, or any of the heresies prevalent in the continental Church. It notices no doctrine or practice of the Church that is not known to have existed before the fifth century. In its style and diction, although written in a different language, there is nothing very dissimilar to the Confession and the Letter about Coroticus, and nothing absolutely inconsistent with the opinion that it may be by the same author.

Add to this, as Dr. Petrie observes, that in the seventh century, when Tirechan composed his annotations, it was certainly believed to be the composition of St. Patrick. That author tells us that in his time there were four honours paid to St. Patrick in all monasteries and churches throughout the whole of Ireland. The first of these was that the festival of St. Patrick in

Antiquity and authenticity of the Hymn.

---

[1] *Salus.* This stanza is in Latin in the original Hymn.
[2] *Hymn.* An admirable poetical translation of this hymn, by the late talented but unfortunate James Clarence Mangan, appeared some years ago in *Duffy's Magazine*. It is founded on Dr. Petrie's version, and retains the error of translating *Atomriug,* 'at Tara.' But it preserves in a wonderful manner the *tone* and spirit of the original. It has been reprinted in a volume of Mangan's collected 'Poems, with Biographical Introduction, by John Mitchell.' New York, 1859, p. 413.

spring, 'sollempnitas dormitationis ejus,' was honoured, for three days and three nights, with all good cheer (except flesh[1] meat), as if Patrick was himself alive at the door. Secondly, that there was a proper Preface for him in the Mass. The third and fourth are thus stated:—

> ' iii. Ymnum ejus per totum tempus cantare.
> iiii. Canticum ejus Scotticum semper canere.'[2]

'To sing his Hymn for the whole time,' and 'to sing his Scotic Hymn always.' 'His Hymn' here mentioned is undoubtedly the Latin Hymn by Sechnall or Secundinus, and 'his Irish or Scotic Hymn' is that of which we have just given a translation. The former was sung during the whole time of his festival, the latter always, or at all times.

Internal evidence is in favour of the antiquity and authenticity of this composition. The prayer which it contains for protection against 'women[3], smiths, and Druids,' together with the invocation of the power of the sky, the sun, fire, lightning, wind, and other created things, proves that notwithstanding the undoubted piety and fervent Christian faith of the author, he had not yet fully shaken off all Pagan

---

[1] *Except flesh.* Because the 17th of March falls within the limits of Lent. As there were other feasts of St. Patrick, our author distinguishes the 17th of March by calling it the 'Solempnitas dormitationis ejus in medio veris.'

[2] *Canere.* See *Book of Armagh*, fol. 16, *a. a.* Petrie, *On Tara*, p. 68. *Irish Book of Hymns*, p. 50.

[3] *Women.* See above, p. 122. The magical powers supposed to belong to aged women and blacksmiths are well known. A belief in them continues to prevail in some parts of Ireland and Scotland to the present day. Petrie, *On Tara*, p. 69.

prejudices. But this class of superstitions lingered longer than any other in men's minds, and was with greater difficulty eradicated. Dr. Petrie suggests that, on this account, the Hymn may have been formerly regarded as of doubtful orthodoxy, and therefore, he says, no allusion to it occurs in the later Lives of St. Patrick. Colgan, he adds, notices it only in his list of St. Patrick's writings. But it is doubtful whether the authors of the later Lives had ever heard of it. From its language it was inaccessible to Joceline. The author of the Tripartite Life speaks of it very distinctly. 'Then,' he says[1], 'St. Patrick composed in the vernacular language that Hymn which is commonly called *Fedh Fiadha*, and by others the *Lorica* of Patrick: and it is held in great esteem by the Irish ever since; for it is believed, and proved by long experience, to preserve from imminent dangers both of soul and body those who devoutly recite it.' These words show no distrust in the orthodoxy of the Hymn, and were evidently written when it was well known, and the recitation of it still generally practised with faith in its efficacy. A belief in the magical power of witches, blacksmiths, and Druids would scarcely have been deemed inconsistent with orthodoxy in the age when the Lives were written, and not even perhaps in the time of Colgan.[2]

[1] *He says.* Quoted by Petrie, *On Tara*, p. 55.
[2] *Colgan.* It is more than probable that Colgan had never seen the text of this hymn; for it is not found in the *Irish Book of Hymns*, now in the library of St. Isidore's Convent, at Rome, which was the copy that Colgan used.

The Hymn exhibits the real character of St. Patrick's teaching.

We may not, therefore, err very much in taking this Hymn as a fair representation of St. Patrick's faith and teaching. Whether it was actually written by him or not, it was certainly composed at a period not very distant from his times, with a view to represent and put forth his sentiments. It exhibits in a much more probable and favourable light the character of the missionary from whom Ireland received the faith, than that in which he is made to appear in the Legendary Lives. In them he stands before us as a great magician, bringing down judgements from heaven, causing sudden destruction to fall upon his enemies, terrifying, not persuading; a magus more powerful than the magi of the Pagan king. But in the Hymn, notwithstanding some tincture of superstition, we find the pure and undoubted truths of Christianity, a firm faith in the protecting providence and power of God; and Christ made all and in all.

The conversion of King Laoghaire not sincere.

King Laoghaire, we are told, was influenced by carnal fear and not by conviction in his submission to the new doctrines. Patrick, if we credit the biographers, had caused the death of both his most eminent Magi. The Druid Lochru was miraculously lifted up into the air, and his brains dashed out upon a stone. Lucetmael, the other magus, having submitted to an ordeal by fire, was defeated and consumed.[1] No

---

[1] *Consumed.* The story is this:— A hut was constructed partly of green partly of dry wood: the magus was placed in the part made of green wood: the boy Binen, who had followed St. Patrick, was placed in the part made of dry wood. The boy had on the magical garment of the

wonder that the king should have been greatly enraged, and should have rushed upon Patrick with intent to kill him.

'But God,' says the old biographer Muirchu, in the Book of Armagh,

Patrick curses King Laoghaire.

'—— but God hindered him, at the prayer of Patrick; for at Patrick's word, the wrath of God fell upon his head, and the King feared greatly, and his heart was troubled, and all the city with him. Therefore, calling together the elders and his whole senate, King Laoghaire said unto them, 'It is better for me to believe than to die.' They then took counsel, and at the advice of his people, he believed on that day, and turned to the Lord, the everlasting God; and many others believed there. And Saint Patrick said unto the King, 'Because thou didst resist my teaching and hast been a stumbling-block unto me, although the days of thine own reign may be prolonged, none of thy seed shall be King for ever.' Then Saint Patrick according to the command of the Lord Jesus, teaching the gentiles, and baptising them in the name of the Father, and of the Son, and of the Holy Ghost, went forth from Temoria, and preached, the Lord working with him and confirming the word with signs following.'[1]

The prediction that none of Laoghaire's descendants should sit upon his throne was not verified. His son Lugaidh was King of Ireland for five and twenty years. The Tripartite Life[2] endeavours to account for this failure by adding to the story, that an exception was made in favour

The prediction not fulfilled.

Druid: Lucetmael was clothed in the garment (casula) of St. Patrick. The hut was then set on fire, but the result was, 'orante Patricio,' that the magus, in the green wood chamber, was burnt to death, the casula of Patrick remaining untouched by the fire; and the boy Binen came forth uninjured, 'secundum quod de tribus pueris dictum est, non tetigit eum ignis neque contristatus est,' &c., although the garment of the magus, in which he was clothed, was utterly consumed. *Book of Armagh*, fol. 5, b.a. fol. 10. a.a.

[1] *Following. Ibid.* fol. 5, b.b. Here we have an imitation of St. Mark, xvi. 20.

[2] *Tripartite Life.* Lib. i. c. 67. *Tr. Th.*, p. 128.

of Lugaidh, then in his mother's womb: the Queen, his mother, having begged on her knees an exemption from the malediction for the unborn babe. Patrick replied that the malediction should not hurt him, provided by his own demerits he did not bring upon himself a further and special curse.

But this is a mode of meeting the difficulty which can scarcely be deemed satisfactory. It is not mentioned in the other Lives, not even in the modern one by Joceline. Were the other biographers ignorant that Lugaidh was the son of King Laoghaire? Or have they transferred to King Laoghaire a prophecy which was originally spoken of his son Lugaidh?

The story probably tampered with. That there has been some tampering with this part of the story, will be evident from the following account of St. Patrick's interview with the last-named sovereign. It occurs in a Tract, of which we have already spoken, 'On the Kings of Ireland since Christianity,' preserved in the Book of Lecan[1]:—

> 'It was in the time of Lugaidh that Patrick came into Ireland. And he went to Temur (Tara) to the place where Lugaidh was, and offered unto him wheat without tillage, and constant milk with cattle during his time, and heaven at the end of his life, and that he should have luck of hounds and horses, and of a queen. But Lugaidh did not consent to this, and because he did not, Patrick cursed him and cursed his queen, namely, Aillinn, daughter of Aengus Mac Nadfraich, King of Munster; so that from that time there is ill luck of queens in Temur, and

---

[1] *Book of Lecan.* See above, p. 396. An extract from this Tract was first printed in the original Irish, with a translation by Dr. Petrie, *Tara Hill*, p. 86.

CHAP. III.] *Lugaidh, son of Laoghaire.* 435

Temur has also been without success in hounds. And Lugaidh son of Laoghaire, died at Achadh Farcha[1], in consequence of the curse of the Tailcend, for a flash of lightning struck him dead from heaven for having rejected the Tailcend.'

Here it is expressly stated that Patrick came to Ireland in the reign of Lugaidh. This is contrary to all the authorities, and would place the arrival of Patrick after the year 463, when Lugaidh succeeded to the throne. But this is much too late; and the suspicion arises that we should read 'in the time of Laoghaire,' instead of 'in the time of Lugaidh,' in this passage. Dr. Petrie, indeed, has suggested that there may have been two missionaries both named Patrick, one of whom appeared in the reign of Laoghaire, and the other in that of his son Lugaidh. But if we give any weight to this document, we must take it according to what the author intended; and it is evident that the author intended to speak only of the great St. Patrick. The Patrick who appeared before Lugaidh is called 'the Tailcend,' or 'Shaven-head,' the well-known name[2] of the apostle Patrick; and there cannot be a doubt that the Patrick whose denunciation of Laoghaire we have just noticed, was, according to all the authorities in which the transaction is recorded, the apostle St. Patrick also.

Patrick's interview with Lugaidh.

The truth seems to be that the similarity of two transactions has led to confusion; the denunciation of King Laoghaire became mixed up

A confusion between the two interviews.

---

[1] *Achadh Farcha*, i.e. 'The Field of Lightning.' See *Four Masters*, A.D. 503, and O'Donovan's note. [2] *Name.* See above, p. 411.

F F 2

with some particulars taken from the denunciation of King Lugaidh, son of Laoghaire. In the shorter and older form of the Tract 'On the Kings of Ireland since Christianity,' preserved in the Book of Leinster[1], the only mention of St. Patrick in the reign of Lugaidh is the notice of his death, '[Quies] Patricii Scotorum episcopi.' We have, therefore, good reason to conclude that the transcriber and interpolater of the same tract in the Book of Lecan made some clerical blunder when he said that Patrick came to Ireland in the reign of Lugaidh.[2]

Both kings unbelievers. Be this, however, as it may, it is evident that both kings, although generally counted among the Christian kings of Ireland, did in fact continue to the end of their lives obstinate unbelievers. It does not appear that Lugaidh ever so much as professed Christianity. His father Laoghaire is represented as having hypocritically submitted to receive baptism from motives of political expediency. But we happen to have very strong and conclusive evidence that he died nevertheless in Paganism.

King Laoghaire died a Pagan. The claim made by the kings of the Hy Neill race to exact from the kings of Leinster an

---

[1] *Leinster.* See above, p. 184.
[2] *Lugaidh.* Dr. Petrie (*Tara*, p. 88) suggests that O'Flaherty and others, who must have been acquainted with this passage in the *Book of Lecan,* suppressed all notice of it designedly, from the impossibility of making it square with the received history and chronology of St. Patrick's life. But it is much more likely that they regarded it as a passage corrupted by mistakes of transcription, and therefore unworthy of notice. Such mistakes are of very common occurrence in the *Book of Lecan*; and the passage in question might be set right either by reading Laoghaire for Lugaidh, as already suggested, or else by omitting the words 'to Ireland.'

annual tribute of cattle, called the Boromean tribute, was a perpetual source of feud and bloodshed.[1] The year before his death, Laoghaire, in an attempt to enforce this tribute, was taken prisoner at a place called Ath-dara[2], a ford on the river Barrow. To obtain his liberty he 'gave the guarantees,' we are told[3], 'of the sun, and of the wind, and of the elements, to the men of Leinster, that he would never again come against them.' But the next year, in violation of his engagement, he renewed the war; 'and the sun and the wind killed him,' say the Annalists, 'because he had outraged them,' or violated the oath made upon them.

Killed by the Sun and Wind.

Perhaps this may not be considered an absolute proof of the King's Paganism. To swear by the sun and wind was apparently no doubt Paganism. But is it not also Paganism to represent the sun and wind as taking vengeance for the king's breach of his oath, and visiting him with death for his perjury? Yet this is the language copied by all the monastic Annalists, and even by the Four Masters, Franciscan friars, writing in the seventeenth century.[4]

---

[1] *Bloodshed.* See *Four Masters*, A.D. 106, and Dr. O'Donovan's note; *Hy Fiachrach*, p. 32.

[2] *Ath-dara*, 'Ford of the oak tree.' This place is not to be confounded with another of the same name, now *Adare*, in the County of Limerick. See the more full account of this transaction, quoted by Dr. Petrie from the *Leabhar na huidhre*, *Tara Hill*, p. 169.

[3] *Told.* See *Four Masters*, at A.D. 457. The *Annals of Ulster*, at 458,

thus record this event: 'Cath Athodara for Laighaire re Laignibh [the battle of Ath-dara was gained over Laoghaire by the Leinster-men], in quo et ipse captus est, sed tunc dimissus est jurans per solem et ventum se boves eis dimissurum' [i.e. that he would remit the tribute]. These annals also assign another date, A.D. 461, to the battle of Ath-dara, and 462 (= 463) to the death of Laoghaire.

[4] *Century.* We have here a proof

438   *King Laoghaire buried*   [CHAP. III.

Laoghaire buried after the customs of the heathen.

But we have stronger and more conclusive evidence. Tirechan, in his 'Annotations,' preserved in the Book of Armagh[1], mentions a second visit of Patrick to King Laoghaire in the following words:—

'And he [Patrick] went again to the city of Tara[2], to Laoghaire son of Niall, because he had made a covenant with him that he should not be put to death in his reign[3]; but he could not believe, saying, 'For Niall my father did not permit me to believe, but [commanded] that I should be buried on the ramparts of Tara (*in cacuminibus Temro*), as men stand up in battle;' for the gentiles are wont to be buried in their sepulchres armed, with weapons ready, face to face, until the day of *Erdathe*, as the Magi call it, that is, the Day of Judgment of the Lord. 'I the son of Niall [must be buried] after this fashion, as the Son of Dunlaing [was buried] at Maistin, in the plain of Liffey, because of the endurance of our hatred.'[4]

Another version of the same story, first printed by Dr. Petrie, from the antient Irish Manuscript

of the remark already made, that this class of superstitions, like the belief in witchcraft, lingered in the Church to a late period, and that an invocation of the sky, the sea, the sun, and wind, such as we find in the Hymn of St. Patrick, would not have been necessarily regarded two centuries ago as inconsistent with orthodoxy.

[1] *Book of Armagh*, fol. 10, *a. b.* Petrie, *On Tara*, p. 170.

[2] *Tara*. 'Ad civitatem Temro,' the city of Temur; *Temro* being the genitive case: we have also *Temrach*, another form of the genitive. See above, p. 416 *n*, 418 *n*.

[3] *Reign*. Or in his kingdom, 'in regno illius.'

[4] *Hatred*. 'Pro duritate odivi,' i.e. odii: *odivum* for *odium*. The Dunlaing (genitive *Dunlinge*) here mentioned was the King of Leinster, by whom the royal girls were murdered at the place called Claenferta,

at Tara, A.D. 222 (Tigh.) or 241 (4 M.). This outrage laid the foundation of the *odium* spoken of. Petrie, *On Tara*, p. 36. O'Flaherty, *Ogyg.*, p. 335. Maistin is the place now called Mullaghmast, antiently a palace or rath of the Kings of Leinster. The concluding clause is obscure. 'Ego filius Neill et filius Dunlinge imMaistin in campo Liphi pro duritate odivi, ut est hoc.' *Duritas* signifies perpetuity, everlastingness; but it might mean, hardness, bitterness. His enemy having been buried in his armour in his royal fortress, Laoghaire felt bound to follow the injunctions of his father, and to be buried at Tara in the same way, to show the implacability of the feud. This Pagan mode of interment continued to a late period. Eoghan Beul, King of Connaught, ordered himself to be so buried, A.D. 537. O'Donovan, *Hy Fiachrach*, p. 472.

called the *Leabhar na huidhre*, gives this commentary on the foregoing passage of Tirechan, which the author evidently had before him:—

'The body of Laoghaire was brought afterwards from the South[1], and interred with his armour of valour[2], in the south-east of the outer rampart of the royal Rath of Laoghaire at Tara, with his face turned southwards upon the men of Leinster, as fighting with them, for he was the enemy of the Leinster-men in his lifetime.'

There is curious internal evidence of authenticity in these traditions. It is clear that King Laoghaire never was a real convert to Christianity; and that the historians who have reckoned him among the Christian kings of Ireland have mistaken or corrupted[3] the facts of history.

Leaving the court of King Laoghaire, Patrick, we are told, went to Aonach[4] Tailltenn, now Telltown, in the County of Meath, where there was at the time a great concourse of people, with games and sports of various kinds. There Carbri, or Cairpri, son of Niall, brother of Laoghaire, sought to kill him, and caused his attendants to be beaten in the river Sele, now the Blackwater. Patrick denounced him as 'the enemy of God,' and said to him, 'Thy seed shall serve the seed

Patrick's interview with Carbri Mac Neill.

---

[1] *South.* That is from Athdara, which, if it was on the Barrow, must have been south of Tara.

[2] *Armour of valour.* 'Co narm gaiscuid,' *lit.* 'With arms of heroship or championship.'

[3] *Corrupted.* Colgan (*Tr. Th.*, p. 173, *col.* 2, *n.* 28) questions the story of Laoghaire having been buried as a heathen. But his reasons are singularly weak. He goes so far as to maintain, on the authority of the Scholia on Aengus, that Niall, the father of King Laoghaire, had died a Christian, and was even regarded as a saint. But there is nothing of the kind in the Dublin or Brussels copies of those Scholia.

[4] *Aonach.* This word signifies a fair, or assembly. It is rendered *Agon regale* by Tirechan. *Book of Armagh*, fol. 10, *a. b.*

of thy brethren, and there shall be no king of thy race for ever. Moreover, there shall never hereafter be large fish in the river Sele.'

<small>Another unfulfilled prophecy.</small>
It is remarkable that we have here also a prophecy that was not fulfilled. For Tuathal Maelgarb, the grandson of Carbri, was king of Ireland from A.D. 533 to 544. It is difficult to account for such oversights in the inventors of these legends. The author of the Tripartite Life endeavours to explain this by a story too silly to require notice.[1]

<small>Conversion of Conall Mac Neill.</small>
Patrick next met with Conall mac Neill, surnamed *Gulban*[2], the youngest brother of King Laoghaire, who received him in his own house with great joy, and was baptised. He gave the site of a church, sixty feet long, for the God of Patrick, measuring it with his own feet. It was afterwards called 'the Great Church of Patrick;' and Patrick blessed him, saying, ' The seed of thy brethren shall serve thy seed for ever; and thou must shew kindness to my successors after me for ever, and thy children and children's children to

---

[1] *Notice.* See *Vit. Trip.*, lib. ii. c. 27. The story is briefly this:— The mother of King Tuathal, then pregnant, is brought to Patrick; he raises his hand to bless her, but stops short, perceiving by inspiration that the child in her womb is of the accursed family of Carbri. But inasmuch as he had raised his hand to bless, Tuathal succeeded to the throne, and was the last king of his race. See Colgan, *Vit.* 3*a*, note 45, *Tr. Th.* p. 31. This story is exactly similar to the explanation given of the failure of St. Patrick's prophecy against the posterity of King Laoghaire. See above, p. 433.

[2] *Gulban.* He had this name from the mountain called Binn Gulban, now corruptly Binn Bulbin, in the parish of Drumcliffe, County of Sligo, where he was fostered. *Battle of Magh Rath*, p. 312 *n*. From him the antient tribes inhabiting the County of Donegal were called Cinel-Conaill, and Tir-Conaill. He was the ancestor of St. Columba and many saints, as well as of many of the kings of Ireland, down to the eleventh century.

Baptism of Ercc.

my believing children, must do what is legitimate for ever.'[1] He added, 'If this church be encroached on (*diminuatur*), thy reign shall not be long nor durable.'

These words are worthy of notice. It appears from them that this prophecy had for its object to support the jurisdiction of the see of Armagh. The legend must have been written at a time when that jurisdiction was called in question, or at least was not universally received in Ireland.

We must now pass over all that we find in the Lives of St. Patrick of his missionary labours in Bregia, and other parts of the territory belonging to the Southern Hy Neill. We have the names of a great number of Churches said to have been founded by him in that district. Many of these, however, are undoubtedly of later date. The bishops said to have been ordained by him, and left in those churches, belong for the most part, to the century, or second century, after his death. The dates[2] of their obits recorded in the Irish annals have betrayed the truth. But some of them may have been real disciples and contemporaries of St. Patrick.

Churches founded in Bregia.

The conversion of Ercc mac Dego, who afterwards became an eminent bishop of Slane, has been already[3] mentioned. Tirechan gives the following account of his baptism:—

Baptism of Ercc.

---

[1] *For ever.* This passage is obscure. 'Et tu misericordiam debes facere heredibus meis post me in seculum, et filii tui et filiorum tuorum filiis meis credulis legitimum sempiternum.' *Book of Armagh,* fol. 10, *a.b.*

[2] *The dates.* See Lanigan, vol. i. p. 237, *sq.* Many of them appear to have died at the end of the 6th or middle of the 7th century.

[3] *Already.* See above, p. 422.

'And he [Patrick] entered into the King's Palace, and they rose not up before him, except one man only, namely, Hercus Sacrilegus.[1] And he said unto him, 'Why didst thou alone rise up to me in honour of my God?' And Hercus said, 'Why I know not — I see sparks of fire going up from thy lips to my lips.' Then the Saint said unto him, 'Wilt thou receive the Baptism of the Lord, which I have with me?' He answered, 'I will receive it.' And they came to the fountain *Loigles* (as it is in the Scotish tongue, with us the *Calf of the Cities*[2];) and when he had opened his book, and had baptised the man Hercus, he heard men behind his back mocking him one to another, about that matter; for they knew not what he had done. And he baptised many thousand[3] men on that day. And between some of the baptismal sentences, behold, he overheard two chieftains conversing together behind him; and one said to the other, 'It is true what thou saidst to me a year ago, that thou wouldst come here at this time. Tell me, I pray thee, thy name, and the name of thy father, and of thy territory, and of thy land, and where thy home is.' And the other answering, said, 'I am [Endeus] son of Amolngid[4], son of Fiachra, son of Eochaidh, from the western regions, from the plain of Domnon, and from the Wood of Fochloth.' And when Patrick heard the name of the Wood of Fochloth, he rejoiced greatly, and said unto Endeus, son of Amolngid, 'I also will go with thee, if I be alive, because the Lord said unto me to go.' And Endeus said, 'Thou shalt not go forth with me, lest we be both slain.' And the Saint said, 'On the contrary, thou shalt never reach thine own country alive unless I go with thee, and thou shalt not

---

[1] *Sacrilegus.* This word is generally used in a bad sense. Dr. Petrie suggests that it may here mean a lawyer. *Tara Hill*, p. 167. Erc is called a magus, *Book of Armagh*, fol. 4, *a. b.* He died, according to Tighernach, A.D. 513. Tirechan says, 'in qua [ecclesia Cerne] sepultus est Hercus qui portavit mortalitatem magnam.' *Ibid.*, fol. 10, *a. a.* This seems to mean that he died of the great pestilence, which first appeared about A.D. 530.

[2] *Calf of the Cities.* 'Vitulus civitatum.' *Laog*, a calf; *Les*, a fort or civitas. This was a well within the fort or enclosure of Tara. See Petrie, *Tara*, p. 166.

[3] *Many thousand.* 'Tot milia hominum.' This seems a quotation from the Confession, sect. 22. *Villan.* p. 206. *Ware*, p. 19.

[4] *Amolngid.* Or Amalgaidh; pronounced Awley. From him the barony of Tir-awley, Co. of Mayo, takes its name. See his genealogy, *Introd.* Table I. p. 249. Magh Domnon, in Iorrus Domhnann, is now the barony of Erris, in the N.W. of the Co. of Mayo. See O'Donovan's *Tribes and Customs* of *Hy Fiachrach*, p. 462, *sq.* For Endeus or Enna and his descendants, see p. 15, *ibid.* His name is there spelt *Eunda*.

have eternal life ; for it was on my account thou camest hither, like Joseph[1] before the children of Israel.' And Endeus said unto Patrick, 'Give baptism unto my son, for he is of tender years; but I and my brothers cannot believe until we come to our own people, lest they should mock us.'[2] So Conall[3] was baptised; and Patrick pronounced a blessing upon him, and took him by the hand, and gave him to Cethiac the bishop, and Cethiac and Mucne the brother of Bishop Cethiac, whose relics are in the Great Church of Patrick in the Wood of Fochloth[4], brought him up and taught him. Wherefore Cethiac gave over his own island to Conall, and it belongs to his family to the present day, for he was a layman[5] after the death of St. Cethiac.'

Our author then goes on to tell us that the appearance of the sons of Amalgaidh at the court of King Laoghaire was owing to a dispute about their inheritance. Enna is said to have been the eldest son, and six of his brothers[6], for what reason we do not know, questioned his right to succeed to the property. They resolved to submit the question to the supreme king at Tara, and this was the business which brought them there when Patrick met them. It is evident,

Patrick meets with the sons of Amalgaidh.

---

[1] *Like Joseph.* The meaning is, 'The providence of God has brought thee here to meet me, as the same providence sent Joseph into Egypt, to save the lives of his father and brethren.'

[2] *Mock us.* Meaning not 'lest our own people should mock us,' but, 'lest the people amongst whom we now are, should mock us,' as they did Hercus.

[3] *Conall*: viz. the son of Endeus.

[4] *Fochloth.* 'In sylva Fochlithi.' It will be observed that *Fochlithi*, or *Fochlothi*, is the genitive of Fochluth. The Great Church, or Domhnach mór of St. Patrick, no longer exists, but the name is still preserved. O'Donovan, *Hy Fiachrach*, p. 463,

n. For St. Mucne, or Mucna, see Colgan, *Actt. SS.* (4 March), p. 457. For Cethiach, or Cethech, see *Mart. of Donegal*, at 16 of June. *Vit. Trip.* ii. 41 ; and Colgan's note, *Tr. Th.*, p. 176, n. 81.

[5] *A layman.* This is a curious proof that the celibacy of the clergy was the rule of the Irish Church in our author's time.

[6] *Of his brothers.* Amalgaidh is said to have had eight sons (of whom Endeus or Enna was the eldest) by his wife Tresi, sister of Aengus Mac Nadfraich, King of Munster; and seven sons by another wife, Erca, daughter of Eochaidh, King of Leinster. O'Donovan, *Hy Fiachrach*, p. 5. 9.

therefore, that at this time their father was dead. It is difficult to imagine that any dispute about inheritance could have arisen amongst the sons during their father's lifetime. Tirechan says nothing about Amalgaidh, or of his conversion to Christianity. The meeting of Patrick with Enna and his brethren must therefore have taken place after the year 449, in which year, according to the Four Masters, their father died; and the story[1] that Amalgaidh was the first Christian king of Connaught is a mistake.

The decision of Laoghaire, in which Patrick concurred, was this, that the seven sons of Amalgaidh should divide the inheritance equally amongst them, with recognition, however, of Enna's right to the chieftainship. Our author proceeds:—

'And Enna said, 'I dedicate (*immolo*) my son and my portion of the inheritance to the God of Patrick and to Patrick.' For this reason, some say that we are the servants of Patrick to the present day.'

These last words are obscure. It does not appear of whom Tirechan speaks when he says 'that *we* are the servants of Patrick.' Nothing is known of his genealogy or history, except what he tells us himself, that he was the disciple of St. Ultan[2] of Ardbraccan. If he was a descendant

---

[1] *Story.* The *Tripartite Life*, ii. 87, says, ' Eo die septem Amalgadii filios cum ipso rege et duodecim millibus hominum Christo lucrifecit, et in fonte qui *Tobur-enadharc* nuncupatur omnes baptizavit.' Jocelin,

c. 59, says nothing of the baptism of Amalgaidh.

[2] *St. Ultan.* Ultan was Bishop of the Dal-Conchobhar, a tribe of the O'Connors of Meath, and a branch of the Desii of Bregia. See above,

CHAP. III.]   *Patrick visits Tirawley.*   445

of Enna, and connected by clanship with the district of Tirawley, the foregoing words may mean, that, in consequence of Enna's donation, he and the tribe, or perhaps the monastic family to which he belonged, ought to be under the jurisdiction of Armagh. The passage deserves notice as proving (if this be its meaning) that in the seventh century the jurisdiction of Armagh extended only to those districts or churches which had been granted in fee, or were alleged to have been so granted, to St. Patrick or his successors.

Tirechan further tells us that Patrick made a league with the sons of Amalgaidh, for a safe passage to their country. This agreement was sanctioned by the authority of King Laoghaire, and Patrick set out accompanied by a body of laymen and holy bishops. He paid also, says our author[1], a sum of money in gold and silver, equal to 'the price of fifteen souls of men, as he himself in his writing declares, *ut in scriptione sua affirmat*, to protect his company from the attacks of bad men, in his passage straight across all Ireland.'

He travels to Tirawley.

There is here an evident reference to the Confession as the undoubted work of St. Patrick. The passage alluded to is as follows; after

p. 213. He is generally supposed to have been himself of that family. But the *Mart. Donegal* (4 Sept.) makes him a descendant of Irial, son of Conall Cearnach. He is always called Mac Ua Conchobhair, or Mac Ui Conchobhair See *Vit. Trip.* i. c. 69. (*Tr. Th.* p. 129.) O'Curry's *Lectures*, App. cvi. p. 607—8.

[1] *Our author.* 'Et extendit [? expendit] Patricius etiam pretium .xu. animarum hominum' [i.e. perhaps the price of 15 slaves], ' ut in scriptione sua adfirmat, de argento et auro, ut nullum malorum hominum impederet eos in via recta transeuntes totam Hiberniam.' *Book of Armagh*, fol. 10, *b. b.*

indignantly repudiating the charge[1] of taking money from his converts, the author adds:—

'Nay, I rather expended money for you as far as I was able[2]; and I went among you, and everywhere, for your sakes, in many dangers, even to those extreme[3] regions, beyond which no man was, and whither no man had ever gone to baptise or ordain clergy, or confirm the people, where, by the gift of the Lord, I did all things diligently, and most gladly, for your salvation. At the same time I gave presents to the Kings, besides the cost of keeping their sons who walked with me, in order that they should not seize me with my companions.[4] And on that day (*in illa die*) they most eagerly desired to kill me, but the time was not yet come: yet they plundered everything they found with us, and bound me in irons; but on the fourteenth day the Lord delivered me from their power: and whatever was ours was restored to us, through God, and by the help of the close friends whom we had before provided. But you know how much I expended upon those who were judges[5] throughout all the districts which I used more frequently to visit. And I think I paid them the price of not less than fifteen men, that so you might enjoy me, and that I may always enjoy you in the Lord. I do not repent of it, yea, it is not enough for me. I still spend, and will spend more. The Lord is mighty to give me more hereafter, that I may spend myself for your souls.[6] (2 Cor. xii. 15.)'

---

[1] *Charge.* See above, p. 409, *n.*
[2] *As far as I was able.* So I venture to translate 'ut me caperet.' The Bollandist text reads 'caperent,' which makes no sense.
[3] *Extreme.* 'Usque ad exteras partes, ubi nemo ultra erat.' Another reading is 'extremas partes.'
[4] *Companions.* I have paraphrased this passage according to what seems the meaning, 'Interea præmia dabam regibus propter [præter, *Boll.*] quod dabam mercedem filiis ipsorum qui mecum ambulabant, et nihil [*al.* non] comprehenderunt me [et nihilominus comprehenderunt me, *Boll.*], cum comitibus meis.' Read, 'Ut non comprehenderent me.' It does not appear on what day he was plundered, and put in chains as he says he was. Perhaps 'in illa die' may mean no more than 'one day,' as Mr. Olden renders it.
[5] *Judges.* 'Qui judicabant.' The Bollandist copy reads, 'indigebant,' which spoils the argument.
[6] *For your souls.* Ware, *Opusc.*, p. 19, 20. *Villan.*, sect. 22, 23. The foregoing passage is not in the Book of Armagh: but, as it is so plainly referred to by Tirechan, it must have been in his copy of the Confession in the seventh century, when the original autograph was in existence. We must, therefore, be cautious in rejecting the evidence of what I have for convenience-sake called 'the interpolations,' that is the passages not in the Book of Armagh.

It is highly probable that by the extreme or distant regions mentioned in this passage, to which no Christian missionary had penetrated, the western coasts of Connaught were intended; and we may well believe that the journey across the island to those wild and uncivilized tribes was fraught with danger of no ordinary kind. *His danger in travelling to Connaught.*

The Tripartite Life records many imminent dangers escaped by St. Patrick during his journey westward, caused by the malice of the Druids, and by the disappointment of the brethren of Enna, who had lost their cause in the court of King Laoghaire. In crossing the Shannon, he discovered the antient altar with the glass chalices, of which we have already[1] spoken. This story assumes that Christianity had penetrated into the eastern borders of Connaught before St. Patrick. But it may, nevertheless, have been true that no missionary had ever before reached the distant region around Croach-aigli[2], or the territories of Iorrus, Tir-Fhiachrach, and Tir-Amalgaidh, which it was his purpose now to visit.

Having crossed the river Moy, he entered this last-named district, and made his way to the wood of Fochlut, of which he had dreamt many years before, and which had clung ever since to his imagination. There, Tirechan tells us, two *He arrives at the wood Fochlut.*

---

[1] *Already.* See above, p. 222.
[2] *Croach-aigli.* 'Hill of the Eagle,' now Croagh Patrick, or Patrick's *Rick*, in the S.W. of the Co. of Mayo. *Iorrus* is now Erris. *Tir-Fhiachrach,* and *Tir-Amalgaidh,* are the baronies of Tireragh and Tirawley.

virgins[1] met him, to whom he gave the veil, and whom he established in a place over the wood Fochlut. More recent legend-makers say that these were the children whose voices were heard in Italy, and, according to one authority[2], by Pope Celestine himself, calling out of their mothers' wombs to Patrick to come and baptise them. Their names were Crebrea and Lassair; they were the daughters of a chieftain named Gleran, son of Cumin. Their relics were preserved at the church of Kil-fhorclann[3], on the western banks of the Moy, about a mile west of Crosspatrick.

He preaches to the Clan Amalgaidh.

Patrick then went to the place of assembly of the clan Amalgaidh, which was called *Forrach*[4] *meic nAmalgaidh*, near the wood of Fochlut, and not far from the present town of Killala. Here, according to the Tripartite Life[5], he found a great

---

[1] *Two virgins.* 'Et ecce ii. filiæ venierunt ad Patricium et acciperunt pallium de manu ejus &c.' *Book of Armagh*, fol. 14, *b. b.*

[2] *Authority.* Namely, the Scholiast on Fiacc, *Tr. Th.*, p. 5; and see also *Vit. Trip.* ii. c. 86. Jocel. c. 38. The names of these virgins do not occur in the Irish Calendars, nor in the Sanctilegium Genealogicum. In some forms of the Legend they are called *pueri* and *infantuli.* See above, p. 313, 327.

[3] *Kil-fhorclann.* So we learn from the Scholia on Fiacc's Hymn, and the Tripartite Life. Dr. O'Donovan has ascertained the site of this church, of which no ruins now exist. See his Correspondence from Mayo (June 2, 1838), *Ordnance MSS. Royal Irish Acad.*, p. 235. *Hy Fiachrach*, p. 467.

[4] *Forrach.* This word signifies a piece of ground in which the meetings or assemblies of a clan were held. *Forrach meic nAmalgaidh* is the assembly-ground of the tribe Mac-Amalgaidh. Tirechan spells the word *Forrgea.* Dr. O'Donovan has shown that this place is in the present parish of Ballisakeery, near the mouth of the Moy, between Ballina and Killala. The name still survives in the townland of *Farragh*, within that parish; and there are two hills (he says) in the neighbourhood whose names indicate that they were antiently places of assembly; viz., *Mullach Fharraidh* (Hilltop of the assembly), and *Cnoc-a-tionol* (Hill of the meeting). *Correspondence, Mayo,* (*Ordnance MSS.*) 17 May, 1838, p. 59. *Hy Fiachrach*, p. 467.

[5] *Tripartite Life.* Lib. ii. c. 87.

assemblage of the people, with their chieftains. He stood up and addressed the multitude. 'He penetrated the hearts of all,' says our author, 'and led them to embrace cordially the Christian faith and doctrine.' The seven sons of Amalgaidh, with the king himself[1] and twelve thousand men, were baptised.[2] They were baptised in a well called *Tobur-ên-adarc*.[3] And St. Patrick left with them as their pastor St. Manchen[4], surnamed *the Master*, a man of great sanctity, well versed in Holy Scripture.

There is mention also of a great baptism[5] of some thousands at Tara, at the baptism of Erc mac Dego; and St. Patrick, in his writings, speaks more than once of having baptised large numbers of men. It was evidently believed that his preaching was followed on more than one occasion by the simultaneous conversion of great multitudes. This may have given occasion to the institution of the festival which we find in the Irish Calendars of the ninth and tenth

Festival of the Baptism of Patrick.

---

[1] *The king himself.* Not the father of the seven sons, who, as we have seen, must have been dead, but as Colgan suggests, the new chieftain, namely, Enna, who had succeeded to his father's rights. *Tr. Th.*, p. 180, *n.* 138.

[2] *Baptised.* Tirechan, although he mentions the visit of St. Patrick to *Foirrgea filiorum Amolngid*, says nothing of the great baptism there. He tells us that Patrick went there 'ad dividendum inter filios Amolngid,' to divide their inheritance among them; and that he built there *a square* church of earth, 'aeclesiam terrenam de humo qua-

dratam,' because there was no wood (sylva) near. *Book of Armagh*, fol. 14, *b.b.* The earthen churches of that age were, therefore, most probably round.

[3] *Tobur-ên-adarc.* 'The well of one horn,' so called, as the Irish Tripartite Life tells us, from a horn-like hill in the vicinity. The more correct spelling would be *Tobur-oen-adharca*.

[4] *St. Manchen.* If this was the Manchen who lived to 652, he could not have been a contemporary of St. Patrick. See Colgan, *Tr. Th.*, p. 111, *n.* 67. Ussher, *Works*, vi. 426.

[5] *Baptism.* See above, p. 442.

centuries on the 5th of April. The Calendar[1] of Aengus on that day has the lines,

> BAITHES PATRAIC PRIMDA
> ATTRANNED INERI.
>
> The Baptism of noble Patrick
> Was ignited[2] in Erinn.

and the Martyrology of Tamlacht interprets this, 'Baptisma Patricii venit in Hiberniam.'

It is evident, therefore, that this festival was not the day on which Patrick was himself baptised, but the day on which 'his baptism,' that is to say, his ministry as a missionary, was found to be preeminently successful. The Scholiast on the Calendar of Aengus says that it was the day on which Sinell[3], his first convert, was baptised. But it is much more probable that it was intended to commemorate the simultaneous baptism of large numbers of men of which he himself speaks in the Confession.[4]

---

[1] *Calendar.* See also Martyrol. of Donegal, at 5th April.

[2] *Ignited.* Or reading *Adroined*, 'was performed.'

[3] *Sinell.* See above, p. 344.

[4] *Confession.* See Lanigan, *Eccl. Hist.* i. 233: a tradition quoted by Ussher from the Book of Sligo, states that Patrick's 'birth, baptism, and death took place on a Wednesday.' From this Lanigan has endeavoured to prop up the year 433 as the year of the first Easter in Ireland, because on that year the 5th April fell on Wednesday. But the Wednesday tradition has nothing to do with the festival of the 5th of April; and Ussher has rightly interpreted it. It was the general opinion, founded perhaps on antient tradition, that Patrick died in the year 493, and it was observed that in that year the 17th of March fell on Wednesday. This fact seems to have given birth to the story that Patrick was born and baptised and died on the same day of the week—'Tri ceadaine Patraic, a gen, a bathais, a bas'— which is literally, 'The three Wednesdays of Patrick, his birth, his baptism, his death.' See Ussher, *Works*, vi. p. 444. A similar legend is told of S. Columba, that he was born, baptised, and died on Whitsunday. Reeves, *Adamnan*, p. 311. So also St. Brigid was born, veiled, and died on Wednesday, *Tr. Th.*, p. 619, which is given in another form, *Book of Lecan*, fol. 45, *a.b.* It would be ridiculous to treat such fables as history.

CHAP. III.] *Daughters of King Laoghaire.* 451

The following curious anecdote is recorded by Tirechan, and repeated with more or less variation in the Lives. It is generally told as having taken place before the events just noticed; whilst Patrick was still in Connaught. Whether true or false, it is worthy of being quoted as a specimen of what was believed to have been his manner of teaching.

Story of King Laoghaire's daughters.

It appears that King Laoghaire had two daughters, named Ethne the fair, and Fedelm the ruddy. He had sent them, for what reason is not explained, to his relatives in Connaught, and placed them under the care of two Druids or magi, named Mael and Caplit. Patrick was at Crochan, or Cruachan[1], the royal cemetery of the kings of Ireland of the race of Herimon, and a very antient residence of the kings of Connaught, in the county of Roscommon. There was a well or fountain called *Clebach,* on the side of the fort, looking towards the east. There Patrick and his attendants assembled one morning at sunrise. He selected, perhaps, the place and hour with the hope of conciliating some Pagan superstitions. Tirechan says that the virgins found Patrick at the well with a synod of bishops,

---

[1] *Cruachan.* Now Rath-croghan, near Belanagare. Antiently, Oenach Cruachan. See the Tract called 'History of Cemeteries,' publ. by Dr. Petrie, *Round Towers,* p. 100, 104. The correct orthography of this name is Crochan, so called from Crochan Crobderg [the red hand], wife of Eochaid Feilioc (King of Ireland, A.M. 3922), and mother of the celebrated Medbh, or Maud, Queen of Connaught. O'Flaherty, *Ogyg.* p. 267, *sq.* Rath Croghan was an antient fort of the Gamanradii, a tribe of the Fir-bolg, or Belgæ. It was called, originally, Drum-nandruad [Mount of the Druids], and Tulach Aichne, which may signify ' Hill of Pleaders,' but the meaning of *Aichne* is uncertain. See Dr. O'Donovan's valuable account of this place, *Four Mast.,* A.D. 1223, not. ʳ.

G G 2

senodum sanctorum episcoporum; but it is probable that by this word our author means only an assembly or company, not a synod properly so called. It will be better, however, to tell the story in the exact words of that antient historian[1], translated as closely as possible:—

Then St. Patrick came to the well (*ad fontem*) which is called *Clebach*, on the sides of *Crochan* towards the east; and before sunrise they [i.e. Patrick and his followers] sat down near the well. And lo! the two daughters of King Laoghaire, Ethne the fair (*alba*), and Fedelm the ruddy (*rufa*), came early to the well, to wash[2], after the manner of women, and they found near the well a synod of holy Bishops with Patrick. And they knew not whence they were, or in what form, or from what people, or from what country; but they supposed them to be Duine Sidhe[3] (*viros Sidhe*), or gods of the earth, or a phantasm.

And the virgins said unto them, 'Where are ye? and whence come ye?'

And Patrick said unto them, 'It were better for you to confess to our true God, than to enquire concerning our race.'

The first virgin said[4],

'Who is God?

'And where is God?

'And of what [nature] is God?

'And where is His dwelling-place?

'Has your God sons and daughters, gold and silver?

'Is He everliving?

---

[1] *Historian.* Book of Armagh, fol. 12, *a.a.*

[2] *To wash.* 'More mulierum ad lavandum mane uenierunt.' Whether this means to wash themselves, or to wash their clothes, the reader must decide. O'Flaherty remarks that this passage shows the simplicity of antient manners. The King's daughters go down to wash at a well in the open air, and at break of day. *Ogyg.* p. 200.

[3] *Duine Sidhe.* 'The men of *Sidhe*,' or phantoms, the name given by the Irish to the *fairies*, men of the hills; the word *Sidhe*, or *Siodha*, signifies the habitations supposed to belong to these aerial beings in the hollows of the hills and mountains. *Ogyg. ib.* It is doubtful whether the word is cognate with the Latin *sedes*, or from a Celtic root, *side*, a blast, a wind.

[4] *Said.* The following singular catechism is written in the Book of Armagh, in lines, as here represented. This page is nearly obliterated in the original MS.

'Is He beautiful?
'Did many foster His Son?
'Are His daughters dear¹ and beauteous to men of the world?
'Is He in heaven or in earth?
'In the sea?
'In rivers?
'In mountainous places?
'In valleys?
'Declare unto us the knowledge of Him.
'How shall He be seen?
'How is He to be loved?
'How is He to be found?
'Is it in youth?
'Is it in old age, that He is to be found?'
But St. Patrick, full of the Holy Ghost, answered and said,
'Our God is the God of all men.
'The God of heaven and earth, of the sea and rivers.
'The God of the sun, the moon, and all stars.
'The God of the high mountains, and of the lowly vallies.
'The God who is above heaven, and in heaven, and under heaven.
'He hath a habitation in the heaven² and the earth and the sea, and all that are therein.
'He inspireth all things.
'He quickeneth all things.
'He is over all things.
'He sustaineth all things.
'He giveth light to the light of the sun.
'Lumen noctis et notitias valat.³
'And He hath made springs in a dry ground,
'And dry islands in the sea,
'And hath appointed the stars to serve the greater lights.

---

¹ *Dear.* 'Caræ et pulchræ sunt hominibus mundi.' O'Flaherty reads, or rather interprets, 'Claræ et pulchriores hominibus mundi.' *Ogyg.* p. 201.

² *Heaven.* 'Habet habitaculum erga cœlum et terram, et mare, et omnia quæ sunt in eis.'

³ *Valat.* This line I know not how to translate. Probus (i. 14) reads, 'Lumen noctis splendore suo perlustrat.' The other Lives all evade the difficulty. The Irish Tripartite quotes the whole of this dialogue in the original Latin of Tirechan, but shortens this clause into 'solis lumen illuminat et lumen lunæ,' and Colgan makes it 'Ab ipso mundi luminaria sol et luna suum lumen participant.' *Tr. Th.*, p. 135.

'He hath a Son co-eternal and co-equal (*consimilem*) with Himself.

'The Son is not younger than the Father,

'Nor is the Father older than the Son,

'And the Holy Ghost breatheth in them (*inflat in eis*).

'The Father, and the Son, and the Holy Ghost are not divided (*non separantur*).

'But I desire to unite you to the Heavenly King, inasmuch as you are the daughters of an earthly King — to believe.'[1]

And the virgins said, as with one mouth and one heart —

'Teach us most diligently how we may believe in the Heavenly King. Show us how we may see Him face to face, and whatsoever thou shalt say unto us, we will do.'

And Patrick said,

'Believe ye that by baptism ye put off the sin of your father and your mother?'—They answered, 'We believe.'

'Believe ye in repentance after sin?'—'We believe.'

'Believe ye in life after death? Believe ye the resurrection at the Day of Judgment?'—'We believe.'

'Believe ye the Unity of the Church?'—'We believe.'

And they were baptised; and a white garment put upon their heads. And they asked to see the face of Christ. And the Saint said unto them, 'Ye cannot see the face of Christ, except ye taste of death, and except ye receive the Sacrifice.'

And they answered, 'Give us the Sacrifice, that we may behold the Son our Spouse.'

And they received the Eucharist of God, and they slept in death (*dormierunt in morte*).

And they were laid out on one bed, covered with garments: and [their friends] made great lamentation and weeping for them.

And the Magus Caplit, who had fostered one of them, came and wept, and Patrick preached unto him, and he believed, and the hairs of his head were taken off.

And his brother Mael came and said, 'My brother hath believed in Patrick, but it shall not be so [with me]; yea, I shall bring him back to Paganism, and to Milthous.'[2]

---

[1] *Believe.* 'Credere,' which perhaps ought to be *credite*.

[2] *Milthous.* 'Sed revertam eum in gentilitatem, et ad Milthoum.' This mention of Milthous is omitted in all the Lives. There is no record of any deity of the Pagan Irish called Milthous. Could the meaning be, 'I will bring back Patrick to Paganism, and to his former master Milchu.' Or perhaps, by Milthous, he means Mael, i.e. himself.

CHAP. III.] *to the Daughters of Laoghaire.* 455

And he spake harsh words to Patrick, and Patrick spake to him and preached to him, and converted him to the repentance of God : and the hairs of his head were taken off—that is, the magical rule [1] [which] was seen on his head, as is said, *air bacc giunnæ*.

It was of him was spoken that most celebrated of all Scotic proverbs, ' Calvus [2] is become like Caplit.'

And they believed in God. And the days of mourning (*ululationis*) for the king's daughters were accomplished, and they buried them near the well Clebach; and they made a circular ditch, like to a *Ferta* [3]; because so the Scotic people and gentiles were used to do ; but with us it is called *Reliquiæ* [4], that is, the remains of the virgins. And this *Ferta* was granted (*immolata est*) with the bones of the holy virgins to Patrick and to his heirs (*heredibus*) after him for ever. And he made a Church of earth in that place.

This remarkable story bears internal evidence of high antiquity; it was evidently written when Paganism was not yet extinct in the country. It represents Patrick as consenting to follow the

Authenticity of the story.

[1] *Rule.* ' Et ablati sunt capilli capitis illius i.e. norma magica in capite videbatur, *air bacc* ut dicitur *giunnæ*.' ' The fashion or rule of the magicians was seen on his head.' This seems to allude to a sort of tonsure worn by the Druids or magi, although the Tripartite Life (ii. 46) explains it that both Caplit and Mael on this occasion received the *monastic* tonsure. This cannot possibly be so. The Irish words *air bacc giunnæ* signify ' as a band [or bond] of hell (Gehenna),' meaning that the Druidical tonsure was a symbol of damnation. It seems quite clear that the author intended to say, not that these magi had received any form of Christian tonsure, but that their hair was cut off to remove all remains of their Pagan or Druidical tonsure. Probus is the only one of the biographers who does not suppress this : he says, ' Tunc jubente S. Patricio ablati sunt capilli capitis ejus, id est, norma magica,

quæ prius in capite ejus videbatur.' ii. 16. *Tr. Th.*, p. 58.

[2] *Calvus.* The name of the Druid Mael signifies Calvus, or the bald. Our author gives the proverb thus, ' Similis est Calvus contra Caplit,' where *contra* signifies, in comparison with, one set against the other. There must be some allusion to the shaven heads of the converted magi: the proverb seems applicable to anything strange or unexpected.

[3] *Ferta.* We have had an instance of the use of this word in the antient name of Slane. See p. 420, *supra*. It is employed in Irish to signify a sepulchral mound of clay, covered with grass. See Petrie, *Round Towers*, p. 106. *Ferta* denotes almost always a Pagan cemetery, as the above passage clearly intimates. Reeves, *Churches of Armagh*, p. 49.

[4] *Reliquiæ.* In Irish, *Relic.* See Dr. Petrie's account of the *Relec na righ*, or Cemetery of the Kings at Cruachan. *Round Towers*, p. 104-7.

custom of the pagan Scots, in the form of the tomb erected over the remains of the royal virgins. It speaks of the Druidical tonsure, without any allusion to the existence of a similar custom amongst Christians. The articles of the Creed which it recites are those alone which are to be found in symbols of the very highest antiquity.[1] But the most singular part of the foregoing story is its conclusion, in which the virgins, after their baptism, are represented as having consented to undergo a voluntary death, in order that they might see the face of Christ. Patrick is represented as approving of their design, and, indeed, as having suggested it. He administered to them the holy Eucharist, as their viaticum; and then, we are told, 'they slept in death,' but by what means death was procured we are not informed.

Contains no esoteric doctrine.

A learned writer[2] has appealed to this transaction to show that the early Irish Church—not perhaps St. Patrick himself, but the 'order' of

---

[1] *Antiquity.* O'Flaherty infers (see *Ogyg.* p. 200), from the questions put to St. Patrick by the king's daughters, that the deities of the Pagan Irish were *topical*, genii or aerial beings, supposed to inhabit the mountains, plains, rivers, lakes, and fountains; and we know that the visible objects of their worship, besides the heavenly bodies, were not idols properly so called, but pillar-stones, remarkable hills, wells, and other natural objects. The Irish had no knowledge of the *Dii gentium*, Saturn, Jupiter, Apollo, Mars, &c., or of the female deities, Juno, Venus, Minerva, &c., under any Celtic names or designations.

Lanigan's note (i. 227), although infected with some of the fictions of Vallancey, contains, on the whole, a correct view of this subject. See above, p. 127, *sq.*

[2] *Writer.* See a paper believed to be by my late lamented friend the Hon. A. Herbert, 'On the Peculiarities of Culdeism,' in the *British Magazine*, vol. xxvi. p. 8. This author knew the Book of Armagh only from Sir Wm. Betham's faulty edition of it. He makes a great deal of the phrase 'Eucharistia dormientium in morte,' which is one of Sir William's innumerable blunders, and does not occur in the original.

ecclesiastics that followed him—had *esoteric* as well as *exoteric* doctrines, and that one of their secret doctrines was the efficacy of human sacrifices; the certainty of salvation to those who submitted to a voluntary death. In the present case, however, there is no attempt at secrecy or concealment. The story is told in the plainest and most unequivocal terms. It is repeated by the later biographers, who do not seem to be conscious of any reason for disguise. Nor can the difficulty be removed by the suggestion of Dr. Lanigan, that the death of the royal virgins, immediately after receiving the holy Eucharist, was not their natural, but their spiritual death; no more being intended than that they had taken the veil, and so had become dead to the world.[1] But they are not said to have taken the veil, and we are expressly told that they were laid out and waked; that lamentation was made for them; that they were buried; a tomb of a particular form erected over their remains, and a church built at their tomb. The original author certainly intended to say that their death was a real and literal death.

Neither is there in this story the smallest attempt at disguise.[2] There is no appearance of

No disguise in the story.

---

[1] *World.* Lanigan, i. p. 241. 'The mistake originated,' he says, 'in their having received the veil, as it is mentioned they did.' But although the Tripartite Life (ii. 44) says this, the reader will observe that there is not a word of their having received the veil, in the original narrative. We are told, indeed, that after their baptism, 'a white garment, candida vestis, was put upon their heads,' but this was evidently the white garment of baptism worn by neophytes in the antient church, for eight days after baptism. Selvaggii *Antiqq.* l. iii. 5, § 2 (tom. v. p. 74). The custom is alluded to by Patrick himself as having been practised by him. See p. 352, *supra.*

[2] *Disguise.* The only one of the biographers who attempts to soften

its being regarded as containing a secret doctrine, which was to be revealed to the initiated only. The writer seems quite unconscious that there was anything in the legend to be ashamed of. The daughters of King Laoghaire, having embraced the Christian faith, desired to behold the face of their Saviour. Being informed that so long as they were in the flesh this could not be, they earnestly desired to depart and to be with Christ; and accordingly, by a special miracle, or grace of God, they were removed into the immediate presence of the Lord, after having received the holy Eucharist of His Body and His Blood. This is the story. And there are abundant instances of similar legends, to which the explanation of a figurative death is inapplicable.

Many similar legends.

We have already had occasion to notice the account given of the virgin who preferred death, as the spouse of Christ, rather than become the earthly spouse of St. Enna[1], then a worldly and ungodly chieftain. We have quoted also the legend of St. Oran[2] of Hi, who devoted himself to a voluntary death for the good of his brethren. In neither of these examples, however, is there any mention of the Eucharist. The following

---

down the objectionable part of the story, is the author of the Fourth Life, who makes St. Patrick say, 'Nisi mortem *paululum* gustaveritis, et sacrosancta mysteria accipiatis, faciem Christi videre non eritis dignæ.' He then gives the same account of their death as the other Lives, but adds that St. Patrick raised them from the dead; the virgins however desired again to die, rather than endure the miseries of this life: and so they died again. *Cap.* 57, *Tr. Th.* p. 42. The Tripartite insinuates an apology for Patrick's recommending their death, 'Vir sanctus *divinorum conscius decretorum.*' ii. c. 45, *Ib.* p. 136.

[1] *St. Enna.* See above, p. 125.
[2] *St. Oran. Ibid.*

anecdote occurs in the life of St. Patrick, and may be cited as a case more in point:—Dichu of Saul, the first convert made by St. Patrick's preaching in Dal-aradia, had a brother named Ross, or Rus, the son of the same father, Trichim. This man was of an advanced age, but entirely devoted to worldly things. Notwithstanding the example of his brother Dichu, he vehemently resisted St. Patrick. The saint reasoned with him on the folly of trusting to this world only, when all his senses had failed, and his limbs were tottering to the grave. Patrick promised, if he would believe, to restore him to youth. This argument prevailed. Ross consented willingly; and, on Patrick's prayer, became forthwith a strong and handsome young man. His repentance, however, was sincere, and his faith exemplary. Patrick seeing this, and fearing for him, as Joceline tells us, the danger of his again encountering the temptations of the world, proposed to him this alternative:—' The choice is given thee,' he said, ' either to live again for a long time in this life, or now to go to heaven.' Ross answered, ' I choose now to depart to eternal life.' Then straightway[1], having received the Sacrifice, he departed unto the Lord.

Story of Ross Mac Trichim.

---

[1] *Straightway.* This story is told by two of the Lives only: the *Vita tertia,* cap. 33, and Joceline, who amplifies a little, cap. 34, 35. Ross Mac Trichim is commemorated at Down, or Dundalethglaiss. He is said to have been at a place called Brittan, now Bright, in the county of Down, when Patrick met him. *Vit. Trip.* i. 52. See Reeves, *Down and Connor,* p. 35. *Mart. of Donegal,* at April 7. Many similar anecdotes may be found in the Lives of the Second Order of Saints. It must suffice here to quote some instances from the life of one of them, St. Brendan, the navigator, who died A.D. 576 or 577. On one occasion, he and his companions found a mermaid lying dead from a

460   *Moral Instruction*   [CHAP. III.

We are not concerned with the miraculous embellishments of these legends; nor indeed with the question whether or not the stories themselves

severe wound. The saint restored her to life, baptised her, and then asked her who she was. 'I am of the inhabitants of the sea,' said she, 'i.e. of the people who implore and pray for the resurrection.' Brendan asked her what was her wish, whether she would go to heaven at once, or return to her fatherland. The girl answered, in a language which none but Brendan understood, and said, 'To heaven,' said she, 'for I hear the voices of the angels praising the Almighty Lord.' After the girl had received the Body of Christ and His Blood, she died without anxiety.

Again, Brendan had amongst his crew some carpenters, a smith, and a *Crossan*, or Cross-bearer. (See Irish Nennius, p. 182, *n*.) They arrived at a high and beautiful island, the shores of which were covered with 'sea cats.' St. Brendan informed his followers that the furious animals were come to devour them. He then said to the Cross-bearer, 'Arise, and take the Body of Christ and His Blood, and go then to eternal life, for I hear the choir of the angels calling thee to them.' He liked this, and said, 'O Lord, what good have I done, that I am to be brought at once to heaven!' Now, after the Crossan had taken the Body of Christ and His Blood, he leaped out at once into the sea with great joy, so that the sea cats devoured him, all except a small portion of his bones, which were buried by his companions, 'and his name is written in the Martyrology, for he was a famous martyr.' [His martyrdom appears to have consisted in his having devoted himself to death to save his companions.]

The smith was then seized with a sudden disease, and was at the point of death. Brendan said to him, 'What wonder, go to the heavenly kingdom, as thou art in search of a country, or if thou desirest to be in this world longer, I will pray to God for thee and thou shalt recover health.' The smith answered, 'I hear the voice of the Lord calling me.' And after taking the Body of Christ and His Blood, he went to heaven.

They still sailed westward, and discovered a small but beautiful island, with much excellent fish left behind by the tide in the inlets and bays. As they sailed round the island they saw a stone church upon it, and an old man praying there, who warned them to fly, as there was a huge sea cat on the island as large as an ox, which would destroy them. They took to their ship, and the sea cat swam after them. Brendan prayed, when another sea monster rose up, and fought with the cat. Both were drowned, and never heard of afterwards. Brendan and his people returned to the island. The old man received them with joy. 'I am one of the men of Erinn,' said he, 'and we set out twelve men of us, on our pilgrimage, and brought that monster sea cat with us, when he was a young kitten, and we were very fond of him; he afterwards grew to a great size, but never did us any harm; and eleven of my companions have died, and I am here waiting for thee to give me the Body of Christ, and afterwards to go to heaven.' The old man then pointed out to them the land of which they were in search, i.e. the Land of Promise; and having received the Body of Christ and His Blood, he went to heaven; and he was buried in that place along with his brethren, with great honour and veneration, with psalms and hymns, in the Name of the Father, and of the Son, and of the Holy Ghost.

The foregoing tales are translated from an Irish Life of St. Brendan.

had any foundation in fact. The teaching they represent may have been the teaching of St. Patrick, although we cannot absolutely infer that it was so. The legendary biographies, in which we find such tales, were all composed at a much later time, and in all probability received much colouring from the opinions and superstitions of their authors. It is important, however, to observe, that not even in the latest of these compositions was any attempt made to disguise the facts, or to treat the voluntary death which the legends seem to recommend as an occult doctrine.

Nothing can be more unfair than to represent that doctrine as equivalent to the doctrine of human sacrifice[1], said to have been held by some heretical sects. The Irish stories had for their object no more than to set forth the superior glories of a future life; the blessedness of being delivered from the burden of the flesh, and the miseries of this sinful world; that 'to depart and to be with Christ is far better.' This object was, no doubt, clumsily effected by superstitious and incredible tales; but such tales fitted the taste, and were eagerly, perhaps profitably, received by the credulity of the age for whose edification they were invented. In some of them death is represented as a miraculous

<small>Human sacrifice not taught in these legends;</small>

---

[1] *Sacrifice.* Nevertheless it is upon the strength of these stories that the learned author we have already referred to says, 'The most remarkable incident to *Culdeism* is the idea of human sacrifice.' *Brit. Magaz.* xxvi. p. 7. We may hereafter have an opportunity of explaining what the *Culdees* really were, and how strangely mistaken this writer was respecting them.

gift, sent from above in answer to the prayer or to the earnest desire of the saint. In other cases, from the stupidity or ignorance of the legend-maker, the saint is represented as having committed something like suicide; devoting himself to death for the good of others, and by his own act voluntarily encountering death. But the idea of human sacrifice does not, even in this case, enter into the story. The victim devotes himself to save his brethren from some great and imminent peril. St. Oran of Hi may have been influenced by the superstitious opinion that until a Christian interment took place in that island, the power of the demons[1], who were its former possessors, could not be entirely overcome. The *Crossan*[2] among the followers of St. Brendan may have been persuaded that the 'wild cats' of the island, satisfied with one victim, would leave his master and companions unmolested. But these stories, superstitious as they are, and tinged perhaps with a Paganism not yet extinct, do not inculcate the merit or benefit of human sacrifice.

nor religious suicide.

Still less do they resemble the *Endura*[3], or

[1] *Demons.* Pennant mentions a tradition current among the peasantry, that Oran's tomb was opened; that he was found alive, and uttered the most fearful blasphemies, so that it became necessary to cover him up again. This story seems to imply that not only his body, but his soul, became the prey of the demons. But there is no antient authority for it. It is a fable of modern demonology. See Irish Nennius, p. xxiv. xxv.

[2] *Crossan.* See note, p. 460.

[3] *Endura.* See Du Cange, *in voce.* Mr. Herbert says (*Brit. Mag.* ibid.), 'We have a memorable instance of it [the doctrine of human sacrifice] in the *Endura* of Paulician Manichees of Languedoc. By that rule, the candidates for Albigensian salvation, when dangerously ill, were required to accelerate their death by abstaining from food, and were even sanctioned in still further accelerating it by bleeding.' Let the reader judge whether there is anything of this kind so much as hinted at in the Irish legends. For the *Endura* of the Albigenses, see Maitland, *Facts and Documents,* p. 235, *sq.*

of religious Suicide. 463

religious suicide of the Albigensian heretics, to which a learned writer has compared them. There *suicide,* properly so called, by a slow and painful death, was the essential idea. A voluntary abstaining from all food, accompanied sometimes by bleeding, and hot baths to aid the effects of the bleeding. In this lingering and gradual extinction of life consisted apparently the merit of the sacrifice; whereas the prominent idea in the Irish stories was a death, as speedy as possible after having received the holy Viaticum, not with any notion of a human sacrifice, but lest sin should be committed to neutralize the purifying effects of the blessed Sacrament, and hinder the admission of the believer into the immediate presence of Christ.

We undoubtedly recognise also in these legends a desire to recommend and enforce the necessity of receiving the holy Eucharist as a viaticum before death. Some of the stories have this alone for their object, as in the case of the Mermaid resuscitated by St. Brendan.[1] A similar anecdote is told of St. Aedh Mac Bric[2]:—

Legend of St. Aedh Mac Bric.

' A rich friend, a native of Munster, and a great benefactor to the Church, had sent for St. Aedh in his last illness, but died before Aedh could reach him. St. Aedh sent his deacon (*ministrum suum*) with all speed, commanding him to say in the ear of the dead man, " Shall I go to thee, or wilt thou come to me ? " Immediately the dead man arose, and crossing himself,

---

[1] *St. Brendan.* See above, p. 460, *n.*
[2] *Aedh Mac Bric.* He was a descendant of Fiacc, son of Niall of the Nine Hostages. See Table III. p. 252, *supra.* He was Bishop at Cill- air, now Killare, in Westmeath, and died A.D. 588. Colgan gives his Life at 28 Feb., but he is commemorated in the *Mart. of Donegal* at 10 Nov.

went to St. Aedh, who said to him, " Wilt thou continue in this life, or go now to heaven ?" He preferred the latter alternative : received the Communion of the Lord from the hand of Aedh, and then slept in peace.'[1]

This story can have had no other object than to inculcate the necessity of receiving the holy Viaticum before death.

Story of Oran the charioteer.

The story of Odhran, or Oran, St. Patrick's charioteer[2], can scarcely be said to belong to this class of legends. The only moral it inculcates is the devotion of a faithful servant to his master. St. Patrick had overturned the great pillar stone, worshipped by the Irish, in the plain of Magh Sleacht[3], co. of Cavan. Berraidhe[4], a chieftain of

---

[1] *In peace.* Abridged from Colgan, *Actt. SS.* p. 419, c. 10. Some similar stories may be briefly noticed here. Eochaidh, son of Crimthann Leith, fifth in descent from Colla-da-Crioch, died in infidelity, but requested that Patrick should be sent for before his body was interred ; Patrick came and raised him from the dead. Eochaidh declared to the people what he had seen of the pains of the damned and the blessedness of the righteous. The choice was given him to live and reign for 15 years more on earth, or at once to go to heaven. Eochaidh declared that he regarded all the delights of the world as naught, and as smoke that soon passes away, when compared with the joys of eternity. He was therefore baptised, and immediately 'rested in the Lord.' *Vit. Trip.* iii. c. 8. Again, Eoghan, grandson of Muredach Meith, son of Imchad, son of Colla-da-crioch, requested St. Patrick to resuscitate his grandfather, who had died in Paganism some years before. The saint consented, Muredach was restored to life, instructed in the mysteries of the faith, baptised, and then

'being again delivered from the burden of the flesh, dismissed to eternal life.' *Ibid.* c. 11. Thirdly, Mumessa, or Munessa, daughter of a British king, although not yet baptised, was inspired with an intense desire of seeing God ; her parents brought her to St. Patrick, she was instructed, and baptised, and forthwith died. *Vit.* 4ta. c. 78. Jocelin (c. 159) adds, that she had received the Viaticum immediately after her baptism.

[2] *Charioteer.* See O'Donovan's *Four Masters*, A.D. 448, p. 138. Odhran, or Oran, was a common name in Ireland ; there is therefore no ground to represent the story of St. Oran of Hi as an imitation of this legend. See *Brit. Magazine*, xxvi. p. 11.

[3] *Magh Sleacht.* See above, p. 127.

[4] *Berraidhe.* He was descended from Ros Failghe (Ros of the rings), eldest son of Cathair Mòr, King of Ireland, A.D. 174. From this Ros Failghe, the Ui Failghe, or Offaly, took their name. See O'Flaherty, *Ogyg.* p. 310. Colgan, *Actt.*

the Ui Failghe, or Offaly, in Leinster, resolved to take vengeance for this deed, by putting Patrick to death. His resolution came to the ears of Oran, who soon after, when they were to pass near the fortress of this chieftain, pretended fatigue, and easily induced Patrick to resign his place in the chariot.[1] The stratagem succeeded. Berraidhe cast his javelin at Oran, supposing him to be St. Patrick, and Oran died, with the satisfaction of having saved his master's life by the sacrifice of his own.

Let us resume the narrative of St. Patrick's missionary progress. After his labours in Connaught, where he is said to have spent seven years[2], he is represented to have revisited Ulster. There he erected a great number of churches, in which he left priests and bishops in the districts of Tirconnell (now the county of Donegal), Dalrieda, and Dalaradia. He then visited Meath; and entering Leinster, is said to have baptised at Naas, at that time the residence of the Leinster kings, Illann and Aillill, sons of Dunlaing, king of Leinster, who both afterwards succeeded to the throne[3] of their father. In the county of Wicklow, he sought hospitality from Driuccriu, then chieftain of the Hy Garchon, who was married to a

---

SS. p. 370. For an account of the district originally belonging to this tribe, see O'Donovan, *Book of Rights*, p. 216, *n*.

[1] *Chariot*. The chariot it seems was capable of holding but one person.

[2] *Seven years*. Vit. Trip. ii. 108. Tirechan, *Book of Armagh*, fol. 15, *a. b.*

[3] *Throne*. The Four Masters tells us that Illann died in 506, and Aillill in 526.

daughter of king Laoghaire. Knowing his father-in-law's hostility to Patrick, Driuccriu refused him the usual courtesy[1] due to a traveller; but Patrick was compensated by the cordial reception he received from Cillin, or Killin, a chieftain of another branch of the same family, whose infant son[2] Marcan was blessed by the saint, and his future eminence foretold.

Visits Magh Lifé.

Patrick next visited Magh Lifé, the plain from which the river Liffey takes its name[3], where he founded some churches; and proceeding into the district called Iarthar Lifé, or western Liffey, he entered the territory of the tribe called Laeghis, or Leix[4], now the Queen's County.

Consecration of Fiacc.

There, it is said, he again met with Dubhtach Maccu Lugil, or Lughair, the great bard or poet, whom he had converted[5] to Christianity some years before, at the court of king Laoghaire; and on this occasion, Dubhtach's disciple Fiacc was made bishop of Sletty, with jurisdiction (as we are told) over all Leinster.

---

[1] *Courtesy.* 'Postulanti denegavit charitatis officia.' *Trip.* iii. 17. This is an incidental proof that Laoghaire was not believed to have been sincere in his profession of Christianity.

[2] *Infant son.* 'Adhuc lactans inter ulnas ministrantis tunc ancillæ.' *Trip. ibid.* See above, Table V. No. 87, p. 253.

[3] *Name.* See above, *Introd.* p. 11, *not.* 2.

[4] *Leix.* For the history and boundaries of this tribe, see O'Donovan, *Book of Rights*, p. 216, *n.* In this account of the acts of St. Patrick in Leinster, no mention is made of Dublin. This is a proof that these legends are older than the eleventh century, when Dublin came to be an ecclesiastical town. Joceline, who wrote in the 12th century, tells us (c. 71) that St. Patrick came to Dublin, 'a noble city:' but he betrays the anachronism by adding that it was then inhabited by the Northmen, who were unknown in Ireland before the year 795. He forgot also that a little before (c. 69) he had represented St. Patrick as predicting the future eminence of Dublin in these words, '*Pagus iste, nunc exiguus,* eximius erit.'

[5] *Converted.* See above, p. 424. *Vit. Trip.* iii. 21. *Tr. Th.* p. 152.

CHAP. III.] *Patrick visits Ossory and Munster.* 467

From Leinster, as the author of the Tripartite Life informs us, Patrick entered Ossory, and blessed[1] the whole district, predicting that from it should proceed many eminent men, both in the ecclesiastical and secular life, and that the country should never be subjected to the yoke of strangers so long as the tribes of Ossory continued in obedience to him and to his successors. This seems to show that, in the times of this author, the jurisdiction of Armagh was not universally acknowledged; and we know that the right of visitation in Ossory was claimed by the successors of Columbkille in the seventh century.[2]

Blessing on Ossory.

We next[3] find Patrick in Munster; and as he had spent seven years in Connaught, so we are told he spent seven years also in Munster. He went at once to Cashel, the seat of the kings. As he approached, the idols all fell before him, like Dagon before the Ark. The king of Munster, Aengus, son of Natfraich, came out to meet him, and conducted him into the palace with the highest reverence and honour. Aengus[4] was at

Patrick in Munster.

---

[1] *Blessed.* 'Totam postea terram et gentem Ossoriorum benedixit, prædicens quod ex ea tam in Christi, quam in seculi militia, multi clari prodituri essent duces; et quod exterorum jugo vel potentia non essent opprimendi, quamdiu in suo, suorumque successorum obsequiis essent permansuri.' *Vit. Trip.* iii. 27.

[2] *Century.* See Reeves, *Adamn.* p. 39, note *d.*

[3] *Next.* The exact chronological order of these events is very unsettled. Ussher places the consecration of Fiacc, the baptism of the sons of Dunlaing, and the seven years' sojourn of St. Patrick in Munster, after the foundation of Armagh. See his *Index Chron.* A.D. 445, 448, 449. He dates the foundation of Clogher two years before that of Armagh, i.e. 443, or fifty years before St. Patrick's death; however, Joceline (c.143), as well as the Tripartite (iii. c. 3), tell us that at the foundation of Clogher, Patrick was so feeble with age, 'senio confectum,' that he used to be carried on the shoulders of his disciple St. Maccarthenn.

[4] *Aengus.* King Aengus was killed A.D. 489, by Illann, son of

once baptised, but a singular accident took place at the ceremony. Patrick, without perceiving it, allowed the lower end of his crosier, which was sharp and pointed, to pierce the king's foot. Aengus, imagining that this was a necessary part of the baptismal ceremony, endured the torture without allowing himself to utter the slightest expression of pain. It was not until the baptism was over that the fact was discovered.

All this bears evident marks of fiction. No mention of Cashel, or of Patrick's journey to Munster, is to be found in the Book of Armagh. Emly, not Cashel, was at first proposed as the archiepiscopal see of Munster[1]; nor is there any notice of Cashel in the Irish annals, as a place of ecclesiastical importance, until the middle of the ninth, or beginning of the tenth century. The 'Irish Life'[2] of St. Patrick, supposed to be the original of Colgan's 'Tripartite,' or 'Vita Septima,' betrays the origin of the Munster legend, when it tells us that Patrick on this occasion had enacted,—

'And no man shall be king of Cashel until the comarb [or successor] of Patrick has confirmed him, and consecrated him to his office.'[3]

Foundation of Armagh.

The foundation of Armagh is the next event

Dunlaing, king of North Leinster, at the battle of Cell-Osnada, or Cenn Losnado, now Kellistown, county of Carlow. See *Four Masters*, in anno, and O'Donovan's note. Illann had not long before been baptised by St. Patrick. See p. 465.

[1] *Munster*. Introd. sect. 85, 86, p. 214, *sq*.

[2] *Irish Life*. Still unpublished, MS. Bodleian. Rawlinson, 505. There is another copy among the Egerton MSS., No. 93, Brit. Museum.

[3] *Office*. 'Ni ri Caisel coro nordne comarba Patricc, agus cotarda grad fair.' This passage is not to be found in Colgan's Latin version, *Vit. Trip*. iii. c. 30, p. 155.

CHAP. III.]   *Foundation of Armagh.*   469

which can be regarded as historical[1] in the life of St. Patrick; and here again we are met by the chronological difficulties created by the story of his Roman mission. The Annals of Ulster give the date A.D. 444 [=445], with the parallel date 1194, or according to another reading 1197, from the foundation of Rome.[2] This record, thus doubly dated, occurs in these annals in connection with two other notices, which seem to show that Armagh was founded in the earlier part of St. Patrick's career, when the success of his mission was ascertained, and his fame established. These notices are as follows:—

'A.D. 441. Patrick the bishop is approved (*probatus est*) in the Catholic faith.'

---

[1] *Historical.* There may perhaps be one or two exceptions. The Tripartite Life (iii. c. 66, *Tr. Th.* p. 162) mentions a hill called Ard-Patrick at the east of the town of Louth, where St. Patrick was minded at first to settle. But an angel brought him 'an epistle,' in which he found a 'commonitorium' or commandment of God, to go to Armagh. He left behind him at Ard-Patrick his disciple Mochta, a Briton, who afterwards built the celebrated church and monastery of Lughmagh, now Louth. See above, p. 29, *sq.* The Lives also tell us (see p. 467 *n.*) that the church of Clogher was founded before Armagh, and at a time when St. Patrick had become enfeebled by age; if so the foundation of Clogher, as well as of Armagh, must be assigned to a much later date than Ussher has chosen. Clogher was a place of antient idolatry, celebrated for a pillar-stone which had been an object of worship. (See above, p. 129.) St. Aedh MacCarthenn was left there as bishop, and to him Patrick gave the copy of the Gospels, some fragments of which still remain, preserved in the shrine called *Domnach-airgid*, now in the Museum of the Royal Irish Academy. See *Vit. Trip.* iii. c. 3, Petrie's Essay, *Trans. R. I. Acad.* vol. xviii. O'Curry's Lectures, p. 322, *sq.* The history of St. MacCarthenn of Clogher will be found in Colgan, *Actt. SS.* (24 Mart.) p. 737. It is difficult to say how far these transactions can be regarded as historical. They are not mentioned in the Book of Armagh.

[2] *Rome.* The numeral letters employed in the MSS. render it difficult to distinguish uii. from iiii. The Dublin MS. of these annals seem to read 1197. Ussher quotes the words of the Ulster Annals thus: 'A.D. 444, Ardmacha fundata est; ab urbe condita usque ad hanc civitatem fundatam 1194 anni sunt,' and he adds, ' Et quidem a Roma *condi cœpta*, usque ad annum æræ Christianæ 445 (ei enim respondet annus 444 in annalibus illis notatus), juxta Polybii rationes, anni 1194 revera effluxerunt.' *Antiqq.* c. 17. *Works*, vi. p. 414.

'A.D. 443. Patrick the bishop in the zeal of faith (*ardore fidei*), is flourishing in our Province.'[1]

Date of the Foundation of Armagh. We have here a manifest remnant of the old chronology of which we have already said so much. Armagh was founded after Patrick had been proved in the faith (A.D. 442), and after his 'flourishing' in Ulster, A.D. 444 (for we must add one year to the dates in these annals) that is to say, about A.D. 445. It is evident that the story of the foundation of Trim, twenty-two, or according to another reading, twenty-five years before the foundation of Armagh, is ignored by this author. That story, although contained in the Book of Armagh, is confessedly of later origin; meaning, of course, later, not as compared with the annals, but in reference to the other collections in the Book of Armagh, transcribed in the eighth century. It is therefore, nevertheless, a legend of some antiquity. The Book of Armagh must have been known to the compiler of the Ulster Annals, who was himself a canon of the cathedral in the fifteenth century; therefore the suspicion arises that he has deliberately rejected the Trim legend.[2]

---

[1] *Province.* Dr. O'Conor reads 'in nostra Hibernia;' *Rerum Hib. Scriptt.* iv. p. 2. And this may be the meaning, but it is more probable that our author intended the district around Armagh. The Annals of Ulster were compiled by Cathal Maguire, a native of Fermanagh, canon of Armagh and Dean of Clogher, who died 1498. They were written in the island of Senait MacMaghnusa (now Belle-isle), in the Upper Lough Erne. From this island these Annals are often called *Annales Senatenses*. See O'Donovan (Four Mast.), at 1498. Harris, *Ware's Writers*, p. 90. O'Curry's *Lectures*, p. 85. On the use of the word Provincia, in older writers, see Reeves, *Adamnan, Glossar. in voce*, p. 451; but from the pen of Maguire in the 15th century the word could scarcely have meant anything but the district round Armagh.

[2] *Legend.* See the Trim legend, p. 260, above. The Four Masters,

The district around Armagh, in the middle of the fifth century, was occupied by the Oirgialla[1], tribes descended from Cairell, Muredach, and Aedh, the three sons of Eochaidh Doimhlen, who are better known by the names of Colla Uais, or Colla the noble; Colla da crioch, or Colla of the two countries[2]; and Colla Meann, the illustrious.

The conquest of Oriel.

These chieftains were the nephews[3] of Fiacha Sraibhtine, king of Ireland, A.D. 297, but they rebelled against their uncle, and slew him at the battle of Dubhcomar[4]; after which Colla Uais, the eldest of the three brothers, usurped the throne.

The three Collas.

He enjoyed the sovereignty for four years, and was then expelled by Muredach Tirech, son of the late king Fiacha, who compelled him to take refuge, with his brothers, in Alba, the modern Scotland. Before the end of a year, however, the Collas made a treaty with their cousin Muredach, and came over to his assistance against the king of Ulster. A decisive battle was fought A.D. 332,

Destruction of Emania.

---

assuming 432 as the date of the foundation of Trim (according to the exigencies of the Roman Mission), and adding 25, give 457 as the date of the foundation of Armagh.

[1] *Oirgialla.* This district is called by the English, *Oriel* and *Uriel.* It included the counties of Armagh, Louth, Monaghan, and Fermanagh. The origin of the name is not evident: for the etymology, *or*, gold, and *giall*, hostage (because their hostages were fettered with golden chains), seems palpably fabulous. O'Donovan, *Book of Rights*, p. 140, 141, *n. Topogr. Poems*, p. xix. (103), (104).

[2] *Two countries.* So called from his connection with Scotland.

[3] *Nephews.* See Genealog. Table IV. p. 252, *supra*: where the relationship between these tribes and the great clans of the O'Neill family is shown.

[4] *Dubhcomar.* This is said to have been the name of a Druid of King Fiacha, who was slain in the battle. *Ogyg.* p. 359; *Tighernach*, A. D. 322. But the word *Comar* signifies the confluence of two rivers, and Dr. O'Donovan conjectures, that Dubhcomar is the antient name of the confluence of the river Dubh, or Blackwater, and the Boyne. *Four Masters*, A.D. 322, *n.*

in the barony of Farney, county of Monaghan, in which the king of Ulster was slain. His royal residence Emania, now Navan Fort, near Armagh, was taken and utterly destroyed. Colla Meann, one of the victorious chieftains, perished in the battle; and the country of the vanquished was divided between the two surviving brothers. The original owners were forced to content themselves with a corner of their former territory.[1] At the times of which we speak, some tribes, the descendants of Colla da Crioch, appear to have been settled in the region of Oirghialla[2], and especially in the district round Emania and Armagh.

Donation of Armagh to St. Patrick.

It was from a chieftain of this race, named Daire, that St. Patrick is said to have obtained the site of Armagh, together with the rights of chieftainship, which descended to his successors, and contributed to the subsequent ecclesiastical importance of the place. The legend is told in the antient Life, by Muirchu Maccu-machtheni, preserved in the Book of Armagh.[3] The following is a literal translation of the story:—

Legend as told in the Book of Armagh.

'There was a certain rich and honourable man in the regions of the Orientals[4], whose name was *Daire*. Him St. Patrick

---

[1] *Territory.* The vanquished tribes were of the clanna Rudhraighe, or descendants of Rury Mor, of the race of Hir, son of Milesius. See p. 248. After the destruction of Emania, they retired to the district NW. of the Righe or Newry river, and Loch Neagh. *Four Masters,* A.D. 331. O'Donovan, *Book of Rights,* p. 36, *n.*, p. 156, *n.* Reeves, *Down and Connor, App.* II. p. 352.

[2] *Oirghialla.* It is difficult to fix at any given time the exact position of these tribes, their possessions varied so much, owing to their internal dissensions.

[3] *Armagh.* Fol. 6, *b. a.* See the original of this passage in Reeves's *Churches of Armagh,* p. 45.

[4] *Orientals.* 'In regionibus orientalium.' This district was Oirthear, or Orior, the eastern part of Oirghialla, from *Oirthear* or *Airthear,* eastern. Reeves, *Ibid.* p. 46.

desired to give unto him a place for the exercise of religion (*ad exercendam religionem*). And the rich man said unto the saint, " What place askest thou ? " " I ask," said the saint, " that thou give me that height of land which is called *Dorsum Salicis*, and there I will build a place." But he would not give that high land to the saint; he gave him however another place in lower land, where now is *Fertæ martyrum*, near *Ardd-Machæ*. And there St. Patrick dwelt with his followers (*cum suis*).

'Now after some time the knight[1] of Daire came, leading his horse Miraculum[2] to feed in the grassy place of the Christians; and such letting-loose of the horse into his place offended Patrick; and he said, " Daire has acted foolishly in sending brute animals to disturb the small holy place[3] which he gave to God." But the knight heeded not, like as a deaf man; and as a dumb man that openeth not his mouth, spake nothing; but leaving his horse there for that night he went his way.

' On the next day however, in the morning, the knight coming to see his horse, found him already dead; and returning home sad, he said to his master, " Lo, that Christian hath slain thy horse, for the disturbing of his place hath offended him." And Daire said, " He also shall be slain; go now and kill him." But as they were going forth, sooner than it can be told death fell upon Daire (*dictu citius mors inruit super Daire*). Then his wife said, " This is because of the Christian; let some one go quickly and let his blessings be brought unto us and thou shalt recover: and let them who went forth to kill him be stopped and recalled."

' So two men went forth to the Christian, and concealing what had happened, said unto him, " Lo, Daire is sick: let something be carried unto him from thee, if peradventure he may be healed." But St. Patrick, knowing the things that had happened, said, " Yea." And he blessed water, and gave it unto them, saying, " Go, sprinkle your horse with this water, and take him with you." And they did so, and the horse revived, and they took

---

[1] *Knight.* 'Eques,' i.e. perhaps his equerry, horseman, or groom. The MS. has 'eques Doiri Dairi,' but the repetition of the name is probably a mistake.

[2] *Miraculum.* Whether this was the name of the horse, or whether it should be rendered a fine or wondrous horse, is doubtful. The Lives understand it in the latter sense.

[3] *Small holy place.* 'Parvum' is in the margin of the MS.: but whether it is intended as an addition to be inserted in the text, or as a substitute for 'sanctum,' is uncertain. The former view is adopted in the translation.

him with them. And Daire was healed, when sprinkled with the holy water.

'Then Daire came after these things to honour St. Patrick, bringing with him a wonderful brazen cauldron, from beyond seas, (*eneum mirabilem transmarinum*) which held three firkins. And Daire said unto the saint, "Lo, this cauldron is thine." And St. Patrick said, "*Gratzacham*."[1] Then Daire returned to his own home and said, "The man is a fool, for he said nothing good for a wonderful cauldron of three firkins, except *Gratzacham*." Then Daire added and said to his servants, "Go and bring us back our cauldron." They went and said unto Patrick, "We must take away the cauldron." Nevertheless this time also Saint Patrick said, "*Gratzacham*, take it." So they took it. Then Daire asked his people, saying, "What said the Christian when ye took away the cauldron?" But they answered, "He said *Gratzacham* again." Daire answered and said, "*Gratzacham* when I give, *Gratzacham* when I take away. His saying is so good that with those *Gratzachams* his cauldron shall be brought back to him." And Daire himself went this time and brought back the cauldron to Patrick, saying to him, "Thy cauldron shall remain with thee; for thou art a steady and imperturbable man; moreover also that portion of land which thou didst desire before, I now give thee as fully as I have it, and dwell thou there." And this is the city which is now named Ardd-machæ. And St. Patrick and Daire both went forth, to view the wonderful and well-pleasing gift of the oblation; and they went up to that height of land, and they found there a roe, with her little fawn, which was lying in the place where the altar of the Northern Church in Ardd-machæ now is; and the companions of Patrick wished to catch the fawn and kill it. But the saint would not, nor did he permit it: nay, he himself took up the fawn, carrying it on his shoulders, and the roe, like a very pet lamb, followed him, until he had laid down the fawn in another field, situated at the north side of Ardd-machæ, where to this day, as the learned say, some signs of the miracle (*signa quædam virtutis*) still remain.'

Authenticity of the legend.

This legend, notwithstanding some admixture of fable, bears internal evidence of authenticity.

[1] *Gratzacham.* A corruption of the Latin ' Gratias ago ' or ' agam.' Reeves, *Anc. Churches of Armagh*, p. 50.

It was certainly written before the idea had arisen of making Armagh an archiepiscopal or primatial see, with metropolitical jurisdiction over all Ireland. Patrick is represented as asking from the chieftain Daire a place for the exercise or practice of religion only. Nothing is said of an episcopal see or diocese, much less of a primacy. All that was demanded was a place or site for such buildings as might suffice for the residence of a religious society. The religious life, and the worship of God, were all that St. Patrick had in view.

The chieftain refused to give the higher ground called Druim Sailech, *Dorsum Salicis*, 'the Ridge or Hill of the Sallow,' or Willow Tree. The elevated ground, in which this Dorsum stands, was called *Ardd-Mache*, rendered Altitudo Machæ, and Altimachæ[1] in the Book of Armagh. The word signifies height, or high ground of Macha. Whether *Macha* was a territorial name, or, as is generally supposed, the name of an antient queen, we need not stop to discuss. Daire probably doubted the prudence of committing to a party of strangers a position of such military importance, on which he probably had his own abode; he therefore proposed to give a site for the religious establishment of the new

The high ground refused.

---

[1] *Altimachæ.* Sometimes also called simply Macha; which gives some countenance to the opinion that Macha was the name of the district. For the story of Queen Macha, see Keating, A.M. 3559 (p. 245, *O'Mahony's Translation*); O'Flaherty, *Ogyg.* p. 258. Ussher supposed the word *Ardmagh* to signify 'High plain.' He was misled by the Anglicized spelling, and supposed the second syllable to be the Celtic word *Magh*, a plain. If that had been so, the word would have been Anglicized *Ardmoy*. See Reeves, *Churches of Armagh*, p. 41.

476   *The Fertæ Martyrum.*   [CHAP. III.

The Fertæ Martyrum.

comers on lower ground. The place was called in our author's time *Fertæ Martyrum,* 'the graves of relics'; but had probably the name of *Ferta,* 'graves,' before its consecration to Christianity. The Irish Tripartite Life puts into Daire's mouth this answer to Patrick's request for the high ground—' I will not give that to thee, but I will give thee a place for thy church (*do reclesa*) in the strong rath below where the *Da Ferta* [the two graves] are.' We may, therefore, infer that *Da Ferta* was the antient name[1] of the place. 'The two graves' were in a rath, or circular fort, in accordance with the Pagan custom; and St. Patrick appears to have kept up the sepulchral character of the place, for the Tripartite Irish Life speaks of the church erected by him there as a *Relig,* or *Recles,* the term always applied to a sepulchral church, and of which ' *Fertæ Martyrum* ' is the Latin equivalent.[2]

Dimensions of the buildings there.

The same authority preserves a curious account of the nature and dimensions of the buildings erected by St. Patrick in the Fertæ, the first ecclesiastical establishment founded by him at Armagh. Colgan's Latin version[3] of the Tripartite Life applies this account to the churches

---

[1] *Antient Name.* Dr. Reeves, in his ' Ancient Churches of Armagh,' has abundantly proved this. The word *martair*, in Irish, although evidently the Latin *martyr*, was used to signify the relics of any saints, whether martyrs or not. See Reeves, *Adamnan*, p. 314, not. *m*. Joceline (c. 161) supposed the word *Fertæ* to signify *miracles*; in which error, as Reeves shews, he is followed by Ussher and others.

[2] *Equivalent.* See Reeves, *Adamnan*, p. 283. *Glossary in v.* Reliquiæ, p. 452. *Churches of Armagh*, p. 8.

[3] *Latin version.* Lib. iii. c. 79, *Tr. Th.*, p. 164.

CHAP. III.] *The Buildings erected there.* 477

afterwards built on the high ground; but the Irish original speaks only of the Fertæ :—

'The way in which Patrick made the *Fertæ*,' it says, 'was this: seven score feet[1] in the *Less*, [or Fort], and seven and twenty feet in the *Tigh mor* [or Great House] ; and seventeen feet in the *Cuile* [or Kitchen] ; and seven feet in the *Aregal* [or Oratory]. And it was thus the houses of the Congbail [the Churches] were built always.'

There can be no doubt that this passage is of great antiquity, and that it relates to the *Fertæ*, not to the churches or religious edifices afterwards erected. The terms that are employed in describing the buildings are some of them obsolete, and would be unintelligible to our best Celtic scholars, but for the explanations of them preserved in antient glossaries. The small dimensions also assigned to the buildings, and the remark that the houses of the churches[2] were always such, are striking evidence that the writer must have lived before the age when larger edifices were required. The arrangement described consisted of a '*Less*',[3] that is to say, an earthen circular fort or

---

[1] *Feet.* The word is *Traig*, plur. *Traiged*, a foot, a footprint. See Zeuss, *Gram. Celt.* p. 6.

[2] *Houses of the churches.* In the original *dom na congbala*, ' Domus ecclesiarum.' The word *Congbal* is explained *eclais*, ' ecclesia,' in an antient Glossary (H.3.18, p. 524) in the Library of Trin. Coll. Dublin. The root seems to signify enclosure, bringing together, congregatio, ἐκκλη-σία. The etymology suggested by Dr. Reeves, *Adamnan*, p. 268, *n.*, and *Colton's Visit.* p. 79, is certainly untenable. The use of this antient Celtic word is remarkable evidence of the authenticity of this tradition. Colgan renders this passage, ' Et hæ *sacræ ædes* omnes juxta has mensuras sunt postea erectæ.' (*Tr. Th.*, p. 164.) But this does not express the real meaning of the Irish: which signifies not that these particular buildings were afterwards erected according to the dimensions given, but that all similar ecclesiastical buildings were constructed on the same scale—*do gres*—for ever afterwards.

[3] *Less.* This word, now written *Lios*, is found in topographical names both in Ireland and Scotland, such as Lismore, Lisnagarvy, Listowel, &c.

enclosure, for the protection of the whole settlement: a 'Great House' for the residence of the ecclesiastics: the *Cuile* (Culina) or Kitchen, which was probably also the Refectory: and the *Aregal*, a word which has greatly puzzled our philologists, but which is probably the medieval Latin *Oraculum*[1], used in the sense of an oratory or place of worship. As one dimension only is given, these structures were probably circular.

No remains of the buildings at the Fertæ Martyrum are now to be found. In the fifteenth century, the place had become a nunnery, and so continued to the period of the Reformation, when it was suppressed under the name of Temple-fertagh. Dr. Reeves has recently determined[2] its exact site in the present 'Scotch Street,' at a spot from which a fine view of the hill upon which the cathedral now stands can be obtained.

<small>Conversion of Daire, chieftain of the Hy Niallain.</small> After some time the holy living, the patience, devotion and piety of St. Patrick and his companions, made an impression upon the chieftain Daire. We may reject, if we please, the marvellous part of the story; but the story itself, notwithstanding the incredible particulars introduced into it, may nevertheless have had some

---

It signifies an earthen fort or rampart, generally surrounded with a foss. The radical idea seems enclosure, protection. In the Scotch Gaelic it signifies a garden; in Welsh it is *llys*, a hall or court. See Stokes, *Irish Glosses* (580), p. 81.

[1] *Oraculum.* See Petrie, *Round Towers* (Trans. R. I. Acad. p. 349), and the authorities collected by Du Cange *in voce.* Colgan translates this word *Argyrotheca*, deriving it apparently from *airget*, silver. But this is quite untenable. The word is sometimes used to signify a cell or chamber of any sort. *Four Masters*, A.D. 1592, page 1922. Reeves, *Colton's Visit.* p. 80, *n.*

[2] *Determined.* See Reeves, *Anc. Churches of Armagh*, p. 5, *sq.*

foundation in fact. It is consistent with antient manners; and the surprise caused by St. Patrick's *gratzacham*, which seemed so strange to Celtic ears, has an appearance of truth. Be this, however, as it may, Daire at length consented to give the Hill which Patrick had originally asked for. He gave it with all the rights[1] of chieftainry which he himself possessed; and 'they went forth together,' we are told, 'both Patrick and Daire, to view the wonderful and well-pleasing gift of this oblation,' *mirabile oblationis et beneplacitum munus.* It is not, however, said in the older authority, that on this occasion a church was built by St. Patrick on the high place; but only that there, in the time of the writer, was the *Less*[2], fort, or civitas, called Ardd-machæ, and that within this fort there was a northern church, *sinistralis ecclesia*, which may mean either a church in the northern[3] part of the fort, or a church lying north and south, not east and west, as was usual. The name of Arddmachæ appears to have been given to the fort or circular enclosure, made for the protection of the buildings erected within it.

The Tripartite Life, however, tells us expressly that on this occasion Patrick founded on the Druim, Dorsum, or Hill, a church[4] 'in the place

Foundation of a Church on the Hill.

---

[1] *All the rights.* 'Quantum habeo.'

[2] *Less.* This word is often translated *civitas*. The name of the fountain at Tara called *Loig-les* is rendered by Tirechan 'vitulus civitatum.' See above, p. 442.

[3] *Northern.* It is curious that our author here uses the term *sinistralis*,

speaking of the church: but afterwards, where he tells us that Patrick carried the fawn to a field at the north of Armagh, his words are 'ad *aquilonalem* partem Airdd-mache.'

[4] *A church.* The Irish original expresses this in Latin, 'et fundavit in eo loco ecclesiam cui nomen est Ardd-Machai.' Colgan's Latin, as

which was called Ardd-machæ;' that Daire, with his wife, and the chieftains of Orior, accompanied Patrick to the hill, to mark out the site of the new foundation; and that they discovered a roe and her fawn, lying 'where the *Sabhall* is at the present day'—that is, of course, at the time of the author. In the older narrative, the roe and fawn are said to have been found on the spot afterwards occupied by the altar of the 'sinistralis,' or northern church. The northern church was, therefore, within the rath or fort, and is thus identified with the *Sabhall*[1], or barn church. St. Patrick carried the fawn on his shoulders, and was followed by the roe to a field (*saltus*) on the north side of Armagh, where he laid down the fawn, and where miraculous appearances were said to have remained. For these, however, our author does not vouch; but reports their continuance on the authority of others.[2] This place is called by the Tripartite Life 'a Hill,' and named *Tulach-na-leice*, or 'Hill of the stones.'

Such is the most antient account that has come down to us of the foundation of Armagh. It has evidently embodied authentic traditions[3]; and,

The northern church or Sabhall.

---

we have already observed, transfers to this foundation the description given in the Irish of the buildings at the Ferta. The other particulars are to be found without any essential difference in both copies.

[1] *Sabhall.* This favours the opinion that it was called *Sinistralis* from its position, north and south. See above, p. 412, and Reeves, *Anc. Churches of Armagh*, p. 12.

[2] *Others.* 'Ubi usque hodie signa quædam virtutis esse manentia periti dicunt.' *Book of Armagh*, fol. 7, a. b. Fawns and deer are frequently mentioned in the Lives of Irish Saints; for some examples, see *Irish Nennius*, p. 183, *n.*

[3] *Traditions.* The Tripartite Life, both in the original Irish and in Colgan's Latin, gives the genealogy of Daire, from whom St. Patrick received Armagh. He is represented as descended in the seventh generation from Colla-da-crioch, son of Eochaidh Doimhlen. (See *Table IV.*

although mingled with many evident fables, bears undoubted evidence of high antiquity.

The story told in the Tripartite and some of the other Lives, that St. Patrick, immediately[1] after the foundation of Armagh, went to Rome, and brought from thence a large collection of relics, is unworthy of any attention. It proves, however, the unscrupulous manner in which the lives were interpolated to prop up later superstitions. St. Patrick, we are told, was not long at Rome on this occasion, when he contrived ' by a pious fraud[2] or theft, whilst the keepers of the sacred places were asleep and unconscious,' to carry off a great quantity of relics of apostles and martyrs, a towel stained with our Saviour's blood, and some of the hair of His blessed Mother. It is added that this ' pious theft'

<small>St. Patrick's visit to Rome.</small>

p. 252, *supra*.) He is called Daire Dearg (or the Red), and was son of Finchadh, s. of Eoghan, s. of Niallan, s. of Fiacc, s. of Fiachra Cassan, s. of Colla-da-Crioch. At the conquest of Emania in 332, Colla was probably of mature age, and his son may have been born. The birth of Daire, even after making this allowance, cannot therefore be referred to a much earlier date than 482, and if he was 20 years of age when he met St. Patrick, Armagh could not have been founded before 500. Here again we have a chronology much too late for the received history. The genealogy of Daire is not found in the Book of Lecan, nor in the collections of MacFirbis. O'Flaherty gives it (probably from the Tripartite Life) without noticing the difficulty. *Ogyg.* p. 364. Comp. Reeves, *Churches of Armagh*, p. 47. We cannot, however, depend upon these genealogies. Flann Febla, or Flann of the Foyle, one of Patrick's successors at Armagh, is in the seventh generation from Colla-da-Crioch, and therefore ought to have been contemporary with Daire. But he died A.D. 704. This requires upwards of 50 years to a generation. On the other hand, if Daire's oblation of Armagh is dated 445, as in the Annals of Ulster, we can only allow 18 years to a generation. The genealogy of Flann Febla is undoubtedly too short : that of Daire is probably too long.

[1] *Immediately*. Ussher dates the journey to Rome, A.D. 462, seventeen years after the foundation of Armagh, departing in this from the authority of all the writers who have made any mention of St. Patrick's supposed visit to Rome.

[2] *Fraud*. ' Nec diu Romæ substitit dum pio astu furtove, sacrorum locorum custodibus nescientibus et dormientibus, sed summo, ut creditur, connivente Pontifice, &c.' *Vit. Trip.* iii. 82 (*Tr. Th.* p. 164).

was believed to have been committed with the connivance of the Pope himself; and the writer exclaims in rapture[1], 'O wondrous deed ! O rare theft of a vast treasure of holy things, committed without sacrilege, the plunder of the most holy place in the world!' Nothing, however, is said, even by this author, of an archiepiscopal jurisdiction. His authorities were probably compiled before that claim had been thought of; otherwise we may be sure he would have had no more scruple in making the Pope do all that was necessary, than Joceline had, who tells us[2] that the supreme Pontiff, embracing Patrick, declared him to be the Apostle of Ireland, invested him with the pallium, made him his legate, and confirmed by the authority of the Holy See whatever he had done in Ireland.

St. Patrick's reform of the Pagan laws.

Tradition ascribes to St. Patrick, or to the influence of St. Patrick, the important work of reforming the antient Druidical or Pagan laws of

---

[1] *Rapture.* 'O mirum facinus, rarumque ingentis thesauri ex loco mundi sacratissimo rapti sacrarumque rerum furtum, sine sacrilegio commissum.' *Ibid.* For the history of the relics of Armagh, see *Book of Hymns*, p. 44, *sq.*

[2] *Tells us.* 'Imprimis ergo illum, ut Hiberniæ Apostolum amplexans, ac pronuncians, pallio decoravit, illique vices suas committens, atque legatum suum constituens, quæcumque in Hibernia gesserat, constituerat, disposuerat, authoritatis suæ munimine confirmavit.' *Jocel.* c. 166 (*Tr. Th.*, p. 101). We are informed also by Joceline, that Patrick, on his way back from Rome, travelled through Britain, founded and restored churches, predicted the future eminence of St. David, then in his mother's womb, and returned to Ireland accompanied by thirty foreign bishops. It is strange that Ussher should have given weight to such fables. He assumes the truth of the legend that Patrick, on his way to Ireland with Pope Celestine's commission in 432, visited the *Vallis Rosina*, or Menevia, and predicted that David would be born thirty years afterwards. Colgan, *Actt. SS.* p. 425. Therefore David was born in 462, and therefore in that year, David being in his mother's womb, Patrick was returning from Rome, and predicted the future eminence of the unborn infant, according to Joceline, c. 147. See Lanigan's confutation of these stories; *Eccl. Hist.* i. p. 319, *sq.*

CHAP. III.] *Reform of the Pagan Laws.* 483

Ireland. When king Laoghaire and his nobles had professed Christianity, so runs the story, a council of nine was formed, to examine the laws of the kingdom, and render them consistent with the principles of the Gospel. This council consisted of three kings, three saints or bishops, and three bards or historians. Their names[1] have been recorded; and the work said to have been compiled by them is still extant. It bears the title of *Senchus Mòr*, or 'Great Antiquity.' It has been also called *Cain Patraic*, or 'Patrick's Law,' and *Noi-fis*[2], 'Knowledge of Nine.' So we are expressly told in the antient Prefatory descriptions of this work, first published by Dr. Petrie, from two MSS. in the library of Trinity College, Dublin. These descriptions, as well as the work itself, establish the fact that it is a body of antient laws, ' modified,' as Dr. Petrie[3] concludes, ' at some period subsequent to the

The Senchus Mòr.

[1] *Names.* An antient rann or quatrain, preserved in Cormac's Glossary, and quoted by the Four Masters, A.D. 438, gives the names as follows:—the three kings, Laoghaire [King of Ireland], Corc [King of Munster], Daire [King of Oriel]. Corc was the grandfather of Aonghus mac Natfraich, the first Christian King of Munster. He must have died in paganism, before the time of Patrick. This is therefore a palpable anachronism. Daire is supposed to have been the chieftain from whom Patrick received the grant of Armagh. The three saints were Patrick, Benen (who was only a child at the Feis of Tara), and Cairnech; he may have been Cairnech of Cornwall, who was contemporary with St. Patrick, not the Irish Cairnech, who lived to A.D. 530. (See *Irish Nennius, Append.* No.

xxi. p. ci. *sq.*) The three bards were Ros, Dubhtach mac Ui Lugair, and Fergus. See Petrie, *On Tara Hill*, p. 69, *sq.* The biographers of St. Patrick, with the exception of Joceline, make no mention of the *Senchus Mòr*, and Dr. Lanigan says, ' What has become of the *Seanchus more* is uncertain,' i. p. 371. He was not aware that it was still extant. Keating gives an erroneous account of it. He had evidently never seen it, and imagined it to be a collection of historical traditions, not a Code of Laws. See *O'Mahony's Transl.* p. 410, *sq.*

[2] *Noi-fis.* From *Noi*, ' nine ;' *fis*, ' knowledge ;' less correctly written *No-es*, by dropping the *f.* See Cormac's Glossary by Stokes (Williams and Norgate, 1862), p. 31. Petrie, *On Tara*, p. 71.

[3] Dr. Petrie. Ibid. The name of

introduction of Christianity, to agree with Christian doctrines.' It is not impossible that such a work may have been begun in the times of St. Patrick, but the Senchus Mòr, in its present form, cannot be of so remote an age. It has at least received large interpolations, many of them clearly fabulous; portions of it, however, are of great antiquity, and the remainder, making allowance for comparatively modern alterations, introduced by ignorant or fraudulent transcribers, can scarcely be regarded as of later date than the ninth or tenth century.[1]

St. Patrick's Synods.

Of the other works[2] attributed to St. Patrick,

Senchus Mòr, 'Antiquitas Magna,' misled Colgan, who describes this work as 'Unum grande opus de Hiberniæ antiquitatibus et sanctionibus legalibus.' *Tr. Th.*, p. 214. Colgan's authority seems to have led Lanigan, O'Conor, and others, into similar mistakes. These errors were first corrected by Dr. Petrie. See also O'Donovan's notes, *Four Masters*, A.D. 438.

[1] *Century.* This curious book is now in the press, and the first volume will shortly be published by the Irish Brehon Law Commissioners. See O'Curry's Lectures, p. 16. The unexpected death of Mr. O'Curry, which followed so soon after that of his colleague, Dr. O'Donovan, has greatly retarded the appearance of this work, and will also necessarily diminish its value, as it must now appear without the advantage of their editorial superintendence.

[2] *Other works.* These will be found in the *Opuscula S. Patricii* of Ware and Villanueva, but they are certainly not by St. Patrick. The tracts *De tribus Habitaculis* and *De duodecim abusionibus Seculi*, are in a style of Latinity so far superior to that of the Confessio, and Letter about Coroticus, that it is impossible they could be by the same author. They quote the Hieronymian Vulgate, and they contain no historical or any other allusion to connect their author with Ireland. They have been both attributed to St. Augustine, and the latter of them also to St. Cyprian. The *Three Habitations* described in the former tract are this present world, heaven, and hell. There is not a word of purgatory; nevertheless Casimir Oudin says, 'Attributum hunc Patricio ab Hibernis librum arbitratus sum quod illic de Purgatorio agatur, atque ita cum *Purgatorio Patriciano* apud Hibernos celeberrimo convenire opinati sunt.' *De Scriptt.* tom. i. 1168. It is evident from these words that this learned writer had never taken the trouble to read the tract *De tribus Habitaculis*; and also that he was ignorant of the real meaning of St. Patrick's Purgatory in Ireland, which was in no sense of the word a *Habitaculum*. It was written before the *Purgatorium Patricianum* was heard of. There is no evidence that it was ever attributed to St. Patrick by the Irish. The *Charta S. Patricii, de antiquitate Avalonica*, is a

CHAP. III.] *St. Patrick's Synods.* 485

the most celebrated are the Synods, or ecclesiastical Canons, published under his name, in the great Collections of the Councils.[1] It is scarcely possible, however, to receive these Canons as really his, although some of them were certainly written during the predominance of Paganism in the country; but others bear internal evidence of a much later date.

The Synod said to have been held ' by Patrick, Auxilius, and Iserninus,' has better claims to antiquity than the rest. If genuine, it must have been held before the year 459 [= A.D. 460]; because the annals of Ulster record the death of Auxilius in that year, and the death of Iserninus in

<small>Synod of Patrick, Auxilius, and Iserninus.</small>

---

palpable forgery, intended to prop up the fable of St. Patrick's connexion with Glastonbury, and betraying the modern origin of that legend. See Lanigan, i. p. 328. There are tracts, poems, &c., in the Irish language, attributed to St. Patrick in various MSS.; but none of them have any appearance of authenticity, with the exception of the curious Hymn of which a translation has been given, p. 426, *supra*.

[1] *Councils.* See also Spelman, Wilkins, Ware, and Villanueva. Joceline tells us that Patrick composed a great volume of Canons, called *Canoin Phadruig*, 'the Canons of Patrick,' c. 185. *Tr. Th.*, p. 106. By this great volume, however, it is most probable that the *Senchus mòr* is intended. Its Irish title was not *Canoin*, Canons, or ecclesiastical rules, but *Cain* Patraic, 'the law of Patrick.' This word properly signifies a tax or tribute; and denoted such laws as had reference to the imposition of taxes or tributes. A law for exempting the clergy from military service, which appears to have been enacted about the beginning of the 8th century, was enforced by the influence of the successors of Patrick at Armagh, under the name of 'the *Cain* or law of Patrick.' See Petrie, *On Tara*, p. 172, 173. The *Cain* of Adamnan, at an earlier period, aimed at exempting women from military service. Reeves, *Adamnan*, p. 179. But the name was also given to certain tributes, collected by the see of Armagh, and by the monastic societies. Thus Caencomhrac mac Maeluidhir, monastic bishop and abbot of Derry, is styled *Maor cana Adamnain*, steward (or procurator) of Adamnan's tribute. Colgan renders this phrase 'Conservator canonum,' mistaking *Cana*, the gen. singular of *Cain*, for the gen. plur. of *Canon*. See above, p. 170, 171, and Reeves, *Adamnan*, p. 393, *n*. We may, therefore, pardon Joceline for confounding these words. The word *Canon* was sometimes used to signify the *Canon* of the Old and New Testaments, or parts of it. Thus the Book of Armagh was often called *Canon* of Patrick, because it belonged to Armagh, and contained a copy of the New Testament. Reeves, *ibid.*, p. 359, and see above, p. 103.

468 [= A.D. 469]. Secundinus, Auxilius, and Iserninus, according to the same annals, came as bishops[1], to assist St. Patrick, (that is to say, they probably accompanied him to Ireland) in 439 [= A.D. 440]. Secundinus is not named as having assisted in the Synod. It may have been held after 447 [= A.D. 448], the year of that bishop's death. But a different cause can be assigned for the omission of his name. Auxilius and Iserninus, but not Secundinus, are said to have been ordained, along with St. Patrick, for the Irish mission; perhaps, as Colgan suggests, they were then ordained priests[2], and afterwards consecrated bishops by St. Patrick himself. For this reason, therefore, Auxilius and Iserninus were represented as sitting in synod with Patrick. The history of Secundinus being more purely Irish, may possibly have been unknown to the compiler of this collection of Canons.

Its sixth Canon.

The following Canon[3], the sixth of this Synod, is evidence of a very rude state of society. It seems to have been enacted before the celibacy of the clergy was enforced in Ireland, but after the adoption of the Roman tonsure :—

'What cleric soever, from an ostiarius to a priest, who shall be seen without a tunic, or who does not cover his nakedness,

---

[1] *As bishops.* The words are 'mittuntur et episcopi ipsi in auxilium Patricii.' We are not told by whom they were sent.

[2] *Priests.* See above, p. 317, *n.*, and Colgan's note, 39, 40. *Tr. Th.*, p. 18.

[3] *Canon.* Villanueva, p. 2, can. vi. 'Quicunque clericus, ab ostiario usque ad sacerdotem, sine tunicâ [Martene, adds *femorali*] visus fuerit, atque turpitudinem ventris et nudi tatem non tegat : et si non more Romano capilli ejus tonsi sint, et uxor ejus si non velato capite ambulaverit ; pariter a laicis contempnentur et ab ecclesia separentur.' See Martene's edit. of this Synod, *Thes. Nov. Anecd.* tom. 4, col. 5.

CHAP. III.] *of Patrick, Auxilius, and Iserninus.* 487

or if his hairs are not tonsured after the Roman manner, or if his wife does not walk with her head veiled, let them' [*i.e.* the cleric and his wife] 'be despised by the laity, and also separated from the church.'

This allusion to the Roman tonsure clearly indicates that the canon was as late as the eighth century, and probably not earlier than the tenth. Adamnan, in his conversation with the abbat Coelfrid[1], whilst he allows to the Irish tonsure the opprobrious name of Simon Magus, defends it, nevertheless, as having been down to that time the 'custom of his country,' *ex consuetudine patria.* Tighernach, in his Annals, gives A.D. 718 as the date of the adoption of the Roman tonsure by the community of Hi. The antient catalogue of the three Orders of Saints tells us that the first and second orders agreed in the same tonsure 'from ear to ear,' which was derived from Patrick, and that 'different tonsures' were the characteristic of the third order only. It is clearly impossible, therefore, that St. Patrick[2]

Allusion to the Roman Tonsure.

[1] *Coelfrid.* See this abbat's letter to Naiton, King of the Picts (dated A.D. 710), in Bede, lib. v. c. 21. The Irish tonsure consisted in shaving all the hair in front of a line drawn over the top of the head from ear to ear. Hence Coelfrid's curious argument with Adamnan, 'O, holy brother, who believest that thou art advancing to the crown of a life that knoweth no end, why dost thou wear on thy head, by a custom contrary to thy faith, the figure of a crown which is bounded?' i.e. the circular crown represents a life without end; the Irish tonsure, where but half the head was shaven, was a semi-circle, terminated at the line drawn from ear to ear. Reeves, *Adamnan,* p. xlvii. 350. Cf. D'Achery, *Spicil.* i.

p. 505, *Con. Hibern. lib.* L. c. 6.

[2] *St. Patrick.* Villanueva maintains the contrary, p. 34, *sq.*, and Ware, *Opusc.* p. 124, says that the Catalogue was wrong in attributing to the first and second orders the tonsure from ear to ear. But the Catalogue, which concurs with the Irish Annals, with Tighernach and Bede, with Adamnan, is surely more to be relied upon than a collection of canons which Ware himself admits to be interpolated, and whose date is by no means ascertained. See Dr. Lanigan's remarks on this canon, vol. iv. p. 360, *sq.* Villanueva's learned dissertation is far from satisfactory. It is not clear that he knew what the Irish tonsure was.

could have been the author of a canon[1] enforcing the Roman tonsure on all the Irish clergy.

Many things in these canons seem to imply a more near approach to diocesan jurisdiction, as well as a more settled state of Christianity in the country, than was possible in the days of St. Patrick. We may not, therefore, be greatly in error if we assign this collection, at least in its present form, to the ninth or tenth century. It is probably Irish, as the enactment against the admission of clergy from Britain[2], without letters from their bishops, would seem to prove. And it is possible that this may have been suggested by the similar canons made in England, in the ninth century, to restrain the wandering bishops of the Scoti.[3] We have already noticed[4] the canon in which offerings made to the bishop are mentioned as 'an antient custom'—*mos antiquus*. This could not possibly have been written by St. Patrick; there could have been no such *antient* custom in Ireland in the fifth century.

The second Synod of St. Patrick.

The other Synod attributed to St. Patrick has even less pretension to genuineness. Easter, Pentecost, and the *Epiphany*[5] are spoken of as the

---

[1] *Canon.* Canons 14 and 15 enact a year of penitence only for a Christian who is guilty of murder, fornication, or of consulting an augur (haruspicem), and half a year for a Christian guilty of theft. This can scarcely belong to the fifth century. See Tillemont, *Mem. Eccl.* xvi. p. 786. Canon 16 excommunicates the Christian who believes in a ghost or a witch seen in a mirror, 'qui crediderit esse Lamiam in speculo, quæ interpretatur Striga.'

[2] *Britain.* 'Clericus qui de Britannis ad nos venit sine epistola, etsi habitet in plebe, non licitum ministrare.' *Can.* 33.

[3] *Scoti.* See p. 40, *supra*.

[4] *Noticed.* See above, p. 4, *n*.

[5] *Epiphany.* Can. 19, *Ware*, p. 36. This seems like an usage of the Greek church, where the Epiphany is by some regarded as commemorating the baptism of Christ; *Selvaggii Antiqq.* tom. ii. p. 200. Pope Leo the Great, in his letter xvi., *ad episcopos Siculos*, objects to the custom of baptising on the Epi-

seasons of baptism. Novatianism is mentioned; a heresy which is not known to have ever appeared in Ireland. The 7th canon seems to imply that controversy about rebaptising the lapsed had arisen. Second marriages appear to have been allowed, in case of adultery[1], by the 26th and 29th of these canons; and the 27th renders necessary the consent of the parent before a virgin could contract matrimony, or enter the religious life. This, as Tillemont[2] observes, was not in accordance with the practice usually attributed to St. Patrick. It is, on the whole, very doubtful whether this Synod be Irish; and it is certain that Patrick could not have been its author.

We are now come to the death of St. Patrick. Upon this subject, as was to have been expected, legend has been busy. An angel in a burning bush predicts his approaching dissolution. A light from heaven indicates the spot in which his remains are to be laid. St. Brigid, moved by divine inspiration, embroiders with her own hands the shroud in which his corpse is to be wrapped. For a space of twelve days, or according to some authorities for an entire year[3], the sun stood still

St. Patrick's death.

phany, and designates it 'an unreasonable novelty,' *irrationabilem novitatem*. But the Epiphany was a solemn day for the administration of baptism in the Oriental and African churches; *Selvag. Ibid.* tom. v. p. 47, 48.
[1] *Adultery.* But this is expressly prohibited by can. 5 of another so-called Patrician collection. *Ware*, p. 40.
[2] *Tillemont.* 'Paroist contraire à S. Patrice, qui recevoit les Vierges malgré leurs pères.' *Mem. Eccl.* xvi. p. 787.
[3] *Year.* It is a strong presumption, against the pretensions of the hymn of Fiacc to antiquity, that it has given the legend in this extreme form, 'For an entire year there was light, a continued long day.' *Tr. Th.* p. 3. Lanigan suggests that the multitude of lights kept burning at the tomb by the clergy, may have given birth to this legend, i. p. 364; but this explanation is insufficient.

over his tomb, and the district of Magh-inis, in which he was entombed, enjoyed a perpetual day. The clergy of Ireland, assembled at his obsequies, heard the heavenly hosts assisting to sing the requiem.

Died at Saul, not at Armagh.

The historical fact seems to be that St. Patrick was at Saul when he felt his end approaching. His first wish was to reach Armagh before his death, that his body might be there interred. But perhaps this clause was inserted into the story in compliment to the Armagh clergy. The interposition of an angel compelled him, in obedience to a divine command, to choose Saul, and not Armagh, as the place of his departure; for as he was setting out for Armagh, intending there to die, his guardian angel, Victor, sent another angel to command him to return to Saul. It was announced to him that the four petitions which he had asked of God were granted to him; first, that his jurisdiction[1] should have its seat in

His four petitions.

Joceline (c. 193), the Tripartite (iii. c. 106), and Probus (ii 34), make the duration of the light twelve days only. The author of *Vita 3tia* says (c. 90), that the twelve days' light rendered candles unnecessary, 'ne lucernæ accenderentur juxta corpus;' and that the darkness of the remaining nights of the year was but moderate; 'non erant ibi tenebræ usque ad finem anni nisi modicæ tenebræ,' c. 92. The Book of Armagh says that this was the story told by the people of Ulidia only, 'Et plebs Ulod dixerunt quod usque in finem anni totius in quo obierat numquam noctium tales tenebræ erant quales antea fuerunt,' fol. 8, *a.b.*

[1] *Jurisdiction.* 'Ut in Ardd-machæ fiat ordinatio tua.' *Book of Ar-* *magh*, fol. 8, *a.a.* Fiacc renders this *in Ardmacha fil righi.* 'In Ardmacha est regnum.' *Str.* 22. The Vita 3tia, c. 88, gives it 'Ordinatio gratiæ tuæ in Ardmacha fiet.' Probus (ii. c. 32) 'ut in tota Hibernia fiat a Domino salutis præstatio de meritis tuis.' Jocelin, c. 187, has it, 'in Ardmachiæ urbe quam diligis, [erit] gratiæ tibi collatæ successiva administratio.' The Tripartite says, 'in ea Regni Metropolis fixa, supremaque ecclesiæ Hibernicæ administratio, publicaque auctoritas consistent' (iii.c. 101). But Fiacc has given the true meaning— 'thy kingdom'—'thy chieftainship.' See three other petitions of St. Patrick, D'Achery, *Spicil.* i. p. 50 *Con. Hibern. lib.* lxiv. c. 5.

Armagh; secondly, that whoever, at the hour of death, should sing the hymn composed in his honour, (meaning the hymn by St. Sechnall,) should have Patrick as the judge[1] of his repentance; thirdly, that the descendants of Dichu[2] should receive mercy and not perish; fourthly, that Patrick, as the apostle of Ireland, should be the judge of all the Irish in the last day, according to the promise made to the other apostles— 'ye shall sit upon twelve thrones, judging the tribes of Israel.'

This story bears internal evidence of having been framed with a view to a compromise between the people of Armagh or Orior, and the people of Ulidia. We are told that after the death of St. Patrick, a bitter feud arose between the Hy Neill and the people of Orior, for the possession of his remains. Peace was restored by a circumstance which looks not unlike a contrivance of the clergy to prevent bloodshed. Two untamed oxen[3] were chosen to carry the bier of the saint, and it was arranged that the oxen should be allowed to go forth of their own accord, without human guidance, and that in the spot where they stopped, there the sacred remains

Contest for his body between the Hy Neill and the Orior.

---

[1] *Judge.* The meaning of this doubtless is that Patrick would be a more lenient or indulgent judge than the Almighty.

[2] *Dichu.* 'Ut nepotes Dichon, qui te benigne susciperunt, misericordiam mereantur, et non pereant.' *Book of Armagh, ibid.* It is remarkable that Fiacc, although he enumerates the other petitions (*St.* 25, 26) omits this. He lived, therefore, at a time when it was no longer necessary to conciliate the family of Dichu. And so also Probus (ii c. 32) for ' nepotes Dichon,' substitutes ' qui tuam memoriam benigne celebraverint.'

[3] *Oxen.* This story, like many of the better sort of legends in the Lives of the Saints, is an imitation of the Scriptures. See 1 Sam. vi. 7, *sq.*

should be interred. They rested at Dun-da-leth-glaisse, the site of the present cathedral of Down, a place which had been previously the fortified residence[1] of the chieftains of Ulidia. This fact probably led to the selection of it as an ecclesiastical establishment. But the contention between the two clans was not so easily brought to an end. They met at a place which Muirchu Maccumachtheni, in the Book of Armagh, calls ' a certain strait[2] named *Collum bovis*;' there the tide rose so high that the contending parties were forced to separate. They prepared, however, to meet again; but on marching in arms to the field of battle, were happily deceived[3] by the appearance of a bier borne by two oxen. Each tribe followed the bier, which seemed, by a divine guidance, to carry the relics of Patrick into its respective territory. The armies separated without bloodshed, under the persuasion that each was the possessor of the coveted treasure. The antient narrative intimates[4] that the Orior claimants followed their

The contending tribes separated by an artifice.

[1] *Residence.* The antient earthworks, which are extensive, still remain near the Cathedral. This place was called *Aras Celtchair*, ' House of Celtchar,' *Rath Celtchair*, or *Dun Celtchair*, from Celtchar, or Keltchar, a warrior who flourished about the commencement of the Christian era. Reeves, *Down and Connor*, p. 142.

[2] *Strait.* ' Fretum quoddam quod *Collum bovis* vocatur.' *Book of Armagh*, fol. 8, *b.a.* See Reeves, *Down and Connor*, p. 236. This was probably a ford on the narrow inlet of Strangford Lough, called Quoile, which separates Inch parish from Saul.

[3] *Deceived.* ' Felici seducti sunt fallacia,' *B. of Armagh*, fol. 8, *b, a.*

[4] *Intimates.* ' Putantes se duos boves et plaustrum invenire, et corpus sanctum rapere æstimabant, et cum corpore et tali præparatu et armatura, usque ad fluuium Cabcenne perveniērunt, et corpus tunc illis non comparuit.' *Book of Armagh*, fol. 8, *b.a.* The Vita 3tia (c. 91), says that the Ulidians followed their waggon to Down, and the Oriors theirs to Armagh, both believing themselves to be in possession of the body of the saint. The Vita 4ta says that the waggon of the Oriors disappeared, but that the Ultonians had the real waggon, and buried the remains of St. Patrick at Down (c. 97). Probus follows Muirchu, but gives the triumph to the Ultonians, stating

bier, and proceeded towards Armagh, until, on reaching the river Cabcenna[1], the bier and oxen vanished. Believing the deception to have been a divine interposition, both parties allowed the feud to drop, as neither could claim a triumph. The general opinion, however, was, and it seems to have held its ground undisputed for many years, that Patrick was buried at Down. This opinion is strongly confirmed by the fact that the legend, as above told, is found in the Book of Armagh, which amounts to a concession on the part of Armagh in favour of Down. The Book of Armagh was compiled, as every one who has examined it must see, with the manifest intention of supporting the then growing pretensions of the church of Armagh. It is not easy to conceive, therefore, that a claim to the possession of the tomb and relics of their founder would have been easily conceded by the Armagh clergy, if public opinion or indisputable facts had not been very strongly in favour of Downpatrick. It is true that Tirechan tells us expressly, as one of the similitudes between Patrick and Moses, and the same thing is repeated by Nennius, that the place of his interment was unknown.[2] But this

The possession of the tomb conceded to Downpatrick.

---

that the waggon of the Oriors vanished at the river *Caubene* (ii. c. 40). Joceline (c. 195) and the Tripartite (iii. c. 108) tell the same story.

[1] *Cabcenna.* This river must have been near Armagh; Joceline says (c. 195), 'Donec pervenirent in confinio Ardmachanæ provinciæ, ad quendam fluvium *Caucune* nominatum.' The Tripartite Life says expressly (iii. c. 108), that this river was near the city, 'cum tendentes Ardmacham, civitati appropinquarent, plaustrum illud imaginarium disparuit.' See also Probus (ii. 40). The name Cabcenna, Caucune (i.e. Cavcune), Caubene, is no longer remembered in the district.

[2] *Unknown.* 'Ubi sunt ossa ejus nemo novit.' Tirechan (*Book of Armagh,* fol. 15, *b.b.*) 'Sepulchrum

is an admission that his sepulchre was certainly
not at Armagh, nor even supposed to be there;
and in another place, Tirechan seems to admit
the truth of the other tradition when, he tells us,
that Columbcille, 'by inspiration[1] of the Holy
Ghost,' had pointed out the tomb of St. Patrick at Saul, 'in a church near the sea.'
Downpatrick is probably intended. Muirchu
Maccumachtheni, however, leaves no doubt upon
this point, for he tells us that when a church[2]
was about to be built at Dun-da-leth-glaisse, or
Downpatrick, the workmen coming upon the
relics of St. Patrick, were terrified, and compelled
to desist, by the flames which issued from the
tomb.[3]

Date of St. Patrick's death according to Ussher;

The exact date of St. Patrick's death has been
much disputed; and it is unnecessary here to
discuss the question at any length. Ussher is
strongly in favour of the year 493. The tradition that Patrick was born, baptised, and died on
Wednesday, and the coincidence that the 17th
of March (the day of his death), was Wednes-

illius non invenitur, sed in occulto humatus est, nemine sciente.' *Nennius*, c. 60, p. 102 (ed. Bertram, *Havniæ*, 1758).

[1] *Inspiration.* 'Spiritu sancto instigante.' *Book of Armagh*, fol. 15, *b.b.*, 16, *a.a.* See also Petrie, *On Tara*, p. 115. This passage of Tirechan is very obscure, and no doubt also corrupt. See the proposed emendation of it by Dr. Reeves, *Adamnan*, p. 313.

[2] *Church.* 'Exierunt [boves], Dei nutu regente, ad Dun-leth-glaisse, ubi sepultus est Patricius; et dixit [anguelus] ei ne reliquiæ ex terra reducun-

tur corporis tui et cubitus de terra super corpus fiat; quod jussu Dei factum in novissimis demonstratum est temporibus, quia quando æclessia super corpus facta est, fodientes humum antropi [ἄνθρωποι] ignem a sepulchro inrumpere viderunt, et recedentes flammigeram timuerunt flammæ ignem.' *Book of Armagh*, fol. 8, *b.a.*

[3] *Tomb.* The whole subject of the burial place of St. Patrick is ably treated by Dr. Reeves, *Down and Connor*, p. 223, *sq.* See also the same author's edition of Adamnan, p. 312, *sq.*

CHAP. III.] *Said to have died on Wednesday.* 495

day in 493, seemingly confirm Ussher's opinion. But no great importance can be assigned to the Wednesday tradition; it is not found in any antient authority, and, as we have already suggested[1], it probably originated in the fact that the year 493, in which the 17th of March was Wednesday, had been generally received as the year of Patrick's death.

The Bollandists maintain that Patrick died in 460, aged 82. They assume his mission by Celestine; and on the authority of Joceline, they assume also that he was then (A.D. 432) 55 years of age. They assert, with Baronius and Petau, that instead of 120 or 132, as some have it, we should read 82[2] as the total duration of his life; and therefore they infer that he lived to the beginning of the 28th year after his arrival in Ireland, and died 17th March, 460. {according to the Bollandists;}

To this Dr. Lanigan objects that in 460 the 17th of March fell on Thursday, and not on Wednesday. He proposes, therefore, to follow the authority of the Bodleian MS. of the annals of Inisfallen[3], where we are told that St. Patrick died in the year 432 *from the Passion* of our Lord, a date which corresponds to 465 of the {according to Lanigan;}

---

[1] *Suggested.* See above, p. 450. *n.*
[2] *Read* 82. That is to say, the numerals cxxxii. are to be read lxxxii. This may be what Lanigan means when he says that the Bollandists 'guessed at A.D. 460' (vol. i. p. 463, note 131); but although founded on very arbitrary assumptions their opinion was more than a guess.
[3] *Inisfallen.* See Lanigan, i. 362.

O'Conor, *Rer. Hib. Scriptt.* ii. part. 2, p. 4. The chronology of these annals, however, is not to be depended upon; they tell us here that St. Patrick died in the same year as St. Mac Cuillinn of Lusk. This was 496, according to the Annals of Tighernach and Ulster, the year in which Pope Gelasius I. died, and in which there was an eclipse of the sun.

common era of the Nativity. This allows 33 years for his missionary life in Ireland, supposing him to have come in A.D. 432, and (what to Lanigan was a strong confirmation) the 17th of March, in the year so determined, fell on Wednesday.

But if we adopt this date, it will follow that Patrick died in the reign of Oilioll Molt, eighteen years before Lugaidh, son of Laoghaire, succeeded to the throne; and we must therefore reject all that we find in our antient records of his interview with the latter monarch.

<small>according to the Annals of Ulster.</small> The Annals of Ulster tell us that *the Scoti*[1] supposed the year 491 to have been the date of St. Patrick's death; and in the next year, 492, the same annals again record the death of St. Patrick in these words: 'Patricius archipostulus Scotorum quievit[2].' We are, therefore, justified in drawing the inference that this was the date assigned to the death of St. Patrick in the antient traditions of the country: the *scripta Scotorum* of which Nennius so often speaks. The tradition seems to have varied between the years 491 and 492; a difference of little importance. It should be observed, however, that these years correspond[3]

---

[1] *Scoti.* The words are, 'Dicunt Scoiti hic Patricium archiepiscopum defunctum.'

[2] *Quievit.* They add, to square this with the Roman mission, 'c°.xx°. anno ætatis sue: lx. a quo venit ad Hiberniam anno ad baptizandos Scotos.'

[3] *Correspond.* This appears from the Sunday letters given in the Annals, viz., 491, Kal. Jan. feria 4; and 492, Kal. Jan. feria 6. That is to say, the 1st of Jan. 491 (= A.D. 492) was on Wednesday, and the 1st of Jan. 492 (= A.D. 493) on Friday; the former year being bissextile. The first date in the Annals of Ulster, is 'Anno ab incarnatione Domini .cccc°.xxx°.i°.'

CHAP. III.]   *The most probable Date.*   497

to 492 and 493 of the common era, the dates in the early portion of the annals of Ulster being counted from the Incarnation, and being, therefore, one year before the common era of the Nativity of our Lord.

On the whole, it seems most probable that Ussher's decision in favour of A.D. 493 is correct. It accords with the later date which the evidence of the epistle about Coroticus and of the Confession appears to assign[1] to the arrival of St. Patrick in Ireland. It is undoubtedly the testimony of the Irish annals, derived from antient national traditions. The principal objection[2] to this date is the supposition of a regular succession of bishops, in the modern sense of the word, at Armagh; with the assumption that Secundinus, Benignus, and Jarlath could not have been the successors of St. Patrick if they had died before him. But this is no real objection, and is founded on ignorance of the antient ecclesiastical customs of Ireland. Another objection, that the year 493 is based upon the fable of the four periods of thirty years in Patrick's life, and upon the similitudes to Moses, is more apparent than real. St. Patrick may have died in 493, without having reached the age of 120, and without having spent sixty years in his Irish mission. It was not, therefore, the year 493, as the date of his death, which required the help of the Mosaic similitudes; but that date having been fixed by

The true date most probably A.D. 493.

---

[1] *To assign.* See above, p. 391. *sq.*   [2] *Objection.* See this objection stated by Lanigan, i. p. 355, *sq.*

K K

the tradition of the Scoti, the attempt to make the year of his mission 432 was the real cause of the legends referred to, and of the confusion which exists in the chronology of his life.

<small>St. Patrick first addressed himself to the chieftains.</small>

In reviewing the history of St. Patrick's missionary labours, we are struck by the fact that he appears to have always addressed himself in the first instance to the kings or chieftains. In Dalaradia, where his earliest church was founded, the site was obtained from the chieftain of the country, Dichu. At Tara he attacked Paganism in its head quarters, and succeeded in obtaining from King Laoghaire a reluctant toleration of his ministry, and an outward profession, at least, of Christianity. In Connaught he addressed himself to the chieftains of Tirawley, and preached to the people at the great assembly of the tribe. In Munster, if that part of his story be true, his first convert was King Aengus himself, whom he baptised at Cashel, the seat of the kings. In Armagh he obtained the favour of Daire, chieftain of the Airtheara or Orior, and received from him the 'civitas' which afterwards became the ecclesiastical metropolis of Ireland.

<small>This policy founded on his knowledge of the people.</small>

This policy may have been pursued by St. Patrick as much from necessity as from a knowledge of the character and habits of the people. The chieftain once secured, the clan, as a matter of course, were disposed to follow in his steps. To attempt the conversion of the clan, in opposition to the will of the chieftain, would probably have been to rush upon inevitable death, or at the least to risk a violent expulsion from the district. The people may not have adopted the outward profession of Christianity, which was all perhaps that in the first instance they adopted, from any clear or intellectual appreciation of its superiority to their former religion; but to obtain from the people even an outward profession of Christianity was an important step to ultimate success. It secured toleration at least for Christian institutions. It enabled Patrick to plant in every tribe his churches, schools, and monasteries. He was permitted without opposition to establish among the half Pagan inhabitants of the country societies of holy men, whose devotion, usefulness, and piety soon produced an effect upon the most barbarous and savage hearts.

This was the secret of the rapid success attributed to St. Patrick's preaching in Ireland. The chieftains were at first the real converts. The baptism of the chieftain was immediately followed by the adhesion of the clan. The clansmen pressed eagerly round the missionary who had baptised the chief, anxious to receive that mysterious initiation into the new faith to which their chieftain and father had submitted. The requirements preparatory to baptism do not seem to have been very rigorous; and it is, therefore, by no means improbable, that in Tirawley, and other remote districts where the spirit of clanship was strong, Patrick, as he tells us himself he did, may have baptised some thousands of men.

His toleration of the Pagan superstitions.

In this policy, also, we may perceive the cause of that spirit of toleration which he seems to have shewn towards the old superstitions. Conscious that he had gained only the outward adherence of the adult members of the clan, he was compelled to use great caution in his attempts to overthrow the antient monuments and usages of Paganism. It was only in some rare instances that he ventured upon the destruction of an idol, or the removal of a pillar-stone. Sometimes he contented himself with inscribing[1] upon such stones the sacred names or symbols of Christianity. The very festivals of the Irish were respected, and converted into Christian solemnities or holidays. The *Beltine* and the *Samhain* of our Pagan forefathers are still observed in the popular sports of May-day and All-hallow-e'en. 'Nothing is clearer,' says Dr. O'Donovan[2], 'than that Patrick engrafted Christianity on the Pagan superstitions with so much skill that he won the people over to the Christian religion before they understood the exact difference between the two systems of belief; and much of this half Pagan, half Christian religion will be found not only in the Irish stories of the middle ages, but in the superstitions of the peasantry to the present day.'

[1] *Inscribing.* A curious instance of this is recorded in the Tripartite Life (ii. c. 52). He was in the Co. of Galway, near Lough Hacket, and there he found three pillar-stones, 'quæ gentilitas ibi in memoriam aliquorum facinorum vel gentilitium rituum posuit.' On these Patrick inscribed the name of Christ in three different languages: on one IESUS, on another SOTER, on the third SALVATOR. See O'Flaherty, *Ogyg.* p. 374.

[2] *Dr. O'Donovan.* Four Masters, A.D. 432, note c, p. 131; and see above, p. 128.

CHAP. III.]   *St. Patrick's Success overrated.*   501

But the extent of St. Patrick's success, as well as the rapidity of his conquests, has been greatly overrated by our popular historians. 'While, in other countries,' says Mr. Moore[1], 'the introduction of Christianity has been the slow work of time, has been resisted by either government or people, and seldom effected without a lavish effusion of blood; in Ireland, on the contrary, by the influence of one humble but zealous missionary, and with little previous preparation of the soil by other hands, Christianity burst forth, at the first ray of apostolic light, and with the sudden ripeness of a northern summer, at once covered the whole land. Kings and princes, when not themselves among the ranks of the converted, saw their sons and daughters joining in the train without a murmur. Chiefs, at variance in all else, agreed in meeting beneath the Christian banner; and the proud Druid and Bard laid their superstitions meekly at the foot of the cross; nor, by a singular disposition of Providence, unexampled indeed in the whole history of the Church, was there a single drop of blood shed, on account of religion, through the entire course of this mild Christian revolution, by which, in the space of a few years, all Ireland was brought tranquilly under the influence of the Gospel.'

Unhappily, a deeper insight into the facts of

The success of Saint Patrick overrated.

---

[1] *Mr. Moore.* History of Ireland, i. p. 203, and see also the Abbé MacGeoghegan, *Hist. d'Irlande*, i. p. 262. 'On peut dire avec vérité, que nulle autre nation dans toute la chrétienneté ne reçut les nouvelles du royaume de Dieu, et la foi de Jesus Christ, avec tant de joie.'

His mission not without danger to himself and his followers.

Irish history effaces much of this pleasing picture. It is not true that no blood was shed. It is not true that *all* Ireland was brought tranquilly under the influence of the Gospel. St. Patrick's life was often attempted, and often in danger. On one occasion his charioteer was slain in mistake for himself. When going into Connaught, he took the precaution of providing himself with an escort, and narrowly escaped the efforts of the Druids to destroy him. His ecclesiastical establishments were surrounded by fortifications[1], for the protection of the inmates; and many of the most celebrated of them, as Armagh, Cashel, Downpatrick, Clogher, and others, were built in situations possessing natural advantages for defence, or near the already fortified habitations of the antient chieftains.

Many tribes rejected his teaching.

There were many districts and tribes of Ireland where the teaching of St. Patrick was rejected.[2] The Hi Garchon are particularly mentioned as having resisted both Palladius and Patrick; and the biographers of the saint would, no doubt, have recorded many similar instances, had it been their object to chronicle the failures instead of the triumphs of their hero. The catalogue[3] of the three orders

---

[1] *Fortifications.* See above, p. 478.

[2] *Rejected.* Tirechan speaks of many chieftains of Ireland in his time (the middle of the seventh century), who refused to submit to the jurisdiction of Armagh, lest the whole island should become subject to the successors of St. Patrick: 'quia video dissertores, et archiclocos et milites Hiberniæ quod odio habent paruchiam Patricii, quia substraxerunt ab eo quod ipsius erat; timentque quoniam si quæreret heres Patricii paruchiam illius, potest pene totam insolam sibi reddere in paruchiam quam Deus dedit illi.' *Book of Armagh,* fol. 11, a.b.

[3] *Catalogue.* See above, Introd. sect. 41, sq.

of Irish saints, and many passages in the Book of Armagh, afford undoubted proofs that *all* Ireland did not submit to Patrick's influence; and the partial apostacy which took place during the two centuries following his death, is a convincing evidence that the Christianity he had planted did not strike its roots as deeply as has been popularly supposed. An adhesion to Christianity, which was in a great measure only the attachment of a clan to its chieftain, and in which Pagan usages, under a Christian name, were of necessity tolerated, could not, in the nature of things, be very lasting.

Many of the foundations of St. Patrick appear to have had the effect of counteracting this evil, by creating a sort of spiritual clanship, well calculated to attract a clannish people, and capable of maintaining itself against the power of the secular chieftains. But this was perhaps an accidental result only: it was certainly not the primary design of these institutions. St. Patrick had a much higher object in view. He seems to have been deeply imbued with faith in the intercessory powers of the Church. He established throughout the land temples and oratories for the perpetual worship of God. He founded societies of priests and bishops, whose first duty it was ' to make constant supplications, prayers, intercessions, and giving of thanks for all men, for kings and for all that are in authority;' persuaded, in accordance with the true spirit of antient Christianity, that the intercessions of

_{Ecclesiastical clanship in the monastic foundations.}

the faithful, in their daily sacrifice of praise and thanksgiving, were efficacious, as St. Paul's words imply, for the salvation of mankind, and for bringing to the knowledge of the truth those upon whom appeals to reason, and arguments addressed to the intellect, would have been probably a waste of words.

The religious societies founded by St. Patrick did not exclude women.

The religious societies thus established did not always exclude from their benefits the weaker sex, and were not, perhaps, in the modern sense of the word, strictly speaking, *monasteries*. At Armagh it is recorded[1] that a sister or relative of St. Patrick, called by some authorities Lupait, with Ercnat, daughter of the chieftain Daire, and Cruimtheris, daughter of a king of Britain, were appointed to discharge the duty of making, washing, and repairing the sacred vestments[2] of the Church. Besides these, there were seven daughters of 'a king of the Lombards,' in connection with the society, and others, perhaps, whose names the biographers have not preserved.

The lands granted for the foundation of churches often conveyed the rights of chieftainship.

The lands given by the piety of St. Patrick's converts, for the foundation of these establishments, often conveyed the rights of chieftainship[3], and so secured the allegiance of the clan. When this was the case, many of the causes obstructive to Christianity were removed, and the people were with less difficulty weaned from their

---

[1] *Recorded.* See *Vit. Trip.* iii. c. 72—76.

[2] *Vestments.* Colgan, *Actt. SS.* in *Vit. S. Ergnatæ*, p. 41. These three ladies are mentioned in the poetical list of St. Patrick's household, as his *druinecha*, or embroiderers; *Four Mast.* A.D. 448, p. 139.

[3] *Chieftainship.* See above, *Introd.* p. 152, *sq.*

antient superstitions, and brought the more fully under the influence of the Gospel. But in some places the lay succession continued, and in time swallowed up[1], or became identified with the ecclesiastical authority. In every case, however, it is evident that the spirit of clanship[2] was engrafted upon the institutions of the Church. This, in the earlier ages of Christianity in Ireland, tended to protect the monastic societies from outrage and plunder, as well as to spread their influence amongst the people. This was also the real cause of the great extension[3] of the monastic life in Ireland. The state of society rendered it practically impossible to maintain the Christian life, except under some monastic rule. The will of the chieftain was law. The clansman was liable at any time to be called upon to serve upon some wild foray, in a quarrel or feud with which he had personally no concern. The domestic ties were unknown, or little respected. No man could call his life or property, his wife or children, his own; and yet, such is the inconsistency of human nature, the people clung to their chieftains and to their clan with a fidelity and an affection which continue to the present day. Hence the spirit of clanship readily transferred itself to the monastery. The abbat was sometimes also chieftain, or a near relative of the chieftain,

Causes of the extension and popularity of the monastic life in Ireland.

---

[1] *Swallowed up.* See a valuable paper by Dr. Reeves, in the Proceedings of the Royal Irish Academy, vol. vi. p. 447.
[2] *Clanship.* See what has been said on this subject, Introd. p. 226.
[3] *Extension.* 'L'Irlande a vû presq' aussi-tot des moines que des Chrétiens.' *MacGeoghegan, Hist. d'Irlande,* i. p. 275.

and the welfare or progress of the monastic society was identified with the prosperity of the clan.

Natives of Ireland made priests and bishops by St. Patrick.

St. Patrick seems, in a large majority of instances, to have placed natives of the country as priests and bishops over the ecclesiastical or monastic societies which were founded by him. This may, at first sight, seem difficult to understand. It is not possible (miracle apart) that a lawless chieftain, baptised in adult life, could be at once converted into a devoted priest or a saintly bishop, without any previous preparation or instruction. But it is a prominent feature in St. Patrick's history, that he was at all times accompanied by a body of men under training for the priesthood. The biographers, it is true, sometimes represent him as ordaining a convert, or even consecrating him a bishop, immediately after his baptism; but we are not to interpret such statements too literally. Some time must be understood to have intervened between the baptism of an Irish convert and his ordination. A machinery for his education is spoken of as at hand. The churches and ecclesiastical or collegiate bodies established by St. Patrick throughout the country, must have had considerable educational influences. Every such society, as it was formed, became a school for the education of the clergy. The daily offices of devotion trained the inmates to the correct observance of the ritual of the Church, and prepared them to become the heads, as priests or bishops, of similar establishments.

It is recorded also that Patrick, on several occasions, taught the *abgitorium*[1], that is to say, the alphabet, to such of his converts as were destined for holy orders; this is sometimes expressed by saying that he wrote for them 'the elements,' *scripsit elementa*—by which phrase the alphabet seems also to have been intended. But it may be said, we are not compelled to understand the instruction so designated as confined to the mere alphabet in the literal sense of the word. To teach *letters* is a phrase which is still in use, to denote education generally. The elements of learning may have been included, when we read that Patrick taught the alphabet; and so the biographers seem to have understood the words. The Tripartite Life, following the Book of Armagh, tells us, that when St. Patrick was in Ciarraidhe-LochanArnedha, now the barony of Costello, county of Mayo, he found Ernasc and his son Loarn sitting under a tree:—

The Abgitoria written by St. Patrick.

'with whom he remained, together with his twelve companions, for a week, and they received from him the doctrine of salvation with attentive ear and mind. In the meanwhile he instructed Loarn, for whom he wrote the alphabet, in the rudiments of learning and piety.'[2]

This Loarn, or Locharnach, as he is called in the Book of Armagh, was afterwards made abbat

---

[1] *Abgitorium.* This word is a corruption of *Abecedarium*, in Irish *Aibgitir*, or more correctly *Abcitir*, the ABC, or alphabet. See Du Cange, in vv. *Abgatorium* and *Abctorium*.

[2] *Piety.* 'Loarnum interea, cui et alphabetum scripsit, in litterarum et pietatis instruendo rudimentis.' *Vit. Trip.* ii. c. 57. 'Scripsit illi elimenta,' *B. of Armagh*, fol. 13, *a.b.*

of a church which Patrick founded in that place. He was, therefore, evidently designed for the ecclesiastical life when St. Patrick taught him the alphabet with the rudiments of learning.

The Abgitoria always taught as a preparation for holy orders.

And we may remark, that in every case where mention is made of Patrick having written *abgitoria*, or alphabets, for his converts, it is clearly implied that this was done as a preparation for holy orders. Thus Tirechan, in the Book of Armagh, prefaces his list of the clergy ordained by St. Patrick, in the following words. Having mentioned that Patrick had consecrated three hundred and fifty bishops in Ireland, he adds:[1]—

'of presbyters we cannot count the number, because he used to baptise men daily, and to read letters and *abgatoriæ* with them, and of some he made bishops and presbyters, because they had received baptism in mature age.'

In another place, the same author records the consecration of Senach as bishop at Achad-Fobhair[2], and tells us that Patrick wrote for his son Oengus an abgitorium, on the day on which his father Senach was ordained.[3]

The only other place in which the abgitorium

---

[1] *Adds.* 'De præspiteris non possimus ordinare, quia babtitzavit cotidie homines et illis litteras legebat et abgatorias, et de aliis episcopos ac presbyteros faciebat quia in etate baptismum accieperunt sobria.' *Book of Armagh*, fol. 9, b.a.

[2] *Achad-Fobhair.* Now Aghagower, Co. of Mayo. See O'Donovan, *Hy Fiachrach*, p. 150, 151.

[3] *Ordained.* 'Cui scripsit Patricius abgitorium in die qua ordinatus erat Senachus.' *Book of Armagh*, fol. 13, b.a. 'Quem S. Patricius alphabeto præscripto litterarum fundamenta cœpit docere, eodem die quo ipse S. Senachus episcopus ordinatus est.' *Vit. Trip.* ii. c. 72. It is curious that Nennius, c. 60, represents Patrick to have written 365 abgitoria, or *abietoria*, as most copies read; and to have consecrated also 365 churches and 365 bishops. It will be remembered that the ceremony of writing the Greek and Roman alphabets on the floor was one of the ancient rites used in the consecration of churches.

CHAP. III.] *Abgitoria mistaken for Swords.* 509

is mentioned, is a passage, which is somewhat obscure, but its obscurity does not affect our present argument. St. Patrick was somewhere near the banks of the river Erne, between the cataract of Easroe and the sea. He had there baptised a man and his infant son; and wrote for him, that is for the father, an abgitorium, and blessed him with the blessing of a bishop.[1]

Another curious passage renders it probable that the word abgitorium, although evidently a corrupt form of abecedarium, and in its primary sense an alphabet, may have ultimately come to signify not an alphabet properly so called, but a waxed tablet prepared for writing, such as was used by the antient schoolmasters for teaching their scholars the elements of learning. St. Patrick, with eight or nine companions, 'having *tablets* in their hands, written after the manner of Moses,'[2] was seen by the pagan inhabitants of the country, who mistook the tablets for swords,

The Abgitoria mistaken for swords.

---

[1] *Bishop.* 'Et scripsit illi abgitorium et benedixit eum benedictione episcopi.' *Book of Armagh*, fol. 15, *a.b.* There are three passages (besides that quoted p. 507 *n.*) in the Book of Armagh in which the phrase 'elementa scripsit' is employed, in connection with preparation for holy orders; 'et alteram ecclesiam *Immruig Thuaithe* [fundavit], et scripsit elimenta Cerpano,' fol. 10, *b.a.* 'Et elegit unum filium ex ipsis cui nomen erat Macc Ercæ, et scripsit elementa et benedixit eum benedictione patris.' *Fol.* 14, *b.b.* 'Et benedixit filium, qui est Macc Rime episcopus, et scripserunt elementa illi, &c.' *Fol.* 15, *a a.*

[2] *Of Moses.* 'Et viderunt illum [Patricium], cum viris viii. aut ix. cum tabulis in manibus scriptis more Moysaico, exclamaverunt gentiles super illos ut sanctos occiderent, et dixerunt gladios in manibus habent ad occidendos homines, videntur lignei in die apud illos, sed ferreos gladios æstimamus ad effundendum sanguinem.' *Book of Armagh*, fol. 9, *a.a.* The Tablets were therefore long and narrow. It seems difficult to suppose that tablets intended for writing should have been really mistaken for swords; but there must have been some remote resemblance to the short swords of the antient Irish, to render the pretended mistake plausible.

exclaiming that although seemingly of wood, they were really of iron, and were intended to shed blood. Such a mistake could only have been a pretence to excuse an intended outrage; but 'a merciful man,' *vir misericors*, who was amongst them, named Hercaith, opposed the violent designs of the mob. He and his son Feradach believed, and were baptised. He dedicated his son to Patrick, *immolavit filium Patricio*. Patrick changed the young man's name to Sachell, or Sacellus, and wrote for him a copy of the book of Psalms, which the writer who records this legend says he had seen.[1]

<small>A knowledge of alphabetic writing not first taught to the Irish by St. Patrick.</small>

We cannot give much weight to the argument[2] that Patrick was the first to bring alphabetic characters into the country, and that the Irish before his time had no knowledge of any sort of writing, because he is said to have written alphabets for his converts. If this had been so, it is scarcely possible to doubt that the Irish would have boasted of having learned letters from St. Patrick. The vanity of having known the alphabet before his time, would scarcely have been allowed to deprive him of the glory of having made known to Ireland the foundation of all learning, along with the still greater blessings of the Christian faith. But there does not occur a

---

[1] *Seen.* 'Et scripsit illi librum Psalmorum, quem vidi.' *Book of Armagh*, fol. 9, *a.a.* A copy of the Gospels, said to have been brought into Ireland by St. Patrick, is still preserved in the library of the Royal Irish Academy, although greatly decayed. See p. 469, *n. supra*, and Petrie's Essay on the Domhnach-airgid, Trans. Royal Irish Acad. vol. xviii. Antiq. p. 14, *sq.*

[2] *Argument.* See Bolland. *Actt. SS. ad* 17 *Mart.* p. 517.

single hint in Irish tradition to shew that the knowledge of the alphabet was believed to have been communicated by St. Patrick.

It has been suggested, indeed, by some writers[1], that as the Irish had a peculiar alphabet of their own, the abgitorium or alphabet made known to them by St. Patrick was the Roman alphabet. But this is founded on a mistake. The alphabet now called the Irish alphabet, and supposed to be peculiar to the Irish language, is nothing more than the Roman alphabet, which was used over all Europe in the fifth and some following centuries. The probability, therefore, is, that the Roman alphabet, if not taught by St. Patrick, certainly became known in Ireland about his time; but it does not follow that the Irish were ignorant of written characters before that period. The older alphabet, perhaps, was known only to the bards or Druids, and communicated to the initiated alone. But it is certain that the Gauls, or at least the Druids of Gaul, even in Cæsar's time[2], had written characters; and antient Gaulish inscriptions, long anterior to the fifth century, are extant. There is nothing unreasonable, therefore, in supposing that the Irish Druids, who from very early times had a close connection

---

[1] *Writers.* See Harris's *Ware, Antiq.* p. 25. MacGeoghegan, *Hist. d'Irlande*, i. pp. 28, 29. It is now well ascertained that the Ogham characters are later than the times of St. Patrick, and derived most probably from the Scandinavian Runes. See Dr. Graves's papers *Proceedings of the R. I. Acad.* vol. iv. pp. 177, 361.

[2] *Cæsar's time.* ' Itaque nonnulli [Druides] annos vicenos in disciplina permanent, neque fas esse existimant ea literis mandare, cum in reliquis fere rebus, publicis privatisque rationibus, græcis literis utantur.' *De Bello Gall.* lib. vi. c. 14.

with their brethren of Gaul[1], may have also had the art of writing. St. Patrick is said to have burnt the idolatrous books[2] of the Irish Druids, preparatory to his reformation of the pagan laws. This story is probably a fable; but it proves the tradition or belief of the people that there was a written literature, and an alphabet in pagan times. The truth may lie, as it often does, between two extremes. St. Patrick most probably introduced what was then the alphabet of the rest of Europe, which has since, by a strange reverse of fortune, become peculiar to Ireland; he taught it, without reserve, to those whom he destined for holy orders, and encouraged them to make it known to others. It was the alphabet in which he taught them to write copies of the Holy Scriptures, as well as Missals, and other sacred books, required for the service of the church. The art of writing was no longer an occult piece of learning confined to a particular class. It became known with the Roman alphabet[3] to the Christian converts of St. Patrick,

---

[1] *Gaul.* Tacitus tells us that in the century before Christ the seaports of Ireland were well known to commercial men. 'Aditus portusque per commercia et negociatores cogniti.' *Agricola.* c. 24.

[2] *Books.* See Petrie, *Tara*, p. 81.

[3] *Alphabet.* There is a curious specimen of an Abgitorium carved on a pillar-stone in the cemetery of Kilmalkedar, County of Kerry. Dr. Petrie has given an accurate representation of it in a woodcut, *Round Towers*, p. 133. From the antiquity of the characters it is probable that this inscription may be as old as the sixth or seventh century. On the front of the stone is a cross, within two concentric circles, about one half of which is lost, owing to the upper part of the stone having been broken. Under this is an ornamental processional cross, the shaft of which extends the whole length of the stone. On the left hand side, are the letters, DÑI, which with the cross were no doubt intended to be read, 'Crux Domini.' Over and around these letters, in smaller but coeval characters, is the Roman alphabet, wanting A, owing to the fracture of the

and the alphabet, which had been before that time peculiar to the Druids, and was probably of Greek origin, became extinct.

To pursue this subject, however, would be inconsistent with the purpose of the present work. That a pagan literature existed in Ireland before the coming of St. Patrick, and that some of that literature[1] is still preserved, is highly probable. Several fragments of very high antiquity, and having internal evidence of a pagan origin, are to be found among the remains of the Brehon laws. But we are now concerned only with the fact that St. Patrick appears to have taught letters and alphabets, whatever that may imply, with the express purpose of preparing his converts for holy orders. The priests and bishops to whom he left the important duty of continuing his work, were in almost every instance, as we have already observed, natives of Ireland; and the monastic or collegiate churches established by him were founded with the double object of providing ecclesiastical education, and of keeping up in the Church the perpetual supplications, prayers, intercessions, and giving of thanks, which the apostle commanded as a duty, the 'first of all.'[2]

Hence it was that in Ireland Christianity be-

---

stone just mentioned. The alphabet, including K and Q, is given as far as U, after which are some marks not very legible, and probably injured, which may have been originally X, Y, Z. The Irish Life of St. Columba represents him as having had an *Abgitir*, or alphabet, written *on a cake*. Reeves, *Adamn.* p. 359, note *l*.

[1] *Literature*. See Petrie, *on Tara*, p. 38, *sq*. O'Flaherty, *Ogygia*, iii. c. 30, p. 214.

[2] *First of all*. 1 Tim. ii. 1. Παρακαλῶ οὖν πρῶτον πάντων.

came at once a national institution. It was not looked upon as coming from foreigners, or as representing the manners and civilisation of a foreign nation. Its priests and bishops, the successors of St. Patrick in his missionary labours, were many of them descendants of the antient kings and chieftains so venerated by a clannish people. The surrounding chieftains and men in authority, who still kept aloof in paganism, were softened by degrees, when they perceived that in all the assemblies of the Christian Church fervent prayers were offered to God for them. In this point of view the public incense of prayer and 'lifting up of hands' of the Church in a heathen land, is perhaps the most important engine of missionary success. 'Nothing,' says St. Chrysostom[1], 'is so apt to draw men under teaching as to love, and to be loved,' to be prayed for in the spirit of love.

Missionary character of St. Patrick. On the whole, the biographers of St. Patrick, notwithstanding the admixture of much fable, have undoubtedly pourtrayed in his character the features of a great and judicious missionary. He seems to have made himself 'all things,' in accordance with the apostolic injunction, to the rude and barbarous tribes of Ireland. He dealt tenderly with their usages and prejudices. Although he sometimes felt it necessary to overturn their idols, and on some occasions risked his life, he was guilty of no offensive or unnecessary iconoclasm. A native himself of

---

[1] *St. Chrysostom.* Hom. VI. in 1 Tim. τὸ φιλεῖν καὶ φιλεῖσθαι.

another country, he adopted the language of the Irish tribes, and conformed to their political institutions. By his judicious management, the Christianity which he founded became self-supporting. It was endowed by the chieftains without any foreign aid. It was supplied with priests and prelates by the people themselves; and its fruits were soon seen in that wonderful stream of zealous missionaries, the glory of the Irish Church, who went forth in the sixth and seventh centuries, to evangelize the barbarians of central Europe. In a word, the example and success of St. Patrick have bequeathed to us this lesson, that the great object of the missionary bishop should be to establish among the heathen the true and unceasing worship of God's Church, and to supply that Church with a native ministry.

INDEX

ABBATES laici of Ireland and Wales, 155 *n.*
Abel, Abbat and Bishop of Laubes, a Scot by race, 59
Aberdeen, Breviary of, 299
— its lessons for St. Palladius at variance with its Calendar, 300
Abernethy, antient Bishopric of, transferred to St. Andrews, 44 *n.*
Abgitoria or Alphabets, meaning of the word, 507
— taught by St. Patrick to candidates for the ecclesiastical life, 508
— may signify tablets for writing, 509
— Patrick wrote 365 alphabets according to Nennius, 508 *n.*
— mistaken for swords, 509
— specimen of, carved on stone, 512 *n.*
— written on a cake for St. Columba, 513 *n.*
Achad Fobhair, now Aghagower, co. of Mayo, 508 *n.*
Achad Farcha, 435
Adamnan, Life of Columba, quoted, 6, 7, 118. See *Columba.*
— his *Cain,* or tribute, 405 *n.*
Adelfius, probably Bishop of Caerleon on Usk, 268
Adrian I. See *Hadrian.*
Adrian IV. claims ownership of Ireland and confers it on Henry II., 48 *n.*; his Bull, 231
Aedh, Bishop of Sletty, 401
Aedh Dubh, his ordination and history, 8, 9
Aedh the Great, and Aedh the Less, brothers, 154
Aedh, son of Ainmire, King of Ireland, 133
— measures proposed by him to Convention of Drumceatt, 134 *n.*
— a party in his court hostile to the clergy, 137

Aedh, son of Eochaidh Doimhlen, surnamed Colla Meann, 471
— slain, 472
Aedh (St.), surnamed Mac Carthenn. See *Mac Carthenn*
Aedh, mac Bric, 463
Aengus, son of Natfraich, King of Munster, his conversion, 129 ; baptised, 467, 498
— accident at the baptism, 468
— slain, 467 *n.*
Agapetus I. (Pope), only a Deacon when consecrated Bishop, 87
Aghagower. See *Achad Fobhair*
Agricola, son of Bishop Severianus, introduced Pelagianism into Britain, 271
Ailbe (St.), of Emly, his history, 203
— etymology of his name, 204
— met St. Declan at Rome, *ib.*
— his tutor Hilary, not Pope Hilary, *ib.*
— followed to Rome by fifty Irishmen, 205
— converted the *filii Goill, ib.*
— not a native of Dalaradia, 206
— visits St. Deelan, 211
— date of his death, 206, 211
— constituted Metropolitan of Munster, 218
— Irish stanza on, 219
Ailbe, Presbyter, 222
— date of his death, 225 *n.*
Ailcluaid, 267, 356
Aileran (St.), author of a Life of St. Patrick, 296
Aillil, son of Dunlaing, baptised, 465
Aill mic Cuirr, 404 *n.*
Aillinn, daughter of Aengus Mac Natfraich, 434
Airbhe, meaning of the word, 119 *n.*
Airchinneach, 160
— etymology of the word, 162
Airer Gaedhil, now Argyle, 267

Airer Gaedhil, Bede's description of, 267
Airthear. See *Oirthear*
Albigenses, their doctrine of the *endura*, 463
Alcluith, 267
Alphabet, not first taught to the Irish by St. Patrick, 510
— known to the Druids of Gaul in Cæsar's time, 511
— probably taught to the Irish Druids, 512
— the present Irish alphabet identical with the Roman, 511
— probably taught by St. Patrick, *ib.*
Altimachæ. See *Ardd-Machæ*
Amalgaidh, or Amolngaid, 442 *n.*
— his sons, 443 *n.*
Amand (St.), biographer of St. Boniface, 47
Amator or Amatorex, Bishop of Auxerre, 317, 335
— consecrates St. Patrick, 317, 323, 326
Amhra Coluimcille, 138
— virtues ascribed to, 139
Amolngaid. See *Amalgaidh*
Anat-cailtrin, 343
Andegarius or Audegarius, Bishop of St. Martin's at Tours, 57
Andrews (St.), antiently Cill-Righmonaigh, 44 *n.*
Animosus, his Life of St. Brigid, 19 *n.*
Anna-down (or Enach-Duin), 38
Annals of ecclesiastical events, from the Book of Leinster, 183-188
— Irish, dates assigned by them to St. Patrick's mission and death, 393
Anselm (St.), his letter to Muirchertagh O'Brien, 1, 2
Antioch, Council of (A.D. 341), 45
Aonach, meaning of the word, 439 *n.*
Aonach-Tailltenn, now Telltown, 343, 439
Aondruim, or Nendrum, 412 *n.*
Apostles, Twelve, of Ireland, 99 *n.*, 147
— why so called, 147, 148
— their influence as a body, 149
— sent for to avert the curse on banquet of Dun-na-ngedh, 148
Aquino, Bishop of, subject to the Abbat of Cassino, 67
Aras, a house, 257 *n.*, 258 *n.*
Aras-Celtchair, 492 *n.*
Archbishop, meaning of the term in antient Irish records, 14-19
Arcuil, now valley of the Braid, 374

Ard-comarb, 157
Ardd-machæ, antient name of Armagh, 475
— signification of the word, 475 *n.*
— Ussher's mistake as to, *ib.* See *Armagh*
Ardmor, co. of Waterford, 211
Ard-na-gcaorach, 211
Ard-patrick, a hill near Louth, 469 *n.*
Aregal (oraculum), an oratory, 477, 478
Argyle, signification of name, 267
Arles, Synod of, 268
Armagh, date of its foundation, 468, 469
— legend of, 472 *sq.*
— jurisdiction of, not universally received, 502
— See *Druim Sailech* ; *Ardd-machæ*
Armagh, Book of, history of foundation of Trim, from, 257
— called Canon of Patrick, 485 *n.*
Arnon (Mount), 323, 337
Asciciput, an error, 411 *n.*
Asterius, T. Rufus, collected the works of Sedulius, 196
Athanasius (St.), only a deacon when consecrated bishop, 87
Ath-dara, a ford on the Barrow, 437
Ath-Truim, foundation of, 149, 150 *sq.*
Atomriug, meaning of the word, 426 *n.*
Attigny, Synod of, 68 *n.*
Augustine (St.), speaks with respect of Pelagius and Cœlestius, 192
Augustinus, companion of Palladius, 280, 301, 324, 326
Autbert, Bishop of Avranches, 337
Auxilius, ordained with St. Patrick, 317, 332, 486

BAAL, the Phœnician god, unknown to the Irish, 414 *n.*
Baptism of great numbers by St. Patrick, 449
— festival of St. Patrick's, 450
Bards, favoured by the clergy, 130
— their influence against Christianity, 132
— attempts to suppress the order, 132 *sq.*
— reformation of the order at the convention of Drumceatt, 135, 136
Barses, a bishop, 45, 46
Beatus, Biat, or Bié, first bishop of Lausanne, 193

Index. 519

Bede (St.), his testimony of the subjection of bishops to the abbat in Hi, 10 *n.*
Beg-Eri, now Begery or Begrin Island, 216 *n.*
Belle-isle in Lough Erne, its antient name, 470 *n.*
Beltaine, or Beltine, festival of, 134 *n.*
— — when celebrated, 414
— — still observed, 500
— — meaning of the name, 414 *n.*
Benedict (St.), his rule recognises the monastic bishop, 69
Benedictus, companion of Palladius, 280, 301, 324, 326
Benin, Benen, or Benignus of Armagh, 130, 412 *n.*
Bernard (St.), his complaint of irregularities in the Church of Ireland, 2, 3
— his Life of St. Malachy, 155 *n.*
Berraidhe, chieftain of Offaly, 464
— his descent, *ib. n.*
Betham, Sir W., 309
Biat (St.) or Bie. See *Beatus*
Binn Gulban, or Binn Bulbin, 440 *n.*
Bishops, deference paid to in the Columban monasteries, 6–10
— subject to the abbat in Columban abbeys, 7 *sq.*
— subject to the abbess in Kildare, 13, 14
— multiplication of in Ireland, 27
— independent in Ireland, 27
— number consecrated by St. Patrick, 28
— living together with Mochta of Louth, 31
— seven living together, 32 ; meaning of the institution, 35
— seven, of Cluain-emain, or Clonown, 34, 35
— 141 groups of seven bishops, mentioned by Aengus, 32, 35
— bishops of the Clans, 38
— conciliar laws against Scotic bishops, 40 *sq.*
— episcopi vagantes, laws relating to, 40 *n.*
— pseudo bishops pretending to be Irish, 42 *n.*
— without sees ($\sigma\chi o\lambda \acute{a}\zeta o\nu\tau\epsilon\varsigma$), on the Continent of Europe, 45
— monastic bishop at St. Denis, 51
— at St. Martin's Tours, 56
— at Lobes or Laubes in Belgium, 57

Bishops, monastic, not peculiar to Ireland, 48
— bishops in Ireland before St. Patrick, 198 ; origin of the story, 221 the story unknown to Jocelin, 224
Blackwater, 439
Boethin (St.), 298
Boethius (Hector), his description of the antient episcopal system of Scotland, 44 *n.*
Bonaght, what, 228
Bonavem Taberniæ, 355, 362
Boind, the river Boyne, 257 *n.*, 259, 368 *n.*
— inflexions of the word, 257 *n.*
Bollandists, their date of the death of St. Patrick, 495
Boniface. See *Winfrid*
Books, magical virtues of, 105, 124
Boromean tribute, 437
Boscoi, or grazing monks, had a bishop of their own, 46
Boulogne-sur-mer, not the birthplace of St. Patrick, 358
Braid, valley of, 374
Braighde, or Braid, river, 374
Brechmigh in Ui Dortain, 260
Bregia, or Magh Bregh, 406 *n.*, 420
— St. Patrick founds churches in, 441
Brehon Law Commiffion, 484 *n.*
Brendan, St., the navigator, 459, 460
Brene, strait of, 406
Brettan. See *Brittan*
Brig, mother of St. Etchen, her descent from Cathair Mor, 255
— mother of King Aedh son of Ainmire, 255
Bright. See *Brittan*
Brigid (St.), her monastery of Kildare, 11
— her choice of a bishop, 12
— ordained a bishop by St. Mel, 13 *n.*
— her prophecy of the declension of faith in Ireland, 108
— her relationship to St. Columba, Table IV., 252
— her relationship to her first Bishop Conlaedh, Table V., 253
Britanniæ, 356
Britanny, Armoric, 360
Brittan, or Brettan, now Bright, co. of Down, 293 *n.*, 459 *n.*
Broccaide, abbat or Bishop of Imleach-Each, 152

Broccaide, brother of Lomman, 260
Broccan, brother of Lomman, 260
Brogan (St.) his Life of St. Brigid, 23
Brogsech, mother of St. Brigid, 34
Bruce (Edward), alliance of the Irish with, 240
Buidhe Chonaill, or flava ictericia, 213 *n.*

CABCENNA, river of, 492, *n.*, 493.
Cabilonense Concilium, 40 *n.*
Cadoc, or Cattwg, his original name Cathmael, 99
Cælestius, the Scot alluded to by St. Jerome, 190
— why supposed to be of Irish birth, 192 *n.*
Caencomhrac mac Mael-uidhir, 485 *n.*
Caerleon, upon Usk, 268 *n.*
Caiman (St.) of Dair-inis, 99
Cain Patraic, or Cain Phadruig, the law of Patrick, 483, 485 *n.*
— meaning of the word *Cain*, 485 *n.*
— Cain Adamnain, *ib.*
Cairbre Righfada, 266
Cairel, son of Eochaidh Doimhlen, surnamed Colla Uais, 471
Cairnech, 483 *n.*
Cairpri. See *Carbri* and *Cairbre*
Cake, alphabet written on, 513 *n.*
Calpurnius, father of St. Patrick, 353
'Calvus like Caplit,' a Scotic proverb, 445
Campus Girgin, 296
Campus Taberniæ, 357.
Cannech (St.), or Canice, of Kilkenny, story of, 116
— his adventure with the œconomus of Ducus, 168
Canoin, significations of the word, 485 *n.*
Canoin Phadruigh, not a collection of Canons, 485 *n.*
Canon of Patrick, Book of Armagh so called, 485 *n.*
Canons, rule for consecration by three bishops, 79 *sq.*
— Irish collection of, published by D'Achery, 97, 143, 144; by Martene, 145; MS. of them in the Vallicellian Library, Rome, 145 *n.*
— attributed to St. Patrick, 484
Caolàn. See *Mochaoi*

Caplit, the Druid, 451
— his conversion to Christianity, 454, 455
Carbri, or Cairpri, son of Niall of the nine hostages, 439
Cashel, St. Patrick's visit to, 467; fictitious, 468
— not at first proposed as the Archiepiscopal See of Munster, 468
— not of ecclesiastical importance before the 9th century, 468
— King of, confirmed and crowned by the successor of Patrick, 468
— Psalter of, 173
Catalogue of the Saints of Ireland, 88 *n.*, 503
— proves that St. Patrick's jurisdiction was resisted, 503
Cathach, the book so called, 124
— the battle crozier of St. Grellan, so called, 125 *n.*
Cathair mòr, King of Ireland, 464 *n.*
Cathal, abbat of Ferns, 166
Cathaldus of Tarentum, an Irishman, 195
— a teacher in the school of Lismore, 196
— belonged to the second order of saints, *ib.*
Cathlaid, a pilgrim, 152, 261
— probably not a bishop, 153
Cathmael, otherwise Cadoc, or Cattwg, 99
Caubene, river, 493 *n.*
Cealcythe, Synod of, 41
Ceancroithi, name of an idol, 128 *n.*
Cechtumbria (St.), or Cectamaria, 381 *n.*
Celestine, Pope, sends Germanus to Britain and Palladius to Ireland, 270
Cellair. See *Killare*
Cell-fine. See *Kill-fine*, 294, 295, 297
Cell-Osnada, battle of, 468 *n.*
Cenn-airthir, 290 *n.*
Cennerbhe, name of an idol, 128 *n.*
Cenn-Losnado, 468 *n.*
Celtchar or Keltchar, 492
Cethiac, 443
Cethuberis (St.), 381 *n.*
Cerpanus, 509 *n.*
Chalons sur Saone, Council of, 40
Chieftainry, rights of, transferred to the Ecclesiastical Lord, 149
Chieftains, first addressed by St. Patrick, 498
— loyalty of the Irish to, 230

Index.   521

Chieftains, Irish, remonstrance of, to Pope John XXII., 236 *n.*
Chorepiscopus, Columba did not seek this order from St. Etchen, 76
— chorepiscopi, probably only presbyters, 76 *n.*
Christianity in Ireland before St. Patrick, 189, 221
— proved by the legend of the altar and glass chalices, 222
— by the mission of Palladius, 225
Chronology of St. Patrick's life, altered to make way for his Roman mission, 399
Church of Ireland, its missionary character, 36 *sq.*
— two Churches in Ireland since the eleventh century, 231, 241
Churches, East and West, in Patrick's time 410
— transverse, 410; sinistralis ecclesia, 411 *n.*
Ciaran, or Kieran (St.), of Saigher, 199 *sq.*
— St. Patrick's prophecy of, 200
— said to have been 30 years in Ireland before St. Patrick, 201
— founds Seir-Kieran, *ib.*
— one of the Twelve Apostles of Ireland, 202
— belonged to second order of saints, 202
— said to have been 300 years old, *ib.*
Ciarraidhe Locha nArnedha, 507
Cill Achaidh-droma-foda, 345 *n.*
Cill Dumha-gluinn, or Cill Dumigluinn, now Kilglin, 260
Cillemoinni, now Kilmoone, co. Meath, 170 *n.*
Cill Finnabrach (now Kilfenora), 38
Cill-mhic-Duach (now Killmacduagh), 38
Cill-Righmonaigh, antient name of St. Andrews, 44 *n.*
Cillin or Killin, chieftain of the Hy Garrchu, 466
Cinel Laoghaire, two districts inhabited by, 262
Cinne (St.), 381 *n.*
Clann, meaning of the word, 157
Clanna Rudhraighe, or Clanna Rury, 406 *n.*
Clanship, spirit of, pervaded the Church of Ireland, 226
— key to Irish History, 227
— abolition of, under James I., *ib.*

Clanship, evil consequences of its abolition, 228 *sq.*
— ecclesiastical, 503
Claudian, quoted, 283
Clebach, a well at Crochan, 451, 452
Clogher, meaning of the name, 129, 130 *n.*
— its idol stone, Cermand Celstach, 129
— date of foundation of, 467 *n.*, 499 *n.*
Cloin Lagen, the plain of Leinster, 151, 259
Clon Bronaigh, Nunnery of, near Granard, 408 *n.*
Cluain-emain (now Clonown), seven bishops of, 34
Clugach, meaning of the word, 137 *n.*
Cnoc-a-tionol, 448 *n.*
Coarbs of Patrick, antient lists of, 172 *sq.* See *Comarbs*
Codraige, one of St. Patrick's names, 363
Coelfrid, Abbat, his discussion with Adamnan on the tonsure, 487
— his letter to Naiton, King of the Picts, 487 *n.*
Coinnmeidh, or Coigne. See *Coyne*
Cogitosus, his Life of St. Brigit; its date, 11 *n.*; his Irish name, 402 *n.*
Colla's, the Three, 471
— — their real names, *ib.*
Collum bovis, 492
Colman (St.) of Dromore, his contest with the bards, 131
Colman, a presbyter, afterwards Bishop, converted the parents of St. Declan, 208
— probably the same as Colman of Cloyne, *ib.*
Colony, Scotic, or Gaedhelic, date of, 248
— came from Spain, *ib.*
Columba (St.), or Columkille, deference paid by him to a bishop, 7
— — his attendants to the synod of Drumchett, 28
— — story of his transcript of St. Finnian's Gospels, 106
— — legend of his ordination, 70
— — anecdote of his vocal powers, 118
— — his escape from the Court of King Diarmait, 121, 122
— — his poem on the occasion, 122
— — was himself a bard, 130

Columba (St.), the Amhra or elegy on, 138
—— his family and that of St. Brigid descended from a common ancestor, Table IV., 252
—— his successors claimed right of visitation in Ossory, 467
Columbanus, established a perpetual service of praise to God at Luxeuil, 36 *n.*
— his rule, 166
Comar, meaning of the word, 471 *n.*
Comarbs, meaning of the word, 155, 156
— held visitations, 158
— battles between, 158. See *Coarbs*
Comgall, of Bangor, persuaded by the Saints of Ireland to remain at home, 117 *n.*
Conaille Muirthemne, 361, 406 *n.*
Conall (son of Aedh, King of Ireland) insults the clergy, 137
— his insanity, *ib.*
— cursed by St. Columba, *ib.*
— why called *Clugach*, 137 *n.*
Conall Cearnach, of the Clanna Rudhraighe, 198 *n.*, 406 *n.*
—— his Pictish wife, 407 *n.*
Conall mac Neill, surnamed Gulban, his conversion, 440
Conalnei, 406 *n.*
Conches, or Conchessa, St. Patrick's mother, 353
Conchubhair, or Connor, a branch of the Desi, of Meath, 213
Condlead, or Conlianus, Bishop of Kildare, 19, 20
— meaning of the name, 20; called also Rondchend, *ib.*; date of his death, *ib. n.*
— legend of his vestments, 22
— his disobedience to Brigid, 24; he was Brigid's artist, 25, 26
— his relationship to St. Brigid, Table V., 253
Confession of St. Patrick does not mention his Roman mission, 310
—— editions of, 346 *n.*
—— its authenticity, 347 *n.*
—— written at the close of Patrick's life, 379
—— its concluding paragraph, 381
—— its doctrine, 388
—— St. Patrick's creed in, 388
—— its testimony irreconcilable with the Roman Mission and continental education of St. Patrick, 386

Confession of St. Patrick, Tillemont's judgment of, 382
—— date of St. Patrick's mission deduced from, 392
—— Armagh copy of, 347; apparently abridged, 348 *n.*
Congbal, a church, 477 *n.*
Consecration of bishops by a single bishop, 74 *sq.*, 77
Constantius, of Lyons, 269
— his Life of St. Germain, 336
Contest for the body of St. Patrick, 491
Corbe, not a chorepiscopus, 155 *n.* See *Comarb*
Corca-laidhe, district of, coextensive with the diocese of Ross, 38
Corca-Modruaidh (now Corcomroe), 38
Cormac's Glossary, 483 *n.*
Coroticus, a chieftain of Glamorganshire, 352
— his genealogy, 352 *n.*
— his crimes, *ib.*
— St. Patrick's epistle on, 311—349, 358, 383; editions of, 311; makes no mention of Roman mission, or foreign education, 311; its date, 384; Tillemont's judgment of, 385; date of St. Patrick's mission, deduced from, 391
Cosherings, 228
Costello, co. of Mayo, barony of, 507
Coyne, or Coyney (Coinn-mhiodh or Coinnmedh), what, 134 *n.*, 136, 228
— not derived from the English word *Coin*, 134 *n.*
Crebrea, 448
Creed, St. Patrick's, as given in the Confession, 388
— not homoousian, 390
— its antiquity, *ib.*
Croach-aigli, 447
Crochan, or Cruachan, 451
Crochan Crobderg, wife of Eochaid Feilioc, 451
Crom-cruach, or Cromdubh, idol destroyed by St. Patrick, 128
— not the name of a man, 128 *n.*
Cromdubh Sunday, 128
Crossan, a cross-bearer, 460
Cruachan, now Rath-croghan. See *Crochan*
Cruitheni, or Picts of Dalaradia, 407
— why so called, *ib. n.*

Index. 523

Cualann, territory of, 343 *n.*
Cuile, a kitchen, 477, 478
Cuil-dreimhne, battle of, 119
Cuirene, district of, 260 *n.*
Cumaine, daughter of Dalbronach, 34
Cuolenni, 343 *n.*, 403
Cyprian (St.), ordination per saltum practised in his day, 85

D'ACHERY, Spicilegium, 97 *n.* Irish canons published by, *ib.*
Da-Ferta, 476
Daimhliac Cianain, now Duleek, co. of Meath, 369 *n.*
Daire, chieftain of Hy Niallan, 472
— gives to St. Patrick the site of Armagh, 472
— legend of the donation, 472 *sq.*
— surnamed Dearg, 481 *n.*; his genealogy too long, *ib.*
— his conversion, 478
Dairinne, 38
Dal-araidhe, or Dalaradia, 267 *n.*, 361 *n.*
Dal-Buain, tribe of, in Dalaradia, 374
Dalriada, 266 *n.*
Dalta, meaning of the word, 177 *n.*
Danes, their invasion of Ireland, 39
Darerca, sister of St. Patrick, 150 *n.*, 354
David, of Menevia, connected with the second order of saints, 95
— his œconomus, 167, 168
— his eminence predicted by St. Patrick, 482
— date of his birth, *ib. n.*
Davis (Sir John), his description of the abolition of the clans, 228 *n.*
Death of St. Patrick, its probable date, 494, 497
— objections to this date, *ib.*
Death, voluntary, of St. Oran of Hy, 125
— of the pupil of St. Fanche, 125, 126 *n.*
— of the daughters of King Laoghaire, 126 *n.*
— further instances of, 456 *sq.*
— not an esoteric doctrine, 457
— not figurative, 457
— not the doctrine of human sacrifice, 461
— not a religious suicide, 462
— moral intent of, 460 *sq.*

Declan (St.), a contemporary of St. Ailbe, 206
— his tribe and genealogy, 207
— meets St. Patrick at Rome, 209
— places seven saints in a cell near Lismore, 210
— fails to convert Aengus, King of Cashel, *ib.*
— visits St. David at Menevia, *ib.*
— settles at Ardmór, 211
— survived St. Ailbe, 212
— St. Ultan his disciple, *ib.*
— a pupil of St. Moling, 214
— author of his life, date of, 219
Declension of Faith in Ireland, evidences of, 107. St. Brigid's prophecy of, 108
Decurio, office of, 354 *n.*
Deece, barony of, co. of Meath, 207
Deities of the Pagan Irish, topical, 456
Denis (St.), abbey of, near Paris, 51
— monastic bishops of, 55 *n.*
Desi, or Desii, 207
Diarmait, King, encouraged Druidism, 119—122. In ill odour with the Church, 123
Dichu, chieftain of Dalaradia, first convert of St. Patrick, 344, 407. His descent, 407
Dimma or Dima, tutor of St. Declan, 208
Dimma Dubh, Bishop of Connor, 209
Dioceses, antiently coextensive with the seigniories of the clans, 38
Disibod (St.), or Disen, an Irishman, life of, 109. An episcopus regionarius, 110
Dobda, or Dobdagrecus, the Irish bishop of Virgil of Saltzburgh, 65, *sq.* His Irish name Dubh-da-crioch, 66. Ussher's difficulty about, *ib. n.*
Domhnall, son of Aedh King of Ireland, blessed by St. Columba, 138
Dominatrix, used to translate banabb, or abbess, 157
Domnach-airgid, 469 *n.*, 510 *n.*
Domnach-Arda, or Domnach-Ardacha, 293 *n.*, 294, 295 *n.*, 297
Donald, King of Scots, 266
Dorsum salicis. See *Druim Sailech*
Driucriu, chieftain of the Hy Garrchon, 465

Druidism of the Irish in the times of the second order of saints, 118 *sq.*
Druids predict St. Patrick's coming, 410. See *Magi*
Druim-luchra, 211
Druim Sailech, or Dorsum salicis, antient name of Armagh, 475
Drumchett, St. Columba's attendants to synod of, 28
— convention of, 133; Keating's account of, 134
— situation of, 133 *n.*
Drumcliffe, co. of Sligo, 34
Drum-na-ndruaid, 451 *n.*
Dubh, river, now Blackwater, 471 *n.*
Dubhcomar, battle of, 471
— where, 471 *n.*
Dubh-da-crioch, a common name in Ireland, 66 *n.*
Dubhtach Maccu-lugil, or Maccu Lugair, chief bard, 130, 446. His conversion, 424
Dublin, an insignificant hamlet in St. Patrick's time, 466 *n.*
— Joceline's inconsistency as to, *ib.*
Duine Suidhe, 452
Duleek. See *Daimhliac-Cianain*
Dumha-graidh, altar and glass chalices of, 222
Dunlaing, King of Leinster, 438
— baptism of his sons, 465
— his feud with the kings of Tara, 438
Dun-da-leth-glaisse, burial-place of St. Patrick, 492
— an antient fort of the chieftains of Ulidia, *ib.*
Dumbarton, 356
Dun-na-ngedh, banquet of, 148

EADGAR, assumed the title of King of Scotia in 1098, 41 *n.*
Easdara, now Ballysadare, 34
Easroe, cataract of, 509
Easter, St. Patrick's first Easter in Ireland, 412
— not the day of his interview with King Laoghaire, 413, 418
Eber. See *Heber*
Ebmoria, or Eboria, in France, 280, 318
Eborius, Bishop of York, 268
Ecbatius, or Ochmus, 353
Edessa, monks of, had bishops without sees, 45

Education of St. Patrick on the continent, not mentioned in the Confession, 311
Eimer, or Eimeria, two daughters of Milchu so called, 408 *n.*
El, a name of God, known to the Irish, 372
Elementa, or alphabetic characters, 507
" Elementa scripsit," passages where the phrase occurs in the Book of Armagh, 507 *n.*, 509 *n.*
Eleran (St.), 296
Eliach, territory of, now Ely O'Carroll, 203
Elias, St. Patrick's supposed invocation of,
— festival of, on Mount Carmel (July 20), 371 *n.*
— never invoked as a saint, *ib.*
Eliphius and Eucharius not Irish, 195
Ely O'Carroll, territory of, 203
Emania, residence of the kings of Ulster, destroyed, 472
Enach-Duin (now Anna-down), 38
Endura, 462
Endeus, or Enna, son of Amolngid, 442. Dedicates his son to Patrick, 444
Enda, or Enna (St.), refused to see his sister, 92 *n.*
— his conversion, 125 *n.*
England, Irish hatred of, not caused by religious differences, 242
Enon, villula, 355 *n.*
Eochaidh, son of Crimthann Leith, 464 *n.*
Eochaidh Dallan, or the Blind, 138
— — his mother named Forchell, *ib.*
— — called Eochaidh Forchaill from her name, *ib.*
— — honoured as a saint, although a bard, 139
Eochaidh Doimhlen, father of the three Collas, 471
Eochaidh Finn Fothart, 287
Eochaidh Muighmeadhoin, King of Ireland, table of kings descended from, 249
Eochaidh Uladh, 214 *n.*
Eoghan Beul, King of Connaught, 438 *n.*
Eoghan, grandson of Muredach Meith, 464 *n.*
Eoghanacht of Magh Girgin, 296 *n.*
Epiphany, a season for baptism, 488

Index. 525

Episcopi vagi, or vagantes, 40 *n*. See *Bishops*
Equonimus. See *Oeconomus*
Ercc mac Dego, Bishop of Slane, 422; his baptism, 441 *sq.*
— curses the banquet of Dun-nangeth, 148
Erdathe, the Day of Judgment, 438
Erenachs, meaning of the name, 160
— not archdeacons, 160
— their duties, 161
— modification of their duties in later times, 161
— Colgan's account of the office, 163
Ernasc, his conversion, 507
Ernin (St.), son of Cresine, of Rathnoi, 286 *n.*
Erris, barony of, 442 *n.*
Etchen (St.), Bishop of Clonfad, ordains St. Columba a priest by mistake instead of bishop, 71
— did not intend to consecrate Columba a chorepiscopus, 76
— his diftant relationship to St. Brigid, Table V., 253
Ethembria (St.), 381 *n.*
Ethica Terra, or Tir-itha, now Tiree, 8 *n.*
Ethne, the fair, 451, 452
Eucharius, not Irish, 195
Eulogius, a bishop, 45

FAMILY of a monastery, what, 159. See *Muinnter*
Fanchea (St.) visits her brother Enna to persuade him to return to Ireland, 117
— her exhortations converted St. Enna, 126 *n.*
Fauns found on the site of Armagh Cathedral, 480
— frequent mention of fauns and deer in Irish legends, 480 *n.*
Fecc, see *Fiacc*
Fedelm, the ruddy, 451, 452
Fedh-Fiadha, 426 *n.* 431
Fedlimid, or Feidilmidh of Trim, son of Laogaire, 150, 258 *sq.*
— his ecclesiastical progenies, 262
— his lay progenies, *ib.*
Feis of Tara, not the Beltine, 414
—— celebrated in November, 415
—— three days before and three days after Samhain, 416
— meaning of name, *ib. n.*

Feredach, son of Hercaith, baptised by St. Patrick, 510
— his named changed to Sachell or Sacellus, 510
Fergus mór mac Erca, dynasty founded by him in North Britain, 283
Ferta, or Fertæ, 455
— meaning of the word, 476 *n.*
Ferta-fer-Feic, now Slane, 420
— meaning of the name, *ib. n.*
Fertæ-martyrum, given to St. Patrick, 473; buildings erected at, 476 *sq.*
— its exact site, 478
Fertighis, 166
Fiacc (St.), or Fecc, Bishop of Sletty, 14 *sq.*
— a bard, disciple of Dubhtach Maccu-lugil, 130, 424
— consecrated Bishop of Sletty, 466
— his relics preserved at Sletty, 424
— his hymn in praise of St. Patrick, 306, 424 *n.*
— silent on the Roman commission of St. Patrick, 313
— records the foreign education and travels of St. Patrick, 314
Fiacha Araidhe, 361 *n.*
Fiacha Sraibhtine, King of Ireland, slain by his nephews, 471
Fiacha Suidhe, son of Feidlimidh Rechtmar, 207
Fianachtach, œconomus of Ferns, 166
Filedh, Filedheacht, meaning of the words, 134 *n.*
Findchan, Abbat of Ardchain in Tiree, 7
Finn mac Gormain, bp. of Kildare, 180
Finnen or Finnian, two saints of the name, 98
Finnian (St.) of Cluain Eraird, now Clonard, 98
— his early education, 99
— prevented by an angel from going to Rome, 100, 101
— the faith corrupted in Ireland in his time, 101
— bardic poem to his honour, 140
— his reward to the bard, 140
— his adventure with the œconomus of St. David, 168
Finnian (St.), of Maghbile, 102
—— first brought the Gospels to Ireland, 103 *sq.*
—— notice of him in the Felire of Aengus, 104

Finnian (St.), his copy of the Gospel, celebrated in Irish legends, 105, 106, 121
—— adventure of St. Fintan of Dunflesk and the Gospel of Finnian, 105
—— St. Columkille's transcript of Finnian's Gospel, 106 ; decision of King Diarmait on, 121
—— his wonderful tree, 121 *n.*
—— contest with St. Rodan on, *ib.*
—— praying contest between him and St. Columba at the battle of Cuildruimhne, 120
Fintan (St.), of Dunflesk, anecdote of, 105
Fire, extinguished at feast of Tara, 420
— ecclesiastical custom of blessing new fire, *ib. n.*
Flann Febla, successor of St. Patrick, his genealogy, 481 *n.*; too short, *ib.*
Fochloth or Fochlut, wood of, 313, 332, 442, 447
Foirtchernn, son of Feidilmith, 150, 258 *sq.*
— his conversion, 258
— refuses the bishopric of Trim, 261
Forannan (St.) Life of, 33
—accompanied St. Columba to Drumchett, 34
Fordun, Church of, 291
Forgnidhe in the district of the Cuircne, 260, now Forgney, *ib. n.*
Forrach, meaning of the word, 448 *n.*
Forrach meic nAmalgaidh, 448
Fortification of ecclesiastical establishments, 502
Fortuatha Laighen, 286
Fotharta of Leinster, 286–287
Fulcuin, his 'Gesta abbatum Lobiensium,' 58 *n.*
Fulrad (St.), charter to him from Pope Stephen, sanctioning a monastic bishop, 53

GAEDHELIC, or Scotic, colony, date of, 248
Gamanradii, 451
Geman, a Christian bard, 140
Genealogy of St. Patrick, 353 *n.*
Genealogical tables, 249 *sq.*
Geography, antient, fragments of, in the Lives of St. Patrick, 335

Germain (St.) of Auxerre, his first mission to Britain, 269, 271. Its success, 274. Accompanied by St. Patrick, 318.
— his ordination, 319 *n.*
— commissions St. Patrick, 316, 328
Gertrude (St.), abbess of Nivelles, her death, 306 *n.*
Gessen, for Goshen, 419 *n.*
Gilla-Caemhain, Chronological Poem by, 396
— O'Conor's Latin version of, *ib. n.*
Gilla, or Gildas, connected with Second Order of Saints, 95, 99
— corruption of the faith in Ireland in his time, 111
— why called Badonicus, *ib. n.*
— meaning of the name Gildas or Gilla, *ib.*
— summoned by Ainmire, King of Ireland, to restore the Catholic faith, 111
— his reformation in Ireland, how far to be credited, 112
— Colgan's and Ussher's arguments against its credibility, 113
— not called to Ireland to oppose Pelagianism, 143
— his legislation in Ireland, 143, 144
Girgin, plain of, 296
Glass, chalices of, 222, 223 *n.*
Glastonbury, St. Patrick's connection with, 485 *n.*
Glencullen, 343 *n.*
Gleran, son of Cumin, 448
Gondbaum, mother of St. Patrick, 354 *n.*
Golam-Miles, or Milesius, 248
Gold ornaments found in Ireland, 325 *n.*
Goll, sons of, 205
Gollit, husband of Darerca, 150 *n.*
— father of Lomman, 260
Gospels, copy of, given by St. Patrick to St. Mac Carthenn, 469 *n.* 510 *n.*
— of St. Finnian, 106
Gratzacham, 474
Graves (Dean), his paper on the Life of St. Patrick, 402 *n.*
— his papers on Ogham writing, 511 *n.*
Gregory the Great, his decision as to consecration by a single bishop, 82
— gave St. Ternan a bell, 302 *n.*

Grellan (St.,) his *Cathach*, or battle crozier, 125 *n*.
Guasacht, son of Milchu, bishop of Granard, 408 *n*.
Gulban, meaning of the name, 440 *n*.
Gulford, or Wlfard, abbat of St. Martin's, Tours, 57

HADRIAN I. (Pope), his charter to the Abbey of St. Denis, 54
Hallelujah Victory, 275
Hæres, the Latin equivalent for *comarb*, 157
Hardiman (James), his ed. of O'Flaherty's West Connaught, 38 *n*.
—— his ed. of the Statute of Kilkenny, 136 *n*., 234 *n*.
Hatred of England by the Irish, not from religious differences, 242
Heber, or Eber, son of Milesius, 248
— took the southern half of Ireland, *ib*.
Helias, Patrick's invocation of, 370
— the true reading *Eli*, 371
Henry of Saltrey, 307
Herbert (Hon. A.) his papers called *Palladius restitutus*, 96 *n*. 309 *n*.
Hercaith, baptised by St. Patrick, 510
Hereford, Synod of, A.D. 673, 49
Herenachs. See *Erenachs*
Heribert, Bp. of the Abbey of St. Denis, anecdote of, 51
Heric of Auxerre, 271 *n*.
— his *Miracula S. Germani*, 318 *n*.
Herimon, son of Milesius, 248
— took the northern half of Ireland, *ib*.
— division of Ireland between Heber and Herimon, 248
— almost all the kings of Ireland descended from Herimon, 248
— exceptions, *ib. n*.
Hermon, Mount, 325, 331, 337
Hi, no lay succession in, 154
— genealogical Table of Abbats of, by Dr. Reeves, 154 *n*.
Hiberio, the name given by St. Patrick to Ireland, 358, 362, 367, 377, 380
Hi Garrchon. See *Hy Garrchon*
Hilary (St.) of Arles, Life of, 223 *n*.
— his hymn in praise of Christ, 372
Hildebert, Bp. of Le Mans, 372 *n*.

Hildegardis, Abbess, her testimony to the declension of faith in Ireland, 109
Honorat (St.), island, 336
Honoratus, bishop of Marseilles, 224 *n*.
Honours of St. Patrick, 429
Hy Garrchon, region of, 286, 290, 338
—— the tribe of, rejected St. Patrick's teaching, 502
Hy Neill, Southern, Table III., 252
—— Northern, Table II., 250, 251
Hymn. See *Fiacc*
Hymn of St. Patrick in Irish, 425
—— supposed occasion of, *ib*.
—— translation of, 426
—— not connected with Tara, 426 *n*.
—— translation of, by Mr. W. Stokes, *ib*.
—— poetical translation of, by J. C. Mangan, 429 *n*.
—— its antiquity and authenticity, 429
—— internal evidence, 430
—— never deemed heterodox, 431
—— Hymn, in Latin, by Sechnall or Secundinus, in praise of St. Patrick, 430
Hynneon, 218

IBAR (St.), of the family of Ui Eachach Uladh, 214
— mentioned in Anmchad's Life of St. Brigid, 215
— a disciple of St. Patrick, *ib*.
— date of his death, 216
— his contest with St. Patrick, *ib*.
Iccian Sea, 330 *n*.
Illan, son of Dunlaing, baptized, 465
Imgæ, a place in the Cinèl Laoghaire Midhe, co. of Meath, 262
Imleach Iubhair, now Emly, 211
Imluich-each, in Ciarrighe-Connacht, now Emlagh, co. of Mayo, 260 *n*.
Immruig Thuaithe, church of, 509 *n*.
Inbher Dea, or mouth of the Vartry river, 338, 339, 340, 341, 403, 405
Inbher Domnan, now Malahide, 405 *n*.
Inbher nAinge, month of the Nanny water, 406
Inbher Colptha, mouth of the Boyne, 412, 420

528   *Index.*

Inchaguile, island in Loch Corrib, 365
Inis-Boethin, Inis Boheen, or Inisboyne, 297
Inis-an-ghoill-craibtigh, now Inchaguile in Loch Corrib, 365
Inis-Patrick, 404
Inneoin-na-nDesi, 218 *n.*
Intercessory power of the Church, 503
— recognized by St. Patrick in his religious foundations, *ib.*
Interpolations in the history of St. Patrick, 332, 333
Ioceline, his Life of St. Kentigern, 77 *n.*
— his Life of St. Patrick, 129 *n. et passim*
Johnson (John) confounds the antient Scoti with the modern Scotch, 42 *n.*
John IV., Pope, when consecrated, 142
John XXII. Pope, Remonstrance of Irish chieftains to, 236 *sq.*
— his reply, 240
Iona, an erroneous name, 19 *n.* See *Hi.*
Iorrus, now Erris, 447
Irchard (St.), disciple of St. Ternan, 302 *n.*
Ire, a name of Ireland, 114
Ireland, called Scotia, 41 *n.*
— ports of, well known to commercial men, in the age of Tacitus, 512
Irial Glunmor, King of Ulster, 408 *n.*
Iserninus, 486. Ordained with St. Patrick, 317, 332
Isidore (St.), College of, at Rome, 360 *n.*
Judaism, allegation that the Irish had gone over to, 110
Juvavia, antient name of Saltzburg, 60
Jerome (St.) speaks of a corpulent Scot, 190
Iarthar Life, 466
Iveagh, baronies of, co. of Down, 214. Derivation of the name, *ib. n.*

KEATINGE (Geoffrey), his history of Ireland, 133 *n.*
Kellistown, co. of Carlow, battle of, 468 *n.* Its antient name, *ib.*
Keltchar. See *Celtchar*
Kenneth, King of Scotland, 44

Kenneth transferred the chief bishopric of the Picts from Abernethy to St. Andrew's, 44. *n.*
Kentigern (St.), alias St. Mungo, 302. Consecrated by a single bishop, 77
Kienan (St.) of Duleek, 369 *n.*
Kieran. See *Ciaran*
Kildare, meaning of the name, 21 *n.*
— monastery of, its peculiar constitution, 11 *sq.*
— first bishop of, 19 *sq.*
— bishop of, in what sense called archbishop, 16, 17
— confusion in first bishops of, 21
— jurisdiction of abbey of, 18
Kill. See *Cill.*
Killeigh, King's co., 345 *n.*
Kill-muine, or Menevia, afterwards St. David's, 99
Kill-finé, 291
Kill-fhorclann, 448
Killare, or Cellair, co. of Westmeath, 463 *n.*
Kilglin, co. of Meath, its antient name, 260 *n.*
Kilkenny, statutes of, 233, 239
Killin. See *Cillin*
Kilfenora (Cill Finnabrach), 38
Kilmalkedar, co. of Kerry, pillar-stone of, with abgitorium, 512 *n.*
Kilmacduagh (see Cill mhic Duach), 39
Kilpatrick, 355 *n.*
Kings of Ireland, list of, from Book of Leinster, 184
— list of, from A.D. 164 to A.D. 665, Table VI., 255
King (Rev. Robert), his 'Primacy of Armagh,' 177
— church history of Ireland, 237 *n.*
Knockmeilidown mountains, antient name of, 218 *n.*

LAEGHIS, or Leix, territory of the tribe of, 466
'Lamia in speculo,' belief in denounced, 488 *n.*
Land, St. Patrick accepted grants of, 409 *n.*
Landeric, or Landri, Bishop of Paris, 54
Lanfranc, Abp., his letter to Torloch O'Brien, 3 *n.*
Langforgund, 299, 300
Lanigan (Dr.), his conjecture as to St. Patrick's birthplace, 358

Index. 529

Lanigan (Dr.), his opinion of the date of St. Patrick's death, 495, 496
— explanation of the exclusion of women by second order of saints, 91
— on St. David, Gildas, and Docus, 95
— his remark on the *Seanchus Mor*, 485 *n*.
Laoghaire, King of Ireland, pronunciation of the name, 150 *n*.
— his interview with St. Patrick, 417, *sq*.— an imitation of the Book of Daniel, 419
— Patrick's contest with the Druids of, *ib*.— an imitation of Exodus, *ib*.
— his conversion to Christianity not sincere, 432—cursed by St. Patrick, 433—the malediction not fulfilled,*ib*.
— died a Pagan, 436 *sq*.
— Patrick's second visit to, 438
— his burial with Pagan rites, 439
— length of his reign, 395, 397
— his daughters, 451—Patrick's instructions to, 452 — their burial, 455.
Lasciciput, meaning of the word, 411 *n*.
Lassair, 448
Laubes, or Lobes, in Belgium, had a monastic bishop, 57
Laws, Pagan, reformed by St. Patrick, 482 *sq*.
Laws, Penal. See *Penal Laws*
Lazarus, Bishop of the Boscoi monks, 46
Leabhar Breac, list of coarbs of Patrick from, 176—its real name, *ib. n*.
Leabhar buidhe Lecan (Yellow Book of Lecan), 178
— list of coarbs of Patrick in, 178
Leabhar na huidhre, 439
Leatha, twofold signification of the word, 23 *n*., 25 *n*.
Lecale, barony of, 408
— meaning of the name, *ib. n*.
Lecan, Book of, 390
— Yellow Book of (Leabhar buidhe), 178
Leinster, Book of, 180
— list of coarbs of Patrick in, *ib*.
— list of kings of Ireland since Christianity in, 183
Leo the Great, his opinion on the validity of ordination per saltum, 86
— epistle of Gallican bishops to, 279
Lerins, island of, 336

Less, a fort, 477 *n*.
— rendered *civitas*, 479 *n*.
Leteoc, adjective from Letha, Letavia, or Armorica, 361 *n*.
Letha, sea of, 337
Lleurwg, surnamed Lleufer Mawr, 266 *n*.
Liamain, or Limania, sister of St. Patrick, 364 — her seven sons *ib. n*.
Light over St. Patrick's tomb, 489
Liguge. See *Locociagum*
Limania. See *Liamain*
Lists of Coarbs of Patrick, 172, *sq*.
Loarn, or Locharnach, son of Ernasc, taught letters by St. Patrick, 507
Loarne, Bishop of Brettan (now Bright), 293 *n*.
Lobes, or Laubes, in Belgium, 57
Locharnach. See *Loarn*
Loch Corrib, island of Inchaquile in, 365
Lochan, son of Luidir, 203
Lochru, magus of King Laoghaire, 422—his death, 423—stone of, *ib. n*.
Locociagum (Liguge), first monastery of the Gallican Church, 87 *n*.
Loigles, fountain so called, 442
Loiguire-Breg, 262
Lombard, Peter, 241 *n*.
Lomman (St.), nephew and disciple of St. Patrick, 150—a Briton, *ib*.— his death, 152—history of, 257 *sq*.— race of, 260
Lonnchad, daughter of Eochaidh Echbeoil, 407 *n*.
Lorica, what, 426, 431
Lorica, of Gildas, 124
— of Patrick, 124, 426
Lough Hacket, 500 *n*.
Louth. See *Lughmagh*
Lucetmael, Druid of King Laoghaire, 422
— pours poison into Patrick's cup, 425
— his incantations, and contest with Patrick, *ib*.—story of his death, 432 *n*.
Lucius, King of Britain, 266
Lugaidh, King of Ireland, 433
— exempted from Patrick's curse, 434
— confusion about St. Patrick's interview with him, 435
Lughmagh, now Louth, Monastery of, 469 *n*.
Lugnaed, nephew of St. Patrick, his tomb-stone, 365

M M

Lunanus, son of the King of the Romans, followed St. Declan to Ireland, 209
Lupait, or Lupita, sister of St. Patrick, 354, 361—curious story of, 90 *n.*
Lupus (St.), of Troyes, 269, 271

MAC-CARTHENN (St.), carried St. Patrick on his shoulders, at the foundation of Clogher, 467 *n.* 469 *n.*
— Gospels given to him by St. Patrick, 469 *n.*
Mac Cuillinn (St.), of Lusk, date of his death, 495. *n.*
Macc Ercæ, 509 *n.*
Macc Rime, episcopus, 509 *n.*
Mac Geoghegan, Hist. de l'Irlande, 241 *n.*
Macha, probably a district, *ib.*
Macha, Queen, 475 *n.*
Mâcon, Council of, 45
Mael, the Druid, 451
— his conversion to Christianity, 454
— meaning of his name, 455 *n.*
Maccuchor, Island of, 405, 406
Magh Bregh, or Bregia, 406 *n.*
Magh Domnon, 442 *n.*
Magh Girgin, 296
Magh-inis, 408
Magh Sleacht, a plain in Cavan, 127, 464—idol in, 127
Magh-Lifé, 466
Magi, or Druids of Laoghaire, 422
— their names, *ib.*
— Patrick's contest with, 423
Magical virtues of Hymns, 124, 140
— — of Books, 105, 106, 124
Magonius, or Maun, a name of St. Patrick, 363
Maguire (Cathal), 470 *n.*
Mahee Island, 412, *n.* See *Mochaoi.*
Maistin, now Mullaghmast, 438
Maine-eiges, father of St. Etchen, his genealogy, 253
Malachy (St.), stone churches a novelty in his time, 304 *n.*
Manchen (St.), 449
Manis, Bishop, 260
Mansuetus, or Mansuy, Bishop of Toul, an Irishman, 194
— not a disciple of St. Peter, *ib.*
Maor, office of, at Armagh, 170
Marcan, son of Cillin, his genealogy, 253, 254—blessed by St. Patrick, 466

Martair, the word signifies relics, 476 *n.*
Martin (St.), of Tours, said to have been uncle to St. Patrick, 87
— — date of his death, 319 *n.*
— — Abbey of, at Tours, 56. Monastic Bishops of, 57 *n.*
Mass, different forms of, used by the three orders of Saints, 88 *sq.*
Mathorex, or Amathorex, 317
Maun, or Magonius, a name of St. Patrick, 363
Maud. See *Medhb.*
Medhb, or Maud, Queen of Connaught, 451 *n.*
Mel (St.), curious story of scandal respecting, 91 *n.*
Meuthi (same name as Tathi or Thaddeus), the Irish priest who baptised St. Cadoc, 99
Meyrick (S. R.), History of Cardiganshire, 352 *n.*
Michael (St.), Mount, 337
Michomeris, an Irishman, 318 *n.*
Milchu, Miliuc, or Michul, St. Patrick's master, 373
— St. Patrick's visit to, 407
— his death, 408
— prediction as to his posterity, *ib.*
— his son and daughters, *ib. n.*
Milo, author of Metrical Life of St. Boniface, 47
Milthous, 454
Mis (Mount), now Slemish, 374
Mission of St. Patrick from Rome, not mentioned by Prosper, 309
— — nor in the Confession, 309
— — nor in the Hymn of St. Sechnall, 312
— — nor in Fiacc's Hymn, 313
— — recorded by Scholiast on Fiacc's Hymn, 321
Mochaoi (St.), called also Caolan, 412—conversion of, 412 *n.*
— — Island Mahee named from him, 412 *n.*
Mochta, Abbat of Lughmagh, or Louth, 29
— numbers composing his household, *ib.*
— antient poem on, 30
— Monastery of Louth founded by, 469 *n.*
Modhaidh, 290
Moedhog, or Mogue (St.), Bishop of Ferns, 14
— — meaning of the name, 115

Index. 531

Moedhog, his adventure with the œconomus of St. David, 167
Mogenog or Mugenog, 260 *n.*
Molagga (St.), commanded by an angel to return to Ireland, 117
Molua (St.), legend of, 114
Monasteries of St. Patrick, founded for intercessory and perpetual devotion, 503
—— did not always exclude women, 504
—— chieftainship of the abbats of, 505
—— causes of their popularity in Ireland, 505
Monastic character of Irish Christianity, 87—not due to St. Patrick, 88
Monduirn, mountain, 423
Moore (Mr.), his description of St. Patrick's success, 501
Morion (Mount), 329, 337
Moses, legendary parallel between him and St. Patrick, 418
Mucne, 443
Mugenog, brother of Lomman, 260
Mugint (St.), story of, 91 *n.*
Muinnter, or *family*, of a monastery, 159
Muircheartach O'Brien, nominal King of Ireland, 2
Muirchu Maccumachtene, his life of St. Patrick, 314 *n.*, 401—preface to, 402—Latin form of his name, 402 *n.*
—— ignores the Roman mission of Patrick, 315
Muir-nicht, the English channel, 360 *n.*
Mullaghmast. See *Maistin.*
Murder of an Irishman, not felony, 239
Muredach, son of Eochaidh Doimhlen, surnamed Colla-da-crioch, 471
Muredach Tirech, King of Ireland, 471
Mullach Fharraidh, 448 *n.*
Mumessa, or Munessa, 464 *n.*
Mungo (St.). See *Kentigern*
Munis. See *Manis*
Munster, conversion of, by St. Patrick, 467—fictitious, 468

NAITON, King of the Picts, Abbat Coelfrid's letter to, 487

Nathi, son of Garrchu, his genealogy, 253—his being contemporary with Palladius and Patrick how explained, 254
— opposes St. Patrick, 338, 341
Navan Fort, near Armagh, 472
Nemthur, birthplace of St. Patrick, 355 *sq.*
Nendrum, or Aondruim, 412 *n.*
Nennius, his account of Palladius, 290 *n.*
— Irish version of Nennius, 3 *n.* 394
Newry River, its antient name, 472 *n.*
Niall of the nine hostages, leader of the expedition in which Patrick was captured, 361
Nicæa, first council of, meaning of its Canon IV., 80 *sq.*
Ninian (St.), 282
Noi-fis, 483
Novatianism, 489

OAK, names of places derived from, 21 *n.*
— of Kildare, 21 *n.*
O'Brien, Muircheartach, 2
O'Callaghan (John), his ed. of the Destruction of Cyprus, 231 *n.*
Ocha, battle of, 394
Ochmus, or Ecbatius, 354
O'Clery (John), 173
O'Conor (Dr.), his argument for the coincidence of the feast of Tara with the vernal equinox, 414
—— his mistake respecting the festival, *ib.*
Odhran. See *Oran*
O'Donnell, Baldearg, 230 *n.*
O'Donovan (Dr.), his edition of the Battle of Magh Rath, 148 *n.*
—— his edition of the Circuit of Ireland, 237 *n.*
—— his edition of the Book of Rights, 130, 207 *n.* 471 *n.*
—— his edition of the Topographical poems of O'Dubhagan, 203 *n.* 471 *n.*
—— his edition of the Four Masters, 128 *n. et passim*
—— his Tribes and Customs of Hy Many, 125 *n.*
—— his Tribes and Customs of Hy Fiachrach, 313 *n.* 442 *sq.*
—— his description of St. Patrick's teaching, 500
O'Driscolls, country of, 38

M M 2

Oeconomus, his duty in a monastery, 166, 169
— often resisted the abbat, *ib.*
— instance of a battle between Oeconomi, *ib.*
— favoured by the rule of St. Columbanus as against the abbat, *ib.*
— sometimes abused his power, 167
— anecdotes of, *ib.*
Oengus, son of Senach, 508
O'Flaherty, family of, 38
O'Flaherty (Roderick), his opinion of the length of King Laoghaire's reign, 397
O'Flynn (Eochaidh), his poem quoted, 416 *n.*
Ogham characters, later than St. Patrick's time, 511 *n.*
O'Hanlon (Rev. J.), his life of St. Malachy, 304 *n.*
Oilioll Molt, slain in the battle of Ocha, 394
Oirghialla, tribe of, 215
— district of, now Oriel, 471 *n.*
— legendary etymology of the name, *ib.*
Oirchinnech, see *Airchinneach*
Oirthear, or Orior, district of, 472 *n.*
— why so called, *ib.*
O'Kearney (Nicholas), his edition of the Festivities of Conan, 426 *n.*
Ollamh, meaning of the word, 134 *n.*
Ollamh Fodla, King of Ireland, 416 *n.*
Ondbahum, mother of St. Patrick, 354 *n.*
Oran, or Odhran, St. Patrick's charioteer, 464
Oran (St.) of Hy, his voluntary death, 125
— — legend of, 462 *n.*
Orders, three, of the saints of Ireland, 88 *n.*, *sq.*
— the second order, 98 *sq.*
— the third order of saints, 97
Ordination per saltum, 74, 84
— not peculiar to the Irish Church, 84
— not invalid, 85
Oriel. See *Oirgialla*
Orior. See *Oirthear*
Ossory, district of, blessed by St. Patrick, 467
— coextensive with present diocese of Ossory, 38
— right of visitation in, claimed by the successors of St. Columba, 467

O'Tooles, 286 *n.*
Oudin, Casimir, his opinion of the writings of St. Patrick, 349
— — his mistake about the tract, *De Tribus Habitaculis*, 534 *n.*

PAGAN literature of Ireland, 512, 513. See *Laws*
Palladius, first bp. of the Scoti, a disciple of St. Germain, 270
— not a deacon of Rome, 276
— more probably St. Germain's deacon, *ib.*
— not a Briton, 278
— probably a native of Gaul, 280
— opinions respecting him, *ib. n.*
— his family eminent in Gaul, 279
— sent to the Scots of Ireland, 280, 281, 285
— not sent to oppose Pelagianism, 284
— landed in Wicklow, 286
— account given of him by Muirchu Maccumacthene, 288
— by Tirechan, 289
— by the Scholiast on Fiacc, 289
— by Nennius, 290 *n.*
— in the Vita secunda, 293
— in the Vita quarta, 296
— his martyrdom, 289, 297
— Scotch traditions of him, 298, 300
— his relics placed in a silver shrine, 299
— Lessons for his day in Brev. of Aberdeen, 299
— his short life inconsistent with the Scotch traditions, 303
— probably commemorated at Auvergne, 305
— coincidence of his day with that of St. Patrick, 305
— called also Patrick, 305
— known by the name of Patrick, to the 12th century, 308
— probably accompanied St. Germain to Britain, 318
Palladius, Archbishop of Bourges, 279
Pall-ere, or Pallad-ere, 294
Paparo, Cardinal, 218
Patricius, a name in common use in the 5th century, 305 *n.* 307
Patrick (St.), not mentioned in Bede's writings, 96
— this silence, how explained, 96

Index. 533

Patrick (St.), overturned pillar-stones, 127
— laboured seven years in Munster, 220
— commissioned by St. Germain, 316, 323
— could not have been a disciple of St. Germain, 319
— story of his connection with St. Germain, transferred from Palladius, 320
— commenced his ministry in Ireland as a priest, 326, 327, 343
— story of his landing in Wicklow really belongs to Palladius, 340 *sq.*
— his genealogy, 353 *n.*
— story of his Jewish descent, 362 *n.*
— admits in his confession his want of learning, 353
— his account of his parents and family, 353
— his father a decurio, 354
— his birthplace, 355
— not a native of Ireland, 358
— his family connected with Armorica, 360
— his own account of his captivity, 362
— his original name *Succat*, 363
— why called Patrick, 363
— his brothers and sisters, 364
— his condition in his captivity, 366
— his escape and return to his native country, 367
— his passage through a desert, 369
— the herd of swine relieves him from famine, 369
— his invocation of Elias, 370—true meaning of the passage, 371
— his escape from Milchu, 374
— his second captivity, 375
— his return to his parents, 376
— his call to convert the Irish, 377
— his second vision, 379
— obscurity of his acts, 401
— rejection of him by the tribes of Leinster, 403
— his Creed, 388
— date of his mission, 391
— chronology of his life altered to suit the story of his Roman mission, 391 *sq.*
— his sojourn at Inis-Patrick, 404
— his success in Ulidia, 407
— his first convert Dichu, 408
— his first Church, 409

Patrick (St.), visits his old master, Milchu, 408
— Druids prophesy his coming, 411
— his preaching in Meath and at Tara, 412 *sq.* 420 *sq.*
— his visit to Tara not on the first Easter after his coming to Ireland, 413, 417 *sq.*
— nature of the Pagan festival celebrated at Tara, 414 *sq.*
— his Irish hymn, 425 *sq.*
— his four honours, 429
— curses King Laoghaire, 433
— the malediction not fulfilled, 433
— his interview with King Lugaidh, 435
— confusion between Laoghaire and Lugaidh, *ib.*
— his second visit to Laoghaire, 438
— his interview with Carbri, son of Niall, 439
— converts Conall Gulban, 440
— his meeting with the sons of Amalgaidh, 442
— visits Tirawley, 445
— his danger on the journey, 447
— discovers the wood Fochlut, 447
— preaches to the clan Amalgaidh, 448
— baptises large numbers, 449
— festival of his 'baptism,' *ib.*
— converts the daughters of King Laoghaire, 451 *sq.*
— revisits Ulster, Meath, Leinster, Wicklow, 465
— consecrates Fiacc, 466
— blesses Ossory, 467
— converts Munster, 467
— baptises Aengus, King of Munster, 468
— founds Armagh, 468 *sq.*
— said to have visited Rome after the foundation of Armagh, 481
— his pious theft of the relics, *ib.*
— his reform of the Irish Pagan laws, 482
— his synods, 484
— spurious works, *ib.*
— his death, 489
— died at Saul, 490
— his four petitions, *ib.*
— contest for his body, 491
— buried at Downpatrick, 493
— date of his death, 494 *sq.*
— review of the history of his mission, 498

Patrick (St.), first addressed himself to the chieftains, *ib.*
— cause of his rapid success, 499
— his toleration of Pagan usages, 500
— his success overrated, 501
— his life sometimes in danger, 502
— his ecclesiastical buildings fortified, *ib.*
— resistance to his preaching and authority, *ib.*
— creates ecclesiastical clanship in the monasteries, 503
— ordains, for the most part, natives of the country, 50
— his measures for education of the priesthood, 506
— teaches abgitoria or alphabets, 507—especially to those intended for the ecclesiastical life, 508
— not the first to teach letters to the Irish, 510
— his missionary character, 514
— See *Mission.*
Patrick of Nola, 307 *n.*
Pausavit and Pausatio, meaning of the words, 177 *n.*
Pelagianism, prevalent in England, 140, 271—not in Ireland, 141
— Gildas, not sent to oppose it, 141
— letter from Tomene of Armagh to the clergy of Rome on, 141
Pelagius, the heretic, of Irish birth, 190
— his great stature, 191 *sq.*
— said to have been a Briton, 192
Pelagius, of Tarentum, 192
Penal laws against the mere Irish, 234, 244
— sanctioned by the bishops and court of Rome, 235
Pennant, his story of St. Oran of Hy, 462 *n.*
Peregrinus, the word signifies a pilgrim, 261 *n.*
Periods, two, in Irish church history, 1
— four, of thirty years in St. Patrick's life, 393 *n.*
Petitions, four, of St. Patrick, 490
Petrie (Dr.), his discovery of a tombstone in Loch Corrib, 365
— first published the Irish Hymn of St. Patrick, 425 *n.*
— his mistake as to the meaning of the first word of the hymn, 426 *n.*

Petrie (Dr.), first published the Senchas-na-relec, 197 *n.*
— essay on Tara quoted, 120, 123, 202, *et passim*
— his 'Round Towers' quoted, 198 *n.* 365, 478 *n.* 512 *n.*
— his account of the Senchus Mòr, 483, 484
— essay on the Domnach Airgid, 469 *n.* 510 *n.*
Philosophers, the word used by Sozomen to denote monks, 46
— used as equivalent to the Irish word *filedh*, 134 *n.*
Picts' wall, 268
Picts of Dalaradia, why so called, 407
Pilgrimage, practised by the second order of saints, 114
Pillar-stones inscribed by St. Patrick with the names of Christ, 500 *n.*—inscribed with abgitorium, at Kilmalkedar, 512 *n.*—the idol of Magh Sleacht, 127
— the idol Crom cruach, or Cromdubh, 127
— Leach Phadruig, at Cashel, 128
— Cermand Celstach, at Clogher, *ib.*
Plague, yellow, or straw-coloured, 213
Pledi, name of Palladius at Fordun, 291
Policy of St. Patrick in his mission, 498
Potitus, a priest, grandfather of St. Patrick, 353
Primacy, of Armagh, nature of, in early times, 94
Princeps, the word often means a bishop, 153 *n.*
— used to translate comarb, 157
— and erenach, 165
Probus, his account of the ordination of St. Patrick, 324
Progenies ecclesiastica and plebilis, meaning of, 153, 154
Prophecy, Druidical, of St. Patrick's coming, 410
— not genuine, 411
Proselytus, used to signify a pilgrim, 6 *n.*
Prosper, of Aquitaine, 270
— his chronicle, *ib. n.*
— his book against Cassian, 273
— does not notice a commission to Patrick from Pope Celestine, 309
Proverb, celebrated Scotic, 455

Psalms, Book of, transcribed by St. Patrick, 510
Psalter, meaning of the word in Irish, 173 *n*.—of Cashel, 173—of Mac Richard Butler, 173
Purgatory of St. Patrick, *Pref.* vii. 307, 484 *n*.

QUADRIGA, a name of St. Patrick, 363
Quoile, an inlet of Strangford lough, 492 *n*.

RALPH of Chester, Polychronicon of, 308
Rathbresail, synod of, 2 *n*.
Rath-croghan, 451. See *Croghan*
Rathnoi, or Rathnew, 287
Rechtitutus, or Restitutus, 364
Reformation of religion in Ireland, the object of the second order of saints, 107
Reformation in 16th century rejected as English, 242—indirect political evils caused by, 244
Relatives of St. Patrick, whether any of them were with him in Ireland, 365 *n*.
Relec-na-righ, 455 *n*.
Relics, stolen by St. Patrick from Rome, 481
Relig, or Recles, name of a sepulchral church, 476
Reliquiæ, 455
Remonstrance of Irish chieftains to Pope John XXII. 236 *sq*.
Restitutus, Bishop of London, 268
Restitutus, or Rechtitutus, a Lombard, 364
Rees (Rev. Rice), his 'Welsh Saints' quoted, 205 *n*. 211 *n*. 352 *n*.
Rees (W. J.), ' Lives of Cambro-British Saints,' 99 *n*.
Reeves (Rev. Dr.), his edition of 'Adamnan,' 6, 8, 19, 106, *et passim*
—— his ' Ecclesiastical History of Down and Connor,' 77, 172, 208, *et passim*
—— his ' Antient Churches of Armagh,' 476 *n. sq*.
—— his ' Archbishop Colton's Visitation,' 478 *n*.
Riada (the Route), 267

Ricend, sister of Patrick, 354
Righe, river, now Newry, 472 *n*.
Rights, Book of, 130, 471 *n*.
Rome, Irish saints miraculously hindered from going to, 100, 101, 115, 116
— St. Patrick's theft of relics from, 481
— date of his supposed visit to, *ib. n*.
Ros-Ailithre, now the see of Ross, 38
Ross, or Rus, son of Trichim, his legend, 459
Route, the, 267
Ructi, brother of St. Patrick, 361 *n*.
Rudbert, or Rupert, founder of the Benedictine abbey of Saltzburgh, 60 — his successors at Saltzburgh, 60, 61—his supposed Irish descent, 62, 63
Russ, or Ross, mac Trichim, 412 *n*.

SABHALL, now Saul, county of Down, 344
— first Church founded by St. Patrick, 409
— meaning of the word, *ib. n*.
— donation of, by Dichu, 410
— request of the donor that the Church should be *transverse*, 26.
— St. Patrick died at, 490
Sabhal, a Church at Armagh so called, 412—identified with the *sinistralis ecclesia*, 480
Sacrifice, human, not taught in Irish legends, 461
Saigher, name of a well, 199, 200
Saints, second order of, had faith in charms and incantations, 123
— resisted the banishment of the bards, 135—evils prevalent in their time, 146
— why called *Catholic* Presbyters, 146
— consecrated St. Moedhog, 147
Salonius, or Solinus, companion of Palladius, 295, 297-301
Saltzburgh, its connection with Ireland, 60 *sq*.
Samhain, what, 134 *n*.
— feast of, 416
Sannan, brother of St. Patrick, 360 *n*.
Saul. See *Sabhal*
Schewes (Wm.), Archbishop of St. Andrews, 299
Scholiast on Fiacc's Hymn ; his account of St. Patrick's mission, 321

Sciric Arcaile, now Skerry, antient Church of, 374
Scot, corpulent, spoken of by St. Jerome, 190 *sq.*
Scothnoe, mother of Feidilmidh, son of Laoghaire, 259
Scotia, Scotland not so called until the twelfth Century, 41 *n.*
— signified Ireland before the twelfth century, 41 *n.* 282 *sq.*
Scoti, their tradition of the date of St. Patrick's death, 496. See *Palladius*
Scotic, or Gaedhelic, colony, date of, 248
Scotland, not called Scotia until the 12th century, 41 *n.*
— its ecclesiastical institutions derived from Ireland, 44
Scotnoe, 151
Scots, Colony of, in North Britain, 266
Scuthin (St.), legend of, 91 *n.*
Sechnall, or Secundinus, 364
— his Hymn, 312, 430
— silent on the Roman mission and education of Patrick, 312
— not present at St. Patrick's Synod, 486
Sectmaide, 361
Secundinus. See *Sechnall*
Sedulius, the Poet, an Irishman, 196
Segetius, 316, 323, 326, 328, 335
Sele, River, now Blackwater, 439
Senach, Bishop, at Achad Fobhair, 508
Senait Mac Maghnusa, an island in Loch Erne, 470 *n.*
Senatenses Annales, why so called, *ib.* enchas na Relic, a History of Cemeteries, 197 *n.*
Senchua, Church of, 222, 225 *n.*
Senchus Mòr, its preface, 483—Dr. Petrie's account of it, 483
— — Colgan's error respecting, *ib.*
Senior (St.), Bishop, 325, 336
Serf (St.), or Servanus, 302 *n.*
Sidhe, or Siodha, meaning of the word, 452
Sidonius Apollinarius, 279 *n.*
Simplicius, Archbishop of Bourges, 278 *n.*—his wife, 279 *n.*
Sinai (Mount), Monks of, had a Bishop of their own, 68
Sinell, son of Finncadh, first convert of St. Patrick, 344, 345 *n.*
Sinistralis ecclesia, at Armagh, 479, 480

Sisters of St. Patrick, 354 *n.*, 360
Sister, signifies sometimes a more distant relation, 366 *n.*
Skerries, 404, 405
Slain, River, running into Strangford Lough, 406
Slane, co. of Meath, antient name of, 420
Slemish. See *Sliabh Mis*
Sletty, or Slebte, 424
Sliabh Gua, or Cua, 218 *n.*
Sliabh Cualann, 343 *n.*
Sliabh Mis, now Slemish, 374, 407, 408
Solinus. See *Salonius*
Staff of Jesus, 323, 328
Stephen (Pope), his charter to St. Fuldrad, sanctioning a monastic bishop, 53
Stokes, Whitley, his translation of the Irish Hymn of St. Patrick, 426 *n.*
— — his analysis of the first word of the Hymn, *ib.*
— — his Irish Glosses, 124 *n.*, 156 *n.*
— — his edition of Cormac's Glossary, 413 *n.*
Stone Churches in Ireland, 304 *n.*
Subjection of Bishops to the Abbat, example of, 8
Succat, St. Patrick's baptismal name, 363
Success of St. Patrick, its cause, 499
— over-rated, 501
Sugar-loaf Mountain, antient name of, 343 *n.*
Sui, meaning of the word, 177 *n.*
Suicide, religious, recommended by the Albigenses, 463
Suir, a sister, used in Irish to signify a more distant relative, 354 *n.*, 366
Sun and wind killed Laoghaire, 437
Swidbert (St.), a Bishop without a see, 47
Sylvester, companion of Palladius, 295, 297, 301
Synchronisms of Kings of Ireland and Scotland, Tract on, 394
Synods attributed to St. Patrick, 484 *n.*
— synod of Patrick, Auxilius, and Iserninus, 485
— — second synod attributed to St. Patrick, 488

TABERNÆ, or Taberniæ, not tabernacles or tents, 358

Index. 537

Tables, genealogical, 247
Tacitus, his testimony to the early commerce of Ireland, 512 *n.*
Tailcend, meaning of the name, 411 *n.* 435
Teach-na-Roman, 291, 294, 297
Telltown, 439
Temple-Fertagh, 478
Termon-lands, 160
Tertullian, his testimony to the early Christianity of Britain, 265
Tervanus, or Ternanus, 302
Theodosius II. emperor, 322, 329
Thirty years, periods of, pervade Irish hagiography, 393 *n.*
Tigris, sister of St. Patrick, 354, 361
Tillemont rejects the stories of St. Patrick's sisters, 365
— his judgment of the Epistle about Coroticus, 385
— his judgment of the Confession of St. Patrick, 382
Tir-Amalgaidh, now Tirawley, 442 *n.*, 447
Tir-Fhiachrach, now Tireragh, 447
Tir-Oiliolla, 223 *n.*
Tirechan, his chronology of St. Patrick's life, 395
— his account of the four honours of St. Patrick, 429
— his history, 444
— a disciple of St. Ultan of Ardbraccan, *ib.*
Tirerrill, 223 *n.*
Toaghie, in the county of Armagh, 215
Tobur-ên-adarc, 449
Toleration, St. Patrick's, 500
Tomene, Bishop of Armagh, his letter to the clergy of Rome, 141, 142
Tonsure, allusion to in the Druidical prophecy of St. Patrick's coming, 411
— Druidical tonsure, 455 *n.*, 456
— Roman tonsure alluded to in a canon attributed to St. Patrick, 486
— Roman, when adopted by the monks of Hy, 487
— Adamnan's conference with Coelfrid, on, 487
— Irish tonsure what, 487 *n.*
Torannan (St.), 302 *n.*
Tordhealbach, meaning of the name, 3 *n.*

Tours, Abbey of St. Martin at, 56
Tract on Chronology of the Kings of Ireland in the Book of Lecan, 396
Traig, a foot, 477 *n.*
Transverse position of the Church of Sabhall, 410
Treguier, 369 *n.*
Trim, meaning of word, 150 *n.*
— legend of foundation of, 257—ignored by the Ulster annals, 470
— See *Ath Truim*
Tuath Eochadha, now Toaghie, co. of Armagh, 215
Tuathal Techtmar, King of Ireland, remodels the institutions of Ollamh Fodla, 416 *n.*
Tuathal Maelgarb, King of Ireland, 440
Tulach Aichne, 451 *n.*
Tulach-na-leicc, near Armagh, 480
Turus, a journey or pilgrimage, 360 *n.*

UI CENNSELAIGH, district of, 216 *n.*
Ui Chorra, or grandsons of Corr, 404 *n.*—romantic tale of their voyages, *ib.*
Ui Dortain, or Ui Tortain, 260 *n.*
Ui Dorthini, 260
Ui Eachach Uladh, 214
Ui Oiliolla, country of, 222, 223 *n.*
Ulidia, now the county of Down, 406
Ulster, Annals of, by whom composed, 470 *n.*
— — why called Annales Senatenses, 470 *n.*
— — their dates one year behind the common æra 469 *n.*, 496 *n.*
— — their date of St. Patrick's death, 496
Ultan (St.) of Ardbraccan, a disciple of St. Declan, 212—legend of, *ib.*
— — his date, 213
— — bishop of the Dal-Conchubhair, *ib.*, 444
— — his care of the orphans whose parents died of the plague, 213
Union Legislative, of Great Britain and Ireland, 245—indirect evil produced by, *ib.*
Ursmar, first Abbat and Bishop of Laubes, 57, 58
Uriel, see *Oirgialla*

Ussher, his opinion of the year in which St. Patrick died, 494

VALENTIA, Roman province of, 268
Vermeriense Concilium, held under King Pepin, 40 *n.*
Vernense, seu Vernorense Concilium, 40 *n.*
Verneuil, synod of, 40 *n.*
Victor, St. Patrick's guardian angel, 377
Victoricus, a man from Hiberio, appears in vision to Patrick, 377
Vigilius, Pope, only a deacon when consecrated bishop, 87
Virgil of Saltzburgh, an Irishman, 64
—— his Irish name Fergil or Fergal, 65
—— called the "Geometer," 64
—— propounded the theory of " antipodes," 65
—— brought with him Bishop Dobda from Ireland, 65
Vitalis of Saltzburgh, said to have been an Irishman, 63

WEDNESDAY, the day of St. Patrick's birth, baptism, and death, 495, 450 *n.*
— the day of St. Brigid's birth, being veiled, and death, 450 *n.*
Whitsunday, the day of St. Columba's birth, baptism, and death, 450 *n.*
Wicterbus, Bishop and Abbat of St. Martin's of Tours, 57
Wilde, Mr., his Introduction to the Census of Ireland, 213 *n.*
Winfrid (St.) or Boniface, a bishop without a see, 47
Wlfard, or Gulfard, Abbat of St. Martin's, 57
Women, exclusion of by second order of saints, 91, 92
— not excluded from St. Patrick's religious societies, 504
Wood, churches of, 304 *n.*
Writing, art of, taught by St. Patrick to his converts, 512

ZEUSS, Grammatica Celtica, 16 *n.* 163 *n.*

www.ingramcontent.com/pod-product-compliance
Lightning Source LLC
Chambersburg PA
CBHW052044290426
44111CB00011B/1613